Essentials of

Children's Literature

A Story Is a Doorway

A story is a doorway
That opens on a wider place.
A story is a mirror
To reflect the reader's face.

A story is a question
You hadn't thought to ponder,
A story is a pathway,
Inviting you to wander.

A story is a window,
A story is a key,
A story is a lighthouse,
Beaming out to sea.

A story's a beginning,
A story is an end,
And in the story's middle,
You just might find a friend.

—Richard Peck

Essentials of
Children's Literature

Seventh Edition

Carol Lynch-Brown
Florida State University

Carl M. Tomlinson
Northern Illinois University

Kathy G. Short
University of Arizona

Boston   Columbus   Indianapolis   New York   San Francisco   Upper Saddle River
Amsterdam   Cape Town   Dubai   London   Madrid   Milan   Munich   Paris   Montreal   Toronto
Delhi   Mexico City   Sao Paulo   Sydney   Hong Kong   Seoul   Singapore   Taipei   Tokyo

Vice President, Editor-in-Chief: Aurora Martínez Ramos
Editorial Assistant: Amy Foley
Managing Editor, Literacy: Barbara Strickland
Executive Marketing Manager: Krista Clark
Editorial-Production Service: Omegatype Typography, Inc.
Production Supervisor: Joe Sweeney
Manufacturing Manager: Megan Cochran
Cover Administrator: Linda Knowles
Text Designer: Omegatype Typography, Inc.
Full Service Project Management: Omegatype Typography, Inc.
Composition: Omegatype Typography, Inc.
Printer/Binder: RR Donnelley, Harrisonburg

Credits and acknowledgments borrowed from other sources and reproduced, with permission, in this textbook appear on pages 405–407.

Library of Congress Cataloging-in-Publication Data

Lynch-Brown, Carol.
  Essentials of children's literature / Carol Lynch-Brown, Carl M. Tomlinson, Kathy G. Short. — 7th ed.
      p.   cm.
  Includes bibliographical references and index.
  ISBN-13: 978-0-13-704884-7 (pbk.)
  ISBN-10: 0-13-704884-X (pbk.)
  1. Children's literature—Study and teaching (Higher)   2. Children's literature—History and criticism.
3. Children's literature—Bibliography.   I. Tomlinson, Carl M.   II. Short, Kathy Gnagey.   III. Title.
  PN1009.A1L96   2011
  809'.892820711—dc22

                                                                        2009052225

10 9 8 7 6 5   RRD-VA   14 13 12

www.pearsonhighered.com

ISBN 10: 0-13-704884-X
ISBN 13: 978-0-13-704884-7

Contents

part TWO   Categories of Literature   53

chapter FOUR   Poetry   55

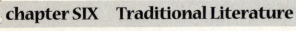

chapter SEVEN   Modern Fantasy   130

chapter TEN   Informational Books   194

part THREE   Literature in the School   243

chapter TWELVE   Planning the Curriculum   245

chapter THIRTEEN   Engaging Children with Literature   279

Features

Excellent Books to Read Aloud

Milestones

Notable Authors and Illustrators

Figures and Tables

Figures

Tables

Preface

Essentials of Children's Literature is a brief, affordable, comprehensive textbook with rich resources—a true compendium of information about children's literature. It is tailored to a survey course in children's literature but, by virtue of its brevity and affordability, is also suitable as a companion text in an integrated language arts course.

The primary focus of a survey course in children's literature should be reading children's trade books, not reading an exhaustive textbook about children's books. Students in such a course need direct experience with these trade books—reading them, reading them aloud to others, discussing them, writing about them, comparing them, criticizing them, evaluating them, applying them to their own lives, and thinking about sharing them with children.

One of our goals is to awaken or reawaken college-level students to the joy of reading. This reawakening can happen only if they experience the pleasure and excitement of reading excellent trade books. At the same time, the body of knowledge about literature and about teaching literature to children can be conveyed most efficiently through a textbook. *Essentials of Children's Literature* presents this body of knowledge in a clear, concise, direct narrative using brief lists, examples, figures, and tables in combination with prose, thus freeing class time for involvement with literature.

The seventh edition of *Essentials of Children's Literature* heralds two milestones. It was two decades ago that we began conceptualizing and planning this book. Much has changed since the first edition to influence the world of children's literature, and although successive editions have reflected these changes, the book remains, in essence, true to our initial concept—a comprehensive but brief alternative to compendium textbooks. The second milestone is the welcome addition of a new co-author, Kathy G. Short, professor of children's literature at the University of Arizona in the Department of Language, Reading, and Culture. Kathy's research in international children's literature and intercultural understanding, children's dialogue about literature, and inquiry-based curriculum is internationally known. We value her contributions to this edition.

Chapter-by-Chapter Changes

Our goals in revising this book were twofold: to make it as fresh and current as possible and to produce a briefer text without sacrificing content. We have added many new children's book titles and retained older titles most likely to be known and appreciated by students. Features within chapters—Milestones, Excellent Books to Read Aloud, Notable Authors and Illustrators, and Issues and Topics for Further Investigation—have been updated as needed to include important developments, recent outstanding children's titles, outstanding new creators of children's books, and current issues and topics related to the field. Revisions to individual chapters are as follows:

Chapter 1: Learning about Children and Their Literature

- Updated table on important studies on literature and reading
- Updated section on the academic value of literature to children
- New examples of children's literature titles appropriate for the various stages of children's development

Chapter 2: Learning about Reading and Literature

- Updated discussion of national reports related to reading and literature

Chapter 3: Learning about Literature

- Updated information on professional associations
- New examples of children's titles

Chapter 4: Poetry

- Full chapter updated to focus solely on poetry, including its elements and types
- Updated examples of poems and types of poetry books
- Updated Recommended Poetry Books list

Chapter 5: Picture Books

- Updated color insert includes illustrations from recent picture books and a graphic novel and examples of computer-generated art
- New section on using the Guide to Illustrations for the color insert
- Artistic media discussion expanded to include computer-generated art
- New section on book design
- Updated Recommended Picture Books list, including a new section on transitional books

Chapter 6: Traditional Literature

- New section on storytelling in the classroom, including digital storytelling
- Updated Recommended Traditional Literature list

Chapter 7: Modern Fantasy

- Updated discussion of fantasy books often challenged by censors
- Updated examples of types of modern fantasy
- Updated Recommended Modern Fantasy Books list

Chapter 8: Realistic Fiction

- Updated discussion of character education and the use of works of realism for character education
- Updated examples of types of realistic fiction
- Updated Recommended Realistic Fiction Books list

Chapter 9: Historical Fiction and Biography

- New section integrating biography with historical fiction

- New pedagogical section, Historical Fiction and Biography in the Classroom, including developing an understanding of historical contexts using jackdaws and other strategies
- Updated Recommended Historical Fiction and Biography Books list, integrated and organized by historical periods to facilitate the creation of text sets

Chapter 10: Informational Books
- Full chapter updated to focus solely on informational literature and its elements
- An emphasis on strategies for teachers to help students comprehend informational literature
- New section on using informational books for bibliotherapy
- New section on series nonfiction
- Updated examples of types of informational books
- Updated Recommended Informational Books list

Chapter 11: Literature for a Diverse Society
- Completely reorganized chapter highlighting a curriculum that is culturally responsive (finding one's own culture within education), culturally expansive (going beyond one's own culture), and culturally critical (addressing critical literacy and social justice education)
- Reorganized presentation of multicultural and international literature

Chapter 12: Planning the Curriculum
- New section on traditional and inquiry approaches to the study of literature
- New section on technology and literature
- New conceptual planning web
- Updated and expanded discussion of censorship

Chapter 13: Engaging Children with Literature
- Completely reorganized chapter now divided into three sections:
  - Reading Widely for Personal Purposes, including reading aloud, independent reading by students, booktalks, shared reading, readers' theatre, and experiencing literature in multimodal texts (audiobooks, films, digital books, plays)
  - Reading Critically to Inquire about the World, including literature discussion, literature response engagements, drama as response, and literature across the curriculum
  - Reading Strategically to Learn about Literacy, including using literary works as writing models
- New table on using literature for multiple perspectives in science and social studies units
- Updated children's book examples and websites

Appendixes
- Appendix A, Children's Book Awards, updated to include award winners and honor books for the years 2007–2009.
- Appendix B, Professional Resources, updated to reflect the latest titles and editions.
- Appendix C, Children's Magazines, updated to include new magazines and to reflect current magazine content, intended audience, website, and ordering information.

Supplements for Instructors and Students

The following supplements comprise an outstanding array of resources that facilitate learning about children's literature. For more information, ask your local Allyn & Bacon Merrill Education representative or contact the Allyn & Bacon Merrill Faculty Field Support Department at 1-800-526-0485. For technology support, please contact technical support directly at 1-800-677-6337 or http://247.pearsoned.com.

Help your students get better grades and become better teachers.

Instructor's Manual and Test Bank

The instructor's manual features multiple syllabi of typical survey courses in children's literature. The test bank includes multiple-choice, matching, fill-in-the-blank, short answer, and essay questions. This supplement has been written by the text authors. (Available for download from the Instructor Resource Center at www.pearsonhighered.com/irc.)

MyEducationKit:
Dynamic Resources Meeting Your Needs

PEARSON myeducationkit™ MyEducationKit is a dynamic website that connects the concepts addressed in the text with effective teaching practice. Plus, it's easy to use and integrate into assignments and courses. Wherever the MyEducationKit logo appears in the text, follow the simple instructions to access a variety of multimedia resources geared to meet the diverse teaching and learning needs of instructors and students. Here are just a few of the features that are available:

- Online study plans, including self-assessment quizzes and resource material
- Gradetracker, an online grade book
- Multimedia resources, including a children's literature database, video clips, student and teacher artifacts, and interviews with children's book authors
- Web links to important national organizations and sites in your field

Study Plan

A MyEducationKit Study Plan is a multiple-choice assessment with feedback that offers opportunities to master sample concepts and information found within chapters. Students can take the multiple-choice quiz as many times as they want. The multiple-choice quizzes provide overall scores for each objective and explain why responses to particular items are correct or incorrect.

Children's Literature Database

A searchable database of thousands of children's literature titles comes with the MyEducationKit for this text. This database allows users to find books in every genre, by hundreds of authors and illustrators, by awards won, by year published, by topic and description, as well as many other search options.

Assignments and Activities

Designed to save instructors preparation time and enhance student understanding, these assignable exercises show concepts in action (through database use, video, and/or student and teacher artifacts). They help students synthesize and apply concepts and strategies they read about in the book.

Multimedia Resources

The media resources you will encounter in MyEducationKit include

- *Videos.* The authentic classroom videos show how real teachers handle actual classroom situations. Discussing and analyzing these videos not only deepens understanding of concepts presented in the text, but also builds skills in observing children and classrooms.
- *Student and teacher artifacts.* Real K–12 student and teacher classroom artifacts—tied to the chapter topics in your text—offer practice in working with the different materials teachers encounter daily in their classrooms.
- *Web links.* On MyEducationKit you don't need to search for the sites that connect to the topics covered in your chapter. Here, you can explore websites that are important in the field and that give you perspective on the concepts covered in your text.
- *Essay questions.* These questions encourage consideration of chapter topics. Hints and feedback are provided.
- *Conversations.* Select chapters provide written interview with children's book authors and illustrators.

General Resources on MyEducationKit

The Resources section is designed to help students pass their licensure exams; put together effective portfolios and lesson plans; prepare for and navigate the first year of their teaching careers; and understand key educational standards, policies, and laws. This section includes

- *Licensure Exams.* Contains guidelines for passing the Praxis exam. The Practice Test Exam includes practice multiple-choice questions, case study questions, and video case studies with sample questions.
- *Lesson Plan Builder.* Helps students create and share lesson plans.
- *Licensure and Standards.* Provides links to state licensure standards and national standards.
- *Beginning Your Career.* Offers tips, advice, and valuable information on:
  - Resume Writing and Interviewing. Expert advice on how to write impressive resumes and prepare for job interviews.
  - Your First Year of Teaching. Practical tips on setting up a classroom, managing student behavior, and planning for instruction and assessment.
  - Law and Public Policies. Includes specific directives and requirements educators need to understand under the No Child Left Behind Act and the Individuals with Disabilities Education Improvement Act of 2004.

  Visit www.myeducationkit.com for a demonstration of this new online teaching resource.

Acknowledgments

We gratefully acknowledge the reviewers of the seventh edition: Dana Duffy Backs, Indiana University; Lisa A. Hazlett, University of South Dakota; Katrina Hunter-Mintz, University of North Alabama; Goldie Johnson, Winona State University; Dianne Koehnecke, Webster University; Ruth Lowery, University of Florida; Caroline S. McKinney, University of Colorado at Boulder; and Billie A. Unger, Blue Ridge Community & Technical College.

We are also indebted to Rafael López for the beautiful wrap-around cover art for this edition of *Essentials of Children's Literature*. His art underscores two of the fundamental messages of this textbook: the magic and wonder in books and the importance of respecting one's cultural roots and those of others.

Children and Literature

Part I provides introductory content for a course on children's literature. This material will help teachers and librarians read, select, and evaluate children's books and integrate them into their classrooms and school library media centers.

Chapter 1 defines children's literature, discusses its personal and academic values for children, and provides research evidence supporting its use with children. General guidelines for the types and topics of literature likely to appeal to children as they develop from year to year complete this chapter.

Chapter 2 considers the relationships between reading and literature as they pertain to the reading process, literature in the reading curriculum, independent reading of free-choice material, accountability and reading, children's reading interests, and the difficulty of reading materials.

Approaches to studying and interpreting literature, elements of fiction, and changes in traditional fictional forms are treated extensively in Chapter 3 and serve as a review for students. An overview of resources for book selection, including review journals, professional websites, and major awards for children's literature, is also discussed in this chapter. The chapter concludes with a discussion of the need for balance and variety in book selection with a table of literary genres and their locations within the book.

Throughout this text, examples of notable books are given as needed, but we include no lengthy plot summaries or book reviews. We believe that more is gained from reading and discussing children's books themselves than reading *about* the books in a lengthy text.

chapter ONE

Learning about Children and Their Literature

Reading

. . . We get no good
By being ungenerous even to a book,
And calculating profits . . . so much help
By so much reading. It is rather when
We gloriously forget ourselves and plunge
Soul-forward, headlong, into a book's profound,
Impassioned for its beauty and salt of truth—
'Tis then we get the right good from a book.

—*Elizabeth Browning*

A child leans forward, head cupped in hands, eyes wide with anticipation, listening to a story: This is an image for all time. Whether that child is seated beside an open fire in the Stone Ages, on a rough bench in a medieval fairground, or in a modern-day classroom, the message of the image is the same: Children love a good story.

Definition of Children's Literature

This book is about literature for children from infancy to adolescence, written for you who will be meeting and working with these children as teachers, librarians, and parents. In these roles, your opportunities to lead children to literature will be unparalleled, if you have the prerequisite knowledge.

Children's literature is good-quality trade books for children from birth to adolescence, covering topics of relevance and interest to children of those ages, through prose and poetry, fiction and nonfiction. This definition contains several key concepts that will be explained in the following sections. Understanding these concepts will help you find your way around the more than 250,000 children's titles published in the last decade and currently in print (*Children's Books in Print, 2009*, 2008) and the more than 25,000 new children's titles being published annually in the United States (*Bowker Annual: Library and Book Trade Almanac* [Bogart, 2008]), as well as the additional thousands of children's books published worldwide each year in English.

Content

Children's books are about the experiences of childhood, both good and bad. Whether these experiences are set in the past, present, or future, they should still be relevant to the child of today. The content of children's books includes amazingly diverse topics that are of interest to children, such as dinosaurs, Egyptian mummies, world records, and fighter planes.

The manner in which content is treated also helps to define children's books. Childhood stories told in a forthright, humorous, or suspenseful manner are appropriate for young readers; stories *about* childhood told in nostalgic or overly sentimental terms are inappropriate. Likewise, when stories show children as victims of natural and human-made disasters, the stories should emphasize the hope for a better future rather than the hopelessness and utter despair of the moment.

The subject matter of children's literature can be expressed in prose or poetry. If the literary work is prose, it must be presented as fiction (a product of the imagination, an invented story), nonfiction (factual), or a combination of the two.

Teachers and librarians distinguish between the terms *textbook* and *trade book.* A **textbook,** by design and content, is for the purpose of instruction. The basal reader used in many classrooms for reading instruction is an example of a textbook. In contrast, a **trade book,** by design and content, is primarily for the purposes of entertainment and information. Trade books are often referred to as *library books* and *storybooks.* The books that we will be discussing in this text will be trade books, not textbooks.

Quality

Not all trade books aimed at young readers are worth attention. Books ranging in quality from excellent to poor are now readily available to parents, teachers, and children through bookstores and libraries as well as online. Look around and you will see racks of children's books in department stores, drugstores, and even grocery stores. But the question is: Are they *good* children's books?

Quality in writing has to do with originality and importance of ideas, imaginative use of language, and beauty of literary and artistic style that enable a work to remain fresh, interesting, and meaningful for many years. The best children's books offer readers enjoyment as well as memorable characters and situations and valuable insights into the human condition. These books have permanent value.

This is not to say that books of good-but-not-great quality, such as series books, have no value. These works win no literary prizes, but many young readers enjoy them, and because books such as these encourage newly independent readers to read more, they have worth. However, you will probably not want to select books of this calibre to read aloud to your students. Why deprive them of the pleasure of reading such easy and enjoyable books independently?

Many so-called children's books today are nothing more than advertisements for film and television characters and associated products, such as candy, clothing, and toys. These books represent the low end of the quality spectrum.

The Personal Value of Literature for Children

Literature for children leads to personal fulfillment and academic gains. Separating the values into personal and academic is an intellectual distinction, because both types benefit the child and are proper parts of a child's schooling. The distinction is useful, however, because teachers and librarians must often justify the benefits of literature in the classroom and find the academic benefits to be the most convincing ones for administrators and parents.

PEARSON
myeducationkit

Go to Activity 1 in the Assignments and Activities section of Chapter 1 in MyEducationKit; view the video on the value of good literature for children and respond to the questions.

Enjoyment

The most important personal gain that good books offer to children is the most obvious one—enjoyment. Those of you who read widely as children will never forget the stories that were so funny that you laughed out loud, the poem that was so lilting that you never forgot it, or the mystery that was so scary that your heart thumped with apprehension. Such positive early experiences often lead to a lifetime of reading enjoyment.

Imagination and Inspiration

By seeing the world around them in new ways and by considering ways of living other than their own, children increase their ability to think divergently. Stories often map the divergent paths that our ancestors might have taken or that our descendants might someday take. Through the vicarious experience of entering a world different from the present one, children develop their imaginations. In addition, stories about people, both real and imaginary, can inspire children to overcome obstacles, accept different perspectives, and formulate personal goals.

Knowledge and Insights

Good books offer both information and wisdom. Informational books provide factual knowledge, whereas realistic fiction, fantasy, and poetry offer insights into life, and historical fiction and biography offer both. When a story is so convincingly written that readers feel as though they have lived through an experience or have actually been in the place and time where the story is set, the book has given them a valuable personal experience. Experiences such as these are broadening for children because they, as readers, are taken to places and times that they could never actually visit—and might not want to! Such experiences can also be good mental exercises for children, because they are asked to view situations from perspectives other than their own.

Understanding and Empathy

Literature helps young people gain an appreciation of the universality of human needs across history, which makes it possible for them to understand that all humans are, to some degree, alike. Walking in someone else's shoes often helps children develop a sense of social justice and a greater capacity to empathize with others. All children can benefit from stories that explain what life is like for people who are restricted by disabilities, politics, or circumstance or whose lives are different from theirs because of culture or geography. Likewise, young people can relate on a more personal level with the events and people of history when reading works of historical fiction told from the point of view of a person their own age.

Heritage and Cultural Identity

Stories that are handed down from one generation to the next connect us to our past, to the roots of our specific cultures, national heritage, and general human condition. Stories are the repositories of culture. Knowing the tales, characters, expressions, and adages that are part of our cultural heritage is part of being culturally literate. In addition, stories based on actual events in the past help young people gain a greater appreciation for what history is and for the people, both ordinary and extraordinary, who made history.

Moral Reasoning

Often, story characters are placed in situations that require them to make moral decisions. Young readers naturally consider what they themselves would do in such a situation. As the story unfolds and the character's decision and the consequences of that choice are disclosed, readers discover whether their own decisions would have had positive outcomes. Regular experience with these types of stories can help young people formulate their own concepts of right and wrong.

Moral reasoning is an integral part of *character education,* a strand in the social studies curricula of many elementary schools today that deals with the principles by which one lives. Character education programs such as "Character Counts" are available for purchase, but reading and discussing well-selected works of literature can serve the same purpose.

Literary and Artistic Preferences

Another valuable result of children's interacting with literature is that they quickly come to recognize the literary and artistic styles of many authors and illustrators. Children who read regularly from a wide variety of children's books soon develop their own personal preferences for types of books and select favorite authors and illustrators. Personal preference and interest as expressed through self-selection of reading materials are powerful reading motivators.

The more children know about their world, the more they discover about themselves—who they are, what they value, and what they stand for. These personal insights alone are sufficient to warrant making good books an essential part of any child's home and school experiences. But literature is also valuable for its academic benefits, as will be discussed in the following section.

The Academic Value of Literature for Children

In addition to the personal benefits of literature for young readers, there are important academic benefits.

Reading

Many of you already may have reached the commonsense deduction that reading ability, like any other skill, improves with practice. Many teachers and librarians believe that regular involvement with excellent and appropriate literature can foster language development in young children and can help them learn to read and value reading. This belief was supported in the landmark study *Becoming a Nation of Readers* (Anderson, Hiebert, Scott, & Wilkinson, 1985), which concludes, "The single most important activity for building the knowledge required for eventual success in reading is reading aloud to children" (p. 23).

In 1997, the National Reading Panel (NRP) was formed, at the request of Congress, to assess the status of research-based knowledge about reading, including the effectiveness of various approaches to teaching children to read. The *Report of the National Reading Panel* (National Reading Panel, 2000) was met with great controversy and skepticism because of its narrow definition of scientific research studies. In this report, the NRP identified the following components of instruction considered to be essential to the teaching of reading: *phonemic awareness* (teaching how to break apart and manipulate the sounds in words); *phonics* (teaching that sounds are represented by letters of the alphabet that blend to form words); and *reading comprehension* (teaching strategies to develop text recall, question generation, and summarizing of information read), including *fluency* (teaching how to read orally with speed, accuracy, and proper expression) and *vocabulary instruction* (teaching the spelling and meaning of new words). Literature-based research studies that support reading aloud to students and independent silent reading by students were not included because they did not meet the NRP's narrow definition of scientific research.

In 2002, the Reading First program was established by the U.S. Department of Education to implement the components of reading instruction approved by the NRP. By 2007, states had awarded subgrants to 1,809 school districts, which had provided funds to 5,880 schools (Institute of Education Sciences National Center for Education Evaluation and Regional Assistance, 2008). In 2008, the Institute of Education Sciences issued an interim report on the impacts of Reading First on classroom reading instruction and student reading comprehension during the 2004–2005 and 2005–2006 school years. The report compared students' reading comprehension scores to estimates of what they would have scored with no Reading First intervention. Evaluators found that, on average, Reading First did *not* have statistically significant impacts on student reading comprehension test scores in grades 1–3 across the 18 study sites. This finding calls into question Reading First and NRP's prediction that a phonics-based approach to reading instruction would produce better readers than other approaches.

Based on our personal and professional experience with children, we contend that reading aloud to children by parents and caregivers and sharing literature with students in the classroom greatly benefit children's acquisition of reading skills and their attitudes toward reading. In addition, we contend that literature-based studies support not only the reading instruction strategies endorsed by the NRP but also the important instructional practices that the NRP report ignores.

Trends in research can be influenced by policy. Following the NRP report and the No Child Left Behind Act of 2001, research in the areas of literature-based reading, literature across the curriculum, and literature and writing decreased considerably from the pace established in the two prior decades.

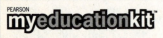

PEARSON

Go to Activity 2 in the Assignments and Activities section of Chapter 1 in MyEducationKit; complete the activity on literature-based research articles.

As educators, you should be aware of research findings about the worth of literature for children. Research studies summarized in Tables 1.1 and 1.2 show that in teaching children to read, two procedures seem especially important: reading excellent literature aloud to children and silent independent reading of free-choice material by children, both on a daily basis, if possible. For a more thorough discussion of literature and the teaching of reading, see Chapter 2 and the section titled Approaches to Teaching Reading with Literature in Chapter 12.

Writing

By listening to and reading excellent literature, children are exposed to rich vocabulary and excellent writing styles, which serve as good models for their own speaking and writing voices. The acquisition of a larger vocabulary through reading offers young writers better word choices for their own stories. Devices found in books such as the use of dialect, dialogue, and precise description are often assimilated into students' own writing. Research studies summarized in Table 1.3 show that skill in reading and skill in writing go hand in hand.

As stated in the previous section, government policies established in the early twenty-first century discouraged research in some literacy-related areas. Scharer, Freeman, and Lehman (2008) found almost no research on the influence of quality children's books on children's writing in their analysis of articles published from 2000 to 2005 in ten scholarly literature-related journals. This finding is supported by Cassidy and Cassidy (2009, 2005), whose annual surveys of literacy leaders have identified writing in general as one of the research topics of least interest to researchers in recent years. We, too, have found no recent notable research studies in this area.

Table 1.1   Landmark Studies on Literature and Reading

Researcher(s)	Subjects	Findings
Carlsen & Sherrill (1988)	College students who had become committed readers	Conditions that promote a love of reading in childhood include: ■ Freedom of choice in reading material ■ Availability of books and magazines ■ Family members who read aloud ■ Adults and peers who modeled reading ■ Role models who valued reading ■ Sharing and discussing books ■ Owning books ■ Availability of libraries and librarians
Eldredge & Butterfield (1986)	1,149 beginning readers in fifty classrooms	Use of children's literature to teach reading has a much greater positive effect on students' achievement and attitudes toward reading than does use of basal readers with traditional homogeneous grouping.
Fielding, Wilson, & Anderson (1986)	Middle-graders	Students who read a lot at home show larger gains on reading achievement tests.
Leinhardt, Zigmond, & Cooley (1981)	Elementary-grade children	The amount of time children spend reading silently in school is associated with their year-to-year gains in reading achievement. Children improve their reading ability by increasing their reading.
Applebee (1978)	Children ages 2 to 17	Children's sense of story grows as they mature. Hearing and reading literature has a positive effect on children's language development.
Butler (1975)	Cushla, severely disabled, from ages 4 months to 3 years	Reading aloud daily to the subject from children's picture books enabled the child to learn to read.
Durkin (1966)	Children who learned to read before attending school	Children who learned to read before attending school were read to regularly from the age of 3. Early reading and early writing are often linked.

Content-Area Subjects

In reading about and discussing children's literature, you will often hear the phrase *literature across the curriculum.* This means using works of literature as teaching materials in the content areas of social studies and history, science, health, and mathematics. Good teachers have always used literature across the curriculum. The logic for this practice is sound. Many trade books contain information that is relevant to the topics studied in school. Moreover, this information is often presented through captivating, sometimes beautifully illustrated, narratives that are interesting to students and

Table 1.2   Important Studies on Literature and Reading, 1990–2005

Researchers(s)	Subjects	Findings
Arya, Martens, Wilson, Altwerger, Jin, Laster, & Lang (2005)	100 urban, low SES second-graders (not special ed. or ESL) in four classes from four schools; two classes used commercial, phonics-based reading programs (Reading Mastery and Open Court); two classes used literature-based instruction (an adaptation of Fountas and Pinnell's *Guided Reading* and a school-designed literature curriculum)	No significant difference was found in measures of students' phonics use within the reading process and in isolation, reading accuracy, or comprehension, regardless of instructional program. These findings contradict the National Reading Panel's predictions that phonics-based reading programs would produce better readers.
Wilson, Martens, Arya, & Altwerger (2004)	Eighty-four urban, low SES second-graders (not special ed. or ESL) taught reading with three different reading programs: Direct Instruction and Open Court, both heavily scripted phonics-based reading programs; and Guided Reading, a literature-based reading program	No significant difference was found in measures of students' phonics use, regardless of instructional program. Guided Reading students could describe settings and characters, retell stories cohesively, form inferences, and make connections. These findings contradict the National Reading Panel's predictions that phonics-based reading programs would produce better readers.
Worthy, Patterson, Salas, Prater, & Turner (2002)	Twenty-four struggling, resistant readers in grades 3 through 5	The most effective factor in increasing these students' motivation to read was a reading instructor who tailored instruction to each student's unique needs, found materials that exactly fit each student's needs and interests, and took time to inspire each student to read.
Ivey & Broaddus (2001)	1,765 sixth-graders in twenty-three diverse schools in mid-Atlantic and northeastern United States	When asked what made them want to read in the classroom, students ranked as most important: ■ Free reading time and teacher read-alouds of literature as part of instructional time ■ Quality and diversity of reading materials and a choice in selecting these materials
Anderson (1996)	Elementary-grade students	Even slight increases (10 minutes a day) in time spent reading independently lead to gains in reading achievement. Amount of free reading in early grades helps determine reading ability in grades 5 and 6.

Table 1.3 Important Studies on Literature and Writing

Researcher(s)	Subjects	Findings
Barrs (2000)	Eighteen fourth-graders in five elementary schools in London whose reading and writing were analyzed over one school year	Children use in their own writing the language and writing styles of books they read. "It seems unlikely that there can be any fundamental writing development without reading development, and vice versa" (p. 59).
Cantrell (1999)	Forty third-graders—twenty-one in four classrooms where teachers adhered to recommended literacy practices (both explicit skill instruction and meaning-centered literacy activities) to a high degree and nineteen in four classrooms where teachers adhered to these practices to a low degree	In classrooms where teachers frequently used children's literature, integrated reading and writing, and taught reading and writing skills in context, students developed reading and writing skills at higher levels than students in classrooms where teachers provided more isolated skill instruction.
Lancia (1997)	Second-graders	Good books are effective models for children's writing. Students "borrowed" plots, plot elements, characters, stylistic devices, and information from books to use in their own writing.
Dressel (1990)	Fifth-graders	Student writing was directly affected by the characteristics of the stories they heard and discussed, regardless of the students' reading abilities. The better the quality of the read-aloud, the better the quality of the student writing. *Which* stories teachers read aloud is important.

therefore are more comprehensible and memorable. When using literature across the curriculum, teachers and students are not confined to the textbook as the sole resource. Using several sources of information has always been considered prudent both in and out of school, because doing so usually provides fuller factual coverage of topics and leads to wiser, more informed decisions on issues. Using literature across the curriculum is particularly appropriate today, given the abundance of masterfully written, information-relevant children's trade books available to teachers and librarians. Scharer and colleagues (2008), despite finding few research studies focusing on literature in the content areas in the years 2000 to 2005, found much evidence in their analysis of classroom experience and conceptual articles that teachers are involved in using literature in the content areas. The articles indicated that teachers are using literature to support the teaching of mathematics and science, using nonfiction with primary-age children, and pairing fiction with informational texts.

Art Appreciation

Illustration in children's picture books can be appreciated for its ability to help tell the story (cognitive value) and for its value as art (aesthetic value). The cognitive value of illustration in picture books will be dealt with in Chapter 5, but the point to be emphasized here is that if you appreciate art for its own sake, there is much that you can do in your classroom to instill in your students a similar appreciation. For example, call to your students' attention particularly striking and unusual picture book illustrations. By doing so, you show them that you value art. Discuss the artist's style, the medium used (watercolor, oils, pastels, etc.), the palette (range of colors), and how the artist's style compares to the styles of other artists. Suggest using picture book art as a model for applied art lessons. By encouraging your students to use media, techniques, and topics suggested by picture book illustrations in their own artwork, you make good use of a handy, valuable resource and in yet another way show that you value this art.

From the foregoing discussion, it should be clear that students are not the only ones in schools who can benefit from children's literature. As a teacher or librarian, you will find that excellent literature is rich in social, historical, and scientific information about the world and its people and that it has great potential for developing the entire elementary and middle-school curriculum.

Children's Development and Literature

In this section we will discuss types of books and general topics most likely to be appreciated by children of different age levels. Children's physical, cognitive, language, and moral development are important considerations in book selection, as is their developing concept of story. By overlaying this general information with the specific interests of any child, you can recognize and make available literature that the children in your care will read with interest and enjoyment.

Ages 0 to 2

Infants can enjoy and benefit from good literature. In choosing books for them, consider the practical aspects of physical development, such as how well infants can see the illustrations and how long they will sit still for a book experience. Most often, these books will be collections of nursery rhymes, which are discussed in Chapter 4, and concept books, board books, and interactive books, which are discussed in Chapter 5. Common features of these book types and formats are relative simplicity of content or story; repetitive text or language patterns; clearly defined, brightly colored illustrations, usually on a plain background; physical durability; and opportunities for the child to participate or interact with the book.

A classic example of a book appropriate for children aged 0 to 2 is Dorothy Kunhardt's interactive book, *Pat the Bunny* (1962/2001). More recent examples are Harriet Ziefert's (2002) *Who Said Moo?*, illustrated by Simms Taback, an interactive board book with lift-the-flaps and language patterns and *Look at You! A Baby Body Book* by Kathy Henderson (2007), illustrated by Paul Howard.

The best baby books, whether wordless or with brief text, invite the reader and listener to "talk the book through." In this way the books promote oral language development, which is the child's first step toward literacy.

Ages 2 to 4

Many of the book types enjoyed by babies are also enjoyed by toddlers, but with slight differences in emphasis. Nursery rhymes, for example, can be committed to memory by many toddlers. Concept books can now include letters (ABC books), numbers (counting books), and more complex concepts such as opposites. Word books, another type of concept book, promote vocabulary development.

Picture storybooks featuring simple plots, illustrations that tell part of the story, and characters who exhibit the physical skills (running, whistling, buttoning clothes, tying shoes) that 2- to 4-year-olds take pride in accomplishing are appropriate for this group. A perennial favorite, *Owen* by Kevin Henkes (1993), and a more recent book, *Will Sheila Share?* by Elivia Savadier (2008), feature protagonists who overcome problems typical of children aged 2 to 4. Other books children enjoy at this stage are wordless books and folktales: the former because children can "read" the pictures and enjoy the books independently, and the latter because of their relatively simple plots, repetitive aspects, and two-dimensional, easy-to-understand characters.

Ages 4 to 7

Increasing independence and enthusiasm for finding out about the world are prominent characteristics of 4- to 7-year-olds. Stories in which children interact with other children, spend time away from home, begin school, and learn interesting facts are popular with this age group. Picture storybooks, folktales, and informational picture books will be at the heart of the literature experience during these years. Rosemary Wells's (2008) *Yoko Writes Her Name* and Marla Frazee's *A Couple of Boys Have the Best Week Ever* (2008) are excellent books for this age group. An informational book that works well with 4- to 7-year-olds is *What Do You Do with a Tail Like This?* by Steve Jenkins and Robin Page (2003).

From ages 4 to 7 most children will acquire the fundamentals of reading. Easy-to-read books or books for beginning readers make use of familiar words, word patterns, illustration clues, and, in some cases, rhyme to make the text easier to read. Often these books appear in series. It is important that books selected for beginning readers precisely match their interests and reading abilities so as not to bore or dishearten them. The classic, easy-to-read Frog and Toad series by Arnold Lobel has been enjoyed by 4- to 7-year-olds for forty years. Also noteworthy are Cynthia Rylant's two more recent easy-to-read series, Henry and Mudge and Mr. Putter and Tabby.

Ages 7 to 9

Most 7- to 9-year-old children become readers, begin to understand and accept others' perspectives, recognize that life and people do not fit into neat "good" and "bad" categories, and develop an understanding of past and future time. They begin to assert their growing abilities to meet their own needs. With these skills they can read or listen to and enjoy books about the lives of other children of the past, present, and future in picture books for older readers, transitional books, and later in novels. Fittingly, books for children aged 7 to 9 often center on the adventures of young characters within their neighborhoods and communities. Jessica Kerrin's

(2005) *Martin Bridge: Ready for Takeoff!*, Lenore Look's (2004) *Ruby Lu, Brave and True,* Sara Pennypacker's Clementine series, and Annie Barrows' Ivy and Bean series will have great appeal for children ages 7 to 9.

Ages 9 to 14

With their rapidly developing physical and mental skills and abilities, 9- to 14-year-olds are ready for more complicated story plots, including such devices as flashback, symbolism, and dialects of earlier times or different cultures. Both historical fiction and science fiction, which are set in the distant past and the distant future, respectively, can be understood and enjoyed. Equally interesting to this age group are stories about their peers who are growing up, asserting themselves, using their new-found skills, moving toward independence, and experiencing growth through meeting challenges, as in survival stories. Because their moral development allows them to recognize the legitimacy of opinions, mores, and lifestyles different from their own, these young people can enjoy stories that present alternative points of view, nontraditional characters, and moral dilemmas. Some good examples include *Esperanza Rising* (historical fiction, Hispanic culture) by Pam Muñoz Ryan (2001), *The City of Ember* (science fiction) by Jeanne DuPrau (2003), and *Red Kayak* (realistic fiction with a moral dilemma) by Priscilla Cummings (2004).

Teachers and librarians who are consistently successful in helping children find books they like rapidly narrow the field of choices by first considering general factors such as age level and types of books appropriate for children of that general age level. Then they consider more personal factors such as the child's current reading interests and reading ability to select specific titles. Knowing children's general reading preferences provides some guidance in book selection, but there is no substitute for knowing the child.

Issues&Topics for FURTHER INVESTIGATION

- In *Cushla and Her Books* Dorothy Butler chronicles the positive impact of literature on a child who is severely disabled. Read this book and reflect on the lessons it has for you and other teachers.

- For an overview of research on the effects of reading aloud to children and an example of a school intervention program that works, see Wood and Salvetti (2001). "Project Story Boost: Read-Alouds for Students at Risk" in *The Reading Teacher*, 55(1), 76–83.

- Investigate responses of teachers, school administrators, parents, and children to the controversial No Child Left Behind program. What is the nature of the controversy?

References

Anderson, R. C. (1996). Research foundations to support wide reading. In V. Greaney (Ed.), *Promoting reading: Views on making reading materials accessible to increase literacy levels* (pp. 55–77). Newark, DE: International Reading Association.

———, Hiebert, E. H., Scott, J. A., & Wilkinson, I. A. G. (1985). *Becoming a nation of readers: The report of the commission on reading.* Washington, DC: National Institute of Education.

Applebee, A. N. (1978). *The child's concept of story.* Chicago: University of Chicago.

Arya, P., Martens, P., Wilson, G. P., Altwerger, B., Jin, L., Laster, B., & Lang, D. (2005). Reclaiming literacy instruction: Evidence in support of literature-based programs. *Language Arts, 83*(1), 63–72.

Barrs, M. (2000). The reader in the writer. *Reading, 34*(2), 54–60.

Bogart, D. (Ed.). (2008). *Bowker annual: Library and book trade almanac* (53rd ed.). Medford, NJ: Information Today.

Browning, E. B. (1902). Reading. In K. D. Wiggins & N. A. Smith (Eds.), *Golden numbers.* New York: Doubleday.

Butler, D. (1975). *Cushla and her books.* Boston: Horn Book.

Cantrell, S. C. (1999). The effects of literacy instruction on primary students' reading and writing achievement. *Reading Research and Instruction, 39*(1), 3–26.

Carlsen, G. R., & Sherrill, A. (1988). *Voices of readers: How we come to love books.* Urbana, IL: National Council of Teachers of English.

Cassidy, J., & Cassidy, D. (2005). What's hot, what's not for 2006: Tenth annual survey examines key topics in reading and discusses trends over the decade. *Reading Today, 23*(3), 1, 3.

———. (2009). What's hot for 2009. *Reading Today, 26*(4), 1, 8, 9.

Children's books in print, 2009. (2008). New Providence, NJ: R. R. Bowker.

Cummings, P. (2004). *Red kayak.* New York: Dutton.

Dressel, J. H. (1990). The effects of listening to and discussing different qualities of children's literature on the narrative writing of fifth graders. *Research in the Teaching of English, 24*(4), 397–414.

Duprau, J. (2003). *The city of Ember.* New York: Random.

Durkin, D. (1966). *Children who read early.* New York: Columbia Teachers College Press.

Eldredge, J. L., & Butterfield, D. (1986). Alternatives to traditional reading instruction. *The Reading Teacher, 40,* 32–37.

Fielding, L. G., Wilson, P. T., & Anderson, R. C. (1986). A new focus on free reading: The role of trade books in reading instruction. In T. Raphael (Ed.), *The contexts of school-based literacy* (pp. 149–160). New York: Random House.

Frazee, M. (2008). *A couple of boys have the best week ever.* New York: Harcourt.

Henderson, K. (2007). *Look at you! A baby body book.* Illustrated by Paul Howard. Cambridge, MA: Candlewick.

Henkes, K. (1993). *Owen.* New York: Greenwillow.

Institute of Education Sciences National Center for Education Evaluation and Regional Assistance. (2008). *Reading First impact study: Interim report.* Retrieved from http://ies.ed.gov/ncee/pubs/20084016/execsumm_program.asp.

Ivey, G., & Broaddus, K. (2001). "Just plain reading": A survey of what makes students want to read in middle school classrooms. *Reading Research Quarterly, 36*(4), 350–377.

Jenkins, S., & Page, R. (2003). *What do you do with a tail like this?* New York: Houghton.

Kerrin, J. (2005). *Martin Bridge: Ready for takeoff!* Toronto, ON: Kids Can.

Kunhardt, D. (1962/2001). *Pat the bunny.* New York: Golden.

Lancia, P. J. (1997). Literary borrowing: The effects of literature on children's writing. *The Reading Teacher, 50*(6), 470–475.

Leinhardt, G., Zigmond, N., & Cooley, W. W. (1981). Reading instruction and its effects. *American Educational Research Journal, 18,* 343–361.

Look, L. (2004). *Ruby Lu, brave and true.* New York: Simon & Schuster.

National Reading Panel. (2000). *Teaching children to read.* NIH Publication No. 00-4769. Washington, DC: U.S. Government Printing Office.

Ryan, P. M. (2001). *Esperanza rising.* New York: Scholastic.

Savadier, E. (2008). *Will Sheila share?* New York: Roaring Brook.

Scharer, P. L., Freeman, E. B., & Lehman, B. A. (2008). Children's literature in the classroom: Essential or marginal? In S. S. Lehr (Ed.), *Shattering the looking glass: Challenge, risk and controversy in children's literature* (pp. 15–26). Norwood, MA: Christopher-Gordon.

Wells, R. (2008). *Yoko writes her name.* New York: Hyperion.

Wilson, G. P., Martens, P., Arya, P., & Altwerger, B. (2004). Readers, instruction, and the NRP. *Phi Delta Kappan, 86*(3), 242–246.

Wood, M., & Salvetti, G. P. (2001). Project story boost: Read-alouds for students at risk. *The Reading Teacher, 55*(1), 76–83.

Worthy, J., Patterson, E., Salas, R., Prater, S., & Turner, M. (2002). "More than just reading": The human factor in reaching resistant readers. *Reading Research and Instruction, 41*(2), 177–202.

Ziefert, H. (2002). *Who said moo?* Illustrated by S. Taback. Brooklyn, NY: Handprint Books.

PEARSON myeducationkit™   Now go to Chapter 1 in the MyEducationKit (www.myeducationkit.com) for your book, where you can:

- Complete Assignments and Activities that can enrich and extend your knowledge of chapter content.

- Expand your knowledge with content-specific Web Links.

- Review the chapter content by going to the Study Plan, taking a chapter quiz, and receiving feedback on your answers.

- Access the Children's Literature Database for your own exploration.

chapter TWO

Learning about Reading and Literature

My Book!

I did it!
I did it!
Come and look
At what I've done!
I read a book!
When someone wrote it
Long ago
For me to read,
How did he know
That this was the book
I'd take from the shelf

And lie on the floor
And read by myself?
I really read it!
Just like that!
Word by word,
From first to last!
I'm sleeping with
This book in bed,
This is the FIRST book
I've ever read!

—*David L. Harrison*

Teachers are fully aware that reading is the most important skill for the future success of the children they teach. Yet some teachers are unsure of literature's role in our schools and in the lives of their students. In Chapter 1 we discussed benefits to be found in literature, but given the current challenges in teaching students to read today, teachers worry that there is time for nothing else but instruction in reading.

What is the intersection between reading and literature? Reading courses provide teachers with instructional strategies that will help children learn how to read and understand what they are reading. Courses in children's literature will acquaint teachers with good-quality reading material and strategies to motivate children to read widely for practice of their reading skills and for developing into lifelong readers. Children need the reading strategies, the motivation, and the practice that literature provides to develop fully in the area of literacy. For these reasons, students in elementary education teacher preparation programs usually take coursework in reading and literature.

In this chapter we will discuss this intersection of reading and literature as it pertains to the reading process, literature in the reading curriculum, accountability and reading, independent reading, resistant readers, children's book choices, children's reading interests, difficulty of reading materials, and reading incentive programs.

Reading Process

Children learn to read at different ages and in different ways, depending on their early experiences with books, their innate abilities, and the quality of their early reading instruction. There is no absolute, lockstep method for learning to read, although some would claim otherwise and subscribe to one of the two prevailing approaches: phonics based and meaning based. Advocates of ***phonics-based reading instruction*** believe that children learn to read by progressing from letter names to letter sounds to words and, finally, to meaning. Emphasis is placed on decoding more than comprehension. Advocates of ***meaning-based reading instruction*** believe that children primarily use their oral language skills—including grammar, the structure of English, and knowledge of the world—to make meaning of written text, and resort to phonetic decoding when other meaning-making strategies fail.

We subscribe to an interactive model of reading that synthesizes aspects of both approaches. Generally, whether they are consciously taught or learn on their own, children come to know that stories can be found in books; that certain formalities, known as ***concepts of print,*** apply in reading (front-to-back, left-to-right, top-to-bottom); that letters represent sounds (sound–symbol relationships); that letters can be used to code spoken language (writing); that words convey meaning; and that finding meaning in the text (comprehension) is the goal of reading.

Literature in the Reading Curriculum

Teaching literature and teaching reading are similar in some respects. Both use similar materials (stories, poetry, plays, and informational texts); both have the purpose of making meaning from texts; and both have the ultimate goal of a greater or deeper understanding of and response to the written text. Because of these similarities, literature and reading can be, and often are, taught simultaneously in the elementary and middle grades. Inservice and preservice teachers will encounter two different approaches to literacy subscribed to in schools and teacher training institutions: the basal reader approach and the literature-based reading approach. (These two philosophies and how each may affect aspects of your teaching are outlined and described in Chapter 12.) Underlying the differences in these two approaches are the different learning theories on which each is based. Your approach to literacy development will depend on your own philosophy of teaching and learning, the ideas you believe in strongly enough to act on.

National Reading Panel Report

Using good, carefully selected literature in the classroom can support many of the findings of the National Reading Panel report (2000) that was discussed in Chapter 1. For example, use of nursery rhymes, pattern books, and poems can help children develop phonemic awareness. *Teacher read-alouds, paired reading, readers' theatre,* and *choral reading* can increase children's reading fluency by giving them models of fluent reading. *Shared reading,* with its emphasis on repeated oral reading, can teach children sound–symbol relationships and increase their reading fluency. Independent *silent reading* of good literature, especially if followed up with some reflection on what was read, can increase children's meaning vocabulary and conceptual knowledge, as well as develop their reading comprehension. For full descriptions and explanations of these strategies, see Chapter 13.

Overemphasis of any one component of reading instruction, such as phonics, to the exclusion of the others in beginning reading instruction would be detrimental to students who are learning to read. Programs advocating heavy emphasis on phonics but no daily teacher read-aloud or daily independent silent reading of excellent books of the students' own choosing should be viewed with suspicion. We strongly advocate daily read-alouds by the teacher and independent silent reading because they give students models of fluency, build meaning vocabulary and conceptual knowledge, offer reading practice, and improve students' attitudes toward reading. As students' reading ability grows, logic would suggest (despite the dictates of any scripted reading program teacher's manual) that teachers shift their emphasis from letter and word decoding toward strategies that involve reading actual stories, poems, and plays. It is important to note that reading aloud and independent silent reading are *not* substitutes for direct reading instruction, however. Primary- and intermediate-grade schedules should include all three every day.

Accountability and Reading

Accountability is a demand by government agencies and the public for school systems and teachers to improve students' school achievement as demonstrated by test scores in the areas of reading, writing, and mathematics. This trend began in the 1980s at the local school district level, then expanded to the state level in many locations, and, with the enactment of the No Child Left Behind Act (NCLB) in 2002, became an important part of federal policy in education. The NCLB Act expanded the original notion of accountability in two important ways: Annual testing of reading and mathematics achievement for all students in grades 3 to 8 became mandatory; and performance data had to be disaggregated according to race, gender, income (as measured by free and reduced-price lunch), and other criteria to demonstrate progress in closing the achievement gap between disadvantaged students and other groups of students.

Under NCLB, each school is graded as Pass or Fail, depending on student achievement by averages for the grade and by subgroups. Schools that receive failing grades are given a period of time to improve student achievement. Failure of a school to do so can result in reduced federal and state funding for the school, vouchers for students to attend another public school or charter school in the case of repeated failures by the school, or replacement of administrators and teachers, depending on state and local policies. States develop the actual tests used, the procedures for implementation of the policy, and timetables for implementation according to federal requirements.

From its inception, NCLB has garnered widespread criticism.

Critics claim that the law's focus on complicated tallies of multiple-choice-test scores has dumbed down the curriculum, fostered a "drill and kill" approach to teaching, mistakenly labeled successful schools as failing, driven teachers and middle-class students out of public schools and harmed special education students and English-language learners through inappropriate assessments and efforts to push out low-scoring students in order to boost scores. Indeed, recent analyses have found that rapid gains in education outcomes stimulated by reforms in the 1990s have stalled under NCLB, with math increases slowing and reading on the decline. (Darling-Hammond, 2007, p. 11)

In light of such criticism, reauthorization of NCLB has been postponed until lawmakers can agree on how to revise it. Although we too question the reliability of a score on a single test as the predominant measure of a student's progress or a teacher's success over the course of a school year, this is the reality educators currently face and within which they must operate. Because it directly affects students, teachers, schools, and school systems, accountability is a high priority issue in education.

The curricular area that is of most concern to parents, teachers, and school administrators is reading, due to its importance for learning in all subjects and because reading scores have been in general decline across the nation for the last twenty-five years, especially at fourth grade through high school levels. The National Association of Educational Progress tracks these trends in reading achievement and reports them in its "Nation's Report Card." Data showing these trends can be seen at http://nationsreportcard.gov/reading_math_grade12_2005/s0203.asp. We believe that a major reason for the decline in reading scores is a decrease in voluntary reading among our students. Partially as a result of NCLB, a large of amount of class time is spent emphasizing basic beginning reading skills, diminishing curricular efforts traditionally spent on other subjects, including the enjoyment and appreciation of literature. Many young people have lost the reading habit.

Reading at Risk: A Survey of Literary Reading in America

Voluntary reading of literature in the United States has been monitored by the Research Division of the U.S. Bureau of the Census and the National Endowment for the Arts (NEA) since 1982. From then until 2002, NEA reports showed a steady decline in voluntary reading across all age groups in the United States, but particularly among the youngest group surveyed, 18- to 24-year-olds. Although the NEA's 2008 report, "Reading on the Rise: A New Chapter in American Literacy" (www.arts.gov/research/Research_brochures.php), has since then shown growth in voluntary reading across all age groups (based on absolute numbers), it is important to note that when the nation's population growth from 2002 to 2008 is factored in, the percentage of 18- to 24-year-old Americans who read declined from 52 percent in 2002 to 50.7 percent in 2008. Moreover, our students do not compare favorably with those in other developed nations, as the Programme for International Student Assessment (PISA; http://nces.ed.gov/surveys/pisa) 2000, 2003, and 2006 reports on the reading, mathematics, and science literacy of 15-year-olds have demonstrated.

The NEA's 2004 report found a correlation between the decline in reading and increased participation in a variety of electronic media, including the Internet, video games, and portable digital devices (Bradshaw & Nichols, 2004, pp. xi–xii). Despite the 9 percent growth in reading from 2002 to 2008 among 18- to 24-year-olds (based on absolute numbers) reported by the NEA in 2008, we believe that it is too early to detect or claim a lasting trend toward more voluntary reading, and we doubt that the use or appeal of electronic media will diminish. It is, nonetheless, important to try to understand the reasons behind the growth in voluntary reading as reported by the NEA in 2008. Dana Gioia, chairman of the NEA, offers the following explanation: "Faced by a clear and undeniable problem, millions of parents, teachers, librarians, and civic leaders took action (inspired by thousands of journalists and scholars who publicized the issues at stake). Reading became a higher priority in families, schools, and communities. Thousands of programs, large and small, were created or significantly enhanced to address the challenge" (www.arts.gov/research/Research_brochures.php, p. 2).

Other findings of the 2008 NEA report of interest to teachers and librarians include the following:

- Young adults read books at a slightly lower rate than older adults, but they also did more reading online than older Americans.
- Greater reading of fiction was responsible for the new growth in adult literary readers.

Much more than falling reading scores and a loss of accountability is at stake when people stop reading voluntarily. Commenting on the effects of a decline in literacy, Dana Gioia, NEA chairman, states that "print culture affords irreplaceable forms of focused attention and contemplation that makes complex communications and insights possible. To lose such intellectual capacity—and the many sorts of human continuity it allows—would constitute a vast cultural impoverishment." He goes on to state that "readers play a more active and involved role in their communities. . . . [A] decline in reading, therefore, parallels a larger retreat from participation in civic and cultural life. The long-term implications of [a decline in literacy] not only affect literature but all of the arts—as well as social activities such as volunteerism, philanthropy, and even political engagement." He concludes by saying, "Advanced literacy is a specific intellectual skill and social habit that depends on a great many educational, cultural, and economic factors. As more Americans lose this capability, our nation becomes less informed, active, and independent-minded. These are not qualities that a free, innovative, or productive society can afford to lose" (Bradshaw & Nichols, 2004, p. vii).

It is little wonder that teachers feel pressured by the demands of accountability to improve their students' reading ability when the population in general is moving away from reading. How do we inspire children to love reading and to become aware of its power to inform, entertain, educate, and change? How do we instill in them the reading habit?

Regardless of students' reading ability, promoting reading is often a matter of helping students select appropriate reading materials. Note the success of various television programs, from *Reading Rainbow* to *Oprah Winfrey,* in convincing people to read books being discussed by saying, "I read this book and loved it. I recommend it to you." To be a successful promoter of reading, you yourself must be a reader. Recommending a book that you have enjoyed is an effective reading motivator. In light of the NEA's "Reading on the Rise" report, there is hope that curricular changes, programs, and strategies as outlined above may have positive results and that students may regain the reading habit.

Independent Reading and Societal Changes

Independent reading—that is, free-choice reading, including sustained silent reading, done voluntarily in and out of school—has been in decline among children and young adults in this country for several decades (Bradshaw & Nichols, 2004; McKenna, Ellsworth, & Kear, 1995; Shapiro & White, 1991). Some national studies report that more than half of today's young people do not engage in independent reading (Bradshaw & Nichols, 2004). This trend is cause for concern, because research findings show that time spent reading correlates with reading achievement (Anderson, Wilson, & Fielding, 1988; Garan & Devoogd, 2008; Krashen, 2005; Moore, Bean, Birdyshaw, & Rycik, 1999; Topping, Samuels, & Paul, 2007) and with attitudes toward reading (Yoon, 2002). Research findings also show that reading practice helps to strengthen the skills learned through reading instruction and that the reading skills of those who do not engage in recreational reading, including good readers, often erode over time (Anderson et al., 1988; Mullis, Campbell, & Farstrup, 1993; Stanovich, 1986).

By the time they are in intermediate and middle-school grades, many children have been turned off from reading. Most often, these students cite irrelevance of teacher-selected reading materials to their lives, disliked instructional practices, too little time, peer pressure, past failures, a preference for electronic media, and a perception of reading as hard work as reasons for not reading. Consequently, the greatest challenge for teachers and librarians who work in primary grades is to provide solid skills instruction and inspire children to love to read and to read voluntarily and regularly. Intermediate-grade teachers must continue these efforts and overcome students' resistance to reading by locating materials appealing to them and by finding ways to get them to read widely and intensively, both at school and at home. (See Padak & Rasinski, 2007.) Teachers and parents need to convince young people of the importance of independent reading and be determined and persistent in guiding them to read better and read more. This determination is essential if we want students to become readers.

Resistant Readers

Children and adolescents resist or reject reading for many different reasons. We will use the term *resistant readers* for young people who can read but choose not to. We have identified five main groups of resistant readers.

Good to Average Readers Who Choose Not to Read

Some children who have good to excellent comprehension, few difficulties in decoding, and average reading rates by third or fourth grade rarely read or do not like to read. They include males and females of all ethnic, racial, and socioeconomic groups. With little or no reading practice, these children eventually lose their former reading achievement levels.

Reasons for this turn of events are multiple: Children perceive the books they must read in school to be irrelevant to their lives and therefore boring. They lack encouragement at home to read for recreational reasons. They seldom or never go to public or school libraries to select books for their reading enjoyment, because the emphasis by their teachers and parents is almost exclusively on improving their reading levels. Neither their parents nor their teachers serve as reading role models, nor do they persist in their efforts to foster a love of reading in these children. Tests and test scores take on tremendous importance to the detriment of other aspects of reading. Yet, in the long run, a passing test score is only a starting point, not an end goal.

Struggling Readers

Struggling readers are those children who struggled with reading from the earliest grades and became discouraged. Most of them can decode, but this skill remains a conscious cognitive act rather than an automatic process. The act of concentrating on decoding words slows the reading rate and fluency of these children, hampers their ability to recall what they have read to make sense of the text, and tires them mentally. Others in this group are fluent decoders who have difficulty comprehending what they read. Experiencing ridicule by their peers and embarrassment in class for their reading difficulties has taught them to avoid reading whenever possible. These are the children for whom regular reading practice is especially important to maintain and improve reading levels.

Ethnic and Racial Minorities Who Resist Reading

Some members of *ethnic and racial minorities* resist reading because of school instructional practices, teacher perceptions, low socioeconomic status, and self-perceptions molded by a cultural disbelief in the importance of intellectual development (Gilbert & Gilbert, 1998; Maynard, 2002; Tatum, 2005). The National Assessment for Educational Progress, since its inception in 1992, has reported a continuing reading achievement gap between whites and Asian Americans on the one hand and American Indians, Hispanics, and African Americans on the other. In 2005, the average reading scores for white and Asian-American eighth-graders was 271 versus 249 for American Indians, 246 for Hispanics, and 243 for African Americans (National Center for Education Statistics, 2005).

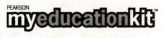

Go to Activity 1 in the Assignments and Activities section of Chapter 2 in MyEducationKit; view the video on English language learners and respond to the questions.

English Language Learners Who Resist Reading

Students learning English as a second language sometimes encounter difficulties in reading. Because they lack strong vocabularies and well-developed sentence structures in English to draw on when encountering English language texts, and because the texts they are asked to read often portray unfamiliar experiences and cultural norms, they have difficulty reading, so they avoid it whenever possible. This group is large and growing. In 2000, about three and a half million children between the ages of 5 and 17 in the United States spoke English less than "very well" (U.S. Census Bureau, 2000).

Boys Who Resist Reading

Boys who resist reading may do so in part because of the preponderance of female teachers in U.S. schools (75% in grades K–12) who tend to select reading materials that do not necessarily appeal to boys, according to Brozo (2005) and Sullivan (2003). Their resistance to reading also may stem from the perception that reading, because it is quiet and passive, is a female activity, or at least not macho. On average, boys exhibit more difficulty in reading and other language areas than girls (National Center for Education Statistics, 2005; Sullivan, 2003).

Not all young people who dislike reading school-based materials are resistant readers. Some, in fact, are avid readers, but of materials that schools do not traditionally recognize, such as magazines, Internet websites, and informational books (Taylor, 2004). Some boys, in particular, fit this profile. Four informative sources about boys and their reading are *Reading Don't Fix No Chevys: Literacy in the Lives of Young Men* (Smith & Wilhelm, 2002); *Teaching Reading to Black Adolescent Males: Closing the Achievement Gap* (Tatum, 2005); *Reluctant Readers: Connecting Students and Books for Successful Reading Experiences* (Jobe & Dayton-Sakari, 1999); and *Connecting Boys with Books 2: Closing the Reading Gap* (Sullivan, 2009).

How do we inspire young people to love reading and to become aware of its power to inform, entertain, educate, and change? How do we instill in them the reading habit?

Assisting Students in Book Selection

The aim of teachers, librarians, and publishers is to bring students to the reading habit by placing in their hands reading materials that will interest and not intimidate them. Publishers, aware of falling test scores in reading and the demand of the public and policymakers for schools to reverse this trend, have produced books written specifically for low-level readers. These include easy-to-read books for beginning readers and transitional books, generally short novels of about 100 pages with high-interest topics.

The points made about quality and content of literature at the beginning of Chapter 1 definitely play a part in any book selection for children. In addition, you will want to consider the following suggestions.

Know the Books

Teachers and librarians who read children's books regularly, who are familiar with a wide variety of genres, and who are informed about recently published books are likely able to interest children in books. In Chapter 3, ways to interpret literature and the elements of fiction will be reviewed in order to assist you in thinking about and evaluating the books you are reading. It is advantageous to have read widely and to be able to share and compare your reactions to a book with children. Other ways to become familiar with a variety of genres include sharing information about books with your fellow teachers and reading book reviews. Chapter 3 lists the major book review journals.

Your own reading program can be made more effective by focusing on award-winning and notable books, as well as those selected for their appeal to individual children under your care. After you have read a number of books from a genre, particularly notable examples, you will develop a framework for thinking about books of that kind, whether or not you have read an individual title. You will, of course, want to have read any book you plan to read aloud to a class.

Know the Child

The best teachers know their students well. For instance, you will find it helpful to know your students—their long-term and short-term interests, their home environment (family makeup, siblings, pets), their friends and social activities, their hobbies, their skills (athletic, academic, artistic), their hopes or plans for the future, and the kind of books they are currently selecting in free-choice situations, such as during library visits and while perusing classroom collections of trade books. Children's interests have been shown to be one of the most powerful motivating forces available to teachers. Because there are now books on almost every topic conceivable and written at varying degrees of difficulty, you should be able to assemble a collection of books from which your students can make satisfying selections.

You will also want to have a grasp of your students' reading and listening levels. Often, children's abilities to read and listen are on different levels. Young children, in particular, are able to listen to and comprehend more difficult material than they are able to read and comprehend. This difference is one that teachers accommodate by reading aloud more challenging books and providing a choice of easier reading material for students' independent reading.

Research on Children's Reading Interests

Research studies on reading interest, reading preference, and reading choice provide useful information to those who purchase books for children and those who encourage them to read the books. Although the terms to describe the various studies and the procedures used in conducting the studies may vary, the studies are trying to infer what students like to read. Generally, a *reading interest* suggests a feeling one has toward particular reading material; a *reading preference* implies making a choice from two or more options; a *reading choice* study investigates "print materials selected and read from a predetermined collection" (Chance, 1999, p. 65). The studies do not always provide an opportunity for students to express their interests. If, for example, the options do not include illustrated books, then students will not be able to select illustrated books. Although the findings from this body of research can be useful, it is important to realize that the results of these studies are based on group data or aggregated data and reflect the reading interests of groups of students, not individuals.

Many studies of children's reading interests have been conducted during the past fifty years. Differences in the choices offered to children and in the ways data were gathered from study to study make extensive generalization difficult, but a few patterns have emerged from these studies:

- There are no significant differences between the reading preferences of boys and girls before age 9.
- The greatest differences in reading preferences of boys and girls occur between ages 10 and 13.
- Boys and girls in the middle grades (ages 10 to 13) share a pronounced preference for mystery and, to a lesser degree, humor, adventure, and animals.
- Preferences of boys in the middle grades include nonfiction, adventure, sports, science fiction, and fantasy stories.
- Preferences of girls in the middle grades include fantasy stories, animal stories, romance, and stories about people.

Certain characteristics of books may matter as much to a young reader as the topic. According to reports (Carter & Harris, 1982; Langerman, 1990; Worthy, 1996; Worthy, Moorman, & Turner, 1999; Worthy, Patterson, Salas, Prater, & Turner, 2002; Worthy, Turner, & Moorman, 1998) and our own observations in working with children, consideration needs to be given to the following characteristics:

- Short books or books with short sections or chapters
- Picture books, illustrated books, comic books, and novels in which illustrations are interspersed throughout the book
- Cover illustrations that suggest the topic of the story
- Episodic plots
- Progressive chronological plots that can be easily followed
- Quick start to the story with action beginning on the first or second page to hook the reader
- Rapid introduction to main characters and only a few main characters
- Characters the age of the reader or slightly older
- Books based on movies and television

In addition, trivia books such as the *Guinness Book of World Records* and *The Dangerous Book for Boys* (Iggulden & Iggulden, 2007), sports statistics books, joke books, and game system guides for video and computer games are very appealing to some boys. Although you will want to motivate your students to enjoy books of excellent quality, the first step is to create an enthusiasm about books and reading. Once they are willing readers, then you can find many opportunities to book-talk and read aloud excellent books that they will come to love and want to read independently.

A teacher or librarian might use the foregoing information to make general predictions about what types of books students of a certain age might enjoy. However, it is inadvisable to depend on the findings of reading interest studies as the sole guide in making specific book recommendations to individuals. General reading preferences do not capture individual reading interests. Knowledge of children's reading interests is personal and individual. Since most teachers and school librarians work with particular groups of children over an extended time, they can learn the interests of each child within the group. In doing this, they gain powerful, effective knowledge to use in successfully matching children and books.

Discovering Reading Interests of Individual Students

Learning your students' reading interests can be accomplished in several ways. One effective method is observing your students' choices of books from the classroom collection or from the school library media center collection and then noting their choices by jotting down authors and titles of books selected. These notes can give you insight to their preferences. Getting to know your students by talking and listening to them in whole-class sharing and in one-to-one conferences are other effective means. All people like to talk about themselves and what interests them, and children are no exception. One or more of the following questions might start a productive dialogue between you and a student:

1. Who is in your family? Tell me about each family member.
2. What are your favorite things to do?
3. Are you very good at doing something? Tell me about it.
4. What would you like to learn more about?
5. What do you like to spend most of your free time doing?
6. Do you like fiction (stories) or nonfiction (information books) better?
7. What kinds of stories do you like to hear?
8. Which subjects do you enjoy reading about in information books?
9. Are there some kinds of books you don't enjoy reading? If so, why?
10. Tell me about a book that you especially enjoyed and why you enjoyed it.

You can also learn about children's interests through their free-choice writing. Journal writing is particularly helpful in this regard. A perfectly valid and more direct approach is to ask children to list their interests or the type of books they like to read. Many teachers keep such lists in their students' writing folders to use during individual conferences.

Yet another way for teachers and librarians to keep current on students' reading interests is to conduct their own *reading interest inventories* several times a year. The following steps show one way to conduct a classroom reading interest inventory:

1. Collect thirty to forty appropriate books that are new to your students and represent a wide variety of genres and topics.
2. Number the books by inserting paper markers with numbers at the top.
3. Note on a master list the number and genre of each book.
4. Design a response form for students, such as the one in Figure 2.1.
5. Place the books in numerical order on tables and shelves around the classroom or media center.
6. Give the students twenty to thirty minutes to make the circuit, peruse the books, and mark their response forms.
7. Collect and tally the students' responses and compare to your master list to arrive at the types of books in which your students are currently most interested.

Figure 2.1   Sample Student Response Form for Reading Interest Inventory

Would You Like to Read This Book?

As you look at each book, answer this question by circling either YES or NO next to the appropriate book number. Be sure to match the book number and the item number before circling your answer. You will not be required to read the books, but your answers will help me select books that you will like for our classroom.

1. YES   NO
2. YES   NO
3. YES   NO
4. YES   NO
5. YES   NO

Classroom reading interest inventories as demonstrated here not only provide teachers and librarians with helpful information about their students' current interests, but they also have the added advantage of introducing children to new genres, topics, and actual titles. Many students will discover a book that they will want to read from the books set out in this manner. Teachers and librarians help accomplish the fundamental tasks of guiding students to good books and expanding their fields of interest and their knowledge bases.

Common sense tells us that children will apply themselves more vigorously to reading or learning something that they are interested in than something that they find uninteresting or boring. Interest generates motivation, and good teachers and librarians put that motivation to work by guiding students to good books on topics that satisfy their individual interests.

Judging the Difficulty of Reading Materials

Two features of books for teachers and librarians to consider are the readability and conceptual difficulty of books. *Readability* is an estimate of a text's difficulty based on its vocabulary (common versus uncommon words) and sentence structure (short, simple sentences versus long, complex sentences). *Conceptual difficulty* pertains to the complexity of ideas treated in the work and how these ideas are presented. Symbolism, abstraction, and lengthy description contribute to the complexity of ideas, just as the use of flashback or shifting points of view contribute to the complexity of plot presentation.

Students' reading levels differ greatly in most classrooms, making it important to provide materials of varying difficulty. Being able to assess the difficulty of reading materials can be helpful to teachers and librarians, especially when locating lower-level materials. However, for independent, leisure reading, students should be encouraged to read books of interest to them regardless of the level, so long as they are capable of comprehending the material and want to read it. As adults, we do not decide to not read a book because it is too easy for us; we should accord the same courtesy to young readers for their leisure reading if we wish to motivate them to be readers.

The long-standing system that has been used in education to assign reading levels to books has been readability formulas, such as the Fry Readability Graph (http://school.discovery education.com/schrockguide/fry/fry.html) and the Lexile Framework (www.lexile.com; Schnick, 2000). *Readability* is defined as "the ease of comprehension because of style of writing" (Harris & Hodges, 1995, p. 203). Syntactic length and vocabulary difficulty are usually measured by a variety of means that vary by readability formula. Generally, texts with shorter, less complex sentences and a predominance of common, high-frequency words, such as *because, little,* and *everyone,* are rated as easier to comprehend. Readability is expressed as a grade level (6.4 = sixth grade, fourth month) or as an age level (11.5 = eleven years and five months) and refers to the approximate grade or age at which an average individual will be able to read the text with comprehension. For example, using the Fry Readability Graph, we estimate that the well-known classic, *Charlotte's Web* (White, 1952), is written at a 5.3 grade level and a 10.4 age level. Using the same formula, we estimate that the Caldecott Award–winning picture book, *The Stray Dog* (Simont, 2001), is written at a 2.1 grade level and an 8.0 age level.

Publishers sometimes place readability information on book covers; some databases also include reading levels. Basal reading programs and reading incentive programs, such as *Accelerated Reader,* grade the books for student reading by such formulas. They tend to use different formulas, however, depending on the publisher.

A teacher who looks carefully at a book can assess its difficulty without using a formula, and most teachers do this with practice. Select a page of uninterrupted text, read the first sentence, count the words in the sentence, then look to see if this length appears to be typical of the rest of the page. Are the sentences generally short or long? Then read the page for word difficulty, noting words your students will likely not know. Are there many or few such words? Readers can, of course, figure out unknown words through context, if they are infrequent. You can estimate a book's difficulty in this way.

Readability is an issue only when the text is at such a high level that the reader cannot comprehend it. The challenge is to find materials for those students whose reading levels are lower. For this, we return to the experts, individual students, in determining what they can read. The teacher can help students decide whether books are too difficult for them by encouraging them to open a book they are considering reading to a middle page and reading through it while counting the number of words they do not understand or cannot read. If they count more than five or six words they cannot read or do not know out of every 100 words, they may want to choose a different book.

Readability formulas may be helpful to teachers, librarians, and parents in selecting books but they are not without their drawbacks. Different readability formulas give different estimates for the same book, so at best they give only a broad estimate of difficulty. Although the two factors of syntactic complexity and word choice are important, other factors make an important difference. A student's prior knowledge on a particular topic cannot be factored into any formula, nor can a student's interest in a topic be measured by formula. Yet we know that students' interest and background knowledge are central to their willingness to read and their ability to comprehend a text.

Conceptual difficulty is another factor not included in a readability formula. Conceptual difficulty pertains to the complexity of the ideas treated in the work and to how these ideas are presented. Symbolism, abstraction, and figurative language contribute to the complexity of ideas, just as the use of nonlinear plots or shifting points of view contribute to the complexity of plot presentation. Consider *Skellig* (Almond, 1999), a work of magical realism in which two young persons become involved with an otherworldly being who is hidden in a garage. The text, having easy vocabulary and short sentences, has a readability of about grade 3.5. Yet the concepts of spirituality, faith, and prejudice cast the conceptual level of this novel at a much higher level, probably appropriate for students aged 11 to 15.

Reading Incentive Programs

Many elementary and middle schools have purchased commercially produced *reading incentive programs* to motivate students to read more widely. Generally, these programs have computerized management components to track students' progress on the tests. These programs, such as *Accelerated Reader,* include a pretest for assigning a reading level to each student for a certain level of books that have a predetermined number of points according to their difficulty as determined by the program developers. After students finish reading a book silently, they complete a multiple-choice test to assess literal comprehension of the book and to earn points based on their score. Students earn prizes according to their performance.

PEARSON
myeducationkit™

Go to Activity 2 in the Assignments and Activities section of Chapter 2 in MyEducationKit; complete the activity on reading incentive programs.

Reports on the success of such programs are mixed. Many teachers and schools report disappointment in the programs. Teachers need to be cautious about whether such programs are having a positive impact on their students' interest in reading. Concerns include the following:

- Students' free choices of books for reading are limited.
- Students value only books in the program's database due to the reward system.
- Extrinsic rewards can diminish the desire of students to read for the pleasure of reading.
- Testing students' literal comprehension can undermine the importance of reading books for vicarious experiences.
- Tests of literal comprehension often emphasize inconsequential material to the detriment of the development of critical thinking in students.
- Many students find ways to gain the rewards without reading the books—for example, by asking other students for the answers, skimming the books for frequently tested details, and seeing the movie.
- Personal enjoyment of literature and reading is often deemphasized.
- These programs are very costly and could be replaced by simply purchasing ample trade books for classroom use and school libraries. The program selections can soon become dated, necessitating additional expenditures.

Teachers can design their own reading incentive programs that avoid these drawbacks and still help students develop as independent readers. In these teacher-developed programs, students usually keep a record of their own free-choice silent reading, have opportunities to respond to books in a variety of ways on a regular basis, and work to achieve individual silent reading goals set by the student and the teacher together. Rewards, such as a special celebration party, are provided for the class for reading, as a group, more total pages or books than were read during the last grading period. Such group rewards avoid the negative consequences of highly competitive programs.

Issues&Topics for FURTHER INVESTIGATION

■ Conduct a reading interest inventory like one shown in this chapter. Analyze your findings, then suggest to individual children appropriate titles for independent reading from books available in the school.

■ Observe and document the reading habits and literary selections of three children over a period of several weeks. Select one avid reader, one typical reader, and one resistant reader for your observations.

■ Consider the effects of NCLB on the schools and education of students in your state. What are the pros and cons of this federal policy in your area? How do you expect this policy to affect you as a teacher?

☆References

Almond, D. (1999). *Skellig.* New York: Delacorte.

Anderson, R., Wilson, P., & Fielding, L. (1988). Growth in reading and how children spend their time outside of school. *Reading Research Quarterly, 23*(3), 285–303.

Bradshaw, T., & Nichols, B. (2004). *Reading at risk: A survey of literary reading in America.* Research Division Report #46. Washington, DC: National Endowment for the Arts.

Brozo, W. G. (2005). Gender and reading literacy. *Reading Today, 22*(4), 18.

Carter, B., & Harris, K. (1982). What junior high students like in books. *Journal of Reading 26*(1), 42–46.

Chance, R. (1999). A portrait of popularity: An analysis of characteristics of novels from Young Adults' Choices for 1997. *The ALAN Review, 27*(1), 65–68.

Darling-Hammond, L. (2007). Evaluating "No Child Left Behind." *The Nation, 284*(20), 11–21.

Garan, E. M., & Devoogd, G. (2008). The benefits of sustained silent reading: Scientific research and common sense converge. *The Reading Teacher, 62*(4), 336–344.

Gilbert, R., & Gilbert, P. (1998). *Masculinity goes to school.* New York: Routledge.

Harris, T. L., & Hodges, R. E. (1995). *The literacy dictionary: The vocabulary of reading and writing.* Newark, DE: International Reading Association.

Harrison, D. L. (1993). My book! In D. L. Harrison (Ed.), *Somebody catch my homework.* Illustrated by Betsy Lewin. Honesdale, PA: Boyds Mills.

Iggulden, C., & Iggulden, H. (2007). *The dangerous book for boys.* New York: Morrow.

Jobe, R., & Dayton-Sakari, M. (1999). *Reluctant readers: Connecting students and books for successful reading experiences.* Markham, ON: Pembroke.

Krashen, S. (2005). A special section on reading research—Is in school free reading good for children? Why the National Reading Panel Report is (still) wrong. *Phi Delta Kappan, 86*(6), 444.

Langerman, D. (1990). Books and boys: Gender preferences and book selection. *School Library Journal 36*(3), 132–136.

Maynard, T. (2002). *Boys and literacy: Exploring the issues.* New York: Routledge.

McKenna, M., Ellsworth, R., & Kear, D. (1995). Children's attitudes toward reading: A national survey. *Reading Research Quarterly, 30*(4), 934–957.

Moore, D. W., Bean, T. W., Birdyshaw, D., & Rycik, J. A. (1999). *Adolescent literacy: A position statement.* Newark, DE: International Reading Association.

Mullis, I., Campbell, J., & Farstrup, A. (1993). *NAEP 1992: Reading report card for the nation and states.* Washington, DC: U.S. Department of Education.

National Center for Education Statistics. (2005). *The nation's report card: Reading 2005.* Retrieved from http://nces.ed.gov/nationsreportcard/pdf/main 2005.

National Endowment for the Arts. (2008). *Reading on the rise: A new chapter in American literacy.* Retrieved from www.arts.gov/research/Research_brochures.php.

National Reading Panel. (2000). *Teaching children to read.* NIH Publication No. 00-4769. Washington, DC: U.S. Government Printing Office.

Padak, N., & Rasinski, T. (2007). Is being wild about Harry enough? Encouraging independent reading at home. *The Reading Teacher, 61*(4), 350–353.

Schnick, T. (2000). *The Lexile framework: An introduction for educators.* Durham, NC: MetaMetrics.

Shapiro, J., & White, W. (1991). Reading attitudes and perceptions in traditional and nontraditional reading programs. *Reading Research and Instruction, 30*(4), 52–66.

Simont, M. (2001). *The stray dog.* New York: Harper-Collins.

Smith, M. W., & Wilhelm, J. D. (2002). *Reading don't fix no Chevys: Literacy in the lives of young men.* Portsmouth, NH: Heinemann.

Stanovich, K. E. (1986). Matthew effects in reading: Some consequences of individual differences in the acquisition of literacy. *Reading Research Quarterly, 21*(4), 360–407.

Sullivan, M. (2003). *Connecting boys with books: What libraries can do.* Chicago: American Library Association.

Sullivan, M. (2009). *Connecting boys with books 2: Closing the reading gap.* Chicago: American Library Association.

Tatum, A. (2005). *Teaching reading to black adolescent males: Closing the achievement gap.* Portland, ME: Stenhouse.

Taylor, D. L. (2004). "Not just boring stories": Reconsidering the gender gap for boys. *Journal of Adolescent & Adult Literacy, 48*(4), 290–298.

Topping, K. J., Samuels, J., & Paul, T. (2007). Does practice make perfect? Independent reading quantity, quality, and student achievement. *Learning and Instruction, 17*(3), 253–264.

United States Census Bureau. (2000). Retrieved from www.census.gov.

White, E. B. (1952). *Charlotte's web.* Illustrated by G. Williams. New York: Harper.

Worthy, J. (1996). Removing barriers to voluntary reading: The role of school and classroom libraries. *Language Arts, 73,* 483–492.

———, Moorman, M., & Turner, M. (1999). What Johnny likes to read is hard to find in school. *Reading Research Quarterly, 34*(1), 12–27.

———, Patterson, E., Salas, R., Prater, S., & Turner, M. (2002). "More than just reading": The human factor in reaching resistant readers. *Reading Research and Instruction, 41*(2), 177–202.

———, Turner, M., & Moorman, M. (1998). The precarious place of free-choice reading. *Language Arts, 75,* 296–304.

Yoon, J.-C. (2002). Three decades of sustained silent reading: A meta-analytic review of the effects of SSR on attitude toward reading. *Reading Improvement, 39*(4), 186–195.

PEARSON myeducationkit™ Now go to Chapter 2 in the MyEducationKit (www.myeducationkit .com) for your book, where you can:

- Complete Assignments and Activities that can enrich and extend your knowledge of chapter content.

- Expand your knowledge with content-specific Web Links.

- Review the chapter content by going to the Study Plan, taking a chapter quiz, and receiving feedback on your answers.

- Access the Children's Literature Database for your own exploration.

chapter THREE

Learning about Literature

A Book

I'm a strange contradiction; I'm new and I'm old,
I'm often in tatters, and oft deck'd in gold;
Though I never could read, yet letter'd I'm found;
Though blind, I enlighten; though loose, I am bound—
I am always in black, and I'm always in white;
I am grave and I'm gay, I am heavy and light.
In form too I differ—I'm thick and I'm thin,
I've no flesh, and no bones, yet I'm covered with skin;
I've more points than the compass, more stops than the flute—
I sing without voice, without speaking confute;
I'm English, I'm German, I'm French and I'm Dutch;
Some love me too fondly; some slight me too much;
I often die soon, though I sometimes live ages,
And no monarch alive has so many pages.

—*Hannah More*

This chapter provides background information on literature, including how to study and interpret literature, and reviews the elements of fiction useful in literary evaluation. Also discussed are sources available for identifying good books, including major children's book awards, review journals, and professional websites. The chapter ends with a discussion of the reasons to select a varied and balanced array of literature for use with children.

Approaches to Studying and Interpreting Literature

The scholarly study of literature generally focuses on the meaning found in a work of literature and how readers construct that meaning. When readers subject a work to deep analysis through exact and careful reading, it is referred to as *New Criticism* or *structural criticism.* In this approach, the analysis of the words and structure of a work is the focus; the goal is to find the "correct" interpretation.

Until the 1960s, structural criticism held sway in most literature classrooms. Many teachers continue to use this method today. Most teachers using this approach take the view that there is one correct interpretation of any work of literature. According to this view, reading is a process of taking from the text only what was put there by the author. Young readers' success with any work of literature is determined by how closely their interpretations match the "authorized" interpretation. Students' responses to literature are thus limited to naming (or guessing) the "right" answers to teachers' questions.

In 1938, Louise Rosenblatt introduced *reader response theory* or the *transactional view of reading.* She asserted that what the reader brings to the reading act—his or her world of experience, personality, and current frame of mind—is just as important in interpreting the text as what the author writes. According to this view, reading is a fusion of text and reader. Consequently, any text's meaning will vary from reader to reader and, indeed, from reading to reading of the same text by the same reader. Almost everyone has experienced reading a book only to discover that a friend has reacted to or interpreted the same book quite differently. Although Rosenblatt (1978) points out that the text of any book guides and constrains the interpretation that is made, an important corollary to her view of reading is that personal interpretations, within reason, are valid, permissible, and in fact desirable.

Beach and Marshall (1990) similarly point out the importance of students' worlds of experience, including (1) knowledge of various genres and literary forms gained from previous reading that can help them understand new, similar works; (2) social relationships that can help them understand and evaluate book characters' actions and motivations; (3) cultural knowledge that influences one's attitudes toward self and others (as in gender roles) and can help readers understand their responses to story events; and (4) topic knowledge or knowledge of the world that can deepen readers' understanding of a text and enrich their response to it.

Another interesting aspect of Rosenblatt's theory is that reading is done for two distinct purposes: to take knowledge from the text *(efferent reading)* and to live through a literary experience, in the sense of assuming the identity of a book character *(aesthetic reading).* Whether people read efferently or aesthetically depends on what they are reading (e.g., a want ad versus a mystery novel) and why they are reading it (e.g., for information versus for pleasure).

Rosenblatt's view of reading has important implications for the way teachers will encourage their students to respond to the literature they share with them. Reader response theory, in accepting different interpretations of the same literary work, accommodates both traditional, genre-specific works as well as genre-eclectic, nonlinear literature with its multiple perspectives and plots and its demands on the reader to act as coauthor. (See Chapter 13 for a detailed discussion, suggestions, and explanations of literature-related response activities.)

Reading is a merging of text and reader, and each reading of a particular literary work results in a different transaction. But if the transaction is unique each time a book is read, how can general assessments of literary merit be made? Rosenblatt believes that although the notion of a single, correct reading of a literary work is rejected, *"given agreed-upon criteria,* it is possible to decide that some readings are more defensible than others" (1985, p. 36). Although each reading of a given literary work will be different, there are certain generally agreed-on interpretations of that work by a community of educated readers.

Traditional literary elements are reviewed next in order to heighten your awareness of literary criticism and to provide a more precise vocabulary for you to express your responses to children's books. Literary terms may also be considered as tools that your students can use to initiate and sustain conversations about literature. In using these terms in the classroom you can help children acquire a literary vocabulary.

Elements of Fiction

Learning to evaluate children's books can best be accomplished by reading as many excellent books as possible. Gradually, your judgment on the merits of individual books will improve. Discussing your responses to these books with children, teachers, and other students and listening to their responses will also assist you in becoming a more appreciative critic. Understanding the different parts, or elements, of a piece of fiction and how they work together can help you become more analytical about literary works; and this, too, can improve your judgment of literature. The elements of fiction are discussed separately in the following sections, but it is the unity of all these elements that produces the story.

Plot

The events of the story and the sequence in which they are told constitute the *plot* of the story. In other words, the plot is what happens in the story. Plot is the most important element of fiction to the child reader. Often, adults believe that a story for children needs only to present familiar, everyday activities—the daily routines of life. Perhaps 2- and 3-year-olds will enjoy hearing narratives such as this, but by age 4, children want to find more excitement in books. A good plot produces conflict to build the excitement and suspense that are needed to keep the reader involved.

The nature of the *conflict* within the plot can arise from different sources. The basic conflict may be one that occurs within the main character, called *person-against-self.* In this type of story, the main character struggles against inner drives and personal tendencies to achieve some goal or overcome a traumatic event. In *Echo* (2006) by Kate Morgenroth, Justin, who has witnessed his younger brother's fatal shooting accident, lashes out at family and friends while struggling with his internal conflict. Stories about adolescence will frequently have this conflict as the basis of the story problem. For example, in *Ghost Boy* (2000) by Iain Lawrence, 14-year-old Harold struggles to find himself and to accept himself and others.

A conflict usually found in survival stories is the struggle the character has with the forces of nature. This conflict is called *person-against-nature.* Worthy examples are *Ice Drift* (2004) by Theodore Taylor, *The Young Man and the Sea* (2004) by Rodman Philbrick, and *Hatchet* (1987) by Gary Paulsen.

In other children's stories, the source of the conflict is found between two characters. Conflicts with peers, problems with sibling rivalries, and stories of children rebelling against an adult are *person-against-person* conflicts. For example, in *Bucking the Sarge* (2004) by Christopher Paul Curtis, 15-year-old Luther's conflict is with his mother, whose views on right and wrong collide with his own.

Occasionally, a story for children presents the main character in conflict with society. This conflict in children's stories is most often either about the environment being destroyed by new technology or changing times or about children caught up in a political upheaval such as war. The conflict is then called *person-against-society.* *How I Found the Strong* (2004) by Margaret McMullan and *Yellow Star* (2006) by Jennifer Roy, both war stories, pose this type of conflict. In the mystery *Hoot* (2002) by Carl Hiaasen, the conflict is between those who want to develop and destroy natural areas and wildlife and those who want to preserve them.

In some stories, the protagonist faces *multiple conflicts* in which, for example, a character may be in conflict with society and also in a conflict with self. In Jean Craighead George's *Julie of the Wolves* (1972), protagonist Julie/Miyax rebels against the societal changes that threaten the wildlife in her native Alaska while at the same time seeking to resolve her own conflicting thoughts about her Inuit traditions and modern society.

Plots are constructed in many different ways. The most common plot structures found in children's stories are *chronological plots,* which cover a particular period of time and relate the events in order within the time period. For example, if a book relates the events of one week, then Monday's events will precede Tuesday's, and so on. *Lizzie Bright and the Buckminster Boy* (2004) by Gary D. Schmidt as well as the classic *Charlotte's Web* (1952) by E. B. White have chronological plots.

Two distinct types of chronological plots are progressive plots and episodic plots. In books with *progressive plots,* the first few chapters are the exposition, in which the characters, setting, and basic conflict are established. Following the expository chapters, the story builds through rising action to a climax. The climax occurs, a satisfactory conclusion (or dénouement) is reached, and the story ends. Figure 3.1 suggests how a progressive, chronological plot might be visualized.

An *episodic plot* ties together separate short stories or episodes, each an entity in itself with its own conflict and resolution. These episodes are typically unified by the same cast of characters and the same setting. Often, each episode comprises a chapter. Although the episodes are usually chronological, time relationships among the episodes may be nonexistent or loosely connected by "during that same year" or "later that month." Examples of short chapter books with an episodic plot structure are *Ramona Quimby, Age 8* (1981) by Beverly Cleary and *My One Hundred Adven-*

Figure 3.1   Diagram of a Progressive Plot

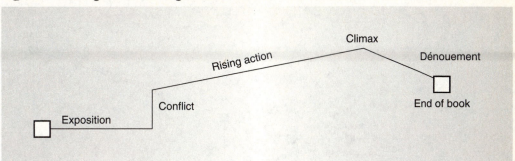

tures (2008) by Polly Horvath. Because episodic plots are less complex, they tend to be easier to read and lend themselves to the recounting of humorous escapades. Thus, the reader who is just making the transition from picture books to chapter books may find these plots particularly appealing. Many easy-to-read books for the beginning reader are also structured in this way. *Frog and Toad Are Friends* (1970) by Arnold Lobel and *Mr. Putter & Tabby Feed the Fish* (2001) by Cynthia Rylant are good examples of an episodic plot in an easy-to-read book. Figure 3.2 suggests how a chronological, episodic plot might be visualized.

Authors use a ***flashback*** to convey information about events that occurred earlier—for example, before the beginning of the first chapter. In this case, the chronology of events is disrupted, and the reader is taken back to an earlier time. Flashbacks can occur more than once and in different parts of a story. The use of a flashback permits authors to begin the story in the midst of the action but later fill in the background for full understanding of the present events. Flashbacks in children's books are mostly found in chapter books for older readers, because such plots can confuse children younger than age 8 or 9. Teachers can help students understand this plot structure by reading aloud good examples of this type of story, such as Jean Craighead George's *My Side of the Mountain* (1959) and *Because of Winn-Dixie* (2000) by Kate DiCamillo. Class discussion can then focus on the sequence of events and why the author may have chosen

Figure 3.2   Diagram of an Episodic Plot

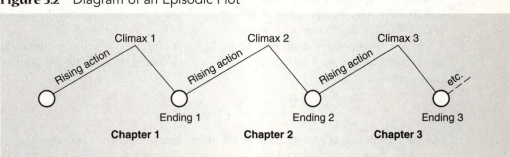

Figure 3.3   Diagram of a Flashback

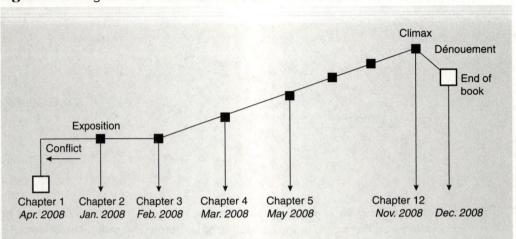

to relate the events in this manner. Figure 3.3 illustrates the structure of a flashback in a book in which some events occurred before the beginning of the book.

With greater frequency, children's novels are appearing with new plot formulations such as *complex multiple plots* in which the traditional chronology is replaced by nonlinear plots that occur simultaneously. In Louis Sachar's *Holes* (1998), a humorous mystery and survival story, two apparently unrelated stories set in two different time periods are developed, yet are gradually revealed to be connected to one another through the unraveling of the mystery. Kathi Appelt's *The Underneath* (2008) relates the events of an animal story set in present-day Louisiana bayou country, while interweaving a fantasy about a centuries-old story of love, betrayal, and revenge.

A stylistic plot device that prepares readers for coming events in a story is *foreshadowing*. This device gives clues to a later event, possibly even the climax of the story. For example, in the first chapter of Kenneth Oppel's *Airborn* (2004), the cabin boy's chance meeting and rescue of a dying balloonist who shares his tales of strange flying creatures foreshadows events to come a year later and prepares readers for the cabin boy's pivotal role in these events. Also, in the classic novel *Tuck Everlasting* (1975) by Natalie Babbitt, the detailed description of the long yellow road in the first chapter foreshadows the long journey the Tuck family members must travel in their lives. You can alert young readers to one of the subtle ways authors prepare them for the outcomes of stories by discussing foreshadowing.

Plot is an important element to all readers, but especially to young readers, who enjoy fast-moving, exciting stories. A well-constructed plot contributes substantially to children's acceptance and enjoyment of stories.

Characters

Memorable characters populate the world of children's literature. Ferdinand the bull, Charlotte the spider, Frances the badger, Little Toot the young tugboat, Karana the Native American girl, and Peter the African-American child with his dog, Willie, are all remembered fondly by generations of readers.

Characters, the "actors" in a story, are another element of fiction vital to the enjoyment of a story. A well-portrayed character can become a friend, a role model, or a temporary parent to a child reader. Although young readers enjoy exciting events, the characters involved in those events must matter to the reader, or the events no longer seem important. How characters are depicted and how they develop in the course of the story are important to the reader. Two aspects to consider in studying a character are characterization and character development.

Characterization refers to the way an author helps the reader know a character. The most obvious way an author can do this is to describe the character's physical appearance and personality. Portraying the character's emotional and moral traits or revealing her relationships with other characters are more subtle and effective techniques. In the most convincing characterizations, we see the character through a combination of his or her own actions and dialogue, the responses of other characters to him or her, and the narrator's descriptions.

Character development refers to the changes, good or bad, the character undergoes during the course of events in the story. If a character experiences significant, life-altering events, we, as readers, expect that the character will somehow be different as a result of those events. For example, Matt, a boy of 11, who was left alone for months in the Maine territory to take care of his family's new cabin, becomes a stronger, more independent young man by the end of *The Sign of the Beaver* (1973) by Elizabeth George Speare. Also, in Nancy Hull's *On Rough Seas* (2008), set in 1939, 14-year-old Alec Curtis decides to go to sea as a galley boy to forget his guilt over the drowning of a cousin. However, when his ship joins the rescue at Dunkirk at the beginning of World War II, Alec gradually recognizes what is important to him, showing his new maturity in unexpected ways.

In a work of fiction for children there are usually one or two main characters and some minor characters. Ideally, each main character, sometimes called the *protagonist,* will be a fully described, complex individual who possesses both good and bad traits, like a real person. Such a character is called a *round character.* For example, in the historical fiction novel *Catherine, Called Birdy* (1994) by Karen Cushman, Birdy, the protagonist whose father is seeking a suitable husband for her, is presented as a complex character with many strengths and weaknesses. In the realistic fiction novel *A Step from Heaven* (2001) by An Na, young Ju, the protagonist whose Korean family immigrates to America, is presented as a round, complex character dealing with the many challenges an immigrant must face.

Minor, or *secondary, characters* may be described in a partial or less complete manner. The extent of description depends on what the reader needs to know about the character for a full understanding of the story. Some of the minor character's traits are described fully, whereas other facets of the character's personality may remain obscure. Because the purpose is to build the story and make it comprehensible, fragmentary knowledge of a minor character may suffice. In the novel *The Ghost of Poplar Point* (2007) by Cynthia DeFelice, Dub, a minor character, is portrayed only as a loyal friend and faithful sidekick to Allie, the 12-year-old protagonist and ghost magnet in this supernatural mystery based on an actual historical Native American massacre in 1779. Another example can be found in *Heat* (2006) by Mike Lupica, in which the secondary character Manny is depicted as the catcher and a loyal mate to talented pitcher Michael Arroyo, the protagonist in this sports novel that portrays a positive image of Hispanic teens competing athletically.

Occasionally, an author will insert a *flat character*—that is, a character described in a one-sided or underdeveloped manner. Although such people do not exist in real life, they may be justified within the story to propel the plot. For example, in Susan R. Vaught's *Big Fat Manifesto* (2008), self-assured and overweight Jamie seeks to be taken seriously in a thin world by writing in the school newspaper about her attitudes about her weight. Other students in the story lack depth and appear as somewhat flat stereotypes. The current importance of the topic presented by a character as well-developed as Jamie will make this an appealing book for many middle-school readers. Sometimes the character is shown as an all-evil or all-frivolous person; for instance, folktales present flat characters as symbols of good and evil. In some stories, a flat character plays the role of *character foil,* a person who is in direct juxtaposition to another character (usually the protagonist) and who serves to highlight the characteristics of the other individual. A character foil may occur as a flat or round character. The character or force that is in direct opposition to the main character is called the *antagonist.* In Avi's *The True Confessions of Charlotte Doyle* (1990), the ship's captain is a frightening antagonist to Charlotte. And in the sports story *Offsides* (2004) by Erik E. Esckilsen, protagonist Tom Gray, the star soccer player, challenges the school's mascot that stereotypes Native Americans and stands up to his coach, one of the antagonists.

The main characters in an excellent work of fiction for children are rounded, fully developed characters who undergo change in response to life-altering events. Because children generally prefer personified animals or children of their own age, or slightly older, as the main characters of their stories, authors of children's books often face a dilemma. Although in real life, children usually have restricted freedom of action and decision making within the confines of a family, the author can develop a more vivid and exciting story if the main characters are "on their own." Thus, in many children's stories, parents are absent, no longer living, or no longer functioning. An example of children on their own can be found in Jeanne Birdsall's *The Penderwicks* (2005), in which four sisters and their absentminded dad spend the summer in a cottage in rural Massachusetts. The spirited, lovable girls' many adventures and near-mishaps could not occur without a preoccupied father. Furthermore, by making up situations, authors are able to focus on just one aspect of life, thereby enabling young readers to see and understand this one facet of life more clearly.

Setting

The time and place in which the story occurs constitute the setting of a story. The setting's importance depends on the story. For example, in historical fiction the authentic re-creation of the period is essential to the comprehension of the story's events. In this situation, the setting, fully described in both time and place, is called an *integral setting.* The story could not be the same if placed in another setting. For example, in the historical fiction mystery novel *The Case of the Missing Marquess* (2006) by Nancy Springer, 14-year-old Enola Holmes, the much younger sister of Sherlock Holmes, unravels the disappearance of her missing mother. Historical facts, British dialect and vocabulary, and Victorian customs create a believable work of historical fiction. The novel, set in nineteenth-century England, also depicts the English countryside and the filth of Victorian London through descriptive imagery.

By contrast, the setting in folktales is often vague and general. For example, "long ago in a cottage in the deep woods" is meant to convey a universal, timeless tale, one that could have happened anywhere and almost anytime except the present or very recent past. This type of setting is called a *backdrop setting.* It simply sets the stage and the mood.

Theme

The literary theme of a story is its underlying meaning or significance. The term *theme* should not be confused with topic or theme as used in the sense of a thematic unit. Although we sometimes think of the literary *theme* as the message or moral of the story, it can just as likely be an aesthetic understanding, such as an appreciation for nature or a viewpoint on a current societal issue. To identify the theme, you may ask yourself what the author's purpose was in writing the story or what the author is saying through this story.

A theme is better expressed by means of a complete sentence than by a single word. For example, students often suggest that a theme found in *Charlotte's Web* (1952) by E. B. White is friendship. A better statement of the theme is "Friendship is one of the most satisfying things in the world," as Wilbur the pig tells us in the story. The single word *friendship* may be a topic found in the story, but it is not an expression of the theme. Similarly, the phrase "race relations during Reconstruction" incompletely expresses the theme of *When I Crossed No-Bob* (2007) by Margaret McMullan. Set in Mississippi ten years after the Civil War, 12-year-old Addy makes a difficult decision when faced with the dilemma of testifying against her own father or keeping silent and letting someone else be hurt. "Doing good is hard, doing nothing is the easiest of all" more clearly states the theme.

Themes in children's books should be worthy of children's attention and should convey truth to them. Furthermore, the themes should be based on high moral and ethical standards. A theme must not overpower the plot and characters of the story, however; children read fiction for enjoyment, not for enlightenment. If the theme is expressed in a heavy-handed, obvious fashion, then the pleasure of the reading experience is diminished. Likewise, overly "teachy" or didactic themes detract from a reader's enjoyment of a story. Certainly a well-written book may convey a moral message, but it should also tell a good story from which the message evolves. In this way the theme is subtly conveyed to the reader. For example, in the novel *Smiles to Go* (2008) by Jerry Spinelli, 14-year-old, self-absorbed perfectionist Will, as a result of a serious accident involving his little sister, discovers that it is worth risking love and friendship even if he can't always be the one in control.

Often, adults write stories not for children's pleasure but to teach morality lessons. Although we think of stories of this sort as the thinly disguised religious tracts found in the early history of children's literature, we must be alert to a tendency for some current authors to use children's literature as a platform to preach about drug abuse, animal rights, and other issues of contemporary interest. If the literary quality of these so-called problem novels is weakened, then the story and characters become secondary to the issue or problem. However, when moral values are embedded within the fabric of a powerful story, children can be led to develop a sense of right and wrong without feeling as if they are being indoctrinated.

Style

Style is the way an author tells the story; it can be viewed as the writing itself, as opposed to the content of the book. However, the style must suit the content of the particular book; the two are intertwined.

Different aspects of style are considered in evaluating a work of fiction. Most obviously, you can look at the *words* chosen to tell the story. Are they long or short, common or uncommon, rhyming or melodic, boring and hackneyed or rich and challenging, unemotional or emotional, standard dialect or regional/minority dialect? The words should be appropriate to the story being told. As an evaluator of books for children, you will want to ask the following questions as you read: Why did the author choose these words? What effect was the author trying to achieve?

The *sentences* may also be considered. Do they read easily? Do they flow without the reader needing to reread to gain the meaning of the text? Sometimes an author chooses to limit the word choices to write a book that can be read by a beginning reader. Yet in the hands of a gifted writer, the sentences will remain no less melodic, varied in length and structure, and enjoyable to read and hear than sentences in the best books for the more advanced reader. Good examples of well-written books for beginning readers are Arnold Lobel's *Frog and Toad Are Friends* (1970), Mo Willems's *I Will Surprise My Friend!* (2008), and Annie Barrows's *Ivy and Bean* (2006), illustrated by Sophie Blackall.

The *organization* of the book may be considered by noting the paragraphs and transitions, length of chapters, headings and chapter titles, preface, endnotes, prologue, epilogue, and length of the book. For the beginning reader it is important whether a story is divided into chapters. After years of looking at, listening to, and reading books without chapters, it is quite an accomplishment for a 6-year-old to move up to so-called chapter books, even if each chapter is only three pages long.

Chapter titles can provoke interest in what will follow, as well as provide the reader with clues to predict story events. Some books provide the readers with a *prologue,* an introductory statement telling events that precede the start of the story. Some authors include an *epilogue,* a concluding statement telling events that occur after the story has ended. Adeline Yen Mah, author of *Chinese Cinderella: The True Story of an Unwanted Daughter* (1999), speaks directly to the reader in an informative prologue about the Chinese language. She invites the reader to become interested in a Chinese girl's language, history, and culture. Another example is found in *Yellow Star* (2006), in which Jennifer Roy places an author's note and a time line of events in the epilogue.

In *Kipling's Choice* (2005) by Geert Spillebeen, an epilogue has been included to provide information on the historical context of World War I in France. Other times, an epilogue resolves questions readers may have regarding what happened after the story's conclusion, as in Marion Dane Bauer's *A Bear Named Trouble* (2005), a story of companionship between a wild bear cub and a lonely boy.

Point of view is another aspect of an author's style. If the story is told through the eyes and voice of a *third-person narrator* (the use of *he, she, it*), then the reader can know whatever the narrator knows about the events of the story. In many stories, the narrator is *omniscient* and can see into the minds of all characters and be at many places at the same time. The reader of Lynne Rae Perkins's *Criss Cross* (2005) can understand and interpret the story from many different perspectives because of Perkins's use of the omniscient point of view. In *Loser* (2002), Jerry Spinelli also draws on the omniscient narrative point of view to relate the story of Donald Zinkoff, whose enthusiasm and exuberance are unabated in spite of being seen as a loser by classmates.

Other stories are narrated from the perspective of only one character in the story. In this case, the story is still told in the third person, but the reader knows only what that particular character can see and understand. This latter technique is called *limited omniscient* point of view. Beverly Cleary's *Dear Mr. Henshaw* (1983) is a realistic story told from the perspective of Leigh, a boy troubled by family difficulties and changes at school, who corresponds with Mr. Henshaw, an author. In *Clay* (2006) by David Almond, disturbing events are told through the point of view of altar boy Davie, who becomes part of those events.

Other times, authors choose to tell the story through a *first-person narrator* (the use of *I*), generally the main character of the story. In such cases the reader gains a sense of closeness to the main character but is not privy to any information unavailable to this character. As you read, you will note that some authors have accomplished a first-person point of view by writing as though their main character were writing a diary or letters, as in *Flight to Freedom* (2002) by Ana Veciana-Suarez; or through narrative poems composed by the main character, as in *Diamond Willow* (2008) by Helen Frost. The story is both an exciting survival adventure and dog story set in Alaska and related through diamond-shaped concrete poems. Occasionally, a story is told in first person through the eyes of a minor character. For example, *We Can't All Be Rattlesnakes* (2009) by Paul Jennings is a humorous animal fantasy about a boy, Gunnar, and his troubled life, told through the point of view of a captured rattlesnake, Crusher.

A *shifting point of view* permits the reader to see events from different characters' points of view. This technique is demanding on young readers' skill. When the point of view shifts, the author must carefully cue readers to the changing point of view, as Avi does in *Nothing but the Truth* (1991) by identifying sender, receiver, or discussants at the beginning of each letter, memorandum, telephone call, or face-to-face conversation. Beverley Naidoo's *Web of Lies* (2006), a sequel to her award-winning *The Other Side of Truth* (2001) about two Nigerian refugee children, relates the story of the children's school experiences in London by shifting between their two points of view.

Symbolism is an artistic invention that authors use to suggest invisible or intangible meanings by analogy to something else through association, resemblance, or convention. Often, a symbol—a person, object, or situation—represents an abstract or figurative meaning in the story in addition to its literal meaning. Some symbols are universal and can be found repeatedly in literary works; others may be particular to the story. For example, a farm usually represents love and security in works of literature. Children often read only on a literal level, but they can be helped by teachers to note more obvious symbols existing in the books they are reading. If the symbolic feature recurs in the story, it is referred to as a *motif*. The number 3 is a common motif in folktales, for example.

A story for children must be more than a plot and a character study; a story integrates all the elements of fiction into a pleasing whole. In drawing together these elements, authors create new worlds for young readers.

Changes in Traditional Fictional Forms

Following World War II, the traditional way of telling stories began to change; some works that no longer fit well-known and accepted patterns of fiction appeared and gained recognition, especially in adult fiction. The postmodern movement in literature emerged. According to *Merriam-Webster's Encyclopedia of Literature, postmodern* refers to "any of several artistic movements that have challenged the philosophy and practices of modern arts or literature since about the 1940s. In literature this has amounted to a reaction against fixed ideas about the form and meaning of texts" (Kuiper, 1995, p. 899). Although it began as a trend in adult literature, postmodernism in works for children and young adults is increasing.

Nikolajeva (1998) points out the defining characteristics of the postmodern literary work, the most recognized of which is genre eclecticism—writing that has aspects of more than one genre and ready acceptance of elements of popular culture such as film and television.

Postmodern literature is also characterized by narrative structures that mirror life. That is, there are not necessarily distinct beginnings, middles, and endings; stories can be emotion driven rather than event driven; and stories may include multiple protagonists, perspectives, and narrators. Some postmodern stories include multiple plots or realities with parallel times and places. Authors of postmodern works encourage readers to take a more active role in the storytelling. Postmodernism has helped broaden the types of literature accepted into the mainstream, including graphic novels, novels in verse, docudramas, and novels of mixed genres.

Balance and Variety in Book Selections

In addition to evaluating the various literary elements that are central to the issue of quality, the child's age and development and the balance and variety among books are also important considerations. Because children in any elementary-grade class have a wide range of reading abilities and reading interests, you need to provide many different types of books, including picture books, easy-to-read books, short chapter books, longer books, and books of prose, poetry, fiction, and nonfiction. Thus, balance among the *genres of literature* as well as *variety in topic* are essential.

Which stories teachers choose to read aloud to students is important. Varying choices for read-alouds will challenge students and enhance the resulting academic benefits for their language and cognitive development, as discussed in Chapter 1. In sharing books with students the *mood* of the books must also be varied to include stories that are sad, humorous, silly, serious, reflective, boisterous, suspenseful, or even a little scary. A steady diet of light, humorous books might appeal to students at first, but eventually, the sameness will become boring. For a teacher to read aloud over many months works of literature with the same predominant emotion is to ignore the rapid change and growth in personal lives and choices that are the hallmark of youth.

PEARSON
myeducationkit™

Go to Activity 1 in the Assignments and Activities section of Chapter 3 in MyEducationKit; view the video on developing a classroom library and respond to the questions.

A balance between male and female main characters over the course of a year is necessary if you are to meet the needs of children of both sexes and to help members of each sex understand more fully the perspectives, problems, and feelings of members of the opposite sex. Classroom and school library collections need to have a wide range of topics with a balance of male and female main characters.

In addition, understanding and empathy for people with physical, emotional, mental, and behavioral disabilities can be gained through portrayals in books of children and adults with impairments. A positive image of people with disabilities needs to be conveyed in these books. Furthermore, children with disabilities need to see characters like themselves in books.

The representation of minorities as main characters is also essential if you are to present a realistic view of society and the world. Through well-written *multicultural literature,* children can see that someone from a different race, ethnic group, or religion has many of the same basic needs and feelings that they themselves have. Literature by and about people different from oneself can help develop an understanding and appreciation for all peoples. Minority children will enjoy reading books in which children from backgrounds similar to their own play the leading, and sometimes heroic, roles. Characters with whom one can identify permit a deeper involvement in literature and at the same time help children understand situations in their own lives.

International literature, literature from other nations and regions of the world, needs to be included in read-aloud choices and in classroom and library collections in order to guide students toward global understanding. Through reading or listening to the favorite books of children from other nations, your children will experience cultural literacy on a worldwide basis.

Classroom libraries are usually limited in scope; therefore, school libraries are necessary to provide adequate balance and variety of books for students' research needs and independent reading. Frequent visits to the library by the class and by individual students need to be arranged by the teacher and librarian.

Book Awards

Several book award programs have been established for the purposes of elevating and maintaining the literary and artistic standards of children's books and for honoring the authors whose work is judged by experts in the field to have the greatest merit. These awards provide teachers and librarians with one source for selecting excellent works of literature to share with children. Table 3.1 lists what are considered to be the major awards for children's books in the United States, Canada, and Great Britain. Lists of actual winners of these major children's book awards listed in Table 3.1 and other awards, such as awards for a specific genre or topic, can be found in Appendix A.

Some book award programs involve children in the selection process. The Children's Choices Project, sponsored by the International Reading Association/Children's Book Council Joint Committee, features newly published books selected by children around the country. The list of winners appears each October in *The Reading Teacher* and is available at www.reading.org.

Most states also have their own state children's choices award and programs. Usually a ballot of book titles is generated for certain age ranges, such as 5–8 and 9–12, from teachers', librarians', or children's nominations. The list is circulated across the state for children to vote on their favorites. Balloting usually occurs in the spring to permit reading time over the course of a school year. More information on state children's book awards and programs, including websites for many of the state programs, can be found at www.childrensbooks.about.com/cs/stateawards.

Another book award program, Teachers' Choices Project, sponsored by the International Reading Association, also develops an annual list of winners. Teachers read and vote for recently published books worthy of use in the classroom, then develop the Teachers' Choices Booklist. The list appears in the November issue of *The Reading Teacher* and is available at www.reading.org.

Review Journals

Journals that review children's books and feature current topics in the field of children's literature are an important source of information for teachers and librarians. Language-related professional teacher journals to which elementary teachers often subscribe, such as *The Reading Teacher* (www.reading.org) and *Language Arts* (www.ncte.org), have columns devoted to reviewing new

Table 3.1 Major U.S., Canadian, and British Children's Book Awards

Award/Country	Period	For/Year Established
Newbery Medal/United States	Annual	The most distinguished contribution to children's literature published in the previous year. Given to a U.S. author. Established 1922.
Caldecott Medal/United States	Annual	The most distinguished picture book for children published in the previous year. Given to a U.S. illustrator. Established 1938.
National Book Award for Young People's Literature/United States	Annual	Outstanding contribution to children's literature, in terms of literary merit, published in the previous year. Given to a U.S. writer. Established 1996.
Coretta Scott King Awards for writing and for illustration/United States	Annual, two awards	Outstanding inspirational and educational contribution to literature for children and young people by an African-American author/illustrator published in the previous year. Established 1970/1974.
Pura Belpré Awards for writing and illustration/United States	Biennial, two awards	Writing and illustration in a work of literature for youth published in the previous two years by a Latino writer and illustrator whose work best portrays, affirms, and celebrates the Latino cultural experience. Established 1996.
Governor General's Literature for Children Award for Writing/Canada	Annual	Best book for children published in the previous year. Separate prizes for works in English and French. Established 1987.
Governor General's Literature for Children Award for Illustration/Canada	Annual	Best illustration in a children's work published in the previous year. Separate prizes for works in English and French. Established 1987.
Carnegie Medal/Great Britain	Annual	The most distinguished contribution to children's literature first published in the United Kingdom the previous year. Given to an author. Established 1936.
Kate Greenaway Medal/Great Britain	Annual	The most distinguished picture book for children first published in the United Kingdom in the previous year. Given to an illustrator. Established 1956.

children's books in each monthly issue. *The Journal of Children's Literature* (www.childrens literatureassembly.org), a journal dedicated solely to children's literature and those involved in it, also has review sections of newly published children's books. In addition, these journals contain articles discussing effective strategies for incorporating literature into reading and content-area instruction and for bringing children and books together.

The review journals listed here offer evaluative annotations and suggested grade-level ranges for books reviewed. These journals are readily available in most university libraries as well as some school and public libraries.

- *Booklist* (www.ala.org). This journal reviews current print and nonprint materials for children and adults that are worthy of consideration for purchase by public libraries and school media centers.
- *The Bulletin of the Center for Children's Books* (http://bccb.lis.illinois.edu). This publication reviews current children's books, assigning a recommendation code to each.
- *The Horn Book Magazine* (www.hbook.com). This magazine includes detailed reviews of children's books deemed worthy in children's literature. The Newbery and Caldecott acceptance speeches are featured in the July/August issue.
- *Kirkus Reviews* (www.kirkusreviews.com). This publication annually reviews approximately 5,000 titles of prepublication books for adults and children.
- *School Library Journal for Children's, Young Adult, and School Librarians* (www.school libraryjournal.com). This journal prints both negative and positive reviews of most children's books published. It also includes articles of interest to school librarians.

Professional Associations and Websites

Major professional associations of benefit to individuals involved in the field of children's literature are listed below.

Association for Library Service to Children (ALSC): www.ala.org/alsc
This professional group is a division of the American Library Association and provides services primarily to librarians and media specialists.

Go to Activity 2 in the Assignments and Activities section of Chapter 3 in MyEducationKit; complete the activity on exploring professional websites.

International Reading Association (IRA): www.reading.org
This professional organization offers services primarily to teachers of language, literacy, and literature.

National Council of Teachers of English (NCTE): www.ncte.org
This professional membership addresses teaching and research in language and literature from preschool through college.

Children's Literature Association (ChLA): www.childlitassn.org
This professional group has many members from the field of English and addresses criticism, research, and teaching of children's literature.

The following websites are helpful in locating professional information about children's literature:

Carol Hurst's Children's Literature Site: www.carolhurst.com
This educational consultant's site provides a collection of book reviews, curriculum ideas, themes, and professional topics for teachers.

Children's Book Council (CBC): www.cbcbooks.org
This nonprofit association of children's book publishers offers book-related literacy materials for children. It also provides updates on National Children's Book Week.

Children's Literature Comprehensive Database: www.childrenslit.com
  Founded in 1993, this independent review-media site includes information about authors and illustrators, special monthly features, recommended book lists, and announcements of book events.

Cooperative Children's Book Center: www.education.wisc.edu/ccbc
  This children's literature examination and research library site provides information about its collections, upcoming events, and publications.

Categories of Literature

In Chapters 4 to 11, the main categories of children's books will be defined and explained, followed by book titles recommended for reading in each of the categories. Chapters 4 and 6 through 10 focus on the literary genres, as presented in Table 3.2 (the number of the chapter in which each genre of literature is discussed is noted next to the genre). For the purposes of this textbook, a genre organization—a traditional, though admittedly imperfect, way of grouping literature—is the most practical choice. It is easy for teachers and librarians to organize learning and to demonstrate the wide spectrum of ideas and emotions that can be found in children's literature. Many students seek and select books for their independent reading by topics, such as mystery, adventure, sports, or friendships. For this reason we have also included subheadings of topics within each genre chapter and have arranged the recommended books by these genres and by the topical subheadings.

Understanding genre characteristics builds a frame of reference for readers of a particular genre and can ease the task of comprehension. Furthermore, as readers encounter postmodern works of literature, which go beyond the traditional boundaries of a genre, knowledge of the traditional literary forms may help them understand what the authors are doing and help them gain new understandings from this shift.

Authors of children's literature have been experimenting with works that blend characteristics of several genres, and, as a result, genre boundaries are increasingly blurred (Kaplan, 2005; Laminack & Bell, 2004). As discussed earlier in this chapter, novels for children written in the style of free verse and other verse forms are being seen with greater frequency. These are referred to in this text as *novels in verse,* a form of literature narrated in free verse or other verse forms. An example is Karen Hesse's *Out of the Dust* (1997), awarded the Newbery Medal and the Scott O'Dell Award for Historical Fiction in the same year. Novels in verse form are listed in this textbook under their particular narrative genre, such as historical fiction, rather than in the chapter about poetry. Works of magical realism, a literary mode that combines realism and fantasy, such as those of Virginia Hamilton (*Sweet Whispers, Brother Rush,* 1982) and David Almond (*Skellig,* 1999), offer their reader new ways to perceive the world. Works of magical realism appear and are discussed in Chapter 7. Historical fantasy blends historical fiction and modern fantasy, as Mary Hoffman does in *Stravaganza: City of Masks* (2002). These works also appear and are discussed in Chapter 7. Other blended genres include

Table 3.2   Genres and Topics of Children's Literature

Poetry (4)	Prose				Nonfiction (10)
	Fiction				
	Fantasy		**Realism**		
	Traditional Literature (6)	*Modern Fantasy (7)*	*Realistic Fiction (8)*	*Historical Fiction and Biographies (9)*	
Nursery rhymes Lyric poems Narrative poems	Myths Epics Legends and tall tales Folktales Fables Religious stories	Modern folktales Animal fantasy Personified toys and objects Unusual characters and situations Worlds of little people Supernatural events and mystery fantasy Historical fantasy Quest stories Science fiction and science fantasy	Families Peers Physical, emotional, mental, and behavioral challenges Communities Animals Sports Mysteries Moral choices Romance and sexuality Coming of age Adventure and survival	Beginnings of civilization Civilizations of the ancient world Civilizations of the medieval world Emergence of modern nations Development of industrial society World wars in the twentieth century Post–World War II	Informational books

works of fictionalized biography and informational books that contain elements of both fiction and nonfiction, as in Russell Freedman's *Confucius: The Golden Rule* (2002) and David Macaulay's *Mosque* (2003); these works appear in Chapters 9 and 10. These blended-genre works offer readers new ways to perceive the world and often provide heightened interest for readers.

Chapter 11 diverges from the organization of genre and presents books organized by culture. Although multicultural and international books have been placed in a separate chapter for emphasis and ready access, many multicultural and international titles are also recommended in the genre chapters.

An overview of the genres, subtopics, and their relationships to one another is displayed in Table 3.2. These genres can be used in making balanced choices for library and classroom reading collections and for choosing books to read aloud.

Issues & Topics for FURTHER INVESTIGATION

- Find and read a book with each of the following characteristics: progressive chronological plot, episodic plot, and plot with flashbacks. Describe each book's plot structure and the age-appropriate target audience for the book.

- Find and read a literary work written from one of the following points of view: third-person omniscient, limited omniscient, first person, or shifting. In your opinion, what effect does the point of view have on the literary work and on the reader? Describe the writing style and your response to the style as a reader.

- Locate your state's children's choices book award and read some of the current nominees or recent winners of the award. Evaluate them for student appeal, literary quality, complexity, curricular value, and illustration quality (if a picture book).

References

Almond, D. (1999). *Skellig*. New York: Delacorte.

———. (2006). *Clay*. New York: Delacorte.

Appelt, K. (2008). *The underneath*. New York: Atheneum.

Avi. (1990). *The true confessions of Charlotte Doyle*. New York: Orchard.

———. (1991). *Nothing but the truth*. New York: Orchard.

Babbitt, N. (1975). *Tuck everlasting*. New York: Farrar.

Barrows, A. (2006). *Ivy and Bean*. Illustrated by S. Blackall. San Francisco: Chronicle.

Bauer, M. D. (2005). *A bear named Trouble*. New York: Clarion.

Beach, R. W., & Marshall, J. D. (1990). *Teaching literature in the secondary school*. Belmont, CA: Wadsworth.

Birdsall, J. (2005). *The Penderwicks*. New York: Knopf.

Cleary, B. (1981). *Ramona Quimby, age 8*. Illustrated by A. Tiegreen. New York: Morrow.

———. (1983). *Dear Mr. Henshaw*. Illustrated by P. O. Zelinsky. Orlando, FL: Harcourt.

Curtis, C. P. (2004). *Bucking the Sarge*. New York: Random.

Cushman, K. (1994). *Catherine, called Birdy*. New York: Clarion.

DeFelice, C. (2007). *The ghost of Poplar Point*. New York: Farrar.

DiCamillo, K. (2000). *Because of Winn-Dixie*. Cambridge, MA: Candlewick.

Eskilsen, E. (2004). *Offsides*. Boston: Houghton.

Freedman, R. (2002). *Confucius: The golden rule*. Illustrated by Frédéric Clément. New York: Arthur A. Levine.

Frost, H. (2008). *Diamond willow*. New York: Farrar.

George, J. C. (1959). *My side of the mountain*. New York: Dutton.

———. (1972). *Julie of the wolves*. Illustrated by J. Schoenherr. New York: Harper.

Hamilton, V. (1982). *Sweet whispers, Brother Rush*. New York: Philomel.

Hesse, K. (1997). *Out of the dust*. New York: Scholastic.

Hiaasen, C. (2002). *Hoot*. New York: Knopf.

Hoffman, M. (2002). *Stravaganza: City of masks*. New York: Bloomsbury.

Horvath, P. (2008). *My one hundred adventures*. New York: Schwartz & Wade.

Hull, N. L. (2008). *On rough seas*. New York: Clarion.

Jennings, P. (2009). *We can't all be rattlesnakes*. New York: HarperCollins.

Kaplan, J. (2005). Young adult literature in the 21st century: Moving beyond traditional constraints and conventions. *The ALAN Review, 32*(2), 11–18.

Kuiper, K. (Ed.). (1995). *Merriam Webster's encyclopedia of literature*. Springfield, MA: Merriam-Webster.

Laminack, L. L., & Bell, B. H. (2004). Stretching the boundaries and blurring the lines of genre. *Language Arts, 81*(3), 248–253.

Lawrence, I. (2000). *Ghost boy.* New York: Delacorte.

Lobel, A. (1970). *Frog and toad are friends.* New York: Harper.

Lupica, M. (2006). *Heat.* New York: Philomel.

Macaulay, D. (2003). *Mosque.* Boston: Houghton.

Mah, A. Y. (1999). *Chinese Cinderella: The true story of an unwanted daughter.* New York: Delacorte.

McMullan, M. (2004). *How I found the strong.* Boston: Houghton.

———. (2007). *When I crossed No-Bob.* Boston: Houghton.

More, H. (1961). A book. In W. Cole (Ed.), *Poems for seasons and celebrations.* Cleveland: World Publishing.

Morgenroth, K. (2006). *Echo.* New York: Simon & Schuster.

Na, A. (2001). *A step from heaven.* Asheville, NC: Front Street.

Naidoo, B. (2001). *The other side of truth.* New York: HarperCollins.

———. (2006). *Web of lies.* New York: HarperCollins.

Nikolajeva, M. (1998). Exit children's literature? *The Lion and the Unicorn, 22*(2), 221–236.

Oppel, K. (2004). *Airborn.* Toronto, ON: HarperCollins.

Paulsen, G. (1987). *Hatchet.* New York: Bradbury.

Perkins, L. R. (2005). *Criss cross.* New York: Greenwillow.

Philbrick, R. (2004). *The young man and the sea.* New York: Blue Sky Press.

Rosenblatt, L. (1978). *The reader, the text, the poem.* Carbondale: Southern Illinois University.

———. (1985). The transactional theory of the literary work: Implications for research. In C. R. Cooper (Ed.), *Researching response to literature and the teaching of literature: Points of departure* (pp. 33–53). Norwood, NJ: Ablex.

Roy, J. (2006). *Yellow star.* New York: Marshall Cavendish.

Rylant, C. (2001). *Mr. Putter & Tabby feed the fish.* Illustrated by A. Howard. San Diego, CA: Harcourt.

Sachar, L. (1998). *Holes.* New York: Farrar.

Schmidt, G. D. (2004). *Lizzie Bright and the Buckminster boy.* New York: Clarion.

Speare, E. G. (1973). *The sign of the beaver.* Boston: Houghton.

Spillebeen, G. (2005). *Kipling's choice.* Illustrated by T. Edelstein. Boston: Houghton.

Spinelli, J. (2002). *Loser.* New York: HarperCollins.

———. (2008). *Smiles to go.* New York: Joanna Cotler.

———. (1997). *Wringer.* New York: HarperCollins.

Springer, N. (2006). *The case of the missing marquess.* New York: Philomel.

Taylor, T. (2004). *Ice drift.* Orlando, FL: Harcourt.

Vaught, S. R. (2008). *Big fat manifesto.* New York: Bloomsbury.

Veciana-Suarez, A. (2002). *Flight to freedom.* New York: Orchard.

White, E. B. (1952). *Charlotte's web.* Illustrated by G. Williams. New York: Harper.

Willems, M. (2008). *I will surprise my friend!* New York: Hyperion.

part TWO

Categories of Literature

Part II presents a broad spectrum of the genres of literature, as outlined in Table 3.2 in Chapter 3. We believe that the organization by genres, topics, and historical eras as found in Chapters 4 through 11 is the most convenient and helpful way for you and your students to locate books. However, from the outset, we acknowledge that literary genres defy absolute definitions. Furthermore, most books can be categorized within genres in more than one way because the stories address more than one topic. For example, stories about peers are often about families, too.

Special features in each chapter of Part II deserve your attention. The Milestones features give you the history of the development of each genre at a glance. The lists of Notable Authors will familiarize you with well-known creators of literature and help you make good choices for in-depth author studies, just as the Excellent Books to Read Aloud features provide help in selecting good read-alouds. The Issues and Topics for Further Investigation features suggest aspects of each chapter's content for in-depth study, issues for discussion, and literature-related activities involving children.

In this edition, as in past editions, we have updated the important Recommended Books section at the end of each genre chapter. Our overall goal has been to include the best books from the recent past as well as some older titles that continue to hold wide appeal for today's children. Inevitably some titles must be dropped from edition to edition, just as libraries periodically remove books from their shelves to make room for newer books. Please note that titles in the Recommended Books lists are organized by the same topics or historical eras as presented in the body of the chapter to make finding specific types of books easier. Following each Recommended Books list is a brief list of films related to the genre. Chapter 11 features multicultural and international literature, the status of the field, and recommended books in this separate chapter in order to highlight the importance of these areas of literature. Please note that we have also integrated multicultural and international titles into the preceding genre chapters.

Other good children's literature titles may be found in Appendix A (Children's Book Awards). Appendix C lists good magazines available for children.

chapter FOUR

Poetry

What's a Poem?

A whisper,
a shout,
thoughts turned
inside out.

A laugh,
a sigh,
an echo
passing by.

A rhythm,
a rhyme,
a moment
caught in time.

A moon,
A star,
a glimpse
of who you are.

—Charles Ghigna

Poetry, in the form of nursery rhymes, is a natural beginning to literature for young children and an enjoyable literary form for all ages. In their earliest years, children acquire language and knowledge of the world around them through listening and observing. Poetry, primarily an oral form of literature that draws heavily on the auditory perceptions of the listeners, is ideally suited to young children. Throughout the elementary- and middle-school years, poetry that relates to topics and issues being explored in the classroom can be shared orally, providing a flash of humor or a new perspective.

Definition and Description

Poetry is the concentrated expression of ideas and feelings through precise and imaginative words carefully selected for their sonorous and rhythmical effects. Originally, poetry was oral, recited by minstrels as they traversed the countryside, sharing poems and songs with listeners of all ages. The musicality of poetry makes it an especially suitable literary form for teachers to read aloud and, at times, to put to music.

Children often believe that rhyme is an essential ingredient of poetry, yet some types of poetry do not rhyme. What, then, distinguishes poetry from prose? The concentration of thought and feeling expressed in succinct, exact, and beautiful language, as well as an underlying pulse or rhythm are the traits that most strongly set poetry apart from prose.

Not all rhyming, rhythmical language merits the label of poetry. *Verse* is a language form in which simple thoughts or stories are told in rhyme with a distinct beat or meter. Mother Goose and nursery rhymes are good examples of well-known, simple verses for children. And, of course, we are all too aware of the *jingle,* a catchy repetition of sounds heard so often in commercials. The most important feature of verses and jingles is their strong rhyme and rhythm. Content is often light or even silly. Although verses and jingles are enjoyable and engage children, poetry enriches children's lives by giving them new insights and fresh views on life's experiences and by bringing forth strong emotional responses.

The term *poetry* is used in this chapter both to refer to a form of language that can evoke great depth of feeling and provoke new insights through imaginative and beautiful language and to refer to favorite verses of childhood.

Types of Poetry Books

Poetry touches our minds and hearts by drawing on all five senses. Children, too, are reached by poetry, even though the subjects that move them may differ from those that move adults. A wide variety of poetry books is available today for use by students and teachers. Selecting books of poetry for use in the classroom as bridges between classroom activities, as materials for reading, and as literature for enjoyment will require teachers to review and evaluate the many types of poetry books: anthologies, Mother Goose and nursery rhyme books, nursery songbooks, books of poems on special topics and by favorite poets, and single illustrated poems in picture book formats.

Mother Goose and Nursery Rhyme Books

Mother Goose and nursery rhyme books are heavily illustrated collections of traditional verse. *Tomie dePaola's Mother Goose,* collected and illustrated by Tomie dePaola, is a good example. Often, a familiar illustration is all a child needs to get her or him to recite one of these well-loved verses. Collected nursery rhymes first appeared in editions of Charles Perrault's *Tales of Mother Goose* in France in the early eighteenth century. These verses are now part of children's literary heritage and are a wonderful introduction to the world of literature for young children. In Western societies in which countless allusions are made every day to the characters and situations found in nursery rhymes, knowledge of this literature is a mark of being culturally literate.

Because so many of these verses exist, the better collections include large numbers of rhymes organized thoughtfully around themes or topics and indexed by titles or first lines. Favorites include *Marguerite de Angeli's Book of Nursery and Mother Goose Rhymes* and *The Arnold Lobel Book of Mother Goose.* These cultural connections can be expanded by collections from other traditions, such as *Rhymes 'Round the World,* selected by Kay Chorao, and *Arrorró, mi niño: Latino Lullabies and Gentle Games,* collected by Lulu Delacre.

Nursery Songs

Nursery songs are heavily illustrated collections of traditional and modern verses with musical notation. Melody emphasizes the innate musicality of these verses and turns some verses into games ("Ring around the Roses") and others into lullabies ("Rock-a-Bye Baby") and finger plays ("Eensy, Weensy Spider"). Collections of songs, like Jane Yolen's *Trot, Trot to Boston* and José-Luis Orozco's *Diez Deditos and Other Play Rhymes and Action Songs from Latin America,* are essential for teachers working with young children. Single illustrated versions of familiar songs provide innovative interpretations, such as the two picture book versions of *Hush, Little Baby* by Brian Pinkney and Marla Frazee.

Anthologies of Poetry

A large, comprehensive *anthology of poetry* for children is a must in every classroom. Anthologies should be organized by subject for easy retrieval of poems appropriate for almost any occasion. In addition, indexes of poets and titles or first lines are usually provided in these texts. Works by contemporary and traditional poets can be found in most of these anthologies; they appeal to a wide age range, providing nursery rhymes for toddlers as well as longer, narrative poems for older readers. Examples include *The Random House Book of Poetry for Children,* edited by Jack Prelutsky, and *The Bill Martin Jr. Big Book of Poetry,* edited by Bill Martin Jr. and Michael Sampson.

Specialized Poetry Books

Specialized poetry books, in which the poems are all by one poet, on one topic, for one age group, or of one poetic form, are readily available. These specialized collections support teachers and children in exploring specific topics, poets, and types of poetry. Beautifully illustrated collections are especially enjoyed by children for independent reading of poetry. Examples include *Dinothesaurus: Prehistoric Poems and Paintings* by Douglas Florian and *Jazz* by Walter Dean Myers.

Single Illustrated Poems

Single illustrated poems that are narratives are frequently presented in picture book formats. These editions make poetry more appealing and accessible to many children, but in some cases the illustrations may remove the opportunity for children to form their own mental images from the language created by poets. *My People,* with photographs by Charles Smith, and *The Negro Speaks of Rivers,* illustrated by E. B. Lewis, provide compelling visual metaphors of classic poems by Langston Hughes.

Elements of Poetry

Just as with a work of fiction, the elements of a poem should be considered if the reader is to understand and evaluate the poem. Each of these parts—meaning, rhythm, sound patterns, figurative language, and sense imagery—work together to express ideas and feelings.

■   *Meaning. Meaning* is the underlying idea, feeling, or mood conveyed through the poem. As with other literary forms, poetry is a form of communication; it is the way a poet chooses to express emotions and thoughts through the choice and arrangement of words.

■   *Rhythm. Rhythm* is the beat or regular cadence of the poem. Poetry, usually an oral form of literature, relies on rhythm to help communicate meaning. A fast rhythm is effected through short lines; clipped syllables; sharp, high vowel sounds, such as the sounds represented by the letters *a, e,* and *i;* and abrupt consonant sounds, such as the sounds represented by the letters *k, t, w,* and *p.* A fast rhythm can provide the listener with a feeling of happiness, excitement, drama, and even tension and suspense. A slow rhythm is effected by longer lines, multisyllabic words, full or low vowel sounds such as the sounds represented by the letters *o* and *u,* and resonating consonant sounds such as the sounds represented by the letters *m, n,* and *r.* A slow rhythm can evoke languor, tranquility, inevitability, and harmony, among other feelings. A change in rhythm during a poem signals the listener to a change in meaning.

In the following poem, the rhythm exhibits the dizzy and increasing speed of a merry-go-round. "Slowly," in contrast, proceeds more slowly in communicating the calm and quiet of summer.

MERRY-GO-ROUND

I climbed up on the merry-go-round.
And it went round and round
I climbed up on a big brown horse
And it went up and down.
 Around and round
 And up and down.
 Around and round
 And up and down.
 I sat high up

On a big brown horse
And rode around
On the merry-go-round

And rode around
On the merry-go-round
I rode around
On the merry-go-round
Around
And round
And
Round.

—Dorothy Baruch

SLOWLY

Slowly the tide creeps up the sand,
Slowly the shadows cross the land.
Slowly the cart-horse pulls his mile,
Slowly the old man mounts the stile.

Slowly the hands move round the clock,
Slowly the dew dries on the dock.
Slow is the snail—but slowest of all
The green moss spreads on the old brick wall.

—James Reeves

■ *Sound Patterns. Sound patterns* are made by repeated sounds and combinations of sounds in the words. Words, phrases, or lines are sometimes repeated in their entirety. Also, parts of words may be repeated, as with **rhyme,** the sound device that children most recognize and enjoy. Rhyme occurs when the ends of words (the last vowel sound and any consonant sound that may follow it) have the same sounds. Examples of rhyming words are *vat, rat, that, brat,* and *flat,* as well as *hay, they, flay, stray,* and *obey. Assonance* is another pattern poets use for effect. In this case, the same vowel sound is heard repeatedly within a line or a few lines of poetry. Assonance is exemplified in these words: *hoop, gloom, moon, moot,* and *boots. Alliteration* is a pattern in which initial consonant sounds are heard frequently within a few lines of poetry. Examples are *ship, shy,* and *shape. Consonance* is similar to alliteration but usually refers to a close juxtaposition of similar final consonant sounds, as in fla*ke,* chu*ck,* and stro*ke. Onomatopoeia* is the device in which the sound of a word imitates its real-world sound. Examples are *buzz* for the sound of a bee and *hiss* for the sound a snake makes.

■ *Figurative Language. Figurative language* takes many different forms, but it involves comparing or contrasting one object, idea, or feeling with another one. A *simile* is a direct comparison, typically using *like* or *as* to point out the similarities. The familiar poem "The Star" includes a simile to compare a star to a diamond.

THE STAR

Twinkle, twinkle little star,
How I wonder what you are!
Up above the world so high,
Like a diamond in the sky.

—Jane Taylor

A *metaphor* is an implied comparison without a signal word to evoke the similarities. In the poem "The Night Is a Big Black Cat," the metaphor implies a comparison between the night sky and a black cat.

THE NIGHT IS A BIG BLACK CAT

The Night is a big black cat
The Moon is her topaz eye,
The stars are the mice she hunts at night,
In the field of the sultry sky.

—G. Orr Clark

Personification is the attribution of human qualities to animals or to inanimate objects for the purpose of drawing a comparison between the animal or object and human beings. In "The Crocus," the flower is personified by human actions and a personal pronoun.

THE CROCUS

The golden crocus reaches up
To catch a sunbeam in her cup.

—Walter Crane

Hyperbole is an exaggeration to highlight reality or to point out ridiculousness. Children often delight in hyperbole because it appeals to their strong sense of the absurd. To show a boy's reluctance to go to school John Ciardi uses hyperbole with good effect in the following stanza from "Speed Adjustments."

Why does a boy who's fast as a jet
Take all day—and sometimes two—
To get to school?

■ ***Sense Imagery.*** A poet will play on one or more of the five senses in descriptive and narrative language. *Sight* may be awakened through the depiction of beauty; *hearing* may be evoked by the sounds of a city street; *smell* and *taste* may be recalled through the description of a fish left too long in the sun; and finally, *touch* can be sensitized through describing the gritty discomfort of a wet swimsuit caked with sand from the beach. After listening to a poem, children can be asked to think about which of the senses the poet is appealing to.

These elements of poetry may be considered to select varied types of poems and to group them for presentation. However, little is gained by teaching each of these elements as a separate item to be memorized or analyzed. Poetic analysis has caused many students to dislike poetry. On the other hand, students whose teachers love poetry, select it wisely, read it aloud well, and share it often and in many enjoyable ways will come to appreciate poetry.

Evaluation and Selection of Poetry

The criteria to keep in mind in evaluating a poem for use with children are as follows:

PEARSON
myeducationkit™

Go to Activity 1 in the Assignments and Activities section of Chapter 4 in MyEducationKit; complete the activity on evaluating a poem you love.

- The ideas and feelings expressed are authentic, fresh, and imaginative.
- The expression of the ideas and feelings is unique, often causing the reader to perceive ordinary things in new ways.
- The poem is appropriate to the experiences of children and does not preach to them.
- The poem presents the world through a child's perspective and focuses on children's lives and activities as well as on activities to which people of all ages can relate.

- Poetry collections should be judged on the quality of the poetry choices first and illustrations and the appearance of the book second. Beautiful illustrations do not ensure a good collection of poems within the covers.
- Children report a preference for narrative poems, and so these poems are a good choice for classroom sharing.
- Although certain poets may be favored by your students, they will also enjoy the poetry of many other writers. Thus, be sure to share poems by a variety of poets.

In selecting poems to read to students, the Golden Age poets listed in the Milestones feature in this chapter, the list of notable poets on page 63, and the list of poets who have won the National Council of Teachers of English (NCTE) Award are good starting points. The NCTE Award was established in 1977 in the United States to honor living U.S. poets whose poetry has contributed substantially to the lives of children. This award is given to a poet for the entire body of writing for children ages 3 through 13 and is now given every three years. In addition, a recent reference book, *Young Adult Poetry: A Survey and Theme Guide* (Schwedt & DeLong, 2002), can be a useful tool for students and teachers in upper elementary and middle grades for locating poems to support the curriculum and to address student interests. This bibliography annotates 198 poetry books and identifies themes in more than 6,000 poems.

PEARSON
myeducationkit™

Go to Activity 2 in the Assignments and Activities section of Chapter 4 in MyEducationKit; complete the activity on evaluating the poetry of an NCTE award–winning poet.

NCTE Excellence in Poetry for Children Award Winners

1977	David McCord	1991	Valerie Worth
1978	Aileen Fisher	1994	Barbara Juster Esbensen
1979	Karla Kuskin	1997	Eloise Greenfield
1980	Myra Cohn Livingston	2000	X. J. Kennedy
1981	Eve Merriam	2003	Mary Ann Hoberman
1982	John Ciardi	2006	Nikki Grimes
1985	Lilian Moore	2009	Lee Bennett Hopkins
1988	Arnold Adoff		

Although more poetry for children is being written, published, and enjoyed by many teachers and their students, some teachers report that they do not share poetry because of their uncertainty about selecting poems for their students. By learning about students' preferences in poetry and some of the best-loved poems and most respected poets, a teacher can become more skillful at selecting poems that engage students.

Children's Poetry Preferences

The findings from surveys of children's poetry preferences can be helpful to teachers in selecting poems for a new group of students. Fisher and Natarella (1982) surveyed primary-grade children and their teachers, and Terry (1974) studied intermediate-grade children. The two age groups were similar, although not identical, in their preferences.

- Both age groups preferred narrative poems over lyric poems.
- Limericks were the favored poetic form of both age groups; free verse and haiku were not well liked by either age group.
- Children of both age groups preferred poems that had pronounced sound patterns of all kinds, but especially enjoyed poems that rhymed.
- Rhythm was an important element to students of both age groups; they preferred poems with regular, distinctive rhythm.
- Children of both age groups liked humorous poems, poems about animals, and poems about enjoyable, familiar experiences.
- The subjects most preferred by primary-grade children were strange and fantastic events, animals, and other children; the older children preferred the realistic contents of humor, enjoyable, familiar experiences, and animals.
- Children in both age groups often found figurative language in poetry confusing.

A study by Kutiper and Wilson (1993) was conducted to determine whether an examination of school library circulation records would confirm the findings of the earlier poetry preference studies. Their findings indicated that the humorous contemporary poetry of Shel Silverstein and Jack Prelutsky dominated the students' choices. The collections of poetry written by the NCTE award winners did not circulate widely; nor were they widely available in the school libraries studied, even though these poets reflect a higher quality of language and usage than is found in the light verse so popular with students. Kutiper and Wilson stated that real interest in poetry must go beyond Prelutsky and Silverstein. This interest needs to be developed by teachers who provide an array of poetry that builds on students' natural interests.

Children's appreciation of poetry can be broadened and deepened by a good teacher, but you may be wise to proceed with caution on less-liked aspects of poetry until your students become fans of poetry. Thus, a good selection of rhyming, narrative poems with distinct rhythms about humorous events, well-liked familiar experiences, and animals is a good starting point for students who have little experience with poetry.

Historical Overview of Poetry

Poetry for children began centuries ago in the form of nursery rhymes that were recited to babies and toddlers by caregivers. These verses were passed along via the oral tradition. The earliest

Notable Authors
of Poetry

Arnold Adoff, recipient of the National Council of Teachers of English (NCTE) Award for Excellence in Poetry for Children. Many poems about relating to people across racial groups. *All the Colors of the Race.* www.arnoldadoff.com

Paul Fleischman, winner of the Newbery Medal for his *Joyful Noise: Poems for Two Voices;* in it and *Big Talk,* the poems are composed and printed for two or four readers to read lines in unison and solo. www.paulfleischman.net

Douglas Florian, poet and illustrator, blends irresistible wordplay, free-flowing poems, interesting facts, and vibrant collage art to create picture book poetry collections. *Dinothesaurus; Comets, Stars, the Moon and Mars; Mammalabilia.* www.douglasflorian.com or see his blog, http://floriancafe.blogspot.com

Kristine O'Connell George, noted for several poetry collections of interest to children from preschool to middle school in which she uses many different poetic forms. *Little Dog Poems; Swimming Upstream: Middle School Poems; Fold Me a Poem.* www.kristinegeorge.com

Nikki Grimes, African-American poet whose poetry celebrates children and their friendships and families. 2006 recipient of the NCTE Award for Excellence in Poetry. *Meet Danitra Brown; A Pocketful of Poems.* www.nikkigrimes.com

Mary Ann Hoberman, recipient of the NCTE Award for Excellence in Poetry, known for her humorous, colorful poetry. *Fathers, Mothers, Sisters, Brothers: A Collection of Family Poems; You Read to Me, I'll Read to You.* www.maryannhoberman.com.

Paul B. Janeczko, contemporary poet and anthologist of poetry that especially appeals to young adults. *Dirty Laundry Pile: Poems in Different Voices; A Poke in the I: A Collection of Concrete Poems; Worlds Afire.* www.pauljaneczko.com

X. J. Kennedy, a favorite creator of nonsense and humorous verse about contemporary themes. *Fresh Brats; Exploding Gravy.* www.xjanddorothymkennedy.com

Naomi Shihab Nye, a poet and anthologist whose meditative poems offer global perspectives and whose edited collections include Mexican, Native American, and Middle Eastern poetry. *This Same Sky: A Collection of Poems from around the World; 19 Varieties of Gazelle: Poems of the Middle East.*

Joyce Sidman, an award-winning poet of picture book collections who uses a range of poetic forms from riddles to concrete poems in celebration of nature. *Song of the Water Boatman and Other Pond Poems; Butterfly Eyes and Other Secrets of the Meadow; Meow Ruff; Red Sings from Treetops.* www.joycesidman.com

Gary Soto, a writer whose poetry captures the experiences of growing up in a Mexican neighborhood in California's Central Valley. *Neighborhood Odes; Worlds Apart: Traveling with Fernie and Me.* www.garysoto.com

Janet Wong, a poet who writes about contemporary American culture and creates free-verse poems based on life experiences, ranging from dreams to growing up Asian-American. *Good Luck Gold and Other Poems; A Suitcase of Seaweed and Other Poems; Night Garden.* www.janetwong.com

published collection of nursery rhymes that survives today is *Tommy Thumb's Pretty Song Book* (1744), which is housed in the British Museum (Gillespie, 1970). This songbook contains familiar rhymes such as "Hickory Dickory Dock" and "Mary Mary Quite Contrary." These rhymes and others like them came to be called *Mother Goose rhymes,* but the term *Mother Goose* was first used in France by Charles Perrault in his *Stories and Tales of Past Times with Morals; or, Tales of Mother Goose* (1697) to refer to his collection of fairy tales. Later editions contained nursery rhymes, which became so popular that Mother Goose became a general name for nursery rhymes. For

MILESTONES *in the Development of Poetry*

Date	Poet	Landmark Work	Country	Characteristic
1846	Edward Lear	*A Book of Nonsense*	England	Father of nonsense poetry, limericks
1864	Lewis Carroll	"Jabberwocky"	England	Nonsense verses, such as those in *Alice's Adventures in Wonderland*
1872	Christina Rossetti	*Sing Song*	England	Poems on children and the small things around them
1885	Robert Louis Stevenson	*A Child's Garden of Verses*	England	Descriptive poems of childhood memories
1888	Ernest Thayer	"Casey at the Bat"	United States	Famous ballad on baseball
1890	Laura E. Richards	*In My Nursery*	United States	Poems with hilarious situations, wordplay, and strong rhythm
1896	Eugene Field	*Poems of Childhood*	United States	Poems reflecting on children and child life
1902	Walter de la Mare	*Songs of Childhood*	England	Musical and imaginative poetry
1920	Rose Fyleman	*Fairies and Chimneys*	England	Imaginative poems about fairies
1922	A. A. Milne	*When We Were Very Young*	England	Poems of fun in which the child's world is observed
1926	Rachel Field	*Taxis and Toadstools*	United States	Poems about city and country through the child's eyes

many, nursery rhymes and poems were the first forms of literature experienced and came to symbolize the reassuring sounds of childhood.

Poems of a moral and religious bent were shared with obvious didactic intent, reflecting the strict attitude toward the rearing of children that held sway in the Western world from the Middle Ages to the late nineteenth century. Fear of death and punishment was instilled as a means of gaining obedience to authority. Ann and Jane Taylor's *Original Poems, for Infant Minds, by Several Young Persons* (1804) provided verse of this kind. Some titles of poems from this early collection are "The Idle Boy," "Greedy Richard," "Meddlesome Matty," and "The Church-Yard."

Poetry for children flourished from the middle of the nineteenth century through the 1920s, a period that can be considered the Golden Age of Poetry for Children. The accompanying Milestones feature lists the poets, countries, landmark works and dates, and characteristics. The Golden Age of Poetry moved away from moralistic poetry and instead provided children with poems describing the beauty of life and nature, with poems of humor, nonsense, and word fun, and with imaginative poems that interpreted life from the child's perspective. Much of the Golden Age poetry retains its appeal for today's children; for example, *A Child's Garden of Verses* (1885) by Robert Louis Stevenson remains a favorite collection of poems among parents and children. This positive shift remains the standard for children's poetry today.

In the 1960s and 1970s, the general trend toward realism in children's literature was also reflected in poetry. More topics were considered suitable for the child audience, resulting in protest poetry, poems about girls in nontraditional roles, and irreverent poems. For example, parents, teachers, and other adults became fair game for ridicule and mockery. Minority poets were more frequently published, and their poetry gained in popularity.

Popularity of poetry in the classroom began in the 1980s and continues to the present day. Developments in the publishing industry attest to this popularity. For example, Boyds Mills Press has a division devoted to children's poetry, called Windsong. Publishers continue to present both single poems and collections of poems in beautifully illustrated book formats. In the 1980s, Nancy Willard's *A Visit to William Blake's Inn: Poems for Innocent and Experienced Travelers* and Paul Fleischman's *Joyful Noise: Poems for Two Voices* received Newbery Medals, indicating greater recognition of poetry for young people in the United States. An increase in the publication of anthologies of poems by and about minorities, such as *Pass It On,* edited by Wade Hudson, and *Cool Salsa,* edited by Lori Carlson, has been noted in the 1990s. This increased publication has also resulted in greater attention to earlier African-American poets, such as Paul Laurence Dunbar, Countee Cullen, and Langston Hughes. A current trend practiced by authors such as Karen Hesse, Helen Frost, Sharon Creech, Jacqueline Woodson, and Margarita Engle involves using poetry to create novels in verse for older children.

Poetry Types and Forms

Poetry can be classified in many ways; one way is to consider two main types that generally differ in purpose: lyric and narrative poetry. *Lyric poetry* captures a moment, a feeling, or a scene and is descriptive in nature, whereas *narrative poetry* tells a story or includes a sequence of events. From this definition, you will recognize the following selection to be a lyric poem.

GIRAFFES

Stilted creatures,
Features fashioned as a joke,
Boned and buckled,
Finger painted,
They stand in the field
On long-pronged legs
As if thrust there.

They airily feed,
Slightly swaying,
Like hammer-headed flowers.

Bizarre they are,
Built silent and high,
Ornaments against the sky.
Ears like leaves
To hear the silken
Brushing of the clouds.

    —Sy Kahn

The next selection is an example of a narrative poem:

AFTER THE PARTY

Jonathan Blake
Ate too much cake,
He isn't himself today;
He's tucked up in bed
With a feverish head,
And he doesn't much care to play.

Jonathan Blake
Ate too much cake,
And three kinds of ice cream too—
From latest reports
He's quite out of sorts,
And I'm sure the reports are true.

I'm sorry to state
That he also ate
Six pickles, a pie and a pear;
In fact I confess
It's a reasonable guess
He ate practically everything there.

Yes, Jonathan Blake
Ate too much cake,
So he's not at his best today;
But there's no need for sorrow—
If you come back tomorrow,
I'm sure he'll be out to play.

    —William Wise

Poetry can also be categorized by its *poetic form,* which refers to the way the poem is structured or put together. *Couplets, tercets, quatrains,* and *cinquains* refer to the number (two, three, four, and five) of lines of poetry in a stanza—a set of lines of poetry grouped together. Couplets, tercets, quatrains, and cinquains usually rhyme, though the rhyme scheme may vary; these poetic forms may constitute an entire poem, or a poem may be comprised of a few stanzas of couplets, tercets, and so on. "Higglety, Pigglety, Pop!" is an example of the cinquain poetic form found in a traditional nursery rhyme.

HIGGLETY, PIGGLETY, POP!

Higglety, pigglety, pop!
The dog has eaten the mop.
The pig's in a hurry,
The cat's in a flurry,
Higglety, pigglety, pop!

—Traditional

Other specific poetic forms frequently found in children's poetry are limericks, ballads, haiku, sijo, free verse, and concrete poetry.

A *limerick* is a humorous, one-stanza, five-line verse form (usually a narrative), in which lines 1, 2, and 5 rhyme and are of the same length and lines 3 and 4 rhyme and are of the same length but shorter than the other lines. The following is an example of a limerick by Edward Lear, the poet who popularized this poetic form in the nineteenth century.

LIMERICK

There was an Old Man with a beard
Who said, "It is just as I feared!—
    Two Owls and a Hen
    Two Larks and a Wren
Have all built their nests in my beard!"

—Edward Lear

A *ballad* is a fairly long narrative poem of popular origin, usually adapted to singing. These traditional story poems are often romantic or heroic, such as "Robin Hood" or "John Henry."

Haiku is a lyric, unrhymed poem of Japanese origin with seventeen syllables, arranged on three lines with a syllable count of five, seven, and five. Haiku is highly evocative poetry that frequently espouses harmony with and appreciation of nature. Here is an example.

    Pigeons masquerade
As wildlife. They can't fool me.
    We're all city folk.

—Nikki Grimes

Sijo is a traditional Korean poetry form with three lines, each with fourteen to sixteen syllables. The first line introduces the topic, the second develops the topic, and the third contains some kind of twist. Unlike haiku, sijo is written about a wide range of topics, including relationships and everyday moments.

POCKETS

What's in your pockets right now? I hope they're not empty;
Empty pockets, unread books, lunches left on the bus—all a waste.
In mine: One horse chestnut. One gum wrapper. One dime. One hamster.

> —Linda Sue Park

Free verse is unrhymed poetry with little or light rhythm. Sometimes words within a line will rhyme. The subjects of free verse are often abstract and philosophical; they are always reflective.

AUTUMN LEAVES

gather in gutters,
pile on walks,
tumble
        from the tips
of toes,
crunching
fall hellos
to back-to-school feet.

> —Rebecca Kai Dotlich

Concrete poetry is written and printed in a shape that signifies the subject of the poem. Concrete poems are a form of poetry that must be seen as well as heard to be fully appreciated. These poems do not usually have rhyme or definite rhythm; they rely mostly on the words, their meanings and shapes, and the way the words are arranged on the page to evoke images. In "Concrete Cat" you will note through the position of the word that the mouse appears to have met with an accident.

CONCRETE CAT

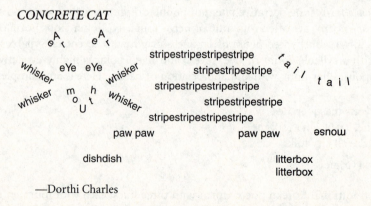

> —Dorthi Charles

Poetry in the Classroom

Young children delight in the sounds and language play of poetry—yet by fifth grade, students typically indicate that poetry is their least favorite genre. What happens to cause this huge shift? School. Poetry is the most misused genre in classrooms, often chosen for memorization and handwriting practice. Poetry tends to be neglected, seldom shared until the dreaded poetry unit comes along and bombards students with abstract poems that they are expected to analyze in order to uncover the "hidden meanings." The result is that students often build a lifelong dislike of poetry, instead of being provided with experiences that create a lifelong love of poetry.

Students' Listening to and Saying Poems

Teachers and librarians can begin by providing even very young students with many opportunities to hear and say poems. Later, when students have developed a love of poetry and an affinity for the language play in poems, students can read poetry by fine poets and by their classmates and can begin to write poems themselves. In other words, poetry needs to be shared in both oral and written forms.

Poetry should be introduced first and often to children in an oral form. Because poetry was originally an oral form of literature, it still relies heavily on the auditory perceptions of listeners. Moreover, children's oral language is the basis for their later acquisition of literacy. These two facts combine nicely to make listening to and saying poems a natural early introduction to literature for children. Some teachers report that they do not share poetry with their students because of their uncertainty about how to read it aloud. By practicing the poems ahead of time and by reading poetry frequently, a teacher can overcome this reluctance. The rewards to both students and teachers are worth the effort.

PEARSON myeducationkit™

Go to the Conversations section of Chapter 4 in MyEducationKit to read the interview with Lee Bennett Hopkins.

Reading Poetry Aloud to Children

Poetry should be read aloud to students on a daily basis. Elster and Hanauer (2002), in examining how kindergarten to fourth-grade teachers shared poems with their students, found that reading poetry aloud with expression is effective in drawing children's attention to literate language. Brief, positive encounters with one to three poems at a time are best. Too many poems in one sitting may overwhelm students or make the reading tedious. Introduce the poem to the class before reading it aloud, either by tying the poem in with something else or by briefly telling why you chose this poem. Then state the title of the poem and begin to read. After reading the poem, be sure to announce the name of the poet so that students discover the writers they especially enjoy. In addition, the following points will help you to read poetry well:

■ Keep in mind that poetry should be read for its meaning. Stress the meaning elements of the poem just as you do when reading prose. The pauses must be determined by the meaning units of the poem, not by the end of the lines.

■ A reader should not overemphasize the beat of the poem. Doing so results in an annoying singsong effect. Let the poetic language provide the rhythm.

■ Poetry should be enunciated clearly. Each sound and each syllable of a poem are important and must be heard to be appreciated. You may need to slow down your normal reading pace to give full value to each sound.

PEARSON
myeducationkit™

Go to Activity 3 in the Assignments and Activities section of Chapter 4 in MyEducationKit; view the artifact on responding to poetry through art and respond to the question.

■ Poetry begs to be performed and dramatized. Try out different effects (using different voices, elongating words, singing, shouting, whispering, pausing dramatically, and so on) as you read poems aloud. Your voice is a powerful tool: You may change it from louder to softer to only a whisper; you may start at a deep, low pitch and rise to a medium and eventually high pitch; you may speak very quickly in a clipped fashion and then slow down and drawl out the words. Sara Holbrook's *Wham! It's a Poetry Jam: Discovering Performance Poetry* (2002) offers good suggestions for performing poetry and running a poetry contest.

■ Some poems may need to be read aloud a number of times for the meaning to be fully understood by listeners. Also, favorite poems can be enjoyed again and again, as teachers and students savor one more reading.

■ Consider recording poems for the listening center and making them available along with the poem in print, on a chart or in a book, for the student to listen to and read. Commercially made recordings of popular poets reading their works, accompanied by music, are available and quite popular with children. Some teachers have asked parents to peruse a poetry anthology, select a favorite poem, and then record their reading of the poem for use in the listening center.

■ After reading a poem aloud, some form of response is usually enjoyed. Some poems warrant discussion, and students can take the opportunity to tell how the poem made them feel or what it made them think about. Ask, "What meaning does the poem have for you?"

Choral Poetry

A time-honored technique for providing opportunities to say and hear poems over and over again is given by choral poetry. *Choral poetry* consists of interpreting and saying a poem together as a group activity. These poems may be practiced and recited or read aloud. Students enjoy this way of experiencing poetry because they have a participatory role in the activity. Most poetry, intended to be listened to, is suitable for choral presentation. The following sections explain how to select choral poems and teach them to students.

1. *Selection.* At first, select a short poem (from one to four stanzas) until your students develop some skill in memorizing, reciting, and performing poems. Humorous narrative poems are good first choices. Later, you will want to experiment with longer poems. Provide students with a copy of the poem.

2. *Arrangements.* Options for reading a poem chorally include unison, two- or three-part, solo voices, cumulative buildup, and simultaneous voices.

■ In unison choral speaking, the students recite the poem together as a group. Two-part or three-part choral poetry is usually based on arranging students into voice types (for example, high, medium, and low) to achieve different effects and by selecting lines of the poem for each group to recite or read.

- Solo voices can be added to either of these presentations and are sometimes used for asking a question or making an exclamation.
- Some poems lend themselves to cumulative buildup presentations. A cumulative buildup is effected by having, for example, only two voices say the first line, then two more join in on the second, and then two more, gradually building to a crescendo until the entire class says the last line or stanza.
- Poems can be presented by simultaneous recitation, which forms a presentation similar to a musical round. In this case, group one begins the poem and recites it all the way through. When group one begins the third line, then group two starts the first line, and the two groups recite simultaneously until the end. Other groups can, of course, be added.
- Poetry selected and arranged for dramatic choral readings on a particular theme infuses an interesting variation into choral poetry. Paul Fleischman's *Joyful Noise: Poems for Two Voices, I Am Phoenix: Poems for Two Voices,* and *Big Talk: Poems for Four Voices* are collections of poetry written in a manner that is already suitable for choral reading. These collections were written to be read aloud by two readers at once, one reading the left half of the page and one reading the right half, as well as certain lines simultaneously. Pairs of students may each take a different poem from the collection.

Many other variations can be developed for use in choral readings. Let imagination be your guide. Words and lines can be spun into ghostly moans, or barked, or sung, or repeated. Choreography adds visual impact, as do simple props. As soon as children learn that poems do not have to be read sedately through exactly as written, they will begin to find excitement and deeper meaning in poetry.

3. *Performance.* Incorporating action, gestures, body movements, and finger plays can produce more interesting and enjoyable presentations. Many of these performances will be informal, with a focus on playing with various arrangements of a poem in a small group or class. More formal peformances involve memorizing a well-loved poem, trying out various arrangements, and then rehearsing the final arrangement for presentation to an audience.

Students' Reading and Writing Poems

Learning to Read Poetry

Children enjoy reading poetry silently and aloud to others. The classroom library corner should have one or two comprehensive poetry anthologies for students to browse through for general purposes. In addition, specialized collections by a single poet, such as *A Pocketful of Poems* by Nikki Grimes, and books of poems on a single topic, such as *Around the World in Eighty Poems* edited by James Berry, are needed as well. Students can be encouraged to make copies of their favorite poems from these various collections to develop personal, individual anthologies. Many students choose to illustrate these and arrange the poems in new and inventive ways. Rotating the poetry books occasionally over the course of the school year will spark renewed interest in reading poetry.

Other activities to encourage the reading of poetry by students follow:

- Place students in pairs to take turns reading favorite poems to one another. Make videotapes or audiotapes of these readings and permit students to listen to or watch their own and other students' readings of poetry.

- Ask each student to select three poems by one poet (for example, a Golden Age poet or an NCTE poet) and find something out about the poet; then place students in groups of five or six to tell briefly about the poet and read the three poems aloud. Paul B. Janeczko's *The Place My Words Are Looking For: What Poets Say about and through Their Work* (1990) and Sylvia Vardell's *Poetry People* (2007) are excellent resources for this purpose. Information about children's authors can also be found on many websites, including www.childrenslit.com.
- Have students find three poems on the same topic, such as dinosaurs, baseball, or friendship; then read them aloud in small groups.
- Encourage students to find poems that are of the same poetic form (cinquains, limericks, etc.), or that exhibit similar poetic elements (rhyme, alliteration, onomatopoeia, etc.), or that have fast or slow rhythms. These poems can then comprise the poems for reading aloud that day or week.

Do	Don't
Read poetry aloud every day	Limit poetry choices to one or two poets or types of poems
Practice reading a poem before reading it aloud for the first time to students	Read poems in a singsong style
Choose poetry the students will like	Choose all poems from one anthology
Have a variety of poetry anthologies and specialized poetry books available in the classroom	Have poetry marathon days or weeks to make up for not sharing poetry regularly
Encourage students to recite and write poems	Force students to memorize and recite poems
Direct choral poetry presentations	Make analysis the focus of poetry study
Invite responses to poetry through art, music, and movement	Have students copy poems for handwriting practice
Feature a notable poet each month	Make the main emphasis of poetry be the writing of formula poems
Begin and end each day with a poem	

Learning to Write Poetry

A rich poetry environment stimulates children's interest in writing their own poems. Children need to be very familiar with poetry of many kinds and by many poets before they should be expected to compose poems. The collection of poems *Inner Chimes: Poems on Poetry,* selected by Bobbye S. Goldstein, may be a natural starting place for helping students to think about poetry and what it is. This collection contains poems by various renowned children's poets writing about creating poetry. Other books that provide suggestions on how to include poetry in the classroom are *Awakening the Heart* (1999) by Georgia Heard and *Poetry Aloud Here!* (2006) by Sylvia Vardell.

Teachers often start the writing of poetry as a collaborative effort. The class brainstorms ideas and composes the poem orally as the teacher writes

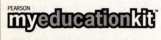

PEARSON
myeducationkit™

Go to Activity 4 in the Assignments and Activities section of Chapter 4 in MyEducationKit; view the video on encouraging students to attend to word choice in writing poetry and respond to the question.

it on the board or on chart paper. As students become comfortable with writing group poetry, they can branch off and compose poems in pairs or individually.

Children should be reminded that poetry is a form of communication and that they should think of an idea, feeling, or event to write about in their poems. They should be reminded that poetry does not have to rhyme and that they may write about something of interest to them. Children's poetry follows no absolute rules; perfection of form should not be a goal. Other suggestions to foster poetry writing include the following:

- Have students compile personal and class anthologies of their own poems or their favorite poems.
- Design bulletin boards with displays of students' own poems as well as copies of poems by favorite poets. Students may also design posters, individually or in groups, to illustrate a favorite poem that is displayed around the school for a few weeks.
- Encourage students to model the works of professional poets by attempting imitation of a whole poem or of specific techniques.
- Read aloud many poems of one poetic form; then analyze the form with the students to reveal the characteristics of its structure. Quatrains, cinquains, haiku, concrete poems, and limericks can all be used as models with students once they have an appreciation for poetry and for the specific poetic form.

Some poets have suggested other models and patterns for students to follow in writing poetry. Kenneth Koch's *Wishes, Lies, and Dreams: Teaching Children to Write Poetry* (1999/1970); M. K. Glover's *A Garden of Poets: Poetry Writing in the Elementary Classroom* (1999); Myra Cohn Livingston's *Poem Making: Ways to Begin Writing Poetry* (1991); Paul Janeczko's *How to Write Poetry* (1999) and *Poetry from A to Z: A Guide for Young Writers* (1994); Ralph Fletcher's *Poetry Matters: Writing a Poem from the Inside Out* (2002); and Jack Prelutsky's *Pizza, Pigs, and Poetry: How to Write a Poem* (2008) are useful resources for teachers who want to encourage students to compose poems.

Issues & Topics for FURTHER INVESTIGATION

- Create a self-portrait anthology by collecting poems that celebrate and explore the different aspects of who you are and what you are doing, thinking, and feeling. Open the anthology by selecting a signature poem for yourself.

- Research the history of Mother Goose or other nursery rhymes within a particular culture.

- Some children see poetry as sentimental and irrelevant to their lives. One way to challenge this viewpoint is to read and discuss poetry that provokes feelings and ideas about issues of social justice. Consider this possible role for poetry by reading about the experiences of children in a classroom (Damico, 2005) and collecting poems that address complex social issues.

✦ References

Baruch, D. (1932). Merry-go-round. In D. Baruch, *I like machines*. New York: Harper.

Charles, D. (1982). Concrete cat. In X. J. Kennedy & D. M. Kennedy (Eds.), *Knock at a star*. Illustrated by K. A. Weinhaus. Boston: Little, Brown.

Ciardi, J. (1996). *The monster den*. Philadelphia: Lippincott.

Clark, G. O. (1983). The night is a big black cat. In J. Prelutsky (Ed.), *The Random House book of poetry for children*. Illustrated by A. Lobel. New York: Random House.

Crane, W. (1983). The crocus. In J. Prelutsky (Ed.), *The Random House book of poetry for children*. Illustrated by A. Lobel. New York: Random House.

Damico, J. (2005). Evoking hearts and heads: Exploring issues of social justice through poetry. *Language Arts, 83*(2), 137–146.

Dotlich, R. K. (2003). Autumn leaves. In R. K. Dotlich (Ed.), *In the spin of things: Poetry of motion*. Illustrated by Karen Dugan. Honesdale, PA: Boyds Mills.

Elster, C. A., & Hanauer, D. I. (2002). Voicing texts, voices around texts: Reading poems in elementary school classrooms. *Research in the Teaching of English, 37*(1), 89–134.

Fisher, C. J., & Natarella, M. A. (1982). Young children's preferences in poetry: A national survey of first, second and third graders. *Research in the Teaching of English, 16*(4), 339–354.

Fletcher, R. (2002). *Poetry matters: Writing a poem from the inside out*. New York: HarperCollins.

Ghigna, C. (2003). What's a poem? In C. Ghigna (Ed.), *A fury of motion: Poems for boys*. Honesdale, PA: Boyds Mills.

Gillespie, M. C. (1970). *Literature for children: History and trends*. Dubuque, IA: Wm. C. Brown.

Glover, M. K. (1999). *A garden of poets: Poetry writing in the elementary classroom*. Urbana, IL: National Council of Teachers of English.

Grimes, N. (2001). Pigeons masquerade. In N. Grimes (Ed.), *A pocketful of poems*. Illustrated by J. Steptoe. New York: Clarion.

Heard, G. (1999). *Awakening the heart: Exploring poetry in elementary and middle school*. Portsmouth, NH: Heinemann.

Holbrook, S. (2002). *Wham! It's a poetry jam: Discovering performance poetry*. Honesdale, PA: Boyds Mills.

Janeczko, P. B., Selector. (1990). *The place my words are looking for: What poets say about and through their work*. New York: Bradbury.

———. (1994). *Poetry from A to Z: A guide for young writers*. New York: Bradbury.

———. (1999). *How to write poetry*. New York: Scholastic.

Kahn, S. (1967). Giraffes. In S. Dunning, E. Lueders, & H. Smith (Eds.), *Reflections on a gift of watermelon pickle*. New York: Lothrop, Lee and Shepard.

Koch, K. (1999/1970). *Wishes, lies, and dreams: Teaching children to write poetry*. New York: Random.

Kutiper, K., & Wilson, P. (1993). Updating poetry preferences: A look at the poetry children really like. *The Reading Teacher, 47*(1), 28–35.

Lear, E. (1946). *The complete nonsense book*. New York: Dodd, Mead.

Livingston, M. C. (1991). *Poem making: Ways to begin writing poetry*. New York: HarperCollins.

McKean, B. (2000–2001). Speak the speech, I pray you! Preparing to read aloud dramatically. *The Reading Teacher, 54*(4), 358–360.

Park, L. S. (2007). Pockets. In L. S. Park, *Tap dancing on the roof: Sijo (poems)*. Illustrated by I. Banyai. New York: Clarion.

Prelutsky, J. (2008). *Pizza, pigs, and poetry: How to write a poem*. New York: Greenwillow.

Reeves, J. (1963). Slowly. In E. Blishen (Ed.), *Oxford book of poetry for children*. Illustrated by B. Wildsmith. Oxford: Oxford University Press.

Schwedt, R., & DeLong, J. (2002). *Young adult poetry: A survey and theme guide*. Westport, CT: Greenwood.

Taylor, J. (1983). The star. In J. Prelutsky (Ed.), *The Random House book of poetry for children*. Illustrated by A. Lobel. New York: Random House.

Terry, A. C. (1974). *Children's poetry preferences: A national survey of upper elementary grades*. Urbana, IL: National Council of Teachers of English.

Vardell, S. (2006). *Poetry aloud here! Sharing poetry with children*. Chicago: American Library Association.

———. (2007). *Poetry people: A practical guide to children's poets.* Santa Barbara, CA: Libraries Unlimited.

Wise, W. (1931/1932). After the party. In W. Wise, *Jonathan Blake.* New York: Knopf.

★ Recommended Poetry Books

Because poetry is usually of interest to a broad age group, entries of poetry books indicate age only for books mainly suitable for older readers.

Mother Goose and Nursery Rhyme Books

Chorao, Kay, compiler. *Rhymes 'Round the World.* Dutton, 2009.

Crews, Nina. *The Neighborhood Mother Goose.* Greenwillow, 2004. Illustrated with photographs in a city setting.

de Angeli, Marguerite. *Marguerite de Angeli's Book of Nursery and Mother Goose Rhymes.* Doubleday, 1954.

Delacre, Lulu, selector. *Arrorró, mi niño: Latino Lullabies and Gentle Games.* Lee & Low, 2004.

dePaola, Tomie, compiler. *Tomie dePaola's Mother Goose.* Putnam, 1985.

Dillon, Leo, and Diane Dillon, compilers. *Mother Goose: Numbers on the Loose.* Harcourt, 2007.

Lobel, Arnold, selector. *The Arnold Lobel Book of Mother Goose.* Knopf, 1997.

Opie, Iona, editor. *Here Comes Mother Goose.* Illustrated by Rosemary Wells. Candlewick, 1999.

———. *Mother Goose's Little Treasures.* Illustrated by Rosemary Wells. Candlewick, 2007.

Nursery Songs

Baum, Maxie. *I Have a Little Dreidel.* Illustrated by Julie Paschkis. Scholastic, 2006.

Frazee, Marla. *Hush, Little Baby.* Harcourt, 2003.

Katz, Alan. *Smelly Locker: Silly Dilly School Songs.* Illustrated by David Catrow. M. K. McElderry, 2008.

Krull, Kathleen. *I Hear America Singing! Folk Songs for American Families.* Illustrated by Allen Garns. Knopf, 2003.

Larrick, Nancy, compiler. *Songs from Mother Goose: With the Traditional Melody for Each.* Illustrated by Robin Spowart. Harper, 1989.

Nelson, Kadir. *He's Got the Whole World in His Hands.* Dial, 2005.

Orozco, José-Luis, selector and translator. *Diez Deditos and Other Play Rhymes and Action Songs from Latin America.* Illustrated by Elisa Kleven. Dutton, 1997.

Pinkney, Brian. *Hush, Little Baby.* Greenwillow, 2006.

Yolen, Jane, editor. *Trot, Trot to Boston: Lap Songs, Finger Plays, Clapping Games, and Pantomime Rhymes.* Illustrated by Will Hillenbrand. Candlewick, 2005.

Anthologies of Poetry

Driscoll, Michael. *A Child's Introduction to Poetry.* Illustrated by Meredith Hamilton. Black Dog & Leventhal, 2003. Ages 9–14. Poetic forms and individual poets, with examples.

Ferris, Helen, compiler. *Favorite Poems Old and New.* Illustrated by Leonard Weisgard. Doubleday, 1957.

Hall, Donald, editor. *The Oxford Illustrated Book of American Children's Poems.* Oxford University, 1999.

Kennedy, X. J., and Dorothy Kennedy, editors. *Knock at a Star: A Child's Introduction to Poetry,* rev. ed. Illustrated by Karen Lee Baher. Little, Brown, 1999.

Martin, Bill Jr., and Michael Sampson, editors. *The Bill Martin Jr. Big Book of Poetry.* Simon & Schuster, 2008.

Prelutsky, Jack, editor. *The Random House Book of Poetry for Children.* Illustrated by Arnold Lobel. Random House, 1983.

———, editor. *The 20th Century Children's Poetry Treasury.* Illustrated by Meilo So. Knopf, 1999.

Yolen, Jane, and Andrew Peters, collectors. *Here's a Little Poem: A Very First Book of Poetry.* Illustrated by Polly Dunbar. Candlewick, 2007.

Specialized Poetry Books

Poetry books by a single poet and thematic poetry books are included.

Adoff, Arnold. *All the Colors of the Race.* Illustrated by John Steptoe. Lothrop, 1982.

———. *Touch the Poem.* Illustrated by Lisa Desimini. Scholastic, 2000.

Agee, Jon. *Orangutan Tongs: Poems to Tangle Your Tongue.* Disney/Hyperion, 2009.

Appelt, Kathi. *Poems from Homeroom: A Writer's Place to Start.* Holt, 2002. Ages 12–18. Includes a bibliography of adult books on writing poems and stories.

Ashman, Linda. *The Essential Worldwide Monster Guide.* Illustrated by David Small. Simon & Schuster, 2003.

Berry, James. *A Nest Full of Stars: Poems.* Pictures by Ashley Bryan. New York: Greenwillow, 2004. Everyday Caribbean language and culture.

———, editor. *Around the World in Eighty Poems.* Illustrated by Katherine Lucas. Chronicle, 2002. Fifty countries represented and many narrative poems.

Brooks, Gwendolyn. *Bronzeville Boys and Girls.* Illustrated by Faith Ringgold. HarperCollins, 2007.

Carlson, Lori, editor. *Cool Salsa: Bilingual Poems on Growing Up Latino in the United States.* Holt, 1994.

Clinton, Catherine, editor. *I, Too, Sing America: Three Centuries of African-American Poetry.* Illustrated by Stephen Alcorn. Houghton, 1998.

———, editor. *A Poem of Her Own: Voices of American Women Yesterday and Today.* Illustrated by Stephen Alcorn. Abrams, 2003. Ages 10–16.

Cullinan, Bernice E., editor. *A Jar of Tiny Stars: Poems by NCTE Award–Winning Poets.* Boyds Mills, 1995.

Dunbar, Paul Laurence. *Jump Back, Honey: The Poems of Paul Laurence Dunbar.* Hyperion, 1999.

Fleischman, Paul. *Big Talk: Poems for Four Voices.* Illustrated by Beppe Giacobbe. Candlewick, 2000. Ages 9–14.

———. *I Am Phoenix: Poems for Two Voices.* Illustrated by Eric Beddows. Harper, 1985.

———. *Joyful Noise: Poems for Two Voices.* Illustrated by Eric Beddows. Harper, 1988.

Florian, Douglas. *Autumnblings.* Greenwillow, 2003. One of his cycles of seasons, including *Handsprings,* 2006; *Summersaults,* 2002; and *Winter Eyes,* 1999.

———. *Comets, Stars, the Moon, and Mars: Space Poems and Paintings.* Harcourt , 2006.

———. *Dinothesaurus: Prehistoric Poems and Paintings.* Atheneum, 2009.

———. *Mammalabilia.* Illustrated. Harcourt, 2000.

Franco, Betsy. *Mathematickles.* Illustrated by Steven Salerno. Simon & Schuster, 2003.

George, Kristine O'Connell. *Fold Me a Poem.* Illustrated by Lauren Stringer. Harcourt, 2005.

———. *Hummingbird Nest: A Journal of Poems.* Illustrated by Barry Moser. Harcourt, 2004.

———. *Little Dog Poems.* Illustrated by June Otani. Clarion, 1999.

———. *Toasting Marshmallows: Camping Poems.* Illustrated by Kate Kiesler. Clarion, 2001.

———. *Up!* Illustrated by Hiroe Nakata. Clarion, 2005.

Ghigna, Charles. *A Fury of Motion: Poems for Boys.* Boyds Mills, 2003. Ages 12–18.

Giovanni, Nikki, editor. *Grand Fathers: Reminiscences, Poems, Recipes, and Photos of the Keepers of Our Traditions.* Holt, 1999. Ages 13–18. Also *Grand Mothers: Reminiscences, Poems, Recipes, and Photos of the Keepers of Our Traditions.* Holt, 1994.

———, editor. *Hip Hop Speaks to Children: A Celebration of Poetry with a Beat.* Illustrated by K. Balouch. Sourcesbooks, 2008.

Goldstein, Bobbye S., editor. *Inner Chimes: Poems on Poetry.* Illustrated by Jane Breskin Zalben. Wordsong/Boyds Mills, 1992.

Grandits, John. *Technically, It's Not My Fault: Concrete Poems.* Clarion, 2004. Ages 9–13.

Greenberg, Jan, editor. *Heart to Heart: New Poems Inspired by Twentieth Century American Art.* Abrams, 2001. Ages 11–15.

Grimes, Nikki. *Meet Danitra Brown.* Illustrated by Floyd Cooper. Morrow, 1994.

———. *A Pocketful of Poems.* Illustrated by Javaka Steptoe. Clarion, 2001.

Hoberman, Mary Ann. *Fathers, Mothers, Sisters, Brothers: A Collection of Family Poems.* Illustrated by Marylin Hafner. Little, 1991.

Holbrook, Sara. *By Definition: Poems of Feelings.* Illustrated by Scott Mattern. Boyds Mills, 2003.

Hopkins, Lee Bennett, selector. *America at War.* Illustrated by Stephen Alcorn. McElderry, 2008.

———, selector. *Behind the Museum Door: Poems to Celebrate the Wonders of Museums.* Illustrated by Stacey Dressen-McQueen. Abrams, 2007.

———, editor. *My America: A Poetry Atlas of the United States.* Illustrated by Stephen Alcorn. Simon & Schuster, 2000. Ages 9–14. Poems evocative of seven geographical regions of the United States.

Hudson, Wade, editor. *Pass It On: African American Poetry for Children.* Illustrated by Floyd Cooper. Scholastic, 1993.

In Daddy's Arms I Am Tall: African Americans Celebrating Fathers. Illustrated by Javaka Steptoe. Lee & Low, 1997.

James, Simon, editor. *Days Like This: A Collection of Small Poems.* Illustrated. Candlewick, 2000.

Janeczko, Paul B., editor. *Dirty Laundry Pile: Poems in Different Voices.* Illustrated by Melissa Sweet. HarperCollins, 2001.

———, editor. *A Foot in the Mouth: Poems to Speak, Sing, and Shout.* Illustrated by Chris Raschka. Candlewick, 2009.

———, selector. *A Kick in the Head: An Everyday Guide to Poetic Forms.* Illustrated by Chris Raschka. Candlewick, 2005. Ages 9–14. Poems of various forms with brief explanations of each form.

———, editor. *A Poke in the I: A Collection of Concrete Poems.* Illustrated by Chris Raschka. Candlewick, 2000.

Katz, Bobbi, editor. *Pocket Poems.* Illustrated by Marylin Hafner. Dutton, 2004.

———. *We, the People.* Illustrated by Nina Crews. Greenwillow, 2000. First-person poems focused on U.S. history; use as dramatic monologues.

Katz, Susan. *Looking for Jaguar and Other Rainforest Poems.* Illustrated by Lee Christiansen. Greenwillow, 2005.

Kennedy, Caroline, editor. *My Favorite Poetry for Children.* Illustrated by Jon J. Muth. Hyperion, 2005.

Kennedy, X. J. *Exploding Gravy.* Little, Brown, 2002. Ages 6–12.

———. *Fresh Brats.* Illustrated by James Watts. Macmillan, 1990.

Kurtz, Jane. *River Friendly, River Wild.* Illustrated by Neil Brennan. Simon & Schuster, 2000.

Kuskin, Karla. *Green as a Bean.* Illustrated by Melissa Iwai. HarperCollins, 2007.

Lewis, J. Patrick. *Doodle Dandies: Poems That Take Shape.* Illustrated by Lisa Desimini. Simon & Schuster, 1998.

———. *Freedom Like Sunlight: Praisesongs for Black Americans.* Creative Editions, 2000.

———. *Vherses: A Celebration of Outstanding Women.* Illustrated by Mark Summers. Creative, 2005. Ages 9–14.

Lillegard, Dee. *Wake Up House! Rooms Full of Poems.* Illustrated by Don Carter. Knopf, 2000.

Liu, Siyu, and Orel Protopopescu. *A Thousand Peaks: Poems from China.* Illustrated by Siyu Liu. Pacific View Press, 2001. Ages 10–18.

Mak, Kam. *My Chinatown.* Illustrated by Kam Mak. HarperCollins, 2002.

Morrison, Lillian, compiler. *It Rained All Day That Night: Autographs, Rhymes & Inscriptions.* Illustrated by Christy Hale. August House, 2003.

Myers, Walter Dean. *Blues Journey.* Illustrated by Christopher Myers. Holiday, 2003. Ages 10–15.

———. *Here in Harlem: Poems in Many Voices.* Holiday, 2004. Ages 12–18.

———. *Jazz.* Illustrated by Christopher Myers. Holiday, 2006.

Nye, Naomi Shihab, editor. *A Maze Me: Poems for Girls.* Illustrated by Terre Maher. Greenwillow, 2005. Ages 11–18.

———. *Come with Me: Poems for a Journey.* Illustrated by Dan Yaccarino. Greenwillow, 2000.

———, editor. *19 Varieties of Gazelle: Poems of the Middle East.* HarperCollins, 2002. Ages 11–18.

———, editor. *The Space between Our Footsteps: Poems and Paintings from the Middle East.* Simon & Schuster, 1998.

———, editor. *This Same Sky: A Collection of Poems from around the World.* Four Winds, 1992. Ages 11–18.

———, and Paul B. Janeczko, editors. *I Feel a Little Jumpy around You: A Book of Her Poems and His Poems Collected in Pairs.* Simon & Schuster, 1996. Ages 12–18.

Park, Linda Sue. *Tap Dancing on the Roof: Sijo (Poems).* Illustrated by Istvan Banyai. Clarion, 2007.

Pearson, Susan. *The Drowsy Hours: Poems for Bedtime.* Illustrated by Peter Malone. HarperCollins, 2002.

Peters, Lisa Westberg. *Earthshake: Poems from the Ground Up.* Illustrated by Cathie Felstead. Greenwillow, 2003. Ages 9–12. Poems about geology.

Prelutsky, Jack. *Behold the Bold Umbrellaphant and Other Poems.* Illustrated by Carin Berger. HarperCollins, 2006.

———. *If Not for the Cat.* Illustrated by Ted Rand. Greenwillow, 2004. Different animals described in haiku.

———, editor. *Read a Rhyme, Write a Rhyme.* Illustrated by Meilo So. Knopf, 2005.

Rex, Adam. *Frankenstein Makes a Sandwich.* Harcourt, 2006. Ages 9–12.

Rochelle, Belinda. *Words with Wings: A Treasury of African-American Poetry and Art.* HarperCollins/ Amistad, 2001.

Roessel, David, and Arnold Rampersad, editors. *Langston Hughes.* Illustrated by Benny Andrews. Sterling, 2006. Ages 10–18.

Ruddell, Deborah. *Today at the Bluebird Cafe: A Branchful of Birds.* Illustrated by Joan Rankin. M. K. McElderry, 2007.

Scieszka, Jon. *Science Verse.* Illustrated by Lane Smith. Viking, 2004.

Sidman, Joyce. *Butterfly Eyes and Other Secrets of the Meadow.* Illustrated by Beth Krommes. Houghton Mifflin, 2006.

———. *Meow Ruff.* Illustrated by Michelle Berg. Houghton Mifflin, 2006.

———. *Red Sings from Treetops: A Year in Colors.* Illustrated by Pamela Zagarenski. Houghton Mifflin, 2009.

———. *Song of the Water Boatman and Other Pond Poems.* Illustrated by Beckie Prange. Houghton, 2005.

Siebert, Diane. *Tour America: A Journey through Poems and Art.* Illustrated by Stephen T. Johnson. Chronicle, 2006. Ages 9–13.

Silverstein, Shel. *Where the Sidewalk Ends: The Poems and Drawings of Shel Silverstein.* Harper, 1974.

Singer, Marilyn. *Central Heating: Poems about Fire and Warmth.* Illustrated by Meilo So. Knopf, 2005. Ages 9–14.

Soto, Gary. *Neighborhood Odes.* Illustrated by David Diaz. Harcourt, 1992. Ages 10–15. Life in a Mexican-American neighborhood.

———. *Worlds Apart: Traveling with Fernie and Me.* Illustrated by Greg Clarke. Putnam, 2005. Ages 9–13.

Strickland, Dorothy S., and Michael R. Strickland, editors. *Families: Poems Celebrating the African American Experience.* Illustrated by John Ward. Wordsong/Boyds Mills, 1994.

Tadjo, Véronique, editor. *Talking Drums: A Selection of Poems from Africa South of the Sahara.* New York: Bloomsbury, 2004. Ages 9–14. A collection of 75 poems from 16 African countries arranged by themes.

Thomas, Joyce Carol. *Crowning Glory: Poems.* Illustrated by Brenda Joysmith. Joanna Cotler, 2002.

Updike, John. *A Child's Calendar.* Illustrated by Trina Schart Hyman. Holiday, 1999.

Vecchione, Patrice, editor. *Truth and Lies.* Holt, 2000. Ages 12–18. A multicultural anthology of 70 poems.

Weatherford, Carole Boston. *Remember the Bridge: Poems of a People.* New York: Philomel, 2002. Ages 10–16.

Willard, Nancy. *A Visit to William Blake's Inn: Poems for Innocent and Experienced Travelers.* Illustrated by Alice and Martin Provensen. Harcourt, 1981.

Wong, Janet. *Good Luck Gold and Other Poems.* M. K. McElderry, 1994.

———. *Night Garden: Poems from the World of Dreams.* Illustrated by Julie Paschkis. M. K. McElderry, 2000.

———. *A Suitcase of Seaweed and Other Poems.* M. K. McElderry, 1996.

Worth, Valerie. *Animal Poems.* Illustrated by Steve Jenkins. Farrar, 2007.

Zolotow, Charlotte. *Seasons: A Book of Poems.* Illustrated by Erik Blegvad. HarperCollins, 2002. Easy-to-read book.

Single Illustrated Poems

Note the distinction between *poems* and *stories told in verse.* Heavily illustrated poems are listed here. Illustrated stories told in verse are included under the heading of Picture Storybooks in Chapter 5.

Bates, Katharine Lee. *America the Beautiful.* Illustrated by Chris Gall. Little, Brown, 2004.

Carroll, Lewis. *Jabberwocky.* Illustrated by Christopher Myers. Jump at the Sun/Hyperion, 2007.

Hughes, Langston. *My People.* Photographs by Charles R. Smith Jr. Atheneum, 2009.

———. *The Negro Speaks of Rivers.* Illustrated by E. B. Lewis. Disney/Jump at the Sun, 2009.

Janeczko, Paul, and J. Patrick Lewis. *Birds on a Wire: A Renga 'Round Town.* Illustrated by Gary Lippincott. Wordsong, 2008.

Longfellow, Henry Wadsworth. *Paul Revere's Ride: The Landlord's Tale.* Illustrated by Charles Santore. HarperCollins, 2003. Ages 9–14. Dramatic illustrations accompany this classic poem.

Nelson, Marilyn. *Fortune's Bones: The Manumission Requiem.* Front Street, 2004. Ages 12–16. An illustrated poetic memorial of an enslaved man who died in 1798.

———. *A Wreath for Emmett Till.* Illustrated by Philippe Lardy. Houghton, 2005. Ages 12–18. An illustrated memorial to the lynched teen through interlocking sonnets.

Shange, Ntozake. *Ellington Was Not a Street.* Illustrated by Kadir Nelson. Simon & Schuster, 2004. Ages 9–13. Memories of a Harlem childhood.

Shore, Diane, and Jessica Alexander. *This Is the Dream.* Illustrated by James Ransome. Amistad, 2006.

Siebert, Diane. *Motorcycle Song.* Illustrated by Leonard Jenkins. HarperCollins, 2002.

Stevenson, Robert Louis. *The Moon.* Illustrated by Tracey C. Pearson. Farrar, 2006.

Thayer, Ernest L. *Casey at the Bat.* Illustrated by Joe Morse. Kids Can, 2006. Ages 9–13. An urban setting.

———. *Casey at the Bat: A Ballad of the Republic Sung in the Year 1888.* Illustrated by C. F. Payne. Simon & Schuster, 2003.

Willard, Nancy. *The Tale I Told Sasha.* Illustrated by David Christiana. Little, Brown, 1999.

PEARSON
myeducationkit™ Now go to Chapter 4 in the MyEducationKit (www.myeducationkit.com) for your book, where you can:

- Complete Assignments and Activities that can enrich and extend your knowledge of chapter content.

- Expand your knowledge with content-specific Web Links.

- Learn how authors and illustrators apply their craft by reading the written interviews in the Conversations section for the chapter.

- Review the chapter content by going to the Study Plan, taking a chapter quiz, and receiving feedback on your answers.

- Access the Children's Literature Database for your own exploration.

chapter FIVE

Picture Books

In the Library

You're right:
I am too old for THIS.
But I like pictures in my book,
And lots of color, easy words—
You needn't give me such a look!
You're wrong:
I am too young for THAT.
The words are long, the type's too small.
I don't find any pictures there—
I'd never get through that at all!

—*Michael Patrick Hearn*

In an era when picture books abound and provide many children with a delightful introduction to the world of books, it is difficult to imagine a time when books had no illustrations. Nonetheless, the picture book as we know it is a product of the twentieth century. The development of different types of picture books over the last century can be seen as a response to our developing awareness of the importance of early learning.

Definition and Description

Picture books are profusely illustrated books in which both words and illustrations contribute to the story's meaning. In a true picture book, the story would be diminished, and in some cases confusing, without the illustrations, and so we say that illustrations in picture books are integral, or essential, to the story. Picture books are written in all genres; they have illustrations on every page or every other page; and, as a general rule, they are thirty-two pages long. A good example of a picture book is *Officer Buckle and Gloria* by Peggy Rathmann.

Books with occasional illustrations that serve to break up or decorate the text, add interest, or depict isolated incidents are called **illustrated books.** Illustrations in these books are said to be incidental, or nonessential, to the content. Illustrated books are not picture books. In *The Curious Adventures of the Abandoned Toys* by Julian Fellowes (2007), illustrated by S. D. Schindler, full-page, full-color illustrations occur about every seventh page and pen-and-ink *vignettes* (small illustrations with no definite border) appear about every other page. The illustrations faithfully represent what is given in the text, but do not add new information to the story.

Evaluation and Selection of Picture Books

Children's first experiences with books must be enjoyable or they will soon not want to be involved with books. Negative experiences could mean that they may never learn to read or to enjoy reading. Over a period of time, evaluation and selection of picture books become a matter of achieving a good balance between what children naturally enjoy and what you want to lead them to enjoy.

The following criteria will help you to identify the best picture books:

- The ideas in picture books should be original or presented in an original way. Picture books on topics that children enjoy and find interesting are preferable to books about childhood, in the sense of nostalgia for or reminiscence of childhood. Books of the latter sort are for adults, not children.
- Picture books should avoid racial, ethnic, or sexual stereotyping in text and illustrations.
- Language and writing style should be rich and varied but not so complicated as to be incomprehensible to the child. It is desirable to feature new or unusual vocabulary within the context of interesting situations and complementary illustrations. Avoid books with overly sentimental and trite language.
- Illustrations should be appropriate in complexity to the age of the intended audience. In picture books for infants, look for relatively uncomplicated pages showing outlined figures against a plain background. Unusual perspectives or page designs in which only parts of a

figure are shown may not be readily understood or appreciated by children younger than age 2.

- Children prefer color in illustrations, but color is not essential in picture book illustrations. The more important point to consider is whether color or black and white is right for the story.

- When a book is to be shared with a large group, the illustrations must be large enough to be seen from a distance.

- Picture books selected for reading aloud, especially by parents and preschool and kindergarten teachers, should offer something to both listener and reader and promote interactive discussion between them (Brabham & Lynch-Brown, 2002). Multiple layers of meaning, child and adult perspectives, and humor are sources of enjoyment found in books that adults willingly read and reread to children. Generally, picture storybooks lend themselves to being read aloud. The titles in the Excellent Picture Books to Read Aloud list provide examples of the sort of book that works well as a read-aloud.

- The amount of text on the pages of a picture book determines how long it will take to read. Generally, the longer the text, the older the intended audience. Note that children's willingness to listen to stories grows with experience, which may result in a younger child who has been read to regularly having a much longer attention span than an older child with no story experience.

Teachers and librarians often rely on the professional judgment of committees that choose what they consider to be the most outstanding picture books published each year in this country and abroad. The most prestigious picture book award in the United States is the Caldecott Medal, sponsored by the Association for Library Service to Children division of the American Library Association. The equivalent award in Great Britain is the Kate Greenaway Medal; in Canada, the Governor General's Award for Illustration; and in Australia, the Picture Book of the Year Award.

★ *Excellent Picture Books* to READ ALOUD

Agee, Jon. *Terrific.* Ages 5–8.
Cole, Brock. *Good Enough to Eat.* Ages 4–8.
DiCamillo, Kate. *Louise, the Adventures of a Chicken.* Illustrated by Harry Bliss. Ages 5–8.
Kasza, Keiko. *The Dog Who Cried Wolf.* Ages 4–7.
Kimmel, Elizabeth C. *The Top Job.* Illustrated by Robert Neubecker. Ages 5–8.
Larochelle, David. *The End.* Illustrated by Richard Egielski. Ages 4–8.
Lloyd, Sam. *Mr. Pusskins: A Love Story.* Ages 4–7.
MacLennan, Cathy. *Chicky Chicky Chook Chook.* Ages 3–6.
Mayo, Margaret. *Choo Choo Clickety Clack!* Illustrated by Alex Ayliffe. Ages 2–5.
McCarthy, Meghan. *Aliens Are Coming! The True Account of the 1938 War of the Worlds Radio Broadcast.* Ages 8–12.
Melling, David. *The Scallywags.* Ages 5–8.
San Souci, Daniel. *Space Station Mars.* Ages 6–9.
Willems, Mo. *Knuffle Bunny: A Cautionary Tale.* Ages 3–5.
———. *Leonardo, the Terrible Monster.* Ages 4–6.
Willis, Jeanne. *Tadpole's Promise.* Illustrated by Tony Ross. Ages 5–9.

(See Appendix A for lists of award winners.) Another reliable source of information about good quality picture books is "The New York Times Best Illustrated Children's Books of the Year," published in early November as a part of *The New York Times Book Review Supplement.*

★ Visual Elements

Go to Activity 1 in the Assignments and Activities section of Chapter 5 in MyEducationKit; view the video on gaining insight into the making of a picture book and respond to the questions.

In many children's books the story is told through both text and pictures. This is particularly true of picture books but is also true of other books for children in which pictures serve an important function. Understanding and assessing the contributions of illustrations in books for children begin with knowing the *visual elements,* or basic elements with which artists and illustrators work. These visual elements are line, color, shape, texture, and composition. Understanding them will help you become more observant of illustrations and more discerning in your selection of picture books to share with children.

Line

The stroke marks that form part of a picture and often define its outline are the *lines.* The line of a picture generally defines the objects within the picture. Artists may choose to use lines that are dark or pale, heavy or light, solid or broken, wide or thin, straight or curved, or have combinations of these elements. The lines may be mostly vertical, horizontal, or on a diagonal. In pictures of the ocean and open prairies, the lines are predominantly horizontal; the impression is one of calm and tranquility. If the ocean is stormy, then the lines are more likely diagonal and upward moving, suggesting action or emotion or both. Each of these choices results in a different visual effect and can help to set a different mood. In evaluating the element of line within a picture, you may ask yourself whether the lines of the picture help to create and convey both the meaning and the feeling of the story. David Shannon's jagged, diagonal lines in *No, David!* convey the constant motion of an exuberant male toddler and the resulting chaos. (See Illustration 1.) The horizontal lines in *Song of the Water Boatmen & Other Pond Poems* by Joyce Sidman, on the other hand, suggest peace and tranquility. (See Illustration 9.)

Color

Color may be observed for its hue and intensity. The predominant colors may be from the cool end of the spectrum (the blues, greens, and gray-violets) or from the warm end (the reds, oranges, and yellows). The colors may be intense or pale (that is, more or less saturated) and may range from diaphanous to opaque. The colors used must first complement the text. For example, the still, quiet mood and cold, dark setting of the story in *Polar Bear Night* by Lauren Thompson are projected in the cool, muted blues, grays, black, and white of the illustrations. (See Illustration 7.) In contrast, the use of bright, loud colors in *Officer Buckle and Gloria* project a jovial, emotionally warm mood and help create the noisy school setting. (See Illustration 10.) If the events and mood of the text change during the course of the story, then the colors will change to reflect and signal the shift occurring in the story. Sometimes illustrations in a picture book will be noteworthy

Eric Carle, author/illustrator. Unusually formatted picture storybooks and concept books about insects and animals. *The Grouchy Ladybug; The Very Busy Spider.* www.eric-carle.com

Bryan Collier, illustrator. Signature watercolor and collage illustrations in picture books with urban settings and predominantly African-American characters. *Uptown; Martin's Big Words.* www.bryancollier.com

Lois Ehlert, author/illustrator. Bold color, use of collage, and engineered pages characterize her informational and concept books. *Color Zoo; Leaf Man.*

Denise Fleming, author/illustrator. Creates pattern books of handmade paper. *In the Small, Small Pond; Mama Cat Has Three Kittens.* www.denisefleming.com

Kevin Henkes, author/illustrator. Creator of family situation animal fantasies featuring mice and simple yet touching picture books about the wonder of life. *Lilly's Purple Plastic Purse; A Good Day; Kitten's First Full Moon.* www.kevinhenkes.com

Steven Kellogg, creator, reteller, and illustrator of a wide range of enduring picture books. Known for his whimsical, action-filled, richly colored illustrations. *Pinkerton, Behave!; If You Decide to Go to the Moon.* www.stevenkellogg.com

Barbara Lehman, illustrator. Uses an uncluttered cartoon style in wordless picture books in which real and imagined worlds blend. *The Red Book; Museum Trip; Rainstorm.*

Kadir Nelson, author/illustrator. Best known for emotional, realistic portrayals of historic African-Americans rendered in oils and other media. *We Are the Ship: The Story of Negro League Baseball; Henry's Freedom Box.* www.kadirnelson.com

Helen Oxenbury, author/illustrator. British. Watercolorist. Best known for baby books in board book format. *Ten Little Fingers and Ten Little Toes; Baby Max and Ruby series of concept books.*

Brian Pinkney, illustrator. Uses distinctive scratchboard technique in folktales and biographies featuring African Americans. *Duke Ellington: The Piano Prince and His Orchestra* (by Andrea Davis Pinkney).

Chris Raschka, illustrator. Spare, expressionist watercolors and brief texts elegantly capture mood. *Yo! Yes?; Mysterious Thelonious.*

Cynthia Rylant, author. Author of Newbery, Newbery Honor, and Caldecott Honor Award–winning books and most recently known for her easy-to-read series involving people and their animals. Henry and Mudge series; Mr. Putter and Tabby series; Annie and Snowball series.

Jon Scieszka, author. Fractured folktales and books for reluctant readers. *The Stinky Cheese Man and Other Fairly Stupid Tales.*

Laura Vaccaro Seeger, author/illustrator. Creator of concept and beginning reader books characterized by bold lines, bright colors, and die-cuts. *First the Egg; One Boy.* www.studiolvs.com

Brian Selznick, author/illustrator. Attention to period detail and unusual perspectives are artistic trademarks in his groundbreaking picture books for older readers. *The Dinosaurs of Waterhouse Hawkins* (by Barbara Kerley); *The Invention of Hugo Cabret.* www.theinventionofhugocabret.com

Maurice Sendak, author/illustrator. Explores the dreams and imagination of children in complex picture storybooks. *Where the Wild Things Are; Outside Over There.*

Uri Shulevitz, author/illustrator. Rich but subtle watercolor illustrations create long-ago settings and exemplify interplay between text and pictures. *Snow; The Treasure.*

Peter Sís, author/illustrator. Noted for intricate pen and ink and watercolor illustrations in picture book biographies for older readers. *Starry Messenger; Tibet through the Red Box.* www.petersis.com

David Small, illustrator. Two-time Caldecott medalist known for his loose style and narrative-rich watercolors. *The Gardener; So You Want to Be President?*

Chris Van Allsburg, author/illustrator. Uses shadow and unusual perspectives to create mysterious moods in picture storybooks for intermediate-grade readers. *Jumanji; The Garden of Abdul Gasazi.* www.chrisvanallsburg.com/flash.html

Rosemary Wells, author/illustrator. Creator of picture books, concept board books, baby books, and beginning readers featuring personified animals. *Max's ABC; Max and Ruby's Snowy Day; Yoko Writes Her Name.* www.rosemarywells.com

David Wiesner, author/illustrator. Creator of wordless fantasy stories. *Tuesday; Sector 7.* www.houghtonmifflinbooks.com/authors/wiesner/home.html

Mo Willems, author/illustrator. Creator of picture books for preschoolers featuring minimalist, childlike art, much humor, and action. *Don't Let the Pigeon Drive the Bus!; Knuffle Bunny: A Cautionary Tale.* www.mowillems.com

for their lack of color, which can be very effective. In *Baseball Hour* by Carol Nevius, illustrated by Bill Thomson, the reader's attention is focused on the brilliant white and red baseball surrounded with muted shades of gray and cream. (See Illustration 4.)

Shape

Shape, or the spatial forms of a picture, is produced by areas of color and by lines joining and intersecting to suggest outlines of forms. Shapes can be evaluated for their simplicity or complexity, their definition or lack of definition, their rigidity (as in geometric shapes) or suppleness (as in organic shapes), and their size. It is easy to see how this visual element can help to create moods or carry messages. Distinctly outlined figures can project security, reality, or permanence, whereas broken or thin outlines might suggest instability, make-believe, or transience. The proportion of one object in an illustration to another and the spaces surrounding the shapes are noteworthy for the nonverbal messages they carry—the bigger, the more important. The use of negative space or blank space may also be observed for its ability to highlight an object or to show isolation or loneliness. For example, consider the proportions of the baseball relative to the human figure in the illustration from *Baseball Hour,* and note that the artist has placed the pitcher on a blank background—all to emphasize the importance of the ball. (See Illustration 4.)

Texture

The tactile surface characteristics of pictured objects comprise the *texture* of a picture. More simply, the impression of how a pictured object feels is its texture. Textures may be rough or slick, firm or spongy, hard or soft, jagged or smooth. Textural effects generally offer a greater sense of reality to a picture, as happens in Barbara Reid's illustrations for *The Subway Mouse,* which feature slightly rounded and textured plasticine for the mice's furry bodies and found objects such as a feather, scraps of newspaper, buttons, and old food labels in their nests. (See Illustration 11.)

Composition

Composition includes the arrangement of the visual elements within a picture and the way in which these visual elements relate one to the other and combine to make the picture. Many artists arrange each illustration around a single focal point, which is often a key to understanding composition. The artist decides on proportion, balance, harmony, and disharmony within the various elements to produce the desired visual impact. The total effect should not overpower the story but rather extend and enrich the meaning and mood of the text. In the illustration from *Knuffle Bunny: A Cautionary Tale* by Mo Willems, the artist places the main characters at the center of the illustration and then further emphasizes them by using color against a nearly monochromatic sepia background. He draws the pair holding hands and sharing a loving look, and he places them in a calm, sunny, urban setting (a digitally-altered photograph). (See Illustration 5.) Although it is not mentioned in the text, the little girl is clutching her stuffed rabbit. This composition indicates to the reader that the story will be about a happy little girl who trusts her father and that whatever happens to them might actually happen in the real world.

Obviously, the details in the illustrations must not conflict with those in the text. Surprisingly, many examples can be cited in which the illustrator was not true to the text in all details. Children are keenly observant of these contradictions and find them distracting. Although children accept illustrations that are varied in all visual elements and artistic styles, they have little tolerance for inaccuracies.

Artistic Styles

Children come to note the distinctive features that identify the work of their favorite illustrators. Although the style of a picture is individual to each artist, artwork in general can be grouped by style similarities. Five broad categories of artistic styles recognized in the Western world are realistic, impressionistic, expressionistic, abstract, and surrealistic. Although an artist's works seldom fit neatly into one single art style, facets of these styles may be merged into the artist's personal expression of the world.

Realistic art represents natural forms and provides accurate representations without idealization. Bill Thomson's almost photographic paintings and Mo Willems's use of actual photographs as backgrounds are excellent examples of realistic art. (See Illustrations 4 and 5.)

Impressionistic art depicts natural appearances of objects by rendering fleeting visual impressions with an emphasis on light. Chris Raschka's rendering of the house in Norton Juster's *The Hello, Goodbye Window,* with its extensive use of white space to create light and lack of detail to suggest a fleeting image, exhibits these qualities. (See Illustration 8.)

Expressionistic art communicates an emotional experience more than an external reality. The intent of the artist is to draw attention to the central message by exaggeration and by eliminating competing details. David Shannon, in the illustration from *No, David!,* distorts the figure of the boy to emphasize his noisy exuberance and keeps background details to a minimum. (See Illustration 1.)

Abstract art uses intrinsic geometric forms and surface qualities with little direct representation of objects to emphasize mood and feeling. Stephen Savage's economy of line and emphasis on elemental triangles and circles in *Polar Bear Night* perfectly suggest the harsh, barren, frozen landscape of the Arctic in winter. (See Illustration 7.)

Surrealistic art emphasizes the subconscious by juxtaposing incongruous dreamlike and fantasy images with realistic ones. In the illustration from *Chester,* Ayano Imai juxtaposes the relatively realistic images of a dog and two humans against the fantasy of flowers growing out of the table (suggesting a positive outcome and a bright future) and smoke coming from the chimney of the dog's house (a visual metaphor for his having found his happy home). (See Illustration 3.)

Folk art, usually seen in picture books set in the distant past or about rural and pre-industrial societies, is supposed to be representative of the artistic style prevalent in the culture featured in the story. Folktales are sometimes illustrated in folk art style to give a sense of the culture and the ancient setting of the story. Folk art is sometimes referred to as *naïve,* in the sense of "untrained." The illustration from Chris Smith's *One City, Two Brothers,* a story based on a folktale shared by Israelis and Palestinians, has this quality. (See Illustration 2.)

Cartoon art features rounded figures, exaggerated action, and simplified backgrounds. Peggy Rathmann's humorous illustrations for *Officer Buckle and Gloria* are reminiscent of those found in comic books and are a good example of cartoon art style. (See Illustration 10.) Nathan Hale uses a slightly more sophisticated cartoon style in the graphic novel *Rapunzel's Revenge,* but the hallmarks of this style are still evident. (See Illustration 6.)

Artistic Media

The *artistic media* refer to the materials and technical means used by artists to create pictures. Although the variety of techniques and materials used by book illustrators is virtually unlimited, some of the more common media found in children's books are listed here.

- *Drawing:* Pen and ink, colored pencils, pastels (colored chalk), charcoal pencils
  Two excellent examples of drawing are Peter Sís's autobiographical *The Wall: Growing Up behind the Iron Curtain,* in which he uses pen and ink and colored markers extensively, and Brian Selznick's *The Invention of Hugo Cabret,* in which he uses charcoal pencil.

- *Collage:* An assemblage of different forms such as real objects and pieces of cut or torn paper to construct an illustration
  The illustration from Barbara Reid's *The Subway Mouse* includes found objects—a feather, torn newspaper, a crayon, fabric, twine, a button. (See Illustration 11.) Steve Jenkins uses cut papers to assemble his dazzling animal collages in such books as *How Many Ways Can You Catch a Fly?* (by Robin Page) and *Living Color.*

- *Print making:* Woodcuts, linoleum prints, block prints, lithography
  Beckie Prange's hand-colored woodcuts in *Song of the Water Boatman & Other Pond Poems* by Joyce Sidman perfectly capture the woodsy spirit of nature and wetland wildlife. (See Illustration 9.) The linocut technique used by Stephen Savage to make the illustrations in *Polar Bear Night* resembles that of woodcuts, except that linoleum is used instead of wood as the relief surface. (See Illustration 7.)

- *Photography:* Black and white, color
  The large, close-up photographs Walter Wick uses to illustrate his book, *A Drop of Water: A Book of Science and Wonder,* support the factual nature of its contents by saying, in effect, "This is real." (See Illustration 12.)

- *Painting:* Oils, acrylics, watercolors, gouache, tempera
  Oils, acrylics, tempera, and gouache paints produce an opaque surface with the possibility of brilliant, rich colors and a solid appearance. Watercolors are more transparent and prized for the luminosity achieved by the white paper surface shining through the paint. Of course, the tools with which the artist applies the paint will affect its look. Tools as varied as brushes, airbrushes, and sponges are used for applying paint. The bold colors in David Shannon's acrylic illustration from *No, David!* enhance the chaotic scene and the character's ebullient personality—a close look at the painting will reveal the artist's actual brush strokes. (See Illustration 1.)

- *Computer:* Digital painting, digital application of color to hand-drawn art, digital manipulation of images such as photographs
  Using software and machines such as scanners, artists can achieve unique artistic effects. In *Knuffle Bunny: A Cautionary Tale,* Mo Willems used a computer to color his hand-drawn characters, create the sepia tone of the background photographs, and even remove some unwanted items from the photographs. (See Illustration 5.)

Artists will generally use one predominant medium in a picture book, drawing from other media for special effects. Occasionally, an artist will choose to combine media more liberally to achieve the desired effect. Brief explanations of the artist's techniques and materials have recently begun to be included on the publishing history page of children's picture books. See the column in the Guide to Illustrations headed "Artistic Style; Media" for examples of illustrations created with mixed media.

Guide to Illustrations

	Source of Book Illustration	Artistic Style; Media	Visual Elements	Elements of Fiction Complemented by Illustrations
1	Shannon, David. *No, David!* Scholastic, 1998.	Expressionist; acrylic paint, colored pencil	Line, shape, color	Character, plot, mood, theme, style
2	Smith, Chris. *One City, Two Brothers.* Illustrated by Aurélia Fronty. Barefoot, 2007.	Folk; acrylic paint	Line, shape/space, color	Setting, theme
3	Imai, Ayano. *Chester.* Penguin, 2007.	Surreal; watercolor with mineral pigments	Composition, color, line	Mood, theme, plot
4	Nevius, Carol. *Baseball Hour.* Illustrated by Bill Thomson. Marshall Cavendish, 2008.	Realistic; oil and acrylic paints, kneaded eraser, colored pencils	Shape/space, line, composition, texture, color	Character, setting, mood
5	Willems, Mo. *Knuffle Bunny: A Cautionary Tale.* Hyperion, 2004.	Cartoon/Realistic; pen and ink, digital photography, computer	Line, color	Character, setting, theme, mood
6	Hale, Shannon, and Dean Hale. *Rapunzel's Revenge.* Illustrated by Nathan Hale. Bloomsbury USA, 2008.	Cartoon/graphic novel format; pencil, ink colored with Photoshop	Line, color	Plot, character, setting, theme, style

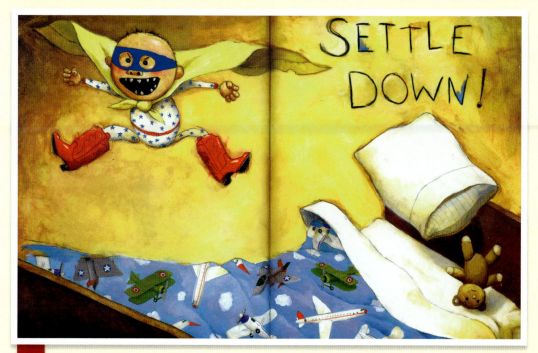

1

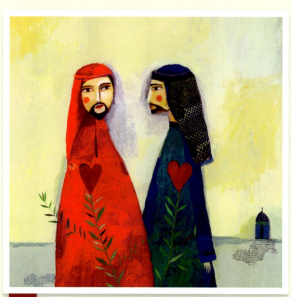

2

3

4

5

6

7

8

9

10

11

12

Guide to Illustrations

	Source of Book Illustration	Artistic Style; Media	Visual Elements	Elements of Fiction Complemented by Illustrations
7	Thompson, Lauren. *Polar Bear Night*. Illustrated by Stephen Savage. Scholastic, 2004.	Abstract; linocut prints	Color, shape, composition	Setting, characters, theme
8	Juster, Norton. *The Hello, Goodbye Window*. Illustrated by Chris Raschka. Hyperion, 2005.	Impressionistic; watercolors, oil pastels, pen and ink, charcoals	Composition, color, line	Character, setting, mood, style
9	Sidman, Joyce. *Song of the Water Boatman & Other Pond Poems*. Illustrated by Beckie Prange. Houghton, 2005.	Woodcut; watercolors	Composition, line, color, mood	Setting, theme
10	Rathmann, Peggy. *Officer Buckle and Gloria*. Putnam, 1995.	Cartoon; watercolors, pen and ink	Line, composition, mood	Plot, character, theme
11	Reid, Barbara. *The Subway Mouse*. Scholastic, 2003.	Cartoon; collage	Texture, color, mood	Character, setting, style
12	Wick, Walter. *A Drop of Water: A Book of Science and Wonder*. Scholastic, 1997.	Realistic; photography	Composition, space	Style, theme

Book Design

Book design is the artful orchestration of all components of a book into a coherent whole. Children's books are more than text or text and pictures combined. In this section we will discuss the other features that are a part of book design.

The *dust jacket* is a removable paper cover wrapped around the book; it serves as protection against soiling. It also attracts purchasers and readers as well as informs them about the book, its author, and its illustrator. The *covers* of a book are usually made of two boards, which make the book more durable and allow it to stand on a shelf. When no dust jacket is on a book, the front cover provides the reader with a first impression of the story. The *title,* an important part of the text—usually first seen by the reader on the dust jacket or front cover—combines with the illustrations of the dust jacket or cover to communicate the nature of the story to young readers who choose books primarily by title and cover. Many titles suggest the topic of the story and can assist readers in deciding whether to read the book. Other titles and covers may not offer as much information about the story. In such cases, some explanation by a teacher or librarian in the form of a booktalk may prove invaluable to young readers seeking just such a book.

The *endpapers* are the pages glued to the inside front and back boards of the cover, and the *flyleaf* is the page facing each endpaper. In many well-designed books, the endpaper and flyleaf are used to provoke curiosity in the reader for what follows, to set a mood, to evoke an affective response in preparation for the story, or to act as a visual prologue and epilogue, as in Emily Gravett's *Orange Pear Apple Bear* and Alan Madison's *Velma Gratch and the Way Cool Butterfly,* illustrated by Kevin Hawkes. When readers turn the flyleaf, they are further prepared by the artist for the story by viewing the title page. The *title page* tells the book's full title and subtitle, if there is one; the names of the author(s) and illustrator(s); and the name and location of the publisher. Occasionally, a book will include a *frontispiece,* an illustration facing the title page, which is intended to establish the tone and to entice the reader to begin the story.

On the reverse side of the title page, often referred to as the *verso* of the title page, is the *publishing history* of the book. On this page is the copyright notice, a legal right giving only the holder permission to produce and sell the work. Others who wish to reproduce the work in any way must request permission from the copyright holder. The copyright is indicated by the international symbol ©. This symbol is followed by the name of the person(s) holding the copyright and the date it takes effect, which is the year the book is first published. Later publications are also listed. The country in which the book was printed, the number assigned to the book by the Library of Congress, the International Standard Book Number (ISBN), and the edition of the book are also included on this page. Many publishers now include on this page cataloguing information for libraries, a very brief annotation of the story, and a statement on the media and techniques used in the illustrations.

The title page typically presents the *typeface,* the style of print to be used throughout the book. The size and legibility of the typeface must be suited to the book's intended audience. In children's books this can be extremely important. Books for the young child who is just learning to read should have large, well-spaced print for easy eye scanning. The print style for an easy-to-read book should be a somewhat larger-than-average standard block print with easily distinguishable and recognizable uppercase and lowercase letters. In children's trade books produced in "big book" size for whole-class or small group reading activities, the print needs to be large enough to be readily seen from a minimum of 10 to 12 feet. Legibility is diminished when background colors are used behind the text, leaving insufficient contrast for easy reading.

The size, shape, and darkness of the print type may vary from book to book. The lines may be heavy and strong or light and willowy. The choice of print type should enhance the overall visual message of the illustrations and fit with the illustrations in style and mood. Note also that the placement of the print on the pages in relation to the illustrations can subtly guide the reader and become a functional part of the story.

Unusual print styles are sometimes selected for a children's book. In a book with a diary format, the use of script print gives the impression of handwriting. In this case, the amount of script print is usually brief, and standard block print is used throughout most of the book for greater ease of reading. In place of print some illustrators choose to hand-letter the text. An example of lettering as part of the illustrative component of a book is found in the classic *Millions of Cats* by Wanda Gág. A more recent example is found in David Larochelle's *The End,* illustrated by Richard Egielski.

The *page layout* is also worth observing. You will notice that illustrations are variously placed one on a page, on facing pages, on alternating pages, or on parts of pages. When the picture extends across the two facing pages, it is called a *doublespread.* A doublespread gives the effect of motion, because the eye is drawn to the next page. It can also give a feeling of grandeur, openness, and expansiveness. Sometimes, a picture will begin on a right-hand page and spill over to the following page, the reverse side. This offers a strong sense of continuity from one part of the story to the next. Some pictures have a *frame.* Framing an illustration can work to distance the reader from the action, lend a sense of order to the story, or make the mood more formal. The frame itself may be anything from a simple line to a broad, ornately decorated ribbon of information. Decorations on a frame may repeat certain images or symbols to reinforce the meaning of the story.

Pages are another part of the book makeup. In evaluating pages, you should note whether the paper is thick enough to be durable and whether textured or colored paper reflects or enhances the story. Similarly, the shape of the pages should be in keeping with the story or concept, particularly if they are unique or unusual (in the shape of a concrete object, fold-out, or engineered, for example).

The *size* of the book is an important design feature. Large picture books are well suited for reading aloud to a class. Smaller picture books are usually not satisfactory choices for read-alouds, unless, of course, you are reading to only one child or to a small group of children.

Book binding, or the way the pages are held together, is important because it helps determine a book's durability. Books may be bound in hardcover, paperback, or in some special-purpose material. For example, books for babies are frequently bound in sturdy cardboard or vinyl to withstand the dual role of toy and book. When buying a hardcover book, determine whether the binding is glued or sewn by carefully opening the book at its midpoint. If the book binding is sewn, you will be able to see the stitches in the gutter of the book. Sewn bindings last much longer than glued ones. Durability relative to cost is the usual trade-off you must weigh in selecting paper or hardcover bindings for classroom or school libraries. Generally speaking, the cost of hardcover books is justified when you expect fairly heavy use.

Observing the Role of Illustrations in Picture Books

The role of illustrations in picture books can best be understood in terms of the literary elements, as defined in Chapter 3, and the visual elements, artistic styles, and artistic media as discussed earlier in this chapter. These roles vary in importance, depending on the type of picture book. In wordless picture books, the illustrations tell the whole story; in picture storybooks, they tell part of the story; in illustrated books, they may serve as mere breaks in the narrative or as decoration.

The Guide to Illustrations found at the beginning and end of the color insert gives a brief analysis of each illustration and how it contributes to the story. To better understand the examples, it would be wise to read the books from which the illustrations were taken and then use the guide as an aid to understanding how artistic styles, visual elements, and elements of fiction found in the illustrations contribute to each story's meaning. For example, in the illustration from David Shannon's *No, David!* (Illustration 1), a pajama-clad little boy, instead of quietly preparing for sleep, careens off his bed imagining that he is a superhero. His mother's presence is found only in her words, "Settle down!" For child and adult reader alike, the boy's exaggerated expression and motion provide humor. Artist David Shannon's use of an expressionistic style, bold colors, and jagged, diagonal lines emphasize the child's wild energy, motion, and zest for life. Seen from his mother's perspective, however, these same artistic attributes could be interpreted as emphasizing the child's naughtiness.

The key to understanding and appreciating the role of illustrations in picture books is to observe them carefully. Look at the illustrations for the messages they contain, in the way children who cannot read words "read" illustrations. Table 5.1 offers tips in what to look for as you read picture storybooks.

PEARSON
myeducationkit™

Go to Activity 2 in the Assignments and Activities section of Chapter 5 in MyEducationKit; complete the activity on examining the relationship between illustrations and text in a picture storybook.

Historical Overview of Picture Books

Orbis Pictus (The World in Pictures), an ABC book written and illustrated by John Amos Comenius in Moravia and published in 1657, is considered to be the first children's picture book. Comenius's emphasis on using pictures to explain and expand the meaning of the text in books for young people was an important first. But since early books were rare and prohibitively expensive, they were seen by very few children. Moreover, until well into the nineteenth century, Europeans and Americans believed that books were for the serious business of educating and soul saving, not for enjoyment! Today's full-color, extravagantly illustrated, highly amusing picture book is the product of the following important developments.

■ Technological advances in color printing made high-quality illustrations in books more affordable.

■ A more understanding attitude toward childhood evolved. During the nineteenth century, society began to accept the notion of childhood as a time for playing and learning. At the same time, the general economy began to be able to afford the average child the leisure time these activities require.

Table 5.1 How Illustrations Contribute to Picture Book Stories: A Summary

Artistic and Literary Aspects		Examples of Illustrations' Contributions to Stories
Literary Elements	Plot	Convey story events not included in the text.
	Character	Show characters not mentioned in the text; contribute to characterization by showing characters' physical descriptions and actions not mentioned in the text.
	Setting	Show the setting (e.g., era as indicated by clothes, cars, architecture). Indicate the passing of time (time of day, seasons, etc.).
	Theme	Underscore the book's theme. Indicate the book's theme (in wordless books).
	Style	Show the author's stance toward the protagonist by viewing the world from the protagonist's perspective. Support a book's literary style to faithfully represent an era or culture.
Visual Elements	Line	Indicate motion or action, story mood (e.g., calm vs. agitated), aspects of plot (e.g., real vs. dreamed), and character (e.g., fragile vs. strong).
	Color	Indicate characters' emotions and personalities, story mood, and aspects of setting (e.g., lush vs. arid, cold vs. warm).
	Shape	Indicate what is most important by relative size. Emphasize contrast by juxtaposing large and small objects.
	Texture	Intensify a sense of character or setting by indicating the feel of objects or surroundings.
	Composition	Focus the eye on what is most important (usually in the center). Indicate a character's perspective (how the character sees the world).
Artistic Styles	Realistic	Emphasize the idea that information in works of nonfiction is factual and that realistic works of fiction could be true or based on fact.
	Impressionistic	Contribute to settings through light-filled scenes of nature.
	Expressionistic	Express characters' feelings and emotions through exaggeration.
	Abstract	Emphasize basic, shared traits of characters; create a nonspecific setting, whether ancient, futuristic, or timeless.
	Surrealistic	Help connect characters' conscious and unconscious thoughts, emotions, and concerns.
	Folk or naïve	Establish and develop settings in the past.
	Cartoon	Provide humor through exaggeration of characters' physical appearance and actions.
Artistic Media	Pen and ink	Help define outlines and distinguish figure from ground in books for the very young; underscore the simplicity of some stories by simplicity of line and absence of color; help explain complicated scientific and technological concepts through precise, detailed drawings.
	Pastels	Contribute to the creation of strong emotions and lush settings with saturated colors.
	Graphite pencils	Focus attention on characters, mood, and actions due to absence of color.

(continued)

Table 5.1 *Continued*

Artistic and Literary Aspects	Examples of Illustrations' Contributions to Stories
Colored pencils	Help create a lighter mood due to transparency of the medium.
Wax crayons	Lend a childlike perspective by using an artistic medium popular with children.
Collages	Contribute to settings and characterization through use of objects with tactile feel; lend a sense of reality through the use of real-world objects.
Woodcuts	Help establish outdoor settings with rough-hewn look; lend a sense of character strength through bold lines.
Photographs	Create a sense of the real world with contemporary photographs; create a sense of the past with period photographs.
Oil paints, gouache	Establish a somber or serious mood due to opaqueness of the medium.
Watercolors	Establish a lighter mood because of transparency of the medium and consequent amount of light reflected.

- Higher standards of excellence in picture book illustrations developed. The beauty, charm, and humor of the illustrations of nineteenth-century illustrators Randolph Caldecott, Kate Greenaway, and Walter Crane brought children's book art to the attention of the general public.
- The establishment of national awards for excellence in children's book illustration in the twentieth century encouraged more artists to enter the children's book field.
- Because of the growth of public school systems and public and school library systems, the demand for books grew. In addition, reading came to be recognized as one of the child's best tools for learning and for gaining a worthy source of entertainment.

Today, the picture book genre is well established, with an ever-widening audience, more multicultural themes, a greater number of bilingual picture books (especially English–Spanish), and more realistic themes such as the effects of war, poverty, immigration, and disabilities on the lives of children. Greater diversity in formats and more illustrated retellings of folktales are available. A trend of the 1990s was to publish picture books with high levels of conceptual difficulty and artistic sophistication intended for middle-grade students. The twenty-first century has witnessed the growth of the graphic novel, a novel-length comic book, originally created for adults, that now includes books for elementary- and middle-grade students.

Types of Picture Books

Today's picture books differ in intended audience, purpose, format, and relative amount of text and illustration. These differences are not absolute, however; quite often, one will find a picture book having characteristics of several specific types. With the understanding that overlap between

MILESTONES *in the Development of Picture Books*

Date	Event	Significance
1484	Publication of *Aesop's Fables,* illustrated by William Caxton	One of the first-known illustrated books enjoyed by children
1657	Publication of *Orbis Pictus,* written and illustrated by John Amos Comenius	Considered to be the first picture book for children
1860–1900	Golden Age of children's book illustration in Great Britain, led by Randolph Caldecott, Walter Crane, and Kate Greenaway	Increased awareness, stature, popularity, and appreciation of children's picture books
1902	Publication of *The Tale of Peter Rabbit* by Beatrix Potter	Early important modern picture storybook in English
1928	Publication of *Millions of Cats* by Wanda Gág	Early important modern American picture storybook
1938	Establishment of the Caldecott Award for illustration in children's books in the United States	Promoted excellence in illustrating for children and encouraged talented artists to illustrate children's books
1940	Publication of *Pat the Bunny* by Dorothy Kunhardt	One of the first books for babies; began the move to supply different types of picture books for different child audiences
1957	Publication of *The Cat in the Hat,* written and illustrated by Dr. Seuss, and *Little Bear,* written by Else Minarik and illustrated by Maurice Sendak	Introduced the easy-to-read genre of picture books
1967	Publication of *A Boy, a Dog, and a Frog,* illustrated by Mercer Mayer	Popularized the wordless book genre
1972	Publication of *Push Pull, Empty Full* by Tana Hoban	Signaled the growing popularity of the concept picture book
1974	Publication of *Arrow to the Sun: A Pueblo Indian Tale* by Gerald McDermott	Signaled the emergence of picture books for older readers as a distinct type of picture book
1981	Publication of "The Baby Board Books" by Helen Oxenbury	Established baby books as a distinct and important type of picture book
1990	*Color Zoo* by Lois Ehlert wins a Caldecott Honor Award	Recognition of the engineered book genre
1991	*Black and White* by David Macaulay wins Caldecott Medal	Denoted influence of postmodernism and acceptance of nontraditional picture book formats
2006	*Henry and Mudge and the Great Grandpas* by Cynthia Rylant, illustrated by Suçie Stevenson, wins the first Theodor Seuss Geisel Award for Beginning Reader Books	Promoted excellence in books for beginning readers

types is inevitable, you will want to learn to recognize the following kinds of picture books (organized by the intended age of the audience from youngest to oldest). Note that poems, nursery rhymes, and songbooks in picture book format are detailed in Chapter 4, folktales in picture book format are discussed in Chapter 6, and informational picture books are covered in Chapter 10.

Baby Books

Baby books are simply designed, brightly illustrated, durable picture books that are intended for use with children aged 0 to 2. Safety is ensured by rounded corners, nontoxic materials, washable pages, and no loose attachments. An example is *Global Babies* by Maya Ajmera in conjunction with the Global Fund for Children. The types of baby books actually denote the material used in their construction. *Board books* are constructed of heavy, laminated cardboard and are either bound as a book with pages or made to fold out in an accordion fashion. *Vinyl books* and *cloth books* are also types of baby books. These books have little or no text. Their content, which deals with the objects and routines that are familiar to the infant and toddler, is presented mainly by the illustrations. The best baby books, such as those produced by Helen Oxenbury, are intelligently designed to emphasize patterns and associations to promote dialogue between the caregiver and the young child, who will often look at these books together.

Interactive Books

Interactive books are picture books that stimulate a child's verbal or physical participation as the book is read. These books ask the child direct questions, invite unison recitation of chants or repeated lines, encourage clapping or moving to the rhythm of the words, or require the child to touch or manipulate the book or find objects in the illustrations. The intended audience is usually children aged 2 to 6, and the books are seen as an extension of their world of play. One classic example of this type of book that is still greatly enjoyed by toddlers today is Dorothy Kunhardt's *Pat the Bunny*. A more recent interactive book worth noting is Mem Fox's *Ten Little Fingers and Ten Little Toes*, illustrated by Helen Oxenbury.

Toy Books

Sometimes called *engineered* or *mechanical books, toy books* use paper that has been engineered (i.e., cut, folded, constructed) to provide pop-up, see-through, movable, changeable, fold-out, or three-dimensional illustrations. Toy books can be found for all ages, but only those that have the simpler types of engineering, such as pages of varying widths or drilled holes for see-through effects (as in Eric Carle's classic, *The Very Hungry Caterpillar,* or Laura Seeger's *First the Egg*), would be appropriate for most young children. Toy books with fragile or elaborate pop-up features, such as Robert Sabuda's amazing pop-up version of *Alice's Adventures in Wonderland*, would not last in the hands of a very young child, but would delight older children (and adults).

Wordless Books

The *wordless book* depends entirely on carefully sequenced illustrations to present the story. There is no text, or the text is limited to one or two pages in the book, so the illustrations must be highly narrative. An outstanding example is Barbara Lehman's *The Red Book,* a fantasy about finding friends in books—literally. Wordless books are generally intended for prereaders, usually children aged 4 to 6. More sophisticated wordless books for older readers, such as David Weisner's *Sector 7,* are also available. When children "read" these illustrations in their own words, they benefit from the book's visual story structure in several ways:

- They develop a concept of story as a cohesive narrative with a beginning and an end.
- They use language inventively, which promotes language development.
- They learn the front-to-back, left-to-right page progression in reading.
- They begin to understand that stories can be found not only in books but in themselves.

Alphabet Books

The *alphabet,* or *ABC, book* presents the alphabet letter by letter to acquaint young children with the shapes, names, and, in some cases, the sounds of the twenty-six letters. For example, see *ABC: A Child's First Alphabet Book* by Alison Jay. Almost all ABC book authors and illustrators choose a theme (animals, elves, fruit, etc.) or device (finding the many objects in the accompanying illustration beginning with the featured letter) to give their books cohesion. In choosing an ABC book, consider the appropriateness of the theme or device for students, whether both uppercase and lowercase letters are displayed, and the use of a simple, easy-to-read style of print.

Most ABC books are intended for the nonreader or beginning reader. Some authors and illustrators use the alphabet itself as a device for presenting information or wordplay. In these cases, the intended audience already knows the alphabet. In *Superhero ABC,* Bob McLeod presents imaginative and wacky superheroes whose names and descriptions begin with the featured letter, inviting readers to invent such characters of their own.

Counting Books

The *counting book* presents numbers, usually 1 through 10, to acquaint young children with the numerals and their shapes (1, 2, 3, . . .), the number names (one, two, three, . . .), the sense of what quantity each numeral represents, and the counting sequence. *Teeth, Tails, & Tentacles: An Animal Counting Book* by Christopher Wormell, with its bold linocut prints clearly depicting the numerals and the objects to be counted, presents lessons in counting and zoology simultaneously. As with alphabet books, authors and illustrators of counting books employ themes or devices to make them more cohesive and interesting. Specific considerations in evaluating a counting book include the appeal to children of the theme and objects chosen to illustrate the number concepts, and the clarity with which the illustrator presents the concept of number.

Illustrators often fill their alphabet and counting books with unusual and intriguing objects for children to name and count, such as aardvarks, barracudas, and chameleons. Children pick up a great deal of interesting information and vocabulary in this way. You will be in the best position to decide whether the novelty of these objects will be motivating or confusing to your students.

Concept Books

A *concept book* is a picture book that explores or explains an idea or concept (e.g., opposites), an object (e.g., a train), or an activity (e.g., working) rather than telling a story. Many concept books have no plot but use repeated elements in the illustrations and text to tie the book together. Laura Seeger combines a simple format, well-known but unexpected objects, and paper cut-outs to create an interesting book about color in *Lemons Are Not Red*. Limited text and clearly understood illustrations in the best concept books stimulate children's exploratory talk about the concepts, objects, and activities presented.

Alphabet and counting books are considered types of concept books. Another variety of the concept book that is popular with 2- to 4-year-olds is the *naming book,* which presents simple, labeled pictures of people, animals, and objects for young children to identify. *My First Word Book* by Angela Wilkes is an example of a naming book.

Picture Storybooks

The *picture storybook* is a book in which a story is told through both the words and pictures. Text and illustration occur with equal frequency in these books, and on most double spreads, both are in view. This is the type of book most people associate with the term *picture book* and is the most common type of picture book. An enduring favorite picture storybook is Chris Van Allsburg's *The Polar Express*. A highly regarded recent example is Kevin Henkes's *Kitten's First Full Moon*. The information and tips found in Table 5.1 are particularly applicable to picture storybooks.

The text of most picture storybooks is meant to be read aloud to the intended audience of 4- to 7-year-olds, at least for the first time or two, and often includes challenging vocabulary. Many of the best picture storybooks are also read and enjoyed independently by children 8 years old and up.

Pattern Books

Picture books that strongly emphasize word patterns are called *pattern books.* They are also called *decodable books* because of their language regularities in which certain phonological features are repeated, as is the line, "Is this the bus for us, Gus?" in Suzanne Bloom's *The Bus for Us*. In addition, *predictable books,* such as Bill Martin Jr. and Eric Carle's perennial favorite *Brown Bear, Brown Bear, What Do You See?* and its companion books, *Polar Bear . . .* and *Panda Bear . . . ,* are sometimes included in this category because of meaning and illustration clues.

Easy-to-Read Books

Easy-to-read books are created to help the beginning reader read independently with success. These books have limited text on each page, large print, double spacing, short sentences, and often occur in series. There is usually an illustration on every other page. Language is often, but not always, controlled, and words are short and familiar. Laura McGee Kvasnosky's *Zelda and Ivy: The Runaways,* with its emphasis on familiar family situations and gentle humor, is a good example. Another is Mo Willems's *Are You Ready to Play Outside?* with its theme of friendship and its story told in dialogue balloons. Easy-to-read books can be used with children whenever they want to learn to read, but the audience for this type of book is usually 5- to 7-year-olds.

The easy-to-read book differs in appearance from the picture storybook in several obvious ways. Because they are intended for independent reading, they do not have to be seen from a distance and may be smaller, the text takes up a greater proportion of each page, and the text is often divided into short chapters.

The importance of the easy-to-read book genre was recognized in 2004 with the establishment of the Theodor Seuss Geisel Award. This annual award, named for the renowned Theodor Geisel, or Dr. Seuss, and sponsored by the American Library Association, is given to the author(s) and illustrator(s) of the most distinguished American book for beginning readers published in English in the United States during the preceding year. The first award was given in 2006.

Picture Books for Older Readers

Picture books for older readers are generally more sophisticated, abstract, or complex in themes, stories, and illustrations and are suitable for children aged 10 and older. This type of picture book began to appear in the 1970s, perhaps in response to our increasingly visual modes of communication, and now artists such as Anthony Browne, D. B. Johnson, David Macaulay, and Peter Sís are known for their work in this area. Peter Sís's autobiographical *The Wall: Growing Up behind the Iron Curtain* has aspects of both picture book and graphic novel. Its serious content and factual, historic base are aimed squarely at middle- and high-school students, making it an excellent example of a picture book for older readers.

Picture books for older readers lend themselves well to use across the middle-school curriculum, including social studies, science, language arts, mathematics, art, music, and physical education. Consider the advantages of using picture books for older readers in middle and secondary schools:

- They can be used as teacher read-alouds for introductions and supplements to textbook-based units of instruction.
- They can be used in text sets (several books on the same topic) for small group in-class reading, analysis, and discussion.
- They can be used by individual students as models of excellent writing.
- They can inject humor and stimulate interest in a topic, and possibly provoke discussion, which would result in a deeper understanding of the content (Albright, 2000, 2002), as David Macaulay's *The Way We Work* could do for the topic of how the human body functions.
- They can demonstrate practical applications of concepts (Alvermann & Phelps, 1998), as D. B. Johnson's *Henry Climbs a Mountain* does for the concept of civil disobedience.
- They often have factual content that reinforces or adds to that found in textbooks, as Margot T. Raven's *Night Boat to Freedom,* illustrated by E. B. Lewis, could do for a history unit of instruction on slavery—as the book is based on narratives from the Federal Writers' Project Slave Narrative Collection.

■ They offer different perspectives on issues, such as the Chinese-American perspectives on immigration to the United States after the passage of the 1882 Chinese Exclusion Act, as recounted in Milly Lee's *Landed,* illustrated by Yangsook Choi.

The traditional notion that picture books are only for younger children no longer applies. Although some adults may persist in guiding older children away from picture books, as Gontarski (1994) found, today's teachers and librarians would be wise to make picture books for older readers an option in any learning situation.

Graphic Novels

The last decade has seen the emergence of *graphic novels* as a book format related to picture books. These novel-length books feature text written in speech bubbles or as captions similar to comic-book illustrations. The term *graphic* refers to stories told through images and does not refer to the nature of the content.

The popularity of these books has grown exponentially in the last decade. Features of graphic novels that appeal to young people and especially to reluctant readers are that they are visually oriented, emphasize dialogue, often occur in series, and have close ties to popular culture such as films and comic-book superheroes. For instance, Shannon and Dean Hale and illustrator Nathan Hale, the creators of the graphic novel featured in the color insert, *Rapunzel's Revenge* (Illustration 6) generate reader interest by recasting the demure folktale heroine as a proactive superwoman and change the setting to the outlaw-ridden U.S. Wild West. A graphic novel appropriate for intermediate-graders is *Babymouse: Queen of the World!* by Jennifer L. Holm and illustrated by Matthew Holm.

Transitional Books

Transitional books are a special type of book for the child who can read but has not yet become a fluent reader. They are not picture books, but lie somewhere between picture books and full-length novels. Characteristics of transitional books are an uncomplicated writing style and vocabulary, illustrations on about every third page, division of text into chapters, slightly enlarged print, and an average length of 100 pages. A good example of a transitional book is *Ruby Lu, Brave and True* by Lenore Look, illustrated by Anne Wilsdorf. Often, books for the transitional reader occur in series, as Donald J. Sobol's much-loved Encyclopedia Brown books and the more recent Ivy and Bean series by Annie Barrows and Martin Bridge series by Jessica Kerrin.

The Center for Children's Books and the Graduate School of Library and Information Science of the University of Illinois at Urbana–Champaign established the Gryphon Award for transitional books in 2004. A $1,000 prize is given annually to the author of the English-language work of fiction or nonfiction published in the preceding year that best exemplifies qualities that successfully bridge the gap in difficulty between picture books and full-length books.

During the twentieth century the picture book was begun and developed as a genre, diversified to meet the demands of an ever-expanding audience and market, and improved as a result of new and refined printing technology. As researchers came to realize the connections between positive early experiences with good literature, reading, and school success, new types of picture books were developed. Today, high-quality picture books on nearly every imaginable topic can enrich the lives and imaginations of young children and the classrooms and libraries where they learn.

Issues & Topics for FURTHER INVESTIGATION

- Investigate the topic of visual symbolism in art. One possible online source is www.umich.edu/~umfandsf/symbolismproject/symbolism.html/index.html. Following your research, read a book noted for its use of visual symbols, such as the Grimm brothers' *Snow White and the Seven Dwarfs,* translated by Randall Jarrell and illustrated by Nancy Ekholm Burkert (1972). How does awareness of visual symbolism enhance a reader's appreciation of stories presented in picture storybook format?

- Select a picture storybook appropriate for the ages of the students you teach. Read the book aloud to the students and then guide them in a discussion of how the illustrations contribute to the story. Use Table 5.1 for ideas.

- Picture books are sometimes viewed as appropriate for primary-graders only. Investigate the pros and cons of using picture books as independent reading options and read-aloud selections in grades 3 and up.

- Investigate the topic of graphic novels for elementary- and middle-grade students in such articles as Brenner's (2006) "Graphic Novels 101: FAQ" and Rudiger's (2006) "Graphic Novels 101: Reading Lessons," both in *The Horn Book Magazine.*

★ References

Albright, L. K. (2000). The effects on attitudes and achievement of reading aloud picture books in seventh-grade social studies classes. Unpublished doctoral dissertation, Ohio University, Athens.

———. (2002). Bringing the Ice Maiden to life: Engaging adolescents in learning through picture book read-alouds in content areas. *Journal of Adolescent and Adult Literacy, 45*(5), 418–428.

Alvermann, D. E., & Phelps, S. F. (1998). *Content reading and literacy: Succeeding in today's diverse classrooms* (2nd ed.). Boston: Allyn & Bacon.

Brabham, E. G., & Lynch-Brown, C. (2002). Effects of teachers' reading aloud styles on vocabulary acquisition and comprehension of students in the early elementary grades. *Journal of Educational Psychology, 94*(3), 465–474.

Brenner, R. (2006). Graphic novels 101: FAQ. *Horn Book Magazine, 82*(2), 123–125.

Fellowes, J. (2007). *The curious adventures of the abandoned toys.* Illustrated by S. D. Schindler. New York: Holt.

Gontarski, M. (1994). Visual literacy as it relates to picture book use by selected fifth grade students. Unpublished doctoral dissertation, Florida State University, Tallahassee.

Grimm, J., & Grimm, W. (1972). *Snow White and the seven dwarfs.* Translated by Randall Jarrell. Illustrated by Nancy E. Burkert. New York: Farrar.

Hearn, M. P. (1984). In the library. In J. Cole (Ed.), *A new treasury of children's poetry.* New York: Doubleday.

Rudiger, H. M. (2006). Graphic novels 101: Reading lessons. *Horn Book Magazine, 82*(2), 126–134.

Recommended Picture Books

Ages indicated refer to approximate concept and interest levels.

Baby Books

Ajmera, Maya, and Global Fund for Children. *Global Babies.* Charlesbridge, 2007. Ages 1–3.

Ashman, Linda. *Babies on the Go.* Illustrated by Jane Dyer. Harcourt, 2003. Ages 2–4.

Burningham, John. *Hushabye.* Knopf, 2001. Ages 1–3.

Frazee, Marla. *Walk On! A Guide for Babies of All Ages.* Harcourt, 2006. Ages 1–2.

Henderson, Kathy. *Look at You! A Baby Body Book.* Illustrated by Paul Howard. Candlewick, 2007. Ages 2–4. (Also an interactive book)

Henkes, Kevin. *Owen's Marshmallow Chick.* Harper-Collins, 2002. Ages 2–5. (Board book)

Lobel, Anita. *Hello, Day!* Greenwillow, 2008. Ages 2–4.

Nye, Naomi Shihab. *Baby Radar.* Illustrated by Nancy Carpenter. Greenwillow, 2003. Ages 2–4.

Oxenbury, Helen. *I Can.* Walker, 2000. Ages 0–3. (See others in the series: *I See, I Touch, I Hear*)

Suen, Anastasia. *Toddler Two.* Illustrated by Winnie Cheon. Lee & Low, 2002. Ages 1–3. Also available in Spanish (*Dos años*) and English/Spanish editions. (Board book)

Uff, Caroline. *Lulu's Busy Day.* Walker, 2000. Ages 0–2. (See also *Happy Birthday, Lulu.*)

Wheeler, Lisa. *Jazz Baby.* Illustrated by R. Gregory Christie. Harcourt, 2007. Ages 2–4.

Ziefert, Harriet. *Who Said Moo?* Illustrated by Simms Taback. Handprint Books, 2002. Ages 1–3. (Board book)

Interactive Books

Beaumont, Karen. *I Ain't Gonna Paint No More!* Illustrated by David Catrow. Harcourt, 2005. Ages 3–7.

Fleming, Denise. *The Cow Who Clucked.* Holt, 2006. Ages 3–6.

Fox, Mem. *Ten Little Fingers and Ten Little Toes.* Illustrated by Helen Oxenbury. Harcourt, 2008. Ages 3–5.

Kunhardt, Dorothy. *Pat the Bunny.* Golden, 2001 (1940). Ages 2–4.

Ljungkvist, Laura. *Follow the Line through the House.* Viking, 2007. Ages 3–7.

Nedwidek, John. *Ducks Don't Wear Socks.* Illustrated by Lee White. Viking, 2008. Ages 3–7.

Schwartz, Amy. *What James Likes Best.* Simon & Schuster, 2003. Ages 3–5.

Slater, Dashka. *Baby Shoes.* Illustrated by Hiroe Nakata. Bloomsbury, 2006. Ages 1–3.

Whybrow, Ian. *The Noisy Way to Bed.* Illustrated by Tiphanie Beeke. Scholastic, 2004. Ages 2–4.

Yee, Wong H. *Who Likes Rain?* Holt, 2007. Ages 3–6.

Yolen, Jane, editor. *This Little Piggy: Lap Songs, Finger Plays, Clapping Games, and Pantomime Rhymes.* Illustrated by Will Hillenbrand. Candlewick, 2006. Ages 2–4.

Zane, Alexander. *The Wheels on the Race Car.* Illustrated by James Warhola. Orchard, 2005. Ages 4–7.

Toy Books

Baum, L. Frank. *The Wonderful World of Oz: A Commemorative Pop-Up.* Illustrated by Robert Sabuda. Simon & Schuster, 2000. Ages 6–9.

Carle, Eric. *The Very Hungry Caterpillar.* World, 1968. Ages 4–6.

Crowther, Robert. *Opposites.* Candlewick, 2005. Ages 4–8. (Also a concept book)

Ehlert, Lois. *Leaf Man.* Harcourt, 2005. Ages 5–8. (Engineered)

Polhemus, Coleman. *The Crocodile Blues.* Candlewick, 2007. Ages 3–7. (Also a picture storybook)

Sabuda, Robert. *Alice's Adventures in Wonderland.* Simon & Schuster, 2003. Ages 8–12.

———, and Matthew Reinhart. *Encyclopedia Prehistorica: Dinosaurs.* Candlewick, 2005. Ages 5–9. (Pop-up)

Seeger, Laura V. *First the Egg.* Roaring Brook, 2007. Ages 3–5. (Also a concept, pattern, and easy-to-read book)

———. *One Boy.* Roaring Brook, 2008. Ages 3–8. (Also a counting and easy-to-read book)

Yorinks, Arthur. *Mommy?* Illustrated by Maurice Sendak. Paper engineering by Matthew Reinhart. Scholastic, 2006. Ages 5–10. (Pop-up)

Zelinsky, Paul O., adapter. *Knick-Knack Paddywhack! A Moving Parts Book.* Dutton, 2002. Ages 5–8.

Wordless Books

Faller, Régis. *The Adventures of Polo.* Roaring Brook, 2006. Ages 4–8. (International/France)

———. *Polo: The Runaway Book.* Roaring Brook, 2007. Ages 4–7.

Fleischman, Paul. *Sidewalk Circus.* Illustrated by Kevin Hawkes. Candlewick, 2004. Ages 5–10.

Geisert, Arthur. *Lights Out.* Houghton, 2005. Ages 5–10.

Lee, Suzy. *Wave.* Chronicle, 2008. Ages 5–8.

Lehman, Barbara. *Museum Trip.* Houghton, 2006. Ages 5–8.

———. *Rainstorm.* Houghton, 2007. Ages 3–7.

———. *The Red Book.* Houghton, 2004. Ages 4–9.

McCully, Emily Arnold. *Four Hungry Kittens.* Dial, 2001. Ages 4–7.

Newgarden, Mark. *Bow-Wow Bugs a Bug.* Illustrated by Megan M. Cash. Harcourt, 2007. Ages 6–8.

Varon, Sara. *Chicken and Cat.* Scholastic, 2006. Ages 4–7.

Vincent, Gabrielle. *A Day, a Dog.* Front Street, 1999. Ages 6–8.

Wiesner, David. *Flotsam.* Clarion, 2006. Ages 4–7.

———. *Sector 7.* Clarion, 1999. Ages 6–10.

Yum, Hyewon. *Last Night.* Farrar, 2008. Ages 3–6.

Alphabet Books

Cronin, Doreen. *Click, Clack, Quackity-Quack: An Alphabetical Adventure.* Illustrated by Betsy Lewin. Atheneum, 2005. Ages 3–6.

Ernst, Lisa Campbell. *The Turn-Around, Upside-Down Alphabet Book.* Simon & Schuster, 2004. Ages 3–6.

Fleming, Denise. *Alphabet under Construction.* Holt, 2002. Ages 4–7.

Floca, Brian. *The Racecar Alphabet.* Atheneum, 2003. Ages 4–8.

Inkpen, Mick. *Kipper's A to Z: An Alphabet Adventure.* Harcourt, 2001. Ages 5–7.

Jay, Alison. *ABC: A Child's First Alphabet Book.* Dutton, 2003. Ages 4–7.

Kalman, Maira. *What Pete Ate from A to Z (Really!).* Putnam, 2001. Ages 5–8.

Lear, Edward, and Suse MacDonald, adapter. *A Was Once an Apple Pie.* Illustrated by Suse MacDonald. Orchard, 2005. Ages 3–7.

Martin, Bill, Jr., and John Archambault. *Chicka Chicka Boom Boom.* Illustrated by Lois Ehlert. Simon & Schuster, 1989. Ages 3–6.

McLeod, Bob. *Superhero ABC.* HarperCollins, 2006. Ages 4–8.

Seeger, Laura Vaccaro. *The Hidden Alphabet.* Roaring Brook, 2003. Ages 4–7.

Spirin, Gennady. *A Apple Pie.* Philomel, 2005. Ages 4–7.

Wells, Rosemary. *Max's ABC.* Viking, 2006. Ages 3–7.

Wood, Audrey. *Alphabet Mystery.* Illustrated by Bruce Wood. Scholastic, 2003. Ages 3–6.

Counting Books

Brown, Ruth. *Ten Seeds.* Knopf, 2001. Ages 3–5.

Carle, Eric. *10 Little Rubber Ducks.* HarperCollins, 2005. Ages 3–6.

Falwell, Cathryn. *Turtle Splash! Countdown at the Pond.* Greenwillow, 2001. Ages 3–6.

Hines, Anna G. *1, 2, Buckle My Shoe.* Harcourt, 2008. Ages 2–5.

Jay, Alison. *123: A Child's First Counting Book.* Dutton, 2007. Ages 4–7.

McMullan, Kate. *I'm Dirty.* Illustrated by Jim McMullan. HarperCollins, 2006. Ages 4–7.

Reiser, Lynn. *Hardworking Puppies.* Harcourt, 2006. Ages 3–7.

Seeger, Laura V. *One Boy.* Roaring Brook, 2008. Ages 3–8. (Also a toy and easy-to-read book)

Wells, Rosemary. *Max Counts His Chickens.* Viking, 2007. Ages 3–5.

Wong, Janet S. *Hide and Seek.* Illustrated by Margaret Chodos-Irvine. Harcourt, 2005. Ages 4–8.

Wormell, Christopher. *Teeth, Tails, & Tentacles: An Animal Counting Book.* Running Press, 2004. Ages 3–8.

Concept Books

Alexander, Claire. *Lucy and the Bully: A Concept Book.* Whitman, 2008. Ages 4–7.

Bang, Molly. *When Sophie Gets Angry—Really, Really Angry. . . .* Scholastic, 1999. Ages 3–6.

Ehlert, Lois. *Color Zoo.* Lippincott, 1989. Ages 3–6.

Fox, Mem. *Where Is the Green Sheep?* Illustrated by Judy Horacek. Harcourt, 2004. Ages 2–5.

Freymann, Saxton, and Joost Elffers. *Fast Food.* Illustrated by Saxton Freymann. Scholastic, 2006. Ages 3–7.

———. *Food for Thought: The Complete Book of Concepts for Growing Minds.* Scholastic, 2005. Ages 3–5.

Gravett, Emily. *Orange Pear Apple Bear.* Simon & Schuster, 2007. Ages 2–4.

Henkes, Kevin. *Old Bear.* Greenwillow, 2008. Ages 3–5.

Hutchins, Hazel. *A Second Is a Hiccup: A Child's Book of Time.* Illustrated by Kady MacDonald Denton. Scholastic, 2007. Ages 3–7.

Jenkins, Emily. *Five Creatures.* Illustrated by Tomek Bogacki. Farrar, 2001. Ages 4–7.

Mayo, Margaret. *Choo Choo Clickety Clack!* Illustrated by Alex Ayliffe. Carolrhoda, 2005. Ages 2–5.

Pittau, Francesco, and Bernadette Gervais. *Elephant, Elephant: A Book of Opposites.* Abrams, 2001. Ages 3–8. (Also an international book)

Prince, April Jones. *What Do Wheels Do All Day?* Illustrated by Giles Laroche. Houghton, 2006. Ages 3–7.

Rohmann, Eric. *A Kitten Tale.* Knopf, 2008. Ages 2–4. (Also a pattern book)

Rosenthal, Amy Krouse. *Cookies! Bite Size Life Lessons.* Illustrated by Jane Dyer. HarperCollins, 2006. Ages 4–7.

Savadier, Elivia. *Will Sheila Share?* Roaring Brook, 2008. Ages 3–5.

Seeger, Laura Vaccaro. *Black? White! Day? Night!* Roaring Brook, 2006. Ages 3–7. (Also a toy book)

———. *First the Egg.* Roaring Brook, 2007. Ages 3–5. (Also a toy, pattern, and easy-to-read book)

———. *Lemons Are Not Red.* Roaring Brook, 2004. Ages 3–7. (Also a toy book)

Wilkes, Angela. *My First Word Book* (3rd edition). DK, 2002. Ages 3–5.

Picture Storybooks

Agee, Jon. *Milo's Hat Trick.* Hyperion, 2001. Ages 5–8.

———. *Nothing.* Hyperion, 2007. Ages 4–8.

———. *Terrific.* Hyperion, 2005. Ages 5–8.

Ahlberg, Allan. *The Pencil.* Illustrated by Bruce Ingman. Candlewick, 2008. Ages 4–7.

Arnosky, Jim. *Grandfather Buffalo.* Putnam, 2006. Ages 5–8.

Bean, Jonathan. *At Night.* Farrar, 2007. Ages 5–7.

Best, Cari. *Three Cheers for Catherine the Great!* Illustrated by Giselle Potter. DK Ink, 1999. Ages 6–9.

Billingsley, Franny. *Big Bad Bunny.* Illustrated by G. Brian Karas. Atheneum, 2008. Ages 4–7.

Bloom, Suzanne. *A Splendid Friend, Indeed.* Boyds Mills, 2005. Ages 2–5.

Brown, Peter. *Chowder.* Little, Brown, 2006. Ages 4–7.

Browne, Anthony. *Voices in the Park.* DK Ink, 1998. Ages 6–10.

———. *Willy the Dreamer.* Candlewick, 1998. Ages 7–10.

Burningham, John. *Edwardo: The Horriblest Boy in the Whole Wide World.* Knopf, 2007. Ages 4–8.

Carle, Eric. *The Grouchy Ladybug.* Crowell, 1971. Ages 5–7.

———. *The Very Busy Spider.* Philomel, 1984. Ages 5–7.

Charlip, Remy. *A Perfect Day.* Greenwillow, 2007. Ages 4–7.

Child, Lauren. *But Excuse Me That Is My Book.* Dial, 2006. Ages 4–6.

———. *Snow Is My Favorite and My Best.* Dial, 2006. Ages 3–5.

Chodos-Irvine, Margaret. *Best Best Friends.* Harcourt, 2006. Ages 3–6.

Coffelt, Nancy. *Fred Stays with Me!* Illustrated by Tricia Tusa. Little, Brown, 2007. Ages 5–7.

Cohen, Miriam. *My Big Brother.* Illustrated by Ronald Himler. Star Bright, 2004. Ages 4–7.

Cole, Brock. *Good Enough to Eat.* Farrar, 2007. Ages 4–8.

Cole, Henry. *On Meadowview Street.* Greenwillow, 2007. Ages 5–8.

Cooper, Elisha. *A Good Night Walk.* Orchard, 2005. Ages 3–6.

Cordsen, Carol Foskett. *The Milkman.* Illustrated by Douglas B. Jones. Dutton, 2005. Ages 3–7.

Cottin, Menena. *The Black Book of Colors.* Illustrated by Rosana Faria. Translated by Elisa Amado. Groundwood, 2008. Ages 5–8. (Also an international book)

Cronin, Doreen. *Click, Clack, Moo: Cows That Type.* Illustrated by Betsy Lewin. Simon & Schuster, 2000. Ages 4–7.

———. *Diary of a Fly.* Illustrated by Harry Bliss. HarperCollins, 2007. Ages 3–8.

———. *Wiggle.* Illustrated by Scott Menchin. Simon & Schuster, 2005. Ages 2–5.

Cruise, Robin. *Little Mama Forgets.* Illustrated by Stacey Dressen-McQueen. Farrar, 2006. Ages 3–7. (Also a multicultural book)

Cunnane, Kelly. *For You Are a Kenyan Child.* Illustrated by Ana Juan. Atheneum, 2006. Ages 5–8.

D'Amico, Carmela. *Ella Takes the Cake.* Illustrated by Steven D'Amico. Scholastic, 2005. Ages 4–6.

Deacon, Alexis. *Beegu.* Farrar, 2003. Ages 3–6.

DiCamillo, Kate. *Great Joy.* Illustrated by Bagram Ibatoulline. Candlewick, 2007. Ages 5–7.

———. *Louise, the Adventures of a Chicken.* Illustrated by Harry Bliss. HarperCollins, 2008. Ages 5–8.

Dillon, Leo, and Diane Dillon. *Jazz on a Saturday Night.* Scholastic, 2007. Ages 5–9.

Dodds, Dayle Ann. *The Prince Won't Go to Bed!* Illustrated by Krysten Brooker. Farrar, 2007. Ages 3–6.

Duval, Kathy. *The Three Bears' Christmas.* Illustrated by Paul Meisel. Holiday, 2005. Ages 3–6.

Falconer, Ian. *Olivia.* Atheneum, 2000. Ages 4–7.

———. *Olivia Saves the Circus.* Atheneum, 2001. Ages 3–7.

Feiffer, Jules. *Bark, George.* HarperCollins, 1999. Ages 3–5.

Flatharta, Antoine Ó. *Hurry and the Monarch.* Illustrated by Meilo So. Knopf, 2005. Ages 4–7.

Fleming, Candace. *Muncha! Muncha! Muncha!* Illustrated by G. Brian Karas. Simon & Schuster, 2002. Ages 3–7.

Foley, Greg. *Thank You, Bear.* Viking, 2007. Ages 3–6.

Ford, Bernette. *First Snow.* Illustrated by Sebastian Braun. Holiday, 2005. Ages 3–7.

Frazee, Marla. *A Couple of Boys Have the Best Week Ever.* Harcourt, 2008. Ages 5–8.

———. *Roller Coaster.* Harcourt, 2003. Ages 4–7.

———. *Santa Claus: The World's Number One Toy Expert.* Harcourt, 2005. Ages 5–7.

Freeman, Don. *A Pocket for Corduroy.* Viking, 1978. Ages 3–5.

Friend, Catherine. *The Perfect Nest.* Illustrated by John Manders. Candlewick, 2007. Ages 5–7.

Gág, Wanda. *Millions of Cats.* Coward-McCann, 1928. Ages 4–6.

George, Kristine O'Connell. *Up!* Illustrated by Hiroe Nakata. Clarion, 2005. Ages 1–4.

Gerstein, Mordicai. *The Man Who Walked between the Towers.* Millbrook, 2003. Ages 5–8.

Goode, Diane. *The Most Perfect Spot.* HarperCollins, 2006. Ages 5–7.

Graham, Bob. *Benny, An Adventure Story.* Candlewick, 1999. Ages 5–8.

———. *Dimity Dumpty: The Story of Humpty's Little Sister.* Candlewick, 2007. Ages 4–7. (Also an international book)

———. *"Let's Get a Pup!" Said Kate.* Candlewick, 2001. Ages 3–6.

———. *Max.* Candlewick, 2000. Ages 4–7.

Gravett, Emily. *Wolves.* Simon & Schuster, 2006. Ages 6–8.

Grey, Mini. *Traction Man Is Here!* Knopf, 2005. Ages 5–7.

———. *Traction Man Meets Turbodog.* Knopf, 2008. Ages 4–7.

Haas, Irene. *Bess and Bella.* Simon & Schuster, 2006. Ages 4–7.

Hamilton, Kersten. *Red Truck.* Illustrated by Valeria Petrone. Viking, 2008. Ages 3–5.

Harper, Charise M. *When Randolph Turned Rotten.* Knopf, 2007. Ages 3–7.

Harrington, Janice N. *The Chicken-Chasing Queen of Lamar County.* Illustrated by Shelley Jackson. Farrar, 2007. Ages 5–7.

Henkes, Kevin. *A Good Day.* Greenwillow, 2007. Ages 3–5.

———. *Kitten's First Full Moon.* Greenwillow, 2004. Ages 3–5.

———. *Lilly's Big Day.* Greenwillow, 2006. Ages 4–7.

———. *Lilly's Purple Plastic Purse.* Greenwillow, 1996. Ages 5–7.

———. *So Happy!* Illustrated by Anita Lobel. Greenwillow, 2005. Ages 6–9.

———. *Wemberley Worried.* Greenwillow, 2000. Ages 5–8.

Hest, Amy. *The Dog Who Belonged to No One.* Illustrated by Amy Bates. Abrams, 2008. Ages 3–6.

Hurst, Carol Otis. *Terrible Storm.* Illustrated by S. D. Schindler. Greenwillow, 2007. Ages 5–7.

Imai, Ayano. *Chester.* Penguin, 2007. Ages 4–6.

Isadora, Rachel. *Yo, Jo!* Harcourt, 2007. Ages 4–7.

Jacobson, Jennifer Richard. *Andy Shane and the Very Bossy Dolores Starbuckle.* Illustrated by Abby Carter. Candlewick, 2005. Ages 5–8.

Jarrett, Clare. *Arabella Miller's Tiny Caterpillar.* Candlewick, 2008. Ages 4–7.

Jeffers, Oliver. *The Incredible Book Eating Boy.* Philomel, 2007. Ages 4–8.

Jenkins, Emily. *That New Animal.* Illustrated by Pierre Pratt. Farrar, 2005. Ages 3–7.

———. *What Happens on Wednesdays.* Illustrated by Lauren Castillo. Farrar, 2007. Ages 4–6.

Juan, Ana. *The Night Eater.* Scholastic, 2004. Ages 4–7.

Juster, Norton. *The Hello, Goodbye Window.* Illustrated by Chris Raschka. Hyperion, 2005. Ages 4–7.

Kasza, Keiko. *The Dog Who Cried Wolf.* Putnam, 2005. Ages 4–7.

Kellogg, Steven. *Pinkerton, Behave!* Dial, 1979. Ages 6–8.

Kimmel, Elizabeth C. *The Top Job.* Illustrated by Robert Neubecker. Dutton, 2007. Ages 5–8.

Kinsey-Warnock, Natalie. *Nora's Ark.* Illustrated by Emily Arnold McCully. HarperCollins, 2005. Ages 5–8.

Kleven, Elisa. *The Apple Doll.* Farrar, 2007. Ages 4–7.

Kloske, Geoffrey. *Once Upon a Time, The End (Asleep in 60 Seconds).* Illustrated by Barry Blitt. Simon & Schuster, 2005. Ages 5–8.

Knudsen, Michelle. *Library Lion.* Illustrated by Kevin Hawkes. Candlewick, 2006. Ages 4–7.

Kohara, Kazuno. *Ghosts in the House!* Roaring Brook, 2008. Ages 3–7.

Kolar, Bob. *Big Kicks.* Candlewick, 2008. Ages 4–8.

Krauss, Ruth. *The Growing Story.* Illustrated by Helen Oxenbury. HarperCollins, 2007. Ages 3–5.

Kulka, Joe. *Wolf's Coming!* Carolrhoda, 2007. Ages 3–7.

Kvasnosky, Laura McGee. *Zelda and Ivy: The Runaways.* Candlewick, 1998. Ages 6–8.

———. *Zelda and Ivy One Christmas.* Candlewick, 2000. Ages 6–8.

Larochelle, David. *The End.* Illustrated by Richard Egielski. Scholastic, 2007. Ages 4–8.

Lee, Ho Baek. *While We Were Out.* Kane/Miller, 2003. Ages 4–7.

Lester, Helen. *Hooway for Wodney Wat.* Illustrated by Lynn Munsinger. Houghton, 1999. Ages 4–7.

Lloyd, Sam. *Mr. Pusskins: A Love Story.* Simon & Schuster, 2006. Ages 4–7.

Lobel, Anita. *Nini Here and There.* Greenwillow, 2007. Ages 3–5.

Long, Melinda. *How I Became a Pirate.* Illustrated by David Shannon. Harcourt, 2003. Ages 5–8.

Loomis, Christine. *Astro Bunnies.* Illustrated by Ora Eitan. Putnam, 2001. Ages 4–7.

Lum, Kate. *What? Cried Granny: An Almost Bedtime Story.* Illustrated by Adrian Johnson. Dial, 1999. Ages 5–8.

MacDonald, Ross. *Bad Baby.* Roaring Brook, 2005. Ages 5–8.

Madison, Alan. *Velma Gratch and the Way Cool Butterfly.* Illustrated by Kevin Hawkes. Random, 2007. Ages 5–8.

Markes, Julie. *Shhhhh! Everybody's Sleeping.* Illustrated by David Parkins. HarperCollins, 2005. Ages 4–6.

McCarty, Peter. *Moon Plane.* Holt, 2006. Ages 3–5.

McClintock, Barbara. *Adèle and Simon.* Farrar, 2006. Ages 5–8.

———. *Dahlia.* Farrar, 2002. Ages 5–7.

McElmurry, Jill. *I'm Not a Baby!* Random, 2006. Ages 4–7.

McFarland, Lyn Rossiter. *Widget.* Illustrated by Jim McFarland. Farrar, 2001. Ages 4–6.

McMillan, Bruce. *The Problem with Chickens.* Illustrated by Gunnella. Houghton, 2005. Ages 4–8.

McMullan, Kate. *I Stink!* Illustrated by Jim McMullan. HarperCollins, 2002. Ages 4–7.

McNulty, Faith. *If You Decide to Go to the Moon.* Illustrated by Steven Kellogg. Scholastic, 2005. Ages 5–8.

Meddaugh, Susan. *The Witch's Walking Stick.* Houghton, 2005. Ages 5–7.

Melling, David. *The Scallywags.* Barron's, 2006. Ages 5–8.

Nakagawa, Chihiro. *Who Made This Cake?* Illustrated by Junji Koyose. Front Street, 2008. Ages 3–5.

Napoli, Donna Jo. *Albert.* Illustrated by Jim LaMarche. Harcourt, 2001. Ages 5–8.

Nevius, Carol. *Baseball Hour.* Illustrated by Bill Thomson. Marshall Cavendish, 2008. Ages 7–9.

Ogburn, Jacqueline. *The Bake Shop Ghost.* Illustrated by Marjorie Priceman. Houghton, 2005. Ages 5–8.

O'Malley, Kevin. *Gimme Cracked Corn & I Will Share.* Walker, 2007. Ages 7–9.

Palatini, Margie. *Three French Hens.* Illustrated by Richard Egielski. Hyperion, 2005. Ages 5–7.

Pearson, Susan. *Slugs in Love.* Illustrated by Kevin O'Malley. Marshall Cavendish, 2006. Ages 5–7.

Pennypacker, Sara. *Pierre in Love.* Illustrated by Petra Mathers. Scholastic, 2007. Ages 4–7.

Perkins, Lynne Rae. *Pictures from Our Vacation.* Greenwillow, 2007. Ages 5–7.

Perl, Erica S. *Chicken Bedtime Is Really Early.* Illustrated by George Bates. Abrams, 2005. Ages 3–5.

Peters, Lisa Westberg. *Cold Little Duck, Duck, Duck.* Illustrated by Sam Williams. Greenwillow, 2000. Ages 1–4.

Pitzer, Susanna. *Not Afraid of Dogs.* Illustrated by Larry Day. Walker, 2006. Ages 5–8.

Prelutsky, Jack. *The Wizard.* Illustrated by Brandon Dorman. Greenwillow, 2007. Ages 5–10. (Also a poetry book)

Pullen, Zachery. *Friday My Radio Flyer Flew.* Simon & Schuster, 2008. Ages 4–7.

Rathmann, Peggy. *The Day the Babies Crawled Away.* Putnam, 2003. Ages 4–7.

———. *Officer Buckle and Gloria.* Putnam, 1995. Ages 6–8.

———. *10 Minutes till Bedtime.* Putnam, 1998. Ages 3–6.

Raven, Margot T. *Night Boat to Freedom.* Illustrated by E. B. Lewis. Farrar, 2006. Ages 6–8. (Also a historical fiction book)

Ray, Jane. *The Apple-Pip Princess.* Candlewick, 2008. Ages 4–7.

Reid, Barbara. *The Subway Mouse.* Scholastic, 2005. Ages 5–7.

Reiss, Mike. *Merry Un-Christmas.* Illustrated by David Catrow. HarperCollins, 2006. Ages 5–7.

Richards, Beah E. *Keep Climbing, Girls.* Illustrated by R. Gregory Christie. Simon & Schuster, 2006. Ages 5–8.

Richardson, Justin, and Peter Parnell. *And Tango Makes Three.* Illustrated by Henry Cole. Simon & Schuster, 2005. Ages 5–8.

Rodman, Mary Ann. *My Best Friend.* Illustrated by E. B. Lewis. Viking, 2005. Ages 5–7.

Roth, Susan L. *Great Big Guinea Pigs.* Bloomsbury, 2006. Ages 5–7.

Sakai, Komako. *Emily's Balloon.* Chronicle, 2006. Ages 2–4.

Samuels, Barbara. *Happy Valentine's Day, Delores.* Farrar, 2005. Ages 5–7.

San Souci, Daniel. *Space Station Mars.* Tricycle, 2005. Ages 6–9.

Schotter, Roni. *The Boy Who Loved Words.* Illustrated by Giselle Potter. Random, 2006. Ages 6–10.

Schwartz, Amy. *Starring Miss Darlene.* Roaring Brook, 2007. Ages 5–7.

Scieszka, Jon. *Cowboy & Octopus.* Illustrated by Lane Smith. Viking, 2007. Ages 5–10.

Sendak, Maurice. *Outside Over There.* Harper, 1981. Ages 7–10.

———. *Where the Wild Things Are.* Harper, 1963. Ages 5–7.

Shannon, David. *David Gets in Trouble.* Scholastic, 2002. Ages 4–6.

———. *Duck on a Bike.* Scholastic, 2002. Ages 3–6.

Shannon, George. *Tippy-Toe Chick, Go!* Illustrated by Laura Dronzek. Greenwillow, 2003. Ages 4–6.

Shulevitz, Uri. *How I Learned Geography.* Farrar, 2008. Ages 5–10.

———. *Snow.* Farrar, 1998. Ages 3–6.

———. *So Sleepy Story.* Farrar, 2006. Ages 2–6.

———. *The Stray Dog: From a True Story by Reiko Sassa.* HarperCollins, 2001. Ages 4–7.

Sís, Peter. *Madlenka.* Farrar, 2000. Ages 5–8.

———. *Madlenka's Dog.* Farrar, 2002. Ages 3–7.

Smith, Chris. *One City, Two Brothers.* Illustrated by Aurélia Fronty. Barefoot, 2007. Ages 5–8. (Also a traditional and religious cultures book)

Smith, Lane. *Madam President.* Hyperion, 2008. Ages 5–7.

Spinelli, Eileen. *Three Pebbles and a Song.* Illustrated by S. D. Schindler. Dial, 2003. Ages 5–8.

Steen, Sandra and Susan. *Car Wash.* Illustrated by G. Brian Karas. Putnam, 2001. Ages 3–7.

Stein, David E. *Leaves.* Putnam, 2007. Ages 3–7.

Stevens, Janet, and Susan Stevens Crummel. *The Great Fuzz Frenzy.* Illustrated by Janet Stevens. Harcourt, 2005. Ages 4–7.

Stewart, Sarah. *The Gardener.* Illustrated by David Small. Farrar, 1997. Ages 4–7.

Stuve-Bodeen, Stephanie. *Elizabeti's Doll.* Illustrated by Christy Hale. Lee & Low, 1998. Ages 3–7.

Swanson, Susan M. *The House in the Night.* Illustrated by Beth Krommes. Houghton, 2008. Ages 3–5.

Teckentrup, Britta. *Grumpy Cat.* Boxer, 2008. Ages 2–5.

Thompson, Lauren. *Polar Bear Night.* Illustrated by Stephen Savage. Scholastic, 2004. Ages 2–5.

Van Allsburg, Chris. *The Garden of Abdul Gasazi.* Houghton, 1979. Ages 6–8.

———. *Jumanji.* Houghton, 1981. Ages 6–10.

———. *The Polar Express.* Houghton, 1995. Ages 5–9.

Van Leeuwen, Jean. *Benny & Beautiful Baby Delilah.* Illustrated by LeUyen Pham. Dial, 2006. Ages 3–5.

Waddell, Martin. *Hi, Harry! The Moving Story of How One Slow Tortoise Slowly Made a Friend.* Illustrated by Barbara Firth. Candlewick, 2003. Ages 3–5.

———. *Tiny's Big Adventure.* Illustrated by John Lawrence. Candlewick, 2004. Ages 4–7.

Wheeler, Lisa. *Boogie Knights.* Illustrated by Mark Siegel. Atheneum, 2008. Ages 5–8.

———. *Castaway Cats.* Illustrated by Ponder Goembel. Atheneum, 2006. Ages 4–7.

———. *Mammoths on the Move.* Illustrated by Kurt Cyrus. Harcourt, 2006. Ages 5–7. (Also a poetry and informational book)

Willems, Mo. *Don't Let the Pigeon Drive the Bus!* Hyperion, 2003. Ages 4–7.

———. *Don't Let the Pigeon Stay Up Late!* Hyperion, 2006. Ages 3–7.

———. *Knuffle Bunny: A Cautionary Tale.* Hyperion, 2004. Ages 3–5.

———. *Knuffle Bunny Too: A Case of Mistaken Identity.* Hyperion, 2007. Ages 3–6.

———. *Leonardo, the Terrible Monster.* Hyperion, 2005. Ages 4–6.

Willis, Jeanne. *Tadpole's Promise.* Illustrated by Tony Ross. Atheneum, 2005. Ages 5–9.

Winthrop, Elizabeth. *Squashed in the Middle.* Illustrated by Pat Cummings. Holt, 2005. Ages 5–8.

Wong, Janet S. *Buzz.* Harcourt, 2000. Ages 3–5.

Yaccarino, Dan. *Deep in the Jungle.* Atheneum, 2000. Ages 5–9.

Pattern Books

Arnold, Marsha Diane. *Roar of a Snore.* Illustrated by Pierre Pratt. Dial, 2006. Ages 2–4.

Becker, Bonny. *A Visitor for Bear.* Illustrated by Kady MacDonald Denton. Candlewick, 2008. Ages 4–7.

Bloom, Suzanne. *The Bus for Us.* Boyds Mills, 2001. Ages 3–6.

Bunting, Eve. *Hurry! Hurry!* Illustrated by Jeff Mack. Harcourt, 2007. Ages 3–6.

Chodos-Irvine, Margaret. *Ella Sarah Gets Dressed.* Harcourt, 2003. Ages 2–5.

Fleming, Denise. *The Cow Who Clucked.* Holt, 2006. Ages 3–6.

———. *In the Small, Small Pond.* Holt, 1993. Ages 5–7.

———. *Mama Cat Has Three Kittens.* Holt, 1998. Ages 2–5.

Gravett, Emily. *Monkey and Me.* Simon & Schuster, 2008. Ages 4–6.

MacLennan, Cathy. *Chicky Chicky Chook Chook.* Boxer, 2007. Ages 3–6. (Also an international book)

Martin, Bill, Jr. *Brown Bear, Brown Bear, What Do You See?* Illustrated by Eric Carle. Holt, 1983. Ages 3–6.

———. *Panda Bear, Panda Bear, What Do You See?* Illustrated by Eric Carle. Holt, 2003. Ages 3–6.

———. *Polar Bear, Polar Bear, What Do You Hear?* Illustrated by Eric Carle. Holt, 1991. Ages 3–6.

Shannon, David. *No, David!* Scholastic, 1998. Ages 2–5.

Smee, Nicola. *Clip-Clop.* Boxer, 2006. Ages 3–5.

Wild, Margaret. *Piglet and Papa.* Illustrated by Stephen M. King. Abrams, 2007. Ages 3–5.

Easy-to-Read Books

Adler, David A. *Young Cam Jansen and the Double Beach Mystery.* Illustrated by Susanna Natti. Viking, 2002. Ages 5–7.

Ahlberg, Allan. *The Children Who Smelled a Rat.* Illustrated by Katharine McEwen. Candlewick, 2005. Ages 7–10.

Arnold, Tedd. *Hi! Fly Guy.* Cartwheel Books/Scholastic, 2005. Ages 5–7.

Bang-Campbell, Monika. *Little Rat Makes Music.* Illustrated by Molly Bang. Harcourt, 2007. Ages 5–7.

Bloom, Suzanne. *A Splendid Friend, Indeed.* Boyds Mills, 2005. Ages 5–7.

Brown, Marc, creator, and Stephen Krensky. *Arthur and the Big Blow-Up.* Illustrated by Marc Brown. Little Brown, 2000. (Representative of others in the lengthy Arthur chapter book series: *Arthur and the Perfect Big Brother; Francine, the Superstar.*) Ages 5–7.

Cammuso, Frank, and Jay Lynch. *Otto's Orange Day.* Illustrated by Frank Cammuso. TOON, 2008. Ages 5–7. (Also a graphic novel)

Cowley, Joy. *Snake and Lizard.* Illustrated by Gavin Bishop. Kane/Miller, 2008. Ages 5–9. (Also an international book)

Danziger, Paula. *Get Ready for Second Grade, Amber Brown.* Illustrated by Tony Ross. Putnam, 2002. Ages 5–7.

———. *It's a Fair Day, Amber Brown.* Illustrated by Tony Ross. Putnam, 2002. Ages 5–7.

dePaola, Tomie. *Hide-and-Seek All Week.* Grosset and Dunlap, 2001. Ages 5–7.

DiCamillo, Kate. *Mercy Watson Goes for a Ride.* Illustrated by Chris Van Dusen. Candlewick, 2006. Ages 5–7.

———. *Mercy Watson to the Rescue.* Illustrated by Chris Van Dusen. Candlewick, 2005. Ages 5–7. (See other titles in the series.)

Dunrea, Olivier. *Gossie.* Houghton, 2002. Ages 3–5. Also *Gossie and Gertie.*

Edwards, Michelle. *Stinky Stern Forever.* Harcourt, 2005. Ages 6–9.

Fine, Anne. *The Jamie and Angus Stories.* Illustrated by Penny Dale. Candlewick, 2002. Ages 5–7.

Fleming, Denise. *Buster.* Holt, 2003. Ages 5–7.

George, Jean Craighead. *Goose and Duck.* Illustrated by Priscilla Lamont. HarperCollins, 2008. Ages 5–7.

Grant, Judyann A. *Chicken Said, "Cluck!"* Illustrated by Sue Truesdell. HarperCollins, 2008. Ages 5–7.

Guest, Elissa Haden. *Iris and Walter.* Illustrated by Christine Davenier. Harcourt/Gulliver, 2000. Ages 6–8.

———. *Iris and Walter: The Sleepover.* Illustrated by Christine Davenier. Harcourt, 2002. Ages 5–7.

Harper, Jessica. *Uh-Oh, Cleo.* Illustrated by Jon Berkeley. Putnam, 2008. Ages 5–8.

Haskins, Lori. *Ducks in Muck.* Illustrated by Valeria Petrone. Random, 2000. Ages 5–7.

Hoberman, Mary Ann. *You Read to Me, I'll Read to You: Very Short Stories to Read Together.* Illustrated by Michael Emberley. Little, Brown, 2001. Ages 5–7.

Holub, Joan. *The Garden That We Grew.* Illustrated by Hiroe Nakata. Viking, 2001. Ages 5–7.

Horowitz, Ruth. *Breakout at the Bug Lab.* Illustrated by Joan Holub. Dial, 2001. Ages 5–8.

Howe, James. *Pinky and Rex and the Just-Right Pet.* Illustrated by Melissa Sweet. Simon & Schuster, 2001. Ages 6–8.

Koss, Amy Goldman. *Where Fish Go in Winter and Other Great Mysteries.* Illustrated by Laura J. Bryant. Dial, 2000. Ages 5–7.

Kvasnosky, Laura McGee. *Zelda and Ivy: The Runaways.* Candlewick, 2006. Ages 5–8.

Livingstone, Star. *Harley.* Illustrated by Molly Bang. North-South, 2001. Ages 5–7.

McDonough, Yona Zeldis. *The Dollhouse Magic.* Illustrated by Diane Palmisciano. Holt, 2000. Ages 7–9.

Paterson, Katherine. *Marvin One Too Many.* Illustrated by Jane Clark Brown. HarperCollins, 2001. Ages 5–7.

Porte, Barbara Ann. *If You Ever Get Lost: The Adventures of Julia and Evan.* Illustrated by Nancy Carpenter. Greenwillow, 2000. Ages 5–7.

Ries, Lori. *Aggie and Ben: Three Stories.* Illustrated by Frank W. Dormer. Charlesbridge, 2006. Ages 4–7.

Rodowsky, Colby. *Not My Dog.* Illustrated by Thomas F. Yezerski. Farrar, 1999. Ages 5–7.

Root, Phyllis. *Mouse Goes Out.* Illustrated by James Croft. Candlewick, 2002. Ages 4–6.

Rylant, Cynthia. *Henry and Mudge and the Great Grandpas.* Illustrated by Suçie Stevenson. Simon & Schuster, 2005. Ages 5–7. (Part of a series)

———. *Mr. Putter & Tabby Feed the Fish.* Illustrated by Arthur Howard. Harcourt, 2001. Ages 5–7. (See other titles in the Mr. Putter & Tabby series.)

———. *Mr. Putter & Tabby See the Stars.* Illustrated by Arthur Howard. Harcourt, 2007. Ages 5–7.

Sachar, Louis. *Marvin Redpost: A Flying Birthday Cake?* Illustrated by Amy Wummer. Random House, 1999. Ages 5–7. (Part of a series)

Seeger, Laura V. *Dog and Bear: Two Friends, Three Stories.* Roaring Brook, 2007. Ages 4–7.

———. *Two's Company.* Roaring Brook, 2008. Ages 4–6.

Silverman, Erica. *Cowgirl Kate and Cocoa.* Illustrated by Betsy Lewin. Harcourt, 2005. Ages 5–7.

Thomas, Shelley Moore. *Good Night, Good Knight.* Illustrated by Jennifer Plecas. Dutton, 2000. Ages 5–8.

Van Leeuwen, Jean. *Amanda Pig and the Really Hot Day.* Illustrated by Ann Schweninger. Dial, 2005. Ages 5–7.

Wallace, Karen. *Wild Baby Animals.* Dorling Kindersley, 2000. Ages 5–8.

Wells, Rosemary. *Yoko Writes Her Name.* Hyperion, 2008. Ages 3–7.

Willems, Mo. *Are You Ready to Play Outside?* Hyperion, 2008. Ages 5–7.

————. *I Am Invited to a Party!* Hyperion, 2007. Ages 5–7.

————. *I Love My New Toy!* Hyperion, 2008. Ages 5–7.

————. *I Will Surprise My Friend!* Hyperion, 2008. Ages 5–7.

————. *There Is a Bird on Your Head!* Hyperion, 2007. Ages 5–7.

Yee, Wong H. *Abracadabra! Magic with Mouse and Mole.* Houghton, 2007. Ages 5–8.

Picture Books for Older Readers

Avi. *Silent Movie.* Illustrated by C. B. Mordan. Atheneum, 2003. Ages 8–12.

Briggs, Raymond. *Ug: Boy Genius of the Stone Age.* Knopf, 2002. Ages 8–12.

Bunting, Eve. *Riding the Tiger.* Illustrated by David Frampton. Clarion, 2001. Ages 8–11.

Cronin, Doreen. *Duck for President.* Illustrated by Betsy Lewin. Simon & Schuster, 2004. Ages 8–10.

Johnson, D. B. *Henry Builds a Cabin.* Houghton, 2002. Ages 9–13.

————. *Henry Climbs a Mountain.* Houghton, 2003. Ages 9–13.

————. *Henry Hikes to Fitchburg.* Houghton, 2000. Ages 9–13.

Kerley, Barbara. *The Dinosaurs of Waterhouse Hawkins.* Illustrated by Brian Selznick. Scholastic, 2001. Ages 8–12.

Lee, Milly. *Landed.* Illustrated by Yangsook Choi. Farrar, 2006. Ages 8–10.

Macaulay, David. *The Way We Work.* Houghton, 2008. Ages 13–18.

McCarthy, Meghan. *Aliens Are Coming! The True Account of the 1938 War of the Worlds Radio Broadcast.* Knopf, 2006. Ages 8–12.

Moss, Marissa. *Brave Harriet: The First Woman to Fly the English Channel.* Illustrated by C. F. Payne. Harcourt, 2001. Ages 8–10.

Myers, Walter Dean. *Blues Journey.* Illustrated by Christopher Myers. Holiday, 2003. Ages 10–14.

Polacco, Patricia. *Pink and Say.* Philomel, 1994. Ages 8–11.

Raven, Margot T. *Night Boat to Freedom.* Illustrated by E. B. Lewis. Farrar, 2006. Ages 8–12.

Rogers, Gregory. *The Boy, the Bear, the Baron, the Bard.* Roaring Brook, 2004. Ages 8–12. (Wordless)

Selznick, Brian. *The Invention of Hugo Cabret.* Scholastic, 2007. Ages 8–12.

Sidman, Joyce. *Butterfly Eyes and Other Secrets of the Meadow.* Houghton, 2006. Ages 6–12.

————. *Song of the Water Boatman and Other Pond Poems.* Illustrated by Beckie Prange. Houghton, 2005. Ages 7–12.

Sís, Peter. *Starry Messenger.* Farrar, 1996. Ages 9–14.

————. *Tibet through the Red Box.* Farrar, 1998. Ages 9–16.

————. *The Wall: Growing Up behind the Iron Curtain.* Farrar, 2007. Ages 8–14. (Partially a graphic novel)

Walter, Mildred Pitts. *Alec's Primer.* Illustrated by Larry Johnson. Vermont Folklife Center, 2004. Ages 7–10.

Graphic Novels

Atagan, Patrick. *The Yellow Jar: Volume I: Two Tales from Japanese Tradition.* NBM, 2002. Ages 11–14.

Cammuso, Frank. *Knights of the Lunch Table, Book 1.* Scholastic, 2008. Ages 9–13.

Crane, Jordan. *The Clouds Above.* Fantagraphics, 2005. Ages 7–9.

Crilley, Mark. *Akiko on the Planet Smoo.* Random, 2000. Ages 9–14.

Czekaj, Jef. *Grampa and Julie: Shark Hunters.* Top Shelf, 2004. Ages 9–14.

Dini, Paul. *Wonder Woman: Spirit of Truth.* Illustrated by Alex Ross. DC Comics, 2001. Ages 9–11.

Eisner, Will. *Sundiata: A Legend of Africa.* NBM, 2003. Ages 10–14.

Frampton, Otis. *Oddly Normal, Vol. 1.* Viper, 2006. Ages 9–12.

Friesen, Ray. *Lookit! A Cheese Related Mishap and Other Stories.* Don't Eat Any Bugs, 2005. Ages 10–13.

Gaiman, Neil. *Coraline: Graphic Novel.* Illustrated by P. Craig Russell. HarperCollins, 2008. Ages 9–12.

————. *The Wolves in the Walls.* Illustrated by Dave McKean. HarperCollins, 2003. Ages 9–12.

Gownley, Jimmy. *Amelia Rules! What Makes You Happy.* ibooks, 2004. Ages 8–12.

————. *Amelia Rules! The Whole World's Crazy.* ibooks, 2003. Ages 8–11.

Hale, Shannon, and Dean Hale. *Rapunzel's Revenge.* Illustrated by Nathan Hale. Bloomsbury USA, 2008. Ages 10–14.

Harper, Charisse M. *Fashion Kitty.* Hyperion, 2005. Ages 9–13.

Hartman, Rachel. *Amy Unbounded: Belondweg Blossoming.* Pug House, 2002. Ages 9–14.

Hayes, Geoffrey. *Benny and Penny: In Just Pretend.* TOON, 2008. Ages 4–6.

Holm, Jennifer L. *Babymouse: Queen of the World!* Illustrated by Matthew Holm. Random, 2005. Ages 9–12. (Part of the Babymouse series.)

———, and Matthew Holm. *Babymouse: Heartbreaker.* Illustrated by Matthew Holm. Random, 2006. Ages 5–7.

Hosler, Jay. *Clan Apis.* Active Synapse, 2000. Ages 10–14.

Huey, Debbie. *Bumperboy and the Loud, Loud Mountain.* Adhouse, 2006. Ages 7–9.

Irwin, Jane, and Jeff Verndt. *Vögelein: A Clockwork Faerie.* Fiery Studio, 2003. Ages 12–16.

Kobayashi, Makoto. *What's Michael? Vol. 10: Sleepless Nights.* Dark Horse, 2005. Ages 10–13.

Kochalka, James. *Monkey vs. Robot.* Top Shelf, 2000. Ages 8–12.

———. *Monkey vs. Robot and the Crystal of Power.* Top Shelf, 2003. Ages 8–12.

———. *Pinky & Stinky.* Top Shelf, 2002. Ages 8–11.

Lat. *Kampung Boy.* First Second, 2006. Ages 9–14. (Autobiography; set in Malaysia; Muslim)

Martin, Ann M., and Raina Telgemeier. *Kristy's Great Idea.* Illustrated by Raina Telgemeier. Scholastic, 2006. Ages 9–11. (From Baby-Sitter's Club series)

Morse, Scott. *Magic Pickle.* Scholastic, 2008. Ages 7–9.

O'Malley, Kevin. *Captain Raptor and the Space Pirates.* Illustrated by Patrick O'Brien. Walker, 2007. Ages 5–9. (Sequel to *Captain Raptor and the Moon Mystery.*)

Renier, Aaron. *Spiral-Bound: Top Secret Summer.* Top Shelf, 2005. Ages 9–12.

Rodi, Rob. *Crossovers.* CrossGeneration, 2003. Ages 11–16.

Roman, Dave, and John Green. *Jax Epoch and the Quicken Forbidden.* Ait/Planet Lar, 2002. Ages 9–14.

Runton, Andy. *Owly, Volume I: The Way Home & the Bittersweet Summer.* Top Shelf, 2004. Ages 5–9.

———. *Owly, Volume II: Just a Little Blue.* Top Shelf, 2005. Ages 5–9.

Sfar, Joann. *Little Vampire Does Kung Fu!* Translated from the French by Mark and Alexis Siegel. Simon & Schuster, 2003. Ages 9–13.

Siegel, Siena Cherson. *To Dance: A Ballerina's Graphic Novel.* Illustrated by Mark Siegel. Simon & Schuster, 2006. Ages 10–14.

Smith, Jeff. *Bone: Out from Boneville.* Graphix, 2005. Ages 9–14.

Spiegelman, Art. *Little Lit: Folklore & Fairy Tale Funnies.* HarperCollins, 2000. Ages 9–14.

Stamaty, Mark Alan. *Alia's Mission: Saving the Books of Iraq.* Knopf, 2004. Ages 9–13.

Steinberg, D. J. *Sound Off!* Illustrated by Brian Smith. Grosset, 2008. Ages 8–10.

Tan, Shaun. *The Arrival.* Scholastic, 2007. Ages 12–18. (Also a wordless book)

Torres, J. *The Collected Alison Dare: Little Miss Adventures.* Illustrated by J. Bone. Oni, 2002. (Vol. 2, 2005). Ages 9–11.

Varon, Sara. *Robot Dreams.* First Second, 2007. Ages 8–14.

Weigel, Jeff. *Atomic Ace (He's Just My Dad).* Albert Whitman, 2004. Ages 9–12.

Yang, Gene L. *American Born Chinese.* First Second, 2006. Ages 12–16. (Also a multicultural book)

Transitional Books

Bang-Campbell, Monika. *Little Rat Rides.* Harcourt, 2004. Ages 6–9.

Barrows, Annie. *Ivy and Bean.* Illustrated by Sophie Blackall. Chronicle, 2006. Ages 6–9. (Part of a series)

Benton, Jim. *Franny K. Stein, Mad Scientist: Lunch Walks among Us.* Simon & Schuster, 2003. Ages 6–9.

Brisson, Pat. *Little Sister, Big Sister.* Illustrated by Diana Cain Blumenthal. Holt, 1999. Ages 6–9.

Delaney, Michael. *Birdbrain Amos.* Putnam, 2002. Ages 6–9.

dePaola, Tomie. *26 Fairmount Avenue.* Putnam, 1999. Ages 6–9.

Doherty, Berlie. *The Famous Adventures of Jack.* Illustrated by Sonja Lamut. Greenwillow, 2001. Ages 6–9.

Edwards, Michelle. *Stinky Stern Forever.* Harcourt, 2005. Ages 6–9.

Fenner, Carol. *Snowed in with Grandmother Silk.* Illustrated by Amanda Harvey. Dial, 2003. Ages 5–7.

Florian, Douglas. *Bow Wow Meow Meow: It's Rhyming Cats and Dogs.* Harcourt, 2003. Ages 6–9.

Fowler, Susi Gregg. *Albertina, the Animals, and Me.* Illustrated by Jim Fowler. Greenwillow, 2000. Ages 6–9.

———. *Albertina the Practically Perfect.* Illustrated by Jim Fowler. Greenwillow, 1998. Ages 6–9.

Graves, Bonnie. *Taking Care of Trouble.* Illustrated by Robin P. Glasser. Dutton, 2002. Ages 6–9.

Greenwald, Sheila. *Rosy Cole's Worst Ever, Best Yet Tour of New York City.* Holt, 2003. Ages 6–9.

Grindley, Sally. *Dear Max.* Illustrated by Tony Ross. Simon & Schuster, 2006. Ages 6–9.

Haas, Jessie. *Jigsaw Pony.* Illustrated by Ying-Hwa Hu. Greenwillow, 2005. Ages 6–9.

———. *Runaway Radish.* Illustrated by Margot Apple. Greenwillow, 2001. Ages 6–9.

Harper, Charise M. *Just Grace.* Houghton, 2007. Ages 7–9.

James, Simon, editor. *Days Like This: A Collection of Small Poems.* Candlewick, 2000. Ages 6–9.

Jenkins, Emily. *Toys Go Out: Being the Adventures of a Knowledgeable Stingray, a Toughy Little Buffalo, and Someone Called Plastic.* Illustrated by Paul O. Zelinsky. Random, 2006. Ages 6–9.

Kerrin, Jessica. *Martin Bridge: Ready for Takeoff!* Illustrated by Joseph Kelly. Kids Can, 2005. Ages 6–9. (Part of a series.)

King-Smith, Dick. *The Nine Lives of Aristotle.* Illustrated by Bob Graham. Candlewick, 2003. Ages 6–9.

Lewis, Maggie. *Morgy Makes His Move.* Illustrated by Michael Chesworth. Houghton, 1999. Ages 6–10.

Levy, Elizabeth. *Big Trouble in Little Twinsville.* Illustrated by Mark Elliot. HarperCollins, 2001. Ages 6–9.

———. *Night of the Living Gerbil.* Illustrated by Bill Basso. HarperCollins, 2001. Ages 6–9.

Look, Lenore. *Ruby Lu, Brave and True.* Illustrated by Anne Wilsdorf. Simon & Schuster, 2004. Ages 6–9.

Marsden, Carolyn. *The Gold-Threaded Dress.* Cambridge, MA: Candlewick, 2002. Ages 6–9.

McEwan, Jamie. *Rufus the Scrub Does Not Wear a Tutu.* Illustrated by John Margeson. Darby Creek, 2007. Ages 7–10.

Nolan, Lucy. *Down Girl and Sit: Smarter Than Squirrels.* Illustrated by Mike Reed. Marshall Cavendish, 2004. Ages 6–9.

Pennypacker, Sara. *Clementine.* Illustrated by Marla Frazee. Hyperion, 2006. Ages 6–9.

———. *Clementine's Letter.* Illustrated by Marla Frazee. Hyperion, 2008. Ages 7–9.

———. *The Talented Clementine.* Illustrated by Marla Frazee. Hyperion, 2007. Ages 7–10.

Roberts, Ken. *The Thumb in the Box.* Illustrated by Leanne Franson. Groundwood, 2001. Ages 6–9.

Sobol, Donald J. *Encyclopedia Brown: Boy Detective.* Illustrated by Leonard Shortall. Bantam, 1985 (originally published by Scholastic, 1968). (Others in this series: *Encyclopedia Brown Tracks Them Down; Encyclopedia Brown and the Case of the Midnight Visitor; Encyclopedia Brown Solves Them All.*) Ages 6–9.

Spinelli, Jerry. *Tooter Pepperday.* Illustrated by Donna Nelson. Random House, 1995. Ages 6–9.

✫ Related Films, Videos, and DVDs

Antarctic Antics. (2000). Author: Judy Sierra (2000). Illustrators: Jose Aruego and Ariane Dewey. 32 minutes.

Diary of a Spider. (2006). Author: Doreen Cronin (2005). Illustrator: Harry Bliss. 9 minutes.

The Dot. (2004). Author/Illustrator: Peter H. Reynolds. (2003) 7.5 minutes.

Giggle, Giggle, Quack. (2003). Author: Doreen Cronin (2002). Illustrator: Betsy Lewin. 9.5 minutes.

Hondo & Fabian. (2006). Author/Illustrator: Peter McCarty (2002). 6 minutes.

I Stink! (2009). Authors/Illustrators: Kate and Jim McMullan (2002). 9 minutes.

Jumanji. (1995). Author/Illustrator: Chris Van Allsburg (1981). 104 minutes.

Knuffle Bunny: A Cautionary Tale. (2006). Author/Illustrator: Mo Willems (2004). 10 minutes.

Lon Po Po. (2006). Author/Illustrator: Ed Young (1989). 12 minutes.

The Man Who Walked between the Towers. (2005). Author/Illustrator: Mordicai Gerstein (2003). 60 minutes.

Max's Words. (2007). Author: Kate Banks (2006). Illustrator: Boris Kulikov. 10 minutes.

Miss Nelson Has a Field Day. (1999). Author: Harry Allard (1985). Illustrator: James Marshall. 13 minutes.

Owen. (1995). Author/Illustrator: Kevin Henkes (1993). 9 minutes.

Seven Blind Mice. (2007). Author/Illustrator: Ed Young (1992). 7 minutes.

So You Want to Be President? (2002). Author: Judith St. George (2000). Illustrator: David Small. 26 minutes.

Sources for Films, Videos, and DVDs

The Video Source Book. Syosset, NY: National Video Clearinghouse, 1979–. Published by Gale Research, Detroit, MI.

An annual reference work that lists media and provides sources for purchase and rental.

Websites of large video distributors:

www.libraryvideo.com

www.knowledgeunlimited.com

http://teacher.scholastic.com/products/westonwoods

PEARSON myeducationkit™ Now go to Chapter 5 in the MyEducationKit (www.myeducationkit.com) for your book, where you can:

- Complete Assignments and Activities that can enrich and extend your knowledge of chapter content.

- Expand your knowledge with content-specific Web Links.

- Review the chapter content by going to the Study Plan, taking a chapter quiz, and receiving feedback on your answers.

- Access the Children's Literature Database for your own exploration.

chapter SIX

Traditional Literature

There Is a Land

There is a land—
a marvelous land—
where trolls and giants dwell;
Where witches
With their bitter brew
Can cast a magic spell;
Where mermaids sing,
Where carpets fly,
Where, in the midst of night,

Brownies dance
To cricket tunes;
And ghosts, all shivery white,
Prowl and moan.
There is a land
Of magic folks and deeds,
And anyone
Can visit there
Who reads and reads and reads.

—*Leland B. Jacobs*

Visual narratives on ancient cave paintings in Europe, Asia, and Australia indicate that prehistoric humans had stories to tell long before they had a written language. For thousands of years, the best of these stories were preserved through the art of storytelling from one generation to the next. Surely these stories survived because people enjoyed hearing them. In folk literature we have our most ancient stories and a priceless literary and cultural heritage that links us to our beginnings as thinking beings.

Definition and Description

Traditional literature is the body of ancient stories and poems that grew out of the oral tradition of storytelling before being eventually written down. Having no known or identifiable authors, these stories and poems are attributed to entire groups of people or cultures. Although some traditional stories are told as cultural or spiritual truths or may contain factual elements, most are considered fantasy.

Because these stories have been preserved over time, they provide insights into the underlying values and beliefs of particular cultural groups and opportunities for comparisons across cultures. Most are considered imaginative stories that provide a window into human nature and cultural beliefs. These traditional stories also provide the basis for many works of modern literature and drama and so children need a strong background in these stories to bring to their later literary experiences.

Traditional literature includes several different types of stories, but because they were all shared orally for so long, they have many features in common:

- *Plots* are short, simple, and direct; all but the essentials disappeared during countless retellings.
- *Action* is concentrated and fast paced, adding interest.
- *Characters* are two-dimensional and easily identified as good or bad.
- *Settings* are unimportant and vague ("In the beginning . . ." or "Long ago in a land far away . . .").
- *Literary style* is characterized by standard beginnings and endings ("Once upon a time . . ."), *motifs* (recurring features such as the number 3), and repeated refrains ("Mirror, mirror, on the wall . . .").
- *Themes* are limited (e.g., good overcomes evil, the small and powerless overcome the powerful, explanations for the ways of the world).
- *Endings* are almost always happy (". . . and they lived happily ever after.").

Folklore is still being created, particularly in cultures and countries where the oral tradition remains an important means of communication. In the United States, urban legends, jokes, and jump-rope rhymes are all part of the constantly evolving body of modern folklore.

Evaluation and Selection of Traditional Literature

For thousands of years, people of all ages were the intended audience for traditional stories. In our scientifically enlightened times, these stories have been relegated to children because of their use of the supernatural and magic. The following list of evaluation criteria was developed with a general child audience in mind:

- A traditional tale, even though written down, should preserve the narrative, or storytelling, style and should sound as though it is being told.
- A traditional tale should preserve the flavor of the culture or country of its origin through the use of unusual speech patterns, a few foreign terms, or proper names common to the culture.
- In illustrated versions, text and illustrations must be of high quality, and illustrations must match the tone of the text and help to capture the essence of the culture of origin.
- Traditional tales employ a simple but rich literary style. Even very young children are fascinated by the chants, stylistic flourishes, and colorful vocabulary that are characteristic of masterful storytelling.
- In evaluating collections of traditional literature, consider the number and variety of tales in the collection and the quality of reference aids, such as tables of contents and indexes.

PEARSON
myeducationkit™

Go to Activity 1 in the Assignments and Activities section of Chapter 6 in MyEducationKit; complete the activity on evaluating several versions of a favorite traditional tale.

Some adults raise concerns that the gruesome violence sometimes found in traditional stories harms or traumatizes children. In recent times, many traditional stories have been rewritten to omit the violence, as in the Disney versions of folktales. In a "softened" version of "Snow White," the evil stepmother is either forgiven by the heroine or banished from the kingdom. Earlier Grimm versions of the tale end with the stepmother dancing to her death in red-hot iron shoes.

Critics of the softened versions of traditional tales claim that altering the stories robs them of their power, their appeal, and their psychological benefit to children, who are reassured that the evil force is gone forever and cannot come back to hurt them. Children should also be made aware of the male chauvinism and poor feminine role models, from ever-sinister stepmothers to ever-helpless princesses, rampant in folktales.

Historical Overview of Traditional Literature

Perhaps the world's first stories grew out of the dreams, wishes, ritual chants, or retellings of the notable exploits of our earliest ancestors. No one knows. Little can be said about the early history of this genre except that these stories existed in oral form for thousands of years.

PEARSON
myeducationkit™

Go to Activity 2 in the Assignments and Activities section of Chapter 6 in MyEducationKit; complete the activity on comparing different cultural variants of the Cinderella story.

Folklorists are intrigued by the startling similarity of traditional tales around the world. Cinderella-type tales, for example, can be found in every culture. One explanation for this is that the first humans created these stories and took them along as they populated the globe. This theory is called *monogenesis,* or "single origin." Another theory credits the fundamental psychological similarity of humans for the similarity of their stories. *Polygenesis,* or "many origins," holds that early humans had similar urges and motives, asked similar fundamental questions about themselves and the world around them, and logically created similar stories in response.

★ *Excellent Traditional Literature* to READ ALOUD

Chen, Jiang Hong. *The Magic Horse of Han Gan.* Ages 5–9. Legend.
dePaola, Tomie. *Strega Nona.* Ages 5–8. Folktale.
Emberley, Rebecca. *Chicken Little.* Illustrated by Ed Emberley. Ages 4–7. Fable.
Fleischman, Paul. *Glass Slipper, Gold Sandal: A Worldwide Cinderella.* Ages 5–9. Folktale.
Hamilton, Virginia, reteller. *In the Beginning: Creation Stories from around the World.* Illustrated by Barry Moser. Ages 9–12. Myths.
Hennessy, B. G., reteller. *The Boy Who Cried Wolf.* Illustrated by Boris Kulikov. Ages 4–7. Fable.
McGill, Alice. *Way Up and Over Everything.* Illustrated by Jude Daly. Ages 8–12. Folktale.
Pinkney, Jerry. *Little Red Riding Hood.* Ages 5–9. Folktale.
Steptoe, John. *Mufaro's Beautiful Daughters: An African Tale.* Ages 6–8. Folktale; Cinderella variant.
Storace, Patricia. *Sugar Cane: A Caribbean Rapunzel.* Illustrated by Raúl Colón. Ages 8–12. Folktale.

Both theories have merit, and since the answer lies hidden in ancient prehistory, neither theory has prevailed over the other.

The popularity of traditional literature with children has continued to grow in the twenty-first century, owing in part to a renewed interest in storytelling. Other trends contributing to the popularity of this genre are the publication of single illustrated retellings of traditional literature, publication of cultural variants of traditional tales from around the world, and publication of ethnic folk literature of Canadian and U.S. minorities in collections and single illustrated works.

Types of Traditional Literature

Classification of traditional literature can be confusing. For instance, not everyone uses the same terms when referring to certain types of traditional stories. Also, modern stories that were written by known authors in the style of the traditional ones but are not of ancient and unknown origin are therefore not "traditional" in the strict sense.

The following terms are commonly used when referring to traditional literature:

- *Traditional Literature.* The entire body of stories passed down from ancient times by the oral tradition. The term *folktales* is sometimes used synonymously with traditional literature, but we see it as a subcategory.
- *Retold Tale.* A version of a tale written in a style that will appeal to a contemporary audience but otherwise remaining true to the ancient tale.
- *Variant.* A story that shares elements of plot or character with other stories and is therefore in the same "story family" but differs mainly by culture. There are hundreds of variants of "Cinderella," for example, from all over the world, that originated in the ancient past.

Myths

Myths are stories that recount and explain the origins of the world and the phenomena of nature. They are sometimes referred to as **creation stories.** The characters in these stories are mainly gods and goddesses, with occasional mention of humans, and the setting is high above earth in the home of the gods. Although often violent, myths nonetheless mirror human nature and the essence of our sometimes primitive emotions, instincts, and desires. Some folklorists believe that myths are the foundation of all other ancient stories. The best-known mythologies are of Greek, Roman, and Norse origin. Many myths are published in collections like Katrin Tchana's *Changing Woman and Her Sisters,* which focuses on goddesses from around the world.

The complexity and symbolism often found in myths make them appropriate for an older audience (9 years and up). Some myths have been simplified for a younger audience, but oversimplification robs these stories of their power and appeal.

Epics

Epics are long stories of human adventure and heroism recounted in many episodes, sometimes in verse. Epics are grounded in mythology, and their characters can be both human and divine. However, the hero is always human or, in some cases, superhuman, as was Ulysses in the *Odyssey,* Beowulf, and Roland in *The Song of Roland.* The setting is earthly but not always realistic. Because of their length and complexity, epics are perhaps more suitable for adolescents, but on the strength of their compelling characters and events, some epics have been successfully adapted and shortened for younger audiences. A good example is Beowulf, retold in three vividly illustrated versions by James Rumford, Gareth Hinds, and Nicky Raven.

Legends and Tall Tales

Legends are stories based on either real or supposedly real individuals and their marvelous deeds. Legendary characters such as King Arthur and Robin Hood and legendary settings such as Camelot are a tantalizing mix of realism and fantasy. Although the feats of the heroes of legend defy belief today, in ancient times these stories were considered factual. Legends, in general, are austere in tone, and, because of their length, seriousness, and complexity, are often suitable for middle-graders.

Tall tales are highly exaggerated accounts of the exploits of persons, both real and imagined, so they may be considered a subcategory of legends. Over time, as each teller embroidered on the hero's abilities or deeds, the tales became outlandishly exaggerated and were valued more for their humor and braggadocio than for their factual content. Well-known North American tall-tale heroes are Pecos Bill, Paul Bunyan, John Henry, and Johnny Appleseed. Lesser-known but equally amazing are such tall-tale heroines as Sally Ann Thunder Ann Whirlwind Crockett. Tall tales can be enjoyed by children age 7 and up.

Folktales

Folktales are stories that grew out of the lives and imaginations of the people, or folk. Folktales have always been a favorite for children from age 3 and up.

Folktales vary in content as to their original intended audiences. Long ago, the nobility and their courtiers heard stories of the heroism, valor, and benevolence of people like themselves—the

MILESTONES *in the Development of Traditional Literature*

Date	Event	Significance
Prehistory–1500s	Oral storytelling	Kept ancient stories alive and provided literature to common people
500 B.C.	Aesop, a supposed Greek slave, wrote classic fables	Established the fable as a type of traditional literature
1484	*Aesop's Fables* published by William Caxton in England	First known publication of traditional literature
1500–1700	Puritan Movement	Prevented the publication of traditional literature by the legitimate press
	Chapbooks emerge	Helped keep interest in traditional heroes alive
Late 1600s	Jean de la Fontaine of France adapted earlier fables in verse form	Popularized the fable
1697	*Tales of Mother Goose* published by Charles Perrault in France	First written version of folktales
1700s	Romantic Movement	Traditional fantasy promoted and embraced in Europe
1812	Wilhelm and Jakob Grimm collected and published *Nursery and Household Tales* in Germany	Helped popularize folk literature
1851	Asbjörnsen and Moe collected and published *The Norwegian Folktales* in Norway	Helped popularize folk literature
1889–1894	Andrew Lang collected and published four volumes of folktales from around the world	Growing popularity and knowledge of folktales worldwide helped popularize folk literature
1894	Joseph Jacobs collected and published *English Fairy Tales* in England; adapted many tales for a child audience	Helped popularize folk literature

ruling classes. In contrast, the stories heard by the common people portrayed the ruling classes as unjust or hard taskmasters whose riches were fair game for those common folk who were quick-witted or strong enough to acquire them. These class-conscious tales are sometimes referred to as *castle* and *cottage* tales, respectively.

Some people use the terms *folktale* and *fairy tale* interchangeably. In fact, the majority of these stories have no fairies or magic characters in them, so to use one term in place of the other can

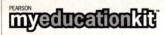

Go to Activity 3 in the Assignments and Activities section of Chapter 6 in MyEducationKit; complete the activity on exploring the categories of traditional literature.

be confusing and erroneous. We categorize fairy tales under *magic tales,* a kind of folktale having magic characters such as fairies.

The following is a list of the most prevalent kinds of folktales. Note that some folktales have characteristics of two or more folktale categories.

Cumulative

The *cumulative tale* uses repetition, accumulation, and rhythm to make an entertaining story out of the barest of plots. Because of its simplicity, rhythm, and humor, the cumulative tale has special appeal to 3- to 5-year-olds. "The Gingerbread Man," with its runaway cookie and growing host of pursuers, is a good example of this kind of tale.

Humorous

The *humorous tale* revolves around a character's incredibly stupid and funny mistakes. These tales are also known as *noodleheads, sillies, drolls,* and *numbskulls.* They have endured, no doubt, for their comic appeal and the guaranteed laughter they evoke. Some famous noodleheads are the Norwegian husband who kept house (and nearly demolished it) and Clever Elsie, who was so addle-brained that she got herself confused with someone else and was never heard from again.

Beast

Beast tales feature talking animals and overstated action. Human characters sometimes occur. Young children accept and enjoy these talking animals, and older children can appreciate that the animals symbolize humans. "Goldilocks and the Three Bears" is a good example.

Magic

Magic tales, also known as *wonder tales* or *fairy tales,* contain elements of magic or enchantment in characters, plots, or settings. Fairies, elves, pixies, brownies, witches, magicians, genies, and fairy godparents are pivotal characters in these stories, and they use magic objects or words to weave their enchantments. Talking mirrors, hundred-year naps, glass palaces, enchanted forests, thumb-sized heroines, and magic kisses are the stuff of magic tales, such as "Aladdin and the Wonderful Lamp."

Pourquoi

Pourquoi tales explain phenomena of nature as in "Why the Sun and Moon Live in the Sky." The word *pourquoi* is French for *why,* and these tales can be understood as explanations for the many "why" questions asked by early humans. The strong connection between these tales and myths is obvious, which is why some folklorists identify pourquoi tales as the simplest myths. However, deities play no role in pourquoi tales as they do in myths and the setting in pourquoi tales is earthly, whereas the setting in myths is the realm of the gods.

Realistic

Realistic tales are those whose characters, plot, and setting could conceivably have occurred. There is no magic in these tales, and any exaggeration is limited to the possible. Only a few realistic tales exist. *Dick Whittington and His Cat* is a good example.

Fables

The *fable* is a simple story that incorporates characters—typically animals—whose actions teach a moral lesson or universal truth. Often, the moral is stated at the end of the story. Fables appeal to adults as well as to children, for the best of these stories are both simple and wise. Moreover, their use of animals as symbols for humans have made them safe, yet effective, political tools. Perhaps because of their adult appeal, fables were put into print far earlier than other forms of traditional literature.

Aesop's fables compose the best-known collection of fables in the Western world, but other collections include the *Panchatantra Tales* from Persia; the *Jataka Tales* from India; and the collected fables of Jean de la Fontaine from France.

Religious Stories

Stories based on religious writings or taken intact from religious manuscripts are considered to be *religious stories.* These stories may recount milestones in the development of a religion and its leadership, or they may present a piece of religious doctrine in narrative form. Stories of the latter sort are usually called *parables.*

Scholars of religion, language, and mythology have found a definite thread of continuity from myth and folk narrative to early religious thinking and writing. Many of the stories, figures, and rituals described in the sacred scriptures of Christianity, Hinduism, and Buddhism, among other religions, have their roots in ancient mythology.

Regardless of whether one considers the religious stories to be fact or fiction, these wonderful stories should be shared with children. Because religion in the classroom is potentially controversial, however, many teachers and librarians do not feel comfortable sharing stories with any religious connection. This is unfortunate, as many excellent stories, characters, sayings, and situations essential to the culturally literate person are therefore missed. Some Indigenous scholars argue that much of their traditional literature is rooted in spiritual beliefs and has been mislabeled as legend.

Traditional literature, the wealth of ancient stories accumulated over the course of human existence, is one of the treasures of our species. We listen to these endlessly fascinating stories, we reflect on them, and they help to tell us who we are. Good companions of our childhood, they easily become part of us and stay with us throughout our lives. Every child deserves access to this wonderful literary and cultural heritage.

Storytelling in the Classroom

Given that traditional literature is rooted in oral tradition, telling these stories in classrooms provides an effective and powerful means for engaging children with this literature. Children are attentive listeners when their teachers tell stories and quickly begin telling stories themselves. By bringing stories to life through personal expression and interpretation, storytellers establish a close communication with their audience.

Notable Retellers and Illustrators
of Traditional Literature

Paul Goble, author and illustrator. Reteller and illustrator of folktales and legends of the North American Indian. *Beyond the Ridge.*

Trina Schart Hyman, reteller and illustrator of classic folktales. *Little Red Riding Hood; The Sleeping Beauty.*

Eric A. Kimmel, storyteller and reteller of folktales from around the world. *Anansi and the Talking Melon; Cactus Soup; Three Samurai Cats.* http://ericakimmel.com

Rafe Martin, storyteller and author who retells stories from a range of cultures. *The Shark God; The Rough-Face Girl; Foolish Rabbit's Big Mistake.* www.rafemartin.com

Jerry Pinkney, Caldecott medalist whose realistic watercolors invigorate folktales, many from the African-American tradition. *Noah's Ark; John Henry; The Ugly Duckling.*

Robert D. San Souci, adapter of obscure or almost-forgotten stories from many different places and ethnic groups. *Cendrillon; The Talking Eggs.* www.rsansouci.com

Ed Young, illustrator and author of Chinese folklore and other folklore from around the world. *Lon Po Po; Yeh-Shen; What about Me?; I, Doko: The Tale of a Basket.* http://edyoungart.com

Paul O. Zelinsky, illustrator whose realistic oil paintings provide insights into the meaning of folktales. *Hansel and Gretel; Rapunzel.* www.paulozelinsky.com/paul.html

Lisbeth Zwerger, illustrator from Vienna with a focus on translated European traditional literature. *Little Red Cap; The Bremen Town Musicians; Aesop's Fables.*

Selection of a Story

To find stories for telling, read through collections of folktales and short stories until you find a few you especially like. Consider these two points:

- Good stories for telling usually have few characters (from two to five), high conflict, action that builds to a climax, and a quick conclusion that ties together all the threads of the story. Humorous elements are also worth seeking.
- The first stories you tell should take no longer than ten minutes. As you develop your storytelling gifts, you may want to tell longer stories.

Good resources for teachers and students in grade 4 and above who want to tell stories more formally is Pellowski's *The Storytelling Handbook* (1995) and Bruchac's *Tell Me a Tale* (1997). Websites also provide stories, storytelling resources, and tips on becoming a good storyteller for you and your students (see www.storyarts.org and www.storynet.org).

Preparation for Telling

Outline the story content in terms of the plot. Many storytellers note the title and source of the tale, the characters' names and story events, and any other information that may be helpful on a 3" × 5" card to consult quickly just before telling a story. Another option is to tape yourself telling stories and use them to refresh your memory for later retellings.

Practice

Tell the story aloud to yourself again and again. Do not memorize the story, but keep in mind the characters and sequence of main story events. Each time you tell the story, it will change a bit, becoming more and more your own story as you include personal touches. Some storytellers use simple props (a hat, a stick-on mustache, or a stuffed toy) or more elaborate ones (a mask, a puppet, or a costume). You can also tell stories through a feltboard, using pictures or objects that are moved around during the story.

Digital storytelling connects the age-old art of storytelling with children's digital worlds through the use of computer-based tools. Digital stories can be personal narratives, traditional tales, or historical recountings that are told by combining computer-based images, text, recorded audio narration, video clips, photographs, drawings, and/or music to tell a brief story. Examples of websites where digital stories are available include the Center for Digital Storytelling (www.storycenter.org) and Educational Uses of Digital Storytelling (http://digitalstorytelling.coe.uh.edu).

Issues&*Topics* for FURTHER INVESTIGATION

- Explore sexism in traditional literature and the subtle messages it conveys to children.

- Engage in a cross-cultural analysis of the "Cinderella" tale. Gather variants from around the world, including Asian, Western European, and American Indian cultures. Compare plot details, themes, and gender messages.

- Disney versions of fairy tales enjoy tremendous popularity and yet are negatively critiqued as stereotyped. Watch the video *Mickey Mouse Monopoly* or locate articles that critique Disney films and books. Use the stereotypes chart in Christensen (2002) to engage in your own analysis.

- Select, learn, and tell (not read) a folktale to a group of children, using props, if appropriate. Note the differences in telling and reading a story to a young audience.

References

Bruchac, J. (1997). *Tell me a tale.* San Diego, CA: Harcourt.

Christensen, L. (2002). Unlearning the myths that bind us. In *Reading, Writing and Rising Up* (pp. 39–51). Milwaukee, WI: Rethinking Schools.

Pellowski, A. (1995). *The storytelling handbook: A young people's collection of unusual tales and helpful hints on how to tell them.* New York: Simon & Schuster.

Pinkney, J. (1999). *The ugly duckling.* New York: Morrow.

✩✦Recommended Traditional Literature

Ages refer to concept and interest levels. Formats other than novels will be coded as follows:

(**PI**) Picture book
(**COL**) Short story collection

Note country, continent, or culture of origin after entries, where applicable.

Myths

Burleigh, Robert. *Pandora.* Illustrated by Raúl Colón. Silver Whistle, 2002. (**PI**) Ages 8–11.

Byrd, Robert, reteller. *The Hero and the Minotaur: The Fantastic Adventures of Theseus.* Dutton, 2005. (**PI**) Ages 8–12.

d'Aulaire, Ingri, and Edgar Parin d'Aulaire. *Book of Greek Myths.* Doubleday, 1962. (**COL**) Ages 8–10.

———. *Norse Gods and Giants.* Doubleday, 1967. (**COL**) Ages 8–10.

Hamilton, Virginia, reteller. *In the Beginning: Creation Stories from around the World.* Illustrated by Barry Moser. Harcourt, 1988. (**COL**) Ages 9–12.

Heaney, Marie. *The Names Upon the Harp: Irish Myth and Legend.* Illustrated by P. J. Lynch. Scholastic, 2000. (**COL**) Ages 10–13.

Hofmeyr, Diane. *The Star-Bearer: A Creation Myth from Ancient Egypt.* Illustrated by Jude Daly. Farrar, 2001. (**PI**) Ages 8–12.

Kimmel, Eric A., reteller. *The McElderry Book of Greek Myths.* Illustrated by Pep Montserrat. M. K. McElderry, 2008. (**COL**) Ages 9–12. (Greece)

McDermott, Gerald. *Creation.* Dutton, 2003. (**PI**) Ages 8–12.

Menchú, Rigoberta, and Dante Liano. *The Honey Jar.* Translated by David Unger. Illustrated by Domi. Groundwood, 2006. (**COL**) Ages 9–12. (Guatemala/Mayan)

Tchana, Katrin Hyman, reteller. *Changing Woman and Her Sisters.* Illustrated by Trina Schart Hyman. Holiday, 2006. (**COL**) Ages 10–14.

Epics

Henderson, Kathy. *Lugalbanda: The Boy Who Got Caught Up in a War.* Illustrated by Jane Ray. Candlewick, 2006. (**PI**) Ages 9–12. (Iraq)

Hinds, Gareth, adapter and illustrator. *Beowulf.* Candlewick, 2007. (**PI**) Ages 10–14. (England)

McCaughrean, Geraldine. *Gilgamesh the Hero.* Illustrated by David Parkins. Eerdmans, 2003. (**PI**) Ages 10–14. (Middle East)

Raven, Nicky, reteller. *Beowulf.* Illustrated by John Howe. Candlewick, 2007. Ages 10–14. (England)

Rumford, James. *Beowulf: A Hero's Tale Retold.* Houghton Mifflin, 2007. Ages 10–14. (England)

Sutcliff, Rosemary. *The Wanderings of Odysseus: The Story of the Odyssey.* Illustrated by Alan Lee. Delacorte, 1996. Ages 10–13. (Greece)

Verma, Jatinder, reteller. *Rama, Sita, and the Story of Divaali.* Illustrated by Nilesh Mistry. Barefoot Books, 2002. (**PI**) Ages 8–14. (India)

Legends and Tall Tales

Bertrand, Lynne. *Granite Baby.* Illustrated by Kevin Hawkes. Farrar, 2005. (**PI**) Ages 5–7. (United States)

Chen, Jiang Hong. *The Magic Horse of Han Gan.* Translated by Claudia Zoe Bedrick. Enchanted Lion, 2006. (**PI**) Ages 5–9. (China)

Demi. *The Legend of Lao Tzu and Tao Te Ching.* M. K. McElderry, 2007. (**PI**) Ages 5–9. (China)

Goble, Paul. *The Girl Who Loved Wild Horses.* Bradbury, 1978. (**PI**) Ages 7–9. (United States)

Hodges, Margaret. *Saint George and the Dragon.* Illustrated by Trina Schart Hyman. Little, Brown, 1984. (**PI**) Ages 8–10. (England)

Hurston, Zora Neale. *Lies and Other Tall Tales.* Illustrated by Christopher Myers. HarperCollins, 2005. (**PI**) Ages 7–10. (Southern United States)

Kellogg, Steven, reteller. *Johnny Appleseed.* Morrow, 1988. (**PI**) Ages 6–8. (United States)

———, reteller. *Paul Bunyan.* Morrow, 1984. Ages 6–8.

———, reteller. *Pecos Bill.* Morrow, 1986. (**PI**) Ages 6–8.

Kimmel, Eric A., reteller. *Gershon's Monster: A Story for the Jewish New Year.* Illustrated by Jon J. Muth. Scholastic, 2000. (**PI**) Ages 6–11. (Jewish)

Lester, Julius. *John Henry.* Illustrated by Jerry Pinkney. Dial, 1994. (**PI**) Ages 8–10. (African-American)

Lindbergh, Reeve. *Johnny Appleseed.* Illustrated by Kathy Jacobsen. Little, Brown, 1990. (**PI**) Ages 6–8. (United States)

Lister, Robin. *The Legend of King Arthur.* Illustrated by Alan Baker. Doubleday, 1990. Ages 8–12. (England)

Maggi, María Elena, reteller. *The Great Canoe: A Kariña Legend.* Translated by Elisa Amado. Illustrated by Gloria Calderón. Groundwood, 2001. (**PI**) Ages 6–11. (Venezuela)

Martin, Rafe. *The World before This One: A Novel Told in Legend.* Illustrated by Calvin Nicholls. Scholastic, 2002. Ages 12–14. (Native American, Seneca)

Nolen, Jerdine. *Big Jabe.* Illustrated by Kadir Nelson. HarperCollins, 2000. (**PI**) Ages 6–10. (African-American)

Osborne, Mary Pope. *American Tall Tales.* Illustrated by Michael McCurdy. Knopf, 1991. (**COL**) Ages 8–11.

Pyle, Howard. *The Merry Adventures of Robin Hood.* Scribner's, 1946 (1883). Ages 9–12. (England)

San Souci, Robert D. *Cut from the Same Cloth: American Women of Myth, Legend, and Tall Tale.* Illustrated by Brian Pinkney. Philomel, 1993. (**COL**) Ages 8–12.

Folktales

Aardema, Verna, reteller. *Why Mosquitoes Buzz in People's Ears.* Illustrated by Leo and Diane Dillon. Dial, 1975. (**PI**) Ages 5–7. (Kenya)

Alley, Zoe. *There's a Wolf at the Door.* Illustrated by R. W. Alley. Roaring Brook, 2008. (**COL**) Ages 5–9. (Western Europe)

Aylesworth, Jim, reteller. *The Tale of Tricky Fox: A New England Trickster Tale.* Illustrated by Barbara McClintock. Scholastic, 2001. (**PI**) Ages 5–8. (United States, New England)

Brown, Marcia. *Stone Soup.* Scribner's, 1975 (1947). (**PI**) Ages 6–8. (France)

Bruchac, James, and Joseph Bruchac, retellers. *The Girl Who Helped Thunder and Other Native American Folktales.* Illustrated by Stefano Vitale. Sterling, 2008. (**COL**) Ages 9–12. (Native American)

Bruchac, Joseph, and James Bruchac, retellers. *Raccoon's Last Race: A Traditional Abenaki Story.* Illustrated by Jose Aruego and Ariane Dewey. Dial, 2004. (**PI**) Ages 4–7. (Native American, Abenaki)

Bryan, Ashley, adapter. *Beautiful Blackbird.* Atheneum, 2003. (**PI**) Ages 5–7. (Zambia)

Cohn, Amy L., editor. *From Sea to Shining Sea: A Treasury of American Folklore and Folk Songs.* Scholastic, 1993. (**COL**) Ages 4–10. (United States)

Corrin, Sara and Stephen Corrin, retellers. *The Pied Piper of Hamelin.* Illustrated by Errol Le Cain. Harcourt, 1989. (**PI**) Ages 7–9. (Germany)

Cummings, Pat. *Ananse and the Lizard: A West African Tale.* Holt, 2002. (**PI**) Ages 4–8. (Ghana)

Demi. *The Hungry Coat: A Tale from Turkey.* M. K. McElderry, 2004. (**PI**) Ages 5–9. (Turkey)

dePaola, Tomie. *Strega Nona.* Prentice Hall, 1975. (**PI**) Ages 5–8. (Italy)

Fleischman, Paul. *Glass Slipper, Gold Sandal: A Worldwide Cinderella.* Illustrated by Julie Paschkis. Holt, 2007. (**PI**) Ages 5–9. (World)

Galdone, Paul. *The Gingerbread Man.* Clarion, 1975. (**PI**) Ages 4–6. (England)

———. *The Little Red Hen.* Seabury, 1973. (**PI**) Ages 5–7. (England)

———. *The Three Billy Goats Gruff.* Seabury, 1973. (**PI**) Ages 5–7. (Norway)

Garland, Sherry. *Children of the Dragon: Selected Tales from Vietnam.* Illustrated by Trina Schart Hyman. Harcourt, 2001. (**COL**) Ages 8–12. (Vietnam)

Gerson, Mary-Joan. *Fiesta Femenina: Celebrating Women in Mexican Folktales.* Barefoot, 2001. (**COL**) Ages 10–13. (Mexico)

Goble, Paul. *Beyond the Ridge.* Bradbury, 1989. (**PI**) Ages 8–10. (Native American)

———, reteller. *Iktomi and the Berries: A Plains Indian Story.* Orchard, 1989. (**PI**) Ages 7–9. (Native American)

———. *Storm Maker's Tipi.* Atheneum, 2001. (**PI**) Ages 7–12. (Native American, Siksika)

Grimm, Jakob, and Wilhelm Grimm. *The Bremen Town Musicians.* Illustrated by Lisbeth Zwerger. Translated by Anthea Bell. Miniedition, 2007. (**PI**) Ages 5–9. (Germany)

———. *Hansel and Gretel.* Illustrated by Anthony Browne. Knopf, 1998 (1981). (**PI**) Ages 8–14. (Germany)

———. *Little Red Cap.* Illustrated by Lisbeth Zwerger. Translated by Elizabeth D. Crawford. Miniedition, 2006. (**PI**) Ages 5–9. (Germany)

———. *Little Red Riding Hood.* Illustrated by Trina Schart Hyman. Holiday, 1982. (**PI**) Ages 6–8. (Germany)

————. *Rumpelstiltskin.* Retold and illustrated by Paul O. Zelinsky. Dutton, 1986. (**PI**) Ages 7–9. (Germany)

————. *Snow-White and the Seven Dwarfs.* Translated by Randall Jarrell. Illustrated by Nancy Ekholm Burkert. Farrar, 1972. (**PI**) Ages 8–10. (Germany)

Hamilton, Virginia. *Bruh Rabbit and the Tar Baby Girl.* Illustrated by James Ransome. Scholastic, 2003. (**PI**) Ages 5–7. (Gullah, South Carolina)

————. *The Girl Who Spun Gold.* Illustrated by Leo and Diane Dillon. Blue Sky, 2000. (**PI**) Ages 5–8. (West Indian)

————. *Her Stories: African American Folktales, Fairy Tales, and True Tales.* Illustrated by Leo and Diane Dillon. Scholastic, 1995. (**COL**) Ages 9–15. (African-American)

————. *The People Could Fly: American Black Folktales.* Illustrated by Leo and Diane Dillon. Knopf, 1985. (**COL**) Ages 8–10. (African-American)

Heo, Yumi, reteller. *The Green Frogs: A Korean Folktale.* Houghton, 1996. (**PI**) Ages 4–7. (Korea)

Hodges, Margaret, reteller. *Dick Whittington and His Cat.* Illustrated by Melisande Potter. Holiday, 2006. (**PI**) Ages 5–9. (England)

Hooks, William H., reteller. *Moss Gown.* Illustrated by Donald Carrick. Clarion, 1987. (**PI**) Ages 7–9. (United States; a Cinderella variant)

Huck, Charlotte. *Princess Furball.* Illustrated by Anita Lobel. Greenwillow, 1989. (**PI**) Ages 6–8. (Germany; a Cinderella variant)

Hughes, Shirley, reteller. *Ella's Big Chance: A Jazz-Age Cinderella.* Simon & Schuster, 2004. (**PI**) Ages 6–9. (England)

Hyman, Trina Schart. *The Sleeping Beauty.* Little, Brown, 1977. (**PI**) Ages 5–8. (Germany)

Isadora, Rachel. *The Twelve Dancing Princesses.* Putnam, 2007. (**PI**) Ages 5–9. (Germany/Africa)

Johnson-Davies, Denys. *Goha the Wise Fool.* Illustrated by Hany El Saed Ahmed and Hag Hamdy Mohamed Fattouh. Philomel, 2005. (**COL**) Ages 6–12. (Middle East)

Kajikawa, Kimiko, adaptor. *Yoshi's Feast.* Illustrated by Yumi Heo. DK Ink, 2000. (**PI**) Ages 5–9. (Japan)

Kilaka, John. *True Friends.* Groundwood, 2006. (**PI**) Ages 5–9. (Tanzania)

Kimmel, Eric A. *Anansi and the Talking Melon.* Illustrated by Janet Stevens. Holiday, 1994. (**PI**) Ages 5–7. (Africa)

————. *Cactus Soup.* Illustrated by Phil Huling. Marshall Cavendish, 2004. (**PI**) Ages 5–9. (Mexico)

————. *Three Samurai Cats.* Illustrated by Mordicai Gerstein. Holiday, 2003. (**PI**) Ages 4–8. (Japan)

Knutson, Barbara. *Love and Roast Chicken: A Trickster Tale from the Andes Mountains.* Carolrhoda, 2004. (**PI**) Ages 4–7. (Peru, Bolivia)

Lesser, Rika. *Hansel and Gretel.* Illustrated by Paul Zelinsky. (**PI**) Ages 5–8. (Germany)

Lester, Julius, reteller. *The Tales of Uncle Remus: The Adventures of Brer Rabbit.* Illustrated by Jerry Pinkney. Dial, 1987. (**COL**) Ages 7–9. (African-American)

Louie, Ai-Ling. *Yeh-Shen: A Cinderella Story from China.* Illustrated by Ed Young. Philomel, 1982. (**PI**) Ages 7–9. (China)

Lunge-Larsen, Lise. *The Hidden Folk: Stories of Fairies, Dwarves, Selkies, and Other Secret Beings.* Illustrated by Beth Krommes. Houghton, 2004. (**COL**) Ages 6–12. (Northern Europe)

————, reteller. *The Troll with No Heart in His Body: And Other Tales of Trolls from Norway.* Illustrated by Betsy Bowen. Houghton, 1999. (**COL**) Ages 7–11. (Norway)

Marcantonio, Patricia Santos. *Red Ridin' in the Hood, and Other "Cuentos."* Illustrated by Renato Alarcão. Farrar, 2005. (**COL**) Ages 7–12. (Latino, United States)

Marshall, James. *Goldilocks and the Three Bears.* Dial, 1988. (**PI**) Ages 5–7. (England)

————. *The Three Little Pigs.* Dial, 1989. (**PI**) Ages 5–7. (England)

Martin, Rafe, reteller. *Foolish Rabbit's Big Mistake.* Illustrated by Ed Young. Putnam, 1985. (**PI**) Ages 6–8. (India)

————. *The Rough-Face Girl.* Illustrated by David Shannon. Putnam, 1992. (**PI**) Ages 8–10. (Native American, Mi'kmaq)

————. *The Shark God.* Illustrated by David Shannon. Scholastic, 2001. (**PI**) Ages 5–9. (Hawai'i)

McClintock, Barbara, reteller. *Cinderella.* Scholastic, 2005. (**PI**) Ages 5–9. (France)

McDermott, Gerald. *Anansi the Spider.* Holt, 1972. (**PI**) Ages 6–8. (Ghana)

————. *Raven: A Trickster Tale from the Pacific Northwest.* Harcourt, 1993. (**PI**) Ages 5–9. (Native American)

McGill, Alice. *Way Up and Over Everything.* Illustrated by Jude Daly. Houghton Mifflin, 2008. (**PI**) Ages 8–12. (African-American)

McKissack, Patricia C. *Flossie and the Fox.* Illustrated by Rachel Isadora. Dial, 1986. (**PI**) Ages 7–9. (African-American)

Milligan, Bryce. *The Prince of Ireland and the Three Magic Stallions.* Illustrated by Preston McDaniels. Holiday, 2003. (**PI**) Ages 6–8. (Ireland)

Mollel, Tololwa. *Subira Subira.* Illustrated by Linda Saport. Clarion, 2000. (**PI**) Ages 5–10. (Tanzania)

Montresor, Beni, adapter. *Little Red Riding Hood.* Doubleday, 1991. (**PI**) Ages 10–14. (Germany)

Morimoto, Junko. *The Two Bullies.* Translated by Isao Morimoto. Crown, 1999. (**PI**) Ages 5–7. (Japan)

Nesbit, E. *Jack and the Beanstalk.* Illustrated by Matt Tavares. Candlewick, 2006. (**PI**) Ages 5–9. (England)

Orgel, Doris, reteller. *The Bremen Town Musicians and Other Animal Tales from Grimm.* Illustrated by Bert Kitchen. Roaring Brook, 2004. (**COL**) Ages 6–9. (Germany)

Parks, Van Dyke, and Malcolm Jones, adaptors and re-tellers. *Jump! The Adventures of Brer Rabbit.* Illustrated by Barry Moser. Harcourt, 1986. (**COL**) Ages 7–9. (African-American)

Paterson, Katherine. *The Tale of the Mandarin Ducks.* Illustrated by Leo and Diane Dillon. Lodestar, 1990. (**PI**) Ages 7–9. (Japan)

Perrault, Charles. *Cinderella.* Illustrated by Marcia Brown. Scribner's, 1954. (**PI**) Ages 6–8. (France)

———. *Puss in Boots.* Illustrated by Fred Marcellino. Farrar, 1990. (**PI**) Ages 6–8. (France)

Pinkney, Jerry. *Little Red Riding Hood.* Little, Brown, 2007. (**PI**) Ages 5–9. (Germany)

Powell, Patricia H. *Frog Brings Rain/Ch'at Tó Yiníló'.* Translated by Peter A. Thomas. Illustrated by Kendrick Benally. Salina Bookshelf, 2006. (**PI**) Ages 5–8. (Bilingual English/Navajo)

Reneaux, J. J. *How Animals Saved the People: Animal Tales from the South.* Illustrated by James Ransome. Morrow, 2001. (**COL**) Ages 9–14. (Rural Southern United States, African-American, Appalachian, Native American)

Sanderson, Ruth, reteller. *The Golden Mare, the Fire-bird, and the Magic Ring.* Little, Brown, 2001. (**PI**) Ages 8–12. (Russia)

San Souci, Robert D., reteller. *Cendrillon: A Caribbean Cinderella.* Illustrated by Brian Pinkney. Simon & Schuster, 1998. (**PI**) Ages 5–7. (Caribbean)

———, reteller. *Sister Tricksters: Rollicking Tales of Clever Females.* Illustrated by Daniel San Souci. August House, 2006. (**COL**) Ages 8–12. (Southern United States)

———. *The Talking Eggs: A Folktale from the American South.* Illustrated by Jerry Pinkney. Dial, 1989. (**PI**) Ages 7–9. (African-American)

Sierra, Judy, selector and reteller. *Can You Guess My Name? Traditional Tales around the World.* Illustrated by Stefano Vitale. Clarion, 2002. (**COL**) Ages 8–10.

———. *The Gift of the Crocodile: A Cinderella Story.* Illustrated by Reynold Ruffins. Simon & Schuster, 2000. (**PI**) Ages 5–9. (Indonesia/Spice Islands)

———. *Tasty Baby Belly Buttons: A Japanese Folktale.* Illustrated by Meilo So. Knopf, 1999. (**PI**) Ages 4–7. (Japan)

Simonds, Nina, Leslie Swartz, and the Children's Museum, Boston. *Moonbeams, Dumplings and Dragon Boats: A Treasury of Chinese Holiday Tales, Activities and Recipes.* Illustrated by Meilo So. Harcourt, 2002. (**COL**) Ages 9–12. (China)

Singer, Isaac Bashevis. *When Shlemiel Went to Warsaw and Other Stories.* Translated by the author and Elizabeth Shub. Illustrated by Margot Zemach. Farrar, 1968. (**COL**) Ages 8–10. (Jewish)

Smith, Chris. *One City, Two Brothers.* Illustrated by Aurélia Fronty. Barefoot Books, 2007. (**PI**) Ages 5–9. (Middle East)

Steptoe, John. *Mufaro's Beautiful Daughters: An African Tale.* Lothrop, 1987. (**PI**) Ages 6–8. (Zimbabwe)

Storace, Patricia. *Sugar Cane: A Caribbean Rapunzel.* Illustrated by Raúl Colón. Jump at the Sun/Hyperion, 2007. (**PI**) Ages 9–12. (Caribbean)

Sweet, Melissa, reteller. *Carmine: A Little More Red.* Houghton, 2005. (**PI**) Ages 4–8. (Germany; also an ABC book)

Taback, Simms, reteller. *Kibitzers and Fools: Tales My Zayda Told Me.* Viking, 2005. (**PI**) Ages 7–12. (Eastern Europe)

———. *This Is the House That Jack Built.* Putnam, 2002. (**PI**) Ages 5–7. (Hebrew)

Tchana, Katrin. *The Serpent Slayer and Other Stories of Strong Women.* Illustrated by Trina Schart

Hyman. Little, Brown, 2000. (COL) Ages 7–12. (World)

Tejima. *Ho-Limlim: A Rabbit Tale from Japan.* Philomel, 1990. (PI) Ages 6–8. (Japan)

Wattenberg, Jane. *Henny-Penny.* Scholastic, 2000. (PI) Ages 7–12. (England)

Yolen, Jane. *Not One Damsel in Distress: World Folktales for Strong Girls.* Illustrated by Susan Guevara. Silver Whistle, 2000. (COL) Ages 8–13. (World)

Young, Ed. *I, Doko: The Tale of a Basket.* Philomel, 2004. (PI) Ages 5–9. (Nepal)

———. *Lon Po Po: A Red-Riding Hood Story from China.* Philomel, 1989. (PI) Ages 7–9. (China)

———. *What About Me?* Putnam, 2002. (PI) Ages 5–8. (Sufi)

Zelinsky, Paul O., reteller. *Rapunzel.* Dutton, 1997. (PI) Ages 5–8. (Germany)

———, reteller. *Rumpelstiltskin.* Dutton, 1986. (PI) Ages 6–8. (Germany)

Zemach, Harve. *Duffy and the Devil.* Illustrated by Margot Zemach. Farrar, 1973. (PI) Ages 6–8. (England)

Zemach, Margot. *It Could Always Be Worse.* Farrar, 1977. (PI) Ages 6–8. (Jewish)

Fables

Aesop's Fables. Illustrated by Jerry Pinkney. North-South/Sea Star, 2000. (COL) Ages 5–9.

Brown, Marcia. *Once a Mouse.* Scribner's, 1961. (PI) Ages 6–8.

Emberley, Rebecca. *Chicken Little.* Illustrated by Ed Emberley. Roaring Brook, 2009. (PI) Ages 4–7.

Goodall, Jane. *The Eagle and the Wren.* Illustrated by Alexander Reichstein. North-South, 2000. (PI) Ages 5–8. (India)

Hennessy, B. G., reteller. *The Boy Who Cried Wolf.* Illustrated by Boris Kulikov. Simon & Schuster, 2006. (PI) Ages 4–7.

Oberman, Sheldon. *The Wisdom Bird: A Tale of Solomon and Sheba.* Illustrated by Neil Waldman. Boyds Mills, 2000. (PI) Ages 5–9. (Also religious story)

Uribe, Verónica, reteller. *Little Book of Fables.* Translated by Susan Ouriou. Illustrated by Constanza Bravo. Groundwood, 2004. (COL) Ages 6–12.

Wormell, Christopher. *Mice, Morals, & Monkey Business: Lively Lessons from Aesop's Fables.* Running Press, 2005. (PI, COL) Ages 5–8.

Zwerger, Lisbeth, selector and illustrator. *Aesop's Fables.* North-South Books, 2006. (COL) Ages 5–9.

Religious Stories

Demi. *Buddha.* Holt, 1996. (PI) Ages 8–12.

Goldin, Barbara Diamond. *Journeys with Elijah: Eight Tales of the Prophet.* Illustrated by Jerry Pinkney. Harcourt, 1999. (COL) Ages 7–14.

Hao, K. T. *Little Stone Buddha.* Translated by Annie Kung. Illustrated by Giuliano Ferri. Purple Bear, 2005. (PI) Ages 4–7.

Johnson, James Weldon. *The Creation.* Illustrated by James E. Ransome. Holiday, 1994. (PI) Ages 6–8.

Muth, Jon J. *Zen Shorts.* Scholastic, 2005. (PI, COL) Ages 5–9. (Buddhist)

Pinkney, Jerry. *Noah's Ark.* North-South, 2002. (PI) Ages 5–8.

Root, Phyllis. *Big Momma Makes the World.* Illustrated by Helen Oxenbury. Candlewick, 2003. (PI) Ages 4–7.

Schwartz, Howard. *Invisible Kingdoms: Jewish Tales of Angels, Spirits, and Demons.* Illustrated by Stephen Feiser. HarperCollins, 2002. (COL) Ages 8–12. (World)

Wisniewski, David. *Golem.* Clarion, 1996. (PI) Ages 6–12.

Young, Ed. *Monkey King.* HarperCollins, 2001. (PI) Ages 5–8. (Buddhist)

Related Films, Videos, and DVDs

American Tall Tales (includes *John Henry, Swamp Angel*). (2006). Retellers: Julius Lester and Paul O. Zelinsky. Illustrators: Jerry Pinkney and Paul O. Zelinsky. 32 minutes.

Favorite Fairy Tales, Volume II (includes *Rapunzel, Princess Furball*). (2006). Retellers: Paul O. Zelinsky and Charlotte Huck. Illustrators: Paul O. Zelinsky and Anita Lobel. 32 minutes.

Hansel and Gretel. (2005). Reteller/Illustrator: James Marshall. 16.5 minutes.

Lon Po Po. (2008). Reteller/Illustrator: Ed Young. 14 minutes.

The Tale of the Mandarin Duck. (1998). Reteller: Katherine Paterson. Illustrators: Leo and Diane Dillon. 16 minutes.

There Was an Old Lady Who Swallowed a Fly. (2002). Illustrator: Simms Tabeck. 8 minutes.

Why Mosquitoes Buzz in People's Ears and Other Caldecott Classics (includes *Why Mosquitoes Buzz in People's Ears; The Village of Round and Square Houses; A Story, A Story: An African Tale*). (2002). Retellers: Verna Aardema, Ann Grifalconi, and Gail E. Haley. Illustrators: Leo and Diane Dillon, Ann Grifalconi, and Gail E. Haley. 32 minutes.

Sources for Films, Videos, and DVDs

The Video Source Book. Syosset, NY: National Video Clearinghouse, 1979–. Published by Gale Research, Detroit, MI.

An annual reference work that lists media and provides sources for purchase and rental.

Websites of large video distributors:

www.libraryvideo.com

www.knowledgeunlimited.com

http://teacher.scholastic.com/products/westonwoods

PEARSON myeducationkit™ Now go to Chapter 6 in the MyEducationKit (www.myeducationkit .com) for your book, where you can:

- Complete Assignments and Activities that can enrich and extend your knowledge of chapter content.

- Expand your knowledge with content-specific Web Links.

- Review the chapter content by going to the Study Plan, taking a chapter quiz, and receiving feedback on your answers.

- Access the Children's Literature Database for your own exploration.

chapter SEVEN

Modern Fantasy

Ladder to the Sky

Do you know
If you try
You really can
Touch the sky?

Lean a ladder
Against the moon
And climb, climb high
Talk to the stars
And leave your handprints
All across the sky

Jump on a cloud
And spend the day

Trampoline-jumping
Through the air
Climb a rainbow
And watch the world
From way up there
Then ride that rainbow slide

Back home.

—*Sheree Fitch*

Modern fantasy has its roots in traditional fantasy, from which motifs, characters, stylistic elements, and, at times, themes have been drawn. Many of the most revered works of children's literature fall into the genre of modern fantasy. *The Adventures of Pinocchio, Alice's Adventures in Wonderland, The Wonderful Wizard of Oz, The Wind in the Willows, Winnie-the-Pooh, Pippi Longstocking,* and *Charlotte's Web* immediately come to mind. The creation of stories that are highly imaginative— yet believable—is the hallmark of this genre.

Definition and Description

Modern fantasy refers to the body of literature in which the events, the settings, or the characters are outside the realm of possibility. A fantasy is a story that cannot happen in the real world, and for this reason this genre has been called "the literature of the fanciful impossible." In these stories, animals talk, inanimate objects come to life, people are giants or thumb-sized, imaginary worlds are inhabited, and future worlds are explored, just to name a few of the possibilities. Modern fantasies are written by known authors, and this distinguishes the genre from traditional literature, in which the tales are handed down through the oral tradition and have no known author. Although the events could not happen in real life, modern fantasies often contain truths that help the reader understand today's world.

The *cycle format,* in which one book is linked to another through characters, settings, or both, is especially prevalent in modern fantasy. Elleman (1987) states, "Events in [fantasy] cycle books are often strung out over three or four volumes. Authors attempt to make each novel self-contained, with varying degrees of success, but usually readers need the entire series for full impact" (p. 418). The cycle format appeals to readers who become attached to certain characters and then delight in reading the next book in the series. An example of the cycle format can be found in the Annals of the Western Shore series by Ursula K. Le Guin.

Evaluation and Selection of Modern Fantasy

The usual standards for fine fiction must also be met by authors of modern fantasy. Believable and well-rounded characters who develop and change, well-constructed plots, well-described settings with internal consistency, a style appropriate to the story, and worthy themes are elements to be expected in all fiction. In addition, the following criteria apply specifically to modern fantasy:

PEARSON myeducationkit

Go to Activity 1 in the Assignments and Activities section of Chapter 7 in MyEducationKit; complete the activity on reading aloud modern fantasies.

■ Authors of modern fantasy have the challenge of persuading readers to open themselves up to believing that which is contrary to reality, strange, whimsical, or magical, yet has an internal logic and consistency. Sometimes, authors will accomplish this through beginning the story in a familiar and ordinary setting with typical, contemporary human beings as characters. A transition is then made from this realistic world to the fantasy world. An example of this literary device is found in C. S. Lewis's *The Lion, the Witch and the Wardrobe,* in which the children in

Excellent Modern Fantasy to READ ALOUD

Appelt, Kathi. *The Underneath.* Ages 9–14.
Avi. *The Seer of Shadows.* Ages 9–14.
———. *Strange Happenings: Five Tales of Transformations.* Ages 10–15.
Babbitt, Natalie. *Jack Plank Tells Tales.* Ages 8–12.
DiCamillo, Kate. *The Miraculous Journey of Edward Tulane.* Ages 8–12.
Finney, Patricia. *I, Jack.* Ages 8–12.
Grey, Mini. *The Adventures of the Dish and the Spoon.* Ages 5–9.
Haddix, Margaret Peterson. *Double Identity.* Ages 10–14.
Jenkins, Emily. *Toy Dance Party.* Ages 6–10.
Jonell, Lynne. *Emmy and the Incredible Shrinking Rat.* Ages 8–11.
Mass, Wendy. *11 Birthdays.* Ages 9–12.
Pullman, Philip. *The Scarecrow and His Servant.* Ages 9–13.
Stanley, Diane. *Bella at Midnight: The Thimble, the Ring, and the Slippers of Glass.* Ages 10–14.
Ullman, Barb Bentler. *The Fairies of Nutfolk Wood.* Ages 8–11.

the story enter a wardrobe in an old house only to discover that the back of the wardrobe leads into the land of Narnia, a fantasy world with unusual characters. Other fantasies begin in the imagined world but manage, through well-described settings and consistent well-rounded characters, to make this new reality believable. Either way, the plot, characters, and setting must be so well developed that the child reader is able to suspend disbelief and to accept the impossible as real.

- For a modern fantasy to be truly imaginative, the author must provide a unique setting. In some stories, the setting may move beyond the realistic in both time (moving to the past or future or holding time still) and place (imagined worlds); in other stories, only one of these elements (place or time) will go beyond reality. Moreover, a modern fantasy author's creation must be original.

- In recent years, partially due to an upsurge of sects whose members refer to themselves as witches, challenges to fantasies for children have increased. Stories with supernatural elements such as magic, Halloween, witches, warlocks, wizards, vampires, and other elements of the occult have been targets of censors. The popular Harry Potter series has topped the American Library Association's Most Frequently Challenged Children's Books list in recent years because some individuals and religious communities disapprove of the book's focus on wizardry and magic. In selecting and recommending stories with these elements, teachers need to be aware of the concerns of their students' parents with regard to the supernatural as a topic in books for children. For a full discussion on censorship, schools' and teachers' responsibilities, and how to address them appropriately, see the section Censorship and the First Amendment in Chapter 12.

Historical Overview of Modern Fantasy

Imaginative literature did not appear until the eighteenth century. These stories were not intended primarily for children but were political satires that came to be enjoyed by children as well as adults. *Gulliver's Travels* (1726) by the Irish clergyman Jonathan Swift is the most noteworthy of such books. In this adult satire ridiculing the antics of the English court and its politics, the hero, Gulliver, travels to strange, imaginary places—one inhabited by six-inch Lilliputians, another inhabited by giants. These imaginary worlds are described in fascinating detail and with sufficient humor to appeal to a child audience.

In England in 1865, Charles Lutwidge Dodgson, an Oxford don who used the pen name Lewis Carroll, wrote *Alice's Adventures in Wonderland,* which tells of a fantastic journey Alice takes to an imaginary world. The total absence of didacticism—replaced by humor and fantasy—resulted in the book's lasting appeal and world fame. Other fantasies that originated in England shortly after the appearance of *Alice* include *The Light Princess* (1867) and *At the Back of the North Wind* (1871) by George MacDonald, and *Just So Stories* (1902) by Rudyard Kipling. This early development of modern fantasy for children in England was unrivaled by any other country and established the standard for the genre worldwide.

Modern fantasy has continued to thrive in England. Noteworthy contributions from England include *The Tale of Peter Rabbit* (1902) by Beatrix Potter, *The Wind in the Willows* (1908) by Kenneth Grahame, *The Velveteen Rabbit* (1922) by Margery Williams, *Winnie-the-Pooh* (1926) by A. A. Milne, *Mary Poppins* (1934) by Pamela Travers, *The Hobbit* (1937) by J. R. R. Tolkien, *The Lion, the Witch and the Wardrobe* (1950) by C. S. Lewis, *The Borrowers* (1953) by Mary Norton, and *The Children of Green Knowe* (1955) by Lucy M. Boston.

Early books of modern fantasy from other countries include *The Adventures of Pinocchio* (1881) by Carlo Collodi (Carlo Lorenzini) from Italy and *Journey to the Center of the Earth* (1864), *Twenty Thousand Leagues under the Sea* (1869), and *Around the World in Eighty Days* (1872) by the Frenchman Jules Verne. Verne's works are considered the first science fiction novels and remain popular today with adults and children. Later in France, Jean de Brunhoff wrote an internationally popular series of animal fantasies about a family of elephants. The first of these was *The Story of Babar* (1937).

Some works of fantasy from Scandinavia also deserve recognition. Hans Christian Andersen, a Dane, published many modern folktales, stories that were very similar in literary elements to the traditional tales. However, Andersen was the originator of most of his tales, for which his own life experiences were the inspiration. "The Ugly Duckling," "The Emperor's New Clothes," and "Thumbelina" are three of the most loved of Andersen's stories. His tales were published in 1835 and are considered the first modern fairy tales. A century later, Swedish author Astrid Lindgren produced *Pippi Longstocking* (1945). Pippi, a lively, rambunctious, and strong heroine who throws caution to the wind, lives an independent life of escapades that are envied by children the world over.

The United States also produced some outstanding early modern fantasies, beginning with *The Wonderful Wizard of Oz* (1900) by L. Frank Baum, which is considered to be the first classic U.S. modern fantasy for children. Other landmark U.S. works of modern fantasy are the memorable animal fantasy *Rabbit Hill* (1944) by Robert Lawson; *Charlotte's Web* (1952) by E. B. White, the best-known and best-loved U.S. work of fantasy; *The Book of Three* (1964), the first of the Prydain Chronicles by Lloyd Alexander; and *A Wrinkle in Time* (1962) by Madeleine L'Engle, which is considered a modern classic in science fiction for children.

Science fiction, the most recent development in modern fantasy, is said to owe its birth to the aforementioned nineteenth-century novels of Jules Verne and H. G. Wells (*Time Machine,* 1895). Adults, not children, were the primary audience for these novels, however. It was not until the twentieth century that science fiction began to be aimed specifically at children. The Tom Swift series by Victor Appleton (collective pseudonym for the Stratemeyer Syndicate), although stilted in style and devoid of female characters, can be considered the first science fiction for

MILESTONES *in the Development of Modern Fantasy*

Date	Event	Significance
1726	*Gulliver's Travels* by Jonathan Swift (England)	An adult novel prototype for children's fantasy adventures
1835	*Fairy Tales* by Hans Christian Andersen (Denmark)	First modern folktales
1864	*Journey to the Center of the Earth* by Jules Verne (France)	First science fiction novel (for adults)
1865	*Alice's Adventures in Wonderland* by Lewis Carroll (England)	First children's masterpiece of modern fantasy
1881	*The Adventures of Pinocchio* by Carlo Collodi (Italy)	Early classic personified toy story
1900	*The Wonderful Wizard of Oz* by L. Frank Baum (United States)	First classic U.S. modern fantasy for children
1908	*The Wind in the Willows* by Kenneth Grahame (England)	Early classic animal fantasy
1910	*Tom Swift and His Airship* by Victor Appleton (United States)	First science fiction novel for children
1926	*Winnie-the-Pooh* by A. A. Milne (England)	Early classic personified toy story
1937	*The Hobbit* by J. R. R. Tolkien (England)	Early quest adventure with a cult following
1950	*The Lion, the Witch and the Wardrobe* by C. S. Lewis (England)	Early classic quest adventure for children; first of the Narnia series
1952	*Charlotte's Web* by E. B. White (United States)	Classic U.S. animal fantasy
1953	*The Borrowers* by Mary Norton (England)	Classic little people fantasy
1962	*A Wrinkle in Time* by Madeleine L'Engle (United States)	Classic U.S. science fiction novel for children
1993	*The Giver* by Lois Lowry (United States)	Popular futuristic fiction novel; Newbery Medal winner
1998	*Harry Potter and the Sorcerer's Stone* by J. K. Rowling (England)	First book in the best-selling quest fantasy series

children. The first Tom Swift book appeared in 1910 (*Tom Swift and His Airship*), with additional titles of the series appearing in rapid succession. The success of the science fiction magazine *Amazing Stories,* launched in 1926, brought formal recognition to the genre of science fiction.

In 1963, Madeleine L'Engle's novel *A Wrinkle in Time* was awarded the Newbery Medal. From this point forward, many science fiction novels for children began to appear. In the late 1960s and 1970s, the theme of mind control was popular. John Christopher's Tripods trilogy and William Sleator's *House of Stairs* (1974) are good examples. Space travel and future worlds were frequent science fiction topics in the 1980s. The accompanying Milestones feature highlights the development of modern fantasy.

Modern fantasy for children remains strong, especially in Great Britain and other English-speaking countries. Although personified toys and animals remain popular and prevalent in children's books, growth in this genre appears to be in stories in which fantasy is interwoven into other genres—science fiction, science fantasy, and historical fantasy. Fractured folktales, traditional tales with a contemporary twist or a tale told from a new perspective, took on new popularity with the publication of Jon Scieszka's *The True Story of the 3 Little Pigs by A. Wolf,* illustrated by Lane Smith and published in 1989. This blurring of traditional genres can also be seen in the interesting mixture of realistic mystery stories with supernatural elements, as in the popular mysteries of John Bellairs and Mary Downing Hahn. Modern fantasy is likely to continue to be a popular genre with children and authors, as evidenced by the extraordinary popularity of the best-selling Harry Potter quest series by J. K. Rowling, whose first novel in the series was published in 1998.

Types of Modern Fantasy

In modern fantasy, as in other genres, the distinctions between types are not totally discrete. The types of modern fantasy in the sections that follow are a starting point for thinking about the variety of fantastic stories, motifs, themes, and characters that gifted authors have created. Additional categories could be listed, and you will find that some stories may fit appropriately in more than one category. For example, Terry Pratchett's *The Wee Free Men,* categorized as a "little people" story, could also be considered a *quest fantasy.*

Modern Folktales

Modern folktales, or *literary folktales* as they are also called, are tales told in a form similar to that of a traditional tale with the accompanying typical elements: little character description, strong conflict, fast-moving plot with a sudden resolution, vague setting, and, in some cases, magical elements. But these modern tales have a known, identifiable author who has written the tale in this form. In other words, the tales do not spring from the cultural heritage of a group of people through the oral tradition but rather from the mind of one creator. However, this distinction does not matter at all to children, who delight in these tales as much as they do in the old folktales.

The tales of Hans Christian Andersen are the earliest and best known of these modern tales. More recently, other authors, including Diane Stanley *(Bella at Midnight* and *Rumpelstiltskin's Daughter)* and Shannon Hale *(Goose Girl* and *River Secrets),* have become known for their modern folktales.

Fractured folktales can be defined as traditional folktales with a contemporary twist or a tale told from a new perspective. A humorous example in which the characters of the well-known nursery rhyme run away to become vaudeville stars is *The Adventures of the Dish and the Spoon* by Mini Grey.

Modern folktales are an important counterbalance to traditional tales. As was noted in Chapter 6, many of the traditional tales present an old-fashioned, stereotypical view of male and female characters. Many of the modern tales present more assertive female characters who are clearly in charge of their own destinies. Examples are *Book of a Thousand Days* by Shannon Hale and *Princess Ben* by Catherine Gilbert Murdock.

Animal Fantasy

Animal fantasies are stories in which animals behave as human beings in that they experience emotions, talk, and have the ability to reason. Usually, the animals in fantasies will (and should) retain many of their animal characteristics. In the best of these animal fantasies, the author will interpret the animal for the reader in human terms without destroying the animal's integrity or removing it from membership in the animal world. For example, a rabbit character in an animal fantasy will retain her natural abilities of speed and camouflage to outsmart her adversaries. At the same time, however, the author will permit the reader to see human qualities such as caring and love by having the rabbit carry on conversations with family members.

PEARSON
myeducationkit

Go to Activity 2 in the Assignments and Activities section of Chapter 7 in MyEducationKit; complete the activity on exploring reasons for animal fantasies.

Animal fantasies can be read to very young children who enjoy the exciting but reassuring adventures in books. Examples are *The Tale of Peter Rabbit* by Beatrix Potter and *Bad Bear Detectives* by Daniel Pinkwater. Books for children in primary grades include somewhat longer stories, often in a humorous vein, such as Beverly Cleary's mouse stories, including *The Mouse and the Motorcycle,* Lynne Jonell's *Emmy and the Incredible Shrinking Rat,* and *The Nine Lives of Aristotle* by Dick King-Smith. Enjoyable animal fantasies for the young reader often have easy-to-follow, episodic plots.

Fully developed novels of modern fantasy with subtle and complex characterizations and a progressive plot are especially suitable for reading aloud to children in their elementary school years. *Charlotte's Web* by E. B. White remains a favorite read-aloud book; *The Tale of Despereaux* by Kate DiCamillo and *I, Jack* by Patricia Finney are also popular. A classic book with richly drawn characterizations is *The Wind in the Willows* by Kenneth Grahame, who describes in artistic detail the life of animal friends along a riverbank. This book features an episodic plot structure but has a challenging style that is appropriate for intermediate-grade students. In *A Coyote's in the House* by Elmore Leonard, the humorous story of a coyote in Hollywood satirizes the movie industry with a style that will be appreciated by many students age 10 and older. *Orwell's Luck* by Richard W. Jennings, a novel with a progressive plot, is also appreciated by intermediate-grade students who enjoy reflecting on what separates reality from fantasy.

Although the interest in animal fantasy peaks at age 8 or 9, many children and adults continue to enjoy well-written animal fantasies. In animal fantasies for older readers, an entire animal world is usually created, with all of the relationships among its members that might be found in a novel portraying human behavior. *The Amazing Maurice and His Educated Rodents* by Terry Pratchett is an example of a complex, fully developed animal fantasy novel for readers in fifth grade through high school.

Personified Toys and Objects

Stories in which admired objects or beloved toys are brought to life and believed in by a child or adult character in the story are the focus of this type of fantasy. An early classic example of these stories is *The Adventures of Pinocchio* by Carlo Collodi (Carlo Lorenzini), in which a mischievous puppet comes to life, runs away from his maker, and has many exciting and dangerous escapades. In these stories, the object, toy, or doll becomes real to the human protagonist and, in turn, becomes real to the child reader (who has perhaps also imagined a toy coming to life). Close family relationships are also demonstrated in *The Doll People* and *The Meanest Doll in the World*

Notable Authors

of Modern Fantasy

Lloyd Alexander, author of quest fantasies based on Welsh mythology, including the Prydain series comprised of *The Book of Three* and four other titles; *The Xanadu Adventure.*

David Almond, British writer noted for magical realism novels for young adults. *Skellig,* Carnegie Medal winner; *Kit's Wilderness; Clay.* www .davidalmond.com

Jane Louise Curry, author known for her historical novels for children, especially historical fantasies. *Dark Shade; The Black Canary.* www.janelouisecurry.com

Kate DiCamillo, author of fantasies and realistic stories for children in primary and intermediate grades. *The Tale of Despereaux,* winner of the Newbery Medal, and *The Miraculous Journey of Edward Tulane.* www.katedicamillo.com

Nancy Farmer, author of young adult novels including *The House of the Scorpion,* National Book Award winner for young people's literature.

Shannon Hale, author of modern folktales. *Goose Girl; Book of a Thousand Days; Rapunzel's Revenge* (co-written with Dean Hale). www .squeetus.com

Dick King-Smith, British author of animal fantasies. *Pigs Might Fly; The Nine Lives of Aristotle.*

Gail Carson Levine, author of modern folktales. *Ella Enchanted; Fairest.*

Lois Lowry, winner of the 1994 Newbery Medal for *The Giver,* a popular work of science fiction. www.loislowry.com

Robin McKinley, author of modern folktales with female protagonists. *Rose Daughter; Spindle's End.* www.robinmckinley.com

Donna Jo Napoli, author of novels for young readers in many genres, especially recognized for her use of myth in modern folktales. *Bound; Crazy Jack; Beast.* www.donnajonapoli .com

Terry Pratchett, British author of the Discworld series that includes *The Wee Free Men.* Winner of the Carnegie Medal for *The Amazing Maurice and His Educated Rodents,* a work of humorous fantasy. www.terrypratchett books.com

Philip Pullman, British creator of His Dark Materials fantasies, a trilogy comprised of *The Golden Compass, The Subtle Knife,* and *The Amber Spyglass.* www.philip-pullman.com

J. K. Rowling, British author of the best-selling series about Harry Potter, a child wizard. *Harry Potter and the Sorcerer's Stone.* www .jkrowling.com

---

PEARSON
myeducationkit™

Go to the Conversations section of Chapter 7 in MyEducationKit to read the interview with Lois Lowry.

by Ann M. Martin and Laura Godwin. Emily Jenkins's *Toys Go Out* and *Toy Dance Party* depict toys who become friends with one another. In Kate DiCamillo's *The Miraculous Journey of Edward Tulane,* a vain china rabbit learns the power of love in this story suitable for intermediate-grade students. Personified toy and object stories appeal to children from preschool through upper elementary grades.

Unusual Characters and Strange Situations

Some authors approach fantasy through reality but take it beyond reality to the ridiculous or exaggerated. Generally, those stories can be best described as having unusual characters or strange situations. Without doubt, *Alice's Adventures in Wonderland* by Lewis Carroll is the best known of this type of modern fantasy. Writers of modern fantasy have described such strange situations as a boy sailing across the Atlantic Ocean in a giant peach (*James and the Giant Peach* by

Roald Dahl) and the daily events of an unlikely school in *Wayside School Gets a Little Stranger* by Louis Sachar.

Modern fantasy appeals to readers of all ages. Shaun Tan's *The Arrival,* a wordless graphic novel, features a hero who leaves his homeland and travels to a bizarre new world where he faces the struggles of being an immigrant, seeks employment, and eventually makes friends in this strange new place. The story is fascinating to students in middle and high school. In Neil Gaiman's *The Graveyard Book,* a young boy is being raised in a cemetery by its ghostly occupants. The topics of life, death, and the power of family can provoke discussion with intermediate-grade students. In *Tuck Everlasting,* Natalie Babbitt explores the theme of immortality and its consequences, a provocative theme for children and adults.

Worlds of Little People

Some authors have written about worlds inhabited by miniature people who have developed a culture of their own in this world or who live in another world. In Barb Bentler Ullman's *The Fairies of Nutfolk Wood,* Willa Jane, the protagonist, defends a band of fairies living in the nearby woods who are threatened by humans. In *The Dark Ground* and *The Black Room,* the first books of a series by Gillian Cross, ant-sized people face psychological adventures, fantasies appealing to students age 11 and older. Stories of little people delight children because they can identify with the indignities foisted on little and powerless people and because the big people in these stories are invariably outdone by the more ingenious little people.

Supernatural Events and Mystery Fantasy

Many recent fantasies evoke the supernatural. One common form of supernatural literature found in children's books is the ghost story. Some ghost stories intrigue younger children, especially when the topic is treated humorously and reassuringly. The goblins of Hilari Bell's *The Goblin Wood* eventually become allies of the protagonist. Ghosts in children's books can be fearful threats or helpful protectors, as is the ghost of Cynthia DeFelice's *The Ghost of Fossil Glen,* who is seeking revenge for a murder. Many authors write mysteries for children in which the solution is partially supernatural or arrived at with supernatural assistance. Vampire stories are gaining in popularity with the success of Stephenie Meyer's vampire novel, *Twilight,* in which a teenage girl falls in love at her new school with a handsome but tortured vampire.

Witchcraft and other aspects of the occult sometimes play a role in children's fantasy books. Witches are often portrayed as the broom-wielding villains of both traditional and modern tales, such as the Russian stories of Baba Yaga. Halloween and its traditions are also frequently presented in children's stories. An example is Frances Hardinge's *Well Witched,* in which three children who steal some coins discover that a witch has endowed the coins with some strange powers. Witchcraft has recently been the focus of criticism because of an upsurge of sects whose members refer to themselves as witches. Also, some parents' groups have attempted to censor children's books featuring witches, Halloween, and other elements of the occult. Chapter 12 has a full discussion on censorship and schools' responsibilities in these situations.

Magical realism, a blend of fantasy and realism, has the appearance of a work of realism but gradually introduces the fantastic as an integral, and necessary, part of the story. The fantastic is merged into these stories such that the distinction between realism and fantasy is blurred, often leaving the reader in some doubt as to what is real and what is fantasy. Magical realism with its origins in Latino literature has stories with the feel of realism, but the magical elements cause them to fall outside of the definition of realistic fiction. Examples are David Almond's works, such as *Skellig, The Fire-Eaters,* and *Clay,* among others. For a discussion on David Almond's works and magical realism, see Latham (2006). These stories of magical realism are placed in the Recommended Books list under Supernatural Events and Mystery Fantasy.

Historical Fantasy

Historical fantasy, sometimes called *time-warp fantasy,* is a story in which a present-day protagonist goes back in time to a different era. A contrast between the two time periods is shown to readers through the modern-day protagonist's discoveries of and astonishment with earlier customs. Historical fantasies must fully and authentically develop the historical setting, both time and place, just as in a book of historical fiction. Mary Hoffman, in *Stravaganza: City of Masks,* succeeds in producing this type of mixed-genre story. Wendy Mass, in *11 Birthdays,* and Jeanette Winterson, in *Tanglewreck,* also present interesting historical fantasies that will appeal to middle-grade students and older.

Quest Stories

Quest stories are adventure stories with a search motif. The quest may be pursuit for a lofty purpose, such as justice or love, or for a rich reward, such as a magical power or a hidden treasure. Quest stories that are serious in tone are called *high fantasy.* Many of these novels are set in medieval times and are reminiscent of the search for the holy grail. In these high fantasies, an imaginary otherworld is fully portrayed: the society, its history, family trees, geographic location, population, religion, customs, and traditions. The conflict in these tales usually centers on the struggle between good and evil. *The Hobbit,* written by J. R. R. Tolkien in 1937, is one of the first of these high fantasies; it retains a cult of followers even today. Because of the greater complexity of these novels, their allure is for children in fifth grade and higher, including adults, of course. Good examples are C. S. Lewis's Chronicals of Narnia series, Philip Pullman's His Dark Materials trilogy, and J. K. Rowling's Harry Potter series.

Many quest fantasies follow a structure similar to that found in traditional myths and described by Joseph A. Campbell (1949) as a *monomyth.* In this structure, sometimes referred to as a *hero cycle,* the hero starts out in the ordinary world and receives a call to enter a strange, dangerous, supernatural world where he must face daunting trials involving a struggle against external forces and internal temptations. If the hero overcomes these trials, he will receive a precious gift. He then has a choice to return to the ordinary world or to remain in the supernatural world. If he chooses to return, he will face more trials on the return journey. After returning successfully, the hero shares the gift to improve the world. The hero cycle represents a journey of self-discovery and personal growth for the protagonist.

Science Fiction and Science Fantasy

Science fiction is a form of imaginative literature that provides a picture of something that could happen based on real scientific facts and principles. Therefore, story elements in science fiction must have the appearance of scientific plausibility or technical possibility. Hypotheses about the future of humankind and the universe presented in science fiction appear plausible and possible

PEARSON
myeducationkit™

Go to Activity 3 in the Assignments and Activities section of
Chapter 7 in MyEducationKit;
view the artifact on student
responses to science fiction and
respond to the questions.

to the reader because settings and events are built on extensions of known technologies and scientific concepts.

In novels of science fiction, such topics as mind control, genetic engineering, space technologies and travel, visitors from outer space, and future political and social systems all seem possible to the readers. For example, in Margaret Peterson Haddix's novel, *Double Identity,* genetic engineering and its implications are explored. These novels especially fascinate many young people because they feature characters who must learn to adjust to change and to become new people, two aspects of living that adolescents also experience. In addition, science fiction stories may portray the world, or one very much like it, that young people will one day inhabit; for this reason, science fiction has sometimes been called *futuristic fiction.*

Science fiction is a type of fiction that you will want to know about because of its growing popularity among children and adolescents. If you are reluctant to read science fiction or have never read it, you may want to start with some books by Nancy Farmer (*The House of the Scorpion*), Andrew Clements (*Things Not Seen*), or Lois Lowry (*The Giver; Messenger*).

The distinction between science fiction and science fantasy is not clearly defined or universally accepted. *Science fantasy* is a popularized type of science fiction in which a scientific explanation, though not necessarily plausible, is offered for imaginative leaps into the unknown. Science fantasy presents a world that often mixes elements of mythology and traditional fantasy with scientific or technological concepts, resulting in a setting that has some scientific basis but never has existed or never could exist. A worthy example is Sylvia Waugh's *Earthborn,* in which the protagonist discovers her parents are space aliens. Science fantasy novels, which usually appear in series, appeal to adolescents and young adults and, like many series, are sometimes formulaic and of mixed quality.

Modern fantasy has appeal for persons with nonliteral minds, who go beyond the letter of a story to its spirit. Children, with their lively imaginations, are especially open to reading fantasies. The many types and topics within this genre—animal fantasies, little people stories, tales of personified toys, mystery fantasies, stories of unusual people and situations, quest tales, science fiction, and so on—offer children a breadth of inspiring and delightful entertainment. Because the level of conceptual difficulty varies considerably in this genre, modern fantasy offers many excellent stories for children, from the youngest to the oldest.

Issues & Topics for FURTHER INVESTIGATION

- Discuss whether you, as a teacher, will include books about wizards and vampires in your curriculum and classroom library. Defend your position.

- Select a classic work of modern fantasy for children, such as *Alice's Adventures in Wonderland, Charlotte's Web, The Wonderful Wizard of Oz,* or *The Wind in the Willows.* Read the work and review articles of literary criticism about the work. Then present your perspectives on the book. Consider whether it remains a valuable book for today's children.

- Select the device of time travel commonly found in historical fantasies. Read two historical fantasies that include time travel, then compare how different authors use this device in telling the story.

⭐ References

Campbell, J. A. (1949). *The hero with a thousand faces.* New York: Pantheon.

Elleman, B. (1987). Current trends in literature for children. *Library Trends, 35*(3): 413–426.

Fitch, S. (1998). Ladder to the sky. In J. Prelutsky (Ed.), *Imagine that!* Illustrated by Kevin Hawkes. New York: Knopf.

Latham, D. (2006). *David Almond: Memory and magic.* Lanham, MD: Scarecrow.

⭐ Recommended Modern Fantasy Books

Ages indicated refer to concept and interest levels. Formats other than novels will be coded as follows:

(**PI**) Picture book
(**COL**) Short story collection
(**GR**) Graphic novel

Modern Folktales

Andersen, Hans Christian. *The Pea Blossom.* Retold and illustrated by Amy Lowry Poole. Holiday, 2005. Ages 5–8.

Datlow, Ellen, and Terri Windling, editors. *A Wolf at the Door and Other Retold Fairy Tales.* Simon & Schuster, 2000. (**COL**) Ages 11–16.

Grey, Mini. *The Adventures of the Dish and the Spoon.* Knopf, 2006. Ages 5–9.

Gruber, Michael. *The Witch's Boy.* HarperCollins, 2005. Ages 11–14.

Hale, Shannon. *Book of a Thousand Days.* Bloomsbury, 2007. Ages 11–15.

———. *Goose Girl.* Bloomsbury, 2003. Ages 11–15.

———. *River Secrets.* Bloomsbury, 2006. Ages 10–15. Adventures of Razo, a character from Hale's *The Goose Girl.*

———, and Dean Hale. *Rapunzel's Revenge.* Illustrated by Nathan Hale. Bloomsbury, 2008. (**GR**) Ages 10–14.

Hopkinson, Deborah. *Apples to Oregon: Being the (Slightly) True Narrative of How a Brave Pioneer Father Brought Apples, Peaches, Pears, Plums, Grapes, and Cherries (and Children) Across the Plains.* Illustrated by Nancy Carpenter. Atheneum, 2004. (**PI**) Ages 6–10.

Isaacs, Anne. *Pancakes for Supper.* Illustrated by Mark Teague. Scholastic, 2006. (**PI**) Ages 4–8.

Lester, Julius. *The Old African.* Illustrated by Jerry Pinkney. Dial, 2005. (**PI**) Ages 9–12.

Levine, Gail Carson. *Ella Enchanted.* HarperCollins, 1997. Ages 10–13.

———. *Fairest.* HarperCollins, 2006. Ages 11–16.

———. *Fairy Dust and the Quest for the Egg.* Illustrated by David Christiana. Disney, 2005. Ages 8–11.

McKinley, Robin. *Rose Daughter.* Greenwillow, 1997. Ages 11–18.

———. *Spindle's End.* Putnam, 2000. Ages 12–18.

McKissack, Patricia C. *Porch Lies: Tales of Slicksters, Tricksters, and Other Wily Creatures.* Illustrated by Andre Carilho. Random, 2006. (**COL**) Ages 8–11.

Mora, Pat. *Doña Flor: A Tall Tale about a Giant Woman with a Great Big Heart.* Illustrated by Raúl Colón. Knopf, 2005. (**PI**) Ages 4–8.

Murdock, Catherine Gilbert. *Princess Ben.* Houghton, 2008. Ages 11–16.

Napoli, Donna Jo. *Beast.* Atheneum, 2000. Ages 11–16.

———. *Bound.* Simon & Schuster, 2004. Ages 10–18.

———. *Crazy Jack.* Delacorte, 1999. Ages 11–15.

———. *Zel.* Dutton, 1996. Ages 13–18.

Osborne, Mary Pope. *Kate and the Beanstalk.* Illustrated by Giselle Potter. Schwartz/Atheneum, 2000. Ages 5–8.

Pattou, Edith. *East.* Harcourt, 2003. Ages 12–16.

Pinkney, Andrea Davis. *Peggony-Po: A Whale of a Tale.* Illustrated by Brian Pinkney. Hyperion, 2006. (**PI**) Ages 5–9.

Pullman, Philip. *The Scarecrow and His Servant.* Illustrated by Peter Bailey. Knopf, 2005. Ages 9–13.

Reeve, Philip. *Here Lies Arthur.* Scholastic, 2008. Ages 12–18.

Sandburg, Carl. *The Huckabuck Family: And How They Raised Popcorn in Nebraska and Quit and Came Back.* Illustrated by David Small. Farrar, 1999. Ages 5–8.

Stanley, Diane. *Bella at Midnight: The Thimble, the Ring, and the Slippers of Glass.* Illustrated by Bagram Ibatoulline. HarperCollins, 2006. Ages 10–14.

———. *Rumpelstiltskin's Daughter.* Morrow, 1997. Ages 5–9.

Animal Fantasies

Anderson, M. T. *Whales on Stilts!* Harcourt, 2005. Ages 9–13. Sequel is *The Clue of the Linoleum Lederhosen,* 2006. Humorous.

Appelt, Kathi. *The Underneath.* Atheneum, 2008. Ages 9–14. Magical realism.

Arkin, Alan. *Cassie Loves Beethoven.* Hyperion, 2000. Ages 9–12. Humorous.

Armstrong, Alan. *Whittington.* Illustrated by S. D. Schindler. Random, 2005. Ages 9–13.

Bruchac, Joseph. *Wabi: A Hero's Tale.* Dial, 2006. Ages 10–15.

Cleary, Beverly. *The Mouse and the Motorcycle.* Illustrated by Louis Darling. Morrow, 1965. Ages 7–11.

DiCamillo, Kate. *The Tale of Despereaux.* Illustrated by Timothy Basil Ering. Candlewick, 2003. Ages 7–10.

Finney, Patricia. *I, Jack.* HarperCollins, 2004. Ages 8–12.

Grahame, Kenneth. *The Wind in the Willows.* Illustrated by E. H. Shepard. Scribner's, 1908. Ages 8–12.

Jennings, Patrick. *We Can't All Be Rattlesnakes.* HarperCollins, 2009. Ages 8–12.

Jennings, Richard W. *Orwell's Luck.* Houghton, 2000. Ages 9–12.

Johnson, D. B. *Henry Builds a Cabin.* Houghton, 2002. (PI) Ages 9–13. Others in the series include *Henry Hikes to Fitchburg,* 2000; and *Henry Climbs a Mountain,* 2003.

Jonell, Lynne. *Emmy and the Incredible Shrinking Rat.* Illustrated by Jonathan Bean. Holt, 2007. Ages 8–11.

King-Smith, Dick. *The Nine Lives of Aristotle.* Candlewick, 2003. Ages 6–9.

———. *Pigs Might Fly.* Illustrated by Mary Rayner. Viking, 1982. Ages 8–11.

Labatt, Mary. *Aliens in Woodford.* Kids Can Press, 2000. Ages 7–10. Humorous.

Leonard, Elmore. *A Coyote's in the House.* Harper-Entertainment, 2004. Ages 9–13.

Palatini, Margie. *The Web Files.* Illustrated by Richard Egielski. Hyperion, 2001. (PI) Ages 9–12. Humorous.

Pinkwater, Daniel. *Bad Bear Detectives.* Illustrated by Jill Pinkwater. Houghton, 2006. (PI) Ages 4–8.

Potter, Beatrix. *The Tale of Peter Rabbit.* Warne, 1902. (PI) Ages 5–9.

Pratchett, Terry. *The Amazing Maurice and His Educated Rodents.* HarperCollins, 2001. Ages 12–16.

Said, S. F. *Varjak Paw.* Illustrated by Dave McKean. Knopf, 2003. Ages 9–12.

Seidler, Tor. *Gully's Travels.* Illustrated by Brock Cole. Scholastic, 2008. Ages 9–12.

White, E. B. *Charlotte's Web.* Illustrated by Garth Williams. Harper, 1952. Ages 8–11.

Personified Toys and Objects

DiCamillo, Kate. *The Miraculous Journey of Edward Tulane.* Illustrated by Bagram Ibatoulline. Candlewick, 2006. Ages 8–12.

Fine, Anne. *The Jamie and Angus Stories.* Illustrated by Penny Dale. Candlewick, 2000. (COL) Ages 5–8.

Jenkins, Emily. *Toy Dance Party.* Illustrated by Paul O. Zelinsky. Schwartz and Wade, 2008. (COL) Ages 6–10.

———. *Toys Go Out: Being the Adventures of a Knowledgeable Stingray, a Toughy Little Buffalo, and Someone Called Plastic.* Illustrated by Paul O. Zelinsky. Random, 2006. Ages 5–8.

Martin, Ann M., and Laura Godwin. *The Doll People.* Illustrated by Brian Selznick. Hyperion, 2000. Ages 8–12.

———. *The Meanest Doll in the World.* Illustrated by Brian Selznick. Hyperion, 2003. Ages 7–11. Sequel to *The Doll People.*

Unusual Characters and Strange Situations

Avi. *Strange Happenings: Five Tales of Transformations.* Harcourt, 2006. (COL) Ages 10–15.

Babbitt, Natalie. *Jack Plank Tells Tales.* Scholastic, 2007. Ages 8–12. Humorous.

———. *Tuck Everlasting.* Farrar, 1975. Ages 10–14.

Dahl, Roald. *James and the Giant Peach.* Illustrated by Nancy Ekholm Burkert. Knopf, 1961. Ages 8–11.

Gaiman, Neil. *The Graveyard Book.* Illustrated by Dave McKean. HarperCollins, 2008. Ages 10–15.

Gonzalez, Julie. *Wings.* Delacorte, 2005. Ages 12–16.

Pullman, Philip. *I Was a Rat!* Illustrated by Kevin Hawkes. Knopf, 2000. Ages 8–12.

Sachar, Louis. *Wayside School Gets a Little Stranger.* Morrow, 1995. Ages 8–12. Humorous.

Tan, Shaun. *The Arrival.* Scholastic, 2007. (**GR**) Ages 11–16. Wordless.

Worlds of Little People

Augarde, Steve. *Celandine.* David Fickling, 2006. Ages 10–14.

———. *The Various.* David Fickling, 2004. Ages 10–14.

———. *Winter Wood.* David Fickling, 2009. Ages 10–14.

Briggs, Raymond. *Ug: Boy Genius of the Stone Age.* Knopf, 2002. (**PI**) Ages 9–16.

Cross, Gillian. *The Dark Ground: Book One of the Dark Ground Trilogy.* Dutton, 2004. Ages 11–15. Sequel is *The Black Room: Book Two,* 2006.

Pratchett, Terry. *The Wee Free Men.* HarperCollins, 2003. Ages 10–15. Sequels are *A Hat Full of Sky,* 2004; and *Wintersmith,* 2006.

Ullman, Barb Bentler. *The Fairies of Nutfolk Wood.* HarperCollins, 2006. Ages 8–11.

Supernatural Events and Mystery Fantasy

Almond, David. *Clay.* Delacorte, 2006. Ages 11–18.

———. *Heaven Eyes.* Delacorte, 2001. Ages 10–13.

———. *Kit's Wilderness.* Delacorte, 2000. Ages 12–18.

———. *Skellig.* Delacorte, 1999. Ages 9–12.

———. *The Fire-Eaters.* Delacorte, 2004. Ages 11–18.

Barry, Dave, and Ridley Pearson. *Peter and the Starcatchers.* Hyperion, 2004. Ages 9–13. Humorous.

Bell, Hilari. *Flame.* Simon & Schuster, 2003. Ages 11–16.

———. *The Goblin Wood.* HarperCollins, 2003. Ages 11–16.

Carey, Janet Lee. *Dragon's Keep.* Harcourt, 2007. Ages 12–16.

Constable, Kate. *The Singer of All Songs.* Scholastic, 2004. Ages 12–16.

Crutcher, Chris. *The Sledding Hill.* Greenwillow, 2005. Ages 11–18.

DeFelice, Cynthia. *The Ghost of Fossil Glen.* Farrar, 1998. Ages 9–12.

Delaney, Joseph. *Revenge of the Witch: The Last Apprentice, Book One.* Illustrated by Patrick Arrasmith. Greenwillow, 2005. Ages 10–14.

Dickinson, Peter. *The Ropemaker.* Delacorte, 2001. Ages 11–18.

———. *The Tears of the Salamander.* Random, 2003. Ages 11–15.

Farmer, Nancy. *A Sea of Trolls.* Atheneum, 2004. Ages 9–14.

Funke, Cornelia. *Dragon Rider.* Translated by Anthea Bell. Scholastic, 2004. Ages 9–14.

———. *Inkheart.* Translated by Anthea Bell. Scholastic, 2003. Ages 12–18. Sequel is *Inkspell,* 2005.

———. *The Thief Lord.* Translated by Oliver Latsch. Scholastic, 2002. Ages 10–14.

Gaiman, Neil. *Coraline.* Illustrated by Dave McKean. HarperCollins, 2002. Ages 10–14.

———. *Coraline: Graphic Novel.* Adapted by P. Craig Russell. HarperCollins, 2008. (**GR**) Ages 10–14. A graphic adaptation of Gaiman's 2002 novel.

Hahn, Mary Downing. *The Old Willis Place: A Ghost Story.* Clarion, 2004. Ages 10–13.

Hardinge, Frances. *Well Witched.* HarperCollins, 2008. Ages 10–14.

Hautman, Pete. *Sweet Blood.* Simon & Schuster, 2003. Ages 12–16.

Hurston, Zora Neale. *The Skull Talks Back and Other Haunting Tales.* Adapted by Joyce Carol Thomas. Illustrated by Leonard Jenkins. HarperCollins, 2004. (**COL, PI**) Ages 9–13.

Ibbotson, Eva. *Island of the Aunts.* Illustrated by Kevin Hawkes. Dutton, 2000. Ages 9–12.

Jones, Diana Wynne. *Dark Lord of Derkholm.* Greenwillow, 1998. Ages 12–16. Sequel is *Year of the Griffin,* 2000.

Lowry, Lois. *Gossamer.* Houghton, 2006. Ages 9–12.

Lubar, David. *Punished!* Darby Creek, 2006. Ages 8–11.

McKinley, Robin. *The Stone Fey.* Illustrated by John Clapp. Harcourt, 1998. (**PI**) Ages 13–18.

———, and Peter Dickinson. *Water: Tales of Elemental Spirits.* Putnam, 2002. (**COL**) Ages 11–16.

Melling, O. R. *The Hunter's Moon.* Abrams/Amulet, 2005. Ages 12–18. First in a trilogy.

Meyer, Stephenie. *Twilight.* Little, Brown, 2005. Ages 13–18.

Noyes, Deborah, editor. *Gothic! Ten Original Dark Tales.* Candlewick, 2004. (**COL**) Ages 12–18.

Prue, Sally. *Cold Tom.* Scholastic, 2003. Ages 10–13.

Slade, Arthur. *Dust.* Random, 2003. Ages 12–16.

Stine, R. L., editor. *Beware! R. L. Stine Picks His Favorite Scary Stories.* HarperCollins, 2002. (**COL**) Ages 9–14.

Historical Fantasy

Avi. *The Seer of Shadows.* HarperCollins, 2008. Ages 9–14.

Buckley-Archer, Linda. *Gideon the Cutpurse: Being the First Part of the Gideon Trilogy.* Simon & Schuster, 2006. Ages 10–14.

Curry, Jane Louise. *The Black Canary.* Simon & Schuster, 2005. Ages 11–14.

———. *Dark Shade.* McElderry, 1998. Ages 11–14.

Etchemendy, Nancy. *The Power of Un.* Front Street, 2000. Ages 9–14.

Gardner, Sally. *I, Coriander.* Dial, 2005. Ages 11–14.

Haddix, Margaret Peterson. *Found.* Simon & Schuster, 2008. Ages 10–14.

Hale, Shannon. *Princess Academy.* Bloomsbury, 2005. Ages 10–14.

Hoffman, Mary. *Stravaganza: City of Masks.* Bloomsbury, 2002. Ages 12–16. Sequel is *Stravaganza II: City of Stars,* 2003.

Mass, Wendy. *11 Birthdays.* Scholastic, 2009. Ages 9–12.

Meyer, Kai. *The Water Mirror.* Translated by Elizabeth D. Crawford. Simon & Schuster, 2005. Ages 10–14.

Myers, Laurie. *Lewis and Clark and Me.* Illustrated by Michael Dooling. Holt, 2002. Ages 8–12.

Pratchett, Terry. *Nation.* HarperCollins, 2008. Ages 11–15.

Smith, Roland. *The Captain's Dog: My Journey with the Lewis and Clark Tribe.* Harcourt, 1999. Ages 12–16.

Thal, Lilli. *Mimus.* Translated by John Brownjohn. Annick, 2005. Ages 11–15. Humorous.

Winterson, Jeanette. *Tanglewreck.* Bloomsbury, 2006. Ages 10–15.

Quest Stories

Alexander, Lloyd. *The Book of Three.* Holt, 1964. Ages 10–15. The first of the Prydain Chronicles series, which includes *The Black Cauldron,* 1965; *The Castle of Llyr,* 1966; *Taran Wanderer,* 1967; and *The High King,* 1968.

———. *The Golden Dreams of Carlo Chuchio.* Holt, 2007. Ages 10–14.

———. *The Xanadu Adventure.* Dutton, 2005. Ages 10–14.

Bass, L. G. *Sign of the Qin.* Hyperion, 2004. Ages 13–15.

Collins, Suzanne. *Gregor the Overlander.* Scholastic, 2003. Ages 9–14.

Cornish, D. M. *Foundling.* Putnam, 2006. Ages 12–16.

———. *Lamplighter.* Putnam, 2008. Ages 12–16.

Crossley-Holland, Kevin. *The Seeing Stone: Arthur Trilogy, Book One.* Scholastic, 2001. Ages 12–16. The first of the Arthur trilogy, which includes *At the Crossing Places,* 2002; and *King of the Middle March,* 2004.

Divakaruni, Chitra Banerjee. *The Conch Bearer.* Millbrook, 2003. Ages 10–14.

Fisher, Catherine. *Day of the Scarab: Book Three of the Oracle Prophecies.* Greenwillow, 2006. Ages 10–14. The third of the Oracle Prophecies Trilogy, which includes *The Oracle Betrayed,* 2004; and *The Sphere of Secrets,* 2005.

Flanagan, John. *The Ruins of Gorlan.* Philomel, 2005. Ages 11–15.

Gavin, Jamila. *The Blood Stone.* Farrar, 2005. Ages 12–16.

Hodges, Margaret. *Merlin and the Making of the King.* Illustrated by Trina Schart Hyman. Holiday, 2004. (**PI**) Ages 9–12.

Lee, Tanith. *Wolf Tower.* Dutton, 2000. Ages 10–13. First in the Claidi Journals series.

Le Guin, Ursula K. *Gifts: Annals of the Western Shore.* Harcourt, 2007. Ages 11–16. The first in the Annals of the Western Shore series, which includes *Voices,* 2006; and *Powers,* 2007.

Lewis, C. S. *The Lion, the Witch and the Wardrobe.* Illustrated by Pauline Baynes. Macmillan, 1950. Ages 9–12. The first in the Chronicles of Narnia series, which includes *Prince Caspian,* 1951; *The Voyage of the Dawn Treader,* 1952; *The Silver Chair,* 1953; *The Horse and His Boy,* 1954; *The Magician's Nephew,* 1955; and *The Last Battle,* 1956.

Morpurgo, Michael. *Sir Gawain and the Green Knight.* Illustrated by Michael Foreman. Candlewick, 2004. Ages 10–14.

Oppel, Kenneth. *Airborn.* HarperCollins, 2004. Ages 11–14.

Pierce, Meredith Ann. *Treasure at the Heart of the Tanglewood.* Viking, 2001. Ages 12–16.

Pullman, Philip. *The Golden Compass.* Knopf, 1996. Ages 12–16. The first of the His Dark Materials trilogy, which includes *The Subtle Knife,* 1998; and *The Amber Spyglass,* 1999.

Riordan, Rick. *The Lightning Thief.* Hyperion, 2005. Ages 10–15. Humorous.

Rodda, Emily. *Rowan of Rin.* Greenwillow, 2002. Ages 8–11. Others in the series include *Rowan and the Zebak,* 2002; and *Rowan and the Travelers,* 2001.

Rowling, J. K. *Harry Potter and the Sorcerer's Stone.* Scholastic, 1998. Ages 9–13. The first in the Harry Potter series, which includes *Harry Potter and the Chamber of Secrets,* 1999; *Harry Potter and the Prisoner of Azkaban,* 1999; *Harry Potter and the Goblet of Fire,* 2000; *Harry Potter and the Order of the Phoenix,* 2003; *Harry Potter and the Half-Blood Prince,* 2005; and *Harry Potter and the Deathly Hallows,* 2007.

Stroud, Jonathan. *The Amulet of Samarkand.* Hyperion, 2003. Ages 11–18. The first in the Bartimaeus trilogy, which includes *The Golem's Eye,* 2004; and *Ptolemy's Gate,* 2006.

Thompson, Kate. *The New Policeman.* Greenwillow, 2007. Ages 12–16.

Tolkien, J. R. R. *The Hobbit.* Houghton, 1937. Ages 12–18.

Turner, Megan Whalen. *The King of Attolia.* Greenwillow, 2006. Ages 11–18. Sequel to *The Queen of Attolia,* 2005.

Yolen, Jane. *Sword of the Rightful King: A Novel of King Arthur.* Harcourt, 2003. Ages 11–15.

Science Fiction and Science Fantasy

Adlington, L. J. *Cherry Heaven.* HarperCollins, 2008. Ages 13–18.

———. *The Diary of Pelly D.* Greenwillow, 2005. Ages 12–18.

Anderson, M. T. *Feed.* Candlewick, 2002. Ages 12–18.

Atwater-Rhodes, Amelia. *Hawksong.* Delacorte, 2003. Ages 12–16.

Bell, Hilari. *A Matter of Profit.* HarperCollins, 2001. Ages 11–16.

Bertagna, Julie. *Exodus.* Walker, 2008. Ages 12–16.

Cart, Michael, editor. *Tomorrowland: Ten Stories about the Future.* Scholastic, 1999. (COL) Ages 11–18.

Clements, Andrew. *Things Not Seen.* Philomel, 2002. Ages 10–14.

DuPrau, Jeanne. *The City of Ember.* Random, 2003. Ages 10–14. Sequel is *The People of Sparks,* 2004.

Farmer, Nancy. *The House of the Scorpion.* Simon & Schuster, 2002. Ages 12–18.

Haddix, Margaret Peterson. *Double Identity.* Simon & Schuster, 2005. Ages 10–14.

———. *Turnabout.* Simon & Schuster, 2000. Ages 9–13.

Hautman, Pete. *Godless.* Simon & Schuster, 2004. Ages 12–18.

———. *Rash.* Simon & Schuster, 2006. Ages 12–18.

Hughes, Ted. *The Iron Giant: A Story in Five Nights.* Knopf, 1999/1968. Ages 9–12.

Kostick, Conor. *Epic.* Viking, 2007. Ages 13–16.

L'Engle, Madeleine. *A Wrinkle in Time.* Farrar, 1962. Ages 11–15.

Lowry, Lois. *Gathering Blue.* Houghton, 2000. Ages 10–15.

———. *The Giver.* Houghton, 1993. Ages 11–15.

———. *Messenger.* Houghton, 2004. Ages 11–15.

Reeve, Philip. *Larklight: A Rousing Tale of Dauntless Pluck in the Farthest Reaches of Space.* Bloomsbury, 2006. Ages 10–15. Humorous.

———. *Mortal Engines.* HarperCollins, 2003. Ages 12–18. The first of the Hungry Cities Chronicles.

Strahan, Jonathan. *The Starry Rift: Tales of New Tomorrows.* Viking, 2008. (COL) Ages 13–18.

Waugh, Sylvia. *Earthborn.* Delacorte, 2002. Ages 9–13.

———. *Space Race.* Delacorte, 2000. Ages 9–12.

★ Related Films, Videos, and DVDs

Borrowers. (1998). Author: Mary Norton (1953). 86 minutes.

Charlotte's Web. (2006). Author: E. B. White (1952). 113 minutes.

The Chronicles of Narnia: The Lion, the Witch and the Wardrobe. (2005). Author: C. S. Lewis (1955). 140 minutes.

The Chronicles of Narnia: Prince Caspian. (2008). Author: C. S. Lewis (1962). 150 minutes.

City of Ember. (2008). Author: Jeanne DuPrau (2003). 95 minutes.

Coraline. (2009). Author: Neil Gaiman (2002). 100 minutes.

Ella Enchanted. (2004). Author: Gail Carson Levine (1997). 96 minutes.

Eragon. (2006). Author: Christopher Paolini (2003). 120 minutes.

Escape to Witch Mountain. (1995). Author: Alexander Key (1968). 97 minutes.

The Golden Compass. (2007). Author: Philip Pullman (1996). 113 minutes.

Harry Potter and the Sorcerer's Stone. (2001). Author: J. K. Rowling (1998). 152 minutes. Five others in the series also available.

The Hobbit. (1991). Author: J. R. R. Tolkien (1938). 76 minutes.

Inkheart. (2008). Author: Cornelia Funke (2003). 106 minutes.

The Iron Giant. (1999). Author: Ted Hughes. (1999/ 1968). 86 minutes.

Redwall: Friends or Foes? (1999). Author: Brian Jacques (1987). 90 minutes.

The Seeker: The Dark Is Rising. (2007). Author: Susan Cooper (1973). 99 minutes.

Shrek. (2001). Author: William Steig (1990). 90 minutes. Also *Shrek 2* (2004) and *Shrek the Third* (2007).

Thief Lord. (2006). Author: Cornelia Funke (2002). 98 minutes.

Tuck Everlasting. (2002). Author: Natalie Babbitt (1975). 88 minutes.

The Water Horse. (2007). Author: Dick King-Smith. (1998). 112 minutes.

A Wrinkle in Time. (2003). Author: Madeleine L'Engle (1962). 128 minutes.

Sources for Films, Videos, and DVDs

The Video Source Book. Syosset, NY: National Video Clearinghouse, 1979–. Published by Gale Research, Detroit, MI.

An annual reference work that lists media and provides sources for purchase and rental.

Websites of large video distributors:
www.libraryvideo.com
www.knowledgeunlimited.com
http://teacher.scholastic.com/products/westonwoods

PEARSON myeducationkit™ Now go to Chapter 7 in the MyEducationKit (www.myeducationkit .com) for your book, where you can:

- Complete Assignments and Activities that can enrich and extend your knowledge of chapter content.

- Expand your knowledge with content-specific Web Links.

- Learn how authors and illustrators apply their craft by reading the written interviews in the Conversations section for the chapter.

- Review the chapter content by going to the Study Plan, taking a chapter quiz, and receiving feedback on your answers.

- Access the Children's Literature Database for your own exploration.

chapter EIGHT

Realistic Fiction

Listening to Grownups Quarreling,

standing in the hall against the
wall with my little brother, blown
like leaves against the wall by their
voices, my head like a pingpong ball
between the paddles of their anger:
I knew what it meant
to tremble like a leaf.

Cold with their wrath, I heard
the claws of the rain
pounce. Floods
poured through the city,
skies clapped over me,
and I was shaken, shaken
like a mouse
between their jaws.

—Ruth Whitman

Children's lives are sometimes sad and harsh. Realistic stories openly address these situations as well as the happy and humorous situations of life. Children of all ages appreciate stories about people who seem like themselves or who are involved in familiar activities. These realistic fiction stories have appealed to children for many years and continue to do so today.

Definition and Description

Realistic fiction refers to stories that could indeed happen to people and animals; that is, it is within the realm of possibility that such events could occur or could have occurred. The protagonists of these stories are fictitious characters created by the author, but their actions and reactions are quite like those of real people or real animals. Sometimes, events in these stories are exaggerated or outlandish—hardly probable but definitely possible. These stories, too, fit under the definition of realistic fiction.

Realism in literature is a complex, multifaceted concept. Marshall (1988) considers various components of realism in literature, including factual, situational, emotional, and social. *Factual*

PEARSON
myeducationkit™

Go to Activity 1 in the Assignments and Activities section of Chapter 8 in MyEducationKit; complete the activity on looking in a mirror through realistic fiction.

realism is provided by the description of actual people, places, and events in a book. When this occurs, the facts need to be recorded accurately. For example, usually in historical fiction and occasionally in realistic fiction, the names and locations of actual places are included in the story, with accurate and complete descriptions. *Situational realism* is provided by a situation that is not only possible but also quite likely, often in an identifiable location with characters of an identifiable age and social class, making the whole treatment believable. Family stories are often examples of stories built on situational realism. *Emotional realism* is provided by the appearance of believable feelings and relationships among characters. Rite-of-passage or growing-up stories often employ emotional realism. *Social realism* is provided by an honest portrayal of society and its conditions of the moment. In almost all good realistic stories, several of these components of realism occur, with varying degrees of emphasis.

Contemporary realism is a term used to describe stories that take place in the present time and portray attitudes and mores of the present culture. Unlike realistic books of several decades ago that depicted only happy families and were never controversial, today's contemporary realism often focuses on current societal issues, such as alcoholism, racism, poverty, and homelessness. Contemporary books still tell of the happy, funny times in children's lives, but they also include the harsh, unpleasant times that are, sadly, a part of many children's lives.

Authors of contemporary realistic fiction set their stories in the present or recent past. But, in time, features of these stories such as dialogue and allusions to popular culture, customs, and dress become dated and the stories are therefore no longer contemporary, though they may still be realistic. Older stories that obviously no longer describe today's world, though they may have once been contemporary realistic fiction, are now simply realistic fiction. Older realistic fiction stories that are considered modern classics are included in this chapter.

Excellent Realistic Fiction to READ ALOUD

Birdsall, Jeanne. *The Penderwicks on Gardam Street.* Ages 9–12.
Cummings, Priscilla. *Red Kayak.* Ages 11–15.
Ellis, Sarah. *The Several Lives of Orphan Jack.* Illustrated by Bruno St-Aubin. Ages 7–11.
FitzGerald, Dawn. *Soccer Chick Rules.* Ages 10–14.
Harper, Charise M. *Just Grace Walks the Dog.* Ages 7–9.
Hautman, Pete, and Mary Logue. *Snatched.* Ages 11–15.
Horvath, Polly. *The Pepins and Their Problems.* Ages 8–12.
Lord, Cynthia. *Rules.* Ages 9–13.
Lowry, Lois. *Gooney Bird and the Room Mother.* Ages 7–9.
McCaughrean, Geraldine. *Smile!* Illustrated by Ian McCaughrean. Ages 10–14.
Nuzum, K. A. *The Leanin' Dog.* Ages 9–12.
Pennypacker, Sara. *Clementine's Letter.* Illustrated by Marla Frazee. Ages 7–10.
Resau, Laura. *Red Glass.* Ages 11–15.
Ritter, John H. *The Boy Who Saved Baseball.* Ages 10–13.
Schusterman, Neal. *Antsy Does Time.* Ages 11–15.
Smith, Hope Anita. *Keeping the Night Watch.* Illustrated by E. B. Lewis. Ages 11–15.
Tarshis, Lauren. *Emma-Jean Lazarus Fell out of a Tree.* Ages 10–14.

Evaluation and Selection of Realistic Fiction

The criteria for evaluating realistic fiction are the same as those for any work of fiction. Well-developed characters who manifest change as a result of significant life events, a well-structured plot with sufficient conflict and suspense to hold the reader's interest, a time and place suitable to the storyline, and a worthy theme are basic literary elements expected of any work of fiction, including works of realistic fiction.

- Even stories that portray adverse and discouraging social situations should permit some cause for optimism. Children need to trust that problems can be overcome or ameliorated and that the world can be a good place in which to live.
- Themes in realistic stories often convey moral values, such as the rewards of kindness and generosity to others. However, these moral values must not be the main reason for the story. At times, adults write books for children with the sole intent of teaching or preaching, and the story itself is nothing more than a thin disguise for a heavy-handed moral lesson. The moral must not overwhelm the story but may be its logical outcome.
- A novel of realistic fiction must be believable, and the events must be possible, even though all aspects may not be probable. Sometimes, an author goes closer to the edge of the believable range to produce a more exciting, suspense-filled story.
- Controversy involving children's books often centers on topics that are found in realistic fiction novels, such as premarital sex, pregnancy, homosexuality, and the use of profanity. Many of these controversial books fall within the types of realism labeled "Moral Choices"

and "Romance and Sexuality" in the recommended reading list at the end of this chapter. Chapter 12 provides a full discussion of issues surrounding censorship and selection.

■ An aspect of writing style that students greatly appreciate is humor. Although humor may be found in stories of any genre, it is more often found in realistic fiction. Humorous stories feature characters caught up in silly situations or involved in funny escapades. *Voss* by David Ives and *The Schwa Was Here* by Neal Schusterman are good examples of humorous stories.

Selection of realistic fiction for classroom and library collections and for read-alouds should be balanced among the different types of realistic stories. A steady diet of humorous read-alouds does not offer the richness of experience to children that they deserve, nor does it provide for the varied reading interests of a group of children. The Edgar Allan Poe Award for Juvenile Mystery Novels can be helpful to you in selecting good mysteries. This award was established in 1961 by the Mystery Writers of America and is awarded annually in order to honor U.S. authors of mysteries for children. The list of winners is included in Appendix A. Intermediate-grade children report on reading interest surveys that realistic fiction is their favorite genre. Of course, some children may prefer other categories, but realistic fiction does hold high appeal for many children at all grade levels.

Historical Overview of Realistic Fiction

The earliest realistic stories were didactic ones that were intended to teach morality and manners to young readers. The characters of the children's stories of the 1700s were usually wooden, lifeless boys and girls whose lives were spent in good works; however, in England during this period, two significant events affecting the future of children's literature occurred. *Robinson Crusoe* by Daniel Defoe, an exciting survival story, was published in 1719 for adults but became a popular book among children. Then in 1744, John Newbery began to publish, expressly for a child audience, books of realistic fiction intended to entertain as well as to educate. These two events laid the groundwork for establishing children's literature as a separate branch of literature. The accompanying Milestones feature highlights the development of realistic fiction.

The first type of realistic fiction for children that avoided the heavy didactic persuasion was the adventure story. Imitators of *Robinson Crusoe* were many, including the very popular *Swiss Family Robinson* by Johann Wyss of Switzerland in 1812. Later adventure stories of renown from England were *Treasure Island* (1883) and *Kidnapped* (1886) by Robert Louis Stevenson; and from the United States, *The Adventures of Tom Sawyer* (1876) and *The Adventures of Huckleberry Finn* (1884) by Mark Twain (pseudonym of Samuel Clemens).

Realistic family stories also came on the scene during the 1800s with *Little Women* (1868) by Louisa May Alcott. The family story remained a favorite in the twentieth century, with early memorable books such as the series *Anne of Green Gables* (1908) by Canadian Lucy Maud Montgomery and *The Secret Garden* (1911) by Frances Hodgson Burnett. Since Anne of *Anne of Green Gables* and Mary of *The Secret Garden* were orphans, the books by Burnett and Montgomery can be considered precursors of adjustment stories that addressed the special needs of children with problems. Stories of happy and often large families continued to thrive and peaked in the 1940s

MILESTONES *in the Development of Realistic Fiction*

Date	Event	Significance
1719	*Robinson Crusoe* by Daniel Defoe (England)	Early survival/adventure on a desert island; many imitators
1812	*Swiss Family Robinson* by Johann Wyss (Switzerland)	Most successful imitation of *Robinson Crusoe*
1868	*Little Women* by Louisa May Alcott (United States)	An early family story of great popularity
1876	*The Adventures of Tom Sawyer* by Mark Twain (United States)	Classic adventure story set along the Mississippi
1877	*Black Beauty* by Anna Sewell (England)	Early horse story deploring inhumane treatment of animals
1880	*Heidi* by Johanna Spyri (Switzerland)	An early international story popular in the United States
1883	*Treasure Island* by Robert Louis Stevenson (England)	Classic adventure story with pirates
1908	*Anne of Green Gables* by Lucy Maud Montgomery (Canada)	Early family story about an orphan and her new family
1911	*The Secret Garden* by Frances Hodgson Burnett (United States)	A classic sentimental novel of two children adjusting to life
1938	*The Yearling* by Marjorie Kinnan Rawlings (United States)	Classic animal story and coming-of-age story
1964	*Harriet the Spy* by Louise Fitzhugh (United States)	The beginning of the new realism movement
1970	*Are You There, God? It's Me, Margaret* by Judy Blume (United States)	Early book with frank treatment of sex
2000	*Monster* by Walter Dean Myers (United States)	First winner of the Michael L. Printz Award for Excellence in Literature for Young Adults

and 1950s in family story series about the Moffat family by Eleanor Estes and about the Melendy family by Elizabeth Enright. These *happy family* stories seem almost lighthearted compared with much of today's contemporary realism for children.

Children from other lands is another theme that can be found in many realistic stories for children. *Hans Brinker, or The Silver Skates* (1865) by Mary Mapes Dodge and *Heidi* (1880) by Johanna Spyri of Switzerland are set in Holland and Switzerland, respectively, and were two of the earliest *other lands* books.

Realistic animal stories for children began to appear in the latter half of the nineteenth century. *Black Beauty* (1877) by Anna Sewell was a plea for humane treatment of animals, and although quite sentimental in places and completely personified (i.e., the animal is given human qualities), it is still appreciated by some readers. Animal stories showing the maturing of the young human protagonist who assists the animal in the story remain popular today.

Regional stories and stories about children of minority groups began to appear with more frequency in the 1940s. *Strawberry Girl* (1945) by Lois Lenski featured rural Florida and was one of the first regional stories. It was only in the 1960s and 1970s that books written by minorities began to achieve national recognition. *Zeely* (1967) by Virginia Hamilton and *Stevie* (1969) by John Steptoe portray African-American childhood experiences and are two of the earliest and most noteworthy books representing this trend toward increased minority authorship—a trend that continues today. For example, Walter Dean Myers has been recognized for his award-winning novel, *Monster* (1999), narrated in the form of a film script by protagonist Steve as he records his experiences in prison and in the courtroom.

A new era in realistic fiction for children was ushered in with the publication of *Harriet the Spy* by Louise Fitzhugh in 1964. This story of an unhappy and, at times, unpleasant girl depicted Harriet, her parents, and her classmates as anything but ideal or sympathetic human beings. This trend toward a more graphic and explicitly truthful portrayal of life and the inclusion of many topics that were previously considered taboo continued in children's books in the 1970s and 1980s and still prevails today. Controversial topics such as death, divorce, drugs, alcoholism, and disabilities, which have always been a part of childhood, became permissible topics in children's books. Parents and other adults began to be portrayed as they truly are, not as one might believe they should be. This newer, franker brand of realism, sometimes referred to as the **new realism,** changed the world of children's books. The new realism books may be less lighthearted than their predecessors, but they are also more truthful and more real. At the present time, censorship of materials for children, including children's trade books, is rampant, in part, because of this trend toward more graphic and explicit writing in children's books.

Types of Realistic Fiction

The subject matter of realistic fiction includes the child's whole world of relationships with self and others: the joys, sorrows, challenges, adjustments, anxieties, and satisfactions of human life. Realistic books will often treat more than one aspect of human life; thus, some realistic fiction books can be categorized by more than one of the following topics.

Families

Stories about the *nuclear family*—children and their relationships with parents and siblings—are a natural subject of books for children. Childhood for most children is spent in close contact with family members. Family stories for younger children often portray a happy child with loving parents. In these stories, everyday activities from brushing teeth to cooking dinner are shown. Easy chapter books appealing to newly independent readers can be found within this type. These stories often show the child at play and sometimes explore sibling relationships as well. *The Quigleys in a Spin* by Simon Mason and *The Pepins and Their Problems* by Polly Horvath are good examples of this type of book.

Extended families can also be found in children's books. Aunts, uncles, grandparents, and cousins are important in the real lives of many children and may also be enjoyed in stories written for children. See *The Same Stuff as Stars* by Katherine Paterson and *The Hello, Goodbye Window* by Norton Juster.

The *alternative family* of today's world is also depicted in family stories. Not all family stories present traditional, intact families. Separation, divorce, single-parent families, adoptive families, foster families, and reconstructed families of stepparents and stepchildren are often the backdrop of stories today. For example, see *Being Bee* by Catherine Bateson and *The Penderwicks on Gardam Street* by Jeanne Birdsall. The difficulty children and adults encounter in adjusting to these new family situations becomes the primary conflict in some stories. It is important for children to see families other than the typical mother, father, and two children portrayed positively in books.

Peers

In addition to adapting to one's family situation, children must also learn to cope with their peers. Many realistic stories show children struggling for *acceptance by peers* in a group situation. School settings are common in these stories. Examples include *Just Grace* by Charise M. Harper and *Fame and Glory in Freedom, Georgia* by Barbara O'Connor.

Bullying by peers can be damaging to the self-esteem of those targeted. Angry outbursts by those being humiliated is not infrequent and, at times, can be frightening. Literature can provide an opportunity to address these issues by developing an awareness and understanding of the harm caused and by encouraging more compassion toward those who are targeted for some real or perceived difference. In Wendelin Van Draanen's *Secret Identity,* Nolan, a fifth-grade outsider, becomes fed up with the school bully and finds an ingenious way to expose the bully's misdeeds. Although the treatment is humorous and lighthearted, the problem can be raised in discussion of the book.

Developing *close friendships* is another focus of stories about peer relationships. Friends may be of the same sex or the opposite sex, of the same age or a very different age, or of the same culture or a different culture. A concern for friendship and how to be a good friend are shared traits of these stories. *Bird Lake Moon* by Kevin Henkes, *Antsy Does Time* by Neal Schusterman, and *Emma-Jean Lazarus Fell out of a Tree* by Lauren Tarshis are good examples of this type of book.

Physical, Emotional, Mental, and Behavioral Challenges

Many children must deal with difficult challenges in their lives. Some children have disabilities; others have a family member or a friend with a disability. These disabilities may be physical, such as scoliosis; emotional, such as bipolar disorder; mental, such as mental retardation or learning disabilities; behavioral, such as hyperactivity; or a combination of these. Yet children do not like to appear different or strange to others. Authors of children's books are becoming increasingly sensitive to the need for positive portrayals of individuals with special challenges. Well-written, honest stories of such individuals in children's books can help other children gain an understanding of disabilities and empathize with people who have disabilities. As inclusion of special education students into regular classrooms becomes a more common practice, this trend in children's literature can be an important educational resource. As examples, Cynthia Lord's *Rules* includes as minor characters an autistic brother and a paraplegic friend of the protagonist, Catherine; and in Sarah Weeks's *So B. It,* the protagonist Heidi lives with her developmentally disabled mother and is cared for by her neighbor, who is agoraphobic.

Communities

Part of growing up involves the discovery of one's membership in a *community,* a group extending beyond the family. In some children's books we find school settings in which students, teachers, administrators, and, at times, parents comprise the community. Helen Frost's novel told through 22 poetic forms, *Spinning through the Universe: A Novel in Poems from Room 214,* shows students, the teacher, and the custodian writing their thoughts about the school and other topics.

In other books the community setting is the neighborhood. Examples are Janet McDonald's novels, *Chill Wind, Twists and Turns,* and *Spellbound,* about a community of teens living in urban housing projects, a community not often featured in juvenile novels.

Community extends beyond country to communities around the world. With increasing interdependence among countries, young people will likely be more connected to an international community than ever before. Books set in foreign countries about life in another culture can help children and adolescents develop an awareness of and kinship toward people from other countries and an appreciation for people whose lives differ from their own. Examples include *Colibrí* by Ann Cameron, *Shabanu: Daughter of the Wind* by Suzanne Fisher Staples, and *Afrika* by Colleen Craig.

Animals

Animal stories remain an ever-popular genre with children, dog and horse stories being the most popular. In realistic animal stories the animal protagonist behaves like an animal and is not personified. Usually, a child is also a protagonist in these stories. Examples are *Because of Winn-Dixie* by Kate DiCamillo and *Diamond Willow* by Helen Frost.

Sports

Sports stories often present a story in which a child protagonist struggles to become accepted as a member of a team and does eventually succeed through determination and hard work. *The Boy Who Saved Baseball* by John H. Ritter is a good example of a sports story. Although traditionally written with boys as the main characters, some sports stories are now available that feature girls as protagonists, such as Dawn FitzGerald's *Soccer Chick Rules.*

Mysteries

Mysteries, popular with boys and girls, range from simple "whodunits" to complex character stories. The element of suspense is a strong part of the appeal of these stories. Mysteries have won more state children's choice awards than any other type of story, a fact that suggests that mysteries are truly favorites of many children. See *Chasing Vermeer* by Blue Balliett and *Evil Genius* by Catherine Jinks.

Three recent series of interest to mystery readers are the Bloodwater Mysteries (beginning with *Snatched*) by Pete Hautman and Mary Logue, the 39 Clues (beginning with *The Maze of Bones*) by Rick Riordan, and the Boy Sherlock Holmes series (beginning with *Eye of the Crow*) by Shane Peacock. An established series with a female protagonist, the Sammy Keyes series (beginning with *Sammy Keyes and the Hotel Thief*) by Wendelin Van Draanen, remains popular, with new mysteries published annually.

Notable Authors
of Realistic Fiction

Sharon Creech, author of novels about girls seeking their families to find themselves. *Walk Two Moons; Ruby Holler; The Wanderer.* www.sharoncreech.com

Helen Frost, author of verse novels and two-time winner of the Lee Bennett Hopkins Award for Poetry. She has also written many information books for children. *Keesha's House; The Braid; Diamond Willow.* www.helenfrost.net

Jack Gantos, author of Joey Pigza novels about a boy with attention deficit disorder, as well as autobiographical books. *Heads or Tails: Stories from the Sixth Grade; Joey Pigza Swallowed the Key.* www.jackgantos.com

Jean Craighead George, author of ecological fiction and survival in nature stories. *Julie of the Wolves; My Side of the Mountain.* www.jeancraigheadgeorge.com

Will Hobbs, author of wilderness-based adventure novels, many set in the Southwest and Mexico, Alaska, and western United States. *Crossing the Wire; The Maze; Jackie's Wild Seattle.* www.willhobbsauthor.com

Polly Horvath, author of realistic and often humorous family stories. *The Trolls* (winner of the Boston Globe/Horn Book Award); *Everything on a Waffle; The Canning Season* (winner of the National Book Award); *My One Hundred Adventures.* www.pollyhorvath.com

Walter Dean Myers, author of novels about African-American adolescents in city settings. *Scorpions; Monster; Slam!* www.walterdeanmyers.net

Katherine Paterson, author of stories featuring relationships with peers and family. *The Great Gilly Hopkins; Bridge to Terabithia.* www.terabithia.com

Gary Paulsen, author of nature survival adventures often set in northern United States or Canada. *Hatchet; The River.* www.garypaulsen.com

Jerry Spinelli, author of realistic novels of peers and their escapades, including Newbery Medal winner *Maniac Magee* and Newbery Honor book *Wringer.* www.jerryspinelli.com

Suzanne Fisher Staples, author of stories that present conflicts within and between diverse cultures. Newbery Honor books *Shabanu* and its sequel *Haveli; Under the Persimmon Tree.* www.suzannefisherstaples.com

Wendelin Van Draanen, author of the popular Sammy Keyes mystery series featuring a funny and clever heroine who has to extricate herself from difficult situations. *Sammy Keyes and the Dead Giveaway; Flipped.* www.randomhouse.com/kids/vandraanen

Nancy Werlin, author of suspenseful mysteries that address difficult situations with sensitivity. *Black Mirror; The Rules of Survival.* www.nancywerlin.com

Jacqueline Woodson, African-American author whose novels often treat sensitive issues of sexuality, abuse, and race. *Locomotion; Hush.* www.jacquelinewoodson.com

---

PEARSON
myeducationkit

Go to the Conversations section of Chapter 8 in MyEducationKit to read the interview with Jerry Spinelli.

Moral Choices

Characters in many realistic fiction novels face moments of crisis, situations of great difficulty, or events in which a decision may change someone's life. These situations are often similar to those that children will face in their lives. Through these stories children can understand the difficult decisions the character is faced with and can discuss the consequences that may result from the choice made. Teachers often select these books for class study with intermediate- and middle-grade students. Using a book in which a character is faced with a difficult moral choice can stimulate lively discussions. An example is Priscilla Cummings's *Red Kayak,* in which a 13-year-old boy faces a conflict between doing the right thing or remaining loyal to his friends.

Realistic stories, both historical and contemporary, in which characters are faced with difficult moral choices, can provide the foundation for programs of *character education,* a process intended to establish important core values in young people and to build awareness of these values among teachers and parents in order to encourage children to adopt them. The Josephson Institute of Ethics, in conjunction with a nonsectarian coalition of legislators, corporate officers, and others, has promoted a framework, *Character Counts,* in which six values with related traits are espoused. Although this program is promoted in schools with accompanying materials available for purchase, these values are often expressed in good literature, which can be the basis for understanding and developing moral reasoning. Stories such as the ones listed below for each of the six values promulgated by *Character Counts* can help children formulate their own concepts of right and wrong.

Trustworthiness
- Bredsdorff, Bodil. *The Crow-Girl: The Children of Crow Cove.* Ages 9–12.
- Park, Linda Sue. *The Firekeeper's Son.* Illustrated by Julie Downing. Ages 8–12.
- D'Amico, Carmela and Steven. *Ella Takes the Cake.* Ages 5–9.

Respect
- DeFelice, Cynthia. *Under the Same Sky.* Ages 12–15.
- Lowry, Lois. *The Silent Boy.* Ages 9–12.
- Lorbiecki, Marybeth. *Jackie's Bat.* Illustrated by Brian Pinkney. Ages 6–9.

Responsibility
- Haas, Jessie. *Jigsaw Pony.* Ages 7–10.
- Johnson, Angela. *The First Part Last.* Ages 12–18.
- Cummings, Priscilla. *Red Kayak.* Ages 11–15.

Fairness
- Fuqua, Jonathan Scott. *Darby.* Ages 9–12.
- Spinelli, Eileen. *Three Pebbles and a Song.* Illustrated by S. D. Schindler. Ages 5–8.

Caring
- Polacco, Patricia. *Mr. Lincoln's Way.* Ages 5–9.
- Paterson, Katherine. *The Same Stuff as Stars.* Ages 10–14.

Citizenship
- Battle-Lavert, Gwendolyn. *Papa's Mark.* Illustrated by Colin Bootman. Ages 6–9.
- Leavitt, Martine. *Tom Finder.* Ages 12–18.

Moralizing and preaching are seldom appreciated by children; literary works for the purpose of character education should meet the same standards for good literature as all other selections. If the moral or lesson overpowers the story, many children will resist the obvious preaching and balk at reading such stories. Children want to read powerful stories that excite them, amuse them, and inspire them.

Romance and Sexuality

Romance stories are popular with preteens and teens, especially girls. Some stories depict boy–girl friendships, as in *Flipped* by Wendelin Van Draanen, *The Possibilities of Sainthood* by Donna Freitas, *Undercover* by Beth Kephart, *Runaround* by Helen Hemphill, and *Deep Down Popular* by Phoebe Stone. Since the 1990s, more stories of characters dealing with pregnancy and teenage parenting have appeared; some realistic examples are Virginia Euwer Wolff's *Make Lemonade,* Sylvia Olsen's *The Girl with a Baby,* and Angela Johnson's *The First Part Last.*

Children become aware of their growing sexuality during preteen and teen years as they begin to mature. Some stories for older teens show attraction between members of the opposite sex as well as members of the same sex, with the beginning of sexual activity sometimes depicted in relationships. Stories that portray the struggle of young people coming to terms with a homosexual or lesbian sexual orientation are seen more frequently than they were in the past; other stories show the cruelty of society toward young homosexuals or lesbians. See *Split Screen* by Brent Hartinger and *So Hard to Say* by Alex Sanchez.

PEARSON myeducationkit™

Go to Activity 2 in the Assignments and Activities section of Chapter 8 in MyEducationKit; view the video on using realistic fiction in a thematic study of discrimination and respond to the questions.

Coming of Age

From birth to age 10, most children's lives revolve around family, friends, and classmates, but during the preteen and teen years a shift toward self-discovery and independence occurs. Rapid growth and change are seen in the physical, emotional, moral, and intellectual domains of life. These changes are reflected in books for adolescents and are referred to as *coming-of-age stories.* Sometimes books that deal with the trials and tribulations encountered during growth from childhood to adulthood are called *rite-of-passage* books. A rite of passage refers to an event in one's life that signals a change from child to adult. Examples of rite-of-passage books are *Olive's Ocean* by Kevin Henkes and *Shift* by Jennifer Bradbury.

Adventure and Survival

Facing physical danger, an external force, also contributes to the maturing process. Stories of *survival and adventure* are ones in which the young protagonist must rely on will and ingenuity to survive a life-threatening situation. Although most survival stories are set in isolated places, a growing number are being set in cities where gangs, drug wars, and abandonment are life threatening. Adventure stories may be set in any environment where the protagonist has freedom of action. *Wilderness* by Roddy Doyle and *The Maze* by Will Hobbs are examples of this type of book.

Stories in the realistic fiction genre present familiar situations with which children can readily identify, often reflect contemporary life, and portray settings not so different from the homes, schools, towns, and cities known to today's children. The protagonists of these stories are frequently testing themselves as they grow toward adulthood; young readers can therefore empathize and gain insight into their own predicaments. Your challenge will be to stay abreast of good realistic stories in order to provide a wide range of books that will entertain, encourage, and inspire your students.

Issues & Topics for FURTHER INVESTIGATION

- Discuss whether teachers and librarians have a responsibility to teach moral values and to develop good character traits in their students. If you believe so, suggest how it should be done. If you do not think so, explain your position.

- Select and read three to five winners of the Edgar Allan Poe Award for Juvenile Mystery Novels. (See Appendix A for the list.) Compare and contrast these novels, considering the source and type of mystery, the devices used to cause suspense, and the elements of realism and fantasy in each story.

- Select fifteen realistic fiction novels suitable for a particular grade level in which you are participating. Booktalk and display these novels for a group of eight students, then ask them to complete an interest ballot on them. What did you discover about their reading preferences from this activity?

References

Marshall, M. R. (1988). *An introduction to the world of children's books* (2nd ed.). Brookfield, VT: Gower.

Whitman, R. (1968). Listening to grownups quarreling. In R. Whitman (Ed.), *The marriage wig and other stories*. Orlando, FL: Harcourt.

Recommended Realistic Fiction Books

Ages indicated refer to content appropriateness and conceptual and interest levels. Formats other than novels will be coded as follows:

(PI) Picture book
(COL) Short story collection
(GR) Graphic novel

Families

Acampora, Paul. *Defining Dulcie.* Dial, 2006. Ages 12–15.

Banks, Kate. *Dillon Dillon.* Farrar, 2002. Ages 10–13.

———. *Walk Softly, Rachel.* Farrar, 2003. Ages 12–15.

Baskin, Nora Raleigh. *What Every Girl (Except Me) Knows.* Little, Brown, 2001. Ages 10–13.

Bateson, Catherine. *Being Bee.* Holiday, 2007. Ages 8–12.

Birdsall, Jeanne. *The Penderwicks on Gardam Street.* Knopf, 2008. Ages 9–12.

———. *The Penderwicks: A Summer Tale of Four Sisters, Two Rabbits, and a Very Interesting Boy.* Knopf, 2005. Ages 9–12.

Bredsdorff, Bodil. *The Crow-Girl: The Children of Crow Cove.* Translated from the Danish by Faith Ingwersen. Farrar, 2004. Ages 9–12.

Budhos, Marina. *Ask Me No Questions.* Simon & Schuster, 2006. Ages 12–16.

Choldenko, Gennifer. *Notes from a Liar and Her Dog.* Putnam, 2001. Ages 10–13.

Cohn, Rachel. *The Steps.* Simon & Schuster, 2003. Ages 9–13.

Creech, Sharon. *Heartbeat.* HarperCollins, 2004. Ages 9–14. Free verse.

———. *Replay.* HarperCollins, 2005. Ages 9–13. Includes a short play featured in the story.

———. *Ruby Holler.* HarperCollins, 2002. Ages 8–11.

———. *Walk Two Moons.* HarperCollins, 1994. Ages 10–13.

Delacre, Lulu. *Salsa Stories.* Scholastic, 2000. (**COL**) Ages 11–14.

Fogelin, Adrian. *Anna Casey's Place in the World.* Peachtree, 2001. Ages 10–13.

———. *The Big Nothing.* Peachtree, 2004. Ages 11–14.

———. *Sister Spider Knows All.* Peachtree, 2003. Ages 11–14.

Fusco, Kimberly Newton. *Tending to Grace.* Knopf, 2004. Ages 12–15.

Gantos, Jack. *What Would Joey Do?* Farrar, 2002. Ages 9–12.

Giff, Patricia Reilly. *Pictures of Hollis Woods.* Wendy Lamb, 2002. Ages 10–12.

Gonzalez, Julie. *Wings.* Delacorte, 2005. Ages 12–16. Two parallel narrators.

Goscinny, René. *Nicholas Again.* Illustrated by Jean Jacques Sempé. Translated by Anthea Bell. Phaidon, 2006. Ages 9–12. Humorous.

Grimes, Nikki. *Dark Sons.* Hyperion, 2005. Ages 11–16.

Hannigan, Katherine. *Ida B: . . . and Her Plans to Maximize Fun, Avoid Disaster, and (Possibly) Save the World.* Greenwillow, 2004. Ages 9–12.

Hicks, Betty. *Out of Order.* Roaring Brook, 2005. Ages 9–12.

Horvath, Polly. *The Canning Season.* Farrar, 2003. Ages 12–16.

———. *Everything on a Waffle.* Farrar, 2001. Ages 9–12.

———. *The Pepins and Their Problems.* Farrar, 2004. Ages 8–12. Humorous.

———. *The Trolls.* Farrar, 1999. Ages 9–13. Humorous.

Jones, Kimberly K. *Sand Dollar Summer.* Simon & Schuster, 2006. Ages 10–14.

Juster, Norton. *The Hello, Goodbye Window.* Illustrated by Chris Raschka. Hyperion, 2005. (**PI**) Ages 4–7.

Koss, Amy Goldman. *The Ashwater Experiment.* Dial, 1999. Ages 9–13.

Leavitt, Martine. *Heck Superhero.* Front Street, 2004. Ages 12–15.

Mackler, Carolyn. *The Earth, My Butt and Other Big, Round Things.* Candlewick, 2003. Ages 12–16.

Mason, Simon. *The Quigleys in a Spin.* Illustrated by Helen Stephens. Random, 2006. Ages 8–11. Humorous.

McKay, Hilary. *Indigo's Star.* Simon & Schuster, 2004. Ages 11–14. Humorous.

———. *Saffy's Angel.* Simon & Schuster, 2002. Ages 9–12.

Naylor, Phyllis Reynolds. *Roxie and the Hooligans.* Atheneum, 2006. Ages 7–10. Humorous.

Nelson, Theresa. *Ruby Electric.* Simon & Schuster, 2003. Ages 10–13.

O'Connor, Barbara. *Moonpie and Ivy.* Farrar, 2001. Ages 10–13.

Paterson, Katherine. *The Great Gilly Hopkins.* Crowell, 1978. Ages 9–12.

———. *The Same Stuff as Stars.* Clarion, 2002. Ages 10–13.

Scieszka, Jon, editor. *Guys Write for Guys Read: Boys' Favorite Authors Write about Being Boys.* Viking, 2005. (**COL**) Ages 10–14.

Smith, Hope Anita. *Keeping the Night Watch.* Illustrated by E. B. Lewis. Holt, 2008. Ages 11–15. Novel in free verse and sonnets.

Spinelli, Jerry. *Smiles to Go.* Joanna Cotler, 2008. Ages 11–14.

Tolan, Stephanie S. *Surviving the Applewhites.* HarperCollins, 2002. Ages 10–14.

Twice Told: Original Stories Inspired by Original Artwork. Illustrated by Scott Hunt. Dutton, 2006. (**COL**) Ages 12–16. Pairs of popular, acclaimed authors respond to the same illustration.

Van Draanen, Wendelin. *Runaway.* Knopf, 2006. Ages 12–16.

Werlin, Nancy. *The Rules of Survival.* Dial, 2006. Ages 12–18.

Williams, Vera B. *Amber Was Brave, Essie Was Smart: The Story of Amber and Essie Told Here in Poems and Pictures.* Greenwillow, 2001. Ages 6–10.

Peers

Castellucci, Cecil. *The Plain Janes.* Illustrated by Jim Rugg. DC Comics, 2007. **(GR)** Ages 12–18.

Creech, Sharon. *Granny Torrelli Makes Soup.* Illustrated by Chris Raschka. HarperCollins, 2003. Ages 9–13. Free verse novel.

———. *Love That Dog.* HarperCollins, 2001. Ages 9–14. Free verse novel.

Dowell, Frances O'Roark. *Chicken Boy.* Atheneum, 2005. Ages 9–13.

Fine, Anne. *Up on Cloud Nine.* Delacorte, 2002. Ages 10–13.

Frost, Helen. *Keesha's House.* Farrar, 2003. Ages 12–16.

Gantos, Jack. *Heads or Tails: Stories from the Sixth Grade.* Farrar, 1994. **(COL)** Ages 10–14. Humorous.

Grindley, Sally. *Dear Max.* Illustrated by Tony Ross. Simon & Schuster, 2006. Ages 7–10.

Gutman, Dan. *The Homework Machine.* Simon & Schuster, 2006. Ages 9–12.

Harper, Charise M. *Just Grace.* Houghton, 2007. Ages 7–9.

———. *Just Grace Walks the Dog.* Houghton, 2008. Ages 7–9.

Henkes, Kevin. *Bird Lake Moon.* HarperCollins, 2008. Ages 9–12.

Howe, James. *The Misfits.* Simon & Schuster, 2001. Ages 10–13.

Lombard, Jenny. *Drita, My Homegirl.* Putnam, 2006. Ages 8–11.

Look, Lenore. *Ruby Lu, Empress of Everything.* Illustrated by Anne Wilsdorf. Simon & Schuster, 2006. Ages 7–9.

Lowry, Lois. *Gooney Bird Greene.* Houghton, 2002. Ages 7–9.

———. *Gooney Bird and the Room Mother.* Houghton, 2005. Ages 7–9.

———. *Gooney, the Fabulous.* Houghton, 2005. Ages 7–9.

Lubar, David. *Sleeping Freshmen Never Lie.* Dutton, 2005. Ages 12–15. Humorous.

O'Connor, Barbara. *Fame and Glory in Freedom, Georgia.* Farrar, 2003. Ages 11–14.

Paterson, Katherine. *Bridge to Terabithia.* Illustrated by Donna Diamond. Crowell, 1977. Ages 9–13.

Pennypacker, Sara. *Clementine.* Illustrated by Marla Frazee. Hyperion, 2006. Ages 7–10. Humorous.

———. *Clementine's Letter.* Illustrated by Marla Frazee. Hyperion, 2008. Ages 7–10. Humorous.

———. *The Talented Clementine.* Illustrated by Marla Frazee. Hyperion, 2008. Ages 7–10. Humorous.

Perkins, Lynne Rae. *All Alone in the Universe.* Greenwillow, 1999. Ages 10–14.

———. *Criss Cross.* Greenwillow, 2005. Ages 11–15.

Schusterman, Neal. *Antsy Does Time.* Dutton, 2008. Ages 11–15.

Spinelli, Jerry. *Wringer.* HarperCollins, 1997. Ages 9–12.

Stauffacher, Sue. *Donuthead.* Knopf, 2003. Ages 9–12.

Tarshis, Lauren. *Emma-Jean Lazarus Fell out of a Tree.* Dial, 2007. Ages 10–14.

Van Draanen, Wendelin. *Secret Identity.* Illustrated by Brian Biggs. Knopf, 2004. Ages 8–12.

Williams, Lori Aurelia. *When Kambia Elaine Flew in from Neptune.* Simon & Schuster, 2001. Ages 12–18.

Physical, Emotional, Mental, and Behavioral Challenges

Duncan, Lois, editor. *On the Edge: Stories at the Brink.* Simon & Schuster, 2000. **(COL)** Ages 12–18.

Gantos, Jack. *I Am Not Joey Pigza.* Farrar, 2007. Ages 10–13. Attention deficit/hyperactivity.

———. *Joey Pigza Loses Control.* Farrar, 2000. Ages 9–12.

———. *Joey Pigza Swallowed the Key.* Farrar, 1998. Ages 9–13.

———. *What Would Joey Do?* Farrar, 2002. Ages 10–12.

George, Madeleine. *Looks.* Viking, 2008. Ages 12–18. Eating disorders.

Hautman, Pete. *Invisible.* Simon & Schuster, 2005. Ages 12–16. Mental health.

Hobbs, Valerie. *Defiance.* Farrar, 2005. Ages 10–14.

Konigsburg, E. L. *Silent to the Bone.* Simon & Schuster, 2000. Ages 11–15. Mutism.

Lord, Cynthia. *Rules.* Scholastic, 2006. Ages 9–13. Autism, paraplegia.

Morgenroth, Kate. *Echo.* Simon & Schuster, 2006. Ages 13–18. Depression, mental health, trauma.

Schumacher, Julie. *Black Box.* Delacorte, 2008. Ages 12–18. Depression.

Schusterman, Neal. *The Schwa Was Here.* Dutton, 2004. Ages 12–15. Humorous.

Sones, Sonya. *Stop Pretending: What Happened When My Big Sister Went Crazy.* HarperCollins, 1999. Ages 12–16. Free verse.

Trueman, Terry. *Stuck in Neutral.* HarperCollins, 2000. Ages 11–16. Cerebral palsy.

Vaught, Susan R. *Big Fat Manifesto.* Bloomsbury, 2008. Ages 12–18. Body image.

Weeks, Sarah. *So B. It.* HarperCollins, 2004. Ages 10–14. Mental retardation, agoraphobia.

Wood, June Rae. *About Face.* Putnam, 1999. Ages 9–12. Birthmark.

Communities

Cameron, Ann. *Colibrí.* Farrar, 2003. Ages 10–16.

Canales, Viola. *The Tequila Worm.* Wendy Lamb, 2005. Ages 11–15.

Cofer, Judith Ortiz. *Call Me Maria.* Orchard, 2004. Ages 11–14.

Craig, Colleen. *Afrika.* Tundra, 2008. Ages 12–15.

Danticat, Edwidge. *Behind the Mountains.* Orchard, 2002. Ages 11–14.

Fogelin, Adrian. *Crossing Jordan.* Peachtree, 2000. Ages 11–14.

Frost, Helen. *Spinning through the Universe: A Novel in Poems from Room 214.* Farrar, 2004. Ages 11–14.

Grimes, Nikki. *Bronx Masquerade.* Dial, 2002. Ages 12–18.

Ives, David. *Voss.* Putnam, 2008. Ages 10–16. Humorous.

Johnston, Tony. *Any Small Goodness: A Novel of the Barrio.* Illustrated by Raúl Colón. Scholastic, 2001. Ages 9–12.

Mah, Adeline Yen. *Chinese Cinderella: The True Story of an Unwanted Daughter.* Delacorte, 1999. Ages 11–15.

Marsden, Carolyn. *Silk Umbrellas.* Candlewick, 2004. Ages 8–12.

McDonald, Janet. *Chill Wind.* Farrar, 2002. Ages 12–18.

———. *Spellbound.* Farrar, 2001. Ages 12–18. Humorous.

———. *Twists and Turns.* Farrar, 2003. Ages 12–18.

Myers, Walter Dean. *145th Street.* Delacorte, 2000. Ages 12–18. (**COL**).

Na, An. *A Step from Heaven.* Front Street, 2001. Ages 13–18.

Naidoo, Beverley. *The Other Side of Truth.* HarperCollins, 2001. Ages 11–14.

———. *Out of Bounds: Seven Stories of Conflict and Hope.* HarperCollins, 2003. Ages 10–14.

———. *Web of Lies.* HarperCollins, 2006. Ages 12–16.

Nye, Naomi Shihab. *Habibi.* Simon & Schuster, 1997. Ages 12–16.

Ochoa, Annette, Betsy Franco, and Tracy L. Gourdine, editors. *Night Is Gone, Day Is Still Coming: Stories and Poems by American Indian Teens and Young Adults.* Candlewick, 2003. (**COL**) Ages 12–18.

Polacco, Patricia. *Mr. Lincoln's Way.* Philomel, 2001. (**PI**) Ages 5–9.

Resau, Laura. *Red Glass.* Delacorte, 2007. Ages 11–15.

———. *What the Moon Saw.* Delacorte, 2006. Ages 10–15.

Saldaña, René, Jr. *The Jumping Tree: A Novel.* Delacorte, 2001. Ages 11–16.

Smith, Hope Anita. *The Way a Door Closes.* Illustrated by Shane W. Evans. Holt, 2003. Ages 10–13. Poetic verse.

Staples, Suzanne Fisher. *Haveli: A Young Woman's Courageous Struggle for Freedom in Present-Day Pakistan.* Knopf, 1993. Ages 12–16.

———. *Shabanu: Daughter of the Wind.* Knopf, 1989. Ages 12–16.

———. *Shiva's Fire.* Farrar, 2000. Ages 12–16.

———. *Under the Persimmon Tree.* Farrar, 2005. Ages 12–16.

Stratton, Allan. *Chanda's Secrets.* Annick, 2004. Ages 12–18.

Whelan, Gloria. *Homeless Bird.* HarperCollins, 2000. Ages 12–16.

Williams-Garcia, Rita. *No Laughter Here.* HarperCollins, 2004. Ages 10–14.

Woodson, Jacqueline. *Locomotion.* Putnam, 2003. Ages 9–12. Free verse.

Animals

Bauer, Marion Dane. *A Bear Named Trouble.* Clarion, 2005. Ages 8–11.

DiCamillo, Kate. *Because of Winn-Dixie.* Candlewick, 2000. Ages 8–11.

———. *The Tiger Rising.* Candlewick, 2001. Ages 8–11.

Frost, Helen. *Diamond Willow.* Farrar, 2008. Ages 11–15. Verse novel.

Haas, Jessie. *Jigsaw Pony.* Illustrated by Ying-Hwa Hu. Greenwillow, 2005. Ages 7–10.

Hearne, Betsy. *The Canine Collection: Stories about Dogs and People.* McElderry, 2003. (**COL**) Ages 10–14.

Hiaasen, Carl. *Hoot.* Knopf, 2003. Ages 10–14.

Nuzum, K. A. *The Leanin' Dog.* Joanna Cotler, 2008. Ages 9–12.

Staples, Suzanne Fisher. *The Green Dog: A Mostly True Story.* Farrar, 2003. Ages 9–12.

Sports

Coy, John. *Crackback.* Scholastic, 2005. Ages 12–18.

Deans, Sis. *Racing the Past.* Holt, 2001. Ages 10–13.

Deuker, Carl. *Gym Candy.* Houghton, 2007. Ages 13–18.

———. *Runner.* Houghton, 2005. Ages 12–18.

Eskilsen, Erik E. *Offsides.* Houghton, 2004. Ages 10–14.

Feinstein, John. *Vanishing Act.* Knopf, 2006. Ages 11–18.

FitzGerald, Dawn. *Soccer Chick Rules.* Roaring Brook, 2006. Ages 10–14.

Johnson, Scott. *Safe at Second.* Philomel, 1999. Ages 11–18.

Koertge, Ron. *Shakespeare Bats Cleanup.* Candlewick, 2003. Ages 11–14.

Lipsyte, Robert. *Yellow Flag.* HarperTeen, 2007. Ages 14–18.

Lupica, Mike. *Heat.* Philomel, 2006. Ages 11–15.

———. *Travel Team.* Philomel, 2004. Ages 10–13.

Myers, Walter Dean. *Slam!* Scholastic, 1996. Ages 12–18.

Powell, Randy. *Run If You Dare.* Farrar, 2001. Ages 12–16.

Ritter, John H. *The Boy Who Saved Baseball.* Philomel, 2003. Ages 10–13.

———. *Under the Baseball Moon.* Philomel, 2006. Ages 11–14.

Roberts, Kristi. *My Thirteenth Season.* Holt, 2005. Ages 10–14.

Mysteries

Abrahams, Peter. *Down the Rabbit Hole.* HarperCollins, 2005. Ages 11–15.

Allison, Jennifer. *Gilda Joyce: Psychic Investigator.* Dutton, 2005. Ages 10–14. Humorous.

Alphin, Elaine Marie. *The Perfect Shot.* Carolrhoda, 2005. Ages 12–18.

Balliett, Blue. *Chasing Vermeer.* Illustrated by Brett Helquist. Scholastic, 2004. Ages 9–14.

———. *The Wright 3.* Illustrated by Brett Helquist. Scholastic, 2006. Ages 9–14.

Broach, Elise. *Shakespeare's Secret.* Holt, 2005. Ages 11–15.

Coman, Carolyn. *The Big House.* Illustrated by Rob Shepperson. Front Street, 2004. Ages 8–12. Humorous.

Curtis, Christopher Paul. *Mr. Chickee's Funny Money.* Random, 2005. Ages 9–13. Humorous.

DeFelice, Cynthia. *Death at Devil's Track.* Farrar, 2000. Ages 10–13.

———. *The Missing Manatee.* Farrar, 2005. Ages 10–14.

Ehrenhaft, Daniel. *Drawing a Blank; or How I Tried to Solve a Mystery, End a Feud, and Land the Girl of My Dreams.* Illustrated by Trevor Ristow. HarperCollins, 2006. Ages 12–18. Alternating chapters of first-person narratives and superhero comic-strip episodes. Humorous.

Fleischman, Sid. *Bo & Mzzz Mad.* Greenwillow, 2001. Ages 10–13. Humorous.

Hautman, Pete, and Logue, Mary. *Doppelganger.* Putnam, 2008. Ages 11–15.

———. *Snatched.* Putnam, 2006. Ages 11–15. The first in the Bloodwater Mysteries series.

Hiaasen, Carl. *Flush.* Knopf, 2005. Ages 10–14.

Jennings, Richard W. *Mystery in Mt. Mole.* Houghton, 2003. Ages 9–12.

Jinks, Catherine. *Evil Genius.* Harcourt, 2007. Ages 12–15.

Peacock, Shane. *Eye of the Crow.* Tundra, 2007. Ages 11–16.

Plum-Ucci, Carol. *The Body of Christopher Creed.* Harcourt, 2000. Ages 13–18.

Riordan, Rick. *The Maze of Bones.* Scholastic, 2008. Ages 9–13. The first in the 39 Clues series.

Sachar, Louis. *Small Steps.* Delacorte, 2005. Ages 10–14. Sequel to *Holes.*

Sorrells, Walter. *Fake ID.* Dutton, 2005. Ages 12–16.

Springer, Nancy. *The Case of the Missing Marquess: An Enola Holmes Mystery.* Philomel, 2005. Ages 10–14.

Valentine, Jenny. *Me, the Missing, and the Dead.* HarperTeen, 2008. Ages 13–18. Humorous.

Van Draanen, Wendelin. *Sammy Keyes and the Cold Hard Cash.* Knopf, 2008. Ages 10–13.

———. *Sammy Keyes and the Hotel Thief.* Knopf, 1998. Sequels include *Sammy Keyes and the Search for Snake Eyes,* 2002; and *Sammy Keyes and the Dead Giveaway,* 2005.

Werlin, Nancy. *Black Mirror.* Dial, 2001. Ages 12–18.

———. *Double Helix.* Dial, 2004. Ages 12–18.

Moral Choices

Battle-Lavert, Gwendolyn. *Papa's Mark.* Illustrated by Colin Bootman. Holiday, 2003. Ages 6–9.

Bauer, Marion Dane. *The Double-Digit Club.* Holiday, 2004. Ages 9–12.

Bredsdorff, Bodil. *The Crow-Girl: The Children of Crow Cove.* Translated by Faith Ingwersen. Farrar, 2004. Ages 9–12.

Cummings, Priscilla. *Red Kayak.* Dutton, 2004. Ages 11–15.

Curtis, Christopher Paul. *Bucking the Sarge.* Random, 2004. Ages 11–16. Humorous.

D'Amico, Carmela, and Steven D'Amico. *Ella Takes the Cake.* Scholastic, 2005. Ages 5–9.

DeFelice, Cynthia. *Under the Same Sky.* Farrar, 2003. Ages 12–15.

Flake, Sharon G. *Money Hungry.* Hyperion, 2001. Ages 12–16.

Fuqua, Jonathan Scott. *Darby.* Candlewick, 2002. Ages 9–12.

Haas, Jessie. *Jigsaw Pony.* Illustrated by Y. Wu. HarperCollins, 2005. Ages 7–10.

Johnson, Angela. *The First Part Last.* Simon & Schuster, 2003. Ages 12–18.

Leavitt, Martine. *Tom Finder.* Red Deer, 2003. Ages 12–18.

Lorbiecki, Marybeth. *Jackie's Bat.* Illustrated by Brian Pinkney. Simon & Schuster, 2003. Ages 6–9.

Lowry, Lois. *The Silent Boy.* Houghton, 2003. Ages 9–12.

Myers, Walter Dean. *Monster.* HarperCollins, 1999. Ages 12–18.

O'Connor, Barbara. *Taking Care of Moses.* Farrar, 2004. Ages 9–12.

Park, Linda Sue. *The Firekeeper's Son.* Illustrated by Julie Downing. Clarion, 2003. Ages 8–12.

———. *Project Mulberry.* Clarion, 2005. Ages 10–13.

Paterson, Katherine. *The Same Stuff as Stars.* Clarion, 2002. Ages 10–14.

Polacco, Patricia. *Mr. Lincoln's Way.* Philomel, 2001. Ages 5–9.

Spinelli, Eileen. *Three Pebbles and a Song.* Illustrated by S. D. Schindler. Dial, 2003. Ages 5–8.

Spinelli, Jerry. *Maniac Magee.* HarperCollins, 1990. Ages 9–12.

Woodson, Jacqueline. *Hush.* Putnam, 2002. Ages 11–15.

Romance and Sexuality

Anderson, Laurie Halse. *Speak.* Farrar, 1999. Ages 12–18.

Deak, Erzsi, and Kristin Embry Litchman, editors. *Period Pieces.* HarperCollins, 2003. (COL) Ages 10–14.

Flake, Sharon G. *Who Am I without Him?* Hyperion, 2004. (COL) Ages 11–18.

Freitas, Donna. *The Possibilities of Sainthood.* Farrar, 2008. Ages 12–16.

Hartinger, Brent. *Geography Club.* HarperTempest, 2003. Ages 12–18.

———. *Split Screen.* HarperTempest, 2007. Ages 12–18.

Hemphill, Helen. *Runaround.* Front Street, 2007. Ages 10–14.

Howe, James. *Totally Joe.* Atheneum, 2005. Ages 10–14.

Johnson, Angela. *The First Part Last.* Simon & Schuster, 2003. Ages 12–18.

Kephart, Beth. *Undercover.* HarperCollins, 2007. Ages 12–16.

Larochelle, David. *Absolutely, Positively Not.* Scholastic, 2005. Ages 12–18. Humorous.

Lawrence, Iain. *Ghost Boy.* Delacorte, 2000. Ages 12–18.

Myers, Walter Dean. *Street Love.* HarperCollins, 2006. Ages 12–18. Verse novel.

———. *What They Found: Love on 145th Street.* Wendy Lamb, 2007. (COL) Ages 13–18.

Naylor, Phyllis Reynolds. *The Grooming of Alice.* Simon & Schuster, 2000. Ages 11–13.

Olsen, Sylvia. *The Girl with a Baby.* Sono Nis Press, 2003. Ages 11–15.

Peters, Julie Anne. *Luna.* Little, Brown, 2004. Ages 13–18.

Sanchez, Alex. *Getting It.* Simon & Schuster, 2006. Ages 13–18.

———. *So Hard to Say.* Simon & Schuster, 2004. Ages 11–15.

Sones, Sonya. *What My Mother Doesn't Know.* Simon & Schuster, 2001. Ages 12–16. Free verse.

Spinelli, Jerry. *Stargirl.* Knopf, 2000. Ages 11–15.

Stone, Phoebe. *Deep Down Popular.* Scholastic, 2008. Ages 10–14.

Van Draanen, Wendelin. *Flipped.* Knopf, 2001. Ages 10–14.

Wild, Margaret. *One Night.* Knopf, 2004. Ages 12–18. Free verse.

Wittlinger, Ellen. *Parrotfish.* Simon & Schuster, 2007. Ages 14–18.

Wolff, Virginia Euwer. *Make Lemonade.* Holt, 1993. Ages 12–18.

Young, Karen Romano. *The Beetle and Me: A Love Story.* Greenwillow, 1999. Ages 11–16.

Coming of Age

Bedard, Michael. *Stained Glass.* Tundra, 2001. Ages 12–18.

Bradbury, Jennifer. *Shift.* Atheneum, 2008. Ages 12–18.

French, Simon. *Where in the World.* Peachtree, 2003. Ages 10–13.

Henkes, Kevin. *Olive's Ocean.* Greenwillow, 2003. Ages 10–13.

Jocelyn, Marthe. *How It Happened in Peach Hill.* Random, 2007. Ages 11–16. Humorous.

Lawrence, Iain. *Ghost Boy.* Delacorte, 2000. Ages 12–18.

Leavitt, Martine. *Tom Finder.* Red Deer Press, 2003. Ages 12–18.

Lynch, Chris. *Me, Dear Dad & Alcatraz.* HarperCollins, 2005. Ages 13–16.

Myers, Walter Dean. *Sunrise over Fallujah.* Scholastic, 2008. Ages 13–18.

Oates, Joyce Carol. *Small Avalanches and Other Stories.* HarperCollins, 2003. (COL) Ages 14–18.

Olsen, Sylvia. *The Girl with a Baby.* Sono Nis, 2004. Ages 12–18.

Peters, Julie Anne. *Mom and Jo.* Little, Brown, 2006. Ages 12–14.

Saldaña, René, Jr. *Finding Our Way.* Wendy Lamb, 2003. (COL) Ages 12–16.

Salisbury, Graham. *Island Boyz: Short Stories.* Wendy Lamb, 2002. (COL) Ages 12–16.

Schmidt, Gary D. *The Wednesday Wars.* Clarion, 2007. Ages 11–15.

Sonnenblick, Jordan. *Notes from the Midnight Driver.* Scholastic, 2006. Ages 12–16. Humorous.

St. Anthony, Jane. *The Summer Sherman Loved Me.* Farrar, 2006. Ages 10–14.

Adventure and Survival

Bauer, Joan. *Backwater.* Putnam, 1999. Ages 12–16.

Couloumbis, Audrey. *The Misadventures of Maude March, or, Trouble Rides a Fast Horse.* Random, 2005. Ages 10–13. Humorous.

Creech, Sharon. *The Wanderer.* HarperCollins, 2000. Ages 11–14.

Doctorow, Cory. *Little Brother.* Tor, 2008. Ages 12–18.

Doyle, Roddy. *Wilderness.* A. A. Levine, 2007. Ages 11–16.

Ellis, Sarah. *The Several Lives of Orphan Jack.* Illustrated by Bruno St-Aubin. Groundwood, 2003. Ages 7–11.

George, Jean Craighead. *Julie.* HarperCollins, 1994. Ages 11–15.

———. *Julie of the Wolves.* Illustrated by John Schoenherr. Harper, 1972. Ages 11–15.

———. *My Side of the Mountain.* Dutton, 1959. Ages 9–12.

Hobbs, Will. *Crossing the Wire.* HarperCollins, 2006. Ages 10–15.

———. *Jackie's Wild Seattle.* HarperCollins, 2003. Ages 10–15.

———. *The Maze.* Morrow, 1998. Ages 11–16.

———. *Wild Man Island.* HarperCollins, 2002. Ages 11–16.

Horvath, Polly. *My One Hundred Adventures.* Random, 2008. Ages 9–12.

Jennings, Richard W. *The Great Whale of Kansas.* Houghton, 2001. Ages 10–13.

Key, Watt. *Alabama Moon.* Farrar, 2006. Ages 11–15.

Lee, Tanith. *Piratica: Being a Daring Tale of a Singular Girl's Adventure Upon the High Seas.* Dutton, 2004. Ages 11–14. Presented in three acts.

McCaughrean, Geraldine. *Smile!* Illustrated by Ian McCaughrean. Random, 2006. Ages 10–14.

———. *The White Darkness.* HarperTempest, 2007. Ages 12–16.

Mikaelsen, Ben. *Touching Spirit Bear.* HarperCollins, 2001. Ages 11–18.

Myers, Walter Dean. *Scorpions.* Harper, 1988. Ages 10–16.

Paulsen, Gary. *Hatchet.* Bradbury, 1987. Ages 9–12.

———. *The River.* Delacorte, 1991. Ages 10–16.

Philbrick, Rodman. *The Young Man and the Sea.* Scholastic, 2004. Ages 10–14.

Salisbury, Graham. *Lord of the Deep.* Delacorte, 2001. Ages 11–15.

Snicket, Lemony. *The End: Book the Thirteenth.* Illustrated by Brett Helquist. HarperCollins, 2006. Ages 10–14.

Stewart, Trenton Lee. *The Mysterious Benedict Society.* Little, Brown, 2007. Ages 10–14.

———. *The Mysterious Benedict Society and the Perilous Journey.* Little, Brown, 2008. Ages 10–14.

Taylor, Theodore. *Ice Drift.* Harcourt, 2004. Ages 9–13.

Wood, Don. *Into the Volcano.* Scholastic, 2008. (GR) Ages 9–14.

Related Films, Videos, and DVDs

Because of Winn-Dixie. (2005). Author: Kate DiCamillo (2000). 106 minutes.

Bridge to Terabithia. (2007). Author: Katherine Paterson (1977). 96 minutes.

The Clique. (2008). Author: Lisi Harrison (2004). 87 minutes.

A Cry in the Wild. (1990). Author: Gary Paulsen, *Hatchet* (1987). 82 minutes.

Finding Buck McHenry. (2000). Author: Alfred Slote (1991). 94 minutes.

Harriet the Spy. (1996). Author: Louis Fitzhugh (1964). 102 minutes.

Holes. (2003). Author: Louis Sachar (1998). 117 minutes.

Homeward Bound. (1993). Author: Sheila Burnford, *The Incredible Journey* (1961). 84 minutes.

Hoot. (2006). Author: Carl Hiaasen (2002). 91 minutes.

Iron Will. (1993). Author: John Reynolds Gardiner, *Stone Fox* (1980). 109 minutes.

Lemony Snicket's A Series of Unfortunate Events. (2004). Author: Daniel Handler, *The Bad Beginning* (1999). 107 minutes.

Maniac Magee. (1992). Author: Jerry Spinelli (1990). 30 minutes.

The Mighty. (1998). Author: Rodman Philbrick, *Freak the Mighty* (1993). 100 minutes.

Shiloh. (1997). Also *Shiloh 2.* (1999). Author: Phyllis Reynolds Naylor, *Shiloh* (1991) and *Shiloh Season* (1996). 93 minutes, 96 minutes.

The Sisterhood of the Traveling Pants. (2005). Also *The Sisterhood of the Traveling Pants 2.* (2008). Author: Ann Brashares (2001, 2005). 117 minutes, 119 minutes.

Summer of the Monkeys. (1998). Author: Wilson Rawls (1976). 101 minutes.

Whale Rider. (2002). Author: Witi Ihimaera (2003/1987). 101 minutes.

Where the Red Fern Grows. (2003). Author: Wilson Rawls (1961). 86 minutes.

Sources for Films, Videos, and DVDs

The Video Source Book. Syosset, NY: National Video Clearinghouse, 1979–. Published by Gale Research, Detroit, MI.

An annual reference work that lists media and provides sources for purchase and rental.

Websites of large video distributors:

www.libraryvideo.com

www.knowledgeunlimited.com

http://teacher.scholastic.com/products/westonwoods

PEARSON
myeducationkit™   Now go to Chapter 8 in the MyEducationKit (www.myeducationkit.com) for your book, where you can:

- Complete Assignments and Activities that can enrich and extend your knowledge of chapter content.

- Expand your knowledge with content-specific Web Links.

- Learn how authors and illustrators apply their craft by reading the written interviews in the Conversations section for the chapter.

- Review the chapter content by going to the Study Plan, taking a chapter quiz, and receiving feedback on your answers.

- Access the Children's Literature Database for your own exploration.

chapter NINE

Historical Fiction and Biography

Ancestors

On the wind-beaten plains
once lived my ancestors.
In the days of peaceful moods,
they wandered and hunted.
In days of need or greed,
they warred and loafed.
Beneath the lazy sun, kind winds above,
they laughed and feasted.
Through the starlit night, under the moon,
they dreamed and loved.
Now, from the wind-beaten plains,
only their dust rises.

—*Grey Cohoe*

Historical fiction and biography bring history to life by placing imaginary child characters in accurately described historical settings or by relating the life stories of actual people who lived in the past. Authors of historical fiction and biography provide young readers with the human side of history, making it more real and more memorable.

Section One: Historical Fiction

In this section the definition, description, evaluation, selection, early books, and trends of historical fiction for children are addressed.

Definition and Description

Historical fiction is realistic fiction set in a time remote enough from the present to be considered history. Stories about events that occurred at least one generation (defined as twenty years or more) prior to the date of the original publication have been included in this chapter and categorized as historical fiction.

Although historical fiction stories are imaginary, it is within the realm of possibility that such events could have occurred. In these stories, historical facts blend with imaginary characters and plot. The facts are actual historical events, authentic period settings, and real historical figures. An imaginary story is constructed around these facts. In the *Reference Guide to Historical Fiction for Children and Young Adults,* Adamson (1987) states:

> Historical fiction recreates a particular historical period with or without historical figures as incidental characters. It is generally written about a time period in which the author has not lived or no more recently than one generation before its composition. For example, fiction written in 1987 must be set, at the latest, in 1967, to be considered historical. Fiction written in 1930 but set in 1925 does not fulfill this criterion for legitimate historical fiction. (p. ix)

In the most common form of historical fiction, the main characters of the story are imaginary, but some secondary characters may be actual historical figures. An example of this type of historical fiction is the classic novel *Johnny Tremain* by Esther Forbes. Set in the U.S. Revolutionary War period, this story tells of Johnny, a fictitious character, who is apprenticed to a silversmith. In the course of the story, Samuel Adams, John Hancock, and Paul Revere are introduced as minor characters. Another example, Carolyn Meyer's *Mary, Bloody Mary,* written from Mary's point of view, is set in sixteenth-century England. Mary Tudor, who was briefly Queen of England, interacts with her father, King Henry, Anne Boleyn, and other court figures.

In another form of historical fiction, the social traditions, customs, morals, and values of the relevant period are described, but with no mention of an actual historical event nor actual historical figures as characters. The physical location is also accurately reconstructed for the readers. An example of this story type is *The Witch of Blackbird Pond* by Elizabeth George Speare. The Puritan way of life in Connecticut in the 1600s is depicted in this story about young Kit from Barbados, who becomes involved in a witchcraft trial. Another example of this type of story is Geraldine

McCaughrean's *Stop the Train!* in which the Oklahoma Land Rush and homesteading in the 1890s are captured in lively detail.

A third type of historical story is one in which elements of fantasy are found, and therefore the story does *not* qualify as historical fiction. For example, time warps and other supernatural features may be found in Jeanette Winterson's *Tanglewreck* and in Margaret Peterson Haddix's *Found.* These stories are **historical fantasy** and are included in Chapter 7.

Evaluation and Selection of Historical Fiction

In evaluating historical fiction for use with children, consider the following criteria:

■ Historical fiction must first tell an engaging story, have rounded, complex characters with whom children can identify, and impart a universal theme that is worthy and thought provoking without being didactic.

PEARSON
myeducationkit

Go to Activity 1 in the Assignments and Activities section of Chapter 9 in MyEducationKit; view the artifact on responding to historical fiction and respond to the question.

■ Historical fiction must present historical facts with as much accuracy and objectivity as books of history. This means that a setting must be described in sufficient detail to provide an authentic sense of time and place without overwhelming the story. Details such as hair and clothing styles, home architecture and furnishings, foods and food preparation, and modes of transportation must be subtly woven into the story to provide a convincing, authentic period setting. The characters must act within the traditions and norms of their times.

■ Expressing the language or dialect of the period presents a particular challenge to the author of historical stories. Dialogue that occurs within the text often becomes problematic for the writer. If the speech of the period is greatly different from that of today, then the author faces a decision: Remain true to the language of the time but cause readers difficulties in comprehending, or present the language in today's dialect but lose the flavor and authenticity of the language of the period. In any case, it seems important that the language not jar the reader by its obvious inappropriateness or lose the reader by its extreme difficulty. Most children's authors strive to attain the middle ground—some flavor of a language difference but modified to be understandable to the child reader.

■ Many adults today are unaware that the history they learned as children may have been biased or one-sided. Some authors attempt to include more modern interpretations of historical events in historical fiction by setting the record straight or adding a minority presence to the story. However, as was previously mentioned, care must be taken that the characters behave in a historically accurate fashion.

The Scott O'Dell Award, established in 1982 by the author Scott O'Dell, honors what is judged to be the most outstanding work of children's historical fiction published in the previous year. The work must be written by a U.S. citizen and be set in the New World. The Scott O'Dell Award winners found in Appendix A can be a source of outstanding historical fiction for use with students. The National Council of Social Studies publishes a list of the most notable trade books in

Excellent Historical Fiction to READ ALOUD

Cushman, Karen. *The Loud Silence of Francine Green.* Ages 11–15.
DeFelice, Cynthia. *Bringing Ezra Back.* Ages 9–13.
Erdrich, Louise. *The Porcupine Year.* Ages 9–14.
Kadohata, Cynthia. *Kira-Kira.* Ages 11–18.
Lee, Milly. *Landed.* Illustrated by Yangsook Choi. Ages 7–11.
Levine, Ellen. *Henry's Freedom Box.* Illustrated by Kadir Nelson. Ages 7–12.
Provensen, Alice. *Klondike Gold.* Ages 7–10.
Roy, Jennifer. *Yellow Star.* Ages 10–15.
Salisbury, Graham. *House of the Red Fish.* Ages 10–15.
Sheth, Kashmira. *Keeping Corner.* Ages 12–18.
White, Ruth. *Little Audrey.* Ages 9–13.
Winters, Kay. *Colonial Voices: Hear Them Speak.* Illustrated by Larry Day. Ages 9–13.

the field of social studies from the preceding year in the April/May issue of its journal, *Social Education*. This list includes many works of historical fiction, as well as nonfiction works, and is a useful source to locate recent books of this genre.

Historical Overview of Historical Fiction

Although historical stories were written for children as early as the 1800s, few titles of interest remain from those early years. The early books placed an emphasis on exciting events and idealized real-life characters—much in the style of heroic legends.

Between World War I and World War II, a few historical stories appeared in which well-developed characters involved in realistic events were portrayed in authentic period settings. Between 1932 and 1943, the first eight books of the Little House series by Laura Ingalls Wilder were published. These stories have continued to grow in popularity, partially as a result of the long-lasting television series based on the books. *Johnny Tremain* by Esther Forbes was awarded the Newbery Medal in 1944 and is considered a children's classic.

The period after World War II saw a flowering of historical fiction for children in both English and U.S. literature. Many outstanding books were published in the fifteen years following the war. Examples are *The Door in the Wall* by Marguerite de Angeli, published in 1949; *Calico Captive* by Elizabeth George Speare, published in 1957; the best-selling, Newbery Medal–winning book *The Witch of Blackbird Pond* by Elizabeth George Speare, published in 1958; and *The Cabin Faced West* by Jean Fritz, published in 1958. In 1954, the Laura Ingalls Wilder Award was awarded to (and named for) Laura Ingalls Wilder, an author of historical fiction. This award, the "Hall of Fame" of children's authors and illustrators, honors an author or illustrator whose books, published in the United States, have made a substantial and lasting contribution to children's literature. By 1960, the genre of historical fiction was well established as a fine resource for children's enjoyment and enrichment. The accompanying Milestones feature highlights the development of historical fiction.

MILESTONES *in the Development of Historical Fiction*

Date	Event	Significance
1888	*Otto of the Silver Hand* by Howard Pyle	Early recognized work of historical fiction
1929	*The Trumpeter of Krakow* by Eric Kelly awarded the Newbery Medal	National recognition for an early work of historical fiction
1932–1943	Publication of the first eight books of **Little House** series by Laura Ingalls Wilder	Classic historical fiction
1944	*Johnny Tremain* by Esther Forbes awarded the Newbery Medal	Classic historical adventure set during the American Revolution era
1949–1960	Many historical novels published, including *The Witch of Blackbird Pond* by Elizabeth George Speare and *The Lantern Bearers* by Rosemary Sutcliff	Dramatic increase in the quality and quantity of historical novels for children
1954	Establishment of the Laura Ingalls Wilder Award, first awarded to Wilder	Recognition of a historical fiction author for the entire body of her work
1961	Scott O'Dell's *Island of the Blue Dolphins* awarded the Newbery Medal	Landmark book of historical fiction with a strong female protagonist from a minority culture
1971	*Journey to Topaz* by Yoshiko Uchida	Early historical work about and by a minority (Japanese American)
1972	Scott O'Dell awarded the Hans Christian Andersen Award	International recognition of a U.S. author of historical novels
1975	*The Song of the Trees* by Mildred Taylor	First in a series of books about an African-American family's struggle starting in the Depression era
1982	Establishment of the Scott O'Dell Award	Award given for outstanding historical novel set in North America brings recognition to the genre
1997	*Out of the Dust* by Karen Hesse awarded the Newbery Medal	Recognition for a novel in verse, setting a trend in children's fiction

Historical fiction continues to flourish today. Some older historical fiction novels have been criticized for portraying some cultural groups in an extremely negative light. For example, two Newbery Medal winners, *Caddie Woodlawn* by Carol Ryrie Brink and *The Matchlock Gun* by Walter D. Edmonds, have been faulted for their negative portrayals of Native Americans. However, minority authors have written a number of excellent works based on the early experiences of their cultural groups in North America; for example, see *The Birchbark House* and its sequels by Louise Erdrich and *Journey to Topaz* by Yoshiko Uchida. The establishment in 1982 of the Scott O'Dell Award for Historical Fiction has begun to offer additional recognition for authors of this genre.

Section Two: Biography

In this section the definition, description, evaluation, selection, types of biographies, and history of biography for children are addressed.

Definition and Description

Biography gives factual information about the lives of actual people, including their experiences, influences, accomplishments, and legacies. An *autobiography* is similar in every respect to biography, except that the author tells about his or her own life. *Memoirs,* although related to autobiographies in that they deal with the authors' lives, focus on the authors' revelations of what events in their lives meant to them, not the events themselves (Barrington, 1997).

The writing in biographies is more narrative in nature than expository and adheres to the elements of fiction, as discussed in Chapter 3. Reading biographies benefits children in several ways. They find inspiration in stories of the lives and accomplishments of people, many of whom overcame hardships and disabilities in their early years to succeed and make their marks on history. They learn history from the context of the lives of historical figures. Readers also recognize the importance of childhood experiences, since many biographies for children emphasize the early years of subjects' lives.

Biographies can also be classified by coverage of the subject's life. In evaluating the following types of biographies, you will want to look for a balance between the need for adequate coverage and the tolerance that the target child audience has for detail.

- The *complete biography* covers the entire life of the subject from birth to death. An example is *Napoléon: The Story of the Little Corporal* by Robert Burleigh.
- The *partial biography* covers only part of the life of the subject. Biographies for very young children will often be of this type, as will, of course, the biographies of living persons. An example is *The Young Hans Christian Andersen* by Karen Hesse, illustrated by Erik Blegvad.
- The *collected biography* includes the life stories of several people in one book, organized into chapters. An example is *Women Daredevils: Thrills, Chills, and Frills* by Julie Cummins, illustrated by Cheryl Harness.
- The *biography series* is a multivolume set of books with each book containing one separate biography. For example, the First Biographies series by David A. Adler includes biographies on such subjects as Thomas Jefferson, Martin Luther King Jr., and Jackie Robinson.

Evaluation and Selection of Biography

In evaluating biography for use with children, consider the following criteria:

- Subjects of biographies should be interesting to children. The subjects' lives or accomplishments should somehow intersect with young readers' lives and interests.
- The facts should be accurate, with no idealization of the subject.

Excellent Biographies to READ ALOUD

Bernier-Grand, Carmen T. *Frida: Viva la Vida! Long Live Life!* Illustrated by Frida Kahlo. Ages 12–18.

Burleigh, Robert. *Napoléon: The Story of the Little Corporal.* Ages 10–14.

Chandra, Deborah, and Madeleine Comora. *George Washington's Teeth.* Illustrated by Brock Cole. Ages 7–11.

Cummins, Julie. *Women Daredevils: Thrills, Chills, and Frills.* Ages 8–12.

Fleischman, Sid. *The Trouble Begins at 8: A Life of Mark Twain in the Wild, Wild West.* Ages 10–15.

Hoose, Phillip. *We Were There, Too! Young People in U.S. History.* Ages 10–13.

McCarthy, Meghan. *Strong Man: The Story of Charles Atlas.* Ages 6–9.

Nivola, Claire A. *Planting the Trees of Kenya: The Story of Wangari Maathi.* Ages 6–9.

Ray, Deborah Kogan. *Down the Colorado: John Wesley Powell, the One-Armed Explorer.* Ages 8–11.

Serrano, Francisco. *The Poet King of Tezcoco: A Great Leader of Ancient Mexico.* Illustrated by Pablo Serrano. Ages 10–14.

Stone, Tanya Lee. *Sandy's Circus: A Story about Alexander Calder.* Illustrated by Boris Kulikov. Ages 5–9.

PEARSON
myeducationkit™

Go to Activity 2 in the Assignments and Activities section of Chapter 9 in MyEducationKit; view the video on students' responding to biographies and respond to the question.

- Biographical selections should include diverse subjects (female and male, people of all ethnicities and abilities).
- The depth of coverage should be at an appropriate level for the intended audience.
- The documentation should be unobtrusive.

Through My Eyes by Ruby Bridges and Margo Lundell fulfills all of these criteria and is particularly appealing to young readers because it is told from the perspective of the author as a 6-year-old.

Types of Biographies

In adult nonfiction, biographies must be completely documented to be acceptable. In biographies for children, more latitude is allowed, and biographers use varying degrees of invention. This invention ranges from choosing what aspect of the subject the biographer wants to emphasize as the theme of the book (e.g., great energy or love of freedom) to actually inventing fictional characters and conversation.

Biographies, then, can be classified by degree of documentation, as discussed next.

Authentic Biography

In *authentic biography,* all factual information is documented through eyewitness accounts, written documents, letters, diaries, and, more recently, audio and video recordings. Details in the lives of people who lived long ago, such as conversations, are often difficult to document, however. So, for the sake of art, biographers must use such devices as interior monologue (telling what some-one probably thought or said to himself or herself based on known actions), indirect discourse (reporting the gist of what someone said without using quotation marks), attribution (interpreta-tion of known actions to determine probable motives), and inference to make their stories lively and appealing and worth the children's time to read. It is advisable to read and compare several biographies of a subject, if possible, to counteract any bias an author might have. *Painting the Wild Frontier: The Art and Adventures of George Catlin* by Susanna Reich is an example of an authentic biography.

Fictionalized Biography

Fictionalized biography is also based on careful research, but the author creates dramatic episodes from known facts by using imagined conversation. The conversation is, of course, carefully struc-tured around the pertinent facts that are known, but the actual words are invented by the author. An example of this type of biography is *The Poet King of Tezcoco: A Great Leader of Ancient Mexico* by Francisco Serrano.

Biographical Fiction

Much artistic license is allowed in *biographical fiction,* including invented dialogue, fictional secondary characters, and some reconstructed action. The known achievements of the biographi-cal subjects are reported accurately, but in other respects these works are as much fiction as fact. Due to a trend toward greater authenticity in children's nonfiction, biographical fiction is rela-tively rare today. An example is *If a Bus Could Talk: The Story of Rosa Parks* by Faith Ringgold.

Historical Overview of Biography

Children's biographies reflect the moral, political, and social values of the times in which they are written. Early U.S. biographies were often didactic and provided life lessons for children to follow. In the mid-1800s, Samuel G. Goodrich (under the pseudonym of Peter Parley) wrote and published for children many idealized biographies of famous men and women. These men and women were treated as heroic figures rather than as human beings with flaws and imperfections. In 1880, Rever-end Mason Weems wrote *The Life and Memorable Acts of George Washington,* a work that set a long-lasting trend of portraying national leaders as paragons of virtue. It was not until the 1920s that some biographers began to draw on the new interest in the fields of psychology and sociology by giving more emphasis to understanding their subjects and examining the early years of their lives.

Examples of children's biographies recognized for their merit from 1930 to 1960 are *Abraham Lincoln* by Ingri and Edgar Parin d'Aulaire; *Daniel Boone* by James H. Daugherty; and *Carry On, Mr. Bowditch* by Jean Lee Latham. In the 1960s and 1970s, children's biographies were affected by the more liberal attitudes and relaxed topic restrictions of the new realism that revolutionized chil-dren's fiction. Before this time certain subjects (women, ethnic minorities, and infamous people) and topics (personal weaknesses, mistakes, tragedies) were seldom found in children's biographies. By the 1970s, this attitude had changed, as Russell Freedman (1988) pointed out in his Newbery

MILESTONES *in the Development of Biographies*

Date	Book	Significance
1939	*Abraham Lincoln* by Ingri and Edgar Parin d'Aulaire	One of the first picture book biographies for younger children; first biography to win the Caldecott Medal
1940	*Daniel Boone* by James H. Daugherty	First biography to win the Newbery Medal
1952	*Diary of a Young Girl* by Anne Frank	Classic autobiography; helped many to understand the tragedy of the Jewish Holocaust
1988	*Lincoln: A Photobiography* by Russell Freedman	First nonfictional photo essay to win a Newbery Medal
1990	First Orbis Pictus Award for Nonfiction (*The Great Little Madison* by Jean Fritz)	Nonfiction as a genre is recognized; first winner is a biography
2001	First Robert F. Sibert Informational Book Medal (*Sir Walter Ralegh and the Quest for El Dorado* by Marc Aronson)	Nonfiction as a genre is further recognized; first winner is a biography

Medal acceptance speech: "The hero worship of the past has given way to a more realistic approach, which recognizes the warts and weaknesses that humanize the great" (p. 447).

Two awards have been established to honor nonfiction works: the Orbis Pictus Award for Nonfiction, first awarded in 1990, and the Robert F. Sibert Award for Nonfiction, first awarded in 2001. Many of the early winners of these awards have been biographies.

Section Three: Historical Fiction and Biography in the Classroom

The importance of understanding and appreciating the contexts found in historical fiction and biography and the value of planning effective strategies for sharing this literature are discussed in this section. Two organizing principles to consider using in planning class presentations of historical literature are suggested. One is to select literature by universal themes that occur over the course of history; the other is to arrange literature chronologically by historical periods.

Developing Understanding and Appreciation for Historical Contexts

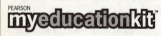

PEARSON

Go to Activity 3 in the Assignments and Activities section of Chapter 9 in MyEducationKit; complete the activity on pairing historical fiction novels and biographies.

Children are often limited in their knowledge of history and *historical context*—the background and environment that surrounded past events, including how people lived and worked. Reading or listening to works of historical fiction and biography are excellent means of helping students understand the past and appreciate the lives of people who lived in earlier times. Many educators are convinced of the benefits students gain through integrating history and literature as part of the social studies curriculum.

Smith, Monson, and Dobson (1992) found that the students in fifth-grade classrooms in which historical novels were used along with standard instructional materials recalled more historical facts and indicated greater enjoyment in their social studies classes than the students in classrooms that had a similar curriculum without the addition of historical novels.

Past events presented in a purely factual manner can seem irrelevant and sometimes unbelievable to students, but by presenting these events as part of a story such as a work of historical fiction or a biographical account and showing how the events affected the lives of characters much like themselves, students better understand the events and are more likely to remember them. Historical stories help children connect to the emotions engendered by past events—the fear of combat and the excitement of exploration. In addition, books set in the past allow children to compare their lives with the lives of characters found in biographies and historical fiction novels and to better understand and appreciate how context affects people's lives, including their own. Students can also begin to consider how their lives may change in the future.

Teachers can encourage students to read works of historical fiction and biography by displaying these books in the classroom, introducing them in booktalks, selecting them for class read-alouds, and presenting them in text sets for independent reading. For ideas of authors to feature for class study, see Notable Authors of Historical Fiction and Biography.

An example of a hands-on activity to help build prior knowledge and to reinforce contextual understandings is the *jackdaw,* a collection of artifacts or copies of realia from a particular historical period or event. Jackdaws are often available in museums for study of a period of history, and some museums lend them to teachers for use in schools. The term *jackdaw* refers to a common European bird that is related to the crow and known to collect colorful objects for its nest. Educators have borrowed the term to refer to a concrete object that can be used to connect historical books with the real events of the times (Devitt, 1970). For example, a teacher may put together a jackdaw based on homesteaders in Oklahoma in the 1800s, then use the jackdaw to build background knowledge to introduce the study of the historical fiction novel *Stop the Train!* by Geraldine McCaughrean.

Jackdaws are made by collecting a wide array of related materials in their original form or in reproductions. Materials that are often collected are regional maps, photographs or models of homes, farms, machines, household furnishings, toys and dolls, kitchen tools, recipes for foods commonly eaten, newspapers and books of the era, clothing, modes of transportation, government of the time (president, congress, political parties, statehood), educational institutions, cultural artifacts such as songs, paintings, and architectural landmarks. After collection the realia are placed in a decorated box with labels and explanations attached, if desired. The jackdaw can be used as an extension activity for a book read in class as well as for building background. Many teachers enlist students in the development of jackdaws and share jackdaws with other teachers who are studying the same historical book.

Presenting Historical Fiction and Biography by Universal Themes

Common themes that extend across time and place in historical stories can be an approach for presenting historical fiction and biography to children. In this case, a theme, such as seeking new frontiers, is explored through a small group of books set in different times and places. Some possible themes for development are listed here, along with historical fiction books and biographies that might be considered for the study of the theme. Other themes may be discovered when you read historical fiction novels and biographies and consider the commonalities to be found among them.

Notable Authors

of Historical Fiction and Biographies

HISTORICAL FICTION

Avi [Wortis], author noted for the Newbery Award–winning historical fiction novel *Crispin: The Cross of Lead* and two Newbery Honor books. www.avi-writer.com

Christopher Paul Curtis, African-American author of two historical novels: the Newbery Medal book, *Bud, Not Buddy,* a Depression era novel, and Newbery Honor book, *The Watsons Go to Birmingham—1963; Elijah of Buxton.* www.christopherpaulcurtis.com

Karen Cushman, author of two Newbery acclaimed historical novels set in the Middle Ages. *Catherine, Called Birdy; The Midwife's Apprentice.* www.karencushman.com

Karen Hesse, author of Newbery Medal winner, *Out of the Dust,* set in Oklahoma in the 1930s. Also noted for historical picture book *The Cats in Krasinski Square.*

Linda Sue Park, Newbery Award–winning author whose novels about historical eras in Korea bring understanding about another culture. *A Single Shard; When My Name Was Keoko; The Kite Fighters.* www.lindasuepark.com

Richard Peck, Newbery Award–winning author noted for his young adult novels and his historical novels set in rural Illinois. *A Year Down Yonder; The River Between Us.*

Graham Salisbury, an author who writes historical and realistic novels set in the Hawaiian Islands where he was raised. *House of the Red Fish; Eyes of the Emperor.* www.graham salisbury.com

Gloria Whelan, winner of the National Book Award for young people's literature for *Home-less Bird,* set in India. Also wrote *Angel on the Square,* set in Russia. www.gloriawhelan.com

BIOGRAPHY

David A. Adler, author of several children's biography series written on different difficulty levels that provide insight to the private and public lives of American leaders and sports figures. *B. Franklin, Printer; A Picture Book of Dwight David Eisenhower; Lou Gehrig: The Luckiest Man.* www.davidaadler.com

Dennis B. Fradin, author of many biographies for middle-grade readers and young adults. *The Signers: The 56 Stories behind the Declaration of Independence; The Founders: The 39 Stories behind the U.S. Constitution; Ida B. Wells: Mother of the Civil Rights Movement* (with Judith B. Fradin).

Russell Freedman, author of biographies of famous Americans and of informational books about U.S. history. *Lincoln: A Photobiography.*

Jean Fritz, biographer of political leaders during the U.S. Revolutionary War era. *Can't You Make Them Behave, King George?; And Then What Happened, Paul Revere?*

Jan Greenberg and **Sandra Jordan,** coauthors of several biographies about renowned artists and their works. *Vincent Van Gogh: Portrait of an Artist; Action Jackson.*

Diane Stanley, author/illustrator of picture book biographies for older readers. *Saladin: Noble Prince of Islam; Joan of Arc.* www.dianestanley .com

---

Seeking New Frontiers

The Braid by Helen Frost. Ages 12–16.

Down the Colorado: John Wesley Powell, the One-Armed Explorer by Deborah Kogan Ray. Ages 8–11.

Theodore Roosevelt: Champion of the American Spirit by Betsy H. Kraft. Ages 10–14.

Onward: A Photobiography of African-American Polar Explorer Matthew Henson by Dolores Johnson. Ages 11–14.

Worth by A. LaFaye. Ages 10–14.
Landed by Milly Lee. Illustrated by Yangsook Choi. Ages 6–10.
The Legend of Bass Reeves by Gary Paulsen. Ages 10–14.
Crooked River by Shelley Pearsall. Ages 10–13.
Double Crossing: A Jewish Immigration Story by Eve Tal. Ages 11–15.
Black Storm Comin' by Diane Lee Wilson. Ages 11–16.

Search for Freedom from Persecution

We Are One: The Story of Bayard Rustin by Larry D. Brimner. Ages 11–16.
A Boy Named Beckoning: The True Story of Dr. Carlos Montezuma, a Native American Hero by Gina
   Capaldi. Ages 7–10.
Emil and Karl by Yankev Glatshteyn. Ages 10–15.
The Cats in Krasinski Square by Karen Hesse. Illustrated by Wendy Watson. Ages 9–12.
Yellow Star by Jennifer Roy. Ages 10–15.
Flight to Freedom by Ana Veciana-Suarez. Ages 11–16.
Colonial Voices: Hear Them Speak by Kay Winters. Illustrated by Larry Day. Ages 9–13.
The Traitor by Laurence Yep. Ages 10–14.

Effects of War

Tasting the Sky: A Palestinian Childhood by Ibtisam Barakat. Ages 12–16.
Soldier Boys by Dean Hughes. Ages 13–18.
Eyes Like Willy's by Juanita Havill. Illustrated by David Johnson. Ages 12–16.
The Brothers' War: Civil War Voices in Verse by J. Patrick Lewis. Ages 10–14.
The Butterfly by Patricia Polacco. Ages 9–12.
Willow Run by Patricia Reilly Giff. Ages 9–12.
Always Remember Me: How One Family Survived World War II by Marisabina Russo. Ages 8–12.
Red Moon at Sharpsburg by Rosemary Wells. Ages 12–15.

Family Closeness in Times of Adversity

Fever 1793 by Laurie Halse Anderson. Ages 11–15.
Bringing Ezra Back by Cynthia DeFelice. Ages 9–13.
Nory Ryan's Song by Patricia Reilly Giff. Ages 9–13.
Going North by Janice N. Harrington. Illustrated by Jerome Lagarrigue. Ages 7–11.
Snow Falling in Spring: Coming of Age in China during the Cultural Revolution by Moying Li. Ages
   12–18.
Esperanza Rising by Pam Muñoz Ryan. Ages 9–13.
House of the Red Fish by Graham Salisbury. Ages 10–15.
The Wall: Growing Up behind the Iron Curtain by Peter Sís. Ages 10–15.
The Floating Circus by Tracie Vaughn Zimmer. Ages 11–16.
Show Way by Jacqueline Woodson. Illustrated by Hudson Talbott. Ages 8–11.

Presenting Historical Fiction and Biography by Periods of History

The natural relationship of historical fiction stories and biographies to the study of history and
geography suggests building whole units of study around periods of world and U.S. history in
which good stories for children are set. The following descriptions of seven historical periods will

give you an idea of how these units might be organized. Historical fiction books and biographies for units on other eras and events can be selected from the lists at the end of the chapter, where you will find both historical fiction stories and biographies arranged by the seven historical periods beginning in 3000 B.C.

Beginnings of Civilization up to 3000 B.C.

This period represents prehistoric cultures and civilizations. Early peoples (Java, Neanderthals, Cro-Magnons) and early civilizations in the Middle East and Asia are included. Egyptians, Syrians, and Phoenicians developed civilizations; and Hebrews produced a religious faith, Judaism, that resulted in the Old Testament. The subcontinent of India was the site of Aryan civilizations. Chinese dynasties were responsible for excellent works of art and agricultural systems of irrigation. Good examples of historical novels set in this time period are Peter Dickinson's *A Bone from a Dry Sea* and Betty Levin's *Thorn*.

Civilizations of the Ancient World, 3000 B.C. to A.D. 600

The era of the Greek city-states was followed by a period of Roman rule in western Europe. Christianity was founded in Jerusalem and spread throughout Europe. Ancient Asia was the site of enduring civilizations that bred two remarkable men born about 560 B.C.: the Indian religious leader Buddha and the Chinese philosopher Confucius. Both have had a lasting influence on their civilizations. Kerrily Sapet's *Cleopatra: Ruler of Egypt* relates the life and times of the legendary Egyptian queen in this illustrated, comprehensive biography. Elizabeth E. Wein's *The Lion Hunter*, a historical novel set in ancient Ethiopia, features King Arthur's half-Ethiopian grandson, who battles political intrigues to survive.

Civilizations of the Medieval World, 600 to 1500

During this era, early African and American civilizations arose independently. The great civilizations of China and Japan continued to flourish throughout these centuries. The eastern part of the Roman Empire maintained its stability and preserved the civilization from the capital of Constantinople. This civilization, the Byzantine Empire, created a distinct culture and branch of the Christian Church—the Orthodox Church—which influenced Russia to adopt both the religion and the culture. The rise of the Islamic religion began in the early 600s with Muhammad preaching in Mecca. Following the fall of the Roman Empire, western Europe dissolved into isolated separate regions without strong governments. Many of the responsibilities of government were carried out by the Christian Church. The Church dominated the economic, political, cultural, and educational life of the Middle Ages in western Europe. These feudal societies eventually gave rise to the separate nations of modern Europe. As examples, K. M. Grant's *Blood Red Horse* and *Blue Flame* portray medieval life in England and France, respectively. Jonah Winter's *The Secret World of Hildegard* relates the remarkable story of the twelfth-century German saint, scientist, and composer.

The Emergence of Modern Nations, 1500 to 1800

The Renaissance, a literary and artistic movement, swept western Europe. Many important developments of this period included the invention of the printing press, a new emphasis on reason, a reformation of the Christian Church, and advances in science. During this same period, central governments throughout Europe increased their power. Spain, and then France, dominated Europe in the 1500s and 1600s. In the 1700s, Russia, Austria, and Prussia rose to power. This was also a time when Europeans explored and settled in Africa, India, and the Americas. The Portuguese and Spanish took the lead in explorations and acquired many foreign colonies. England, the Netherlands, France, and Russia also colonized and influenced East Asia, India, Africa, and the Americas.

Revolutions created new governments and new nations. The American Revolution (1776–1781) created a new nation; the French Revolution in 1789 affected the direction of governments toward democracy in all of Europe. Napoleon built an empire across Europe, resulting in the uniting of European nations to defeat Napoleon. Robert Burleigh's richly illustrated biography, *Napoléon: The Story of the Little Corporal,* describes Napoleon's early childhood in Corsica, his rise to power as a military leader, and his decline. The nations of Latin America also began to gain their independence. China expanded gradually under the Ming and Ch'ing dynasties. Japan prospered under the Tokugawa shogunate. The United States and Canada were the sites of rapid population increases due to immigration; the settlements in North America were predominantly along the eastern coasts. Some westward expansion was beginning in the United States and Canada. Short stories describing the roles of different persons during the Boston Tea Party in 1773 are presented in Kay Winters's *Colonial Voices: Hear Them Speak.*

The Development of Industrial Society, 1800 to 1914

The 1800s were marked by a rapid shift from agricultural societies to industrial societies. Great Britain was an early site for this change. The factory system developed and prospered, while working and living conditions deteriorated for the worker. Three stories about life as a millworker in this period are Katherine Paterson's *Bread and Roses, Too;* Katharine Boling's *January 1905;* and Elizabeth Winthrop's *Counting on Grace.* New technology—railroad trains, steamboats, the telegraph, and the telephone—affected transportation and communications. Advances in science and medicine helped to explain the nature of life and improved the quality of life. Education developed into an important institution in western Europe and North America. Europe underwent revolutions that readjusted boundaries and eventually led to the unification of new nations. The colonization of sub-Saharan Africa by European nations expanded rapidly from 1870 to 1890. Most of the region was under control of the various European nations by the end of this period.

The westward movement was fully realized as pioneers settled across the United States and Canada. The building of railroads hastened the establishment of new settlements. Native Americans struggled for survival in the face of these massive population shifts. Slavery had existed in the American colonies from earliest days, but in the 1800s, slavery became a social and economic issue. Julius Lester's *Day of Tears: A Novel in Dialogue* reconstructs the largest slave auction in American history, which took place in Savannah, Georgia, in 1859. The despair and tragedy of slavery through the personal accounts of the slaves and the slave owners are vividly portrayed. Slavery was abolished as a result of the Civil War (1861–1865) and the Union was preserved at the cost of 600,000 lives and a major rift between the North and the South. Mildred D. Taylor's *The Land* depicts the hardships endured by a biracial boy in the post–Civil War South.

The United States grew in economic and political strength. An age of imperialism resulted in firm control of large areas of the world by other world powers such as England, France, and Belgium. Great Britain dominated India and parts of Africa and continued its influence over Canada, Australia, and New Zealand, while Japan became a powerful force in east Asia.

World Wars in the Twentieth Century, 1914 to 1945

This era includes World War I (1914–1918) in Europe, in which the United States and Canada joined and fought with the Allies (Great Britain, France, Russia, Greece, and Romania); the between-wars period that included the Great Depression; Hitler's rise to power in 1933; and World War II (1939–1945) in Europe and Asia, in which Canada and the United States joined forces with England, France, and Russia to battle Germany, Italy, and Japan. In 1917, the Bolshevik Revolution established a Communist government in Russia. In 1931, Great Britain recognized Canada, Australia, New Zealand, and South Africa as completely independent. However, each nation declared its loyalty to the British monarch and continued its cultural ties with Great Britain. The Holocaust during World War II—the persecution and killing of Jewish and other people by the Nazi regime—stands out as one of the most atrocious periods in modern history. In Jennifer Roy's *Yellow Star,* Sylvia, a Jewish girl, and her family struggle to survive in the Lodz ghetto in Poland during the Nazi occupation from 1939 to 1945. World War II ended shortly after the United States dropped nuclear devices on Hiroshima and Nagasaki, Japan.

Post–World War II Era, 1945 to 1980s

During this era, the United States and western European nations were involved in a struggle for world influence against the Communist nations, particularly the Soviet Union and China. A massive arms buildup, including nuclear weapons, was undertaken by the major nations of both sides. The Korean War (1950–1953) and the Vietnam War (1965–1973) were major conflicts in which the United States fought to contain Communist expansion. The Korean War, combined with the postwar economic recovery of Japan, drew attention to the growing importance of East Asia in world affairs. The Soviet Union launched a series of satellites beginning with *Sputnik I* on October 4, 1957, inaugurating the space age. An explosion of scientific knowledge occurred as a result of increased spending for weapons development and space exploration. The 1950s, 1960s, and 1970s have been described as the Cold War decades because of the increasing hostility between the Soviet Union and the United States, gradually ending with the defeat of the Soviet regime in the early 1990s. In the 1970s, public pressure mounted in the United States to reduce the nation's external military commitments following the Vietnam War.

During the 1960s, a strong Civil Rights Movement, led by Martin Luther King Jr. and other prominent figures of the era, fought for equal treatment of African Americans. The movement led to desegregation of schools, restaurants, transportation, and housing. Another struggle against the policies of racial separation occurred in South Africa in the 1970s and 1980s. The end of apartheid was declared in 1990, followed by free elections in 1994. Equal rights for women were also sought during the feminist movement in the 1970s. Examples of books depicting the civil rights struggle are Robert Sharenow's *My Mother the Cheerleader* and Larry D. Brimner's *We Are One: The Story of Bayard Rustin.*

Many fine works of historical fiction and biography for children can now be found. Children have an opportunity to live vicariously the lives of people from long ago—people from different cultures and different parts of the world.

Issues&Topics for FURTHER INVESTIGATION

- Select and read a historical fiction novel, then research the time period and location of its setting. Contrast the actual historical facts with the events in the story. Develop a time line to display both the historical facts and the story events.

- Choose one of the seven periods of history listed in this chapter. Select five recommended works of historical fiction and biography set in this era and read them to develop a plan for sharing these works with students during a unit of study.

- Pick a theme often found in historical fiction novels and biographies suggested in this chapter. Compare and contrast several books from the list of books exemplifying the theme.

- Discuss whether older works of historical fiction and biography that accurately reflect the white, Euro-American perspective of a past era—even though now viewed as biased—should be included in the classroom or banned from classroom use. Explain your reasoning.

References

Adamson, L. G. (1987). *A reference guide to historical fiction for children and young adults.* Westport, CT: Greenwood Press.

Barrington, J. (1997). *Writing the memoir: From truth to art.* Portland, OR: Eighth Mountain Press.

Cohoe, G. (1972). Ancestors. In T. Allen (Ed.), *The whispering wind: Poetry by young American Indians.* New York: Doubleday.

Devitt, M. (Ed.). (1970). *Learning with jackdaws.* London: St. Paul's Press.

Freedman, R. (1988). Newbery Medal acceptance. *The Horn Book, 64*(4), 444–451.

Smith, J. A., Monson, J. A., & Dobson, D. (1992). A case study on integrating history and reading instruction through literature. *Social Education, 56,* 370–375.

Recommended Historical Fiction and Biography Books

Ages indicated refer to content appropriateness and conceptual and interest levels. Formats other than novels will be coded as follows:

(PI) Picture book
(COL) Short story collection
(GR) Graphic novel

Beginnings of Civilization up to 3000 B.C.

Historical Fiction

Brennan, J. H. *Shiva.* Lippincott, 1990. Ages 11–15. Prehistoric Europe, Neanderthal, and Cro-Magnon tribes. Sequels are *Shiva Accused: An Adventure of the Ice Age,* 1991; and *Shiva's Challenge: An Adventure of the Ice Age,* 1993.

Cowley, Marjorie. *Anooka's Answer.* Clarion, 1998. Ages 10–15. Southern France, Upper Paleolithic era.

———. *Dar and the Spear-Thrower.* Clarion, 1994. Ages 10–15. Southeastern France, Cro-Magnon era.

Craig, Ruth. *Malu's Wolf.* Orchard, 1995. Ages 9–13. Stone Age Europe, domestication of wolves.

Denzel, Justin. *Return to the Painted Cave.* Philomel, 1997. Ages 10–14. France and Spain, Stone Age, cave paintings.

Dickinson, Peter. *A Bone from a Dry Sea.* Delacorte, 1993. Ages 11–15. Prehistoric tribe.

———. *Po's Story.* Putnam, 1998. Ages 8–12. Prehistoric clans. Others in The Kin series include *Suth's Story,* 1998; *Mana's Story,* 1999; and *Noli's Story,* 1999.

Levin, Betty. *Thorn.* Front Street, 2005. Ages 12–16. Prehistoric times, birth defects.

Civilizations of the Ancient World, 3000 B.C. to A.D. 600

Historical Fiction

Hunter, Mollie. *The Stronghold.* Harper, 1974. Ages 9–14. British Isles, 100 B.C.

Lawrence, Caroline. *The Thieves of Ostia: A Roman Mystery.* Millbrook, 2002. Ages 11–14. Roman port city Ostia, A.D. 79.

Sutcliff, Rosemary. *The Light Beyond the Forest: The Quest for the Holy Grail.* Dutton, 1980. Ages 12–18. Re-creation of the times of King Arthur and his knights, c. 520 A.D.

———. *The Road to Camlann: The Death of King Arthur.* Dutton, 1982. Ages 12–18.

Wein, Elizabeth E. *The Lion Hunter: The Mark of Solomon, Book One.* Viking, 2007. Ages 12–16. Ethiopia, sixth century.

Winters, Kay. *Voices of Ancient Egypt.* Illustrated by Barry Moser. National Geographic, 2003. (**PI**) Ages 8–12. Egypt, c. 2686–1029 B.C.

Biography

Bankston, John. *The Life and Times of Alexander the Great.* Lane, 2004. Ages 11–13.

Lasky, Kathryn. *The Librarian Who Measured the Earth.* Illustrated by Kevin Hawkes. Little, Brown, 1994. (**PI**) Ages 7–10.

Sapet, Kerrily. *Cleopatra: Ruler of Egypt.* Morgan Reynolds, 2007. Ages 11–18. Egypt, 30 B.C.

Zannos, Susan. *The Life and Times of Socrates.* Lane, 2004. Ages 11–14.

Civilizations of the Medieval World, 600 to 1500

Historical Fiction

Alder, Elizabeth. *The King's Shadow.* Farrar, 1995. Ages 12–16. England, end of Saxon era, pre-1066.

Avi. *Crispin: At the Edge of the World.* Hyperion, 2006. Ages 10–16. England, 1377.

———. *Crispin: The Cross of Lead.* Hyperion, 2002. Ages 12–16. England, fourteenth century.

Branford, Henrietta. *The Fated Sky.* Candlewick, 1999. Ages 12–16. Norway, Iceland, Viking era.

———. *Fire, Bed, and Bone.* Candlewick, 1998. Ages 10–14. England, fourteenth century.

Cadnum, Michael. *Book of the Lion.* Viking, 2000. Ages 12–16. England, twelfth century.

———. *Raven of the Waves.* Orchard, 2001. Ages 12–16. England, Norsemen, A.D. 794.

Cushman, Karen. *Catherine, Called Birdy.* Clarion, 1994. Ages 11–15. England, manor life, 1290s.

———. *Matilda Bone.* Clarion, 2000. Ages 11–15. Medieval England, medical practitioner.

———. *The Midwife's Apprentice.* Clarion, 1995. Ages 12–16. England, Middle Ages.

Grant, K. M. *Blood Red Horse.* Walker, 2005. Ages 12–16. Crusades, 1185–1193 A.D.

———. *Blue Flame.* Walker, 2008. Ages 11–15. Languedoc region of France, 1242.

Jinks, Catherine. *Pagan's Crusade.* Candlewick, 2003. Ages 12–15. Templar Knights of Jerusalem, 1187. Sequels are *Pagan in Exile,* 2004; *Pagan's Vows,* 2004; and *Pagan's Scribe,* 2005.

Love, D. Anne. *The Puppeteer's Apprentice.* Simon & Schuster, 2003. Ages 9–12. England in the Middle Ages.

McCaughrean, Geraldine. *The Kite Rider: A Novel.* HarperCollins, 2002. Ages 12–16. China, thirteenth century.

Napoli, Donna Jo. *Breath.* Atheneum, 2003. Ages 14–18. Germany, late 1200s.

———. *Daughter of Venice.* Random, 2002. Ages 11–15. Venice, Italy, sixteenth century.

Park, Linda Sue. *The Kite Fighters.* Clarion, 2000. Ages 8–12. Korea, 1473.

———. *A Single Shard.* Clarion, 2001. Ages 9–13. Korean village, 1100s.

Sedgwick, Marcus. *The Dark Horse.* Random, 2003. Ages 12–18. Ancient Britain, Viking tribes.

Shulevitz, Uri. *The Travels of Benjamin of Tudela: Through Three Continents in the Twelfth Century.* Farrar, 2005. (**PI**) Ages 9–14. Journey across southern Europe and the Middle East, 1159.

Skurzynski, Gloria. *Spider's Voice.* Simon & Schuster, 1999. Ages 13–18. Medieval lovers Abélard and Héloïse, France, 1100s.

Tingle, Rebecca. *The Edge on the Sword.* Putnam, 2001. Ages 11–15. Feudal England, late 800s.

Yolen, Jane, and Robert Harris. *Girl in a Cage.* Putnam, 2002. Ages 11–16. England, 1306.

Biography

Demi. *Marco Polo.* Marshall Cavendish, 2008. (**PI**) Ages 9–13. Venetian's trip to China, thirteenth century.

———. *Muhammad.* Simon & Schuster, 2003. (**PI**) Ages 9–13. Life of the prophet and the origins of Islam, 570–632.

Doak, Robin S. *Galileo: Astronomer and Physicist.* Compass Point Books, 2005. Ages 11–15.

Freedman, Russell. *The Adventures of Marco Polo.* Illustrated by Bagram Ibatoulline. Scholastic, 2006. Ages 12–15.

Krull, Kathleen. *Leonardo da Vinci.* Illustrated by Boris Kulikov. Viking, 2005. Ages 10–14. Part of the Giants of Science series.

Serrano, Francisco. *The Poet King of Tezcoco: A Great Leader of Ancient Mexico.* Illustrated by Pablo Serrano. Translated by Trudy Balch and Jo Anne Engelbert. Groundwood, 2007. (**PI**) Ages 10–14. Mexico, 1400s.

Shulevitz, Uri. *The Travels of Benjamin of Tudela: Through Three Continents in the Twelfth Century.* Farrar, 2005. (**PI**) Ages 10–14.

Stanley, Diane. *Joan of Arc.* Morrow, 1998. Ages 11–14.

Winter, Jonah. *The Secret World of Hildegard.* Illustrated by Jeanette Winter. Arthur A. Levine, 2007. (**PI**) Ages 7–12. Germany, 1100s.

The Emergence of Modern Nations, 1500 to 1800

Historical Fiction

Anderson, Laurie Halse. *Chains.* Simon & Schuster, 2008. Ages 11–15. New York City, enslaved sisters, 1776.

———. *Fever 1793.* Simon & Schuster, 2000. Ages 11–16. Philadelphia, yellow fever epidemic, freed slaves' role, 1793.

Bruchac, Joseph. *The Winter People.* Dial, 2002. Ages 11–16. French and Indian War, Abenaki village, 1759.

Duble, Kathleen Benner. *The Sacrifice.* Simon & Schuster, 2005. Ages 11–15. U.S. colonial era, Salem witch hunts, 1692.

Forbes, Esther. *Johnny Tremain.* Houghton, 1943. Ages 10–13. U.S. Revolutionary War era, 1770s.

Hearn, Julie. *The Minister's Daughter.* Atheneum, 2005. Ages 14–18. English village, Christianity, pregnancy, witchcraft, 1645.

Hesse, Karen. *Stowaway.* Simon & Schuster, 2000. Ages 10–15. British sailing ship, Captain Cook's voyage, 1768.

Ketchum, Liza. *Where the Great Hawk Flies.* Clarion, 2005. Ages 10–14. Vermont, relationships between white settlers and Pequot Indians, intermarriage, 1782.

Lawrence, Iain. *The Wreckers.* Delacorte, 1998. Ages 10–14. Adventures on the high seas; pirates, treasure, mystery, 1800s. The trilogy includes *The Smugglers,* 1999; and *The Buccaneers,* 2001.

Lunn, Janet. *The Hollow Tree.* Viking, 2000. Ages 10–14. U.S. Revolutionary War, 1777.

Meyer, Carolyn. *Mary, Bloody Mary.* Harcourt, 1999. Ages 11–15. England, Mary Tudor and the court of her father, Henry VIII, 1500s.

McCully, Emily Arnold. *The Escape of Oney Judge: Martha Washington's Slave Finds Freedom.* Farrar, 2007. (**PI**) Ages 9–12. Washington, D.C., late 1800s.

Park, Linda Sue. *The Firekeeper's Son.* Illustrated by Julie Downing. Clarion, 2003. (**PI**) Ages 8–12. Korea, early 1800s.

Rees, Celia. *Pirates!* Bloomsbury, 2003. Ages 12–16. Swashbuckling adventure, 1725.

Rockwell, Anne. *They Called Her Molly Pitcher.* Illustrated by Cynthia Von Buhler. Knopf, 2002. (**PI**) Ages 8–11. U.S. Revolutionary War, 1778.

Speare, Elizabeth George. *The Witch of Blackbird Pond.* Houghton, 1958. Ages 10–14. U.S. colonial era, 1680s.

Sturtevant, Katherine. *A True and Faithful Narrative.* Farrar, 2006. Ages 11–16. London, seventeenth century.

———. *At the Sign of the Star.* Farrar, 2000. Ages 10–15. London, 1677.

Van Leeuwen, Jean. *Hannah's Helping Hands.* Phyllis Fogelman, 1999. Ages 7–10. Connecticut, U.S. Revolutionary War, 1779.

Winters, Kay. *Colonial Voices: Hear Them Speak.* Illustrated by Larry Day. Dutton, 2008. (**PI**) Ages 9–13. Boston Tea Party, 1773.

Biography

Adler, David A. *B. Franklin, Printer.* Holiday, 2001. Ages 9–13.

Anderson, M. T. *Handel, Who Knew What He Liked.* Illustrated by Kevin Hawkes. Candlewick, 2001. (**PI**) Ages 8–12.

Aronson, Marc. *Sir Walter Ralegh and the Quest for El Dorado.* Clarion, 2000. Ages 12–16.

Burleigh, Robert. *Napoléon: The Story of the Little Corporal.* Abrams, 2007. (**PI**) Ages 10–14. Paintings, drawings, and historic political cartoons in the telling of Napoléon's rise and eventual decline, 1769–1821.

Chandra, Deborah, and Madeleine Comora. *George Washington's Teeth.* Illustrated by Brock Cole. Farrar, 2003. (**PI**) Ages 7–11. Washington's lifelong struggle with bad teeth. Humorous story in verse.

Fleming, Candace. *Ben Franklin's Almanac: Being a True Account of the Good Gentleman's Life.* Atheneum, 2003. Ages 11–14.

Fradin, Dennis B. *The Founders: The 39 Stories behind the U.S. Constitution.* Illustrated by Michael McCurdy. Walker, 2005. Ages 10–15.

———. *The Signers: The 56 Stories behind the Declaration of Independence.* Illustrated by Michael McCurdy. Walker, 2002. Ages 10–15.

Freedman, Russell. *Confucius: The Golden Rule.* Illustrated by Frédéric Clément. Scholastic, 2002. (**PI**) Ages 9–14.

———. *Washington at Valley Forge.* Holiday, 2008. Ages 11–15. Revolutionary War, winter of 1777–1778.

Fritz, Jean. *And Then What Happened, Paul Revere?* Illustrated by Tomie dePaola. Coward/McCann, 1973. Ages 8–10.

———. *Can't You Make Them Behave, King George?* Illustrated by Tomie dePaola. Coward/McCann, 1976. Ages 8–10.

———. *The Great Little Madison.* Putnam, 1989. Ages 9–12.

Giblin, James Cross. *The Amazing Life of Benjamin Franklin.* Illustrated by Michael Dooling. Scholastic, 2000. Ages 8–11.

Harness, Cheryl. *The Remarkable Benjamin Franklin.* National Geographic, 2005. (**PI**) Ages 7–11.

Jurmain, Suzanne Tripp. *George Did It.* Illustrated by Larry Day. Dutton, 2005. (**PI**) Ages 7–11.

Lasky, Kathryn. *The Man Who Made Time Travel.* Illustrated by Kevin Hawkes. Farrar, 2003. (**PI**) Ages 8–12.

Marrin, Albert. *George Washington and the Founding of a Nation.* Dutton, 2001. Ages 11–16.

Murphy, Jim. *The Real Benedict Arnold.* Clarion, 2007. Ages 11–16. Examination of rumors and facts about this military leader, Revolutionary War era.

Price, Sean. *Ivan the Terrible: Tsar of Death.* Scholastic, 2007. Ages 11–15. Russia, 1500s.

Reich, Susanna. *Painting the Wild Frontier: The Art and Adventures of George Catlin.* Clarion, 2008. Ages 12–18. Eighteenth-century painter of Native American life.

Rosen, Michael. *Shakespeare: His Work and His World.* Candlewick, 2001. Ages 10–14.

Sís, Peter. *Play, Mozart, Play!* Greenwillow, 2006. (**PI**) Ages 5–8.

Stanley, Diane. *Michelangelo.* HarperCollins, 2000. (**PI**) Ages 9–14.

———. *Saladin: Noble Prince of Islam.* HarperCollins, 2002. (**PI**) Ages 9–14.

The Development of Industrial Society, 1800 to 1914

Historical Fiction

Avi. *Silent Movie.* Illustrated by C. B. Mordan. Atheneum, 2003. (**PI**) Ages 8–12. New York City, Swedish immigrants, early 1900s.

Bartoletti, Susan Campbell. *No Man's Land: A Young Man's Story.* Blue Sky, 1999. Ages 11–15. Confederate Army, Georgia Okefenokee Regiment, U.S. Civil War, 1860s.

Battle-Lavert, Gwendolyn. *Papa's Mark.* Illustrated by Colin Bootman. Holiday, 2003. (**PI**) Ages 6–9. Post–Civil War South, African-American voting.

Blackwood, Gary. *Second Sight.* Dutton, 2005. Ages 11–15. Civil War, 1864.

Boling, Katharine. *January 1905.* Harcourt, 2004. Ages 9–13. U.S. mill town, child labor, 1905.

Brown, Don. *Kid Blink Beats the World.* Roaring Brook, 2004. (**PI**) Ages 7–11. Striking against newspaper owners, 1899.

Byars, Betsy. *Keeper of the Doves.* Viking, 2002. Ages 9–13. Kentucky, 1899.

Cadnum, Michael. *Blood Gold.* Viking, 2004. Ages 12–18. Adventure, California Gold Rush, 1849.

Carvell, Marlene. *Sweetgrass Basket.* Dutton, 2005. Ages 12–15. Native Americans at an off-reservation boarding school, early 1900s.

Curtis, Christopher Paul. *Elijah of Buxton.* Scholastic, 2007. Ages 11–14. Canada, freed slaves in a refuge house, 1849.

Cushman, Karen. *Rodzina.* Clarion, 2003. Ages 9–14. Trip from Chicago to California, orphan train, 1881.

DeFelice, Cynthia. *Bringing Ezra Back.* Farrar, 2006. Ages 9–13. Ohio frontier, 1830s. Sequel to *Weasel.*

———. *Weasel.* Macmillan, 1990. Ages 9–12. Ohio frontier, 1830s.

Donnelly, Jennifer. *A Northern Light.* Harcourt, 2003. Ages 12–16. Mystery and suspense in upstate New York, 1906.

Draper, Sharon M. *Copper Sun.* Atheneum, 2006. Ages 14–18. Carolinas, slave trade and plantation life, early 1800s.

Erdrich, Louise. *The Birchbark House.* Hyperion, 1999. Ages 8–12. Ojibwe family living in northern Wisconsin along Lake Superior.

———. *The Game of Silence.* HarperCollins, 2005. Ages 10–14. Northern Wisconsin, Ojibwes and white settlers, 1850.

———. *The Porcupine Year.* HarperCollins, 2008. Ages 9–14. Displaced Ojibwe family seeking a home, 1852. Sequel to *The Birchbark House* and *The Game of Silence.*

Frost, Helen. *The Braid.* Farrar, 2006. Ages 12–16. Scotland to Canada, 1850s. Verse novel.

Giff, Patricia Reilly. *Maggie's Door.* Random, 2003. Ages 9–13. Ireland, potato famine, immigration, 1840s.

———. *Nory Ryan's Song.* Delacorte, 2000. Ages 9–13. Ireland, potato famine, 1845.

———. *Water Street.* Random, 2006. Ages 9–14. Brooklyn, Irish-American immigrants, 1876.

Hill, Kirkpatrick. *Minuk: Ashes in the Pathway.* Illustrated by Patrick Faricy. Pleasant, 2002. Ages 10–14. Eskimo village in Alaska, 1890.

Holub, Josef. *An Innocent Soldier.* Translated by Michael Hofmann. Scholastic, 2005. Ages 14–18. Napoleon's Russian campaign, 1812.

Hurst, Carol Otis. *Through the Lock.* Houghton, 2001. Ages 10–13. Connecticut farm community, nineteenth century.

Ibbotson, Eva. *Journey to the River Sea.* Dutton, 2002. Ages 11–14. Brazil, 1910.

———. *The Star of Kazan.* Illustrated by Kevin Hawkes. Dutton, 2004. Ages 10–14. Germany and Austria, late 1800s.

LaFaye, A. *Worth.* Simon & Schuster, 2004. Ages 10–14. Orphan train, Nebraska, late 1800s.

Lee, Milly. *Landed.* Illustrated by Yangsook Choi. Farrar, 2006. (**PI**) Ages 7–11. Southeastern China to Angel Island, San Francisco, early 1900s.

Lester, Julius. *Day of Tears: A Novel in Dialogue.* Hyperion, 2005. Ages 12–18. Savannah, Georgia, largest slave auction in American history, 1859.

Levine, Ellen. *Henry's Freedom Box.* Illustrated by Kadir Nelson. Scholastic, 2007. (**PI**) Ages 7–12. Virginia, slavery, 1849.

Lewis, J. Patrick. *The Brothers' War: Civil War Voices in Verse.* National Geographic, 2007. Ages 10–14. Poems honoring heroes of the U.S. Civil War.

Lowry, Lois. *The Silent Boy.* Houghton, 2003. Ages 9–15. Small New England town character with developmental disability, autism, 1908–1911.

Lyons, Mary E. *Dear Ellen Bee: A Civil War Scrapbook of Two Union Spies.* Simon & Schuster, 2000. Ages 10–13. Richmond, Virginia, Civil War era.

McCaughrean, Geraldine. *Stop the Train!* HarperCollins, 2003. Ages 10–13. Homesteading in Enid, Oklahoma, 1893.

McMullan, Margaret. *How I Found the Strong.* Houghton, 2004. Ages 11–15. Civil War battlefield slaughter.

Myers, Anna. *Assassin.* Walker, 2005. Ages 11–15. Alternating narratives. Assassination of Abraham Lincoln, 1865.

Paterson, Katherine. *Bread and Roses, Too.* Clarion, 2006. Ages 10–14. Massachusetts, mill workers' strike, 1912.

———. *Preacher's Boy.* Clarion. 1999. Ages 10–13. Vermont, turn of the century.

Pearsall, Shelley. *Crooked River.* Knopf, 2005. Ages 10–13. Relations between white pioneers and Indians on the Ohio frontier, 1812.

———. *Trouble Don't Last.* Knopf, 2002. Ages 11–15. Northern Kentucky, slavery, 1859.

Peck, Richard. *Fair Weather.* Dial, 2001. Ages 9–12. Rural Illinois in 1893.

———. *The River Between Us.* Dial, 2003. Ages 12–18. Southern Illinois town, early Civil War era, 1861.

———. *The Teacher's Funeral: A Comedy in Three Parts.* Dial, 2004. Ages 10–14. Rural Indiana, 1904. Humorous.

Provensen, Alice. *Klondike Gold.* Simon & Schuster, 2005. (**PI**) Ages 7–10. Canadian Gold Rush in the Yukon Territory, late 1890s.

Raven, Margot T. *Night Boat to Freedom.* Illustrated by E. B. Lewis. Farrar, 2006. (**PI**) Ages 7–10. Slavery, crossing from Kentucky to Ohio.

Reeder, Carolyn. *Before the Creeks Ran Red.* Harper-Collins, 2003. Ages 11–15. Beginning of the U.S. Civil War, three linked novellas set in different locations.

Rinaldi, Ann. *Numbering All the Bones.* Hyperion, 2002. Ages 12–15. U.S. Civil War, Andersonville Prison in southwest Georgia, slavery, 1864.

Robinet, Harriette Gillem. *Missing in Haymarket Square.* Atheneum, 2001. Ages 10–15. Working conditions, Chicago, 1886.

Schmidt, Gary. *Lizzie Bright and the Buckminster Boy.* Clarion, 2004. Ages 12–18. Maine, race relations, Christian life, 1912.

Siegelson, Kim. *Trembling Earth.* Putnam, 2004. Ages 12–18. Okefenokee Swamp, Georgia, U.S. Civil War era, survival story, 1860s.

Snyder, Zilpha Keatley. *Gib Rides Home.* Delacorte, 1998. Ages 9–12. Taken from an orphanage to work on a farm, early 1900s. Sequel is *Gib and the Gray Ghost,* 2000.

Stolz, Joelle. *The Shadows of Ghadames.* Translated by Catherine Temerson. Delacorte, 2004. Ages 12–15. Muslim traditions, sex roles, Libya, late 1800s.

Tal, Eve. *Double Crossing: A Jewish Immigration Story.* Cinco Puntos, 2005. Ages 11–15. Emigration from the Ukraine, 1905.

Taylor, Mildred D. *The Land.* Phyllis Fogelman, 2001. Ages 11–15. The South, post–U.S. Civil War, 1870s.

Wells, Rosemary. *Red Moon at Sharpsburg.* Viking, 2007. Ages 12–15. Virginia, Civil War Stories interwoven from North and South, Battle of Antietam, 1862.

Whelan, Gloria. *Angel on the Square.* HarperCollins, 2001. Ages 11–15. St. Petersburg, Russia, fall of the Russian Empire, 1913.

Wilson, Diane Lee. *Black Storm Comin'.* Simon & Schuster, 2005. Ages 11–16. Missouri to California, Civil War backdrop, mixed-race family, 1860.

Winthrop, Elizabeth. *Counting on Grace.* Random, 2006. Ages 10–15. Laboring in a Vermont mill, 1910.

Woodson, Jacqueline. *Show Way.* Illustrated by Hudson Talbott. Putnam, 2005. (**PI**) Ages 8–11. African-American women's stories on quilts; slavery through the Civil Rights period.

Yep, Laurence. *Spring Pearl.* Pleasant, 2002. Ages 9–14. Canton, China, Opium Wars, 1857.

———. *The Traitor.* Farrar, 2003. Ages 10–14. Chinese and Western coal miners in the Wyoming Territory, 1885.

Yin. *Coolies.* Illustrated by Chris Soentpiet. Philomel, 2001. (**PI**) Ages 8–12. Chinese Americans, transcontinental railroad, 1860s.

Zimmer, Tracie Vaughn. *The Floating Circus.* Bloomsbury, 2008. Ages 11–16. A circus barge from Pittsburgh to New Orleans, 1850s.

Biography

Adler, David A. *America's Champion Swimmer: Gertrude Ederle.* Illustrated by Terry Widener. Harcourt, 2000. Ages 6–10.

Armstrong, Jennifer. *Photo by Brady: A Picture of the Civil War.* Atheneum, 2005. Ages 12–14. Photoessay.

Basel, Roberta. *Sequoyah: Inventor of Written Cherokee.* Compass Point Books, 2007. Ages 10–14. Invention of a Cherokee syllabary, 1821.

Blumberg, Rhoda. *Shipwrecked! The True Adventures of a Japanese Boy.* HarperCollins, 2001. Ages 10–14.

———. *York's Adventures with Lewis and Clark: An African-American's Part in the Great Expedition.* HarperCollins, 2004. Ages 11–15.

Bolden, Tonya. *Maritcha: A Nineteenth-Century American Girl.* Abrams, 2005. Ages 10–14.

Borden, Louise. *A. Lincoln and Me.* Illustrated by Ted Lewin. Scholastic, 1999. (**PI**) Ages 5–8.

Brown, Don. *Uncommon Traveler: Mary Kingsley in Africa.* Houghton, 2000. Ages 7–10.

Brown, Mónica. *My Name Is Gabriela/Me llamo Gabriela: The Life of Gabriela Mistral/La vida de Gabriela Mistral.* Illustrated by John Parra. Luna Rising, 2005. (**PI**) Ages 5–7. Bilingual English/Spanish.

Burleigh, Robert. *Toulouse-Lautrec: The Moulin Rouge and the City of Light.* Abrams, 2005. (**PI**) Ages 8–14.

Capaldi, Gina. *A Boy Named Beckoning: The True Story of Dr. Carlos Montezuma, a Native American Hero.* Carolrhoda, 2008. (**PI**) Ages 7–10. A kidnapped Yavapi Indian from Arizona, an advocate for Native Americans, late 1800s.

Cohn, Amy L., and Suzy Schmidt. *Abraham Lincoln.* Illustrated by David A. Johnson. Scholastic, 2002. (**PI**) Ages 7–11.

Cummins, Julie. *Women Daredevils: Thrills, Chills, and Frills.* Illustrated by Cheryl Harness. Dutton, 2007. (**PI**) Ages 8–12. Collective biography of stunt performers, 1880–1929.

Debon, Nicolas. *The Strongest Man in the World: Louis Cyr.* Groundwood, 2007. (**GR**) Ages 7–11.

Denenberg, Barry. *Lincoln Shot: A President's Life Remembered.* Illustrated by Christopher Bing. Feiwel & Friends, 2008. Ages 10–15. Oversize book with striking newspaper-format pages on Lincoln's life.

Dooling, Michael. *Young Thomas Edison.* Holiday, 2005. (**PI**) Ages 7–11.

Engle, Margarita. *The Poet Slave of Cuba: A Biography of Juan Francisco Manzano.* Illustrated by Sean Qualls. Holt, 2006. (**PI**) Ages 12–14. Free verse.

Fleischman, Sid. *The Trouble Begins at 8: A Life of Mark Twain in the Wild, Wild West.* HarperCollins, 2008. Ages 10–15.

Fleming, Candace. *The Lincolns: A Scrapbook Look at Abraham and Mary.* Random, 2008. Ages 11–15. Chapters alternate between husband and wife.

Fradin, Dennis B. *Duel! Burr and Hamilton's Deadly War of Words.* Illustrated by Larry Day. Walker, 2008. (**PI**) Ages 8–11. The famous Weehawken, New Jersey, duel, 1804.

———, and Judith B. Fradin. *Ida B. Wells: Mother of the Civil Rights Movement.* Clarion, 2000. Ages 10–15.

Fradin, Judith B., and Dennis B. Fradin. *5,000 Miles to Freedom: Ellen and William Craft's Flight from Slavery.* National Geographic, 2006. Ages 12–15.

———. *Jane Addams: Champion of Democracy.* Clarion, 2006. Ages 12–14.

Freedman, Russell. *Lincoln: A Photobiography.* Clarion, 1987. Ages 9–12.

Giblin, James Cross. *Good Brother, Bad Brother: The Story of Edwin Booth and John Wilkes Booth.* Clarion, 2005. Ages 11–14.

Greenberg, Jan, and Sandra Jordan. *Vincent Van Gogh: Portrait of an Artist.* Delacorte, 2001. Ages 10–18.

Helfer, Ralph. *The World's Greatest Elephant.* Illustrated by Ted Lewin. Philomel, 2006. (**PI**) Ages 7–12.

Hesse, Karen. *The Young Hans Christian Andersen.* Illustrated by Erik Blegvad. Scholastic, 2005. Ages 7–10.

Hopkinson, Deborah. *Fannie in the Kitchen: The Whole Story from Soup to Nuts of How Fannie Farmer Invented Recipes with Precise Measurements.* Illustrated by Nancy Carpenter. Atheneum, 2001. (**PI**) Ages 6–8.

Johnson, Dolores. *Onward: A Photobiography of African-American Polar Explorer Matthew Henson.* National Geographic, 2005. Ages 11–14.

Jurmain, Suzanne. *The Forbidden Schoolhouse: The True and Dramatic Story of Prudence Crandall and Her Students.* Houghton, 2005. Ages 12–14.

Keating, Frank. *Theodore.* Illustrated by Mike Wimmer. Simon & Schuster, 2006. (**PI**) Ages 7–12.

Kerley, Barbara. *Walt Whitman: Words for America.* Illustrated by Brian Selznick. Scholastic, 2006. (**PI**) Ages 9–12.

———. *What to Do about Alice? How Alice Roosevelt Broke the Rules, Charmed the World, and Drove Her Father Crazy.* Illustrated by Edwin Fotheringham. Scholastic, 2008. (**PI**) Ages 5–10. President Theodore Roosevelt's daughter in the White House.

Kraft, Betsy H. *Theodore Roosevelt: Champion of the American Spirit.* Clarion, 2003. Ages 10–14.

Lasky, Kathryn. *Vision of Beauty: The Story of Virginia Breedlove Walker.* Illustrated by Nneka Bennett. Candlewick, 2000. Ages 8–11.

Lutes, Jason, and Nick Bertozzi. *Houdini: The Handcuff King.* Hyperion, 2007. (**GR**) Ages 11–15. Cambridge, Massachusetts, 1908.

Marrin, Albert. *Sitting Bull and His World.* Dutton, 2000. Ages 11–18.

McClafferty, Carla Killough. *Something Out of Nothing: Marie Curie and Radium.* Farrar, 2006. Ages 12–16.

McCully, Emily Arnold. *Marvelous Mattie: How Margaret E. Knight Became an Inventor.* Farrar, 2006. (**PI**) Ages 5–8.

Nelson, Marilyn. *Fortune's Bones: The Manumission Requiem.* Front Street, 2004. Ages 12–18. Poetry.

Old, Wendie C. *To Fly: The Story of the Wright Brothers.* Illustrated by Robert Andrew Parker. Clarion, 2002. (**PI**) Ages 8–11.

Paulsen, Gary. *The Legend of Bass Reeves.* Random, 2006. Ages 11–14.

Place, François. *The Old Man Mad about Drawing: A Tale of Hokusai.* Translated by William Rodarmor. Godine, 2003. Ages 10–14.

Rappaport, Doreen. *Abe's Honest Words: The Life of Abraham Lincoln.* Illustrated by Gary Kelley. Hyperion, 2008. (**PI**) Ages 6–10. Lincoln's life with quotations from his speeches and writings.

Ray, Deborah Kogan. *Down the Colorado: John Wesley Powell, the One-Armed Explorer.* Farrar, 2007. (**PI**) Ages 8–11. Western exploration, 1869.

Rockwell, Anne. *Only Passing Through: The Story of Sojourner Truth.* Illustrated by R. Gregory Christie. Knopf, 2000. (**PI**) Ages 8–13. Slavery and the Abolitionist Movement, mid-1800s.

Rosen, Michael. *Dickens: His Work and His World.* Illustrated by Robert Ingpen. Candlewick, 2005. Ages 11–14.

Rumford, James. *Sequoyah: The Man Who Gave His People Writing.* Houghton, 2004. (**PI**) Ages 6–10.

Sandler, Martin W. *Lincoln through the Lens: How Photography Revealed and Shaped an Extraordinary Life.* Walker, 2008. Ages 12–15. Lincoln's life, 1809–1865.

Silverman, Erica. *Sholom's Treasure: How Sholom Aleichem Became a Writer.* Illustrated by Mordicai Gerstein. Farrar, 2005. (**PI**) Ages 5–9.

Sís, Peter. *The Tree of Life.* Farrar, 2003. (**PI**) Ages 12–16. Charles Darwin.

Varmer, Hjørdis. *Hans Christian Andersen: His Fairy Tale Life.* Translated by Tiina Nunnally. Illustrated by Lillian Brøgger. Groundwood, 2005. Ages 10–14.

Weatherford, Carole B. *Moses: When Harriet Tubman Led Her People to Freedom.* Illustrated by Kadir Nelson. Jump at the Sun, 2006. (**PI**) Ages 7–11.

White, Linda Arms. *I Could Do That! Esther Morris Gets Women the Vote.* Illustrated by Nancy Carpenter. Farrar, 2005. (**PI**) Ages 7–10.

World Wars in the Twentieth Century, 1914 to 1945

Historical Fiction

Adler, David A. *The Babe and I.* Illustrated by David Widener. Harcourt, 1999. (**PI**) Ages 9–13. Bronx, New York, Depression era.

Bat-Ami, Miriam. *Two Suns in the Sky.* Front Street, 1999. Ages 13–16. World War II in New York state, relations among European refugees and U.S. citizens.

Cormier, Robert. *Frenchtown Summer.* Delacorte, 1999. Ages 11–14. Monument, Massachusetts, post–World War I.

Currier, Katrina Saltonstall. *Kai's Journey to Gold Mountain.* Illustrated by Gabhor Utomo. Angel Island, 2005. Ages 9–13. (**PI**) Emigration from China, internment on Angel Island, 1934.

Curtis, Christopher Paul. *Bud, Not Buddy.* Delacorte, 1999. Ages 9–13. Michigan, Depression era.

Doucet, Sharon Arms. *Fiddle Fever.* Clarion, 2000. Ages 9–13. Cajun life in southern Louisiana, World War I.

Dowell, Frances O'Roark. *Dovey Coe.* Atheneum, 2000. Ages 9–13. North Carolina, 1928 murder trial.

Fuqua, Jonathon Scott. *Darby.* Candlewick, 2000. Ages 9–12. South Carolina, racism, 1926.

Giff, Patricia Reilly. *Willow Run.* Random, 2005. Ages 9–12. World War II, homefront deprivations.

Glatshteyn, Yankev. *Emil and Karl.* Translated by Jeffrey Shandler. Roaring Brook, 2006. Ages 10–15. Pre–World War II Vienna, Nazi persecution, 1930s.

Hartnett, Sonya. *Thursday's Child.* Candlewick, 2002. Ages 12–16. Australia, Great Depression.

Havill, Juanita. *Eyes Like Willy's.* Illustrated by David Johnson. HarperCollins, 2004. Ages 12–16. Austrian and French friends on opposite sides, World War I era.

Hesse, Karen. *The Cats in Krasinski Square.* Illustrated by Wendy Watson. Scholastic, 2004. (**PI**) Ages 9–12. Nazi occupation of Warsaw, Jewish ghetto, World War II era. Free verse.

———. *Out of the Dust.* Scholastic, 1997. Ages 11–18. Oklahoma, 1930s. Free verse.

———. *Witness.* Scholastic, 2001. Ages 10–18. Vermont, Ku Klux Klan, 1924. Told in a series of poems in five acts.

Hughes, Dean. *Soldier Boys.* Atheneum, 2001. Ages 13–18. An American and a German in World War II era. Chapters alternate point of view.

Hull, N. L. *On Rough Seas.* Clarion, 2008. Ages 9–13. England to Dunkirk, World War II, 1939.

Janeczko, Paul B. *Worlds Afire.* Candlewick, 2004. Ages 12–15. Hartford, Connecticut, fire, 1944. Narrative poems.

Kadohata, Cynthia. *Weedflower.* Simon & Schuster, 2006. Ages 10–14. An internment camp in Arizona desert, Japanese American family, World War II era.

Larson, Kirby. *Hattie Big Sky.* Delacorte, 2006. Ages 11–15. Homesteading in Montana, discrimination toward Germans during World War I, 1918.

Lawrence, Iain. *B for Buster.* Delacorte, 2004. Ages 12–18. Canadian Air Force, World War II, deployment to England for raids over Germany, 1943.

———. *Land of the Nutcracker Men.* Delacorte, 2001. Ages 11–15. England and France, World War I.

Lisle, Janet Taylor. *The Art of Keeping Cool.* Simon & Schuster, 2000. Ages 10–13. United States and Canada, World War II.

Maguire, Gregory. *The Good Liar.* Clarion, 1999. Ages 9–12. Occupied France, World War II.

Mazer, Norma Fox. *Good Night, Maman.* Harcourt, 1999. Ages 10–14. Oswego, New York, Holocaust survivors, Jewish refugees, World War II era.

Mikaelsen, Ben. *Petey.* Hyperion, 1998. Ages 11–15. Cerebral palsy and its treatment, 1920s.

Morpurgo, Michael. *Private Peaceful.* Scholastic, 2004. Ages 13–18. England and France, World War I era.

Park, Linda Sue. *When My Name Was Keoko: A Novel of Korea in World War II.* Clarion, 2002. Ages 10–14. Japanese occupation of Korea, 1940s.

Parkinson, Siobhan. *Kathleen: The Celtic Knot.* Pleasant, 2003. Ages 10–14. Ireland, poverty in Dublin, 1937.

Peck, Richard. *Here Lies the Librarian.* Dial, 2006. Ages 11–16. Rural Indiana, 1914. Humorous.

———. *A Year Down Yonder.* Dial, 2000. Ages 10–15. Southern Illinois, Depression era, 1937. Humorous.

Peck, Robert Newton. *Horse Thief.* HarperCollins, 2002. Ages 13–18. Florida, Depression era, 1930s.

Polacco, Patricia. *The Butterfly.* Philomel, 2000. (**PI**) Ages 9–12. French Resistance, persecution of Jews, World War II.

Ray, Delia. *Ghost Girl: A Blue Ridge Mountain Story.* Clarion, 2003. Ages 10–13. Virginia, 1929–1932.

Roy, Jennifer. *Yellow Star.* Marshall Cavendish, 2006. Ages 10–15. Poland, Nazi occupation of the Lodz ghetto, 1939–1945.

Ryan, Pam Muñoz. *Esperanza Rising.* Scholastic, 2000. Ages 9–13. Mexico and United States, Depression era.

Salisbury, Graham. *Eyes of the Emperor.* Random, 2005. Ages 12–18. Japanese American in World War II, prejudice, training scout dogs.

———. *House of the Red Fish.* Random, 2006. Ages 10–15. Sequel to *Under the Blood-Red Sun.*

Selznick, Brian. *The Invention of Hugo Cabret.* Scholastic, 2007. Ages 9–13. Paris, illustrated cinematic mystery, 1930s.

Sheth, Kashmira. *Keeping Corner.* Hyperion, 2007. Ages 12–18. Rural India, 1918.

Spillebeen, Geert. *Kipling's Choice.* Translated by Terese Edelstein. Houghton, 2005. Ages 12–16. France, World War I, with an epilogue that provides historical context.

Spinelli, Jerry. *Milkweed.* Random, 2003. Ages 11–16. Warsaw, persecution of Jews, 1940s.

Uchida, Yoshiko. *Journey to Topaz.* Illustrated by Donald Carrick. Scribner's, 1971. Ages 10–14. United States, internment of Japanese Americans, World War II.

Wells, Rosemary. *Wingwalker.* Illustrated by Brian Selznick. Hyperion, 2002. Ages 8–11. Oklahoma, Depression era, 1930s.

Whelan, Gloria. *Burying the Sun.* HarperCollins, 2004. Ages 10–14. World War II, German occupation, Leningrad, 1941.

———. *The Impossible Journey.* HarperCollins, 2003. Ages 10–14. Opposition to Stalin, journey into Siberia, 1934.

Wolf, Joan M. *Someone Named Eve.* Clarion, 2007. Ages 11–16. Czechoslovakian survivor in a German family, World War II, 1942.

Woodson, Jacqueline. *Coming On Home Soon.* Illustrated by E. B. Lewis. Putnam, 2004. (**PI**) Ages 5–9. African-American mother in Chicago for the war effort, World War II.

Zusak, Markus. *The Book Thief.* Knopf, 2006. Ages 13–18. Munich, Germany, German foster girl, World II.

Biography

Adler, David A. *Lou Gehrig: The Luckiest Man.* Illustrated by Terry Widener. Harcourt, 1997. Ages 8–11.

Anderson, M. T. *Strange Mr. Satie.* Illustrated by Petra Mathers. Viking, 2003. (**PI**) Ages 8–12.

Barbour, Karen. *Mr. Williams.* Holt, 2005. (**PI**) Ages 5–8.

Bartoletti, Susan Campbell. *Hitler Youth: Growing Up in Hitler's Shadow.* Scholastic, 2005. Ages 11–14.

Bausum, Ann. *Dragon Bones and Dinosaur Eggs: A Photobiography of Explorer Roy Chapman Andrews.* National Geographic, 2000. Ages 9–15.

Bernier-Grand, Carmen T. *Frida: Viva la Vida! Long Live Life!* Illustrated by Frida Kahlo. Marshall Cavendish, 2007. (**PI**) Ages 12–18. Mexican artist, 1907–1954. Free verse.

Bolden, Tonya. *George Washington Carver.* Abrams Books, 2008. (PI) Ages 8–12. African-American scientist and inventor, 1864–1943.

Brown, Don. *Mack Made Movies.* Millbrook, 2003. (PI) Ages 6–10.

Christensen, Bonnie. *Woody Guthrie: Poet of the People.* Knopf, 2001. (PI) Ages 6–8.

Cline-Ransome, Lesa. *Satchel Paige.* Illustrated by James Ransome. Simon & Schuster, 2000. (PI) Ages 7–10.

Currier, Katrina Saltonstall. *Kai's Journey to Gold Mountain: An Angel Island Story.* Illustrated by Gabhor Utomo. Angel Island Association, 2004. (PI) Ages 9–13.

Denenberg, Barry. *Shadow Life: A Portrait of Anne Frank and Her Family.* Scholastic, 2005. Ages 12–14.

dePaola, Tomie. *26 Fairmount Avenue.* Putnam, 1999. Ages 7–9.

Fleischman, Sid. *Escape! The Story of the Great Houdini.* Greenwillow, 2006. Ages 10–14.

Fleming, Candace. *Our Eleanor: A Scrapbook Look at Eleanor Roosevelt's Remarkable Life.* Atheneum, 2005. Ages 11–14.

Grimes, Nikki. *Talkin' about Bessie: The Story of Aviator Elizabeth Coleman.* Illustrated by E. B. Lewis. Scholastic/Orchard, 2002. (PI) Ages 8–13.

Krinitz, Esther N., and Bernice Steinhardt. *Memories of Survival.* Hyperion, 2005. Ages 10–12.

Maurer, Richard. *The Wright Sister.* Millbrook, 2003. Ages 12–16.

McCarthy, Meghan. *Strong Man: The Story of Charles Atlas.* Knopf, 2007. (PI) Ages 6–9. Transformation of a weakling to a fitness legend.

Millman, Isaac. *Hidden Child.* Farrar, 2005. (PI) Ages 11–14. Autobiography.

Nelson, Marilyn. *Carver: A Life in Poems.* Front Street, 2000. Ages 12–16. Free verse.

Nobleman, Marc Tyler. *Boys of Steel: The Creators of Superman.* Illustrated by Ross MacDonald. Knopf, 2008. (PI) Ages 6–8. Inventors of the fictional cartoon character, 1930s.

Parker, Robert Andrew. *Piano Starts Here: The Young Art Tatum.* Schwartz & Wade, 2008. (PI) Ages 6–10. African-American jazz musician, 1910–1956.

Partridge, Elizabeth. *This Land Was Made for You and Me: The Life and Songs of Woody Guthrie.* Viking, 2002. Ages 11–16.

Poole, Josephine. *Anne Frank.* Illustrated by Angela Barrett. Knopf, 2005. (PI) Ages 11–13.

Rubin, Susan Goldman, with Ela Weissberger. *The Cat with the Yellow Star: Coming of Age in Terezin.* Holiday, 2006. Ages 9–13.

Russo, Marisabina. *Always Remember Me: How One Family Survived World War II.* Atheneum, 2005. Ages 8–12.

Ryan, Pam Muñoz. *When Marian Sang: The True Recital of Marian Anderson.* Illustrated by Brian Selznick. Scholastic, 2002. (PI) Ages 6–10.

Stone, Tanya Lee. *Sandy's Circus: A Story about Alexander Calder.* Illustrated by Boris Kulikov. Viking, 2008. (PI) Ages 5–9. Artist Calder's wire sculptures, Paris, 1920s.

Whiteman, Dorit Bader. *Lonek's Journey: The True Story of a Boy's Escape to Freedom.* Star Bright, 2005. Ages 11–14.

Yoo, Paula. *Sixteen Years in Sixteen Seconds: The Sammy Lee Story.* Illustrated by Dom Lee. Lee & Low, 2005. (PI) Ages 6–10.

Post-World War II Era, 1945 to 1980s

Historical Fiction

Clinton, Catherine. *A Stone in My Hand.* Candlewick, 2002. Ages 11–16. Palestine, 1980s.

Curtis, Christopher Paul. *The Watsons Go to Birmingham—1963.* Delacorte, 1995. Ages 8–12. Flint, Michigan, to Birmingham, Alabama, Civil Rights Movement.

Cushman, Karen. *The Loud Silence of Francine Green.* Clarion, 2006. Ages 11–15. McCarthyism in Los Angeles, 1950s.

Going, K. L. *The Liberation of Gabriel King.* Putnam, 2005. Ages 9–12. Georgia, facing prejudice, 1976.

Harrington, Janice N. *Going North.* Illustrated by Jerome Lagarrigue. Farrar, 2004. (PI) Ages 7–11. African-American family leaves Alabama for jobs, 1964.

Herrera, Juan Felipe. *Downtown Boy.* Scholastic, 2005. Ages 10–14. Free verse. Migrant workers in California, 1958–1959.

Hobbs, Valerie. *Sonny's War.* Farrar, 2002. Ages 12–16. California, Vietnam War era, 1966.

Holt, Kimberly Willis. *Dancing in Cadillac Light.* Putnam, 2001. Ages 11–14. Texas, small town life, 1968.

———. *When Zachary Beaver Came to Town.* Holt, 1999. Ages 10–14. Small-town Texas, Vietnam War era, 1971.

Houston, Julian. *New Boy.* Houghton, 2005. Ages 13–18. Civil rights struggle, first black student in a Connecticut boarding school, late 1950s.

Johnston, Tony. *Bone by Bone by Bone.* Roaring Brook, 2007. Ages 11–16. Race relations in Tennessee, 1950s.

Kadohata, Cynthia. *Kira-Kira.* Simon & Schuster, 2004. Ages 11–18. Small-town Georgia, Japanese Americans, late 1950s.

Lawrence, Iain. *Ghost Boy.* Delacorte, 2000. Ages 13–18. Death of a parent in World War II, joining a circus, late 1940s.

Levine, Ellen. *Catch a Tiger by the Toe.* Viking, 2005. Ages 10–14. McCarthy hearings, Communism, issues of freedom of expression, 1953.

Lorbiecki, Marybeth. *Jackie's Bat.* Illustrated by Brian Pinkney. Simon & Schuster, 2003. (**PI**) Ages 6–9. Jackie Robinson and the Brooklyn Dodgers, 1947.

Lyon, George Ella. *Sonny's House of Spies.* Simon & Schuster, 2004. Ages 12–15. Alabama, family secrets, homosexual father, 1940s and 1950s.

Mah, Adeline Yen. *Chinese Cinderella: The True Story of an Unwanted Daughter.* Delacorte, 1999. Ages 12–18. China, 1940s and 1950s.

Mankell, Henning. *Secrets in the Fire.* Translated by Anne Connie Stuksrud. Annick, 2003. Ages 11–14. Southern Africa, land mines, poverty, Mozambique civil war, 1970s and 1980s.

Martin, Ann M. *Belle Teal.* Scholastic, 2001. Ages 9–12. Rural South, 1962.

———. *A Corner of the Universe.* Scholastic, 2002. Ages 9–13. Small town, 1960.

Nuzum, K. A. *A Small White Scar.* HarperCollins, 2006. Ages 11–14. Colorado rodeo life, 1940s.

Sharenow, Robert. *My Mother the Cheerleader.* HarperTeen, 2007. Ages 12–15. A court-ordered integration of a school, New Orleans, 1960.

Veciana-Suarez, Ana. *Flight to Freedom.* Orchard, 2002. Ages 11–16. Cuban immigrant to Miami, 1967.

White, Ruth. *Little Audrey.* Farrar, 2008. Ages 9–13. Poverty in a Virginia coal-mining camp, 1948.

———. *Memories of Summer.* Farrar, 2000. Ages 13–18. Virginia and Michigan, 1950s.

———. *The Search for Belle Prater.* Farrar, 2005. Ages 10–15. Sequel to *Belle Prater's Boy,* 1996.

———. *Tadpole.* Farrar, 2003. Ages 10–15. Appalachian mountains, 1950s.

Biography

Adler, David A. *A Picture Book of Dwight David Eisenhower.* Holiday, 2002. Ages 7–9.

Aldrin, Buzz. *Reaching for the Moon.* Illustrated by Wendell Minor. HarperCollins, 2005. (**PI**) Ages 7–10. Autobiography.

Barakat, Ibtisam. *Tasting the Sky: A Palestinian Childhood.* Farrar, 2007. Ages 12–16. Memoir of a life under military occupation in Palestine, 1961–1987.

Bausum, Ann. *Freedom Riders: John Lewis and Jim Zwerg on the Front Lines of the Civil Rights Movement.* National Geographic, 2005. Ages 12–15.

Bernier-Grand, Carmen T. *César: ¡Sí, Se Puede!/Yes, We Can!* Illustrated by David Diaz. Marshall Cavendish, 2005. (**PI**) Ages 9–12.

Bridges, Ruby, and Margo Lundell. *Through My Eyes.* Scholastic, 1999. Ages 9–16.

Brimner, Larry D. *We Are One: The Story of Bayard Rustin.* Boyds Mills, 2007. Ages 11–16. Civil rights activist from 1940s to 1980s.

Budhos, Marina. *Ask Me No Questions.* Simon & Schuster, 2005. Ages 12–15.

Chin-Lee, Cynthia. *Amelia to Zora: Twenty-Six Women Who Changed the World.* Charlesbridge, 2005. Ages 9–13.

Cline-Ransome, Lesa. *Young Pelé: Soccer's First Star.* Illustrated by James E. Ransome. Random, 2007. (**PI**) Ages 5–9. Small-town Brazilian soccer star, 1950s–1970s.

Delano, Marfé F. *Genius: A Photobiography of Albert Einstein.* National Geographic, 2005. Ages 11–14.

Dendy, Leslie, and Mel Boring. *Guinea Pig Scientists: Bold Self-Experimenters of Science and Medicine.* Holt, 2005. (**COL**) Ages 11–14.

Ellis, Deborah. *Our Stories, Our Songs: African Children Talk about AIDS.* Fitzhenry & Whiteside (Canada), 2005. Ages 12–15.

Fradin, Dennis Brindell. *With a Little Luck: Surprising Stories of Amazing Discovery.* Dutton, 2006. (**COL**) Ages 12–14.

Freedman, Russell. *Babe Didrikson Zaharias: The Making of a Champion.* Clarion, 1999. Ages 10–15.

———. *The Voice that Challenged a Nation: Marian Anderson and the Struggle for Equal Rights.* Clarion, 2004. Ages 11–14.

Giovanni, Nikki. *Rosa.* Illustrated by Bryan Collier. Holt, 2005. (**PI**) Ages 8–11.

Govenar, Alan. *Osceola: Memories of a Sharecropper's Daughter.* Illustrated by Shane W. Evans. Jump at the Sun, 2000. Ages 8–12.

Greenberg, Jan, and Sandra Jordan. *Action Jackson.* Illustrated by Robert Andrew Parker. Millbrook, 2002. (**PI**) Ages 7–10.

———. *Frank O. Gehry: Outside In.* DK Ink, 2000. Ages 9–14.

———. *Runaway Girl: The Artist Louise Bourgeois.* Abrams, 2003. Ages 12–16.

Hoose, Phillip. *We Were There, Too! Young People in U.S. History.* Farrar, 2001. Ages 10–13. A collective biography of 60 young people of all ages, colors, and historical eras who influenced their times.

Howard, Helen. *Living as a Refugee in America: Mohammed's Story.* World Almanac Library, 2005. Ages 12–14. Part of Children in Crisis series.

Levine, Ellen. *Rachel Carson.* Viking, 2007. Ages 10–16. Marine biologist and author of *Silent Spring*, 1962. Part of the Up Close biography series.

Li, Moying. *Snow Falling in Spring: Coming of Age in China during the Cultural Revolution.* Farrar, 2008. Ages 12–18. Memoir, 1966–1976.

McDonough, Yona Zeldis. *Hammerin' Hank: The Life of Hank Greenberg.* Illustrated by Malcah Zeldis. Walker, 2006. (**PI**) Ages 7–12.

Niven, Penelope. *Carl Sandburg: Adventures of a Poet.* Illustrated by Marc Nadel. Harcourt, 2003. (**PI**) Ages 7–11.

Nivola, Claire A. *Planting the Trees of Kenya: The Story of Wangari Maathi.* Farrar, 2008. (**PI**) Ages 6–9. Environmental leader in East Africa who led a reforestation project in the 1980s.

Pinkney, Andrea Davis. *Duke Ellington: The Piano Prince and His Orchestra.* Illustrated by Brian Pinkney. Hyperion, 1998. (**PI**) Ages 8–11.

Rappaport, Doreen. *Martin's Big Words: The Life of Dr. Martin Luther King, Jr.* Illustrated by Bryan Collier. Hyperion, 2001. (**PI**) Ages 8–10.

Rembert, Winfred. *Don't Hold Me Back: My Life and Art.* Cricket, 2003. (**PI**) Ages 9–13. Autobiography.

Ringgold, Faith. *If a Bus Could Talk: The Story of Rosa Parks.* Simon & Schuster, 1999. Ages 5–9.

Scieszka, Jon, editor. *Guys Write for Guys Read: Boys' Favorite Authors Write about Being Boys.* Viking, 2005. (**COL**) Ages 11–14.

Sís, Peter. *The Wall: Growing Up behind the Iron Curtain.* Farrar, 2007. Ages 10–15. (**PI/GR**) Autobiography.

Winter, Jonah. *Dizzy.* Illustrated by Sean Qualls. Scholastic, 2006. (**PI**) Ages 8–14.

———. *Roberto Clemente: Pride of the Pittsburgh Pirates.* Illustrated by Raúl Colón. Atheneum, 2005. (**PI**) Ages 7–11.

Related Films, Videos, and DVDs

Historical Fiction

The Boy in the Striped Pajamas. (2008). Author: John Boyne (2006). 90 minutes.

Civil War Diary. (1991). Author: Irene Hunt, *Across Five Aprils* (1964). 82 minutes.

The December Boys. (2007). Author: Michael Noonan (1990/2008). 105 minutes.

The Devil's Arithmetic. (1999). Author: Jane Yolen (1988). 97 minutes.

Lyddie. (1995). Author: Katherine Paterson (1991). 90 minutes.

A Midwife's Tale. (1997). Author: Laurel Ulrich (1990). 88 minutes.

My Louisiana Sky. (2001). Author: Kimberly Willis Holt (1998). 98 minutes.

A Picture of Freedom. (1999). Author: Patricia McKissack (1997). Dear America Series. 30 minutes.

Sarah, Plain and Tall. (1991). Author: Patricia MacLachlan (1985). 98 minutes.

Seabiscuit. (2003). Author: Laura Hildenbrand (2001). 141 minutes.

The Sign of the Beaver. (1996). Author: Elizabeth George Speare (1983). 100 minutes.

Skylark. (1999). Author: Patricia MacLachlan (1994). 98 minutes.

So Far from Home. (1999). Author: Barry Denenberg (1997). Dear America Series. 30 minutes.

Sounder. (2003). Author: William H. Armstrong (1969). 90 minutes.

Standing in the Light. (1999). Author: Mary Pope Osborne (1998). Dear America Series. 30 minutes.

Winter of the Red Snow. (1999). Author: Kristiana Gregory (1996). Dear America Series. 30 minutes.

Biography

The Diary of Anne Frank. (1959). Author: Anne Frank (1953). 171 minutes.

Just a Few Words, Mr. Lincoln. (1999). Author: Jean Fritz (1993). Illustrator: Charles Robinson. 21 minutes.

The Man Who Walked between the Towers. (2005). Author/Illustrator: Mordicai Gerstein (2003). 10 minutes.

Snowflake Bentley. (2003). Author: Jacqueline Briggs Martin (1998). Illustrator: Mary Azarian. 16 minutes.

What's the Big Idea, Ben Franklin? (1993). Author: Jean Fritz (1996). Illustrator: Margot Tomes. 30 minutes.

Will You Sign Here, John Hancock? (1997). Author: Jean Fritz (1997). Illustrator: Trina Schart Hyman. 30 minutes.

Sources for Films, Videos, and DVDs

The Video Source Book. Syosset, NY: National Video Clearinghouse, 1979–. Published by Gale Research, Detroit, MI.

An annual reference work that lists media and provides sources for purchase and rental.

Websites of large video distributors:
www.libraryvideo.com
www.knowledgeunlimited.com
http://teacher.scholastic.com/products/westonwoods

PEARSON
myeducationkit™ Now go to Chapter 9 in the MyEducationKit (www.myeducationkit .com) for your book, where you can:

- Complete Assignments and Activities that can enrich and extend your knowledge of chapter content.

- Expand your knowledge with content-specific Web Links.

- Learn how authors and illustrators apply their craft by reading the written interviews in the Conversations section for the chapter.

- Review the chapter content by going to the Study Plan, taking a chapter quiz, and receiving feedback on your answers.

- Access the Children's Literature Database for your own exploration.

chapter TEN

Informational Books

Questions at Night

Why
Is the sky?

What starts the thunder overhead?
Who makes the crashing noise?
Are the angels falling out of bed?
Are they breaking all their toys?

Why does the sun go down so soon?
Why do the night-clouds crawl
Hungrily up to the new-laid moon
And swallow it, shell and all?

If there's a bear among the stars,
As all the people say,
Won't he jump over those pasture-bars
And drink up the Milky Way?

Does every star that happens to fall
Turn into a firefly?
Can't it ever get back to Heaven at all?
And why
Is the sky?

—*Louis Untermeyer*

Children are naturally curious. Their interest in the world around them is boundless. Teachers, librarians, and parents want to nourish that curiosity with lively, intelligent answers, provocative questions, and stimulating books that provide answers and a thirst for further knowledge. Today's innovative, colorful, and intriguing informational books are excellent resources for children and the adults who guide their learning.

Definition and Description

Informational books give factual information about or explain any aspect of the biological, social, or physical world, including what is known of outer space. They can be further defined in terms of emphasis: The content emphasis of children's informational literature is documented fact about the natural or social world. Its primary purpose is to inform. In contrast, the content of fictional literature is largely, if not wholly, a product of the imagination, and its purpose is to entertain. Writing in informational books is often referred to as *expository writing,* or writing that explains, whereas fiction writing is called *narrative writing,* or writing that tells a story.

   Some countries now recognize a type of literature that has elements of both fiction and nonfiction, called *faction.* Faction presents accurate factual information on an entertaining ribbon of fiction. The popular, science-based Magic School Bus books by Joanna Cole are excellent examples of faction. In North America, faction is treated as a part of informational literature.

Elements of Informational Literature

Understanding the parts, or elements, of informational books and how they work together can help you become more analytical about this kind of literature. This knowledge can also improve your judgment when evaluating and selecting informational literature.

Structure

Structure has to do with how the author organizes the information to be presented. Most informational literature is structured in one or more of the following ways:

- *Description.* The author gives the characteristics of the topic (e.g., *Spiders* by Nic Bishop).
- *Sequence.* The author lists items in order, usually chronologically or numerically (e.g., *All Stations! Distress! April 15, 1912: The Day the Titanic Sank* by Don Brown).
- *Comparison.* The author juxtaposes two or more entities and lists their similarities and differences (e.g., *Wild Tracks! A Guide to Nature's Footprints* by Jim Arnosky).
- *Cause and Effect.* The author states an action and then shows the effect, or result, of this action (e.g., *Blizzard! The Storm That Changed America* by Jim Murphy).
- *Problem and Solution* (also referred to as *Question and Answer*). The author states a problem and its solution or solutions (e.g., *What Do You Do with a Tail Like This?* by Steve Jenkins and Robin Page).

Some informational books will employ a single text structure; others, particularly longer works, will employ several.

Theme

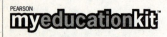

Go to the Conversations section of Chapter 10 in MyEducationKit to read the interview with James Cross Giblin.

Theme in informational literature is the main point made in the work. Although an informational book may communicate hundreds of facts about a topic, the theme of the work will answer the question "What's the point?" (Colman, 1999, p. 221). Sometimes the theme will be a cognitive concept, such as the way viruses multiply; in other cases it will be an emotional insight, such as a new or deepened awareness of the social injustices that are a part of the history of the United States (e.g., slavery, child labor), as revealed in Deborah Hopkinson's *Up Before Daybreak: Cotton and People in America*.

Style

Style is how authors and illustrators, with their readers in mind, express themselves in their respective media. Sentence length and complexity, word choice, and formal versus conversational tone are part of the expository style, as are use of technical vocabulary, captions, and graphic elements such as tables, charts, illustrations, photographs, diagrams, maps, and indexes. Shelley Tanaka's colorful language and use of large, richly colored photographs, maps, sidebars, and a time line in *Mummies: The Newest, Coolest, and Creepiest from Around the World* demonstrate how style can make informational literature more interesting.

Reading Informational Literature

An interesting contradiction concerning informational literature exists in today's schools. Although school and public library records indicate that informational literature makes up 50 to 85 percent of the circulation of children's libraries, reading achievement test scores and research studies indicate that U.S. students in the elementary grades score better on literary reading (i.e., narrative text) than on informational reading (i.e., expository text). This can be explained in part because of a lack of classroom experience with informational literature in the early grades. See Table 10.1 for research evidence supporting the reading of informational books in the elementary grades.

Go to Activity 1 in the Assignments and Activities section of Chapter 10 in MyEducationKit; view the artifacts on students' responses to listening to informational literature read aloud and respond to the question.

Studies such as the ones reported in Table 10.1 reveal several critical points about children and reading informational literature. First, it is only through repeated experience with a specific genre that one learns how to read or write that genre. Second, all children, even primary-graders, benefit from learning how to read and enjoy informational books, since from middle grades through adulthood, most day-to-day reading demands (textbooks, news reports, instructions, recipes, etc.) are expository. Third, a key factor in comprehending expository text is that readers learn to relate new informa-

Table 10.1 Important Studies on Reading and Informational Literature

Researcher(s)	Subjects	Findings
Mullis, Martin, Kennedy, & Foy (2007)	200,000 fourth-graders from forty countries	U.S. students scored lower in informational reading than in literary reading and ranked fifteenth overall among forty participating countries.
Duke (2000)	Twenty first-grade classrooms, ten each from very high and very low SES groups	Presence of nonfiction texts and use of nonfiction in class were rare to nonexistent. Consequently, students were unable to read and write informational texts successfully. Findings applied particularly to low-SES students.
Campbell, Kapinus, & Beatty (1995)	National sample of fourth-graders	Students with experience reading magazines and nonfiction had higher average reading proficiencies than those who never read these types of materials.

tion found in the text to their own *schemata,* or prior knowledge on the topic stored in their minds.

Particularly in the early grades, teachers and librarians may have to take the lead in introducing informational literature to their students, since parents and caregivers traditionally select only fiction as read-aloud material. Selecting excellent works of informational literature for reading aloud and suggesting similar works to parents for at-home reading is a good way to begin. Calling attention to students' prior knowledge on a subject and noting the various text structures while reading will help students learn to read and appreciate this genre. In addition, informational books can be included and promoted as options in students' self-choice reading, added to classroom library collections (Moss & Hendershot, 2002), and used across the curriculum in various ways.

Evaluation and Selection of Informational Books

It is important to remember that not every informational book needs to meet every criterion to be worthy and that no one book can cover a topic completely. By offering children a variety of satisfactory books on the same topic to be read and compared, you more than compensate for the shortcomings of a good-but-not-great book. Selection criteria include the following:

- Children's informational literature must be written in a clear, direct, easily understandable style. In recent years, a tight, compressed, but conversational, writing style has come to be favored in nonfictional text.
- Facts must be accurate and current. A reliable check is to compare the information with that found in other recently published sources on the topic.

- Captions and labels must be clearly written and informative.
- Informational literature must distinguish between fact, theory, and opinion. When not clearly stated as such, theories or opinions are flagged by carefully placed phrases such as "maybe," "is believed to be," or "perhaps."
- *Personification*—attributing human qualities to animals, material objects, or natural forces—should be avoided because the implication is factually inaccurate.
- Works of informational literature must be attractive to the child. An intriguing cover, impressive or humorous illustrations, and balance of text and illustrations make books look interesting to a child.
- Presentation of information should be from known to unknown, general to specific, or simple to more complex to aid conceptual understanding and encourage analytical thinking. Reference aids such as tables of contents, indexes, pronunciation guides, glossaries, maps, charts, and tables make information in books easier to find and retrieve, more comprehensible, and more complete.
- Stereotyping must be avoided. Positive images of cultural diversity should be offered in text and illustrations.
- Format and artistic medium should be appropriate to the content. For example, engineered paper or pop-up illustrations are appropriate when three dimensions are required to give an accurate sense of placement of the parts of a whole, as in human anatomy.
- Depth and complexity of subject treatment must be appropriate for the intended audience. If an explanation must be simplified to the extent that facts must be altered before a child can begin to understand, perhaps the concept or topic should be taken up when the child is older.

Two award programs offer sources of good informational titles. The NCTE's Orbis Pictus Award for Outstanding Nonfiction for Children and the ALA's Robert F. Sibert Informational Book Medal spotlight what are considered to be the best works of nonfiction published in the preceding year.

For a complete listing of the Orbis Pictus and Sibert Award winners, see Appendix A.

Formats of Informational Books

Informational book format has to do with how information is presented on the book page, rather than with the information itself. The most common distinct formats in which informational books for children are currently being produced are as follows:

- *Informational Chapter Book.* This format features a large amount of text that is organized into chapters. Graphics and illustrations are common in the more recent nonfiction chapter books but are still less important than the text. Examples include *Blizzard! The Storm That Changed America* by Jim Murphy and *Life on Earth—and Beyond* by Pamela Turner.
- *Informational Picture Book.* This format features large, uncomplicated illustrations and brief text. The illustrations help to convey the information as discussed in Chapter 5. Examples include *Ox, House, Stick: The History of Our Alphabet* by Don Robb, illustrated by Anne Smith, and *The Story of Salt* by Mark Kurlansky, illustrated by S. D. Schindler.

Excellent Informational Literature to READ ALOUD

Bartoletti, Susan Campbell. *Black Potatoes: The Story of the Great Irish Famine, 1845–1850.* Ages 12–16.

Butterworth, Chris. *Sea Horse: The Shyest Horse in the Sea.* Illustrated by John Lawrence. Ages 4–8.

Cowley, Joy. *Chameleon, Chameleon.* Photographs by Nic Bishop. Ages 4–7.

Hopkinson, Deborah. *Up Before Daybreak: Cotton and People in America.* Ages 9–14.

Jenkins, Steve, and Robin Page. *How Many Ways Can You Catch a Fly?* Illustrated by Steve Jenkins. Ages 4–8.

Krupp, Edwin. *The Rainbow and You.* Illustrated by Robin Krupp. Ages 5–7.

Sayre, April Pulley. *Stars Beneath Your Bed: The Surprising Story of Dust.* Ages 5–10.

Schlitz, Laura A. *Good Masters! Sweet Ladies! Voices from a Medieval Village.* Illustrated by Robert Byrd. Ages 9–13.

Strauss, Rochelle. *One Well: The Story of Water on Earth.* Illustrated by Rosemary Woods. Ages 9–14.

Winters, Kay. *Colonial Voices: Hear Them Speak.* Illustrated by Larry Day. Ages 9–12.

- *Science and Social Science Concept Picture Book.* Originally conceived for 4- to 8-year-olds, this type of book presents one or two scientific or social concepts via brief, uncomplicated text accompanied by numerous, large illustrations. It also encourages participation by including an experiment or hands-on activity. These books are now available for older children as well. *Bugs Are Insects* by Anne Rockwell, illustrated by Steve Jenkins, exemplifies the science concept picture book and is part of the well-known "Let's-Read-and-Find-Out" series of books of this kind.

- *Photo Essay.* Presentation of information in the photo essay is equally balanced between text and illustration. Excellent, information-bearing photographs and crisp, condensed writing style are hallmarks of this format. Photo essays are generally written for children in the intermediate grades and up. A good example is *Sneeze!* by Alexandra Siy, with photographs by Dennis Kunkel.

- *Fact Books.* Presentation of information in these books is mainly through lists, charts, and tables. Examples include almanacs, books of world records, and sports trivia and statistics books. For example, see *The Guinness Book of World Records.*

- *Informational Book Series.* These consist of a number of titles that all share a general topic (e.g., world cultures), format, writing style, and reading level. A few series, such as the Eyewitness Books published by Dorling Kindersley, take an omnibus approach and include a wide range of topics. A series can have a sole author–illustrator team, as is the case with Scholastic's well-known Magic Schoolbus series by Joanna Cole, illustrated by Bruce Degen; or each book in the series can be created by a different author–illustrator team, as in Houghton Mifflin's Scientists in the Field series. Informational series are published for all age groups and on topics tailored to school curricula. See the Informational Book Series section at the end of the Recommended Informational Books list for some of the best entries in this essential category.

Historical Overview of Informational Literature

The history of children's informational literature begins in 1657 with the publication of John Amos Comenius's *Orbis Pictus (The World in Pictures)*. Not only was this the first children's picture book, but it was also an informational book. This auspicious beginning for informational literature was cut short, however, by the Puritan Movement. For nearly 200 years the vast majority of books published for and read by children were intended more for moralistic instruction than for information.

Although informational books continued to be written in the eighteenth and nineteenth centuries, much of the growth and development of this genre occurred in the latter half of the twentieth century.

Rapid development of informational literature as a genre began in the 1950s and 1960s in response to the launching of *Sputnik*, the first artificial space satellite, by the former Soviet Union. Competing in the race for space exploration and new technology, the U.S. Congress funneled money into science education, and publishers responded with new and improved science trade books. (See Milestones in the Development of Informational Literature.) Particularly noteworthy are the introduction of informational picture books for primary grades and the trend toward more illustrations and less text in informational books for all levels.

As the stature of informational literature rose and more top-flight authors and illustrators were engaged in its production, the quality of research, writing, and art in these books improved. A lighter, yet factual, tone balanced with high-quality, informative illustrations and graphics emerged as the preferred nonfiction style (Elleman, 1987).

In 1990, the National Council of Teachers of English established the Orbis Pictus Award for Outstanding Nonfiction for Children. Named in honor of Comenius's book written some 300 years earlier, this award program signaled how far children's nonfiction had come. In 2001, the Robert F. Sibert Informational Book Medal, sponsored by the American Library Association, was established, further documenting the acceptance of informational literature as an equal player in the field of children's literature. One of the most noticeable and significant trends in the development of informational books in the last decade is the burgeoning growth of informational series books. With so many informational titles available to support school curricula, perhaps U.S. students will increase their proficiency in informational reading.

Topics of Informational Books

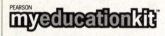

Go to Activity 2 in the Assignments and Activities section of Chapter 10 in MyEducationKit; complete the activity on selecting informational books.

Although informational literature is confined to just one chapter in this book, it is one of the largest single genres in children's literature, in that everything known to humankind is a conceivable topic. Organization of such an enormous variety of topics could, of course, be done in a variety of ways, one of which is the scientific approach used here. The world of information is divided into the biological, the physical, the social, and the applied sciences; the humanities are dealt with separately.

MILESTONES *in the Development of Informational Literature*

Date	Book	Significance
1657	*Orbis Pictus* by John Amos Comenius	First known work of nonfiction for children
1683	*New England Primer*	First concept book for American children; reflected didacticism of the Puritan era
1922	*The Story of Mankind* by Hendrik Van Loon	Won the first Newbery Medal; greatly influenced children's books with its lively style and creative approach
1960	Let's-Read-and-Find-Out series by Franklyn Branley and Roma Gans	Introduced the science concept picture book for young children
1990	Orbis Pictus Award for Nonfiction established	Informational literature as a genre is recognized
2001	Robert F. Sibert Informational Book Medal established	Informational literature as a genre is further recognized

Biological Science

Biological science deals with living organisms and the laws and phenomena that relate to any organism or group of organisms. Topics within this field that interest primary- and intermediate-graders are dinosaurs, pets, wild animals, ecology, and the environment. *A Dinosaur Named Sue: The Story of the Colossal Fossil: The World's Most Complete T. Rex* by Pat Relf is a good example.

A subtopic of biological science that deserves special attention is human anatomy and sexuality. Young children are naturally interested in their bodies, and as they grow into puberty, they become interested in sex. Experts in the field of sex education suggest that honest, straightforward answers to children's questions about their bodies, bodily functions, sex, and sexual orientation are best. Books on these topics are not necessarily appropriate for use in schools in the elementary grades, but rather for use by parents who want a resource to share with their children. Teachers and librarians should be able to recommend age-appropriate books on these topics, if asked by parents. Robie Harris's book, *It's Not the Stork! A Book about Girls, Boys, Babies, Bodies, Families, and Friends* illustrated by Michael Emberley, is a good example.

Physical Science

Physical science, sometimes referred to as *natural science,* deals primarily with nonliving materials. Rocks, landforms, oceans, the stars, and the atmosphere and its weather and seasons are all likely topics that children could learn about within the fields of geology, geography, oceanography, astronomy, and meteorology. Not only will children be able to satisfy their curiosity about such topics as volcanoes and earthquakes, but teachers will also find the many books about the planets and our solar system helpful in presenting these topics in class. Christopher Harbo's *The Explosive World of Volcanoes with Max Axiom, Super Scientist,* is an interesting example presented in comic book format.

Notable Authors and Illustrators
of Informational Literature

Nic Bishop, author/illustrator known for extreme close-up photographs of inhabitants of the natural world. *Spiders; Frogs; Red-Eyed Tree Frog* (with Joy Cowley). www.nicbishop.com

Susan Campbell Bartoletti, author of informational books about young people during historic periods of oppression. *Hitler Youth: Growing Up in Hitler's Shadow; Black Potatoes: The Story of the Great Irish Famine, 1845–1850.* www.scbartoletti.com

Joanna Cole, author of a variety of informational books for beginning independent readers. Magic School Bus series.

Russell Freedman, author of informational books about U.S. history. *Who Was First? Discovering the Americas; Children of the Wild West.*

James Cross Giblin, author of informational books about the social implications of cultural developments and inventions. *Secrets of the Sphinx; When Plague Strikes: The Black Death, Smallpox, AIDS.*

Steve Jenkins, author/illustrator known for colorful, textural cut-paper collage illustrations in informative picture books about living creatures. *Living Color; Dogs and Cats.* www.stevejenkinsbooks.com

David Macaulay, author/illustrator of several books of faction about construction of monumental buildings and informational picture books for older readers. *Cathedral: The Story of Its Construction; Building Big.* www.davidmacaulay.com

Jim Murphy, author of informational chapter books about events in U.S. history. *An American Plague: The True and Terrifying Story of the Yellow Fever Epidemic of 1793; The Great Fire.* www.jimmurphybooks.com

Stuart J. Murphy, creator of the MathStart series of informational picture books on the subject of mathematics. www.stuartjmurphy.com

Social Science

Social science deals with the institutions and functioning of human society and the interpersonal relationships of individuals as members of society. Through books in this field children can learn about various forms of government, religions, different countries and their cultures, money, and transportation. Most children have a natural interest in books about careers, family relationships, and leisure activities and will appreciate finding answers to their questions without always having to ask an adult. An example is *What the World Eats* by Faith D'Aluisio and Peter Menzel.

Bibliotherapy is the use of books by professionally trained therapists to treat emotionally disturbed individuals. Most teachers and librarians are not trained as psychologists, and misguided bibliotherapy may be unhelpful or even harmful to students. On the other hand, we know that students benefit psychologically from reading and talking about powerful stories and the thoughts, feelings, and actions of characters in these stories. Discovering that others, real or imaginary, have faced problems similar to their own is reassuring to children. Furthermore, we all benefit from knowing what to do when faced with troubling or problematic situations.

Books offering help, support, and guidance to young people can be found in all genres. Fictional stories, particularly realistic fiction, show how imaginary children overcome or cope with their problems; biographies often present real examples of the same. Informational books help children by naming and defining problems and problematic behaviors and telling them what actions to take to get help or to cope with the problem. The How Can I Deal With . . . series (Smart Apple Media) offers case studies and helpful advice to children on the subjects of bullying, new babies in the family, divorce, stepfamilies, death, and racism. Two outstanding series for older students, Issues in Focus Today (Enslow) and Issues that Concern You (Greenhaven), discuss the problems associated with abortion, addictions, body image and obesity, abuse, bullying, discrimination, gangs, and sexuality, among others.

Books shared by sensitive and caring teachers and librarians may help students to develop understanding and empathy for others or acknowledge their own unkind behaviors. Bibliotherapy as a professional treatment, however, should be left to trained therapists.

Applied Science

Applied science deals with the practical applications of pure science that people have devised. All machines, for example—from simple levers to supercomputers, from bicycles to space rockets—are part of this field, and many children are naturally interested in finding out how they work. Interest in the applied sciences can be developed in children by pointing out how their lives are affected by these applications. For example, children get sick, and medicine helps to cure them. How? Children get hungry, and food appears. What are the processes by which the food is produced, prepared, packaged, and marketed? Children like toys and buy them in stores. Who designs the toys and how are they manufactured? The answers to questions like these can be found in today's informational literature. For example, see *Skyscrapers* by Lynn Curlee and *Go! The Whole World of Transportation* by Andrea Mills and Phil Hunt.

A specific type of book within the applied sciences—the *experiment* or *how-to book*—capitalizes on children's natural curiosity and fondness for hands-on activities. Its contents range from directions for conducting various scientific experiments to cookbooks, guides to hobbies, and directions for small construction projects, like clubhouses. For example, see *Chemistry Science Fair Projects Using French Fries, Gumdrops, Soap, and Other Organic Stuff* by Robert Gardner and Barbara G. Conklin.

Humanities

The *humanities* deal with the branches of learning that primarily have a cultural or artistic character. Of greatest interest to children and their teachers are books about the fine arts of drawing, painting, and sculpture; the performing arts of singing, dancing, making instrumental music, and acting; and handicrafts of all sorts. Since many children are artistically creative and often study dance, music, and drawing, they can be led to read about the arts and artists to learn new techniques or to draw inspiration from the experiences of others. Some might read these books to decide whether they are interested in trying to develop their artistic talents. Some books make the arts more accessible or real to children by explaining what to look for in paintings, for example, or by revealing the hard work required of an artist to achieve a spectacular performance or an intriguing work of art, as in *Artist to Artist: 23 Major Illustrators Talk to Children about Their Art* published by the Eric Carle Museum of Picture Book Art.

Today's nonfictional literature for children is able to meet the needs and interests of young readers in quality, variety, and reader appeal. With these books, children's appetites for learning can be fed while their curiosity for more information is piqued.

Issues&Topics for FURTHER INVESTIGATION

- Select an age-appropriate text set of informational books on a science- or math-related topic under study in a classroom. Booktalk these titles to the class, then make the books available for browsing. Note students' responses to these books through observation and interviews.

- Investigate all books in one of the informational book series listed in the Recommended Informational Books list. Evaluate these books in terms of their support of the curricular area indicated, their content, and their likely appeal to children.

- Books for young people about evolution are met with opposition in some communities. Explain your stand on the issue of making books on this subject available to children.

- Locate and read books for elementary and middle-school students on the subject of sex that are available in your local school or public library. What is your stand on whether these books should be made available to young people?

- Investigate the idea of pairing informational books with other genres as part of a literature unit. Choose a topic and grade level and generate a text set of 10–12 age-appropriate books containing a balance of fiction, biography, and informational books.

References

Campbell, J. R., Kapinus, B., & Beatty, A. S. (1995). Interviewing children about their literacy experiences. Data from NAEP's integrated reading performance record at grade 4. Washington, DC: U.S. Department of Education.

Colman, P. (1999). Nonfiction is literature, too. *The New Advocate, 12*(3), 215–223.

Duke, N. K. (2000). 3.6 minutes a day: The scarcity of informational texts in first grade. *Reading Research Quarterly, 35*(2), 202–225.

Elleman, B. (1987). Current trends in literature for children. *Library Trends, 35*(3), 413–426.

Jansen, M. (1987). *A little about language, words, and concepts—Or what may happen when children learn to read.* Translated by Lotte Rosbak Juhl. Dragør, Denmark: Landsforeningen af Læsepædagoger.

Moss, B., & Hendershot, J. (2002). Exploring sixth graders' selection of nonfiction trade books. *The Reading Teacher, 56*(1), 6–17.

Mullis, I. V. S., Martin, M. O., Kennedy, A. M., & Foy, P. (2007). *IEA's Progress in International Reading Literacy Study in Primary School in 40 Countries: PIRLS 2006 International Report.* Boston, MA:

TIMSS & PIRLS International Study Center, Boston College. (Retrievable at http://timssandpirls.bc.edu/pirls2006/intl_rpt.html)

Untermeyer, L. (1985). Questions at night. In L. Untermeyer (Selector), *Rainbow in the sky.* San Diego: Harcourt.

★ Recommended Informational Books

Ages indicated refer to content appropriateness and conceptual and interest levels. Formats other than informational chapter books will be coded as follows:
  (**PI**) Picture book
  (**COL**) Short story collection
  (**GR**) Graphic novel

Biological Science

Arnosky, Jim. *Wild Tracks! A Guide to Nature's Footprints.* Sterling, 2008. Ages 7–11.

Bishop, Nic. *Digging for Bird Dinosaurs: An Expedition to Madagascar.* Houghton, 2000. Ages 9–14.

———. *Frogs.* Scholastic, 2008. (**PI**) Ages 5–7.

———. *Spiders.* Scholastic, 2007. (**PI**) Ages 8–10.

Bonner, Hannah. *When Fish Got Feet, Sharks Got Teeth, and Bugs Began to Swarm: A Cartoon Prehistory of Life Long Before Dinosaurs.* National Geographic, 2007. (**PI**) Ages 8–11.

Butler, Dori Hillestad. *My Mom's Having a Baby.* Illustrated by Carol Thompson. Albert Whitman, 2005. (**PI**) Ages 7–9.

Butterworth, Chris. *Sea Horse: The Shyest Horse in the Sea.* Illustrated by John Lawrence. Candlewick, 2006. (**PI**) Ages 4–8.

Cole, Joanna. *The Magic Schoolbus Explores the Senses.* Illustrated by Bruce Degen. Scholastic, 1999. Ages 7–9.

Collard, Sneed. *Pocket Babies and Other Amazing Marsupials.* Darby Creek, 2007. Ages 8–12.

———. *The Prairie Builders: Reconstructing America's Lost Grasslands.* Houghton, 2005. Ages 10–14.

Cowley, Joy. *Chameleon, Chameleon.* Photographs by Nic Bishop. Scholastic, 2005. (**PI**) Ages 4–7.

———. *Red-Eyed Tree Frog.* Photographs by Nic Bishop. Scholastic, 1999. Ages 6–9.

Davies, Nicola. *Extreme Animals: The Toughest Creatures on Earth.* Illustrated by Neal Layton. Candlewick, 2006. (**PI**) Ages 8–10.

Farrell, Jeanette. *Invisible Allies: Microbes That Shape Our Lives.* Farrar, 2005. Ages 12–18. Also *Invisible Enemies: Stories of Infectious Disease,* 2005.

Fisher, Aileen. *The Story Goes On.* Illustrated by Mique Moriuchi. Roaring Brook, 2005. (**PI**) Ages 4–7.

Fleischman, John. *Phineas Gage: A Gruesome but True Story about Brain Science.* Houghton, 2002. Ages 12–14.

Frost, Helen. *Monarch and Milkweed.* Illustrated by Leonid Gore. Atheneum, 2008. (**PI**) Ages 4–7.

Gamlin, Linda. *Eyewitness Science: Evolution.* DK Publishing, 2000. Ages 8–12.

Harris, Robie H. *It's Not the Stork! A Book about Girls, Boys, Babies, Bodies, Families, and Friends.* Illustrated by Michael Emberley. Candlewick, 2006. Ages 5–9. For parents to use with children.

———. *It's Perfectly Normal: A Book about Changing Bodies, Growing Up, Sex, and Sexual Health.* Illustrated by Michael Emberley. Candlewick, 1994. Ages 11–14.

———. *It's So Amazing! A Book about Eggs, Sperm, Birth, Babies and Families.* Illustrated by Michael Emberley. Candlewick, 1999. Ages 7–12. For parents to use with children.

Hatkoff, Isabella, Craig Hatkoff, and Paula Kahumbu. *Owen & Mzee: The True Story of a Remarkable Friendship.* Photography by Peter Greste. Scholastic, 2006. Ages 5–12. Photoessay. Sequel is *Owen & Mzee: The Language of Friendship,* 2007.

Jenkins, Steve. *Almost Gone: The World's Rarest Animals.* HarperCollins, 2006. (**PI**) Ages 5–8.

———. *Dogs and Cats.* Houghton, 2007. (**PI**) Ages 5–11. (Also a toy book.)

———. *Life on Earth: The Story of Evolution.* Houghton, 2002. (**PI**) Ages 8–11.

———. *Living Color.* Houghton, 2007. (**PI**) Ages 5–10.

———. *Prehistoric Actual Size.* Houghton, 2005. (**PI**) Ages 5–10.

————, and Robin Page. *How Many Ways Can You Catch a Fly?* Illustrated by Steve Jenkins. Houghton, 2008. (**PI**) Ages 4–8.

————. *Move!* Illustrated by Steve Jenkins. Houghton, 2006. (**PI**) Ages 4–7.

————. *What Do You Do with a Tail Like This?* Houghton, 2003. (**PI**) Ages 4–7.

Kurlansky, Mark. *The Cod's Tale.* Illustrated by S. D. Schindler. Penguin, 2001. (**PI**) Ages 8–12.

Larson, Peter, and Kristin Donnan. *Bones Rock! Everything You Need to Know to Be a Paleontologist.* Invisible Cities, 2004. Ages 11–14.

Mannis, Celeste D. *Snapshots: The Wonders of Monterey Bay.* Viking, 2006. Ages 6–10.

Markle, Sandra. *Little Lost Bat.* Illustrated by Alan Marks. Charlesbridge, 2006. (**PI**) Ages 6–10.

Montgomery, Sy. *Search for the Golden Moon Bear: Science and Adventure in the Asian Tropics.* Houghton, 2004. Ages 11–18.

————. *The Tarantula Scientist.* Photography by Nic Bishop. Houghton, 2004. Ages 11–14.

Page, Robin, and Steve Jenkins. *Sisters and Brothers: Sibling Relationships in the Animal World.* Illustrated by Steve Jenkins. Houghton, 2008. (**PI**) Ages 7–9.

Pericoli, Matteo. *The True Story of Stellina.* Knopf, 2006. (**PI**) Ages 4–9.

Relf, Pat. *A Dinosaur Named Sue: The Story of the Colossal Fossil: The World's Most Complete T. Rex.* Scholastic, 2000. Ages 12–14.

Rockwell, Anne. *Bugs Are Insects.* Illustrated by Steve Jenkins. HarperCollins, 2001. (**PI**) Ages 3–6.

Romanek, Trudee. *Squirt! The Most Interesting Book You'll Ever Read about Blood.* Illustrated by Rose Cowler. Kids Can, 2006. Ages 9–12.

Sayre, April Pulley. *Stars Beneath Your Bed: The Surprising Story of Dust.* Illustrated by Ann Jonas. Greenwillow, 2005. (**PI**) Ages 5–10.

Schlosser, Eric, and Charles Wilson. *Chew on This: Everything You Didn't Want to Know about Fast Food.* Houghton, 2006. Ages 12–14.

Schulman, Janet. *Pale Male: Citizen Hawk of New York City.* Illustrated by Meilo So. Knopf, 2008. (**PI**) Ages 5–10.

Simon, Seymour. *Guts: Our Digestive System.* HarperCollins, 2005. (**PI**) Ages 9–14.

Singer, Marilyn. *What Stinks?* Darby Creek, 2006. (**PI**) Ages 9–12.

Siy, Alexandra. *Sneeze!* Photographs by Dennis Kunkel. Charlesbridge, 2007. Ages 9–18.

Sloan, Christopher. *The Human Story: Our Evolution from Prehistoric Ancestors to Today.* Photography by Kenneth Garrett. Illustrated by Alfons Kennis and Adrie Kennis. National Geographic, 2004. Ages 11–18.

Turner, Pamela S. *Gorilla Doctors: Saving Endangered Great Apes.* Houghton, 2005. Ages 10–14.

————. *Life on Earth—and Beyond.* Charlesbridge, 2008. Ages 10–13.

Walker, Sally M. *Fossil Fish Found Alive: Discovering the Coelacanth.* Carolrhoda, 2002. Ages 10–13.

Physical Science

Arnosky, Jim. *Wild and Swampy.* HarperCollins, 2000. (**PI**) Ages 7–10.

Branley, Franklyn M. *The Planets in Our Solar System.* Illustrated by Kevin O'Malley. HarperCollins, 1998. (**PI**) Ages 6–8.

Burns, Loree G. *Tracking Trash: Flotsam, Jetsam, and the Science of Ocean Motion.* Houghton, 2007. Ages 10–13.

Godkin, Celia. *Fire!* Fitzhenry & Whiteside, 2006. (**PI**) Ages 6–9.

Gore, Al. *An Inconvenient Truth: The Crisis of Global Warming.* Adapted by Jane O'Connor. Viking, 2007. Ages 10–13.

Grace, Catherine. *Forces of Nature: The Awesome Power of Volcanoes, Earthquakes, and Tornadoes.* National Geographic, 2004. Ages 11–14.

Harbo, Christopher L. *The Explosive World of Volcanoes with Max Axiom, Super Scientist.* Capstone, 2008. (**GR**) Ages 9–12.

Krupp, Edwin. *The Rainbow and You.* Illustrated by Robin Krupp. HarperCollins, 2000. Ages 5–7.

Murphy, Jim. *Blizzard! The Storm That Changed America.* Scholastic, 2000. Ages 10–14.

Prager, Ellen J. *Sand.* Illustrated by Nancy Woodman. National Geographic, 2000. Ages 4–8.

Strauss, Rochelle. *One Well: The Story of Water on Earth.* Illustrated by Rosemary Woods. Kids Can, 2007. (**PI**) Ages 9–14.

Treaster, Joseph B. *Hurricane Force: In the Path of America's Killer Storms.* Kingfisher, 2007. Ages 9–13.

Wick, Walter. *A Drop of Water: A Book of Science and Wonder.* Scholastic, 1997. Ages 8–11.

Social Science

Adkins, Jan. *What If You Met a Pirate?* Roaring Brook, 2004. (**PI**) Ages 7–10.

Allen, Thomas B. *George Washington, Spymaster: How the Americans Outspied the British and Won the Revolutionary War.* National Geographic, 2004. Ages 11–14.

Ambrose, Stephen E. *The Good Fight: How World War II Was Won.* Atheneum, 2001. Ages 11–14.

Ancona, George. *Charro: The Mexican Cowboy.* Harcourt, 1999. Ages 8–10.

Armstrong, Jennifer. *The American Story: 100 True Tales from American History.* Illustrated by Roger Roth. Knopf, 2006. Ages 9–13.

Bartoletti, Susan Campbell. *Black Potatoes: The Story of the Great Irish Famine, 1845–1850.* Houghton, 2001. Ages 12–16.

———. *Kids on Strike.* Houghton, 1999. Ages 11–16.

Bial, Raymond. *Tenement: Immigrant Life on the Lower East Side.* Houghton, 2002. Ages 9–14.

Blacklock, Dyan. *The Roman Army: The Legendary Soldiers Who Created an Empire.* Illustrated by David Kannett. Walker, 2004. (**PI**) Ages 11–14.

Blumenthal, Karen. *Let Me Play: The Story of Title IX: The Law That Changed the Future of Girls in America.* Atheneum, 2005. Ages 12–14.

Bober, Natalie S. *Countdown to Independence: A Revolution of Ideas in England and Her American Colonies: 1760–1776.* Atheneum, 2001. Ages 12–16.

Brown, Don. *All Stations! Distress! April 15, 1912: The Day the Titanic Sank.* Roaring Brook, 2008. (**PI**) Ages 6–12.

D'Aluisio, Faith, and Peter Menzel. *What the World Eats.* Tricycle, 2008. Ages 9–13.

Deems, James M. *Bodies from the Ash: Life and Death in Ancient Pompeii.* Houghton, 2005. Ages 10–14.

Ellis, Deborah. *Our Stories, Our Songs: African Children Talk about AIDS.* Fitzhenry & Whiteside, 2005. Ages 12–14.

Floca, Brian. *Lightship.* Atheneum, 2007. (**PI**) Ages 5–7.

Fradin, Dennis Brindell. *Let It Begin Here! Lexington and Concord: First Battles of the American Revolution.* Illustrated by Larry Day. Walker, 2005. (**PI**) Ages 6–10.

Frank, Mitch. *Understanding the Holy Land: Answering Questions about the Israeli-Palestinian Conflict.* Viking, 2005. Ages 12–14.

Freedman, Russell. *Children of the Great Depression.* Clarion, 2005. Ages 11–14.

———. *In Defense of Liberty: The Story of America's Bill of Rights.* Holiday, 2003. Ages 10–14.

———. *Freedom Walkers: The Story of the Montgomery Bus Boycott.* Holiday, 2006. Ages 9–13.

———. *Kids at Work: Lewis Hine and the Crusade against Child Labor.* Photos by Lewis Hine. Clarion, 1994. Ages 9–12.

———. *Who Was First? Discovering the Americas.* Clarion, 2007. Ages 10–14.

Gaskins, Pearl Fuyo. *What Are You? Voices of Mixed-Race Young People.* Holt, 1999. Ages 13–16.

Gibbons, Gail. *My Baseball Book.* HarperCollins, 2000. (**PI**) Ages 4–8.

Giblin, James Cross. *Secrets of the Sphinx.* Illustrated by Bagram Ibatoulline. Scholastic, 2004. Ages 9–12.

———. *When Plague Strikes: The Black Death, Smallpox, AIDS.* Illustrated by David Frampton. HarperCollins, 1995. Ages 12–16.

Goodman, Joan Elizabeth. *A Long and Uncertain Journey: The 27,000-Mile Voyage of Vasco da Gama.* Illustrated by Tom McNeely. Mikaya/Firefly, 2001. (**PI**) Ages 11–14.

Greenfield, Howard. *After the Holocaust.* Greenwillow, 2001. Ages 12–16. Oral histories.

The Guinness Book of World Records. Guinness Media, Inc. Published annually. Ages 7–13.

Hill, Laban C. *Harlem Stomp! A Cultural History of the Harlem Renaissance.* Little, Brown, 2004. Ages 11–14.

Hinds, Kathryn. *The City.* Cavendish, 2000. Ages 11–14. See others in Life in the Middle Ages series.

Hoose, Phillip. *The Race to Save the Lord God Bird.* Farrar, 2004. Ages 11–14.

———. *We Were There, Too! Young People in U.S. History.* Farrar, 2001. Ages 10–13.

Hopkinson, Deborah. *Shutting Out the Sky: Life in the Tenements of New York 1880–1924.* Scholastic, 2003. Ages 11–14.

———. *Up Before Daybreak: Cotton and People in America.* Scholastic, 2006. Ages 9–14.

Janeczko, Paul B. *Top Secret: A Handbook of Codes, Ciphers, and Secret Writing.* Illustrated by Jenna LaReau. Candlewick, 2004. Ages 9–14.

Jenkins, Steve. *The Top of the World: Climbing Mount Everest.* Houghton, 1999. Ages 9–12.

Kalman, Maira. *Fireboat: The Heroic Adventures of the John J. Harvey.* Putnam, 2002. (**PI**) Ages 6–8.

Kuklin, Susan. *Families.* Hyperion, 2006. (**PI**) Ages 5–10.

Kurlansky, Mark. *The Story of Salt.* Illustrated by S. D. Schindler. Putnam, 2006. (**PI**) Ages 8–11. (Also a physical science book.)

Lauber, Patricia. *Who Came First? New Clues to Prehistoric Americans.* National Geographic, 2003. Ages 10–14.

Macy, Sue. *Swifter, Higher, Stronger: A Photographic History of the Summer Olympics.* National Geographic, 2004. Ages 11–14.

Markle, Sandra. *Rescues!* Lerner, 2006. Ages 9–13.

Marrin, Albert. *Oh, Rats! The Story of Rats and People.* Illustrated by C. B. Mordan. Dutton, 2006. Ages 8–12.

Martin, Bill, Jr., and Michael Sampson. *I Pledge Allegiance: The Pledge of Allegiance.* Illustrated by Chris Raschka. Candlewick, 2002. (**PI**) Ages 6–9.

McWhorter, Diane. *A Dream of Freedom: The Civil Rights Movement from 1954 to 1968.* Scholastic, 2004. Ages 10–14.

Meyer, Don, editor. *The Sibling Slam Book: What It's Really Like to Have a Brother or Sister with Special Needs.* Woodbine, 2005. Ages 12–14.

Morris, Ann. *Families.* HarperCollins, 2000. Ages 4–7. Photoessay.

Murphy, Jim. *An American Plague: The True and Terrifying Story of the Yellow Fever Epidemic of 1793.* Clarion, 2003. Ages 9–14.

———. *The Great Fire.* Scholastic, 1995. Ages 10–14.

———. *Inside the Alamo.* Delacorte, 2003. Ages 9–14.

National Children's Book and Literary Alliance. *Our White House: Looking In and Looking Out.* Candlewick, 2008. (**PI**) Ages 9–13.

Nelson, Kadir. *We Are the Ship: The Story of Negro League Baseball.* Hyperion, 2008. (**PI**) Ages 9–13.

Nevius, Carol. *Karate Hour.* Illustrated by Bill Thomson. Marshall Cavendish, 2004. (**PI**) Ages 5–10.

Olson, Tod. *How to Get Rich in the California Gold Rush: An Adventurer's Guide to the Fabulous Riches Discovered in 1848.* Illustrated by Scott Allred. National Geographic, 2008. Ages 9–13.

Osborne, Mary Pope. *Pompeii: Lost & Found.* Illustrated by Bonnie Christensen. Knopf, 2006. (**PI**) Ages 7–12.

Patent, Dorothy Henshaw. *The Buffalo and the Indians: A Shared Destiny.* Illustrated by William Muños. Clarion, 2006. Ages 9–14. Photoessay.

Peters, Stephanie T. *The Battle Against Polio.* Benchmark, 2004. Ages 10–14. Also in the proposed five-part Epidemic! set are *The 1918 Influenza Pandemic; Smallpox in the New World;* and *The Black Death.*

Philbrick, Nathaniel. *Revenge of the Whale: The True Story of the Whaleship Essex.* Putnam, 2002. Ages 12–14.

Philip, Neil. *The Great Circle: A History of the First Nations.* Clarion, 2006. Ages 11–15.

Rappaport, Doreen. *Lady Liberty: A Biography.* Illustrated by Matt Tavares. Candlewick, 2008. (**PI**) Ages 7–10.

Robb, Don. *Ox, House, Stick: The History of Our Alphabet.* Illustrated by Anne Smith. Charlesbridge, 2007. (**PI**) Ages 9–12.

Schlitz, Laura A. *Good Masters! Sweet Ladies! Voices from a Medieval Village.* Illustrated by Robert Byrd. Candlewick, 2007. Ages 9–13.

Sloan, Christopher. *Bury the Dead: Tombs, Corpses, Mummies, Skeletons and Rituals.* National Geographic, 2002. Ages 10–14.

St. George, Judith. *The Journey of the One and Only Declaration of Independence.* Illustrated by Will Hillenbrand. Philomel, 2005. (**PI**) Ages 10–13.

———. *So You Want to Be President?* Illustrated by David Small. Philomel, 2000. Ages 7–10. (Also a biography.)

Tanaka, Shelley. *Mummies: The Newest, Coolest, and Creepiest from Around the World.* Abrams, 2005. Ages 9–13.

Walker, Sally M. *Secrets of a Civil War Submarine: Solving the Mysteries of the H. L. Hunley.* Carolrhoda, 2005. Ages 12–14.

Winters, Kay. *Colonial Voices: Hear Them Speak.* Illustrated by Larry Day. Dutton, 2008. (**PI**) Ages 9–12.

Applied Science

Abramson, Andra S. *Heavy Equipment Up Close.* Sterling, 2008. (**PI**) Ages 7–9.

Ball, Johnny. *Go Figure! A Totally Cool Book about Numbers.* DK Publishing, 2005. Ages 10–14.

Carson, Mary Kay. *Exploring the Solar System: A History with 22 Activities.* Chicago Review, 2006. Ages 11–14.

Curlee, Lynn. *Capital.* Atheneum, 2003. (**PI**) Ages 7–11.
———. *Parthenon.* Atheneum, 2004. (**PI**) Ages 11–14.
———. *Skyscrapers.* Atheneum, 2007. Ages 9–13.
Dash, Joan. *The Longitude Prize.* Illustrated by Dušan Petricic. Farrar, 2000. (**PI**) Ages 6–13.
Fisher, Valorie. *How High Can a Dinosaur Count? And Other Math Mysteries.* Random, 2006. (**PI**) Ages 6–10.
Gardner, Robert, and Barbara G. Conklin, *Chemistry Science Fair Projects Using French Fries, Gumdrops, Soap, and Other Organic Stuff.* Enslow, 2004. Ages 11–14.
Giblin, James Cross. *Secrets of the Sphinx.* Illustrated by Bagram Ibatoulline. Scholastic, 2004. Ages 11–14.
Hakim, Joy. *The Story of Science: Aristotle Leads the Way.* Smithsonian, 2004. Ages 11–14. Also in The Story of Science series is *Newton at the Center,* 2005.
Jackson, Donna M. *ER Vets: Life in an Animal Emergency Room.* Houghton, 2005. Ages 12–14.
Katzen, Mollie. *Salad People and More Real Recipes.* Tricycle Press, 2005. Ages 5–8.
Leedy, Loreen. *The Great Graph Contest.* Holiday, 2005. (**PI**) Ages 6–8.
Macaulay, David. *Building Big.* Houghton, 2000. (**PI**) Ages 12–16.
———. *Cathedral: The Story of Its Construction.* Houghton, 1973. (**PI**) Ages 10–16.
———. *Mosque.* Houghton, 2003. (**PI**) Ages 12–16.
———. *The Way Things Work.* Houghton, 1988. Ages 10–15. [CD-ROM version: Dorling Kindersley, 1995.]
Mills, Andrea, and Phil Hunt. *Go! The Whole World of Transportation.* Dorling Kindersley, 2006. Ages 8–12.
Ridley, Sarah. *A Metal Can.* Gareth Stevens, 2006. Ages 7–9.
Ross, Val. *The Road to There: Mapmakers and Their Stories.* Tundra, 2003. Ages 12–16.
Severance, John. *Skyscrapers: How America Grew Up.* Holiday, 2000. Ages 10–14.
Skurzynski, Gloria. *Are We Alone? Scientists Search for Life in Space.* National Geographic, 2004. Ages 10–14.
Sullivan, George. *Built to Last: Building America's Amazing Bridges, Dams, Tunnels, and Skyscrapers.* Scholastic, 2005. Ages 12–16.

Humanities

Aliki. *Ah, Music!* HarperCollins, 2003. (**PI**) Ages 6–9.
Bull, Jane. *The Crafty Art Book.* Dorling Kindersley, 2004. Ages 8–10.
Christelow, Eileen. *What Do Illustrators Do?* Clarion, 1999. Ages 6–10.
Cummings, Pat, compiler–editor. *Talking with Artists,* Vol. 1. Illustrated by various artists. Bradbury, 1992. Ages 8–12. Vol. 2, 1995; Vol. 3, 1999.
Eric Carle Museum of Picture Book Art. *Artist to Artist: 23 Major Illustrators Talk to Children about Their Art.* Philomel, 2007. Ages 9–18.
Fritz, Jean. *Leonardo's Horse.* Illustrated by Hudson Talbot. Putnam, 2001. Ages 9–13.
Govenar, Alan. *Extraordinary Ordinary People: Five American Masters of Traditional Arts.* Candlewick, 2006. Ages 12–15.
Helsby, Genevieve. *Those Amazing Musical Instruments!* Sourcebooks, 2007. Ages 9–14. (Includes CD.)
Levine, Gail Carson. *Writing Magic: Creating Stories That Fly.* HarperCollins, 2006. Ages 9–12.
Lipsey, Jennifer. *I Love to Finger Paint!* Sterling/Lark, 2006. Ages 6–8.
Marcus, Leonard S. *The Wand in the Word: Conversations with Writers of Fantasy.* Candlewick, 2006. Ages 11–14.
Raczka, Bob. *Here's Looking at Me: How Artists See Themselves.* Lerner, 2006. Ages 8–11.
Ruggi, Gilda W. *The Art Book for Children.* Phaidon, 2005. Ages 7–9.
Sayre, Henry. *Cave Paintings to Picasso: The Inside Scoop on 50 Art Masterpieces.* Chronicle, 2004. Ages 11–14.
Swett, Sarah. *Kids Weaving: Projects for Kids of All Ages.* Photography by Chris Hartlove. Illustrated by Lena Corwin. Stewart, Tabori & Chang, 2005. Ages 7–13.
Todd, Mark, and Esther P. Watson. *Whatcha Mean, What's a Zine? The Art of Making Zines and Mini-Comics.* Houghton, 2006. Ages 11–18.
Warhola, James. *Uncle Andy's: A Faabbbulous Visit with Andy Warhol.* Putnam, 2003. (**PI**) Ages 5–8.
Wolf, Allan. *Immersed in Verse: An Informative, Slightly Irreverent & Totally Tremendous Guide to Living the Poet's Life.* Illustrated by Tuesday Mourning. Lark Books, 2006. Ages 12–14.

Informational Book Series

Art
My Very Favorite Art Book series. Sterling/Lark. Ages 6–8.
Start-Up Art and Design series. Cherrytree. Ages 7–10.

Bilingual
Animal Clues/¿Adivina de quién es? series. Rosen. Ages 4–7.
Animales opuestos/Animal Opposites series. Capstone. Ages 4–7.
Everyday Wonders/Maravillas de todos los días series. Rosen. Ages 4–7.

Environment
One Small Step series. Smart Apple Media. Ages 7–10.
Saving Our Living Earth series. Lerner. Ages 10–14.

Geography
America the Beautiful series. Children's Press. Ages 9–13.
Meet Our New Student series. Mitchell Lane. Ages 7–9.
World of Colors series. Capstone. Ages 5–7.

Global Issues
Changing World series. Arcturus. Ages 10–13.

Health and Personal Problems
Head-to-Toe Health series. Marshall Cavendish. Ages 7–9.
How Can I Deal with . . . series. Smart Apple Media. Ages 7–10.
Issues in Focus Today series. Enslow. Ages 12–18.
Issues That Concern You series. Greenhaven. Ages 12–16.

History
America's Living History series. Enslow. Ages 9–14.
Kids' Translations series. Capstone. Ages 8–12. (The "translations" are of important American historical documents.)

Mathematics
Count the Critters series. ABDO. Ages 5–7.
Real World Math series. Cherry Lake. Ages 9–11.
Sir Cumference Math Adventures series. Charlesbridge. Ages 9–11.

Science
Discovery! series. Lerner. Ages 11–15.
Face to Face with Animals series. National Geographic. Ages 7–10.
How It's Made series. Gareth Stevens. Ages 7–9.
Max Axiom series. Capstone. Ages 9–12.
Nic Bishop Science series. Scholastic. Ages 5–7.
Scientists in the Field series. Houghton. Ages 8–12.

Social Studies
How to Get Rich series. National Geographic. Ages 9–13. (Also a History and Mathematics series.)
People in the Community series. Heinemann. Ages 4–6.
Up Close series. Sterling. Ages 7–12.

World Cultures
Cultures of the World series. Marshall Cavendish. Ages 10–13.

Wide Range of Topics
Eyewitness Books series. Dorling Kindersley. Ages 11–15.

Related Films, Videos, and DVDs

Building Big. (2000, miniseries). Author: David Macaulay. 327 minutes.
Dinosaur Bones. (2006). Author: Bob Barner (2001). 12 minutes.
The Emperor's Egg. (2005). Author: Martin Jenkins (1999). 10 minutes.

Magic School Bus. Author: Joanna Cole. 52 videos based on the book series available online at www .scholastic.com/magicschoolbus/tv/video.htm#
Open Wide: Tooth School Inside . . . and Other Stories. (2007). Author: Laurie Keller (2000). 54 minutes.

Sources for Films, Videos, and DVDs

The Video Source Book. Syosset, NY: National Video Clearinghouse, 1979–. Published by Gale Research, Detroit, MI.

An annual reference work that lists media and provides sources for purchase and rental.

Websites of large video distributors:

www.libraryvideo.com
www.knowledgeunlimited.com
http://teacher.scholastic.com/products/westonwoods

PEARSON myeducationkit™ Now go to Chapter 10 in the MyEducationKit (www.myeducationkit.com) for your book, where you can:

- Complete Assignments and Activities that can enrich and extend your knowledge of chapter content.

- Expand your knowledge with content-specific Web Links.

- Learn how authors and illustrators apply their craft by reading the written interviews in the Conversations section for the chapter.

- Review the chapter content by going to the Study Plan, taking a chapter quiz, and receiving feedback on your answers.

- Access the Children's Literature Database for your own exploration.

chapter ELEVEN

Literature for a Diverse Society

Oh, the Places You'll Go

Uh-huh, I've travelled
By car, train, boat, plane
To Kenya, Uganda
France, Italy, Spain.

Still many a country
I plan to explore
Here's how you do it
I've done it before.

Weather won't stop you
Nor cost of the flight
You'll fly the world over
By day and by night.

The means are at hand
You've not far to look
Oh, the places you'll go
When you travel by book.

—*Ashley Bryan*

This chapter is presented in two parts. The first part, An Education That Is Multicultural and Intercultural, focuses on ways teachers can make their teaching relevant to students and to the interconnected world in which they live. The second part, Multicultural and International Literature, identifies literature that supports a culturally-based curriculum.

Section One: An Education That Is Multicultural and Intercultural

A serious mismatch exists in U.S. schools today. On one hand, school curricula and textbooks present predominantly mainstream, European-American perspectives. Moreover, the cadre of U.S. teachers is predominantly (84.3% in 1999–2000) from European-American, suburban backgrounds (U.S. Department of Education, 2000). They have been taught to teach in ways that work best with people with similar backgrounds and often have not had close, sustained relationships with individuals from ethnic, cultural, and socioeconomic backgrounds that differ from their own. On the other hand, school populations in the United States are becoming increasingly diverse, as evidenced by the prediction that the school-aged minority populations will be the majority by 2010 (U.S. Department of Education, 2002).

The resulting mismatch has contributed to an education system that is not working for many students. The Office of National Assessment for Educational Progress reports a continuing reading achievement gap between whites and Native Americans, Latinos, and African Americans. In 2007, the average reading score for white eighth-graders was 272, versus 247 for Native Americans and Latinos and 245 for African Americans (National Center for Education Statistics, 2007). School dropout rates provide further evidence of the problem, indicating that in 2005, the dropout rate was 22.1 percent for Latinos and 10 percent for African Americans, as compared to 5.8 percent for whites (U.S. Department of Education, 2008). Clearly, teachers need to become more familiar with the influence of culture on teaching and learning.

At the same time, U.S. classrooms are experiencing the largest influx of immigrants since the early 1900s, further increasing the diversity of students. More than 13 million legal immigrants (along with an undetermined number of those undocumented) settled in the United States between 1990 and 2000, coming from all parts of the world (U.S. Census Bureau, 2000).

Teachers in all parts of the country are increasingly likely to have students from diverse ethnic, racial, national, and language groups in their classrooms, whether in urban, suburban, or rural areas. This diversity is reflected in the global nature of our lives. Children will live and work in a world that is vastly different from the one in which we grew up. Rapid economic, technological, and social changes are connecting us across the globe. Knowledge of the world and of diverse cultures is no longer a luxury, but a necessity. Children need understandings of both the diverse cultural groups within their own country and of global cultures that cross outside of their borders.

An education that is multicultural and intercultural is one in which diverse cultural perspectives are woven throughout the curriculum and school life, instead of being the focus of a special book or unit (Sleeter & Grant, 1987). This orientation includes the following:

- Understanding one's own personal cultural identity
- Valuing the unique perspectives of diverse cultural groups
- Connecting to the univeral experiences that cut across cultures

- Critiquing the inequities and injustices experienced by specific cultural groups
- Developing a commitment to taking action to create a more just and equitable world

An education that is multicultural and intercultural is culturally responsive, culturally expansive, and culturally critical. Children's literature plays a crucial role by providing students with the opportunity to immerse themselves into story worlds and gain insights into how people feel, live, and think. They go beyond a tourist's perspective of simply gaining information about particular cultures to live *within* these cultures through their experiences with literature.

Culturally Responsive Curriculum

All students need to find their lives and cultural experiences reflected within classrooms and the books they read, but this is much more likely to occur for students from mainstream, European-American families. Culturally responsive curriculum focuses on the need to develop teaching strategies and materials that are more consistent with the cultural orientations of ethnically and globally diverse students. Geneva Gay (2000) points out that using the cultural knowledge, experiences, frames of reference, and performance styles of ethnically diverse students makes learning more relevant and effective (p. 29).

Teachers can become more culturally responsive in their use of literature by following these suggestions:

- *Find Reading Materials That Are Relevant to Students' Lives.* Supporting all students as learners means becoming personally acquainted with students and knowledgeable about books that are culturally relevant to their lives. For ethnically and globally diverse students this may be literature about young people whose lives and cultures are similar to their own. For second-language learners this may be bilingual literature in the student's native tongue, so as to make learning English easier and to signal the value of the student's first language. Students who rarely find their lives reflected in a book may dismiss literacy as irrelevant or even a threat to their cultural identities.

- *Ensure That School and Classroom Literature Collections Reflect the Cultural Diversity of the Classroom, School, Community, and World.* Even when schools and communities are culturally homogeneous, librarians and teachers should select books that reflect the diversity of the greater world. To do so, they may need to search for books from small presses that focus on particular ethnic groups and for translated books originating from other countries.

- *Give Students a Choice in Their Reading Material.* This may require teachers and librarians to broaden the scope of what they consider appropriate reading material to include less conventional formats, such as picture books for older readers and graphic novels, as well as nonfiction materials such as manuals, magazines, and audiobooks. Giving students a choice in what they read acknowledges their lives and interests as significant and relevant within the walls of the classroom.

- *Conference with Students about Their Reading as Often as Possible.* These one-on-one discussions give teachers an opportunity to learn about their students' individual reading interests and needs, to express their interest in what the students are currently reading, and to suggest other books they might like to read.

The search for culturally relevant literature recognizes that all children have multiple cultural identities, including gender, social class, family structure, age, religion, and language, as well as ethnicity and nationality. This broad understanding of culture as ways of living and being in the world that influence our actions, beliefs, and values is essential to understanding why culture matters in our lives. Culture influences how each of us think about ourselves and the world around us. Students from all cultures, including the mainstream, must recognize that they have a particular perspective on the world in order to value as well as critically examine that perspective. This understanding, in turn, supports them in exploring other cultural perspectives.

Culturally Expansive Curriculum

A culturally expansive curriculum builds from awareness of students' own cultural identities to considering points of view that go beyond their own. Literature provides a window to ethnic and global cultures through in-depth inquiries into a particular culture and the integration of multiple cultural perspectives into every classroom study.

An inquiry into a particular culture should include a range of books that reflect the diversity and complexity of that culture. In exploring Navajo culture, for example, students can read historical fiction, such as *Little Woman Warrior Who Came Home* by Evangeline Parsons-Yazzie, along with traditional literature, such as *Ma'ii and Cousin Horned Toad* by Shonto Begay. They can also examine images of contemporary Navajo life both off and on the reservation in *Alice Yazzie's Year* by Ramona Maher and *Racing to the Sun* by Paul Pitts. This range of literature challenges students to go beyond stereotypes to examine the shared values and beliefs within a culture as well as the diversity of views and lives that are integral to every cultural group.

A culturally expansive curriculum becomes inclusive of multiple cultural perspectives across all content areas through the integration of literature. The perspectives of those long neglected—Native Americans, African Americans, and Asian Americans, to name a few—can be included in the social studies and history curriculum. Important contributions by scientists, such as George Washington Carver, can be included in the science curriculum. Works by authors who reflect a range of ethnic and global backgrounds can be included in the reading and literature curriculum. For example, a literature unit could focus on Francisco Jiménez, a Mexican American whose works describe the struggles of immigrants and their families who work in the California fields. Often teachers choose one of the featured author's works to read aloud while students discuss others by that author in literature circles.

The goal of those who write, publish, and promote multicultural and international children's literature is to help people learn about, understand, and ultimately accept those different from themselves, thus breaking the cycles of prejudice and oppression among peoples of different cultures. Progress toward this goal may well begin when young people read multicultural or international literature and realize how similar they are to children of different cultures and how interesting their differences are. They are also challenged not to consider their own culture as the "norm" against which others are judged as strange or exotic. These books help build bridges and cross borders between people of different nationalities and cultures (Lepman, 2002; Rochman, 1993).

The books that are selected for read-alouds, booktalks, book displays, and text sets for classroom studies or independent reading should reflect the diversity of cultural experiences in the classroom as well as invite exploration of broader ethnic and global cultures. Booktalks, for example, might be used to connect students who read mainstream books with literature from a wider range of cultures that have a similar theme or genre. A collection of picture books on families, a common topic investigated in the primary grades, might include the following.

> *Families* by Ann Morris and *Families* by Susan Kuklin (Cross-cultural)
> *I Love Saturdays y Domingos* by Alma Flor Ada, illustrated by Elivia Savadier (Mexican-American)
> *Mayeros: A Yucatec Maya Family* by George Ancona (Mayan Indian, Mexico)
> *My Mei Mei* by Ed Young (Chinese-American)
> *Where's Jamela?* by Niki Daly (South African)
> *My Two Grannies* by Floella Benjamin, illustrated by Margaret Chamberlain (British)

Culturally Critical Curriculum

Although multicultural education celebrates diversity and cross-cultural harmony, its more important goal has always been to transform society and ensure greater voice, equity, and social justice for marginalized groups (Gay, 2000). Raising issues of inequality, power, and discrimination is central to an education that is multicultural and intercultural. Paulo Freire (1970) believes that students need to critically read the world by questioning "what is" and "who benefits," instead of accepting inequity as just the way things work. Students need to examine why these social problems exist and who benefits from keeping inequities in place. They also need to consider new possibilities by asking "what if" and taking action for social change. Through these questions, students develop a critical consciousness about their everyday world and the ways in which power plays out in their relationships and society.

Literature plays a significant role in social justice education by documenting the history and contemporary stories of marginalized peoples, presenting their perspectives, and providing a way for their voices to be heard. These perspectives are rarely included within textbooks and the standard curriculum. Literature can support students in considering multiple perspectives on complex social issues such as undocumented immigrants, as in *Friends from the Other Side* by Gloria Anzaldúa, *The Circuit* by Francisco Jiménez, *Ask Me No Questions* by Maria Budhos, *Ziba Came on a Boat* by Liz Lofthouse, and *The Arrival* by Shaun Tan.

A critical literacy or social justice curriculum has four dimensions (Lewison, Leland, and Harste, 2008), all of which can be supported by literature:

- Disrupting the commonplace by looking at the everyday through new lenses that challenge assumptions (e.g., *The Other Side* by Jacqueline Woodson or *Wringer* by Jerry Spinelli)
- Considering multiple perspectives that may be contradictory or offer alternative interpretations of history or current issues (e.g., *Voices in the Park* by Anthony Browne or *Seedfolks* by Paul Fleischman)
- Focusing on sociopolitical issues to examine societal systems and unequal power relationships and to get at the root causes of social problems (e.g., *Freedom Summer* by Deborah Wiles or *Nory Ryan's Song* by Patricia Reilly Giff)
- Taking action and promoting social justice by taking a stand against oppression and acting to create change (e.g., *The Lady in the Box* by Ann McGovern or *Iqbal* by Francesco D'Adamo)

SECTION TWO: Multicultural and International Literature

Two bodies of literature support a curriculum that is multicultural and intercultural. Multicultural literature and international literature are not separate genres; rather, they occur in all genres. You will have noted many references to these books and authors throughout the previous chapters in discussions of trends and issues, notable author and illustrator lists, and recommended booklists. In an ideal, culturally integrated world, such inclusion would be sufficient. But the groups and perspectives represented in multicultural literature have, until recently, been absent or misrepresented in books for children and remain underrepresented today. Furthermore, neither multicultural nor international literature is well known or fully recognized by the educational mainstream. Changing demographics in the United States and globalization of society require school curricula and materials that will prepare young people to live in a changing and ever more diverse world.

Definitions and Descriptions

Multicultural literature is defined in various ways by educators and scholars. Some define it broadly as all books about people and their individual or group experiences within a particular culture, including mainstream cultures. Most define it more narrowly as literature by and about groups that have been marginalized and disregarded by the dominant European-American culture in the United States. This definition includes all racial, ethnic, religious, and language minorities, those living with physical or mental disabilities, gays and lesbians, and the poor. In this chapter, we highlight literature by and about the racial, religious, and language groups in the United States who have created a substantial body of children's literature. This includes literature by and about African Americans, Asian/Pacific Americans (including people of Chinese, Hmong, Japanese, Korean, and Vietnamese descent), Latinos (including Cuban Americans, Mexican Americans, Puerto Ricans, and others of Spanish descent), religious cultures (including Buddhist, Hindu, Jewish, and Muslim), and Native Americans (a general term referring to the many tribes of American Indians). Examples of books about other marginalized groups are found throughout the genre chapters, especially in the lists of recommended books.

International literature in the United States refers to books that are set in countries outside of the United States. The focus of this chapter is on books originally written and published in countries other than the United States for children of those other countries and then published in this country. These books can be subdivided into three categories:

- *English Language Books.* Books originally written in English in another country and then published or distributed in the United States. Examples include *How to Heal a Broken Wing* by Bob Graham (Australia) and the Harry Potter series (U.K.).
- *Translated Books.* Books written in a language other than English in another country, then translated into English and published in the United States. Examples include *The Friends* by Kazumi Yumoto (Japan) and *The Zoo* by Suzy Lee (Korea).
- *Foreign Language Books.* Books written and published in a language other than English in another country, then published or distributed in the United States in that language. One example is *Le Petit Prince* by Antoine de Saint-Exupéry (France).

Many authors and illustrators of books set in international contexts are from the United States. These books are written and published in the United States primarily for an audience of U.S. children, rather than written for children of that specific culture. Many of these books, often referred to as *global literature,* have been integrated into other chapters and so are not highlighted in this chapter. Categories of these books include:

- Books written by immigrants from another country who now reside in the United States and write about their country of origin; for example, *The Red Scarf Girl* by Ji-Li Jiang (China).
- Books written by American authors who draw from their family's heritage in their country of origin, but whose own experiences have been in the United States; for example, *When My Name Was Keoko* by Linda Sue Park (Korea).
- Books written by an author who lived in another country for a significant period of time; for example, *Colibrí* by Ann Cameron (Guatemala).
- Books written by authors who research a particular country and who may or may not have visited that country as part of their research; for example, *The Day of the Pelican* by Katherine Paterson (Kosovo).

The Value of Multicultural and International Literature for Children

Multicultural and international literature builds bridges of understanding across countries and cultures, connecting children to their home cultures and to the world beyond their homes. This literature benefits children in the following ways:

- Gives young people who are members of marginalized groups or recent immigrants the opportunity to develop a better sense of who they are, improve their self-esteem, and consequently take social action for a better future.
- Develops an understanding of and appreciation for other cultures, bringing alive those histories, traditions, and people.
- Addresses contemporary issues of race, religion, poverty, exceptionalities, and sexual orientation from the perspectives of members of those groups to provide a more complete understanding of current issues and of the people who belong to these groups, thus challenging prejudice and discrimination.
- Adds the perspective of marginalized groups and global cultures to the study of history, thereby giving students a more complete understanding of past events.
- Helps young people realize the social injustices endured by particular peoples in the United States and abroad, both now and in the past, to build a determination to work for a more equitable future.
- Builds students' interest in the people and places they are reading about and paves the way to a deeper understanding and appreciation of the geographical and historical content encountered in textbooks and later content-area studies.
- Provides authenticity through literature written by insiders to a country, region, or ethnic group and allows members of that group to define themselves. These portrayals challenge the typical media coverage of violence and crises.

- Develops a bond of shared experience with children of other ethnicities and nations and enables students to acquire cultural literacy with a global perspective.

In a study by Monson, Howe, and Greenlee (1989), 200 U.S. children, ages 9 to 11, were asked what they wanted to know about children in other countries. Their responses, categorized into nine questions, then formed the basis for a comparison of eight social studies textbooks and fifteen works of children's fiction about Australia. It was found that both textbooks and trade books gave information about the country. However, the novels answered more of the children's questions and were richer in details of daily life and human emotion than the textbooks. The social studies texts gave many facts about the country, whereas the novels showed the implications of the facts for children's lives and helped the readers "live in" the country for a time.

Evaluation and Selection of Multicultural and International Literature

In addition to the requirement that literature have high literary merit, multicultural and international books need to be examined for *cultural authenticity,* an analysis of the extent to which a book reflects the core beliefs and values and depicts the details of everyday life and language for a specific cultural group. Given the diversity within all cultural groups, there is never one image of life within any culture and so underlying world views are often more important to consider. Readers from the culture depicted in a book need to be able to identify and feel affirmed that what they are reading rings true in their lives; readers from another culture need to be able to identify and learn something of value about cultural similarities and differences (Fox & Short, 2003). The following criteria should be considered when evaluating and selecting multicultural and international books for school and classroom libraries:

- *Authenticity of Cultural Beliefs and Values from the Perspective of That Group.* Research the background of the author and illustrator to determine their experiences or research related to this story (check their websites). Examine the values and beliefs of characters and whether they connect to the actual lives of people from within that culture.
- *Accuracy of Cultural Details in Text and Illustrations.* Examine the details of everyday life, such as food, clothing, homes, speech patterns, and so on, represented in the book and whether they fit within the range of experiences of that culture.
- *Integration of Culturally Authentic Language.* Look for the natural integration of the language or dialect of a specific cultural group, especially within dialogue. Some terms or names in the original language of translated books, for example, should be retained. Check whether a glossary is included if needed.
- *Power Relationships between Characters.* Examine which characters are in roles of power or significance in a book, with a particular focus on how the story is resolved and who is in leadership and action roles.
- *Perspectives and Audience.* Look at whose perspectives and experiences are portrayed and who tells the story. In particular, consider whether the story is told from a mainstream or European-American perspective about ethnically or globally diverse characters. Also consider

whether the intended audience is children from within that culture or if the book was written to inform a mainstream audience about a particular culture.

■ *Balance between Historic and Contemporary Views of Groups.* The majority of literature about global and ethnic cultures is found in the genres of traditional literature and historical fiction, creating stereotypes of these cultures as dated and set in the past. Search for books that reflect contemporary images to add to your collection.

■ *Adequate Representation of Any Group within a Collection.* No one book can definitively describe a culture or cultural experience. Look for a range of books that provide multiple representations of a culture and be aware of particular images that are overrepresented—for example, almost all of the picture books on Korean Americans depict them as newly arrived immigrants to the United States. These overrepresentations and generalizations reflect stereotypes of a particular group.

Book awards can guide teachers and librarians toward high-quality multicultural and international books. The best known of these is the Coretta Scott King Award, given annually to an African-American author and illustrator whose books are judged to be the most outstanding inspirational and educational literature for children. The Américas Award and the Pura Belpré Award honor outstanding Latino authors and illustrators of children's books and are good resources for locating authentic literature for this rapidly growing population. Recently established awards include the Asian Pacific American Award for Literature, honoring outstanding work of Asian-American authors and illustrators, and the American Indian Youth Literature Awards, honoring the very best writing and illustrations by and about American Indians. Awards such as these encourage the publication of more and better-quality multicultural literature.

Awards for international literature are plentiful but often more difficult to locate. The Mildred L. Batchelder Award is given to a U.S. publisher of the most distinguished translated children's book, encouraging the translation and publication of international books in the United States (see Appendix A). Two annual award lists are the Outstanding International Books List (www.usbby.org) and Notable Books for a Global Society (www.tcnj.edu/~childlit). Also, many countries have their own national awards, similar to the Newbery and Caldecott awards in the United States. The Hans Christian Andersen award winners and nominees are a good source of the most outstanding authors and illustrators from around the world (www.ibby.org). Worlds of Words (www.wowlit.org) has a searchable database of international literature available in the United States and several online journals discussing the use of this literature in classrooms and reviews of cultural authenticity.

In recent years, small presses have been a source of multicultural and international books that are particularly valuable for their cultural points of view.

Asian American Curriculum Project. Publishes and distributes Asian-American books from other small and large presses. www.asianamericanbooks.com (Another distributor is Asia for Kids at www.afk.com)

Children's Book Press. Publishes folktales and contemporary picture books, often bilingual, for Native American, Asian-American, and Latino children. www.childrensbookpress .org

Cinco Puntos. Focuses on the U.S./Mexico border region, the Southwest, and Mexico. www .cincopuntos.com

Piñata Books/Arte Público. Publishes children's books with a Latino perspective. www .latinoteca.com/arte-publico-press/pinata-books

Just Us Books. Produces Afrocentric books that enhance the self-esteem of African-American children. www.justusbooks.com

Lee & Low Books. Asian-American–owned company that stresses authenticity in stories for Asian-American, Latino, and African-American children. www.leeandlow.com

Oyate. A Native American organization that critically evaluates books with Native themes and distributes books with an emphasis on those written and illustrated by Native people. www .oyate.org

Evaluating, selecting, and bringing multicultural and international literature to your classroom, although essential, is not enough to ensure that your students will actually read the books. Without adult guidance, children tend to choose books about children like themselves, so invite students to explore these books through reading them aloud, giving booktalks, and encouraging discussion in literature circles.

Multicultural Literature

Historical Overview of Multicultural Literature

Many cultures living in the United States were long ignored within children's books or portrayed as crudely stereotyped characters, objects of ridicule, or shadowy secondary characters. Books with blatant racism, such as Helen Bannerman's *The Story of Little Black Sambo* (1900) and Hugh Lofting's *The Voyages of Dr. Dolittle* (1922) have today either been rewritten to eliminate the racism or have disappeared from libraries.

PEARSON
myeducationkit™

Go to Activity 1 in the Assignments and Activities section of Chapter 11 in MyEducation-Kit; complete the activity on examining the *Little Black Sambo* controversy.

The first harbinger of change came in 1949 when an African-American author, Arna Bontemps, became the first member of a minority group to win a Newbery Honor Award, for *Story of the Negro.* A more sympathetic attitude toward diverse ethnic cultures emerged in the 1950s, as evidenced by the positive, yet somewhat patronizing, treatment of multicultural characters in such Newbery Medal winners as *Amos Fortune, Free Man* by Elizabeth Yates (1950) and *. . . And Now Miguel* by Joseph Krumgold (1953).

The Civil Rights Movement of the 1960s focused attention on the social inequities and racial injustices that prevailed in the United States. The spirit of the times resulted in two landmark publications. The first of these was *The Snowy Day* by Ezra Jack Keats (1962), the first Caldecott Medal book with an African-American protagonist. The second publication was a powerful article in 1965 by Nancy Larrick, "The All-White World of Children's Books." Larrick reported that African Americans either were omitted entirely or were scarcely mentioned in nearly all U.S. children's books. American trade book publishers, the education system, and the public library system were called on to fill this void.

The Coretta Scott King Award was established in 1969 to recognize African-American authors, but it was not until 1975 that an author of color, Virginia Hamilton, won a Newbery Medal. The prevailing opinion among U.S. children's book publishers and professional reviewers shifted to focus on members of a group as the ones most able to write authentically about their own cultures and experiences. European-American authors were no longer as likely to win major awards for writing about minorities as they were in the early 1970s.

MILESTONES *in the Development of Multicultural Literature*

Date	Event	Significance
1932	*Waterless Mountain* by Laura Armer wins Newbery Medal	One of the few children's books about minorities in the first half of the twentieth century
1946	*The Moved-Outers* by Florence C. Means wins Newbery Honor	A departure from stereotyped depiction of minorities begins
1949	*Story of the Negro* by Arna Bontemps wins Newbery Honor	First minority author to win a Newbery Honor
1950	*Song of the Swallows* by Leo Politi wins Caldecott Medal	First picture book with a Latino protagonist to win the Caldecott Medal
1963	*The Snowy Day* by Ezra Jack Keats wins Caldecott Medal	First picture book with an African-American protagonist to win the Caldecott Medal
1965	"The All-White World of Children's Books" by Nancy Larrick published in *Saturday Review*	Called the nation's attention to the lack of multicultural literature
1969	Coretta Scott King Award founded	African-American literature and authors begin to be promoted and supported
1975	*M. C. Higgins, the Great* by Virginia Hamilton wins Newbery Medal	First book by a minority author to win the Newbery Medal
1976	*Why Mosquitoes Buzz in People's Ears* illustrated by Leo and Diane Dillon wins Caldecott Medal	First picture book by an African-American illustrator to win the Caldecott Medal
1990	*Lon Po Po: A Red-Riding Hood Story from China* translated and illustrated by Ed Young wins Caldecott Medal	First picture book by a Chinese-American illustrator to win the Caldecott Medal
1993	Américas Award founded	Encouraged authors and illustrators to publish excellent books portraying Latin America, the Caribbean, and Latinos in the United States
1994	*Grandfather's Journey* written and illustrated by Allen Say wins Caldecott Medal	First picture book by a Japanese-American illustrator to win the Caldecott Medal
1996	Pura Belpré Award founded	Promoted Latino literature, authors, and illustrators
2001	*The Trip Back Home* by Janet S. Wong, illustrated by Bo Jia, wins first Asian Pacific American Award for Literature	Promoted Asian-American literature, authors, and illustrators

The late 1990s saw much-needed development in Latino literature. Bilingual books published in response to the demands of ESOL/ELL (English for speakers of other languages/English language learners) programs and the founding of the Américas Award and the Pura Belpré Awards contributed to this growth.

Although the last several decades have seen positive changes in the status of multicultural literature in the United States, there is still a marked shortage of both books and of authors and illustrators from within those cultures. The Cooperative Children's Book Center (Horning, Lindgren, Michaelson, & Schliesman, 2009) reported the following statistics from approximately 3,000 new children's and young adult books they reviewed in 2008:

- 5.7 percent (172 books) had significant African or African-American content (48% created by black authors/illustrators).
- 3.3 percent (98 books) had significant Asian/Pacific or Asian-/Pacific-American content (79% created by authors/illustrators of Asian/Pacific heritage).
- 2.6 percent (79 books) had significant Latino content (61% created by Latino authors/illustrators).
- 1.3 percent (40 books) featured American Indian themes, topics, or characters (22% created by American Indian authors/illustrators).

A broader indication of the shortage is to note that approximately 13 percent of the new books published for children in 2008 were by or about people of color, even though these groups represented more than 35 percent of the population in 2005 (National Center for Educational Statistics, 2007). In addition to not enough books, subtle issues of racism and stereotypes continue to be problematic. All children have the right to see themselves within a book; to find the truth of their experiences, rather than misrepresentations, and so many challenges remain in the writing and publication of multicultural literature.

Types of Multicultural Literature

Each ethnic group contains subgroups that differ remarkably from one another in country of origin, language, race, traditions, and present location. Teachers must be especially conscious of and sensitive to these differences and guard against presenting these groups as uniform or selecting literature that does so. Gross overgeneralization is not only inaccurate but also a form of stereotyping.

African-American Literature

Of all multicultural groups living in the United States, African Americans have produced the largest and most rapidly growing body of children's literature (Bishop, 2007). Every genre is well represented in African-American literature, but none better than poetry. Because it is so personal, poetry portrays a culture well, as is evident in the sensitive yet powerful work of poets Nikki Giovanni, Nikki Grimes, Eloise Greenfield, Langston Hughes, Marilyn Nelson, and Joyce Carol Thomas. For example, see *The Blacker the Berry* by Joyce Carol Thomas.

Tapping into their rich oral tradition, African Americans have contributed Anansi the Spider, Brer Rabbit, and John Henry the Steel Drivin' Man to the list of favorite U.S. folklore characters. Even today, authors are bringing folktales to the United States from Africa. Examples include *Beautiful Blackbird* by Ashley Bryan and *The Girl Who Spun Gold* by Virginia Hamilton, illustrated by Leo and Diane Dillon.

In some cases, African Americans have reclaimed their tales by retelling (without racist elements) stories that were first written by European-American authors, as Julius Lester has done in his retelling of Joel Chandler Harris's *The Tales of Uncle Remus: The Adventures of Brer Rabbit.*

Excellent Multicultural Literature to READ ALOUD

Canales, Viola. *The Tequila Worm.* Ages 12–15. (Mexican-American)
Curtis, Christopher Paul. *Elijah of Buxton.* Ages 9–12. (African-American)
English, Karen. *Hot Day on Abbott Avenue.* Illustrated by Javaka Steptoe. Ages 5–8. (African-American)
Jaramillo, Ann. *La línea.* Ages 11–15. (Mexican-American)
Levine, Ellen. *Henry's Freedom Box.* Illustrated by Kadir Nelson. Ages 5–8. (African-American)
Morales, Yuyi. *Just a Minute.* Ages 5–8. (Mexican-American)
Na, An. *A Step from Heaven.* Ages 13–18. (Korean-American)
Nislick, June Levitt. *Zayda Was a Cowboy.* Ages 9–13. (Jewish)
Park, Linda Sue. *Mulberry Project.* Ages 10–14. (Korean-American)
Soto, Gary. *Chato and the Party Animals.* Illustrated by Susan Guevara. Ages 5–8. (Mexican-American)
Tingle, Tim. *Crossing Bok Chitto.* Illustrated by Jeanne Rorex Bridges. Ages 8–11. (Choctaw/Native American)

More recent modern folktales include *Thunder Rose* by Jerdine Nolen and *Porch Lies* by Patricia McKissack.

African Americans have told the stories of their lives in the United States through both historical and realistic fiction. The stories for older readers often include painfully harsh but accurate accounts of racial oppression, as in *Elijah of Buxton* by Christopher Paul Curtis or Mildred Taylor's historical fiction saga of the close-knit Logan family, including *Roll of Thunder, Hear My Cry.* Teachers can balance these stories with more positive, encouraging contemporary novels such as Jacqueline Woodson's *Locomotion* and Angela Johnson's *Heaven.*

Many picture books focus on stories based on historical events, particularly slavery or civil rights, but the range of themes and topics in historical and contemporary picture books is expanding. The works of illustrators Leo and Diane Dillon, Jerry Pinkney, Brian Pinkney, E. B. Lewis, Bryan Collier, and Kadir Nelson deserve special notice. Examples include *Henry's Freedom Box* by Ellen Levine, illustrated by Kadir Nelson, and *The Moon over Star* by Dianna H. Aston, illustrated by Jerry Pinkney.

African-American nonfiction is mainly biography, featuring sports heroes as well as those from a broader spectrum of achievement—for example, see *Becoming Billie Holiday* by Carole Boston Weatherford, illustrated by Floyd Cooper, and *Carver: A Life in Poems* by Marilyn Nelson.

Asian-/Pacific-American Literature

Asian-/Pacific-American children's literature is mainly represented in the United States by stories about Chinese Americans, Japanese Americans, and Korean Americans, possibly because these groups have lived in this country longer than others, such as Vietnamese Americans. A major theme in much of the fiction and nonfiction for older readers is the oppression that drove the people out of their homelands or the prejudice and adjustments that they faced as newcomers in this country. A more positive theme is learning to appreciate one's cultural heritage while adjusting to life in the United States. A good example is An Na's *A Step from Heaven.*

AFRICAN-AMERICAN

Leo and Diane Dillon, illustrators of two Caldecott Medal books. Leo is the first African American to win a Caldecott Medal. *Why Mosquitoes Buzz in People's Ears; Ashanti to Zulu.*

Angela Johnson, author of books on family relationships, longing, and loss. *Tell Me a Story, Mama; Heaven.*

Patricia McKissack, author of modern African-American folktales and historical books. *Goin' Someplace Special.*

Walter Dean Myers, author of sometimes gritty contemporary realistic fiction about African Americans growing up. *Scorpions; Monster.* www.walterdeanmyers.net

Kadir Nelson, illustrator and author of historical picture books with dramatic expressive paintings. *We Are the Ship; Henry's Freedom Box.* www.kadirnelson.com

Brian Pinkney, illustrator who uses swirling lines and intricate scratchboard renderings. *Cendrillon: A Caribbean Cinderella; Boycott Blues.* www.brianpinkney.net

Mildred Taylor, award-winning author of historical fiction about growing up black in southern United States in the 1940s and 1950s. *Roll of Thunder, Hear My Cry.*

Jacqueline Woodson, author of introspective novels dealing with adversity and loss. *Miracle's Boys; Feathers; Locomotion.* www.jacqueline woodson.com

ASIAN-/PACIFIC-AMERICAN

Lenore Look, author of contemporary picture books and short chapter books on Chinese-American family life. *Henry's First-Moon Birthday; Ruby Lu, Empress of Everything.*

Linda Sue Park, author of historical and contemporary fiction about Korean and Korean-American experiences. *Keeping Score; Project Mulberry.* www.lindasuepark.com

Allen Say, illustrator and author of picture books who uses soft, evocative watercolors to focus on the cultural struggles of Japanese-American and Japanese characters. *Grandfather's Journey; Tea with Milk.*

Kashmira Sheth, author of historical and contemporary fiction about India and the experiences of Indian Americans. *Keeping Corner; Blue Jasmine.* www.kashmirasheth.typepad.com

LATINO

Francisco Jiménez, author of autobiographical stories of his childhood as an undocumented Mexican immigrant farm worker in California. *The Circuit; Breaking Through; Reaching Out.* www.scu.edu/cas/modernlanguages/faculty staff/jimenezhomepage.cfm

Pat Mora, author of picture storybooks, biographies, and poems about the Mexican-American experience. *Tomás and the Library Lady; Doña Flor.* www.patmora.com

Yuyi Morales, illustrator and author of picture books combining storytelling and glowing images from Mexican traditions. *Just a Minute; Just in Case.* www.yuyimorales.com

Gary Soto, author of contemporary stories about the Mexican-American experience. *Chato and the Party Animals; Baseball in April.* www.garysoto.com

NATIVE AMERICAN

Joseph Bruchac, Abenaki author of Native American historical and contemporary novels as well as traditional literature. *Buffalo Song; Hidden Roots; Code Talker.* www.josephbruchac.com

Louise Erdrich, author of historical fiction about an Ojibwa tribe on Lake Superior. *The Birchbark House; The Game of Silence; The Porcupine Year.*

Paul Goble, reteller and illustrator of Great Plains folktales and legends. *The Girl Who Loved Wild Horses.*

S. D. Nelson, illustrator and author of traditional and historical picture books with a focus on Lakota images and stories. *Crazy Horse's Vision; Quiet Hero: The Ira Hayes Story.* www .sdnelson.net

RELIGIOUS CULTURES

Adèle Geras, anthologist of folktales and other stories celebrating the Jewish tradition. *My Grandmother's Stories: A Collection of Jewish Folk Tales.* www.adelegeras.com

Asma Mobin-Uddin, Pakistani-American author of picture books about Muslim-American experiences and Islamic religious traditions. *My Name Is Bilal; A Party in Ramadan.* www .asmamobinuddin.com

Traditional stories from Asia retold in English have contributed many interesting folktales and folktale variants to children's libraries. Characters who are generally thought of as European, such as Little Red Riding Hood and Cinderella, have their Asian counterparts. Examples are *Lon Po Po: A Red-Riding Hood Story from China,* translated and illustrated by Ed Young, and *Yeh-Shen: A Cinderella Story from China* by Ai-Ling Louie, illustrated by Ed Young.

Asian-American artists have brought the sophisticated style and technical artistry of Asia to U.S. children's book illustration. Ed Young's use of screenlike panels and exotic, textured paper and Allen Say's precision are especially noteworthy. Examples are *Tea with Milk* by Allen Say and *My Mei Mei* by Ed Young.

> **PEARSON**
> **myeducationkit**™
>
> Go to the Conversations section of Chapter 11 in MyEducationKit to read the interview with Allen Say.

The body of Asian-/Pacific-American children's literature is rapidly expanding, particularly in realistic and historical fiction, through authors such as Linda Sue Park, Cynthia Kadohata, Lenore Look, Grace Lin, and Kashmira Sheth. The Asian Pacific American Award for Literature, along with small presses and distributors, has also expanded this body of literature. The Pacific is still not represented well in this body of literature, although Hawai'i has a long history of small presses with a strong focus on traditional literature. A notable recent Hawaiian title is *Surfer of the Century* by Ellie Crowe, illustrated by Richard Waldrep.

Latino Literature

Few Latino children's books are published in the United States, despite the fact that Latinos represent an estimated 13 percent of the population and are considered the fastest-growing segment of the population (U.S. Census Bureau, 2000). The books that are available mainly focus on the experiences of Mexican Americans and Puerto Ricans, with a few books based on Cuban-American experiences. This body of literature continues to be filled with stereotyped portrayals of Latinos living in poverty and struggling to learn English, with their problems typically solved by European Americans. Many of the books focus on superficial aspects of culture, such as festivals and food, rather than the everyday lives and struggles of Latino children. A recent development has been the natural integration of Spanish phrases and words into books written in English to reflect the cognitively complex codeswitching of bilingual speakers.

Recent developments hold promise for improvement in the amount and quality of Latino literature. One exciting development is the number of outstanding Latino authors and illustrators who are creating books for children, including Alma Flor Ada, George Ancona, Lulu Delacre, Gary Soto, Yuyi Morales, Francisco Jiménez, Juan Felipe Herrera, Maya Christina González, and Margarita Engle. Good examples are *Just in Case* by Yuyi Morales and *The Circuit: Stories from the Life of a Migrant Child* by Francisco Jiménez.

The Américas Award (honoring a U.S. work that authentically presents Latino experiences in Latin America, the Caribbean, or the United States) and the Pura Belpré Award (honoring outstanding Latino authors and illustrators) promote more high-quality Latino literature for children. Another resource is the Barahona Center for the Study of Books in Spanish for Children and Adolescents at the University of California San Marcos (www.csusm.edu/csb), which contains lists of books in English about Latinos, as well as Spanish books.

Native American Literature

Almost from the moment that European explorers landed on this continent some 500 years ago, Native Americans have suffered at the hands of European Americans. Consequently, books written from a Native American perspective often focus on oppression and racism, ranging from historical novels, such as *Sweetgrass Basket* by Marlene Carvell, to contemporary novels, such as *The Absolutely True Diary of a Part-Time Indian* by Sherman Alexie. *Shin-Chi's Canoe* by Nicola I. Campbell, illustrated by Kim LaFave, is an example of these themes in picture books. Appreciation, celebration, and protection of nature—central tenets of Native American cultures—are other recurrent themes in this body of literature. Examples are *Buffalo Song* by Joseph Bruchac, illustrated by Bill Farnsworth, and *The Birchbark House* by Louise Erdrich.

Although much has been written about Native Americans, relatively little has been written by members of this culture, such that this body of literature is dominated by outsider perspectives and problems of authenticity. Another imbalance is that the majority of books published continue to be traditional literature and historical fiction, with few contemporary books to challenge stereotypes of Native Americans as existing "long ago." A further issue is that many tribal nations have few or no children's books available about their specific nation, while others, such as the Navajos, have a larger body of work. Small press publishers specializing in literature by Native Americans may help to change these imbalances.

Native Americans who are known for their children's books include Cynthia Leitich Smith for her novels, Joseph Bruchac for his historical and realistic novels and retold stories, Tim Tingle for his retold stories, and S. D. Nelson and Shonto Begay for their illustrations. Examples are *Rain Is Not My Indian Name* by Cynthia Leitich Smith, *Hidden Roots* by Joseph Bruchac, and *Crossing Bok Chitto* by Tim Tingle, illustrated by Jeanne Rorex Bridges.

PEARSON
myeducationkit™

Go to the Conversations section of Chapter 11 in MyEducationKit to read the interview with Joseph Bruchac.

PEARSON
myeducationkit™

Go to Activity 2 in the Assignments and Activities section of Chapter 11 in MyEducationKit; complete the activity on evaluating and selecting Native American literature.

Religious Cultures Literature

As the mainstream religious culture in the United States, Christianity dominates children's books. Books that portray other religious cultures in the United States, including Buddhist, Hindu, Jewish, and Muslim cultures, are difficult to find. Good, contemporary children's fiction set within the context of a religious culture and written from the perspective of a member of that religion is especially scarce. An example is Asma Mobin-Uddin's *My Name Is Bilal,* a picture book for older readers illustrated by Barbara Kiwak, which explores fitting into the U.S. mainstream while remaining true to one's Islamic culture and heritage. Nonfiction and folklore on the subject of religion are somewhat more plentiful. Author–illustrator Demi, for example, is known for her picture book biographies and story collections about Buddha and Muhammed.

The body of Jewish children's literature is by far the largest produced by any nonmainstream religious culture in this country and mainly focuses on the Jewish Holocaust in Europe during the 1930s and 1940s. The prejudice and cruelty that led to the Holocaust and the death camps are recurring themes in both fiction and nonfiction for older readers. Since many Jewish people immigrated to the United States as the Nazi threat grew in Europe, much Holocaust literature has been written by eyewitnesses or by those whose relatives were victims. Examples are *Thanks to My Mother* by Schoschana Rabinovici and *Always Remember Me* by Marisabina Russo.

Illustrated Jewish folktales offer excellent, witty stories of high literary quality to complement the strong information books about Jewish holidays and traditions. One major concern is the lack of picture books and novels reflecting contemporary Jewish-American experiences, although a few are emerging, such as *I Wanna Be Your Shoebox* by Cristina García.

The Jewish community has produced a number of excellent authors and illustrators of children's books. Literary creativity is promoted through two book award programs: the National Jewish Book Awards and the Association of Jewish Libraries' Sydney Taylor Awards for children's and young adult literature.

Bilingual Literature

Bilingual books provide the text in two languages, frequently English/Spanish to reflect the rapid growth of the Latino population in the United States. Picture books and shorter chapter books predominate, since longer books in two languages would be bulky and costly and are not generally useful for advanced readers. These books, if well done, are helpful to children in ESOL/ELL and world language programs. They also provide a way to value and maintain literacy in a child's first language. However, not all bilingual books have artful or even accurate translations, so careful selection is advisable. The concept book *My Colors, My World/Mis colores, mi mundo* by Maya Christina González involves a child's search for the colors hidden in her desert environment through poetic text in English and Spanish. Bilingual books reflecting Asian languages, particularly Japanese and Chinese, are also being published.

International Literature

Historical Overview of International Literature

Much of the children's literature that was available in the United States during the seventeenth, eighteenth, nineteenth, and early twentieth centuries came from Europe. These early children's books are an important part of our cultural heritage, but we seldom think of the fact that they were originally published in other countries and languages. They are so familiar that we consider them our children's classics, and indeed they have become so. The accompanying Milestones feature lists a sampling of international children's classics published from the end of the seventeenth century up to World War II.

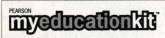

Go to Activity 3 in the Assignments and Activities section of Chapter 11 in MyEducationKit; complete the activity on examining award-winning international books.

With the rapid growth in the U.S. children's book field in the twentieth century, the flow of books from other countries became overshadowed by large numbers of U.S. publications. In addition, during World War II, little cultural exchange occurred across international borders. The end of World War II saw a change in the international mood, and two developments occurred that had far-reaching effects on the children's book field: (1) children's books in translation began to be published in unprecedented numbers and (2) the international children's book field was established. Prominent features of the international children's book field include:

- The International Board on Books for Young People (www.ibby.org), an organization involving people from many nations who are involved in all aspects of the children's book field. The U.S. affiliate organization is the United States Board on Books for Young People (www.usbby.org).

✦ *Excellent International Literature* to READ ALOUD

Boyce, Frank Cottrell. *Millions*. Ages 11–14. England.
Carmi, Daniella. *Samir and Yonatan*. Ages 9–12. Israel.
Chen, Zhiyuan. *Guji, Guji*. Ages 5–8. Taiwan.
Dowd, Siobhan. *The London Eye Mystery*. Ages 8–11. U.K.
Goscinny, René. *Nicholas*. Illustrated by Jean Jacques Sempé. Ages 9–12. France.
Graham, Bob. "*Let's Get a Pup!" Said Kate*. Ages 3–8. Australia.
Skármeta, Antonio. *The Composition*. Illustrated by Alfonso Ruano. Ages 8–12. Venezuela.
Valckx, Catharina. *Lizette's Green Sock*. Ages 3–6. France.
Wild, Margaret. *Fox*. Illustrated by Ron Brooks. Ages 6–8. Australia.
Yumoto, Kazumi. *The Friends*. Ages 10–14. Japan.

- Book award programs, the most prominent of which are the Hans Christian Andersen Award and the Batchelder Award. (See Appendix A.)
- A biennial IBBY world congress and a biennial USBBY conference.
- A journal, *Bookbird: Journal of International Children's Literature.*

We are all citizens of an ever-changing world. Our lives are going global, connected by the stories we share across cultures. International literature immerses children in stories to gain insights into how people live, think, and feel in other times and places. We need to promote more literary exchanges with countries whose bodies of literature are growing rapidly to bring more of the world's best literature to our children's attention. We also must encourage the development of stronger literature from countries that have not had the resources to support the writing and publication of their own national literature.

International Literature by World Regions

The international books that are most often available in the United States have been and continue to be books from other English-speaking countries. The largest numbers come from Great Britain, Australia, and Canada. Although the books do not require translation, they are often published in the United States with changes in spelling, character and place names, and sometimes titles and cover illustrations. The major awards and award winners from English-speaking countries are listed in Appendix A.

Translated books come to the United States from around the world, but the largest numbers come from Western Europe. Today, many books come from Sweden, Norway, Denmark, Switzerland, the Netherlands, Germany, France, and Belgium. A few books come from Italy and Spain. An example from Sweden is *In Ned's Head* by Anders Jacobsson and Sören Olsson.

Most translated children's books from the Middle East are novels for middle-graders or young adults and come to the United States from Israel. Books from or set in other countries in this region—such as *Tasting the Sky* by Ibtisam Barakat, set in Palestine, and *Persepolis* by Marjane Satrapi, set in Iran—are all the more welcome for their rarity.

MILESTONES

in the Development of International Children's Literature

Date	Event	Signficance
1657	*Orbis Pictus* by John Amos Comenius	Earliest nonfiction picture book
1697	*Tales of Mother Goose* by Charles Perrault	Earliest folktales from France
1719/ 1726	*Robinson Crusoe* by Daniel Defoe and *Gulliver's Travels* by Jonathan Swift	Two early adult adventure books from England adopted by children
1812	*Nursery and Household Tales* by Jakob and Wilhelm Grimm	Traditional folktales from Germany
1836	*Fairy Tales* by Hans Christian Andersen	Early modern folktales from Denmark
1846	*Book of Nonsense* by Edward Lear	Early humorous poetry from England
1865	*Alice's Adventures in Wonderland* by Lewis Carroll	Classic English modern fantasy
1880	*Heidi* by Johanna Spyri	Early realistic story from Switzerland
1881	*The Adventures of Pinocchio* by Carlo Collodi	Modern fantasy from Italy
1883	*Treasure Island* by Robert Louis Stevenson	Adventure tale by a Scottish author
1885	*A Child's Garden of Verses* by Robert Louis Stevenson	Classic collection of Golden Age poems from England
1894	*The Jungle Book* by Rudyard Kipling	Animal stories set in India by an English author
1901	*The Tale of Peter Rabbit* by Beatrix Potter	Classic English picture book
1906	*The Wonderful Adventures of Nils* by Selma Lagerlöf	A fantasy trip around Sweden
1908	*The Wind in the Willows* by Kenneth Grahame	Animal fantasy from England
1908	*Anne of Green Gables* by Lucy Maud Montgomery	Realistic family story from Canada
1926	*Winnie-the-Pooh* by A. A. Milne	Personified toy story from England
1928	*Bambi* by Felix Salten	Personified deer story from Germany
1931	*The Story of Babar* by Jean de Brunhoff	Personified elephant story from France
1945	*Pippi Longstocking* by Astrid Lindgren	Classic fantasy from Sweden

Translated children's literature from Asia originates mostly in Japan, but books from Korea, China, and Taiwan are increasingly available. Japan and Korea have a sophisticated field of book illustrating, and many beautifully illustrated picture books are making their way into the U.S. market. An example from South Korea is *While We Were Out* by Ho Baek Lee.

African nations, with the exception of the Republic of South Africa, have produced little children's literature that has been exported to the United States. The reasons for this are many,

Notable Authors and Illustrators
of International Literature

David Almond, British Carnegie Medal–winning author of novels often described as magical realism. *Skellig; Kit's Wilderness.* www.davidalmond.com

Anthony Browne, British author/illustrator whose stark surrealism reveals modern social ills. *Voices in the Park; Little Beauty.*

Mem Fox, Australian author of picture storybooks for beginning readers. *Wilfrid Gordon McDonald Partridge; Ten Little Fingers and Ten Little Toes.* www.memfox.com

Cornelia Funke, German author of award-winning fantasy novels, including the Inkheart trilogy. *The Dragon Rider; The Thief Lord.* www.corneliafunke.de/en

Bob Graham, Australian author and illustrator of whimsical picture books. *How to Heal a Broken Wing.*

Emily Gravett, British author and illustrator of award-winning picture books full of intricate details and dry humor. *Little Mouse's Big Book of Fears; Wolves.* www.emilygravett.com

Beverley Naidoo, South African author and Carnegie Medalist whose novels deal with the effects of political injustice on children. *The Other Side of Truth; Burn My Heart.* www.beverleynaidoo.com

Philip Pullman, British creator of His Dark Materials trilogy, comprised of *The Golden Compass, The Subtle Knife,* and *The Amber Spyglass.* www.philip-pullman.com

J. K. Rowling, British author of the best-selling series about Harry Potter, a child wizard. *Harry Potter and the Sorcerer's Stone* and its sequels. www.jkrowling.com

Shaun Tan, Malaysian-Australian author and illustrator who explores social and political issues through surreal, dreamlike imagery. *The Arrival; Tales from Outer Suburbia.* www.shauntan.net

Margaret Wild, Australian author of picture books about friendship and its power to heal. *Fox; The Very Best of Friends.*

Tim Wynne-Jones, Canadian author of humorous and suspenseful novels for middle-graders and young adults. *The Maestro; Rex Zero, King of Nothing.* www.timwynne-jones.com

but the most influential one is that of economics. Publishing books is expensive, especially in full color; therefore, the publishing industry is not firmly established in these countries. Books of realistic fiction in which contemporary life in an African country is portrayed are rare. Beverley Naidoo's *The Other Side of Truth,* for example, is set in Nigeria, then London, and addresses political persecution.

One of the challenges for those who work with children is combating the ignorance that is at the root of racial, cultural, and religious prejudice and intolerance. Children's literature, particularly the rich multicultural and international selections that are currently available, is a powerful tool in this effort, for it shows that the similarities between all people are much more fundamental than the differences. We are connected by a shared humanity and by the uniqueness that each culture contributes to a richly diverse world. Children need to find their own lives reflected within a book as well as imagine cultural ways of living and thinking beyond their own. Integrating a literature that is multicultural and intercultural into classrooms builds bridges of understanding across cultures.

Issues & Topics for FURTHER INVESTIGATION

- Select a minority group whose perspectives have been omitted or inadequately covered in the study of U.S. history. Examples include Native Americans and their forced removal to reservations in the 1800s, Japanese Americans and their internment in prison camps during World War II, and Chinese Americans and their role in the construction of the transcontinental railroad in the 1860s. Read several works of age-appropriate historical fiction or nonfiction about that era written from the perspective of that group. Discuss how including these books in the study of U.S. history is likely to change students' understanding of the particular historical era.

- Choose a global issue, such as violence, conservation, child labor, or hunger, and pull together a text set of ten to fifteen books that explore this issue across multiple cultures. Compare the various perspectives on this issue from these different cultures.

- Select a country or region outside the United States that you will likely have to teach about. Compile an annotated bibliography of ten to twenty children's books, both fiction and nonfiction, that could promote interest in and help young people learn more about the country or region.

References

Bishop, R. S. (2007). *Free within ourselves: The development of African American children's literature.* Portsmouth, NH: Heinemann.

Bryan, A. (1998). Oh, the places you'll go. In *Book poems.* New York: The Children's Book Council.

Fox, D., & Short, K. (2003). *Stories matter: The complexity of cultural authenticity in children's literature.* Urbana, IL: National Council of Teachers of English.

Freire, P. (1970). *Pedagogy of the oppressed.* New York: Continuum.

Gay, G. (2000). *Culturally responsive teaching.* New York: Teachers College Press.

Horning, K. T., Lindgren, M. V., Michaelson, T., & Schliesman, M. (2009). *CCBC Choices, 2009.* Madison: University Publications, University of Wisconsin-Madison.

Larrick, N. (1965, September 11). The all-white world of children's books. *Saturday Review,* 63–65, 84–85.

Lepman, J. (2002). *A bridge of children's books.* Dublin, Ireland: O'Brien Press.

Lewison, M., Leland, C., & Harste, J. (2008). *Creating critical classrooms.* New York: Erlbaum.

McGovern, A. (1997). *The lady in the box.* Illustrated by Marni Backer. Madison, CT: Turtle Books.

Monson, D. L., Howe, K., & Greenlee, A. (1989). Helping children develop cross-cultural understanding with children's books. *Early Child Development and Care, 48* (special issue), 3–8.

National Center for Education Statistics. (2007). *The nation's report card: Reading 2007.* Retrieved June 27, 2009, from http://nces.ed.gov/nationsreportcard/reading_2007.

Paterson, K. (2009). *The Day of the Pelican.*

Rochman, H. (1993). *Against borders.* Chicago: ALA Books.

de Saint-Exupéry, A. (2001). *Le petit prince.* New York: Marnier.

Sleeter, C., & Grant, C. (1987). An analysis of multi-cultural education in the United States. *Harvard Education Review, 57,* 421–444.

U.S. Census Bureau. (2000). www.census.gov.

U.S. Department of Education. (2000). *School and staffing survey: 1999–2000 public school teacher questionnaire and public charter school teacher questionnaire.* Washington, DC: NCES.

U.S. Department of Education. (2002). *Minority population growth.* Washington, DC: Author.

U.S. Department of Education. (2008). *Dropout rates in the United States.* Washington, DC: NCES.

✰ Recommended Multicultural Books

Ages refer to approximate interest levels.

(**PI**) Picture book
(**COL**) Short story collection

African-American Literature

Aston, Dianna H. *The Moon over Star.* Illustrated by Jerry Pinkney. Dial, 2008. (**PI**) Ages 5–8.

Bridges, Ruby, and Margo Lundell, editors. *Through My Eyes.* Scholastic, 1999. Ages 9–15.

Bryan, Ashley. *Ashley Bryan: Words to My Life's Song.* Photographs by Bill Meguinness. Atheneum, 2009. (**PI**) Ages 8–12.

———. *Beautiful Blackbird.* Atheneum, 2003. (**PI**) Ages 5–8.

Cline-Ransome, Lesa. *Satchel Paige.* Illustrated by James Ransome. Simon & Schuster, 2000. Ages 7–10. (Also a biography.)

Curtis, Christopher Paul. *Elijah of Buxton.* Scholastic, 2007. Ages 9–12.

English, Karen. *Hot Day on Abbott Avenue.* Illustrated by Javaka Steptoe. Clarion, 2004. (**PI**) Ages 5–8.

Fradin, Dennis Brindell, and Judith Bloom Fradin. *Ida B. Wells: Mother of the Civil Rights Movement.* Clarion, 2000. Ages 10–16. (Also a biography.)

Grimes, Nikki. *Bronx Masquerade.* Dial, 2002. Ages 12–18.

———. *Danitra Brown, Class Clown.* Illustrated by E. B. Lewis. HarperCollins, 2005. (**PI**) Ages 7–10.

Hamilton, Virginia. *Many Thousand Gone: African Americans from Slavery to Freedom.* Illustrated by Leo and Diane Dillon. Random, 1992. Ages 10–14.

———. *The People Could Fly: The Picture Book.* Illustrated by Leo and Diane Dillon. Knopf, 2004. (**PI**) Ages 11–15.

Howard, Elizabeth Fitzgerald. *Virgie Goes to School with Us Boys.* Illustrated by E. B. Lewis. Simon & Schuster, 2000. (**PI**) Ages 6–9.

Hudson, Wade, and Cheryl W. Hudson, compilers. *In Praise of Our Fathers and Our Mothers: A Black Family Treasury of Outstanding Authors and Artists.* Just Us Books, 1997. Ages 9–14.

Johnson, Angela. *Heaven.* Simon & Schuster, 1998. Ages 12–16.

———. *Tell Me a Story, Mama.* Illustrated by David Soman. Scholastic, 1992. (**PI**) Ages 3–7.

Lester, Julius. *Day of Tears: A Novel in Dialogue.* Hyperion, 2005. Ages 12–14.

———. *John Henry.* Illustrated by Jerry Pinkney. Dial, 1994. (**PI**) Ages 7–10.

Levine, Ellen. *Henry's Freedom Box.* Illustrated by Kadir Nelson. Scholastic, 2007. (**PI**) Ages 5–8.

McKissack, Patricia. *Goin' Someplace Special.* Illustrated by Jerry Pinkney. Scholastic, 2001. (**PI**) Ages 6–9.

———. *Porch Lies: Tales of Slicksters, Tricksters, and Other Wily Characters.* Illustrated by André Carrilho. Schwartz & Wade, 2006. (**PI**) Ages 7–10.

Myers, Walter Dean. *Malcolm X: A Fire Burning Brightly.* Illustrated by Leonard Jenkins. HarperCollins, 2000. (**PI**) Ages 7–11. (Also a biography.)

———. *Scorpions.* Harper, 1988. Ages 9–12.

Nelson, Kadir. *We Are the Ship: The Story of Negro League Baseball.* Jump at the Sun/Hyperion, 2008. (**PI**) Ages 7–10.

Nelson, Marilyn. *Carver: A Life in Poems.* Front Street, 2000. Ages 12–15. (Also a biography.)

Nolen, Jerdine. *Thunder Rose.* Illustrated by Kadir Nelson. Harcourt, 2003. (**PI**) Ages 5–8.

Pinkney, Andrea D. *Boycott Blues: How Rosa Parks Inspired a Nation.* Illustrated by Brian Pinkney. Greenwillow, 2008. (**PI**) Ages 5–8.

Shange, Ntozake. *Coretta Scott.* Illustrated by Kadir Nelson. Amistad, 2009. (**PI**) Ages 5–8.

Taylor, Mildred. *Roll of Thunder, Hear My Cry.* Dial, 1976. Ages 9–12.

Thomas, Joyce Carol. *The Blacker the Berry: Poems.* Illustrated by Floyd Cooper. Joanna Cotler Books, 2008. (**COL**) Ages 5–8.

Weatherford, Carole Boston. *Becoming Billie Holiday.* Illustrated by Floyd Cooper. Wordsong, 2008. Ages 12–15.

Wiles, Deborah. *Freedom Summer.* Illustrated by Jerome Lagarrigue. Atheneum, 2001. (**PI**) Ages 7–10.

Woodson, Jacqueline. *Feathers.* Putnam, 2007. Ages 11–14.

———. *Locomotion.* Putnam, 2003. Ages 9–12.

———. *Miracle's Boys.* Putnam, 2000. Ages 10–16.

———. *The Other Side.* Illustrated by E. B. Lewis. Putnam, 2001. (**PI**) Ages 5–8.

———. *Show Way.* Illustrated by Hudson Talbott. Putnam, 2005. (**PI**) Ages 7–12.

Asian-/Pacific-American Literature

Barasch, Lynne. *Hiromi's Hands.* Lee & Low, 2007. (**PI**) Ages 5–8. (Japanese-American)

Brown, Jackie. *Little Cricket.* Hyperion, 2004. Ages 11–14. (Hmong)

Budhos, Marina. *Ask Me No Questions.* Atheneum, 2006. Ages 10–14. (Bangladeshi-American)

Cha, Dia. *Dia's Story Cloth: The Hmong People's Journey to Freedom.* Stitchery by Chue and Nhia Thao Cha. Lee & Low, 1996. (**PI**) Ages 8–11. (Hmong)

Crowe, Ellie. *Surfer of the Century: The Life of Duke Kahanamoku.* Illustrated by Richard Waldrep. Lee & Low, 2007. (**PI**) Ages 8–11. (Hawaiian)

Gilmore, Rachna. *A Gift for Gita.* Illustrated by Alice Priestley. Tilbury, 2002. (**PI**) Ages 6–9. (Indian-Canadian)

Heo, Yumi. *Ten Days and Nine Nights: An Adoption Story.* Schwartz & Wade, 2009. (**PI**) Ages 5–8. (Korean-American)

Kadohata, Cynthia. *Kira-Kira.* Atheneum, 2004. Ages 11–14. (Japanese-American)

———. *Weedflower.* Atheneum, 2006. Ages 11–14. (Japanese-American)

Krishnaswami, Uma. *Chachaji's Cup.* Illustrated by Sumeya Sitaraman. Children's Book Press, 2003. (**PI**) Ages 5–9. (Indian-American)

Lin, Grace. *The Year of the Dog.* Little Brown, 2006. Ages 8–11. (Taiwanese-American)

Look, Lenore. *Henry's First-Moon Birthday.* Illustrated by Yumi Heo. Atheneum, 2001. (**PI**) Ages 4–8. (Chinese-American)

———. *Ruby Lu: Empress of Everything.* Atheneum, 2006. Ages 6–9. (Chinese-American)

———. *Uncle Peter's Amazing Chinese Wedding.* Illustrated by Yumi Heo. Atheneum, 2006. (**PI**) Ages 5–8. (Chinese-American)

Ly, Many. *Roots and Wings.* Delacorte, 2008. Ages 12–16. (Cambodian-American)

Mochizuki, Ken. *Baseball Saved Us.* Illustrated by Dom Lee. Lee and Low, 1993. (**PI**) Ages 7–10. (Japanese-American)

Na, An. *A Step from Heaven.* Front Street, 2001. Ages 13–18. (Korean-American)

Park, Linda Sue. *Keeping Score.* Clarion, 2008. Ages 9–12. (Korean-American)

———. *Project Mulberry.* Clarion, 2005. Ages 10–14. (Korean-American)

Salisbury, Graham. *Night of the Howling Dogs.* Wendy Lamb Books, 2007. Ages 8–11. (Hawaiian)

Say, Allen. *Grandfather's Journey.* Houghton, 1993. (**PI**) Ages 7–9. (Japanese-American)

———. *Tea with Milk.* Lorraine/Houghton, 1999. (**PI**) Ages 6–9. (Japanese-American)

Sheth, Kashmira. *Blue Jasmine.* Hyperion, 2004. Ages 11–14. (Indian-American)

Strom, Yale. *Quilted Landscape: Conversations with Young Immigrants.* Simon & Schuster, 1996. Ages 11–14. (Varied cultures)

Uchida, Yoshiko. *Journey to Topaz.* Scribner's, 1971. Ages 9–12. (Japanese-American)

Wong, Janet S. *Alex and the Wednesday Chess Club.* Illustrated by Stacey Schuett. M. K. McElderry, 2004. (**PI**) Ages 5–8. (Chinese-American)

Yep, Laurence. *Dragon's Gate.* HarperCollins, 1993. Ages 12–14. (Chinese-American)

———. *Dragonwings.* Harper, 1975. Ages 9–12. (Chinese-American)

Young, Ed. *My Mei Mei.* Philomel, 2006. (**PI**) Ages 4–7. (Chinese-American)

Latino Literature

Ada, Alma Flor. *I Love Saturdays y Domingos.* Illustrated by Elivia Savadier. Atheneum, 2002. (**PI**) Ages 4–8. (Mexican-American)

Ancona, George. *Barrio: José's Neighborhood.* Harcourt, 1998. Ages 6–9.

———. *Capoeira: Game! Dance! Martial Art!* Lee & Low, 2007. Ages 10–14. (Brazilian-American)

———. *Fiesta U.S.A.* Lodestar, 1995. Ages 8–10.

Canales, Viola. *The Tequila Worm.* Random, 2005. Ages 12–15. (Mexican-American)

Freedman, Russell. *In the Days of the Vaqueros: America's First True Cowboys.* Clarion, 2001. Ages 10–14. (Mexican-American)

González, Lucia M. *The Storyteller's Candle.* Illustrated by Lulu Delacre. Children's Books Press, 2008. (**PI**) Ages 5–8. (Puerto Rican–American)

Hayes, Joe. *Dance, Nana, Dance/Baila, Nana, baila: Cuban Folktales in English and Spanish.* Illustrated by Mauricio Trenard Sayago. (**COL**) Ages 8–11. (Cuban-American)

Jaramillo, Ann. *La línea.* Roaring Brook, 2006. Ages 11–15. (Mexican-American)

Jiménez, Francisco. *The Circuit: Stories from the Life of a Migrant Child.* Houghton, 1999. (**COL**) Ages 10–14. (See also *Breaking Through* and *Reaching Out.*)

———. *La mariposa.* Illustrated by Simón Silva. Houghton, 1998. (**PI**) Ages 8–11. (Mexican-American)

Joseph, Lynn. *The Color of My Words.* HarperCollins, 2000. Ages 10–14. (Dominican)

Mora, Pat. *Doña Flor.* Illustrated by Raúl Colón. Knopf, 2005. (**PI**) Ages 5–8. (Mexican-American)

———. *Tomás and the Library Lady.* Illustrated by Raúl Colón. Knopf, 1997. (**PI**) Ages 6–8. (Mexican-American)

Morales, Yuyi. *Just a Minute.* Chronicle Books, 2003. (**PI**) Ages 5–8. (Mexican-American)

———. *Just in Case.* Roaring Brook Press, 2008. (**PI**) Ages 5–8. (Mexican-American)

Resau, Laura. *What the Moon Saw.* Delacorte, 2006. Ages 11–15. (Mexican-American)

Ryan, Pam Muñoz. *Becoming Naomi León.* Scholastic, 2004. Ages 11–15. (Mexican-American)

Soto, Gary. *Chato and the Party Animals.* Illustrated by Susan Guevara. Putnam, 2000. (**PI**) Ages 5–8. (Mexican-American)

———. *Fearless Fernie: Hanging Out with Fernie and Me: Poems.* Illustrated by Regan Dunnick. Putnam, 2002. (**COL**) Ages 10–14. (Mexican-American)

Veciana-Suarez, Ana. *Flight to Freedom.* Orchard, 2002. Ages 12–14. (Cuban-American)

Native American Literature

Alexie, Sherman. *The Absolutely True Diary of a Part-Time Indian.* Little, Brown, 2007. Ages 14–16. (Spokane/Coeur d'Alene)

Ancona, George. *Mayeros: A Yucatec Maya Family.* Lothrop, 1997. Ages 7–11. (Mayan/Mexico)

Begay, Shonto. *Ma'ii and Cousin Horned Toad.* Scholastic, 1992. (**PI**) Ages 6–9. (Diné/Navajo)

Bruchac, Joseph. *Buffalo Song.* Illustrated by Bill Farnsworth. Lee & Low, 2008. (**PI**) Ages 8–11. (Nez Percé)

———. *Code Talker.* Dial, 2005. Ages 12–15. (Diné/Navajo)

———. *Crazy Horse's Vision.* Illustrated by S. D. Nelson. Lee & Low, 2000. (**PI**) Ages 6–10. (Lakota)

———. *Hidden Roots.* Scholastic, 2006. Ages 8–11. (Abenaki)

———. *Wabi: A Hero's Tale.* Dial, 2006. Ages 12–14.

Campbell, Nicola I. *Shin-Chi's Canoe.* Illustrated by Kim LaFave. Groundwood, 2008. (**PI**) Ages 5–8. (Interior Salish/Métis/Canada)

Carvell, Marlene. *Sweetgrass Basket.* Dutton, 2005. Ages 10–14. (Mohawk)

Erdrich, Louise. *The Birchbark House.* Hyperion, 1999. Ages 8–12. (See also *The Game of Silence; The Porcupine Year*) (Ojibwe)

Goble, Paul. *The Girl Who Loved Wild Horses.* Bradbury, 1978. (**PI**) Ages 6–8.

Maher, Ramona. *Alice Yazzie's Year.* Illustrated by Shonto Begay. Tricycle, 2003. (**PI**) (Diné/Navajo)

Medicine Crow, Joseph. *Counting Coup: Becoming a Crow Chief on the Reservation and Beyond.* National Geographic, 2006. Ages 10–14. (Absarokee)

Messinger, Carla, & Susan Katz. *When the Shadbush Blooms.* Illustrated by David Kanietakeron Fadden. Tricycle, 2007. (**PI**) Ages 5–8. (Lenape)

Nelson, S. D. *Quiet Hero: The Ira Hayes Story.* Lee & Low, 2006. (**PI**) Ages 8–11. (Pima)

Nicholson, Caitlin Dale, & Leona Morin-Neilson. *Niwechihaw = I Help.* Illustrated by Caitlin Dale

Nicholson. Groundwood, 2008. (PI) Ages 5–8. (Cree)

Parsons-Yazzie, Evangeline. *Dzani Yazhi Naazbaa': Little Woman Warrior Who Came Home: A Story of the Navajo Long Walk.* Illustrated by Irving Toddy. Salina Bookshelf, 2005. (PI) Ages 8–11. (Diné/Navajo)

Pitts, Paul. *Racing to the Sun.* HarperCollins, 1988. Ages 9–12. (Navajo)

Smith, Cynthia Leitich. *Rain Is Not My Indian Name.* HarperCollins, 2001. Ages 10–14. (Muskogee)

Tingle, Tim. *Crossing Bok Chitto: A Choctaw Tale of Friendship and Freedom.* Illustrated by Jeanne Rorex Bridges. Cinco Puntos, 2006. (PI) Ages 8–11. (Choctaw)

Religious Cultures Literature

Bunting, Eve. *One Candle.* Illustrated by Wendy Popp. HarperCollins, 2002. (PI) Ages 6–9. (Jewish)

Demi. *Buddha.* Henry Holt, 1996. (PI) Ages 5–8. (Buddhist)

———. *Muhammad.* M. K. McElderry, 2003. (PI) Ages 8–11. (Muslim)

Ferber, Brenda. *Julia's Kitchen.* Farrar, 2006. Ages 10–14. (Jewish)

García, Cristina. *I Wanna Be Your Shoebox.* Simon & Schuster, 2008. Ages 8–11. (Jewish)

Geras, Adèle. *My Grandmother's Stories: A Collection of Jewish Folk Tales.* Illustrated by Anita Lobel. Knopf, 2003 (1990). (PI) Ages 8–10. (Jewish)

Hershenhorn, Esther. *Chicken Soup by Heart.* Illustrated by Rosanne Litzinger. Simon & Schuster, 2002. (PI) Ages 4–7. (Jewish)

Hesse, Karen. *The Stone Lamp: Eight Stories of Hanukkah through History.* Illustrated by Brian Pinkney. Hyperion, 2003. (COL) Ages 9–13. (Jewish)

Kimmel, Eric A., reteller. *Gershon's Monster: A Story for the Jewish New Year.* Illustrated by Jon J. Muth. Scholastic, 2000. Ages 6–11. (Jewish) (legend)

———. *Wonders and Miracles: A Passover Companion.* Scholastic, 2004. (COL) Ages 11–14. (Jewish)

Krishnaswami, Uma. *The Closet Ghosts.* Illustrated by Shiraaz Bhabha. Children's Book Press, 2005. (PI) Ages 6–8. (Hindu)

Lingen, Marissa. *The Jewish Americans.* Mason Crest, 2009. Ages 10–14. (Jewish)

Littman, Sarah. *Confessions of a Closet Catholic.* Dutton, 2005. Ages 10–14. (Jewish)

Millman, Isaac. *Hidden Child.* Illustrated. Farrar, 2005. Ages 9–14. (Jewish)

Mobin-Uddin, Asma. *The Best Eid Ever.* Illustrated by Laura Jacobsen. Boyds Mills, 2007. (PI) Ages 5–8. (Muslim)

———. *My Name Is Bilal.* Illustrated by Barbara Kiwak. Boyds Mills, 2005. (PI) Ages 9–12. (Muslim)

———. *A Party in Ramadan.* Illustrated by Laura Jacobsen. Boyds Mills, 2009. (PI) Ages 5–8. (Muslim)

Nislick, June Levitt. *Zayda Was a Cowboy.* Jewish Publication Society, 2005. Ages 9–13. (Jewish)

Rabinovici, Schoschana. *Thanks to My Mother.* Penguin, 1988. Ages 10–14. (Jewish)

Rocklin, Joanne. *Strudel Stories.* Delacorte, 1999. Ages 7–12. (Jewish)

Rubin, Susan Goldman. *Fireflies in the Dark: The Story of Friedl Dicker-Brandeis and the Children of Terezin.* Holiday, 2000. (PI) Ages 11–14. (Jewish)

Russo, Marisabina. *Always Remember Me: How One Family Survived World War II.* Atheneum, 2005. (PI) Ages 8–11. (Jewish)

Schmidt, Gary. *Mara's Stories: Glimmers in the Darkness.* Holt, 2001. Ages 11–14. (Jewish)

Bilingual Literature

Ada, Alma Flor. *Gathering the Sun: An Alphabet in Spanish and English.* Translated by Rosa Zubizarreta. Illustrated by Simón Silva. Lothrop, 1997. Ages 5–9. (Also a poetry book.) (English/Spanish)

Alarcón, Francisco X. *Animal Poems of the Iguazú: Poems/Animalario del Iguazú: Poemas.* Illustrated by Maya Christina González. Children's Book Press, 2008. (COL) Ages 9–12. (English/Spanish)

———. *Poems to Dream Together/Poemas para soñar juntos.* Illustrated by Paula Barragán. Lee & Low, 2005. (COL) Ages 8–12. (English/Spanish)

Anzaldúa, Gloria. *Friends from the Other Side/Amigos del otro lado.* Illustrated by Consuelo Mendez. Children's Book Press, 1993. (PI) Ages 6–9. (English/Spanish)

Argueta, Jorge. *A Movie in My Pillow/Una película en mi almohada: Poems.* Illustrated by Elizabeth

Gómez. Children's Book Press, 2001. (**PI**) Ages 8–12. (Also a poetry book.) (English/Spanish)

Brown, Mónica. *Pelé, King of Soccer/Pelé, el rey del fútbol.* Translated by Fernando Gayesky. Illustrated by Rudy Gutierrez. Rayo, 2009. (**PI**) Ages 5–8. (English/Spanish)

———. *My Name Is Celia: The Life of Celia Cruz/Me llamo Celia: La vida de Celia Cruz.* Illustrated by Rafael López. Rising Moon, 2004. (**PI**) Ages 8–11. (English/Spanish)

Carlson, Lori, editor. *Red Hot Salsa: Bilingual Poems on Being Young and Latino in the United States.* Henry Holt, 2005. (**COL**) Ages 10–14. (English/Spanish)

Cohn, Diana. *¡Sí, se puede!/Yes, We Can!: Janitor Strike in L.A.* Translated by Sharon Franco. Illustrated by Francisco Delgado. Cinco Puntos, 2002. (**PI**) Ages 6–8. (English/Spanish)

Colato Laínez, Rene. *Playing Lotería/El juego de la lotería.* Illustrated by Hill Arena. Luna Rising, 2005. (**PI**) Ages 5–8. (English/Spanish)

Cumpiano, Ina. *Quinito, Day and Night/Quinito, día y noche.* Illustrated by José Ramírez. Children's Book Press, 2008. (**PI**) Ages 5–8. (English/Spanish)

———. *Quinito's Neighborhood/El vecindario de Quinito.* Illustrated by José Ramírez. Children's Book Press, 2005. (**PI**) Ages 4–7. (English/Spanish)

Garza, Carmen Lomas, with Harriet Rohmer. *In My Family/En mi familia.* Edited by David Schecter. Translated by Francisco X. Alarcón. Children's Book Press, 1996. (**PI**) Ages 5–12. (English/Spanish)

González, Maya Christina. *My Colors, My World/Mis colores, mi mundo.* Children's Book Press, 2007. (**PI**) Ages 5–8. (English/Spanish)

Guy, Ginger Foglesong. *Siesta.* Illustrated by René King Moreno. Greenwillow, 2005. (**PI**) Ages 3–6. (Also a concept book.) (English/Spanish)

Herrera, Juan Felipe. *Grandma and Me at the Flea/Los meros meros remateros.* Illustrated by Anita DeLucio-Brock. Children's Book Press, 2002. (**PI**) Ages 4–8. (English/Spanish)

———. *The Upside Down Boy/El niño de cabeza.* Illustrated by Elizabeth Gómez. Children's Book Press, 2000. (**PI**) Ages 8–11. (English/Spanish)

Ho, Minfong. *Maples in the Mist: Children's Poems from the Tang Dynasty.* Illustrated by Jean and Mousien Tseng. Translated by Minfong Ho. Lothrop, 1996. Ages 8–14. (Also a poetry book.) (English/Chinese)

Kitsao, Jay. *McHeshi Goes to the Market.* Illustrated by Wanjiku Mathenge. Jacaranda Designs, 1995. (**PI**) Ages 3–5. (English/Swahili) (See others in the McHeshi series.)

Lee, Jeanne. *Song of Mu Lan.* Front Street, 1995. (**PI**) Ages 5–8. (English/Chinese)

Lee-Tai, Amy. *A Place Where Sunflowers Grow.* Translated by Marc Akio Lee. Illustrated by Felicia Hoshino. Children's Book Press, 2006. (**PI**) Ages 5–8. (English/Japanese)

MacDonald, Margaret Read. *The Girl Who Wore Too Much: A Folktale from Thailand.* Thai text by Supaporn Vathanaprida. Illustrated by Yvonne LeBrun Davis. August House, 1998. (**PI**) Ages 4–8. (English/Thai)

Medina, Jane. *The Dream on Blanca's Wall/El sueño pegado en la pared de Blanca.* Illustrated by Robert Casilla. Boyds Mills/Wordsong, 2004. Ages 11–12. (English/Spanish)

Nye, Naomi Shihab, editor. *The Tree Is Older Than You Are: A Bilingual Gathering of Poems and Stories from Mexico with Paintings by Mexican Artists.* Simon & Schuster, 1995. (**COL**) Ages 8–16. (English/Spanish)

Pérez, Amada Irma. *My Diary from Here to There/Mi diario de aquí hasta allá.* Illustrated by Maya Christina González. Children's Book Press, 2002. (**PI**) Ages 8–10. (English/Spanish)

Robles, Anthony. *Lakas and the Makibaka Hotel/Si Lakas at ang Makibaka Hotel.* Translated by Eloisa D. de Jesús. Illustrated by Carl Angel. Children's Book Press, 2006. Ages 7–9. (English/Tagalog)

Shin, Sun Yung. *Cooper's Lesson.* Translated by Min Paek. Illustrated by Kim Cogan. Children's Book Press, 2004. (**PI**) Ages 5–8. (English/Korean)

Song, Ha. *Indebted as Lord Chom: The Legend of the Forbidden Street/No nhu Chua Chom.* Illustrated by Ly Thu Ha. East West Discovery Press, 2006. (**PI**) Ages 5–8. (English/Vietnamese)

Stewart, Mark, and Mike Kennedy. *Latino Baseball's Finest Fielders/Los más destacados guantes del béisbol latino.* Translated by Manuel Kalmanovitz. Millbrook, 2002. (**COL**) Ages 9–13. (English/Spanish) (See companion volume, *Latino Baseball's Hottest Hitters,* 2002.)

Tran, Truong. *Going Home, Coming Home/Ve Nha, Tham Que Huong*. Illustrated by Ann Phong. Children's Book Press, 2003. (**PI**) Ages 5–8. (English/Vietnamese)

Zepeda, Gwendolyn. *Growing Up with Tamales/Los tamales de Ana*. Translated by Gabriela Baeza Ventura. Illustrated by April Ward. Piñata Books, 2008. (**PI**) Ages 5–8. (English/Spanish)

✪ Recommended International Books

Ages refer to approximate interest levels. Country of original publication is noted.
  (**PI**) Picture .book
  (**COL**) Short story collection

English Language Books

Ahlberg, Janet, and Allan Ahlberg. *Each Peach Pear Plum*. Viking, 1979. Ages 3–6. (U.K.)

———. *The Jolly Postman*. Little, Brown, 1986. Ages 5–8. (U.K.)

Alborough, Jez. *Fix-It Duck*. HarperCollins, 2002. (**PI**) Ages 2–5. (U.K.)

Asare, Meshack. *Sosu's Call*. Kane/Miller, 2002. (**PI**) Ages 6–9. (Ghana)

Baker, Jeannie. *Home*. Greenwillow, 2004. (**PI**) Ages 5–8. (Australia)

Barakat, Ibtisam. *Tasting the Sky: A Palestinian Childhood*. Farrar, 2007. Ages 10–14. (Palestine)

Base, Graeme. *The Water Hole*. Abrams, 2001. (**PI**) Ages 4–8. (Australia)

Bateson, Catherine. *Stranded in Boringsville*. Holiday House, 2005. Ages 10–14. (Australia)

Benjamin, Floella. *My Two Grannies*. Illustrated by Margaret Chamberlain. Francis Lincoln, 2008. (**PI**) Ages 6–9. (U.K.)

Boyce, Frank Cottrell. *Framed*. HarperCollins, 2006. Ages 11–14. Humorous. (U.K.)

———. *Millions*. HarperCollins, 2004. Ages 11–14. Humorous. (U.K.)

Briggs, Raymond. *The Snowman*. Random House, 1978. (**PI**) Ages 5–8. (U.K.)

Browne, Anthony. *Little Beauty*. Candlewick, 2008. (**PI**) Ages 5–8. (U.K.)

———. *Voices in the Park*. DK, 2001. (**PI**) Ages 8–11. (U.K.)

Brugman, Alyssa. *Being Bindy*. Delacorte, 2006. Ages 12–15. (Australia)

Burgess, Melvin. *Kite*. Farrar, 2000. Ages 12–16. (U.K.)

Child, Lauren. *I Will Never Not Ever Eat a Tomato*. Candlewick, 2000. (**PI**) Ages 3–8. (U.K.)

Clarke, Judith. *Kalpana's Dream*. Front Street, 2005. Ages 12–15. (Australia)

Colfer, Eoin. *Artemis Fowl*. Hyperion, 2001. Ages 10–12. (Ireland)

Crossley-Holland, Kevin. *The Seeing Stone*. Scholastic, 2001. Ages 10–15. (U.K.)

Daly, Niki. *Once Upon a Time*. Farrar, 2003. (**PI**) Ages 4–8. (South Africa)

———. *Where's Jamela?* Farrar, 2004. (**PI**) Ages 5–8. (South Africa)

Dhami, Narinder. *Bindi Babes*. Delacorte, 2004. Ages 11–14. Humorous. (U.K.)

Dowd, Siobhan. *The London Eye Mystery*. David Fickling, 2008. Ages 8–11. (U.K.)

Doyle, Brian. *Mary Ann Alice*. Douglas & McIntyre, 2002. Ages 9–13. (Canada)

Fensham, Elizabeth. *Helicopter Man*. Bloomsbury, 2005. Ages 12–14. (Australia)

Fine, Anne. *The Jamie and Angus Stories*. Illustrated by Penny Dale. Candlewick, 2002. Ages 7–9. (U.K.)

Foreman, Michael. *Saving Sinbad*. Kane/Miller, 2002. (**PI**) Ages 4–8. (U.K.)

Fox, Mem. *Ten Little Fingers and Ten Little Toes*. Illustrated by Helen Oxenbury. Harcourt, 2008. (**PI**) Ages 5–8. (Australia)

———. *Wilfrid Gordon McDonald Partridge*. Illustrated by Julie Vivas. Kane/Miller, 1985. (**PI**) Ages 5–8. (Australia)

French, Jackie. *Hitler's Daughter*. HarperCollins, 2003. Ages 9–12. (Australia)

Gardner, Lyn. *Into the Woods*. Illustrated by Mini Grey. David Fickling, 2007. (**PI**) Ages 8–11. (U.K.)

Gavin, Jamila. *Coram Boy.* Farrar, 2001. Ages 11–16. (U.K.)

Gay, Marie-Louise. *Caramba.* Anansi, 2005. (**PI**) Ages 5–8. (Canada)

Gilmore, Rachna. *A Group of One.* Holt, 2001. Ages 11–15. (Canada)

Gleeson, Libby. *Half a World Away.* Illustrated by Freya Blackwood. Scholastic, 2007. (**PI**) Ages 5–8. (Australia)

Graham, Bob. *How to Heal a Broken Wing.* Candlewick, 2008. (**PI**) Ages 5–8. (Australia)

———. *"Let's Get a Pup!" Said Kate.* Candlewick, 2003. (**PI**) Ages 3–8. (Australia)

Gravett, Emily. *Little Mouse's Big Book of Fears.* Simon & Schuster, 2008. (**PI**) Ages 5–8. (U.K.)

———. *Wolves.* Simon & Schuster, 2006. (**PI**) Ages 5–8. (U.K.)

Grey, Mini. *Traction Man Meets Turbodog.* Knopf, 2008. (**PI**) Ages 5–8. (U.K.)

Horacek, Petr. *Silly Suzy Goose.* Candlewick, 2006. (**PI**) Ages 4–6. (U.K.)

Horne, Constance. *The Tenth Pupil.* Ronsdale Press, 2001. Ages 8–11. (Canada)

Ibbotson, Eva. *Journey to the River Sea.* Illustrated by Kevin Hawkes. Dutton, 2001. Ages 9–12. (U.K.)

———. *The Star of Kazan.* Dutton, 2004. Ages 11–13. (U.K.)

Ihimaera, Witi. *Whale Rider.* Harcourt, 2003. Ages 12–15. (New Zealand)

King-Smith, Dick. *Lady Lollipop.* Illustrated by Jill Barton. Candlewick, 2001. (**PI**) Ages 8–11. (U.K.)

Little, Jean. *Willow and Twig.* Viking, 2003. Ages 11–14. (Canada)

Lester, Alison. *Are We There Yet? A Journey around Australia.* Kane/Miller, 2005. (**PI**) Ages 5–8. (Australia)

Lofthouse, Liz. *Ziba Came on a Boat.* Illustrated by Robert Ingpen. Kane/Miller, 2007. Ages 8–12. (**PI**) (Australia/Afghanistan)

Loyie, Larry, with Constance Brissenden. *As Long as the Rivers Flow.* Illustrated by Heather D. Holmlund. Douglas & McIntyre, 2002. (**PI**) Ages 8–12. (Canada)

Lunn, Janet. *Laura Secord: A Story of Courage.* Illustrated by Maxwell Newhouse. Tundra, 2001. Ages 9–12. (Canada)

Matas, Carol. *Sparks Fly Upward.* Clarion, 2002. Ages 9–13. (Canada)

McKay, Hilary. *Saffy's Angel.* McElderry, 2002. Ages 9–12. (U.K.)

Morpurgo, Michael. *Kensike's Kingdom.* Scholastic, 2003. Ages 8–11. (U.K.)

Murray, Martine. *The Slightly True Story of Cedar B. Hartley (Who Planned to Live an Unusual Life).* Scholastic, 2003. Ages 9–13. (Australia)

Naidoo, Beverley. *Burn My Heart.* Amistad, 2009. Ages 10–14. (Kenya)

———. *The Other Side of Truth.* HarperCollins, 2001. Ages 10–15. (South Africa)

———. *Out of Bounds: Seven Stories of Conflict and Hope.* HarperCollins, 2003. Ages 10–14. (South Africa)

Nicholls, Sally. *Ways to Live Forever.* Scholastic, 2008. Ages 8–11. (U.K.)

Overend, Jenni. *Welcome with Love.* Illustrated by Julie Vivas. Kane/Miller, 2000. Ages 5–8. (Australia)

Parkinson, Siobhan. *Something Invisible.* Roaring Brook Press, 2006. Ages 10–13. (Ireland)

Pendziwol, Jean. *Marja's Skis.* Illustrated by Jirina Marton. Groundwood, 2007. (**PI**) Ages 5–8. (Canada)

Pratchett, Terry. *The Amazing Maurice and His Educated Rodents.* HarperCollins, 2001. Ages 11–15. (U.K.)

Pullman, Philip. *The Golden Compass.* Knopf, 1996. Ages 12–15. The first of His Dark Materials trilogy, which includes *The Subtle Knife,* 1997; and *The Amber Spyglass,* 1999. (U.K.)

Rodda, Emily. *The Key to Rondo.* Scholastic, 2008. Ages 8–11. (Australia)

———. *Rowan of Rin.* Greenwillow, 2001. Ages 8–12. The first in a series. (Australia)

Rosen, Michael. *Michael Rosen's Sad Book.* Illustrated by Quentin Blake. Candlewick, 2005. (**PI**) Ages 8–11. (U.K.)

Rosoff, Meg. *Meet Wild Boars.* Illustrated by Sophie Blackall. Holt, 2005. (**PI**) Ages 4–8. (U.K.)

Rowling, J. K. *Harry Potter and the Sorcerer's Stone.* Scholastic, 1998. Ages 9–13. The first in a series of quest fantasies. (U.K.)

Sheth, Kashmira. *Keeping Corner.* Disney/Hyperion, 2009. Ages 12–16. (India)

Slade, Arthur. *Dust.* Wendy Lamb, 2003. Ages 11–15. (Canada)

Stanley, Elizabeth. *The Deliverance of Dancing Bears.* Kane/Miller, 2002. (**PI**) Ages 5–9. (Australia)

Tan, Shaun. *The Arrival.* Scholastic, 2007. (**PI**) Ages 10–14. (Australia)

———. *Tales from Outer Suburbia.* Scholastic, 2009. (**PI**) Ages 13–16. (Australia)

Thompson, Kate. *Wild Blood.* Hyperion, 2000. Ages 11–15. Last in a trilogy. (Ireland)

Updale, Eleanor. *Montmorency.* Scholastic, 2004. Ages 12–16. Part of a series. (U.K.)

Waddell, Martin. *Farmer Duck.* Illustrated by Helen Oxenbury. Candlewick, 1992. (**PI**) Ages 4–6. (U.K.)

Wallace, Ian. *Boy of the Deeps.* DK Ink, 1999. (**PI**) Ages 8–11. (**PI**) (Canada)

———. *The Naked Lady.* Roaring Brook, 2002. (**PI**) Ages 6–12. (Canada)

Walsh, Alice. *Heroes of Isles aux Morts.* Illustrated by Geoff Butler. Tundra, 2001. Ages 4–8. (Canada)

Waugh, Sylvia. *Space Race.* Delacorte, 2000. Ages 9–12. (U.K.)

Wild, Margaret. *Fox.* Illustrated by Ron Brooks. Kane/Miller, 2001. (**PI**) Ages 6–8. (Australia)

———. *The Very Best of Friends.* Illustrated by Julie Vivas. Harcourt, 1990. (**PI**) Ages 4–9. (Australia)

———. *Woolvs in the Sitee.* Illustrated by Anne Spudvilas. Front Street, 2007. (**PI**) Ages 10–14. (Australia)

Wilson, Jacqueline. *Candyfloss.* Illustrated by Nick Sharratt. Roaring Book Press, 2007. Ages 10–14. (U.K.)

Wynne-Jones, Tim. *The Maestro.* Orchard, 1996. Ages 10–14. (Canada)

———. *Rex Zero and the End of the World.* Farrar, 2007. Ages 8–11. (Canada)

———. *Rex Zero, King of Nothing.* Farrar, 2008. Ages 9–12. (Canada)

Translated Books

Arcellana, Francisco. *The Mats.* Illustrated by Hermès Allègre. Kane/Miller, 1999. Ages 5–9. (Philippines)

Ashbé, Jeanne. *What's Inside.* Kane/Miller, 2000. (**PI**) Ages 2–5. (Belgium)

Björk, Christina. *Vendela in Venice.* Illustrated by Inga-Karin Eriksson. Translated from Swedish by Patricia Crampton. R & S, 1999. Ages 9–12. (Sweden)

Bluitgen, Kåre. *A Boot Fell from Heaven.* Illustrated by Chiara Carrer. Kane/Miller, 2003. (**PI**) Ages 5–9. (Denmark)

Bredsdorff, Bodil. *The Crow-Girl: The Children of Crow Cove.* Translated from Danish by Faith Ingwersen. Farrar, 2004. Ages 11–12. (Denmark)

Buchholz, Quint. *The Collector of Moments.* Translated from German by Peter F. Niemeyer. Farrar, 1999. (**PI**) Ages 9–12. (Germany)

Carmi, Daniella. *Samir and Yonatan.* Translated from Hebrew by Yael Lotan. Scholastic, 2000. Ages 9–12. (Israel)

Chen, Zhiyuan. *Guji, Guji.* Kane/Miller, 2004. (**PI**) Ages 5–8. (Taiwan)

D'Adamo, Francesco. *Iqbal: A Novel.* Translated from French by Ann Leonori. Atheneum, 2003. Ages 9–12. (Pakistan)

de Mari, Silvana. *The Last Dragon.* Translated from Italian by Shaun Whiteside. Hyperion, 2006. Ages 10–14. (Italy)

Eriksson, Eva. *A Crash Course for Molly.* Translated from Swedish by Elisabeth Dyssegaard. Farrar, 2005. (**PI**) Ages 5–7. (Sweden)

Filipovic, Zlata. *Zlata's Diary: A Child's Life in Wartime Sarajevo.* Translated from French by Fixot et editions Robert Laffont. Penguin, 1994/2006 (revised edition). Ages 12–18. (Bosnia)

Frank, Anne. *Anne Frank: The Diary of a Young Girl.* Translated from Dutch by B. M. Mooyaart. Doubleday, 1967. Ages 13–18. (Netherlands)

Funke, Cornelia. *Dragon Rider.* Translated from German by Anthea Bell. Scholastic, 2004. Ages 10–14. (Germany)

———. *Inkheart.* Translated from German by Anthea Bell. Scholastic, 2003. Ages 10–14. (Germany)

———. *The Thief Lord.* Translated from German by Oliver Latsch. Scholastic, 2002. Ages 10–14. (Germany)

Goscinny, René. *Nicholas.* Illustrated by Jean Jacques Sempé. Translated from French by Anthea Bell. Phaidon, 2005. (**COL**) Ages 9–12. (France)

Gündisch, Karin. *How I Became an American.* Translated from German by James Skofield. Cricket, 2001. Ages 9–12. (Germany)

Harel, Nira. *The Key to My Heart.* Illustrated by Yossi Abulafia. Kane/Miller, 2002. (**PI**) Ages 4–7. (Israel)

Highet, Alistair. *The Yellow Train.* Based on a story by Fred Bernard. Illustrated by François Roca. Creative, 2000. (**PI**) Ages 4–7. (Canada)

Hogeweg, Margriet. *The God of Grandma Forever.* Translated from Dutch by Nancy Forest-Flier. Front Street, 2001. Ages 9–13. (Netherlands)

Hole, Stian. *Garmann's Summer.* Translated from Norwegian by Don Bartlett. Eerdmans, 2008. (**PI**) Ages 5–8. (Norway)

Holtwijz, Ineke. *Asphalt Angels.* Front Street, 1999. Translated from Dutch by Wanda Boeke. Ages 12–16. (Set in Rio de Janeiro)

Jacobsson, Anders, and Sören Olsson. *In Ned's Head.* Translated from Swedish by Kevin Read. Atheneum, 2001. Ages 9–12. (Sweden)

Jung, Reinhard. *Dreaming in Black and White.* Translated from German by Anthea Bell. Phyllis Fogelman Books, 2003. Ages 10–14. (Germany)

Kruusval, Catarina. *Ellen's Apple Tree.* Translated from Swedish by Joan Sandin. R & S Books, 2008. (**PI**) Ages 5–8. (Sweden)

Landström, Lena. *Boo and Baa Have Company.* Illustrated by Olof Landström. Translated from Swedish by Joan Sandin. Farrar, 2006. (**PI**) Ages 4–7. (Sweden) (Part of the Boo and Baa series.)

Lat. *Kampung Boy.* First Seconds, 2006. Ages 10–12. (Malaysia)

Lee, Ho Baek. *While We Were Out.* Kane/Miller, 2003. (**PI**) Ages 3–6. (South Korea)

Lee, Suzy. *The Zoo.* Kane/Miller, 2007. (**PI**) Ages 5–8. (Korea)

Léonard, Marie. *Tibili, the Little Boy Who Didn't Want to Go to School.* Translated from French. Illustrated by Andrée Prigent. Kane/Miller, 2001. (**PI**) Ages 5–8. (Set in Africa)

Liu, Jae Soo. *Yellow Umbrella.* Kane/Miller, 2002. (**PI**) Ages 2–6. (Companion CD with music composed by Sheen Dong Il.) (South Korea)

Morgenstern, Susie. *A Book of Coupons.* Translated from French by Gil Rosner. Illustrated by Serge Bloch. Viking, 2001. Ages 9–12. (France)

Orlev, Uri. *Run, Boy, Run.* Translated from Hebrew by Hillel Halkin. Houghton, 2003. Ages 10–13. (Israel)

Sakai, Komako. *Emily's Balloon.* Translated from Japanese. Chronicle, 2006. (**PI**) Ages 3–5. (Japan)

Satrapi, Marjane. *Persepolis.* Pantheon, 2003. Ages 10–14. (Iran)

Sellier, Marie. *Legend of the Chinese Dragon.* Illustrated by Catherine Louis. Translated from French by Sibylle Kazeroid. NorthSouth, 2007. (**PI**) Ages 5–8. (Set in China)

Singh, Vandana. *Younguncle Comes to Town.* Illustrated by B. M. Kamath. Viking, 2006. Ages 8–11. (India)

Skármeta, Antonio. *The Composition.* Illustrated by Alfonso Ruano. Translated from Spanish by Elisa Amado. Groundwood, 2000. (**PI**) Ages 8–12.

Stolz, Joelle. *The Shadows of Ghadames.* Translated from French by Catherine Temerson. Delacorte, 2004. Ages 11–14. (Set in Libya)

Uehashi, Nahoko. *Morbito: Guardian of the Spirit.* Illustrated by Yuko Shimizu. Translated from Japanese by Cathy Hirano. Scholastic, 2008. Ages 10–14. (Japan)

Valckx, Catharina. *Lizette's Green Sock.* Translated from French. Clarion, 2005. (**PI**) Ages 3–6. (France)

Vejjajiva, Jane. *The Happiness of Kati.* Translated from Thai by Prudence Borthwick. Atheneum, 2006. Ages 10–12. (Thailand)

Weninger, Brigitte. *Special Delivery.* Illustrated by Alexander Reichstein. Translated from German by J. Alison James. North-South, 2000. (**PI**) Ages 3–5. (Austria)

Xiong, Kim. *The Little Stone Lion.* Translated from Chinese. Heryin, 2006. (**PI**) Ages 4–7. (China)

Yan, Ma. *The Diary of Ma Yan: The Struggles and Hopes of a Chinese Schoolgirl.* Translated from Mandarin by He Yanping. HarperCollins, 2005. Ages 10–14. (China)

Yumoto, Kazumi. *The Friends.* Translated from Japanese by Cathy Hirano. Farrar, 1996. Ages 10–14. (Japan)

Zullo, Germano. *Marta and the Bicycle.* Illustrated by Albertine. Translated from French. Kane/Miller, 2002. (**PI**) Ages 4–8. (Switzerland)

⭐ Related Films, Videos, and DVDs

I Hate English! (2006). Author: Ellen Levine (1989). 14 minutes. (Asian-American)

I Love Saturdays y Domingos. (2002). Author: Alma Flor Ada. Illustrated by Elvivia Savadier (2002). 18 minutes. (Bilingual)

Millions. (2005). Author: Frank Cottrell Boyce (2004). 98 minutes. (England)

The Thief Lord. (2006). Author: Cornelia Funke (2002). 99 minutes. (Germany/Australia)

Sources for Films, Videos, and DVDs

The Video Source Book. Syosset, NY: National Video
   Clearinghouse, 1979–. Published by Gale Research,
   Detroit, MI.

   An annual reference work that lists media and provides sources for purchase and rental.

Websites of large video distributors:
   www.libraryvideo.com
   www.knowledgeunlimited.com
   http://teacher.scholastic.com/products/
   westonwoods

PEARSON myeducationkit™   Now go to Chapter 11 in the MyEducationKit (www.myeducationkit
.com) for your book, where you can:

- Complete Assignments and Activities that can enrich and extend your knowledge of chapter content.

- Expand your knowledge with content-specific Web Links.

- Learn how authors and illustrators apply their craft by reading the written interviews in the Conversations section for the chapter.

- Review the chapter content by going to the Study Plan, taking a chapter quiz, and receiving feedback on your answers.

- Access the Children's Literature Database for your own exploration.

part THREE

Literature in the School

Chapters 12 and 13 focus on curriculum and teaching strategies. Planning for and evaluating a literature curriculum as it pertains to a specific lesson, a unit of instruction, a yearlong classroom plan, and a schoolwide literature program are explained in Chapter 12. The two main approaches to teaching reading—basal reading programs and literature-based reading—are discussed here in terms of strategies for incorporating literature into the teaching of reading. Features such as sample planning webs, evaluation checklists, sample focus books for a yearlong curriculum, and literature-related activities to help preservice teachers in school practicums gain experience with literature provide practical procedural suggestions and advice. Chapter 12 concludes with a discussion of censorship, selection, and First Amendment rights.

Chapter 13 presents strategies for engaging children with literature and eliciting their responses to it. The chapter and strategies are organized under three headings. The first, Reading Widely for Personal Purposes, includes strategies for teacher read-alouds, student independent reading, booktalks, readers' theatre, and experiencing literature as multimodal texts. The second, Reading Critically to Inquire about the World, includes literature discussions, a variety of literature response engagements, using drama as response, and literature across the curriculum. The third, Reading Strategically to Learn about Literacy, focuses on using literature to learn about writing.

chapter TWELVE

Planning the Curriculum

Close your eyes and look inside,
A mirror shines within;
To find where you are going,
First see where you have been.

—*Charles Ghigna*

This chapter deals with long-range planning for literature instruction. Short-range planning is discussed in Chapter 13. First, the literature curriculum is defined, and approaches to teaching and organizing such a curriculum are presented. Guidelines for developing the literature curriculum and a discussion of how literature can be integrated into a school's reading program follow. The latter part of the chapter includes sections on evaluating a literature program; implementing a schoolwide literature program; gaining experience with literature as a preservice teacher; and learning about censorship, selection, and First Amendment rights (primarily free speech) as they pertain to literature in the schools.

Defining the Literature Curriculum

Literature is more than a collection of well-written stories and poems. Literature also has its own body of knowledge. A term that is sometimes used to label this treatment of literature is *discipline-based literature instruction.* The object of such a course of study is to teach children the mechanics of literature: the terms used to define it, its components or elements, its genres, and the craft of creating it. The terms and elements of fiction are presented in Chapter 3; the terms and elements of nonfiction are presented in Chapter 10; and the genres and their characteristics are presented in Chapters 4 through 11.

Choosing the Approach

Two approaches to instruction prevalent in today's schools are the traditional approach and the inquiry approach. You must determine which approach to instruction best suits you and your students, and then you must decide how to organize your literature instruction.

The *traditional approach* to instruction focuses on mastery of content. It places the teacher at the center, in that the teacher decides the agenda, dispenses the information, asks the questions, and often supplies the answers. The goal of this approach is for students to learn what the teacher tells them about the literature under study.

The *inquiry approach* to instruction, which shares some features of problem-based learning and constructivist learning, focuses on how one learns. Teachers who choose this approach want their students to become aware of the power of literature to explain the human condition. The inquiry approach is characterized by the following precepts:

- Students' inquiry is guided by their *own* questions related to a work of literature—questions they honestly care about. During the inquiry process, students refine or alter their questions as they learn and discuss, debate, and share information with other students. Collaborative learning, team projects, and small group discussions are emphasized.
- Emphasis is placed on the process of how one gets and makes sense of information about literature so that knowledge gained will have wide application.
- Teachers operate as facilitators rather than dispensers of knowledge. They ask leading questions rather than tell answers.

This approach to literature instruction can be managed as a whole-class inquiry into one question, small group inquiries into various questions, or independent inquiries into questions selected by each student.

Most often, elementary and middle-school teachers organize the literature curriculum by genre, theme or topic, author or illustrator, literary element or device, or notable books. An alternative is to create a hybrid literature curriculum by including aspects of several of these approaches in the plan.

Genre

By organizing a literature curriculum around literary genres, teachers provide a context for students to learn about the various types of literature and the characteristics of each. In the beginning, the teacher will have to direct students' attention to similarities in books of like genre—for example, the students will learn that works of historical fiction are always set in the past or that characters in folktales are two-dimensional. Soon, however, students will begin to read with more genre awareness and will enjoy finding common elements within and differences between genres.

One advantage of this plan is that students over the school year can be exposed to a wide variety of literature. Knowledge of different genres gives students useful *schemata*—frameworks for understanding born of prior knowledge and experience—for story types. A genre approach can work in all grade levels, given thoughtful selection of titles and delivery of literary concepts. Planning involves choosing the genres to be studied, selecting the representative children's books for each, and determining the order in which the genres will be studied.

Theme or Topic

Organizing a study of literature by theme or topic works particularly well with the inquiry approach to literature. Focusing on a book's meaning or message gives students an opportunity to relate what they learn to their own lives. Themes and topics will vary according to ages and circumstances of students. For example, primary-grade children will be interested in themes and topics having to do with school and family life. Those in the middle grades, on the other hand, will be more intrigued by themes and topics dealing with the discovery and use of inner resources to become more independent or even to survive.

Possible themes that a seventh- or eighth-grade class might explore through a year include the following:

Effects of Poverty
Staying Healthy
Alienation and Acceptance by Peers
Coping with Parents and Younger Siblings
Teenagers through History: The Same Old Problems?
Dependence and Independence
The Future World
Accepting Those Who Are Different from Ourselves
Community Involvement and Activism
Walking in Someone Else's Shoes: The Importance of Perspective

Possible themes and topics for a younger group might include these:

Families Come in All Shapes and Sizes
School Now and in the Past
What It Means to Be a Good Friend
The Problem of Bullying and Teasing
Stories from Other Countries
Protecting Our Environment
Famous People Were Children, Too

In this method, each child reads or listens to the book or books chosen by the teacher to accompany each theme. After the reading, students explore the theme through questioning, journaling, reflecting, discussing, writing, responding through drama and art, and further reading on the theme or topic.

Themes and topics are chosen by the teacher on the basis of students' needs and interests, current events, and prior successes with previously developed thematic units. The length of time spent on any one theme or topic can vary from a school year to a day, but several weeks' duration is the norm.

Two pitfalls of thematic curriculum models must be avoided:

1. Do not choose a theme or topic just because a few related books are at hand. Remember: The unit theme or topic drives literature selection, not vice versa.
2. Do not choose literature because it relates to the theme or topic but with no regard to its quality or appropriateness for the students. Boring books make boring thematic instructional units.

Author or Illustrator

The goal of a curriculum in literature organized by author or illustrator is to make students more familiar with the works and styles of selected children's book authors and illustrators. An additional goal may be knowledge of the authors' or illustrators' lives insofar as these life experiences influenced the subjects' works. The choice of authors and illustrators will naturally be guided both by students' reading interests and the teacher's desire to introduce students to important authors and illustrators and their works. The number of works chosen to represent an author or illustrator will vary, but even when an author's books are lengthy, more than one work is recommended.

As a class experiences a sampling of the chosen author's or illustrator's work, attention will be focused on trademark stylistic elements such as unusual use of words, color, or media, as well as themes, characters, character types, or settings common to these works. Later, information about the person's life can be introduced through reports, audiotaped and videotaped interviews, and even guest appearances by the author or illustrator. Websites, biographies, and biographical reference volumes, such as *Something about the Author* (Gale Research, 2006) and *Children's Literature Review* (Gale Research, 2006), provide information about children's book authors and illustrators. Note also series biographies and autobiographies of children's book authors and illustrators offered by publishers, such as Richard C. Owen's Meet the Author series for 7- to 10-year-olds (www.rcowen.com/MTABkList.htm).

Success of author and illustrator studies is not necessarily defined by wholesale student approval of the featured artists. Students must be allowed to decide whether they like a person's work or not and should be encouraged to discover why they have these feelings. Wholesale *disapproval* by students of the works of a featured author or illustrator, however, is an important form of teacher evaluation that should not be ignored. In such a case, the teacher's choice of author or books to be studied was not appropriate for this purpose and should be reconsidered. Students are evaluated informally through observation of their recognition of featured authors' or illustrators' works and their ability to compare literary and artistic styles of various authors and illustrators.

Literary Element and Device

When teachers say that their teaching of literature is organized by literary element, they are usually referring to the elements of fiction and nonfiction, as presented in Chapters 3 and 10, respectively. Other elements, such as artistic styles, media, and book format, could be addressed as well. A *literary device* is "any literary technique deliberately employed to achieve a special effect" (Baldick, 1990, p. 55). Irony, symbolism, parody, and foreshadowing are examples of devices that add richness to stories.

The goal of a literature curriculum organized by literary elements and devices is to give students a better understanding of the craft of writing so that they can read more perceptively and appreciatively and possibly apply this knowledge to their own writing. Since this approach is analytical and somewhat abstract, it is more appropriate for students in the fourth grade or above.

Careful selection of children's books to accompany the investigation of each literary element or device is crucial to the success of this approach. The featured element must be prominent and must have been used by the author with extraordinary skill. In addition, the story itself must captivate young readers. Note that in this approach, books of various genres can be grouped to demonstrate the same literary element. Note also that picture books are particularly good at presenting literary elements and devices clearly and in relatively simple contexts so that they can be understood more easily. An excellent resource for selecting picture books for this use is Hall's *Using Picture Storybooks to Teach Literary Devices*, Vols. 1–4 (1990, 1994, 2001, 2007).

Students' acquaintance with the literary elements and devices can go far beyond mere definition. Close reading of key passages reveals the author's craft at developing character, establishing mood, authenticating setting, or using such devices as inference, symbolism, or foreshadowing. Re-creation of these elements and devices in their own art, drama, and writing not only gives students a personal and more complete understanding of these concepts, but it also gives teachers a way to evaluate their students' grasp of these concepts.

Notable Book

Notable, in this context, means any exemplary work for children. Notable books can be classic or contemporary and can include works from several different genres, including biography and informational literature. The books are read and analyzed for the features that contribute to their excellence, such as their relevance to readers, unique perspectives or insights, treatment of topics, memorable characters, or illustrations.

In the primary grades, teachers will most likely read the notable books aloud to students. Reading aloud by teachers works for intermediate and middle grades as well, but an alternative at these levels is independent reading of the selected books by students. Analysis of notable books can be conducted through discussion (whole class, small group, teacher led, or student led), dialogue journal writing (with the teacher or a friend who is reading the same book), or reading logs. Regardless of the method students use to respond to these books, they should be encouraged to relate the books to their own lives and to compare them to other books they have read. Even if students are responding in more independent ways, such as journal writing, it is a good idea to invite them to share their thoughts with one another from time to time.

Teachers who organize their literature curriculum by notable books must be careful to remain flexible in book selections from year to year so that the list of notable books reflects students' current interests and reading preferences. A list of notable books that never varies can result in student disinterest and stale teaching.

Developing the Literature Curriculum

Planning for a literature curriculum involves two practical considerations: building a classroom library collection and outlining a yearlong literature curriculum.

Building a Classroom Library Collection

Most, if not all, of the responsibility for acquiring a sufficiently large and varied collection of books in your classroom will be yours. With perseverance, it can be done. Most good classroom libraries have a permanent collection as well as a collection that comes from the school or public library and changes regularly. Beginning teachers who are willing to plan ahead with their school and public librarians can borrow enough books for adequate temporary classroom libraries while they build their own collections. Even after a large permanent collection is established, a rotating selection from the school and public library can be coordinated with specific units of study, providing depth and breadth to the unit content and to the students' learning experience.

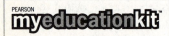

PEARSON

Go to Activity 1 in the Assignments and Activities section of Chapter 12 in MyEducationKit; complete the activity on exploring teacher tools available on the Internet.

Careful selection of titles for the classroom library makes the most of limited resources. Children's librarians can provide invaluable advice in selecting titles for a classroom library and should be consulted. If this is not an option, browsing a well-stocked children's bookstore and consulting publishers' catalogs are alternative ways of finding out what is available. Publishers of children's books issue one or two catalogs annually in which they describe their new publications and list their previous publications that are currently available (the backlist). If your school or public librarian does not have these catalogs, publishers will supply them on request. Some teachers use catalogs to get an overview of what is available before going to a bookstore.

Your own permanent trade book collection can be built inexpensively by using several proven approaches. These include the following:

- Requesting an allocation from your principal or PTO for purchase of books
- Submitting a small grant proposal ($250–$1,000) to your school district or professional organization for purchase of trade books
- Taking advantage of bonus books offered by student paperback book clubs
- Informing students' parents that you are building a collection and would like to have first refusal of any children's books that they plan to discard
- Establishing a "give a book to the classroom" policy for parents who want to celebrate their child's birthday or a holiday at school in some way
- Frequenting garage sales and library book sales, where good books can often be purchased for pennies

Most bookstores offer a 20 percent discount to teachers who use their own money to buy books to add to their classroom collections. An alternative to the bookstore is the book jobber, or wholesale dealer for many publishers. Jobbers offer even greater discounts to teachers, sometimes up to 40 percent, but it is important to remember that most jobbers do not carry small-press publications. Your school librarian probably uses a jobber and can assist you in setting up a staff account with the same firm. Some of the larger firms include Baker & Taylor, Brodart, and Ingram Book Company. One of the most popular of these is Follett Library Resources, with its *Titlewave* selection tool.

With these methods and sources, classroom collections grow quickly. From the beginning, you will need to devise a coding system for your permanent collection to streamline shelving and record keeping. Many teachers find that color coding their books by genre with colored tape on the spines works well. If at all possible, students should be trained and given the responsibility for color coding, checking in and out, repairing, and reshelving books.

Remember that the whole point of building a classroom library is to promote reading, not to provide a handsome display. Inevitably, if children use their classroom library, books will be lost and damaged. Severe reprimands for losing or damaging a book may work against your ultimate goal.

Outlining a Yearlong Literature Curriculum

Outlining a yearlong literature curriculum helps teachers determine a practical scope of content and logical sequence of presentation and gives them time to gather the necessary resources by the time they are needed. Recommended steps in outlining for a yearlong literature curriculum are reviewed in the following subsections.

Establish Goals
Goals in a literature curriculum are those aims one expects to accomplish by the end of the course of study. Central to this part of the planning process is deciding on the literary concepts to be taught. Because goals largely determine the parameters of the curriculum, they must be established early in the planning process.

Goals for a literature curriculum are established by individual teachers and sometimes by schools or school districts. Goals for a primary-grade teacher who has chosen a mixed genre/author organization to teaching literature would include the following:

- Students will enjoy reading a variety of genres of literature.
- Students will be familiar with the characteristics of folktales, modern fantasy, contemporary realistic fiction, and nonfiction and will be able to classify a book as belonging to one of the featured genres when reading it.
- Students will become familiar with several leading authors (or collectors in the case of folktales) of each of the genres and will be able to identify characteristics of the writing of each author.

Determine Literature Units

After goals have been identified and set, the next step in outlining a literature curriculum is to determine the units of study through which the literature content will be delivered. In this way, a tentative schedule can be set in order to foresee needs in terms of time and materials and to coordinate delivery of the units with the school calendar.

Select Focus Books

Early selection of unit titles is important for several reasons. Balance in the overall book selection, for instance, is achieved much more easily in the planning stages. Balance, as presented in Chapter 3, means that the books selected present a diversity of characters who have relevance to children's lives (type, gender, age, ethnicity, place of origin), settings (urban, rural, familiar, foreign), and themes. Another advantage of early selection is being able to estimate the time necessary for each unit. Some units will take longer than others, depending on such variables as the extent of content to be covered, the length and difficulty of books to be read, the type and complexity of planned book extension activities, and the ability to locate and obtain the books and related resources such as films and guest speakers. A sample list of units, books, and featured authors for a fifth-grade teacher who is implementing a combined genre/author organization for teaching literature is shown in the accompanying box.

Unit 1: Traditional Literature

(Females in Traditional Literature)

Mythology
Changing Woman and Her Sisters: Stories of Goddesses from Around the World by Katrin Hyman Tchana, reteller, illustrated by Trina Schart Hyman (2006)
The Gods and Goddesses of Olympus retold and illustrated by Aliki (1994)

Legends and Tall Tales
Cut from the Same Cloth: American Women of Myth, Legend, and Tall Tale retold by Robert D. San Souci, illustrated by Brian Pinkney (1993)
Clever Beatrice: An Upper Peninsula Conte, by Margaret Willey, illustrated by Heather Solomon (2001)

Folktales

Cinderella retold by Ruth Sanderson (2002)
Rapunzel's Revenge by Shannon and Dean Hale, illustrated by Nathan Hale (2008)

Read-Aloud

Not One Damsel in Distress: World Folktales for Strong Girls retold by Jane Yolen, illustrated by Susan Guevara (2000)

Unit 2: Modern Fantasy

(Unusual Characters and Strange Situations)

Finders Keepers by Emily Rodda (1991)
The Power of Un by Nancy Etchemendy (2000)
Things Not Seen by Andrew Clements (2002)

Read-Aloud

Tuck Everlasting by Natalie Babbitt (1975)
Featured Author: Natalie Babbitt

Unit 3: Informational Literature

(Current World Issues)

An Inconvenient Truth: The Crisis of Global Warming by Al Gore, adapted by Jane O'Connor (2007)
Child Labor Today: A Human Rights Issue by Wendy Herumin (2007)
One Well: The Story of Water on Earth by Rochelle Strauss, illustrated by Rosemary Woods (2007)

Read-Aloud

What the World Eats by Faith D'Aluisio and Peter Menzel (2008)

Unit 4: Contemporary Realistic Fiction

(Cultural Diversity)

Crossing Jordan by Adrian Fogelin (2000)
The Tequila Worm by Viola Canales (2005)
Rules by Cynthia Lord (2006)
Show Way by Jacqueline Woodson (2005)

Read-Aloud

Locomotion by Jacqueline Woodson (2003)
Featured Author: Jacqueline Woodson

Unit 5: Mystery

(Young Sleuths)

Down the Rabbit Hole by Peter Abrahams (2005)
Holes by Louis Sachar (1998)
Hoot by Carl Hiaasen (2003)

(continued)

Read-Aloud
Sammy Keyes and the Hotel Thief by Wendelin Van Draanen (1998)
Featured Author: Wendelin Van Draanen

Unit 6: Science Fiction

(Future Worlds)

The City of Ember by Jeanne DuPrau (2003)
Turnabout by Margaret Peterson Haddix (2000)
The House of the Scorpion by Nancy Farmer (2002)

Read-Aloud
Messenger by Lois Lowry (2004)
Featured Author: Lois Lowry

Developing Literature Units

Thinking through, organizing, and writing down the details of daily lessons and activities in the various units are the final steps in planning for a literature curriculum. Two helpful tools in organizing the details of literature units are webs and lesson plans.

Webs

A *web*—a graphic planning tool that reveals relationships between ideas—can help you create a visual overview of a literature unit, including its focus, concepts, related book titles, and activities. A web is like a map in that it helps teachers and students find their way to their goals and objectives; but unlike a map, it can be changed easily to encompass new ideas, be adapted for different uses, or meet special needs and circumstances.

Ideas for a web are generated through brainstorming. The main advantage of webbing is that the process clarifies and even suggests ties or associations between concepts, books, and activities. Activities can be drawn from all content areas and all skill areas—writing, reading, listening, thinking, speaking, art, crafts, drama, and music. Involving students in creating webs benefits everyone: Students are motivated by being given a voice in planning the learning unit, and teachers benefit when students have original ideas and see new relationships that improve the overall plan. The web in Figure 12.1 shows ideas for a unit of study on the literary element, character. The web in Figure 12.2 is built around concepts relating to the topic of immigration.

A disadvantage of a web is that it gives no indication of the chronology of events or time allotments. The set of daily or weekly lesson plans that can be developed from a web provides the more linear format preferred by most teachers.

Lesson Plans

Lesson plans are organized by day or week. Specificity will vary according to the needs and experience of the teacher, but each day's or week's lesson plan usually includes the following components:

- *Objectives,* which are short-range aims to be accomplished day by day or week by week. An objective for a teacher conducting a literature unit on the topic of immigration, as found in

Figure 12.1 Web Demonstrating Investigation of a Literary Element, Grades 2–4

Small Group Reading

Note whether the characters in these stories changed or remained the same. If they changed, how?

Realistic Fiction
Morgy Makes His Move
  by Maggie Lewis
Rosy Cole's Worst Ever, Best Yet Tour of New York City
  by Sheila Greenwald

Modern Fantasy
Clever Beatrice: An Upper Peninsula Conte
  by Margaret Willey
Good Enough to Eat by Brock Cole

Traditional Literature
The Sleeping Beauty
  by Trina Schart Hyman
Cinderella by Ruth Sanderson

Read-Aloud

Listen for ways that the author helps you get to know the main character.

Clementine by Sara Pennypacker
Rowan of Rin by Emily Rodda

Independent Reading

Look for protagonists, antagonists, secondary characters, and character foils in these stories.

Hot Fudge Hero by Pat Brisson
Amber Was Brave, Essie Was Smart by Vera B. Williams
The Gold-Threaded Dress
  by Carolyn Marsden
Tooter Pepperday by Jerry Spinelli
Finders Keepers by Emily Rodda
Just Grace by Charise M. Harper
Martin Bridge: Ready for Takeoff!
  by Jessica Kerrin
Ruby Lu, Brave and True by Lenore Look
Rufus the Scrub Does Not Wear a Tutu by Jamie McEwan
Snowed In with Grandmother Silk
  by Carol Fenner
Stinky Stern Forever by Michelle Edwards
The Talented Clementine by Sara Pennypacker

Characterization

Character Development

Character Types

CHARACTER

Discussion

How are characters in works of realistic fiction different from characters in works of traditional literature?

How would you describe the female characters in the works of traditional folktales you read? How do they compare with the female characters in the modern folktales?

Find a paragraph in a book you read that describes the protagonist. Why is this a good description?

How do you learn about characters in the books you read?

Writing

List the ways that a character in a book you read changed from the beginning to the end of the story.

Select as many adjectives as you can to accurately describe a character in one of the books you read.

With a partner, write interview questions for a story character. Write answers to these questions as if you were that character. Make sure that your answers are in keeping with the character's personality.

Art

Using descriptions found in the story, draw a portrait of a character you liked.

Draw a scene from the story that, in your opinion, caused the protagonist to change the most.

Drama

Select a scene that shows character development from a story you read with a small group. Adapt this scene for readers' theatre. Make an audiorecording of your reading for others in your class to enjoy.

Figure 12.2   Conceptual Web on Immigration, Grades 5–8

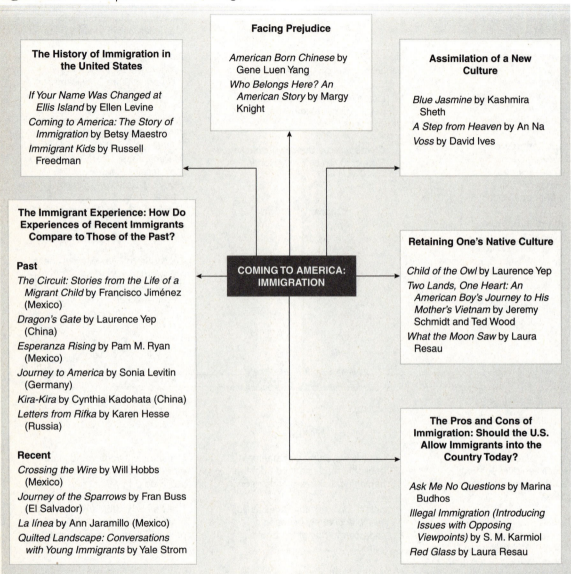

Facing Prejudice

American Born Chinese by Gene Luen Yang
Who Belongs Here? An American Story by Margy Knight

The History of Immigration in the United States

If Your Name Was Changed at Ellis Island by Ellen Levine
Coming to America: The Story of Immigration by Betsy Maestro
Immigrant Kids by Russell Freedman

Assimilation of a New Culture

Blue Jasmine by Kashmira Sheth
A Step from Heaven by An Na
Voss by David Ives

The Immigrant Experience: How Do Experiences of Recent Immigrants Compare to Those of the Past?

Past
The Circuit: Stories from the Life of a Migrant Child by Francisco Jiménez (Mexico)
Dragon's Gate by Laurence Yep (China)
Esperanza Rising by Pam M. Ryan (Mexico)
Journey to America by Sonia Levitin (Germany)
Kira-Kira by Cynthia Kadohata (China)
Letters from Rifka by Karen Hesse (Russia)

Recent
Crossing the Wire by Will Hobbs (Mexico)
Journey of the Sparrows by Fran Buss (El Salvador)
La línea by Ann Jaramillo (Mexico)
Quilted Landscape: Conversations with Young Immigrants by Yale Strom

COMING TO AMERICA: IMMIGRATION

Retaining One's Native Culture

Child of the Owl by Laurence Yep
Two Lands, One Heart: An American Boy's Journey to His Mother's Vietnam by Jeremy Schmidt and Ted Wood
What the Moon Saw by Laura Resau

The Pros and Cons of Immigration: Should the U.S. Allow Immigrants into the Country Today?

Ask Me No Questions by Marina Budhos
Illegal Immigration (Introducing Issues with Opposing Viewpoints) by S. M. Karmiol
Red Glass by Laura Resau

Figure 12.2, might be for students to realize that most Americans or their ancestors are immigrants and deserve respect regardless of how recently they have arrived in this country.

■ *Procedures and methods,* which tell what the teacher does, in what order and with what materials, what tasks or assignments students will be given, and what the teacher expects of them. Procedures of the teacher conducting the immigration unit in Figure 12.2 in order to fulfill the objective stated above might be to read aloud Margy Knight's book, *Who Belongs*

Here? An American Story (1999/2003), then ask students to share in small groups their own or their families' stories of how they came to this country.

■ *Evaluation,* in which teachers must consider how they intend to evaluate their students and themselves in terms of how well the students met the objectives and how well their plans worked. *Student evaluation* can take the form of written examinations, oral questions, listening to students' comments during whole-class or small group discussions, reading students' journals, and examining students' written, oral, artistic, and dramatic responses to literature. *Self-evaluation by the teacher* can be in terms of student interest in the lesson, student success in meeting the stated objectives, and the plan's success in predicting time and materials needed and effectiveness of methods and procedures. At regular intervals during the literature unit teachers will want to evaluate their students' progress in meeting the unit and year-long goals and, if necessary, revise the plans or the goals.

Because literature units are several weeks long, they usually include a culminating activity that gives students an opportunity to reflect on what they have learned, review major points, and sometimes celebrate the focus of the unit in some way. An overall unit evaluation is valuable to teachers, particularly if they intend to use the unit with another group of students. The unit should indicate the method of evaluation. Revisions can make the unit even more successful in succeeding years.

Approaches to Teaching Reading with Literature

Nowhere in the school curriculum is literature more important than in the reading program. In the primary grades literature can be instrumental in helping teach children to read, and in the intermediate and middle grades it can keep young people's interest in reading alive, helping struggling readers strengthen their reading skills and encouraging all students to become lifelong readers. In the following sections the two most common approaches to teaching reading in the United States will be presented while demonstrating literature's role in each.

Basal Reading Program Supplemented by Children's Literature

Just as children bring a variety of learning styles and needs to the task of learning, so do teachers bring a variety of teaching styles and needs to teaching. A single approach to teaching reading cannot suit all teachers or all students. The most common approach to the teaching of reading is the *basal reading approach supplemented by children's literature.*

The basal reading program has been the traditional approach to teaching reading in U.S. elementary schools for decades. According to Durkin (1987), it is "composed of a series of readers said to be written at successively more difficult levels" (p. 417). The core materials include a student reader, a teacher's manual, student workbooks, and tests. The strength of the basal program is that it provides teachers with an organized instructional framework on which to build (Lapp, Flood, & Farnan, 1992). In other words, the teacher using this approach does not develop a reading program by selecting materials and planning the related activities. Basal reading programs offer teachers considerable guidance and help with the decisions and challenges involved in teaching children to read.

Guided reading, a program used primarily with English language learners and children who have reading difficulties, is intended to bring students up to their grade-level competency in reading. The main features of guided reading are small group instruction, close attention to assessment of students' reading levels, matching students with books that are incrementally "leveled" by reading difficulty, explicit instruction on reading strategies to improve comprehension, and short-term intervention. One widely used guided reading program is the Fountas and Pinnell Leveled Books Program, K–8, published by Heinemann.

The learning theory on which basal reading materials have been based for the last century holds that learning complex skills begins with mastering the simplest components of that skill before attempting the next larger components, and so on until the whole skill is learned. In terms of learning to read, this means that the letters of the alphabet are learned first, followed by letter–sound patterns, words, and then sentences. Finally, when the components of reading are learned, whole works of literature, such as stories, plays, and poems, are read.

In the 1980s, U.S. publishers of basal readers made an effort to improve the quality of stories written specifically for the basal readers. Multicultural characters began to appear in basal stories with more frequency than in the past. Most important, excerpts from high-quality trade books and some whole, albeit brief, literary works were integrated into basal readers. These changes were incorporated while retaining the skill-based instruction (particularly phonics instruction for beginning readers) that researchers regard as important to well-rounded reading programs (Anderson, Hiebert, Scott, & Wilkinson, 1985).

Even with these changes, basal readers are not designed to be a complete substitute for trade books. Even though some basal stories are good literature, not excerpted or adapted, the brevity of these selections is a problem for intermediate grades. Most students in these grades are capable of reading novel-length chapter books and should be doing so regularly in their school reading program. Students in classes where anthologies and basal readers are used exclusively are denied the all-important self-selection of reading material from a wide variety of books.

Ideally, each teacher should be allowed to choose the approach to teaching reading that best suits his or her philosophy of learning and teaching style. In many school districts across the United States, however, the use of a basal approach to teach reading is mandated. Even more restrictive is mandated Direct Instruction (DI), a lockstep method of teaching reading relying on highly scripted, prescribed teacher plans that must be followed to the letter, accommodating no teacher or student variation. School administrators would be wise to note Ryder, Sekulski, and Silberg's (2003) three-year study of methods of teaching reading that showed that DI has limited applicability, should not be used as the main method of reading instruction, and is not as effective as traditional teaching methods that allow teachers a more flexible approach.

Many teachers, despite mandates, have begun to move away from a slavish, "read-every-page-or-bust" attitude toward these programs. They have found ways to improve their teaching of reading by using their basal programs in innovative ways that eliminate some of the skills exercises of this approach and allow time for literature as well. Some guidelines drawn from the example of these teachers are as follows:

- Use only the best literary selections the basal offers. Substitute good trade literature for the rest.
- Let students read some of the better-written basal selections simply for enjoyment. It is the joy and wonder of reading marvelous tales or interesting information that motivate children to learn to read, not the tests on their comprehension of these stories. Use the time saved from skill, drill, and comprehension questions for silent reading.

■ Eliminate the stigma of ability grouping by forming one whole-class, heterogeneous reading group. Use the time saved from planning and conducting three or four different reading lessons to hold individual reading conferences.

■ Use basal readers' phonics lessons and drills only when, in the teacher's opinion, an individual student or group of students will benefit from them. (This need is exhibited by students in their individual reading conferences and in their writing.) Children do not learn according to an imposed schedule, but only when they are ready to learn. Use the time saved from ineffective exercises to read aloud from good books or for silent reading from self-choice books.

■ Avoid comprehension questions at the end of basal reading lessons that trivialize the stories or demean the students. Use the time saved to allow children to share their personal reactions to the story, to offer literary criticisms of the selection, or to respond to the story in writing, drama, or art.

■ Make phonics instruction a regular but brief (10–15 minutes) part of primary-grade reading instruction. Avoid letting phonics instruction become the main attraction of reading. That role should be reserved for good stories.

Basal readers are most effective when used in concert with a wide variety of trade books that reflect students' interests and reading abilities. In this arrangement, the basal reader provides guidance and structure to both teaching and learning, while the trade books provide the variety, opportunity for self-selection, and interest that motivate children to want to read.

Literature-Based Reading

Literature-based reading is an approach to teaching reading through the exclusive use of trade books. The learning theory in which literature-based reading is grounded holds that children learn by searching for meaning in the world around them, constantly forming hypotheses, testing them to determine whether they work, and subsequently accepting or rejecting them.

Teachers using the literature-based approach to reading will structure a classroom environment that immerses children in good literature. In these classrooms, children hear literature read aloud several times a day, they see good readers reading voluntarily, they discover that good books can entertain them and tell them things they want to know, and they constantly practice reading books that they themselves have chosen because they are interested in the topics. Frequent student–teacher conferences allow teachers to check students' comprehension, discover skills weaknesses, and prescribe remediation.

As in basal reading programs, explicit reading instruction is an important feature of literature-based reading, particularly in the primary grades. Phonics, concepts of print, and vocabulary are taught in literature-based reading, but within the context of interesting literature. Unlike basal reading programs, these skills are never taught in isolation, where they have no real meaning, are never the focus of the entire reading period, and are taught only when needed.

As noted in Chapter 1, literature-based reading instruction addresses the components of instruction considered essential to the teaching of reading by the National Reading Panel: phonemic awareness, phonics, and reading comprehension, including fluency and vocabulary instruction. By including daily teacher read-alouds and self-choice independent reading, this method of teaching reading is more likely to engender some valuable intrinsic behaviors in students that cannot be taught: a positive attitude toward reading, self-motivation to read, and a lifelong reading habit.

Key elements of the literature-based reading classroom include the following:

- Daily reading aloud of good literature by the teacher
- Reading skills taught when needed and then within meaningful contexts, never in isolation
- Quantities of good trade books in the classroom (five or more books per child) selected to match specific interests and approximate reading abilities of the students in the class
- Daily silent reading by students of self-selected books
- Daily opportunities for students to share their reactions to books orally
- Daily opportunities for students to respond to literature in a variety of ways, including writing, drama, and art
- Frequent individual student–teacher reading conferences (see the discussion of individual conferences in Chapter 13)

Decisions about what to teach, when to teach it, and what materials to use are made by the teacher in the literature-based reading classroom. These decisions and the responsibility for materials selection and acquisition may make literature-based reading more demanding of teachers' professional judgment than other reading instruction methods; however, when it is managed well, this approach has proven to be effective not only in teaching students to read but also in creating a positive attitude toward reading. Moreover, the stimulus of new and exciting materials and students' unique personal responses to them can make teaching more exciting and enjoyable.

The absence of a prescribed, lockstep program is one of the greatest strengths of literature-based reading, but it also makes this approach vulnerable to many abuses. The following practices have no place in the literature-based reading classroom:

- Using mediocre literature in the reading program solely on the basis of having it at hand with no regard to its appeal to students or its suitability to curricular goals
- Regularly using class sets of single trade books with a predetermined reading schedule and fill-in-the-blank worksheets (a practice referred to as the "basalization of literature")
- Reading works of literature by round-robin reading
- Selecting and assigning every title read by students
- Assigning book reports regularly under the guise of book response to check comprehension
- Excluding multicultural and international titles, poetry, and a balance of genres and character types from the classroom selection

There is no one right way to teach literature-based reading. The method cannot be packaged. Your best protection against bogus claims, materials, and practices is to have a complete understanding of the theory behind the practice. *Transitions* and *Invitations* by Routman (1988, 1991); *Literature-Based Reading Programs at Work,* edited by Hancock and Hill (1987); and *How to Teach Reading with Children's Books* by Veatch (1968) are a few of the excellent, practical resources that have stood the test of time.

Technology and Literature

The phenomenal growth in availability, capability, and use of electronic devices that enable users to read, write, communicate, gather, and share information makes technological development a topic worthy of attention by teachers. In this section, we will address technologies that have in-school applications and are currently affecting instruction and learning in schools.

The computer, handheld devices, and cell phones with Internet browsing, e-mail, and text messaging capabilities are currently the most frequently used technological devices. These technologies have already shown their potential for assisting in effective language and literature instruction and learning consistent with curricular goals; however, guidelines for the appropriate use of these instructional devices in the classroom will need to be set by teachers to prevent socializing or game playing. Some of the predominant educational uses of technology follow.

The Internet

The Internet is very useful for research and lesson planning—teachers can use information they find on the Internet to corroborate information from other sources, develop overviews of content being studied, and update information found in textbooks. Online professional sources can also assist in lesson planning; see, for example, ReadWriteThink (www.readwritethink.org) and Web English Teacher (www.webenglishteacher.com) for lessons developed by teachers. Such lessons, if they meet teachers' curricular goals, can provide new ideas and resources.

Teachers can use closed Internet networks to have students share their responses to literature being studied in class or drafts of writing with partners or to require or encourage student journaling. In our experience, middle-school students are more willing to share their responses to literature if it can be done on a computer, through the Internet, or by text messaging. In-school use of interactive websites, weblogs, and class-created chat rooms must, of course, be operated within the safety guidelines of the school system.

Students can use the Internet to research topics for literature-related units of study, locate websites for author studies, or identify sources for further research on a theme. Students often enjoy finding books on topics of interest and reading others' comments about them. The American Library Association's Great Sites for Kids (www.ala.org/gwstemplate.cfm?section=greatwebsites&template=/cfapps/gws/default.cfm) has links to several such sites in the Literature and Languages category. Students can also access many free audiobooks through websites such as http://librivox.org and www.gutenberg.org. Auditory learners especially appreciate audiobooks, and even very young children are capable of learning how to download audiobooks onto CDs or MP3 players.

Promising Newer Technologies

E-Book Readers

A device growing in popularity is the *electronic book (e-book) reader,* an electronic device used to read *e-books* (the digital equivalent of a conventional printed book). Although e-books are not yet widely used in schools, they are growing in popularity among the general public and appear to have potential for use in classrooms as the technology develops and becomes more affordable. E-books are generally cheaper than paper books, take up less space, are environmentally less wasteful to produce, and are more easily distributed. They have the potential to make the concept of an out-of-print book obsolete and to make virtually any book available to readers who have access to the Internet. Access to full-text books is also becoming possible on smartphones such as the iPhone and BlackBerry.

Furthermore, e-book readers provide access not only to books, but also to newspapers, magazines, and blogs. As a result, teachers may have greatly expanded choices of reading material for their students and of literature for text sets and in-class reading. An important disadvantage of some e-book readers that are currently available is the lack of color graphic capability, making picture books, illustrated informational books, and graphic novels using color ineffective as e-books.

Capabilities of e-book readers such as Amazon's Kindle2 and the Sony Reader that may facilitate reading include the following:

- A built-in dictionary so that readers can get a definition of a word simply by clicking on it
- Automatic searching and cross-referencing of text (useful for finding earlier references to characters or events)
- Nonpermanent highlighting
- Text-to-speech software that can convert e-books to audiobooks automatically

Our interest is in how e-books will affect the teaching of literature in schools. Will they permit teachers to make more choices for text sets available? Will the cost of books decrease and availability increase as more e-books are produced? Will these technologies change the way people read and think? Will they enable readers to improve their reading ability or motivate them to read more?

Supporters of reading on the Internet say that ease of access to books on the Internet may increase the time young people spend reading, therefore helping them to become better readers. Critics say that Internet reading is reducing readers' attention spans and diminishing literacy. Teacher observation and research into these questions will, in time, provide some answers.

Interactive Electronic Whiteboards

The *interactive electronic whiteboard* is, in essence, a computer with a screen large enough to be seen by everyone in a normal-sized classroom. Software enables teachers to download and present interactive lessons on any subject. One software source, for example, offers recent news articles from the AP Wire Service accompanied by guides to interpretation, vocabulary, and comprehension. Various interactive programs assist students in brainstorming, mapping, writing, and editing their written responses to literature. Interactive electronic whiteboards, such as Smartboard, allow instructors to add interest and depth to their lessons by accessing photographs, drawings, maps, video and audio clips, and related sources of information.

With the field of technology changing rapidly, it is important for teachers to stay informed about newer technologies that have potential for teaching. Information sources include school technology managers who offer assistance and workshops for teachers on promising new instructional technologies available for use in their school system, educational technology conferences, and professional organizations such as NCTE and IRA. These organizations provide conference workshops, Internet newsletters such as the NCTE Inbox, and publications that include information on emerging technologies.

Evaluating the Literature Program

Ongoing evaluation is part of responsible teaching, because it reveals students' strengths and weaknesses in learning and teachers' strengths and weaknesses in instruction and indicates where intervention or revision is needed. In today's schools, reading and mathematics skills are given the lion's share of attention in standardized evaluation programs, and all too often, no attention is paid to children's growth in literary understanding. This section focuses on how to evaluate a literature program from both students' and teachers' perspectives.

Well-known student assessment methods include traditional paper-and-pencil testing, portfolio assessment, conferencing, and observing. Teachers have found the latter three most informative in assessing how well a literature program is meeting children's needs. Portfolio assessment and conferencing can leave information gaps, however, and do not necessarily assess the teacher's performance or the program itself. We find that observation, when carefully directed, provides a full description of the students' progress, the teacher's strengths and weaknesses, and the literature program. It is also the most efficient method of assessment, since it can be done while one is engaged in other tasks.

Observation and Assessment of Student Learning

Evaluation of students in relation to a literature curriculum will focus mainly on the curriculum's effect on student behaviors rather than on the students' grasp of concepts. Consequently, the evaluation will be accomplished primarily by observing students rather than by testing them. An important principle to remember in planning for evaluation of teaching and learning is that evaluation must parallel the goals and objectives of the instructional plan. To look for conceptual understandings or behaviors in students when those concepts or behaviors have not been taught or encouraged is to invite failure and disappointment.

Experienced teachers often develop checklists to use in observation and assessment of various aspects of their literature programs. Also, generic checklists can be developed by teams of teachers and librarians at each grade level in a school and then tailored by individual teachers to fit their own specific plans.

Checklist for Student Involvement with Books

Some of the behaviors that teachers look for in their students' interaction with literature will vary by grade level and the students' development. Other behaviors will show up on checklists for all grade levels. For example, preschool or first-grade teachers would be likely to look for evidence that their students know the terms *author* and *illustrator*, use the terms correctly in their discussions of books, and recognize the work of specific authors and illustrators. Middle-grade teachers, on the other hand, would be more likely to look for evidence that students are choosing and reading novel-length stories independently. Teachers at all grade levels will be looking for evidence that their students are enjoying reading and voluntarily choosing to read. Figure 12.3 gives an idea of what such an evaluation instrument might look like.

Observation and Assessment of Teacher Effectiveness

Regular self-assessment is an important part of a teacher's professional development. The following two checklists were conceived with preservice teachers in mind, mainly for the purposes of self-evaluation and guiding their observation of the classrooms they visit during their school participation experiences.

Figure 12.3 Checklist for Student Involvement with Literature

Evaluator: _____   Date: _____

Behavior	Yes	No	Comment
Reading and Listening			
Student reads voluntarily and willingly	___	___	_____
Student enjoys reading and listening to literature	___	___	_____
Student reads during silent reading time	___	___	_____
Student reads and listens to literature for entertainment	___	___	_____
Student reads for information	___	___	_____
Student reads and listens to a variety of fiction, nonfiction, and poems	___	___	_____
Response to Literature			
Student talks intelligently about books read or heard	___	___	_____
Student shares responses to books with peers	___	___	_____
Student is attentive during read-aloud sessions	___	___	_____
Student is able to discuss a work of fiction in terms of			
character	___	___	_____
plot	___	___	_____
setting	___	___	_____
theme	___	___	_____
style	___	___	_____
Student is able to discuss a work of informational literature in terms of			
structure	___	___	_____
theme	___	___	_____
style	___	___	_____
Student is able to accept that different people may have different responses to the same story	___	___	_____
Student is able to relate stories to personal experience, where applicable	___	___	_____
Student is able to compare and contrast stories, authors' writing styles, and illustrators' artistic styles	___	___	_____
Selection of Literature			
Student knows how to select appropriate books for independent reading	___	___	_____
Student knows how to use a computer to find, read about, and select books from the school library	___	___	_____
Student keeps a log of books read independently	___	___	_____
Student is developing personal preferences in literature	___	___	_____
Student tries new book genres	___	___	_____

Checklist for Classroom Environment

The environment of a classroom is determined mainly by what the resident teacher values in learning and teaching. These values, in turn, determine how the classroom is arranged, which materials are available, and what sorts of events and activities are regularly scheduled. Figure 12.4 incorporates all of these features.

Checklist for Teaching Activities

Success in making children lovers of books and reading certainly does not depend on generous supplies of equipment or a certain physical layout, although these can facilitate the job. In the end, it is what the teacher does with literature that makes the biggest impression on children. Activities that make the learning experience positive and nonthreatening are generally the most successful with children. This point of view is evident in Figure 12.5.

Implementing a Schoolwide Curriculum in Literature

Having a schoolwide curriculum in literature benefits teachers and students and is worth pursuing. The main benefit to students is that their teachers' efforts will be coordinated from year to year. Repetition of content and titles will be avoided and continuity will be improved. The main benefits to teachers are that ideas, expertise, and materials will be shared and planning will be facilitated by knowing what experiences with literature incoming students have had or should have. The task of developing a schoolwide literature curriculum should be shared by a committee that has a representative from each grade level and the library media specialist.

A literature curriculum committee's function is to determine what literature content will be presented at each grade level. A set of trade books appropriate for delivering the literature curriculum at each grade level can also be suggested by the committee, although the ultimate choice of books to be used in a classroom will be the individual teacher's decision. Literature curriculum committees often select and update their schoolwide read-aloud list. Such a list helps to prevent duplication of teachers' read-aloud choices at different grade levels and to assure that students hear a well-balanced selection of books over the years. Having such a list may also convince some teachers to begin a read-aloud program.

Supporting Resources and Activities

Effective planning for a literature curriculum includes resources and activities beyond the classroom. School library media centers, publisher-owned book clubs, bookfairs, parents, guest authors and illustrators, and local public libraries offer invaluable resources and supports.

- *School Library Media Center.* The well-stocked, efficiently run library media center is the heart of a school. Ideally, library media specialists and teachers have a shared responsibility for teaching. Teachers tell librarians their resource needs, and librarians help teachers by identifying and locating appropriate resources, keeping teachers updated with the newest literature, and suggesting ways to present books to students. The librarian should be encouraged to play a key role in planning and developing a schoolwide curriculum in literature.

Figure 12.4 Checklist for Promoting Literature through Classroom Environment

Evaluator: _____   Date: _____

Behavior	Yes	No	Comment
Physical Layout			
Desks are arranged to promote student-to-student discussion	___	___	_____
Classroom has a computer center with several computers	___	___	_____
Room arrangement provides quiet areas for reading and thinking	___	___	_____
Reading area is well lighted	___	___	_____
Reading area has comfortable seating	___	___	_____
Reading area has adequate and convenient shelving for books	___	___	_____
Reading area is well organized and orderly	___	___	_____
Student response projects are displayed	___	___	_____
Materials			
Classroom has a trade book and audiobook library	___	___	_____
Classroom library is adequate in			
scope (variety of genres, both fiction and nonfiction)	___	___	_____
depth (variety of books within a genre)	___	___	_____
quality (light reading for entertainment to excellent quality for study)	___	___	_____
providing for varying reading abilities	___	___	_____
recent books	___	___	_____
multicultural and international books	___	___	_____
poetry collections	___	___	_____
Classroom has an adequate number of audiobook players, some for take-home use	___	___	_____
Classroom has a temporary collection	___	___	_____
Temporary collection			
addresses gaps in permanent collection	___	___	_____
is exchanged regularly	___	___	_____
provides for varying student interests	___	___	_____
is coordinated with topics of study	___	___	_____
Classroom library materials are			
easy for students to reach and reshelve	___	___	_____
coded and organized logically	___	___	_____
Scheduling			
Time is provided for self-choice reading every day	___	___	_____
Time is provided for browsing and selecting books regularly	___	___	_____
Time is provided for response to literature	___	___	_____

Figure 12.5   Checklist for Promoting Literature through Teaching Activities

Evaluator: _____   Date: _____

Behavior	*Yes*	*No*	*Comment*
Making Literature Enjoyable			
Read aloud daily (high-quality literature)	——	——	_____
Select books for read-aloud that			
reflect students' interests	——	——	_____
represent a wide variety of genres	——	——	_____
represent outstanding examples of each genre	——	——	_____
Share poetry orally on a regular basis	——	——	_____
Popular poets	——	——	_____
NCTE Award–winning poets	——	——	_____
Golden Age poets	——	——	_____
Share stories through storytelling	——	——	_____
Motivating Students to Read			
Introduce books regularly through booktalks	——	——	_____
Introduce students to interactive computer versions of books and audiobooks	——	——	_____
Encourage students to listen to audiobooks and read along in print versions	——	——	_____
Encourage student response to literature			
by asking open-ended or divergent questions	——	——	_____
by encouraging varied responses	——	——	_____
through oral response	——	——	_____
through written response	——	——	_____
through graphic response	——	——	_____
Allow students to choose books for independent reading	——	——	_____
Make both fiction and nonfiction options for independent reading	——	——	_____
Take class to school library weekly or more frequently for book browsing or selection	——	——	_____
Take class to public library for a field trip	——	——	_____
Invite a librarian to your class to booktalk and tell stories	——	——	_____

(continued)

Figure 12.5   *Continued*

Modeling Reading Behaviors

Read during silent reading time

Talk enthusiastically about books read

Show students how to select books

Showing the Relevance of Literature

Include literature that is culturally relevant to students

   in read-aloud selections

   in booktalks

   in text sets for group reading

Integrate literature across the curriculum

   in health/science

   in social studies/history

   in language arts/reading

   in mathematics

Encouraging Literature Appreciation

Present a yearlong literature curriculum

Reaching beyond the Classroom

Send read-aloud suggestions to parents

Encourage parents to visit library with
their children

Invite parents and community leaders to be guest
readers for read-alouds

Evaluation

Record student growth

   in understanding literary concepts

   in choices of books to read

   in attitude toward reading

   in quality of responses (verbal, written, artistic)

■ *Publisher-Owned Book Clubs.* These clubs offer inexpensive paperback books representing a full range of quality, from award-winning books to joke books and stickers, so children benefit from teacher guidance in making their selections. Participant teachers often use their bonus points derived from student purchases to build their classroom book collections. Children and teachers who lack access to well-stocked libraries especially benefit from these clubs.

■ *Bookfairs.* A bookfair is a book sale that is organized by a book vendor and held in the school building for one or more days. Bookfairs always call attention to literature and reading and can even be considered a reading motivator. They are especially appropriate in areas where there are no children's bookstores or well-stocked libraries.

Bookfairs send strong messages to children and their parents about a school's stance on reading and about what sorts of reading materials teachers and librarians in the school endorse. When selecting book vendors, make sure that they offer and prominently display good quality literature.

■ *Parent Involvement.* Parent involvement in literature begins with getting support for the school reading program at home. Parents are almost always willing to promote their children's academic efforts at home if they are told how to do it. Many teachers give parents lists of activities that support reading, including brief, carefully worded explanations where necessary. Some typical suggestions include reading to their children at night, listening to their children read aloud, and taking their children to the library to select books. Some parents are willing to help in classrooms on a regular basis. Ways in which parents can help teachers include listening to children read orally, reading aloud to small groups or individual students, and recording stories and poems on audiotapes for listening.

■ *Guest Authors and Illustrators.* Professional children's authors and illustrators often visit schools to speak to children about their careers and their books. Such visits are powerful reading motivators. The procedure for setting up an author visit can often be found on the publisher's website. In any case, the first step is to contact the marketing director of the author's publisher. Since established authors' expenses can be high, schools within a system often share the author and expenses.

■ *Local Public Library.* The community has no more valuable resource than its public library. Public libraries provide many important services in addition to loaning books, including the interlibrary loan system, summertime reading programs for children, and story hours for young children. Teachers can help to make the public library more effective by making students and their parents aware of the library and its programs and services.

Gaining Experience with Literature in School Practicums

Many elementary and early childhood education programs include multiweek, school-based practicum experiences. These school participation experiences give preservice teachers opportunities to observe teaching and classroom management styles, acquire firsthand experience working with children, and test the theories and ideas presented in their teacher training courses, such as those involving the use of good literature with young people.

An important part of practicum assignments involving literature is the selection of age- and content-appropriate books that will interest young readers. Although testing one's own ability to select appropriate books is important, it is advisable in school-based practicums to ask the classroom teacher to approve books prior to their use with children.

In the accompanying box are sample literature activities that we have found to work in school-based practicums. Observations and lessons learned are even more valuable when shared with other preservice teachers for similarities and differences.

Learning about Children as Readers

1. Interview three children in the classroom, preferably at three different levels of reading ability, to find their exposure to literature, their attitudes toward reading, their purposes for reading, and their sources of reading material.
2. Interview a number of students about their reading interests. Based on your findings, suggest to students appropriate titles for independent reading from books available in the school.
3. Conduct a class survey of reading interests. Use the procedure described on pages 27–28. Compile and analyze findings. Suggest titles for independent reading.

Learning How to Help Children Experience Literature

1. Booktalk a set of four or five books appropriate for students in the class. (See Chapter 13, pages 284–285.) Be sure to include works of informational and multicultural literature. (See Chapters 10 and 11.) After the booktalk, display the books in the classroom and observe students' interest in reading them.
2. Read aloud one or two picture books and a chapter book. After each read-aloud session, allow students to give their reactions. Compare your experiences of reading aloud from the two types of books. Compare students' responses to the two types of books. For example, how much attention do children pay to illustrations in a picture storybook?
3. Select a poem, guide students in arranging it for choral reading, rehearse the students, and present the choral reading to any available audience. (See Chapter 4, pages 70–71.) Note students' response to this activity and to the poem selection.
4. Introduce students to a specific children's book author or illustrator by demonstrating how to give an author or illustrator profile. These profiles are often required of preservice teachers, but they can be done by students as well and have merit as reading motivators. *Author and illustrator profiles* generally include interesting facts about the author, perhaps a recent picture, the one or two most distinguishing characteristics of the author's work (such as favorite topic, themes, style of illustration, or writing style), what the presenter liked about the author's work, and other books the author has written. A one-page handout summarizing this information and listing major works by the author will be appreciated by other preservice teachers and the cooperating teacher. Elementary- and middle-grade students presenting author or illustrator profiles can post their summary sheets on the class bulletin board.

    Traditionally, author and illustrator reports are presented orally to the class. Interesting variations include:

    ■ Presenting the profile in first-person format as the author or illustrator (costumes or props can be used)
    ■ Presenting the profile as a biographical skit about the author (presentation by a pair of students or a small group)

- Making a poster or bulletin board display about the author or illustrator
- Presenting the profile as a pretend interview (one student is the interviewer and one student pretends to be the author)

Learning about Student Response to Literature

1. Select a picture book or a chapter from a novel that involves four to six characters. Read it aloud to a group of students. Lead the children in a creative drama, readers' theatre, or graphic arts response to the book you have shared. (See Chapter 13 for ideas and guidance.) Note students' insights into the work as revealed in their responses.
2. Help students design and construct a literature-related bulletin board. This could range from a mural based on a whole-class read-aloud selection to response to books read independently by students in the class. This display can be mounted in the school hallway for observation by students in other classrooms. Note students' interest in the book(s) featured in the display.

Censorship and the First Amendment

The First Amendment to the United States Constitution guarantees to all citizens the right to free speech and freedom of the press, among other rights. Teaching children about their First Amendment rights is important because there are those who would take these rights away through censorship. *Censorship* is "the actual removal, suppression, or restricted circulation of literary, artistic, or educational materials . . . on the grounds that they are morally or otherwise objectionable" (Reichman, 2001). When a person or persons attempt to remove material from the curriculum or library, thereby restricting the access of others, it is called a *challenge.* Most book challenges occur locally, and most fail. When a challenge is successful and materials are removed from the curriculum or library, it is called a *banning* (www.ala.org/ala/issuesadvocacy/banned/about bannedbooks/index.cfm).

Our position regarding censorship is:

- *Teachers and schools have the right and the obligation to select reading materials suitable for the education of their students. With this right comes the professional responsibility to select good quality literature that furthers stated educational goals while remaining appropriate for the age and maturity level of the respective students.*
- *Parents are within their rights to protect their children from materials or influences they see as potentially damaging to their children. In the instance that a parent believes that material selected by a school or teacher is potentially harmful to his or her child, that parent has the right to bring this to the attention of the school and request that his or her child not be subjected to this material. Parents must indicate the reason for their concern.*
- *The school must take the parent's objection seriously and provide a reasonable substitute for the material of concern. If an alternative procedure is necessary in order to effect the substitution (for example, the student will listen to a different book in the library while the teacher is reading aloud), the alternative provided should respect the student and be sensitive to his or her feelings.*

■ *The parent does not have the right to demand that the material in question be withheld from other students. This would interfere with the right and professional duty of the teacher and school to educate the students. Once a student is given a reasonable alternative, the school has fulfilled its obligation and should not interfere with the First Amendment rights of other students.*

As adults, we cherish our right to choose our reading material and use it nearly every day of our lives. Elementary and middle-school social studies and civics textbooks proudly proclaim the freedom of choice that citizens of the United States have in their daily lives. But do we, as parents, teachers, and librarians, actually extend these rights to our children? Specifically,

■ Do we allow ourselves to be bullied by outspoken special-interest groups into taking good, but controversial, books off the library shelves, or do we stand by our convictions and book selections?
■ Do we self-censor by only selecting books on "safe" topics, or do we select books on the basis of quality and age appropriateness?
■ Do we listen to young readers' ideas about the books that they have read, or do we only ask them comprehension questions?
■ Do we allow children to reject books that they do not like, or do we force them to read what we have chosen for them to read?

In other words, do we actually teach students, by our actions as well as by our words, about their First Amendment rights?

According to the censorship database of the American Library Association's Office of Intellectual Freedom (OIF), from 2001 to 2008 the most censorship attempts came from parents (51%), other library patrons (11%), and school administrators (6%) (www.ala.org/ala/issues advocacy/banned/frequentlychallenged/21stcenturychallenged/index.cfm). Of the 3,736 challenges reported to the OIF in these eight years, 32 percent were based on material perceived to be "sexually explicit"; 27 percent were based on material perceived to have "offensive language"; and 19 percent were based on material perceived to be "unsuited to the age group." It should be noted that the OIF estimates that 75 to 80 percent of censorship attempts are not reported, so these figures are approximate.

Another unlikely, but significant, source of censorship is teachers themselves. A study by Wollman-Bonilla (1998) of pre- and inservice teachers' ideas about acceptable and unacceptable children's books reveals a tendency toward teacher bias in book selection for children. The researcher found that teachers "commonly objected to texts that reflect gender, ethnic, race, or class experiences that differed from their own" (p. 289). This subtle form of censorship is made worse by the fact that most teachers are unaware of their own biases in text selection (Jipson & Paley, 1991; Luke, Cooke, & Luke, 1986). Wollman-Bonilla makes a strong point in favor of First Amendment rights for children when she concludes, "If we are to know how books actually affect children, we need to hear *children's* voices and understand *their* experiences before, during, and after reading" (p. 293).

Teaching the First Amendment

Teaching students about their First Amendment rights might begin by posting a copy of the First Amendment, having students read it, and then discussing what this amendment means to them and what its loss might mean to them. Lists of children's books that some have declared "objectionable" could be posted. Children who have read the books could discuss why they might have been found objectionable and why banning these books would violate their First Amendment rights. Children's and young adults' fiction about censorship could be read and discussed. Good examples for younger readers are *Arthur and the Scare-Your-Pants-Off Club* by Marc Brown and Stephen Krensky (1998) and *The Landry News* by Andrew Clements (1999); for older readers, see *The Sledding Hill* by Chris Crutcher (2005), *The Last Safe Place on Earth* by Richard Peck (1995), *The Trials of Molly Sheldon* by Julian Thompson (1995), and *Save Halloween!* by Stephanie Tolan (1993). As teachers and librarians, we should do everything possible to promote the kinds of books that encourage critical thinking, inquiry, and self-expression, while maintaining respect for the views of others.

Dealing with Censorship Attempts

The American Library Association's Office of Intellectual Freedom monitors the challenges made against children's books in the United States. Most adults and children who have read the highly regarded books that often appear on these "most challenged books" lists find the reasons given for the challenges perplexing, if not incredible. The following titles, for example, appeared on one or more of the ALA's "Top 10 Most Frequently Challenged Books of the Year" lists from 2003 to 2008:

Alice (series) by Phyllis Reynolds Naylor (1985) for offensive language and being sexually explicit

And Tango Makes Three by Justin Richardson and Peter Parnell (2005) for anti-ethnic and anti-family content, homosexuality, having a religious viewpoint, and being unsuited to the age group

Bridge to Terebithia by Katherine Paterson (1977) for occult/Satanist content and offensive language

Captain Underpants (series) by Dav Pilkey (1997) for anti-family content, being unsuited to the age group, and violence

Harry Potter (series) by J. K. Rowling (1998) for occult/Satanist content

His Dark Materials (trilogy) by Philip Pullman (1996) for political and religious viewpoints and violence

In the Night Kitchen by Maurice Sendak (1970) for nudity, offensive language, and being sexually explicit

It's Perfectly Normal by Robie H. Harris (1994) for sex education and being sexually explicit

It's So Amazing! A Book about Eggs, Sperm, Birth, Babies, and Families by Robie H. Harris (1999) for sex education and sexual content

Julie of the Wolves by Jean Craighead George (1972) for being unsuited to the age group and violence

Olive's Ocean by Kevin Henkes (2003) for offensive language and being sexually explicit

Roll of Thunder, Hear My Cry by Mildred D. Taylor (1976) for offensive language

Scary Stories (series) by Alvin Schwartz (1981) for occult/Satanist content, religious viewpoint, and violence

Summer of My German Soldier by Bette Greene (1973) for offensive language, racism, and being sexually explicit

Often, individuals challenge books on the basis of a single word or phrase, or on hearsay, and have not read the book at all. Teachers and library media specialists have found that a written procedure is helpful for bringing order and reason into discussions with parents who want to censor school materials. Most procedures call for teachers and librarians to give would-be censors a complaint form and ask them to specify their concerns in writing. There are advantages to such a system: Both teachers and parents are given time to reflect on the issue and to control their emotions; and the would-be censor is given time to read the book in its entirety, if he or she has not done so already. Developing written procedures and complaint forms for dealing with a would-be censor are important tasks for the literature curriculum committee. Figure 12.6 presents a model form produced by the National Council of Teachers of English (NCTE) for reconsideration of a work of literature.

The American Library Association's Office for Intellectual Freedom has several publications about censorship, such as Reichman's *Censorship and Selection: Issues and Answers for Schools* (2001), that provide important and helpful information to schools on this topic. (For a catalog of all ALA publications, go to www.ala.org.) People for the American Way, an organization that provides advice and assistance in combating school censorship, can be contacted at www.pfaw.org.

The National Council of Teachers of English also offers a valuable document about censorship, *The Students' Right to Read* (Committee on the Right to Read, 1982), which explains the nature of censorship, the stand of those opposed to it, and ways to combat it. This document and the *Citizen's Request for Reconsideration of a Work* are available free of charge at www.ncte.org/positions/statements/righttoreadguideline.

Issues&Topics for FURTHER INVESTIGATION

- Investigate the issue of censorship of children's books further by reading the statement *Guideline on the Students' Right to Read* published by the National Council of Teachers of English online at www.ncte.org/positions/statements/righttoreadguideline.

- Investigate the nature of book challenges by reading several of the American Library Association's most frequently challenged books listed on pages 273–274. Analyze them for the reasons the would-be censors found them objectionable. Develop an argument for or against the censorship attempt for each book.

- Investigate the inquiry approach to teaching by finding and reading articles explaining the approach and comparing it to the traditional approach to teaching. Consider whether this approach suits you.

Figure 12.6   Citizen's Request for Reconsideration of a Work

Author _____ Paperback _____ Hardcover _____
Title _____
Publisher (if known)_____
Request initiated by_____
Telephone _____
Address _____ City _____ Zip Code _____
Complainant represents:
___ Himself/Herself
___ (Name Organization) _____
___ (Identify other group) _____

1. Have you been able to discuss this work with the teacher or librarian who ordered it or used it?
   _____ Yes _____ No
2. What do you understand to be the general purpose for using this work?
   a. Provide support for a unit in the curriculum? _____ Yes _____ No
   b. Provide a learning experience for the reader in one kind of literature? _____ Yes _____ No
   c. Other _____

3. Did the general purpose for the use of the work, as described by the teacher or librarian, seem a suitable
   one to you? _____ Yes _____ No
   If not, please explain. _____
   _____
4. What do you think is the general purpose of the author in this book? _____
5. In what ways do you think a work of this nature is not suitable for the use the teacher or librarian wishes
   to carry out? _____
   _____
6. Have you been able to learn what is the students' response to this work? _____ Yes _____ No
7. What response did the students make? _____
   _____
8. Have you been able to learn from your school library what book reviewers or other students of literature
   have written about this work? _____ Yes _____ No
9. Would you like the teacher or librarian to give you a written summary of what book reviewers and other
   students have written about this book or film? _____ Yes _____ No
10. Do you have negative reviews of the book? _____ Yes _____ No
11. Where were they published? _____
12. Would you be willing to provide summaries of the reviews you have collected? _____ Yes _____ No
13. What would you like your library/school to do about this work?
    ___ Do not assign/lend it to my child.
    ___ Return it to the staff selection committee/department for reevaluation.
    ___ Other—Please explain
    _____
14. In its place, what work would you recommend that would convey as valuable a picture and perspective of
    the subject treated? _____
    Signature _____ Date _____

Source: Committee on the Right to Read. (1982). *The students' right to read.* Urbana, IL: National Council of
Teachers of English.

✦ References

Abrahams, P. (2005). *Down the rabbit hole*. New York: HarperCollins/Laura Geringer.

Aliki. (1994). *The gods and goddesses of Olympus*. New York: HarperCollins.

American Library Association. (2009). *Frequently challenged books of the 21st century*. Retrieved from www.ala.org/issuesadvocacy/banned/frequently challenged/21stcenturychallenged/index.cfm.

Anderson, R. C., Hiebert, E. H., Scott, J. A., & Wilkinson, I. A. (1985). *Becoming a nation of readers: The report of the commission on reading*. Champaign, IL: Center for the Study of Reading.

Babbitt, N. (1975). *Tuck everlasting*. New York: Farrar.

Baldick, C. (1990). *The concise Oxford dictionary of literary terms*. New York: Oxford University Press.

Brisson, P. (1997). *Hot fudge hero*. Illustrated by D. K. Blumenthal. New York: Holt.

Brown, M., & Krensky, S. (1998). *Arthur and the scare-your-pants-off club*. Illustrated by Marc Brown. New York: Little, Brown.

Budhos, M. (2006). *Ask me no questions*. New York: Atheneum.

Buss, F. L. (1991). *Journey of the sparrows*. New York: Lodestar.

Canales, V. (2005). *The tequila worm*. New York: Random.

Children's literature review: Excerpts from reviews, criticism, and commentary on books for children and young people, vols. 1–117. (1976–2008). Detroit: Thomson Gale.

Clements, A. (1999). *The Landry News*. New York: Simon & Schuster.

———. (2002). *Things not seen*. New York: Putnam.

Cole, B. (2007). *Good enough to eat*. New York: Farrar.

Committee on the Right to Read. (1982). *The students' right to read*. Urbana, IL: National Council of Teachers of English.

Crutcher, C. (2005). *The sledding hill*. New York: HarperCollins.

D'Aluisio, F., & Menzel, P. (2008). *What the world eats*. Berkeley, CA: Tricycle.

Duprau, J. (2003). *The city of Ember*. New York: Random.

Durkin, D. (1987). *Teaching young children to read* (4th ed.). Boston: Allyn & Bacon.

Edwards, M. (2005). *Stinky Stern forever*. New York: Harcourt.

Etchemendy, N. (2000). *The power of un*. Asheville, NC: Front Street.

Farmer, N. (2002). *The house of the scorpion*. New York: Simon & Schuster.

Fenner, C. (2003). *Snowed in with Grandmother Silk*. Illustrated by Amanda Harvey. New York: Dial.

Fogelin, A. (2000). *Crossing Jordan*. Atlanta: Peachtree.

Freedman, R. (1980). *Immigrant kids*. New York: Dutton.

George, J. C. (1972). *Julie of the wolves*. New York: Harper.

Ghigna, C. (2003). In sight. In *A fury of motion: Poems for boys*. Honesdale, PA: Boyds Mills.

Gore, A. (2007). *An inconvenient truth: The crisis of global warming*. Adapted by Jane O'Connor. New York: Viking.

Greene, B. (1973). *Summer of my German soldier*. New York: Dial.

Greenwald, S. (2003). *Rosy Cole's worst ever, best yet tour of New York City*. New York: Holt.

Haddix, M. P. (2000). *Turnabout*. New York: Simon & Schuster.

Hale, S., & Hale, D. (2008). *Rapunzel's revenge*. Illustrated by Nathan Hale. New York: Bloomsbury.

Hall, S. (1990). *Using picture storybooks to teach literary devices: Recommended books for children and young adults* (Vol. 1). Phoenix: Oryx. (Vol. 2, 1994; Vol. 3, 2001; Vol. 4, 2007; Santa Barbara, CA: Libraries Unlimited)

Hancock, J., & Hill, S. (1987). *Literature-based reading programs at work*. Portsmouth, NH: Heinemann.

Harper, C. M. (2007). *Just Grace*. Boston: Houghton.

Harris, R. H. (1994). *It's perfectly normal: A book about changing bodies, growing up, sex, and sexual health*. Illustrated by Michael Emberley. New York: Candlewick.

———. (1999). *It's so amazing! A book about eggs, sperm, birth, babies and families*. Illustrated by Michael Emberley. New York: Candlewick.

Henkes, K. (2003). *Olive's ocean*. New York: Greenwillow.

Herumin, W. (2007). *Child labor today: A human rights issue*. Berkeley Heights, NJ: Enslow.

Hesse, K. (1992). *Letters from Rifka*. New York: Holt.

Hiaasen, C. (2003). *Hoot*. New York: Knopf.

Hobbs, W. (2006). *Crossing the wire.* New York: Harper-Collins.

Hyman, T. S. (1977/2001). *Sleeping beauty.* New York: Little, Brown.

Ives, D. (2008). *Voss.* New York: Putnam.

Jaramillo, A. (2006). *La línea.* New York: Roaring Brook.

Jiménez, F. (1999). *The circuit: Stories from the life of a migrant child.* Boston: Houghton.

Jipson, J., & Paley, N. (1991). The selective tradition in children's literature: Does it exist in the elementary classroom? *English Education, 23,* 148–159.

Kadohata, C. (2004). *Kira-kira.* New York: Atheneum.

Karmiol, S. M. (2007). *Illegal immigration (Introducing issues with opposing viewpoints).* Farmington Hills, MI: Greenhaven.

Kashmira, S. (2004). *Blue jasmine.* New York: Hyperion.

Kerrin, J. S. (2005). *Martin Bridge: Ready for take-off!* Illustrated by Joseph Kelly. Toronto: Kids Can.

Knight, M. B. (1993/2003). *Who belongs here: An American story.* Illustrated by A. S. O'Brien. Gardiner, ME: Tilbury House.

Lapp, D., Flood, J., & Farnan, N. (1992). Basal readers and literature: A tight fit or a mismatch? In K. D. Wood & A. Moss (Eds.), *Exploring literature in the classroom: Content and methods* (pp. 33–57). Norwood, MA: Christopher-Gordon.

Levine, E. (1993). *If your name was changed at Ellis Island.* Illustrated by W. Parmenter. New York: Scholastic.

Levitin, S. (1970). *Journey to America.* New York: Atheneum.

Lewis, M. (1999). *Morgy makes his move.* Illustrated by Michael Chesworth. Boston: Houghton.

Look, L. (2004). *Ruby Lu, brave and true.* Illustrated by Anne Wilsdorf. New York: Simon & Schuster.

Lord, C. (2006). *Rules.* New York: Scholastic.

Lowry, L. (2004). *The messenger.* Boston: Houghton.

Luke, A., Cooke, J., & Luke, C. (1986). The selective tradition in action: Gender bias in student teachers' selections of children's literature. *English Education, 18,* 209–218.

Maestro, B. (1996). *Coming to America: The story of immigration.* Illustrated by S. Ryan. New York: Scholastic.

Marsden, C. (2002). *The gold-threaded dress.* Cambridge, MA: Candlewick.

McEwan, J. (2007). *Rufus the scrub does not wear a tutu.* Illustrated by John Margeson. Plain City, OH: Darby Creek.

Na, A. (2001). *A step from heaven.* Asheville, NC: Front Street.

Naylor, P. R. (1985). *The agony of Alice.* New York: Simon & Schuster. (13-book series published between 1985–2001.)

Paterson, K. (1977). *Bridge to Terabithia.* New York: Crowell.

Peck, R. (1995). *The last safe place on earth.* New York: Delacorte.

Pennypacker, S. (2006). *Clementine.* Illustrated by Marla Frazee. New York: Hyperion.

———. (2007). *The talented Clementine.* Illustrated by Marla Frazee. New York: Hyperion.

Pilkey, D. (1997). *The adventures of Captain Underpants.* New York: Scholastic. (Multi-volume series published from 1997–present.)

Pullman, P. (1996). *The golden compass.* New York: Knopf. (Others in His Dark Materials trilogy: *The subtle knife,* 1998; *The amber spyglass,* 1999.)

Reichman, H. (2001). *Censorship and selection: Issues and answers for schools.* Chicago: American Library Association Editions.

Resau, L. (2007). *Red glass.* New York: Delacorte.

———. (2006). *What the moon saw.* New York: Delacorte.

Richardson, J., & Parnell, P. (2005). *And Tango makes three.* Illustrated by Henry Cole. New York: Simon & Schuster.

Rodda, E. (1991). *Finders keepers.* New York: Greenwillow.

———. (2001). *Rowan of Rin.* New York: Greenwillow.

Routman, R. (1988). *Transitions: From literature to literacy.* Portsmouth: Heinemann.

———. (1991). *Invitations: Changing as teachers and learners K–12.* Portsmouth: Heinemann.

Rowling, J. K. (1998). *Harry Potter and the sorcerer's stone.* New York: Scholastic. (Seven-book series published between 1998–2007.)

Ryan, P. M. (2000). *Esperanza rising.* New York: Scholastic.

Ryder, R. J., Sekulski, J. L., & Silberg, A. (2003). Results of direct instruction reading program evaluation longitudinal results: First through third grade, 2000–2003. Madison: Wisconsin Department of Public Instruction.

Sachar, L. (1998). *Holes.* New York: Farrar.

San Souci, R. D. (1993). *Cut from the same cloth: American women of myth, legend, and tall tale.* Illustrated by B. Pinkney. New York: Philomel.

Sanderson, R. (2002). *Cinderella.* New York: Little, Brown.

Schmidt, J., & Wood, T. (1995). *Two lands, one heart: An American boy's journey to his mother's Vietnam.* New York: Walker.

Schwartz, A. (1981). *Scary stories to tell in the dark.* New York: HarperCollins. (Part of a three-book series published between 1981–1991.)

Sendak, M. (1970). *In the night kitchen.* New York: Harper.

Something about the author: Facts and pictures about authors and illustrators of books for young people, vols. 1–169 (1971–2006). Detroit: Thomson Gale.

Spinelli, J. (1995). *Tooter Pepperday.* Illustrated by D. Nelson. New York: Random.

Strauss, R. (2007). *One well: The story of water on Earth.* Illustrated by Rosemary Woods. Toronto: Kids Can.

Strom, Y. (1996). *Quilted landscape: Conversations with young immigrants.* New York: Simon & Schuster.

Taylor, M. (1976). *Roll of thunder, hear my cry.* New York: Dial.

Tchana, K. H. (2006). *Changing woman and her sisters: Stories of goddesses from around the world.* Illustrated by Trina Schart Hyman. New York: Holiday.

Thompson, J. (1995). *The trials of Molly Sheldon.* New York: Holt.

Tolan, S. (1993). *Save Halloween!* New York: HarperCollins.

Van Draanen, W. (1998). *Sammy Keyes and the hotel thief.* New York: Knopf.

Veatch, J. (1968). *How to teach reading with children's books* (2nd ed.). New York: Richard C. Owen.

Willey, M. (2001). *Clever Beatrice: An Upper Peninsula conte.* Illustrated by Heather Solomon. New York: Atheneum.

Williams, V. B. (2001). *Amber was brave, Essie was smart: The story of Amber and Essie told here in poems and pictures.* New York: Greenwillow.

Wollman-Bonilla, J. E. (1998). Outrageous viewpoints: Teachers' criteria for rejecting works of children's literature. *Language Arts, 75*(4), 287–295.

Woodson, J. (2003). *Locomotion.* New York: Putnam.
———. (2005). *Show way.* New York: Putnam.

Yang, G. L. (2007). *American born Chinese.* New York: First Second.

Yep, L. (1977). *Child of the owl.* New York: Harper.
———. (1993). *Dragon's gate.* New York: HarperCollins.

Yolen, J. (2000). *Not one damsel in distress: World folktales for strong girls.* Illustrated by S. Guevara. New York: Silver Whistle.

PEARSON myeducationkit™ Now go to Chapter 12 in the MyEducationKit (www.myeducationkit.com) for your book, where you can:

- Complete Assignments and Activities that can enrich and extend your knowledge of chapter content.
- Expand your knowledge with content-specific Web Links.
- Review the chapter content by going to the Study Plan, taking a chapter quiz, and receiving feedback on your answers.
- Access the Children's Literature Database for your own exploration.

chapter THIRTEEN

Engaging Children with Literature

I Meant to Do My Work Today

I meant to do my work today—
But a brown bird sang in the apple tree,
And a butterfly flitted across the field,
And all the leaves were calling me.

And the wind went sighing over the land
Tossing the grasses to and fro,
And a rainbow held out its shining hand—
So what could I do but laugh and go?

—*Richard LeGallienne*

Engagement with literature highlights the potential of a book to capture children's attention and invite their participation in a story world. Authentic, well-written books are the first step, but they must be supported by significant experiences that bring children and books together for a variety of purposes. These experiences include reading widely for personal purposes, reading critically to inquire about the world, and reading strategically to learn about literacy.

Teachers are the key to effectively engaging children in these three types of experiences with literature throughout the school day. Gabriela, a 9-year-old, begins her day by pulling *To Dance: A Ballerina's Graphic Novel* (Siegel, 2006) out of her desk to pursue her personal inquiry on becoming a ballerina. After independent reading, the class moves into reading instruction and guided reading. The teacher works with Gabriela's group in a guided inquiry to analyze how authors use dialogue for character development in *Wishes Don't Come True* (Bellingham, 2000). After lunch, the teacher reads aloud from *Iqbal* (D'Adamo, 2001), the fictionalized story of a boy who led an influential movement against child labor in Pakistani carpet factories, as part of a collaborative inquiry on human rights. Students discuss the protagonist's anger and fear and his willingness to take action for freedom, despite the risks. They explore his strategies for taking action and their concerns about whether kids can really make a difference in a world controlled by adults.

Balancing these experiences supports children's development as readers and as human beings, although the emphasis may shift as children become proficient readers and gain life experiences. Older readers may primarily focus on using reading to inquire, whereas young children focus more on reading for personal purposes and to learn about literacy. This shift in emphasis does not exclude the other types; all three should be integrated into the experiences offered to children, no matter what their age. Each serves a different purpose and highlights different books and roles for adults and children.

Reading Widely for Personal Purposes

Reading literature widely for personal purposes highlights choice and extensive reading for purposes that are significant to children's own lives, ranging from enjoyment to personal inquiries on topics of interest. Reading widely involves engagement and demonstration; students are not focused on writing or talking about the book or using it for an activity. They just immerse themselves in reading alongside other readers. The goal is to create a lifelong habit of reading for purposes that matter to the reader—not because the teacher said so.

Students should have the opportunity to choose from a wide range of reading materials. Wide reading provides children with a broad background from which to develop comprehension and interpretation strategies, promotes positive attitudes about reading, and encourages the development of lifelong reading habits. Many adults stop engaging with books once they leave school and view reading as boring because of the lack of choice in schools. In addition, reading many materials with ease increases children's fluency and the integration of reading strategies.

The experiences that encourage reading widely for personal purposes include reading aloud, independent reading, shared reading, and experiencing literature through multimodal texts. The role of the teacher is to provide regularly scheduled reading time and a variety of materials and to read alongside their students.

Reading Aloud by Teachers

Reading aloud to children by family members and teachers is essential for children's acquisition of reading strategies and positive attitudes toward reading. It is the centerpiece of a curriculum in literature. Beginning in their infancy and throughout the elementary- and middle-school years and beyond, children should hear books and poems read aloud on a daily basis. This teaching strategy is just as important in the intermediate grades as it is in primary grades.

Some important reasons that teachers read aloud are as follows:

■ To increase students' abilities to think critically and comprehend connected discourse

Go to Activity 1 in the Assignments and Activities section of Chapter 13 in MyEducationKit; complete the activity on finding read-aloud books that encourage movement.

■ To help students understand literary devices and the conventions of story, such as genres, characters, settings, themes, and plot
■ To expand and enrich vocabulary
■ To provide a model of expressive, fluent reading
■ To build background and interest in topics and issues related to classroom inquiries and content-area units
■ To share exciting and stimulating literature that is beyond students' reading ability, but well within their listening ability
■ To encourage students to love reading and literature

Three distinct aspects of the read-aloud experience need to be examined to make it as effective a teaching strategy as possible. Those aspects are (1) selecting the literature to read, (2) preparing the students for read-aloud time, and (3) reading the book aloud. Each aspect needs to be taken into consideration for a successful read-aloud experience.

Book Selection

No matter which book you choose to read aloud, it is essential that you first read the book to determine whether the story is enjoyable and worthy of children's time and whether it is appropriate for your students. You also can note ways in which the story lends itself to student response.

Over the course of a school year you will want to read aloud a variety of literature: poems, short stories, picture books, and chapter books of different genres and moods. You will also want to ensure that there is a balance of males and females as main characters in the books and that the main characters come from different backgrounds and cultural settings.

Lists of Excellent Books to Read Aloud are provided in Chapters 5 through 11. You may also want to look at two reference works that suggest books for reading aloud: Judy Freeman's *Books Kids Will Sit Still for, 3: A Read-Aloud Guide* (2006) and Jim Trelease's *The Read-Aloud Handbook* (2006).

The most recognized works in children's literature, though sometimes complex, deserve to be shared with students over the course of their elementary school years. When a book or poem is challenging for students, you need to be prepared to support their understanding. Without this help, many children would never experience and enjoy some of the more difficult but worthwhile pieces of literature. Conversely, you will want to avoid choosing books for reading aloud that students can and will consume eagerly on their own, reserving those books for students' independent reading.

When first reading aloud to a new class, however, you will want to start with shorter and easier works that are popular with students, and gradually build to longer and more challenging works as you become better acquainted with your students, their interests, and their abilities.

Preparation

For students to profit from read-aloud experiences, they need to be attentive. You can prepare students for reading aloud by having them remove distractions, such as pencils and other objects, from their immediate vicinity; by having them sit quietly in the designated place for read-aloud time; and by asking them to be ready to listen. If the book has concepts that you believe will baffle your students, you may want to quickly establish a context for the book before beginning to read.

Introduce the book by stating the title, author, and illustrator of the book, even with the smallest children. This will teach children that books are written and illustrated by real people called authors and illustrators. For international and multicultural literature, use the book jacket to briefly tell students how the author's and illustrator's backgrounds relate to the book's focus—for example, "This author lives in the United States, but her parents are from Korea, so she talked with them about their experiences and did research in libraries." You may need to look at the author's website to get this information, but first check the book jacket and look for an author's note or acknowledgment in the book.

Sometimes you may want to ask the students to predict what they believe the story will be about from looking at the cover and the title; other times you may want to explain briefly why you chose this book to read to them. For example, you may say that you are going to read this book because "it's another story by one of our favorite authors, Anthony Browne" or that "the book will tell us more about what it was like to live in Korea right after World War II." Some teachers read aloud several picture books by the same author over the course of a week to make students aware of a notable author. Book introductions should be kept short. They serve the purpose of inviting students to enter into the world of the story with you.

Reading Picture Books Aloud Effectively

Consider the following steps:

- Position yourself close to the class so that all students can see the pictures.
- Show the pictures as you read the book. Remember that the text and pictures are carefully integrated in a picture book to convey the story as a whole. Hearing and seeing picture books should be simultaneous.
- After the introduction, read the book aloud, placing emphasis on the meaning of the story. Think of reading aloud as a type of dramatic performance.
- Your body movements and facial expressions can enhance the drama of the read-aloud experience. Leaning forward during a scary, suspenseful part of a story and smiling or chuckling during a funny part can convey your involvement in the story.
- Maintain eye contact with your students. Be sure you are aware of their nonverbal responses to this reading experience to determine if a word of explanation is needed.
- Read fiction from beginning to end without interruptions except on an as-needed basis. Some books, such as concept books, informational books, and interactive books, do call for interruptions in the read-aloud process.

Reading Chapter Books Aloud Effectively

Many of the same considerations hold true with chapter book read-alouds. Of course, chapter books have few, if any, illustrations, so holding the book for students to see the pictures is not necessary. In addition, chapter books are usually read aloud over a relatively long period of time, from a few days to many weeks.

Practices that teachers have used successfully during chapter book read-alouds to help hook the students on the book and to keep them tuned in and involved include the following:

- Keep a chart of the characters—their names, relationships, and roles in the story—as the characters appear. This strategy is especially helpful if the story has a large number of characters. For example, in *The Westing Game* (1978) by Ellen Raskin, the many characters of this mystery must be remembered for the plot to make sense.
- Design and display a map of the story setting to track the events of the story in sequence. In most quest fantasies this visual aid can assist students in following the characters' journey.
- Develop a time line on which the dates are set at intervals above the line and the story events placed below the line at the appropriate date. For historical fiction and biographies, a time line can also include a third tier of historic events.

Sharing Literature from Oral Traditions through Storytelling

Telling stories to students is particularly important for sharing literature from oral traditions. Many Native American tribal nations, for example, have long traditions of oral literature. Some traditional stories are meant to be told only at certain times of the year or to particular audiences, and so it is not appropriate for these stories to be published as a book that could be read at the wrong times and places. These stories should be shared in their oral form.

Teachers bring oral stories to life through personal expression and interpretation and can use them to establish a close connection with students. Oral storytelling should be a regular part of classroom read-aloud experiences. Suggestions and resources for storytelling are in Chapter 4.

Independent Reading by Students

Another way for students to experience good literature is to read it to themselves. Indeed, the ultimate goal of a literature program is to turn students into readers who, of their own free will, read self-selected literature with enjoyment, understanding, and appreciation. To assist students in becoming independent, lifelong readers, teachers in grades K–8 need to set aside time each day for students to read independently. Kindergarten and first-grade students may spend only five to ten minutes reading independently, and often a quiet hum occurs as beginning readers say the words aloud as they read or tell their own stories based on the illustrations. Fourth- and fifth-grade students will often read silently for up to an hour.

Many schools have instituted *sustained silent reading (SSR)* programs on a schoolwide basis to promote the reading habit in students. A certain time each day is set aside for all students, teachers, librarians, coaches, principals, custodians, and office and kitchen staff to take a "reading break." The philosophy behind SSR programs is that students need to see adults who read and who place a high priority on reading. Students read materials of their own choosing and are not usually required to write book reports or give oral reports on these materials.

If your school utilizes a commercial reading incentive program, you may take advantage of the availability of the literature that is provided as part of the program. Use the program flexibly in ways that develop intrinsic motivation for reading, avoid the negative competitive aspects of the program, and help students achieve individual goals set for their independent reading.

Whether or not your school that has an SSR program, you will want to provide your students with an independent reading time each day. Remember that the goal is to have the students read as many different books and materials as possible, so they should not be required to write long responses. At most, they might be asked to keep a simple record sheet of what they have read. Tips for establishing a successful independent reading time include the following:

- Have a well-stocked classroom collection of books—poetry, plays, picture books, novels, and information books, along with graphic novels and magazines.
- Conduct booktalks regularly so that students become aware of books they may wish to read.
- Display new books attractively in the classroom and show videos of notable authors talking about their books and craft. These techniques are effective in "selling" books to children.
- Schedule the same time each day for independent reading. Allow enough time for students to get well into their books and to achieve some level of satisfaction from the reading.
- Insist on attentiveness to books during this time. With primary-grade students, quiet talking in pairs about books or individual lipreading aloud may be on-task behavior. Children in intermediate grades can read silently and usually prefer to do so, although recent research indicates some boys prefer social interaction while reading.
- Spend the independent reading period engrossed in books, setting yourself as an example of a reader. Be knowledgeable of and interested in the books the students are reading.

Retellings and dramatic play are another way that students engage in independent exploration of literature to make the stories their own. As young children tell and retell stories, they develop their concept of story and expand their oral language. Teachers can encourage retellings by creating a conducive environment in one area of the classroom with props, such as story puppets, feltboards with cut-out story figures, toys that can be used as characters (stuffed animals, dolls, plastic figures), wordless books, and favorite picture books. Some children take a book shared by the teacher during a class read-aloud and page through it, retelling the story from the pictures; others take puppets and re-create the story or make up an entirely new adventure with the same characters.

Audio or video recorders can inspire younger students to record and listen to their favorite stories, and older students can use the recorder to develop radio or television shows based on favorite books or to record their readers' theatre performances.

Booktalks

A *booktalk* is an oral presentation by a teacher, a librarian, or a student who tells about a book to interest other students in reading it. Booktalks are not book reports, analyses of the author's style, or old-fashioned discussion of characters, setting, theme, and plot. Booktalks have been used effectively for years by librarians who developed this strategy into an art for the purpose of encouraging students to check out books from the library. Teachers can give booktalks on five to ten books each week from their classroom and school library collections; in this way, they can entice students to read and experience good literature.

Some teachers who give frequent booktalks also encourage students to give booktalks to induce other students to read the suggested books. A regular feature of *Reading Rainbow,* the public television program about children's books, is children giving booktalks. One teacher taped two or three of these *Reading Rainbow* booktalks and showed them in class to help her students learn how to give good booktalks. For more tips on booktalks, see www.thebooktalker.com and www.nancykeane.com/booktalks.

The following are our recommendations for giving a good booktalk:

- Read the book before trying to do a booktalk.
- Choose books that you have liked or that you think your students will enjoy. Sincere enthusiasm for a book is stimulating and infectious.
- Have the book available to show to the students as you give the booktalk. Format aspects—such as cover illustrations, length, size, and shape of the books—which also influence book choices, can be weighed by students only if they can see the book.
- Keep the booktalk brief, generally no more than two or three minutes. Do not tell too much about the book or the students will see no reason to read it. For most books, four to six sentences will suffice.
- Tell the topic and something about the action in the story, but *do not tell the plot*. Feature a scene or character that the story revolves around, but do not discuss the scene that gives away the ending.
- Booktalk a group of books that share the same theme; in this case you will want to talk briefly about each book and how it fits with the others.

The following is an example of a booktalk on *The House of the Scorpion* (2002) by Nancy Farmer:

If you ever think about what life will be like in the future, 100 years from now, you will enjoy reading *The House of the Scorpion,* a novel about young Matt, who has spent his life locked away in a hut because he is a clone and clones are outcasts hated by human society. As Matt comes of age he discovers that he is the clone of El Patrón, the cruel ruler of Opium, a drug kingdom farmed by "eejits," brain-dead clones. Opium is located between the United States and Aztlán, once called Mexico. In El Patrón's household, Matt finds support from a cook and a bodyguard, and eventually Maria, who begins to care about Matt. When Matt realizes that his life is at risk, he makes a break for freedom and escapes to Aztlán, only to face more hardships and adventures. Matt wonders who he is, why he exists, and whether, as a clone, he has free will. *The House of the Scorpion* by Nancy Farmer has received many honors, including winning the National Book Award for young people's literature.

After you have given the booktalk, place the book on the reading table for students to peruse and to consider. Over time, give booktalks on a variety of books at different levels of reading difficulty, on different topics, and with male and female protagonists from many cultures. In this way, you will appeal to the wide range of interests and abilities that exist among students in a classroom.

Shared Reading

Shared reading is a term we use to describe teaching strategies that attempt to draw on the natural literacy learning that has long occurred in book-loving homes around the world. These various strategies—*shared-book experience, choral reading,* and *paired reading*—provide children with opportunities to experience good literature as they are learning to read. The strategies have in common a modification of the parent–child interaction with repeated readings of favorite books as the child gradually acquires an understanding of print and its relationship to our sound system or to the words we speak. A list of pattern books suitable for use in shared reading activities can be found at the end of Chapter 5.

The *shared-book experience* is an adaptation of a natural home-learning strategy used with groups of beginning readers in school settings. Enlarged-text books of 24" × 30" or larger, called *Big Books,* usually well-loved and predictable books like Eric Carle's *The Very Hungry Caterpillar* (1968), are presented to groups of beginning readers in a sequence proposed by Holdaway (1982). First, favorite, well-known poems and songs are repeated in unison by the students and the teacher while the teacher points to the text of the Big Book. A review story is then used to teach skills in context. Following this activity, the teacher involves the students in language play, such as alphabet games, rhymes, and songs that use letter names. Then a new story in Big Book format is presented by the teacher. Students participate by repeating the story, line by line, after the teacher. Later, students read independently from a wide selection of favorite books and compose original stories, often modeled after the new story.

Choral reading is reading aloud in unison or parts with a whole class, small group, or individual students so that students hear the text at the same time they read it. Choral reading can involve arranging a poem into speaking parts as a way to enjoy and interpret the poem (see Chapter 4). Choral reading a range of texts can provide support for students who are struggling as readers, typically by having less proficient students read in unison with more fluent readers or having a struggling student read chorally with a recorded version of the text. Teachers can also read one-on-one with a child, so that the teacher initially takes the lead in the choral reading and then gradually quiets her/his voice as the child gains confidence and takes over the lead.

Paired reading, also known as partner reading or buddy reading, involves two people sharing the reading of a text in some way. Two children can share a text by reading back and forth to each other, changing off every other page or section of the book or taking different voices or parts of the text. Another variation, often used with struggling readers, involves the teacher and child reading side by side. The child reads aloud until she or he has difficulty, at which point the adult supplies the word so that the reading can continue fluently.

In all of these strategies, well-chosen literature is important; the nature of the experience is companionable, not authoritative; and the child reader must see the text and hear the words simultaneously. Sometimes, the adult places a finger under each word as it is being read to draw the child's attention to the print. Selecting favorite, loved stories as well as meaningful, predictable stories is essential because the success of these strategies is contingent on frequent rereadings of the same book.

All of these variations of shared reading focus on the role of fluent reading experiences and multiple rereadings in teaching a child to read. As students read stories over and over, they are able to attend to different aspects of the print and the story, learning something different about the text each time. They also develop a feeling of competence in themselves as readers, which is especially important for struggling readers who may not have experienced fluent reading.

Readers' Theatre

Readers' theatre is the oral presentation of literature by two or more actors, and usually a narrator, reading from a script. Unlike plays, there is little or no costuming or movement, no stage sets, and no memorized lines. Literature becomes a living experience for readers through the use of facial expressions, voice, and a few gestures. Students engage in multiple rereadings of the script to develop a fluent, expressive interpretation of the story to share with an audience. Features typically associated with readers' theatre include the following:

- The readers and narrator typically remain on the "stage" throughout the production.
- Readers use little movement; instead, they suggest action with simple gestures and facial expressions.
- Readers and narrator sit on chairs or stools, and performers usually remain seated throughout the performance. Sometimes, certain readers sit with their backs to the audience to suggest that they are not in a particular scene.
- No costumes or stage settings are necessary and, at most, should be suggestive, rather than complete or literal, to encourage the imaginations of the audience. The use of sound effects may enhance the performance and give the impression of a radio play.

Scripts can be developed for readers' theatre by the teacher or by older students adapting a work of literature enjoyed by the class. Picture books readily lend themselves to adaptation, as do short stories. Some teachers have successfully adapted well-selected scenes from a favorite chapter book for readers' theatre (see Figure 13.1). Alan Armstrong's novel *Whittington* (2005), a Newbery Honor Book, is an animal fantasy that intertwines three plots: the contemporary barnyard, the medieval folktale, and Ben's reading problems. The qualities to seek in a promising story are natural-sounding dialogue, strong characterization, drama or humor, and a satisfactory ending. If the original work has extensive dialogue, the script writing is a very easy activity. The script begins with the title of the book, the name of the author, a list of characters, and usually an opening statement by the narrator. Following the introduction, the dialogue is written into script form, with the narrator scripted for the remaining nondialogue, narrative parts.

Scripts can also be purchased, but finding scripts that are both well written and adapted from the literature you are using in your classroom may prove difficult. If you decide to develop readers' theatre scripts from the literature you are using, remember that developing the first script is the most difficult. Once you have created the first one, you will find out how easy the process is. Intermediate-grade students take readily to script development once they have a model to imitate. Aaron Shepard's RT Page (www.aaronshep.com/rt) is a website guide to readers' theatre with tips on scripting, staging, and performing.

Choice of literature to use can include virtually any literary genre—picture storybooks, novels, biographies, long poems, letters, diaries, and journals. See Figures 13.2 and 13.3 for books suitable for script development. Another example, Paul Fleischman's *Bull Run* (1993), a historical novel set during the Civil War, is written as a series of episodes told by different characters at different stages of the war. At the end of the book, the author provides a list of each character's

Figure 13.1   Sample Page of a Script Developed for Readers' Theatre

Whittington (adapted from Chapter 1, pp. 2–5)
by Alan Armstrong
Random House, 2005.

CHARACTERS:
Narrator
Whittington (cat)
The Lady (duck)
Other characters appear later in the story

Narrator:	This scene takes place in the barnyard.
Whittington:	Hello.
The Lady:	Who are you?
Whittington:	Whittington.
The Lady:	Whittington? That's a funny name for a cat. It's more like the name of a town.
Whittington:	Doesn't it mean anything to you?
The Lady:	No.
Whittington:	Then you don't know history. Whittington is a person in history. He's in books. Anyway, what's your name?
The Lady:	They call me Lady because I'm in charge.
Narrator:	Whittington, the cat, explains that he needs a place to live.
The Lady:	You don't have a home?
Whittington:	I did. A boy took me in when I was a kitten. Then they sent him away because he read things backwards. They were ashamed. They sent him to a special school out west. He was going to take me along but they said no.
The Lady:	So what do you want from me?
Whittington:	A place in the barn.
Etc.	

Figure 13.2   Picture Books Adaptable for Readers' Theatre Scripts

Buttons by Brock Cole
Chrysanthemum by Kevin Henkes
Dog and Bear: Two Friends, Three Stories by Laura Vaccaro Seeger
Duck on a Bike by David Shannon
Frog and Toad Are Friends by Arnold Lobel
The Great Kapok Tree: A Tale of the Amazon Rainforest by Lynne Cherry
I Am the Dog, I Am the Cat by Donald Hall
The Three Little Wolves and the Big Bad Pig by Eugene Trivizas
Tommy at the Grocery Store by Bill Grossman

Figure 13.3   Novels Adaptable for Readers' Theatre Scripts

Bud, Not Buddy by Christopher Paul Curtis
Dave at Night by Gail Carson Levine
Ella Enchanted by Gail Carson Levine
The Giver by Lois Lowry
Out of Order by Betty Hicks
Seedfolks by Paul Fleischman
Whittington by Alan Armstrong
Witness by Karen Hesse

entries that can be used to produce readers' theatre performances. Variations on readers' theatre can be accomplished through the addition of background music, choral poems, and brief scenes from different stories tied together by a common theme.

Preparation for a readers' theatre presentation gives students a good opportunity to strengthen their oral reading abilities and to try out their expressive skills. The group typically reads through the script once or twice and then works on refining the interpretive aspects of each performer. Decisions need to be made on the arrangement of chairs and speakers for greatest visual effect. Following each presentation, an evaluation is made by the group with the goal of improving future performances.

Readers' theatre is well suited to classroom reenactments of literary experiences. Students have the opportunity to construct meaning for a literary work in a new medium—the medium of drama—with considerable ease and pleasure.

Experiencing Literature as Multimodal Texts

Children in today's world are immersed in mass media, including video games, iPods, and the Internet, that provide them with interactive digital, visual, auditory, and dramatic texts. Children's literature is increasingly available in a range of media, providing important points of access for many children. These multimodal texts include audiobooks, films, and digital books.

Audiobooks of children's literature, available today on CDs, provide readings by well-known actors and professional readers. Reviews of excellent-quality audiobooks can be found in the major review journals (listed in Chapter 3). The following are websites of publishers of substantial numbers of audiobooks:

www.randomhouse.com
www.recordedbooks.com
www.scholastic.com

Audiobooks are an excellent teaching tool. Consider some of the following uses:

- Listen to an audiobook as a class instead of using a teacher read-aloud. The novelty of the performance—something different from the teacher's reading—may add interest.
- Use audiobooks at a listening center where a group of children can work independently. Provide each child with a copy of the book to follow the narration.

■ When assigning homework reading to students, offer students who have difficulties in reading the option of listening to the audiobook while following the narration in a copy of the book. Students who otherwise would be unable to participate in class discussions of the book with their peers will be able to contribute.

Films based on children's books provide students with a multimedia experience of a story. Teachers can engage students in comparing how film is similar to and different from text. Both have plots, characters, settings, themes, styles, and points of view. Both are edited and both can have dialogue and narration. However, film differs from text in that it has sound (spoken words, music, and sound effects) and photography (its use of color or black and white, angles, close-ups, and panoramas). Additionally, films have actual people or animated characters inhabiting the character roles and actual settings, whereas books ask readers to form their own images of characters and settings.

> **PEARSON**
> **myeducationkit™**
>
> Go to Activity 2 in the Assignments and Activities section of Chapter 13 in MyEducationKit; complete the activity on comparing a picture book with its film adaptation.

With this quick background in the elements of cinema, students can become better "readers" of film, equipped to discuss or write their personal responses to films based on literature. Films that support or contradict the content of the book may be suitable for classroom use depending on the teacher's intent. Generally, teachers show a film based on a book after the book has been read and discussed. The film then provides an opportunity to compare and contrast the book and the film while considering the advantages and limitations of the two media. For some students the movie experience may be motivation to read the book or others in the same series or by the same author.

At the end of Chapters 5 through 11, lists of films related to book categories are provided. The American Library Association has an annual award, the Andrew Carnegie medal for Excellence in Children's Video, given to the producer of the video. Teachers will want to select films based on children's books that are appropriate to the age level and are connected to classroom inquiries.

Some sources for films, videos, and DVDs are as follows:

■ *The Video Source Book* (Syosset, NY: National Video Clearinghouse), published by Gale Research, Detroit, MI. This annual reference work lists media and provides sources for purchase and rental.

■ Two websites of large video distributors are www.libraryvideo.com and www.knowledge unlimited.com.

■ The Internet Movie Database (www.imdb.com) is a large film database with production, ratings, and other movie details with links to external reviews.

Digital books are an increasingly popular format for accessing literature. Digital books are available on websites such as the International Children's Digital Library (www.en.childrens library.org), which makes books available in different languages, as well as from a range of children's publishers and software suppliers (see www.childrenssoftwareonline.com). Many of these books provide interactive components, allowing children to click on a particular character or part of the setting to get additional information, dialogue, or sound effects, as well as narration that students can read along with. Digital books are discussed in more detail in Chapter 12.

Plays, as a literary genre, are written, dramatic compositions or scripts intended to be acted. A play may be divided into parts called *acts;* in turn, each act may be divided into *scenes.* The script usually has set design, costumes, and stage directions, as well as dialogue provided for each actor. Plays are usually published in *playbooks* that can be purchased as a set for use in group reading situations.

A good play has a subject that appeals to children, an interesting character or two, and a problem that worsens before being resolved satisfactorily. Humor always appeals to children and conflict between characters is needed for interest and drama. Some children's plays are adaptations of children's books, while others are *original plays*—stories originating in play form. The following resources can be used to locate plays:

- *Children's Book and Play Review,* an online journal of play reviews (http://cbpr.lib.byu.edu)
- International Association of Theatre for Children and Young People (U.S. national section is Theatre for Young Audiences, www.assitej-usa.org)
- American Alliance for Theatre and Education (www.aate.com)
- Smith and Kraus, publisher of plays and play anthologies (www.smithandkraus.com)
- Eldridge Publishing, one of the oldest children's play publishers (www.histage.com)

Several children's authors have written play scripts. Examples include *Skellig: The Play* by David Almond (2005), *Zap* by Paul Fleischman (2005), *Monster* by Walter Dean Myers (1999), *Novio Boy: A Play* by Gary Soto (2006), and *Pushing up the Sky* by Joseph Bruchac (2000). Sharon Creech's *Replay* (2005) has a play included at the end of the novel.

Children create a unique literary experience by performing a play, one that immerses them in creating a story while building on their natural enjoyment of play. Plays can be read independently or in small groups, performed as readers' theatre, or performed as a drama for an audience.

Reading Critically to Inquire about the World

Reading literature critically to inquire about the world involves reading to consider issues and ideas in children's lives, broader society, and the content areas. These experiences support children in becoming critical and knowledgeable readers and thinkers. Readers are encouraged to engage deeply with the text and then to step back to share their connections and reflect critically with others about the text and their responses.

This focus on the intensive reading of a few books to think deeply and critically balances the extensive reading of many books. The books chosen for intensive reading have multiple layers of meaning and invite readers to linger longer. These books invite social interaction and discussion, as students need others to think with as they struggle with interpretation and understanding. Because the focus is on dialogue and thinking, the literature may be beyond their reading ability, so the text should be read aloud to them, particularly in the case of young children and struggling readers.

When students experience a story, they often want to respond or express their reactions to the experience in some way. Sharing their responses can involve thinking about the experience through a new form or medium; they develop a better understanding of what they experienced by organizing and deepening their feelings and thought, and they discover that other readers' experiences with the same book may have been different. Although it is important to give students opportunities to respond to books, not every book needs or merits a lengthy response. Rosenblatt (1978) reminds us that no two people have the same life experiences and that it is the transaction that occurs between the text, the reader, and the present context that provokes a particular response. Teachers can offer opportunities for students to respond to their literary experiences in many different ways.

In addition, children can engage with literature as part of thematic studies or inquiries within content areas, such as math, science, and social studies. They read critically to compare information and issues across these books, learn facts about the topic, and consider conceptual issues. Literature becomes a tool for understanding the world and considering broader social and scientific issues, as well as a means of facilitating children's interest in a topic.

Literature Discussion

Whole-class discussion usually accompanies a read-aloud. In these discussions, comprehension is assumed and the discussion centers on the different ways students feel and think about the book, characters, events, themes, and outcome. Teachers invite students to share their connections by asking "What are you thinking?" instead of asking questions to check comprehension. In a class discussion, the teacher often has the pivotal role as discussion leader. However, only some of the students will have an opportunity to express their viewpoints because of the group size.

Another format for students to discuss their responses to literature is a *literature circle,* where students meet in small groups to share their responses about a book they have read as a group or a book read aloud by the teacher to the whole class. One of the goals of literature circles is for children to learn to work and think with one another and to value the opinions and views of others. The small group format is student led and provides more opportunities for dialogue. The following features are typically found in literature circles:

- The books are organized around a particular theme as either *shared book sets* (multiple copies of the same text) or *text sets* (ten to fifteen conceptually related picture books). Each small group reads a different shared book or text set related to the same broad theme (see Figures 13.4 and 13.5).
- Students are introduced to the selections through short booktalks and given time to browse the books. They list their first and second choices on ballots that are used to organize students into heterogeneous groups of four to six students.
- Students read the books and prepare for literature discussion.
  - Students reading chapter books determine how many pages to read a day in order to finish the book in one or two weeks. Reading goals that are not completed at school are considered homework. Students meet in a mini-circle for ten to fifteen minutes daily to check in with each other on their reading goals and share connections and confusions. Students who are struggling with the book can partner with another student from the group or listen to an audiorecording of the book.
  - Young children may not be able to independently read the more complex picture books that support literature discussion. The books can be read aloud to them by a teacher, an older buddy reader, or a family member, or they can listen to an audiorecording. Young

Figure 13.4   Shared Book Sets on Journeys for Literature Circles

Picture Books

Each literature circle has multiple copies of one of these titles.

Amelia's Road by Linda Altman
Fox by Margaret Wild
Goin' Someplace Special by Patricia McKissack
Going Home by Eve Bunting
John Patrick Norman McHennessy: The Boy Who Was Always Late by John Burningham
The Pink Refrigerator by Tim Egan
Sebastian's Roller Skates by Jeanne de Déu Prats
Something Beautiful by Sharon Wyeth

Chapter Books

Each literature circle has multiple copies of one of these titles.

Becoming Naomi León by Pam Muñoz Ryan
Elijah of Buxton by Christopher Paul Curtis
The Golden Compass by Philip Pullman
Journey by Patricia MacLachlan
The Last Dragon by Silvana de Mari
Lizzie Bright and the Buckminster Boy by Gary Schmidt
When My Name Was Keoko by Linda Sue Park
Wringer by Jerry Spinelli

children benefit from hearing the book read aloud several times. One option is to have the books read aloud at home for several days before the school discussion.

- As students read, they respond by writing or sketching their connections, questions, and concerns to be ready to share with group members. The responses may be in a literature log, on Post-its placed in the book, or on a graffiti board (see p. 296).
- Encourage students who finish reading ahead of the rest of the group to read an independent reading book thematically related to their literature circle books.

- Students complete the book and meet in literature circles for extended discussions. These discussions typically occur after students have read the entire book. Students may need to meet in literature circles along the way if a chapter book is particularly difficult or if students are struggling readers or English language learners. Literature circles typically last anywhere from two days to two weeks, depending on the length of the book and the depth of the discussion about the book. The discussions are open-ended and provide time for readers to share their initial responses with each other and then dialogue about several issues in more depth.

- Students create a web or consensus board to brainstorm the issues that they could explore further, based on their initial sharing.
- Students identify a focused anomaly or concern that they want to inquire about together as a group.

Figure 13.5   Text Sets on War and Conflict for Literature Circles

Conditions That Lead to War

Baseball Saved Us by Ken Mochizuki
The Butter Battle Book by Dr. Seuss
I Hate You! I Like You! by Tomek Bogacki
In the Rainfield by Isaac Olaleye
The Island of the Skog by Steven Kellogg
The Mightiest by Keiko Kasza
Terrible Things by Eve Bunting
Tusk Tusk by David McKee
When I Grow Up, I Will Win the Nobel Peace Prize
    by Isabel Pin
The Wild Wombat by Udo Weigelt

War as an Institution

The Araboolies of Liberty Street by Sam Swope
The Conquerors by David McKee
The Day Gogo Went to Vote by Eleanor Sisulu
The End of War by Irmela Wendt
The Monkey Bridge by Rafe Martin
The Roses in My Carpets by Rukhsana Khan
Sami and the Time of the Troubles by Florence P.
    Heide and Judith Heide Gilliland
The War by Anais Vaugelade
War and Peas by Michael Foreman
*When the Horses Ride By: Children in the Times of
    War* by Eloise Greenfield

Consequences of War

The Bracelet by Yoshiko Uchida
Faithful Elephants by Yukio Tsuchiya
Gleam and Glow by Eve Bunting
My Secret Camera by Mendel Grossman
The Orphans of Normandy by Nancy Amis
Rose Blanche by Roberto Innocenti
Sadako by Eleanor Coerr
Shin's Tricycle by Tatsuharu Kodama
So Far from the Sea by Eve Bunting
Star of Fear, Star of Hope by Jo Hoestlandt

Overcoming War

Alia's Mission: Saving the Books of Iraq by Mark
    Stamaty
The Brave Little Parrot by Rafe Martin
The Cello of Mr. O by Jane Cutler
Gandhi by Demi
Hiroshima No Pika by Toshi Maruki
Let the Celebrations Begin! by Margaret Wild
Oasis of Peace by Laurie Dolphin
A Place Where Sunflowers Grow by Amy Lee-Tai
Rebel by Allan Baillie
*The Yellow Star: The Legend of King Christian X of
    Denmark* by Carmen Deedy

- Students prepare for the discussion of the identified issue by rereading sections of the book, writing or sketching in their logs, marking relevant quotations with Post-its, engaging in further research, or using a particular response engagement.
- Students share their ideas and connections related to the identified issue and engage in dialogue around differing interpretations and perspectives.
- Students can continue their literature circles by returning to their web multiple times to identify another issue for discussion.
- Text set discussions begin with each student reading one or two books from the set and meeting to share their books. Students often move between reading and sharing for a week or two and then web the connections and differences across the books in their set. They choose one of these issues to discuss in greater depth through inquiry and critique.
- Teachers do not need to be in a group, but if they join a group, they participate as a reader and group member, sharing their thoughts.
- When students complete their literature circles, they can present the key ideas from their discussions to pull together their thinking about the book or text set.

- They may share informally by talking about their book and showing their web of connections and issues to the class.
- They can prepare a formal presentation by listing the most important ideas they want to share with others about their book and discussion. They then brainstorm different ways to present these ideas (murals, skits, posters, dioramas, etc.) and choose the one that best fits the ideas they want to share.
- They can create a classroom newsletter/newspaper in which each literature group writes about the books they are reading and includes visual sketches, webs, or charts.

The discussions in literature circles are more complex and generative if teachers embed these circles within a broad class theme, such as identity or journeys, around which they have planned a range of engagements, including class read-alouds and browsing of other books on that theme. This theme may be connected to a unit of inquiry within the curriculum or to issues students are exploring in their lives.

When students have the opportunity to converse and dialogue about what they are reading, they explore their "in-process" understandings, consider alternative interpretations, and become critical inquirers. Literature circles support reading as a transactional process in which readers actively construct understandings of a text by bringing meaning to, as well as from, that text. They come to understand that there is no one meaning to be determined, but many possible interpretations to explore and critique. The primary intent of these discussions is to provide a space for readers to think about life from multiple perspectives, not to learn about literary elements or comprehension strategies.

Literature Response Engagements

Requiring students to list the author, title, date, genre, setting, main characters, and summary of the plot seldom causes students to delve more deeply into literature. Students usually view traditional book reports as tedious busywork and as a punishment for reading a book. Although teachers assign book reports to get students to read, students often report that they never read the book, but instead read the bookflap and a page or two at the beginning and end.

Recently, some so-called literature response forms or worksheets have been published for use by teachers who adopt literature-based reading approaches. These worksheets are often little more than disguised book report forms. Such comprehension assessment may be occasionally useful for reading instruction, but is of no use if your interest is students' responses to literature.

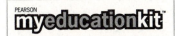

Go to Activity 3 in the Assignments and Activities section of Chapter 13 in MyEducationKit; complete the activity on investigating several response engagements to the books you are reading.

Readers deepen and extend their interpretations of literature when they respond in a variety of ways. When readers move from reading to writing, art, or drama, they take a new perspective on the piece of literature. In the process of exploring their thinking about a book through various sign systems, they discover new meanings and expand their understandings of that book.

The following response engagements provide structures to encourage students to push their thinking about a book. These engagements stand in contrast to activities where students write a summary, retell a book, answer comprehension questions, or make a "cute" art project. Response engagements challenge students to find and explore the issues that they find significant within a book, rather than answer the teacher's questions about the book. (See *Creating Classrooms for Authors and Inquirers* by Kathy G. Short and Jerome Harste, 1996, for more information and examples of these engagements.)

- **Freewrites.** At the beginning of a group meeting, set a timer for five minutes and write continuously about your thoughts on the book, then turn and talk in the group. If the group is still not sure how to begin, one person can read aloud all or part of their freewrite. The group discusses the ideas in that freewrite and then moves on to the next person.

- **Post-ful Thinking.** Put Post-its on pages where you have a significant connection as you read and jot a quick comment. Share these when your group meets to find issues to discuss together. You can also use Post-its to revisit the book when the group decides to examine a particular issue. Mark pages relevant to the issue as a way to prepare for the discussion.

- **Literature Logs.** Stop periodically as you read and respond to what you are thinking about, including questions and connections. These entries can take the form of a written response, a sketch, a web, a chart, quotes you want to remember, and so on. Reread your literature log right before beginning a group discussion so the issues are fresh in your mind.

- **Collage Reading/Text Rendering.** Mark quotes that are significant to you as you read. In collage reading, group members read aloud quotes to each other. One person reads a quote, then someone else reads another quote, and the reading continues in no particular order. Readers choose when to read a quote in order to build off of what someone else has read, but no comments are made about the quotes. Text rendering is similar, except the reader states why they chose the quote. There is no discussion until after the text rendering is finished.

- **Graffiti Boards.** Put a large sheet of paper on the table. Each group member takes a corner of the paper to write, web, and sketch their thoughts about the book or text set. The comments, sketches, quotes, and connections are not organized; the major focus is on recording initial responses during or immediately after reading a book. Group members share from their graffiti to start the dicussion. Webbing or charting can then be used to organize the connections.

- **Save the Last Word for Me.** As you read, note passages or quotes that catch your attention because they are interesting, powerful, confusing, or contradictory and put the quote on a 3" × 5" card. On the back of the card, write why you found that particular passage noteworthy. In the group, one person shares a quote and the group briefly discusses their thinking while the initial person remains silent. When the discussion dies down, the person who chose the quote tells why he/she chose it. That person has the last word, then the group moves on to the next person. Young children can show a page from a picture book instead of reading a quote.

- **Sketch to Stretch.** After reading a book, make a sketch (a quick graphic/symbolic drawing) of what the story meant to you or your connections to the book (not an illustration of the story). In the group, show your sketch and discuss its symbols and ideas. After sharing the sketches, choose issues to explore in more depth as a group.

- **Webbing What's on My Mind.** After sharing initial responses to a book, your group brainstorms a web of issues, themes, and questions that could be discussed from the book or text set. Using the web, your group decides on the one issue that is most interesting or causes the most tension to begin discussion. You can continue your discussion by choosing from other ideas on the web. New ideas are added as they develop from the discussion.

- **Consensus Board.** Divide a large board into four sections with a circle in the middle. The circle contains the book's title or key theme. In the individual sections, each of you writes or sketches personal connections to the book or theme. The group discusses these individual connections and comes to consensus on the issues or big ideas to explore further. These are written in the middle of the board for further discussion.

- *Comparison Charts/Venn Diagrams.* Read a text set and discuss similarities and differences across the books. From these discussions, develop broad categories that you want to compare more closely. Make a chart with the books listed on the side and the categories across the top. Both pictures and words are used to make the comparisons in the boxes. A Venn diagram (two circles that overlap in the center) focuses the comparison on one major issue at a time.

- *Story Ray.* You each receive a three-foot strip of paper (a ray) on which to create a visual essence of a selected chapter using colors, images, and a few words with various art media and little or no white space. Share your rays in the groups and explain their symbolism. The rays are then assembled on a large mural or wall in the shape of sun rays to reflect the unfolding of the novel.

- *Mapping.* Maps provide a way to organize your thinking and explore relationships among ideas, people, and events. They can take a range of forms to show visual relationships, explore processes and change, and record movement of people or ideas. Consider using maps to show the following:
  - The journey of change for a character within a book or of an idea/issue over the course of the book
  - Symbols that show the heart (the values and beliefs) or the mind (the thoughts and ideas) of a particular character
  - A cultural "x-ray" in the shape of a person that show a character's inner values and beliefs and outer actions and qualities
  - A flowchart that explores how certain decisions made by a character create particular consequences

- *Time Lines and Diagrams.* Time lines can help you think about how particular historical events influenced the characters in your story. Draw a line on a long strip of paper, placing the dates below the line on scaled intervals. Note the story events above the line and the events from history below the line. Time lines are also useful with text sets of historical sources.

Students who are new to working in groups often find that working in pairs is an easier way to become comfortable with discussion. Any of these response engagements may be used with partners, rather than in a small group. There are also several response engagements that are particularly designed for partners.

- *Say Something.* Two people share the reading of a short story. The first person reads aloud a chunk of text (several paragraphs or a page) to the other person. When the reader stops, both of them "say something" by making a prediction, sharing personal connections, asking questions, or commenting on the story. The second person then reads aloud a chunk of text and again both "say something." The two readers continue alternating the reading of the story, commenting after each reading, until the story is completed.

- *Written Conversation.* Have a silent conversation by talking on paper. Two people share a piece of paper and a pencil, talking about a book by writing back and forth to each other. No talking is allowed, except with young children, who often need to write and then read what they have written aloud in order for the other child to write back.

Drama as Response

Creative drama is informal drama that involves the reenactment of story experiences (McCaslin, 1990). It is improvisational and involves the actors creating dialogue and movement as they engage in the drama. Props may be used, but not scenery or costumes. Because of its improvisational nature and simplicity, creative drama places importance on the experience of the participants, not on performance for an audience.

A picture book, short story, or single scene from a chapter book may be dramatized. The most suitable stories to start with are relatively simple, involving two to six characters and high action. Many folktales fit this description. The steps in guiding creative drama in the classroom are as follows:

- Students select a story they want to act out, and listen to or read it independently several times, paying attention to the characters and story scenes.
- Students list the characters and the scenes on the chalkboard or on chart paper.
- Students assign parts to actors. If enough students are interested in dramatizing the same story, two or more casts of actors can be assigned. Each cast of characters can observe the performances of the others and learn from them.
- Each cast uses the list of scenes to review the plot, ensuring that all actors recall the events. Discuss the characters, having students describe the actions, dialogue, and appearance for each.
- Give the cast of characters a few minutes to decide how to handle the performance. Then run through it several times to work out the bumpy parts. Lines are improvised, not memorized.

The Fantastic Plays for Kids website (www.childdrama.com) also has useful ideas and lesson plans for creative drama.

Dramatic inquiry, also known as *Drama in Education,* involves the use of drama to create an imaginative space or drama world around critical moments in a story, rather than acting out a story (Heathcote, 1984). Students develop characters and situations and take on diverse perspectives that go beyond the book. Discussion supports readers in standing back and talking about events that happened to other people in a different world. Dramatic inquiry puts students in the middle of events and within the world of the story as they explore their tensions and issues. Students explore multiple perspectives within and beyond the story boundaries through strategies such as the following:

- *Tableaus.*   Each small group of students creates a frozen image without talk or movement to represent an idea or moment related to the story.
- *Writing-in-Role.*   Students assume the identity of a character and write a text from that perspective, such as a reflection on events or a journal entry.
- *Hot Seat.*   Students take on the roles of different characters and sit on the hot seat to respond to questions about their perspective on an issue from the story.
- *News Program.*   Students take on the role of television or newspaper reporters and interview characters from the book to retell an event from a range of perspectives.
- *Perspective Switch.*   Each student shifts perspectives, trying out the perspectives of characters who are opposed, supportive, or ambivalent to an issue.

These drama strategies take readers beyond reenactments of a story to their own drama worlds, giving them a lens for critically examining the events and margins of a story. *Action Strate-*

gies for Deepening Comprehension (Wilhelm, 2002) offers examples of these drama strategies in responding to literature.

Literature across the Curriculum

Literature across the curriculum refers to the use of literature to replace or supplement textbooks in social studies, science, health, and mathematics. Literature provides more interesting and well-written accounts and perspectives on historical events and scientific information. In addition, textbooks often superficially cover large amounts of information, whereas nonfiction literature focuses on a particular topic in more depth, providing a context for inquiry into broader social and scientific issues. Students who struggle as readers can benefit from attractively illustrated and more accessible nonfiction literature. A collection of nonfiction literature of varying lengths and difficulties can meet the needs of students at different reading levels, unlike textbooks written on a single readability level.

Literature makes social studies content more memorable because the stories are presented from a child's point of view, allowing children to see the world through a narrative framework. Children are more likely to understand and remember history when it is presented as a story with characters, settings, and events. They can then move from an interest in the narrative to an interest in the history itself.

Literature also permits students to examine multiple perspectives on a topic, which helps develop critical thinking. By comparing historical information from various sources, students encounter differing perspectives on a particular era of history. In addition, literature often relates political and social events to relevant moral issues. Children can see how these events affected the lives of real people and understand the morality underlying their choices. Unlike textbook authors, who must write to satisfy all viewpoints, authors of children's literature are more likely to face controversial issues head-on. For ideas on planning social studies units incorporating fiction and nonfiction, see the immigration web in Figure 12.2. Examples of literature offering a range of perspectives for a social studies inquiry on Japanese-American internment camps and for a science unit about the moon can be found in Figure 13.6.

Trade books in science and health present different sources of information as a means to verify facts. Students can compare the facts presented in the textbook with those found in various books on the same topic. Global warming, a topic frequently in the news, is addressed in a number of books. For example, Laurence Pringle's *Global Warning: The Threat of Earth's Changing Climate* (2001) and David Laurie and Cambria Gordon's *The Down-to-Earth Guide to Global Warming* (2007) are two fairly short, well-written informational books, while Marcus Sedgwick's science fiction novel *Floodland* (2001) features a girl who searches for her parents after the sea has risen as a result of global warming, causing cities to become islands. Another work of science fiction, *The House of the Scorpion* (2002) by Nancy Farmer, can become the basis for investigations into cloning and its ramifications.

Many nonfiction books on health and science present information in interesting ways through graphs, tables, figures, photographs, and other visual presentations, coupled with a lively writing style. Comparison of information from different sources can be readily provided when students are not limited to a single source for their information. Teachers who draw on various types of texts for their instruction have discovered that literature has the power to educate the mind while enlightening the spirit.

Figure 13.6 Text Sets for Multiple Perspectives in Science and Social Studies Units

The Moon

And if the Moon Could Talk by Kate Banks, illustrated by Georg Hallensleben (Realistic fiction)

Comets, Stars, the Moon, and Mars: Space Poems and Paintings by Douglas Florian (Poetry)

The Dog Who Loved the Moon by Cristina Gárcia, illustrated by Sebastia Serra (Fantasy, Cuba)

If You Decide to Go to the Moon by Faith McNulty, illustrated by Steven Kellogg (Fantasy/science)

Many Moons by James Thurber, illustrated by Louis Slobodkin (Fable)

The Moon by Robert Louis Stevenson, illustrated by Tracey C. Pearson (Poem)

The Moon by Seymour Simon (Science)

Moon Man by Tomi Ungerer (Fantasy, France)

The Moon over Star by Dianna H. Aston, illustrated by Jerry Pinkney (Historical fiction)

Moon Plane by Peter McCarty (Fantasy)

Moonshot: The Flight of Apollo 11 by Brian Floca (History)

Moontellers: Myths of the Moon from around the World by Lynn Moroney, illustrated by Greg Shed (Myths, world)

One Giant Leap by Robert Burleigh, illustrated by Mike Wimmer (History)

Japanese-American Internment Camps/World War II

Baseball Saved Us by Ken Mochizuki, illustrated by Dom Lee (Historical fiction picture book)

Bat 6: A Novel by Virginia Euwer Wolff (Historical fiction novel)

The Children of Topaz: The Story of a Japanese American Internment Camp by Michael Tunnell and George Chilcoat (History)

Dear Miss Breed: True Stories of the Japanese American Incarceration during World War II and a Librarian Who Made a Difference by Joanne Oppenheim (History)

Fighting for Honor: Japanese Americans and World War II by Michael Cooper (History)

Flowers from Mariko by Rick Noguchi, illustrated by Michelle R. Kumata (Historical fiction picture book)

Home of the Brave by Allen Say (Modern fable, picture book)

Journey to Topaz and *Journey Home* by Yoshiko Uchida (Historical fiction novels, memoir)

A Place Where Sunflowers Grow by Amy Lee-Tai, illustrated by Felicia Hoshino (Historical fiction picture book)

Under the Blood-Red Sun by Graham Salisbury (Historical fiction novel, Hawai'i)

Weedflower by Cynthia Kadohata (Historical fiction novel)

Content-area reading is the ability to read to acquire, understand, and connect to new content in a particular discipline. In content-area classes students are often assigned textbooks, a type of expository text, which they frequently have more difficulty reading and understanding than narrative texts. Teachers can make reading textbooks easier if they teach students how such texts are structured and explain their specialized features. In Chapter 10, the elements of nonfiction are explained with examples. Stead (2005) and Hoyt, Mooney, and Parkes (2003) provide many practical ideas on teaching reading strategies for informational texts.

Reading Strategically to Learn about Literacy

Reading literature to learn about literacy creates strategic readers who reflect on their reading processes and text knowledge. Adults should encourage these engagements by helping children develop a repertoire of strategies to use when they encounter difficulty, either in figuring out words or in comprehending, and to gain knowledge of text structures and literary elements. Adults guide children's reflections on their reading processes by teaching lessons on strategies, literary elements, and text structures and by having students read literature that highlights particular reading strategies based on teacher knowledge of children's needs. Students who have a range of effective reading strategies and text knowledge can problem solve when encountering difficulty so as to develop reading proficiency.

PEARSON
myeducationkit™

Go to Activity 4 in the Assignments and Activities section of Chapter 13 in MyEducationKit; view the video on teaching students to read like a writer and respond to the question.

Many schools use commercial materials for reading instruction rather than literature. Although children are taught how to read through these materials, they do not necessarily develop the desire or habit of reading. They are capable of reading but are not engaged readers who are motivated, knowledgeable, and strategic.

Engagements with literature that focus on learning about literacy include guided reading, guided comprehension, conferencing, and mini-lessons in which students read books in order to examine their current reading strategies and develop new strategies. Teachers carefully assess which readers are on the "edge of knowing" and form small groups of students who share similar needs for guided reading (see Chapter 12). Reading strategies are taught within the context of reading a book for meaning and then pulling back to talk about the strategies students used to make sense of that book or to figure out unfamiliar words.

Often literary instruction takes the form of worksheets where students list story elements, such as character, plot, and conflict, rather than thoughtfully considering how these elements influence meaning. Recently there has been a strong emphasis on genre studies (see Chapter 12). Some of these genre studies are formulaic, whereas others involve students in an inquiry approach to construct their understandings of the genre. (See Cruz and Pollock, 2004, for an example of how they immersed their students in an inquiry around fantasy.) These genre studies can be an excellent way for students to explore literary elements and genre within a meaningful context and can involve the following:

- Gathering and sorting a wide range of texts to determine which belong to the genre
- Reading aloud picture books and novels to discuss excellent examples of the genre
- Independently reading many books in the genre
- Charting student observations about the genre in various ways
- Discussing selected books in the genre in small group literature circles
- Writing their own stories based on their knowledge of the genre

Author studies, in which students immerse themselves in reading and examining an author's whole body of work, provide another meaningful context in which students can examine particular literary elements and genres to learn about literature (see Chapter 12).

Writing often provides an effective way for students to explore language and text structure, particularly if they use literary works as writing models. When children read and listen to stories, they accumulate vocabulary, sentence structures, stylistic devices, and story ideas and structures. Well-written stories and poems, such as those in Tables 13.1 and 13.2, serve as models for children in their own writing. When an 8-year-old boy who wrote extremely well-developed, interesting stories was asked how he learned to make up such good stories, he replied, "It's really a secret, but

Table 13.1 Using Literary Works as Writing Models in Grades 2–4

Literary Device or Element	Suggested Books
Characterization	*Olivia* by Ian Falconer *Sheila Rae, the Brave* by Kevin Henkes *Farmer Duck* by Martin Waddell *Duck on a Bike* by David Shannon
Dialogue	*Something Beautiful* by Sharon Wyeth *John Patrick Norman McHennessy* by John Burningham *The Wild Wombat* by Udo Weigelt
Episodic Plot	*Starring Grace* by Mary Hoffman *Dog and Bear: Two Friends, Three Stories* by Laura Vaccaro Seeger *When Mules Flew on Magnolia Street* by Angela Johnson
Journal Writing	*The Journey* by Sarah Stewart *Diary of a Fly* by Doreen Cronin
Setting	*Miss Rumphius* by Barbara Cooney *The Pink Refrigerator* by Tim Egan *Goin' Someplace Special* by Patricia McKissack

Table 13.2 Using Literary Works as Writing Models in Grades 5–8

Literary Device or Element	Suggested Books
Characterization	*Becoming Naomi León* by Pam Muñoz Ryan *Lizzie Bright and the Buckminster Boy* by Gary Schmidt
Dialogue	*Ruby Holler* by Sharon Creech *Don't You Know There's a War On?* by Avi
Metaphor	*Uptown* by Bryan Collier *Dovey Coe* by Frances O'Roark Dowell
Mood	*Dawn* by Uri Shulevitz *Don't Let the Pigeon Drive the Bus!* by Mo Willems *The Wolves in the Walls* by Neil Gaiman *Star of Fear, Star of Hope* by Jo Hoestlandt
Journal Writing	*Diary of a Wimpy Kid* by Jeff Kinney *Ways to Live Forever* by Sally Nicholls *The Diary of Ma Yan* by Ma Yan *Stowaway* by Karen Hesse
Point of View	*Faith and the Electric Dogs* by Patrick Jennings *When My Name Was Keoko* by Linda Sue Park *Flipped* by Wendelin Van Draanen *The Misfits* by James Howe
Flashbacks	*Who Is Jesse Flood?* by Malachy Doyle *Racing the Past* by Sis Deans *Hush* by Jacqueline Woodson *Pictures of Hollis Woods* by Patricia Reilly Giff

I'll tell you if you won't tell my teacher. I don't really make up the stories. When I was little, my mother read lots of books to me; then in school my teachers read a lot more. So what I do is take a beginning from one of the stories, a middle from another, and the end from another. And then I make up a title." Children who have a rich literary background have a well-stocked storehouse of ideas and structures to put to use in their storytelling and writing.

Writing a story modeled after another story can be an enjoyable way to explore constructing meaning through particular text structures. In modeling, the student adapts a story form or idea into a new creation. Examples include the following:

- Students create another episode using the same characters.
- Students write a different ending to the story.
- Students recast the story from the perspective of another character. Examples of a change in point of view can be found in Jon Scieszka's *The True Story of the 3 Little Pigs by A. Wolf* (1989), which gives the Big Bad Wolf's version, and Scieszka's *The Frog Prince Continued* (1991), which tells the shocking truth about "happily ever after."
- Students write a prequel to a story.
- Students take a story set in the past and rewrite it with a modern-day setting. Alternatively, a character from the historical narrative can become a visitor to modern times.

Many cultures view reading as necessary to a well-ordered society and to the moral well-being of the individual. Engagement with literature invites children to make meaning of texts in personally significant ways in order to facilitate learning of content and to develop positive lifelong reading attitudes and habits. In addition, children gain a sense of possibility for their lives and for society, along with the ability to consider others' perspectives and needs. Engagement with literature thus allows them to develop their own voices and, at the same time, go beyond self-interest to an awareness of broader human consequences.

Issues & Topics for FURTHER INVESTIGATION

- Select a picture book or scene from a novel to rewrite into a script for readers' theatre. If possible, try the piece with a group of children and reflect on their engagement.

- Read aloud a picture book to a group of students and engage them in a discussion using one of the literature response engagements. Reflect on this experience and what you learned from the students' responses. Read teacher vignettes from *WOW Stories* (www.wowlit.org/on-line-publications/stories), in which teachers reflect on their use of these engagements with students.

- Put together a group of text sets around a theme, such as power, conflict, change, journeys, identity, or relationships. Include a range of perspectives, genres, and cultures within your set of books. You might also include multimodal texts and oral literature as well as written literature.

★ References

Almond, D. (2005). *Skellig: The play.* New York: Delacorte.

Altman, L. J. (1995). *Amelia's road.* Illustrated by E. Sanchez. New York: Lee & Low.

Amis, N. (2003). *The orphans of Normandy.* New York: Atheneum.

Armstrong, A. (2005). *Whittington.* New York: Random House.

Aston, D. (2008). *The moon over star.* Illustrated by J. Pinkney. New York: Dial.

Avi. (2001). *Don't you know there's a war on?* New York: HarperCollins.

Baillie, A. (1994). *Rebel.* Illustrated by D. Wu. Boston: Houghton Mifflin.

Banks, K. (1998). *And if the moon could talk.* Illustrated by G. Hallensleben. New York: Frances Foster.

Bellingham, B. (2000). *Wishes don't come true.* New York: Mondo.

Bogacki, T. (1997). *I hate you! I like you!* New York: Farrar.

Bruchac, J. (2000). *Pushing up the sky: Seven Native American plays for children.* New York: Dial.

Bunting, E. (2001). *Gleam and glow.* Illustrated by P. Sylvada. San Diego, CA: Harcourt.

———. (1998). *Going home.* Illustrated by D. Diaz. New York: HarperCollins.

———. (1998). *So far from the sea.* Illustrated by C. Soentpiet. New York: Clarion.

———. (1989). *Terrible things.* Illustrated by S. Gammell. Philadelphia: Jewish Publication Society.

Burleigh, R. (2009). *One giant leap.* Illustrated by M. Wimmer. New York: Philomel.

Burningham, J. (1987). *John Patrick Norman McHennessy: The boy who was always late.* New York: Knopf.

Carle, E. (1968). *The very hungry caterpillar.* New York: Philomel.

Cherry, L. (1990). *The great kapok tree: A tale of the Amazon rainforest.* San Diego: Harcourt.

Coerr, E. (1993). *Sadako.* Illustrated by E. Young. New York: Putnam.

Cole, B. (2000). *Buttons.* New York: Farrar.

Collier, B. (2000). *Uptown.* New York: Holt.

Cooney, B. (1982). *Miss Rumphius.* New York: Viking.

Cooper, M. (2000). *Fighting for honor: Japanese Americans and World War II.* New York: Clarion.

Creech, S. (2005). *Replay: A new book.* New York: Joanna Cotler Books.

———. (2002). *Ruby Holler.* New York: HarperCollins.

Cronin, D. (2007). *The diary of a fly.* Illustrated by H. Bliss. New York: Joanna Cotler Books.

Cruz, M., & Pollock, K. (2004). Stepping into the wardrobe: A fantasy genre study. *Language Arts, 81*(3), 184–195.

Curtis, C. P. (1999). *Bud, not Buddy.* New York: Delacorte.

———. (2007). *Elijah of Buxton.* New York: Scholastic.

Cutler, J. (1999). *The cello of Mr. O.* Illustrated by G. Couch. New York: Puffin.

D'Adamo, F. (2001). *Iqbal.* New York: Aladdin.

David, L., & Gordon, C. (2007). *The down-to-earth guide to global warming.* New York: Orchard.

Deans, S. (2001). *Racing the past.* New York: Holt.

De Deu Prats, J. (2005). *Sebastian's roller skates.* Illustrated by F. Rovira. LaJolla, CA: Kane/Miller.

Deedy, C. A. (2000). *The yellow star: The legend of King Christian X of Denmark.* Illustrated by H. Sørensen. Atlanta, GA: Peachtree.

de Mari, S. (2006). *The last dragon.* New York: Hyperion.

Demi. (2001). *Gandhi.* New York: M. K. McElderry.

Dolphin, L. (1993). *Oasis of peace.* Illustrated by B. Dolphin. New York: Scholastic.

Dowell, F. O. (2000). *Dovey Coe.* New York: Atheneum.

Doyle, M. (2002). *Who is Jesse Flood?* New York: Bloomsbury.

Dr. Seuss. (1984). *The butter battle book.* New York: Random House.

Egan, T. (2007). *The pink refrigerator.* Boston: Houghton Mifflin.

Falconer, I. (2000). *Olivia.* New York: Atheneum.

Farmer, N. (2002). *The house of the scorpion.* New York: Atheneum.

Fleischman, P. (1993). *Bull Run.* New York: HarperCollins.

———. (1997). *Seedfolks.* New York: HarperCollins.

———. (2005). *Zap.* New York: Candlewick.

Floca, B. (2009). *Moonshot: The flight of Apollo 11.* New York: Atheneum.

Florian, D. (2007). *Comets, stars, the moon, and Mars: Space poems and paintings.* New York: Harcourt.

Foreman, M. (2002). *War and peas.* Atlanta, GA: Andersen Press.

Freeman, J. (2006). *Books kids will sit still for, 3: A read-aloud guide.* Portsmouth, NH: Libraries Unlimited.

Gaiman, N. (2003). *The wolves in the walls.* New York: HarperCollins.

Garcia, C. (2008). *The dog who loved the moon.* Illustrated by S. Serra. New York: Atheneum.

Giff, P. R. (2002). *Pictures of Hollis Woods.* New York: Wendy Lamb.

Greenfield, E. (2006). *When the horses ride by: Children in the times of war.* Illustrated by J. S. Gilchrist. New York: Lee & Low.

Grossman, B. (1989). *Tommy at the grocery store.* Illustrated by V. Chess. New York: Harper.

Grossman, M. (2000). *My secret camera.* San Diego, CA: Gulliver.

Hall, D. (1994). *I am the dog, I am the cat.* Illustrated by Barry Moser. New York: Dial.

Heathcote, D. (1984). *Dorothy Heathcote: Collected writings on education and drama.* London: Hutchinson.

Heide, F. P., & Gilliland, J. H. (1992). *Sami and the time of the troubles.* Illustrated by T. Lewin. New York: Clarion.

Henkes, K. (1991). *Chrysanthemum.* New York: Greenwillow.

———. (1987). *Sheila Rae, the brave.* New York: Greenwillow.

Hesse, K. (2000). *Stowaway.* New York: McElderry.

———. (2001). *Witness.* New York: Scholastic.

Hicks, B. (2005). *Out of order.* New Milford, CT: Roaring Brook.

Hoestlandt, J. (1995). *Star of fear, star of hope.* Illustrated by J. Kang. Translated by M. Polizzotti. New York: Walker.

Hoffman, M. (2000). *Starring Grace.* Illustrated by C. Binch. New York: Fogelman.

Holdaway, D. (1982). Shared book experience: Teaching reading using favorite books. *Theory Into Practice, 21,* 293–300.

Howe, J. (2001). *The misfits.* New York: Atheneum.

Hoyt, L., Mooney, M., & Parkes, B. (2003). *Exploring informational texts.* Portsmouth, NH: Heinemann.

Innocenti, R. (1985). *Rose Blanche.* Minneapolis, MN: Creative Education.

Jennings, P. (1996). *Faith and the electric dogs.* New York: Scholastic.

Johnson, A. (2000). *When mules flew on Magnolia Street.* Illustrated by J. Ward. New York: Knopf.

Kadohata, C. (2006). *Weedflower.* New York: Atheneum.

Kasza, K. (2001). *The mightiest.* New York: Putnam.

Kellogg, S. (1973). *The island of the Skog.* New York: Dial.

Khan, R. (1998). *The roses in my carpets.* Illustrated by R. Himler. New York: Holiday.

Kinney, J. (2007). *Diary of a wimpy kid.* New York: Amulet.

Kodama, T. (1992). *Shin's tricycle.* Illustrated by N. Ando. New York: Walker.

Laurie, D., & Gordon, C. (2007). *The down-to-earth guide to global warming.* New York: Orchard.

Lee-Tai, A. (2006). *A place where sunflowers grow.* Illustrated by F. Hoshino. San Francisco: Children's Book Press.

LeGallienne, R. (1969). I meant to do my work today. In L. Untermeyer (Ed.), *The Golden treasury of poetry.* Illustrated by J. W. Anglund. New York: Golden Press.

Levine, G. (1999). *Dave at night.* New York: HarperCollins.

———. (1997). *Ella enchanted.* New York: HarperCollins.

Lobel, A. (1970). *Frog and Toad are friends.* New York: Harper.

Lowry, L. (1993). *The giver.* New York: Houghton.

MacLachlan, P. (1993). *Journey.* New York: Yearling.

Martin, R. (1998). *The brave little parrot.* Illustrated by S. Gaber. New York: Putnam.

———. (1997). *The monkey bridge.* Illustrated by F. Amiri. New York: Knopf.

Maruki, T. (1980). *Hiroshima no pika.* New York: Lothrop, Lee & Shepard.

McCarty, P. (2006). *Moon plane.* New York: Holt.

McCaslin, N. (1990). *Creative drama in the classroom* (5th ed.). New York: Longman.

McKee, D. (2004). *The conquerors.* New York: Handprint.

———. (1990). *Tusk tusk.* LaJolla, CA: Kane/Miller.

McKissack, P. (2001). *Goin' someplace special.* Illustrated by J. Pinkney. New York: Atheneum.

McNulty, F. (2005). *If you decide to go to the moon.* Illustrated by S. Kellogg. New York: Scholastic.

Mochizuki, K. (1993). *Baseball saved us.* Illustrated by D. Lee. New York: Lee & Low.

Moroney, L. (1995). *Moontellers: Myths of the moon from around the world.* Illustrated by G. Shed. Flagstaff, AZ: Northland.

Myers, W. D. (1999). *Monster.* New York: HarperCollins.

Nicholls, S. (2008). *Ways to live forever.* New York: Scholastic.

Noguchi, R. (2001). *Flowers from Mariko.* Illustrated by M. R. Kumata. New York: Lee & Low.

Olaleye, I. O. (2000). *In the rainfield.* Illustrated by A. Grifalconi. New York: Blue Sky.

Oppenheim, J. (2006). *Dear Miss Breed: True stories of the Japanese American incarceration during World War II and the librarian who made a difference.* New York: Scholastic.

Park, L. S. (2002). *When my name was Keoko.* New York: Clarion.

Pin, I. (2005). *When I grow up, I will win the Nobel Peace Prize.* New York: Farrar.

Pringle, L. (2001). *Global warming: The threat of earth's changing climate.* New York: SeaStar.

Pullman, P. (1996). *The golden compass.* New York: Knopf.

Raskin, E. (1978). *The westing game.* New York: Dutton.

Rosenblatt, L. M. (1978). *The reader, the text, the poem: The transactional theory of the literary work.* Carbondale: Southern Illinois University Press.

Ryan, P. M. (2005). *Becoming Naomi León.* New York: Scholastic.

Salisbury, G. (1994). *Under the blood-red sun.* New York: Delacorte.

Say, A. (2002). *Home of the brave.* New York: Houghton Mifflin.

Schmidt, G. (2004). *Lizzie Bright and the Buckminster boy.* New York: Clarion.

Scieszka, J. (1991). *The frog prince continued.* Illustrated by S. Johnson. New York: Viking.

———. (1989). *The true story of the 3 little pigs by A. Wolf.* Illustrated by L. Smith. New York: Viking.

Sedgwick, M. (2001). *Floodland.* New York: Delacorte.

Seeger, L. V. (2007). *Dog and bear: Two friends, three stories.* New York: Roaring Brook.

Shannon, D. (2002). *Duck on a bike.* New York: Blue Sky.

Short, K., & Harste, J. (1996). *Creating classrooms for authors and inquirers.* Portsmouth, NH: Heinemann.

Shulevitz, U. (1974). *Dawn.* New York: Farrar.

Siegel, S. (2006). *To dance: A ballerina's graphic novel.* Illustrated by M. Siegel. New York: Simon & Schuster.

Simon, S. (2003). *The moon.* New York: Simon & Schuster.

Sisulu, E. B. (1996). *The day Gogo went to vote.* Illustrated by S. Wilson. Boston: Little, Brown.

Soto, G. (1997). *Novio boy: A play.* New York: Harcourt.

Spinelli, J. (2004). *Wringer.* New York: Harper.

Stamaty, M. A. (2004). *Alia's mission: Saving the books of Iraq.* New York: Knopf.

Stead, T. (2005). *Reality checks: Teaching reading comprehension with nonfiction K–5.* Portland, ME: Stenhouse.

Stevenson, R. L. (2006). *The moon.* Illustrated by T. C. Pearson. New York: Farrar.

Stewart, S. (2001). *The journey.* Illustrated by D. Small. New York: Atheneum.

Swope, S. (1989). *The Araboolies of Liberty Street.* Illustrated by B. Root. New York: Sunburst.

Thurber, J. (1971). *Many moons.* Illustrated by L. Slobodkin. New York: Harcourt.

Trelease, J. (2006). *The read-aloud handbook* (6th ed.). New York: Penguin.

Trivizas, E. (1993). *The three little wolves and the big bad pig.* Illustrated by H. Oxenbury. New York: Macmillan.

Tsuchiya, Y. (1988). *Faithful elephants.* Illustrated by T. Lewin. Boston: Houghton Mifflin.

Tunnell, M., & Chilcoat, G. (1996). *The children of Topez: The story of a Japanese American internment camp.* New York: Holiday.

Uchida, Y. (1993). *The bracelet.* Illustrated by J. Yardley. New York: Philomel.

———. (1978). *Journey home.* New York: Aladdin.

———. (1971). *Journey to Topaz.* New York: Aladdin.

Ungerer, T. (2009). *Moon man.* London: Phaidon.

Van Draanen, W. (2001). *Flipped.* New York: Knopf.

Vaugelade, A. (2001). *The war.* Minneapolis, MN: Carolrhoda.

Waddell, M. (1992). *Farmer Duck*. Illustrated by H. Oxenbury. Cambridge, MA: Candlewick.

Weigelt, U. (2001). *The wild wombat*. Illustrated by A. K. Piepenbrink. New York: North-South.

Wendt, I. (1991). *The end of war*. Illustrated by A. Boratynski. New York: Pitspopany.

Wild, M. (2006). *Fox*. Illustrated by R. Brooks. LaJolla, CA: Kane/Miller.

———. (1991). *Let the celebrations begin!* Illustrated by J. Vivas. New York: Orchard.

Wilhelm, J. (2002). *Action strategies for deepening comprehension*. New York: Scholastic.

Willems, M. (2003). *Don't let the pigeon drive the bus*. New York: Hyperion.

Wolff, V. (1998). *Bat 6: A novel*. New York: Scholastic.

Woodson, J. (2002). *Hush*. New York: Putnam.

Wyeth, S. (2002). *Something beautiful*. Illustrated by C. Soentpiet. New York: Dragonfly.

Yan, M. (2005). *The diary of Ma Yan*. New York: HarperCollins.

PEARSON myeducationkit™ Now go to Chapter 13 in the MyEducationKit (www.myeducationkit .com) for your book, where you can:

- Complete Assignments and Activities that can enrich and extend your knowledge of chapter content.

- Expand your knowledge with content-specific Web Links.

- Review the chapter content by going to the Study Plan, taking a chapter quiz, and receiving feedback on your answers.

- Access the Children's Literature Database for your own exploration.

Children's Book Awards

Some of the following awards were established prior to 1988. For access to the complete lists of winners and honor books for these awards, go to the websites as indicated.

 ## National, General Awards

The United States

Caldecott Medal

This award, established in 1938 and sponsored by the Association for Library Service to Children division of the American Library Association, is given to the illustrator of the most distinguished picture book for children published in the United States during the preceding year. Only U.S. residents or citizens are eligible for this award. Award winners and honor books since 1988 are listed here. For the complete list of winners and honor books, go to www.ala.org/ala/mgrps/divs/alsc/awardsgrants/bookmedia/caldecotthonors/caldecottmedal.cfm.

2009   *The House in the Night* by Susan Marie Swanson. Illustrated by Beth Krommes. Houghton (Fantasy, ages 3–5).

HONOR BOOKS
A Couple of Boys Have the Best Week Ever by Marla Frazee. Harcourt (Realism, ages 5–8).
How I Learned Geography by Uri Shulevitz. Farrar (Mixed genre, ages 5–10).
A River of Words: The Story of William Carlos Williams by Jen Bryant. Illustrated by Melissa Sweet. Eerdmans (Biography, ages 3–5).

2008   *The Invention of Hugo Cabret* by Brian Selznick. Scholastic (Fantasy, novel-length, ages 8–12).

HONOR BOOKS
Henry's Freedom Box: A True Story from the Underground Railroad by Ellen Levine.

Illustrated by Kadir Nelson. Scholastic (Biography [1849]/Multicultural [African-American], ages 7–10).
First the Egg by Laura Vaccaro Seeger. Roaring Brook (Pattern/Concept/Easy-to-read/Toy book, ages 3–5).
The Wall: Growing Up Behind the Iron Curtain by Peter Sís. Farrar (Autobiography/Partial graphic novel, ages 8–14).
Knuffle Bunny Too: A Case of Mistaken Identity by Mo Willems. Hyperion (Realism, ages 3–6).

2007   *Flotsam* by David Wiesner. Clarion (Fantasy/Wordless, ages 5–9).

HONOR BOOKS
Gone Wild: An Endangered Animal Alphabet by David McLimans. Walker (ABC/Nonfiction, ages 8–14).
Moses: When Harriet Tubman Led Her People to Freedom by Carole Boston Weatherford. Illustrated by Kadir Nelson. Hyperion/Jump at the Sun (Biography, ages 7–11).

2006   *The Hello, Goodbye Window* by Norton Juster. Illustrated by Chris Raschka. Hyperion (Realism, ages 4–7).

HONOR BOOKS
Rosa by Nikki Giovanni. Illustrated by Bryan Collier. Holt (Biography, ages 8–11).
Zen Shorts by Jon J. Muth. Scholastic (Traditional/Religious, ages 5–9).

Hot Air: The (Mostly) True Story of the First Hot-Air Balloon Ride by Marjorie Priceman. Atheneum (Historical fiction [1783], ages 4–8).

Song of the Water Boatman and Other Pond Poems by Joyce Sidman. Illustrated by Beckie Prange. Houghton (Poetry, ages 7–12).

2005 *Kitten's First Full Moon* by Kevin Henkes. Greenwillow (Animal fantasy, ages 3–5).

HONOR BOOKS

The Red Book by Barbara Lehman. Houghton (Fantasy/Wordless, ages 4–9).

Coming on Home Soon by Jacqueline Woodson. Illustrated by E. B. Lewis. Putnam (Historical fiction [Rural U.S., World War II], ages 5–8).

Knuffle Bunny: A Cautionary Tale by Mo Willems. Hyperion (Realism, ages 3–6).

2004 *The Man Who Walked between the Towers* by Mordecai Gerstein. Roaring Brook/Millbrook (Realism, ages 5–9).

HONOR BOOKS

Ella Sarah Gets Dressed by Margaret Chodos-Irvine. Harcourt (Realism, ages 3–5).

What Do You Do with a Tail Like This? by Steve Jenkins and Robin Page. Houghton Mifflin (Informational, ages 4–7).

Don't Let the Pigeon Drive the Bus! by Mo Willems. Hyperion (Fantasy, ages 4–7).

2003 *My Friend Rabbit* by Eric Rohmann. Roaring Brook/Millbrook (Animal fantasy, ages 4–8).

HONOR BOOKS

The Spider and the Fly by Mary Howitt. Illustrated by Tony DiTerlizzi. Simon & Schuster (Poetry, ages 6–12).

Hondo and Fabian by Peter McCarty. Holt (Realism, ages 3–6).

Noah's Ark by Jerry Pinkney. SeaStar/North-South (Traditional, ages 6–10).

2002 *The Three Pigs* by David Wiesner. Clarion/Houghton Mifflin (Traditional, ages 5–7).

HONOR BOOKS

The Dinosaurs of Waterhouse Hawkins by Barbara Kerley. Illustrated by Brian Selznick. Scholastic (Informational, ages 7–10).

Martin's Big Words: The Life of Dr. Martin Luther King, Jr. by Doreen Rappaport. Illustrated by Bryan Collier. Hyperion (Biography, ages 5–9).

The Stray Dog by Marc Simont. HarperCollins (Realism, ages 4–7).

2001 *So You Want to Be President?* by Judith St. George. Illustrated by David Small. Philomel (Informational/Biography, ages 7–10).

HONOR BOOKS

Casey at the Bat: A Ballad of the Republic Sung in the Year 1888 by Ernest L. Thayer. Illustrated by Christopher Bing. Handprint (Poetry, ages 7–12).

Click, Clack, Moo: Cows That Type by Doreen Cronin. Illustrated by Betsy Lewin. Simon & Schuster (Animal fantasy, ages 6–9).

Olivia by Ian Falconer. Atheneum (Animal fantasy, ages 4–8).

2000 *Joseph Had a Little Overcoat* by Simms Taback. Viking (Traditional/Pattern, ages 4–7).

HONOR BOOKS

When Sophie Gets Angry—Really, Really Angry . . . by Molly Bang. Scholastic (Realism, ages 4–6).

A Child's Calendar by John Updike. Illustrated by Trina Schart Hyman. Holiday (Poetry, ages 5–9).

The Ugly Duckling adapted and illustrated by Jerry Pinkney. Morrow (Modern folktale, ages 4–7).

Sector 7 by David Weisner. Clarion (Modern fantasy/Wordless, ages 5–9).

1999 *Snowflake Bentley* by Jacqueline Briggs Martin. Illustrated by Mary Azarian. Houghton (Biography, ages 8–12).

HONOR BOOKS

Duke Ellington: The Piano Prince and His Orchestra by Andrea Davis Pinkney. Illustrated by Brian Pinkney. Hyperion (Biography, ages 8–10).

No, David! by David Shannon. Scholastic. (Realism/Pattern, ages 3–5).

Snow by Uri Shulevitz. Farrar (Realism, ages 4–6).

Tibet through the Red Box by Peter Sís. Farrar (Biography/Magic realism, ages 7 and up).

1998 *Rapunzel* by Paul O. Zelinsky. Dutton (Traditional, ages 7–10).

HONOR BOOKS

The Gardener by Sarah Stewart. Illustrated by David Small. Farrar (Realism, ages 7–10).

Harlem by Walter Dean Myers. Illustrated by Christopher Myers. Scholastic (Poetry, ages 10–14).

There Was an Old Lady Who Swallowed a Fly by Simms Taback. Viking (Folk poem/Engineered, ages 5–7).

1997 *Golem* by David Wisniewski. Clarion (Traditional, ages 6–12).

HONOR BOOKS

Hush! A Thai Lullaby by Minfong Ho. Illustrated by Holly Meade. Orchard (Poetry, ages 2–6).

The Graphic Alphabet by David Pelletier. Orchard (ABC/Art, ages 7–10).

The Paperboy by Dav Pilkey. Orchard (Realism, ages 8–10).

Starry Messenger by Peter Sís. Farrar (Biography, ages 9–14).

1996 *Officer Buckle and Gloria* by Peggy Rathmann. Putnam (Animal fantasy, ages 5–7).

HONOR BOOKS

Alphabet City by Stephen T. Johnson. Viking (Concept, ages 7–9).

The Faithful Friend by Robert D. San Souci. Illustrated by Brian Pinkney. Simon & Schuster (Traditional, ages 10–14).

Tops & Bottoms by Janet Stevens. Harcourt (Traditional, ages 6–8).

Zin! Zin! Zin! A Violin by Lloyd Moss. Illustrated by Marjorie Priceman. Simon & Schuster (Concept, ages 5–7).

1995 *Smoky Night* by Eve Bunting. Illustrated by David Diaz. Harcourt (Realism/Multicultural, ages 6–8).

HONOR BOOKS

Swamp Angel by Anne Isaacs. Illustrated by Paul O. Zelinsky. Dutton (Modern folktale, ages 6–9).

John Henry by Julius Lester. Illustrated by Jerry Pinkney. Dial (Traditional, ages 6–9).

Time Flies by Eric Rohmann. Crown (Wordless, ages 6–9).

1994 *Grandfather's Journey* by Allen Say. Houghton (Biography, ages 7–9).

HONOR BOOKS

Peppe the Lamplighter by Elisa Bartone. Illustrated by Ted Lewin. Lothrop (Realism, ages 7–9).

In the Small, Small Pond by Denise Fleming. Holt (Pattern, ages 5–7).

Owen by Kevin Henkes. Greenwillow (Animal fantasy, ages 5–7).

Raven: A Trickster Tale from the Pacific Northwest by Gerald McDermott. Harcourt (Traditional [Native American], ages 7–9).

Yo! Yes? by Chris Raschka. Orchard (Realism/Multicultural, ages 5–7).

1993 *Mirette on the High Wire* by Emily Arnold McCully. Putnam (Realism, ages 7–9).

HONOR BOOKS

Seven Blind Mice by Ed Young. Philomel (Modern folktale, ages 6–10).

The Stinky Cheese Man and Other Fairly Stupid Tales by Jon Scieszka and Lane Smith. Illustrated by Lane Smith. Viking (Modern folktales, ages 7–11).

Working Cotton by Sherley Anne Williams. Illustrated by Carole Byard. Harcourt (Realism [African-American], ages 7–9).

1992 *Tuesday* by David Wiesner. Clarion (Fantasy/Wordless, ages 7–10).

HONOR BOOK

Tar Beach by Faith Ringgold. Crown (Multicultural [African-American], ages 6–9).

1991 *Black and White* by David Macaulay. Houghton (Mystery, ages 8–12).

HONOR BOOKS

Puss in Boots by Charles Perrault. Illustrated by Fred Marcellino. Farrar (Traditional, ages 5–7).

"More, More, More." Said the Baby: 3 Love Stories by Vera Williams. Greenwillow (Realism, ages 3–5).

1990   *Lon Po Po: A Red-Riding Hood Story from China* translated and illustrated by Ed Young. Philomel (Traditional, ages 5–8).

HONOR BOOKS
Hershel and the Hanukkah Goblins by Eric A. Kimmel. Illustrated by Trina Schart Hyman. Holiday (Modern folktale, ages 7–10).
The Talking Eggs adapted by Robert D. San Souci. Illustrated by Jerry Pinkney. Dial (Traditional, ages 6–9).
Bill Peet: An Autobiography by Bill Peet. Houghton (Biography, ages 7–10).
Color Zoo by Lois Ehlert. Lippincott (Concept, ages 3–6).

1989   *Song and Dance Man* by Karen Ackerman. Illustrated by Stephen Gammell. Knopf (Realism, ages 7–10).

HONOR BOOKS
Free Fall by David Wiesner. Lothrop (Fantasy/Wordless, ages 7–10).
Goldilocks and the Three Bears retold and illustrated by James Marshall. Dial (Modern folktale, ages 5–8).
Mirandy and Brother Wind by Patricia McKissack. Illustrated by Jerry Pinkney. Knopf (Traditional, ages 7–9).
The Boy of the Three-Year Nap by Diane Snyder. Illustrated by Allen Say. Houghton (Traditional, ages 7–10).

1988   *Owl Moon* by Jane Yolen. Illustrated by John Schoenherr. Philomel (Realism, ages 5–8).

HONOR BOOK
Mufaro's Beautiful Daughters retold by John Steptoe. Lothrop (Traditional, ages 6–9).

Newbery Medal

This award, established in 1922 and sponsored by the Association for Library Service to Children division of the American Library Association, is given to the author of the most distinguished contribution to children's literature published during the preceding year. Only U.S.

citizens or residents are eligible for this award. Award winners and honor books since 1988 are listed here. For the complete list of winners and honor books, go to www.ala.org/ala/mgrps/divs/alsc/awardsgrants/bookmedia/newberyhonors/newberymedal.cfm.

2009   *The Graveyard Book* by Neil Gaiman. Illustrated by Dave McKean. HarperCollins (Fantasy, ages 10–14).

HONOR BOOKS
The Underneath by Kathi Appelt. Illustrated by David Small. Atheneum (Animal fantasy, ages 9–13).
The Surrender Tree: Poems of Cuba's Struggle for Freedom by Margarita Engle. Holt (Poetry, ages 11–18).
Savvy by Ingrid Law. Dial (Fantasy, ages 10–12).
After Tupac & D Foster by Jacqueline Woodson. Putnam (Realism/Multicultural [African-American], ages 11–14).

2008   *Good Masters! Sweet Ladies! Voices from a Medieval Village* by Laura Amy Schlitz. Candlewick (Informational, ages 9–13).

HONOR BOOKS
Elijah of Buxton by Christopher Paul Curtis. Scholastic (Historical fiction [mid-eighteenth-century Ontario]/Multicultural [African-American], ages 9–13).
The Wednesday Wars by Gary D. Schmidt. Clarion (Realism, ages 10–13).
Feathers by Jacqueline Woodson. Putnam (Historical fiction [1971], ages 9–12).

2007   *The Higher Power of Lucky* by Susan Patron. Illustrated by Matt Phelan. Simon & Schuster (Realism, ages 9–12).

HONOR BOOKS
Penny from Heaven by Jennifer L. Holm. Random (Mixed genre: Realism/Autobiography/Historical fiction [Brooklyn, 1953], ages 11–14).
Hattie Big Sky by Kirby Larson. Delacorte (Historical fiction [Montana, 1918], ages 12–16).
Rules by Cynthia Lord. Scholastic (Realism/Special challenges [Autism], ages 9–13).

2006   *Criss Cross* by Lynne Rae Perkins. Greenwillow (Realism, ages 12–15).

HONOR BOOKS

Whittington by Alan Armstrong. Illustrated by S. D. Schindler. Random (Traditional/Animal fantasy/Special challenges [Dyslexia], ages 9–14).

Hitler Youth: Growing Up in Hitler's Shadow by Susan Campbell Bartoletti. Scholastic (Collected biography, ages 11–15).

Princess Academy by Shannon Hale. Bloomsbury (Modern fantasy, ages 12–14).

Show Way by Jacqueline Woodson. Illustrated by Hudson Talbott. Putnam (Multicultural [African-American], ages 7–12).

2005   *Kira-Kira* by Cynthia Kadohata. Atheneum (Historical fiction [Georgia, 1950s]/ Multicultural [Japanese-American], ages 11–14).

HONOR BOOKS

Al Capone Does My Shirts by Gennifer Choldenko. Putnam (Realism/Special challenges [Autism], ages 11–14).

The Voice That Challenged a Nation: Marian Anderson and the Struggle for Equal Rights by Russell Freedman. Clarion (Photobiography, ages 11–14).

Lizzie Bright and the Buckminster Boy by Gary D. Schmidt. Clarion (Historical fiction [Maine, 1912], ages 13–16).

2004   *The Tale of Despereaux: Being the Story of a Mouse, a Princess, Some Soup, and a Spool of Thread* by Kate DiCamillo. Illustrated by Timothy Basil Ering. Candlewick (Modern fantasy, ages 5–8).

HONOR BOOKS

Olive's Ocean by Kevin Henkes. Greenwillow (Realism, ages 9–12).

An American Plague: The True and Terrifying Story of the Yellow Fever Epidemic of 1793 by Jim Murphy. Clarion (Informational, ages 9–14).

2003   *Crispin: The Cross of Lead* by Avi. Hyperion (Modern fantasy, ages 8–12).

HONOR BOOKS

The House of the Scorpion by Nancy Farmer. Atheneum (Modern fantasy, ages 11–14).

Pictures of Hollis Woods by Patricia Reilly Giff. Random House (Realism, ages 10–13).

Hoot by Carl Hiaasen. Knopf (Realism, ages 9–12).

A Corner of the Universe by Ann M. Martin. Scholastic (Realism, ages 11–14).

Surviving the Applewhites by Stephanie S. Tolan. HarperCollins (Realism, ages 12–16).

2002   *A Single Shard* by Linda Sue Park. Clarion/ Houghton (Realism, ages 10–14).

HONOR BOOKS

Everything on a Waffle by Polly Horvath. Farrar (Realism, ages 12–14).

Carver: A Life In Poems by Marilyn Nelson. Front Street (Poetry/Biography, ages 12–14).

2001   *A Year Down Yonder* by Richard Peck. Dial (Historical fiction [U.S., 1930s], ages 10–14).

HONOR BOOKS

Because of Winn-Dixie by Kate DiCamillo. Candlewick (Animal realism, ages 8–12).

Hope Was Here by Joan Bauer. Putnam (Realism, ages 12–14).

Joey Pigza Loses Control by Jack Gantos. Farrar (Realism, ages 9–12).

The Wanderer by Sharon Creech. HarperCollins (Realism, ages 12–14).

2000   *Bud, Not Buddy* by Christopher Paul Curtis. Delacorte (Multicultural [African-American], ages 9–12).

HONOR BOOKS

Getting Near to Baby by Audrey Couloumbis. Putnam (Realism, ages 10–12).

26 Fairmount Avenue by Tomie dePaola. Putnam (Biography, ages 7–9).

Our Only May Amelia by Jennifer L. Holm. HarperCollins (Historical fiction [U.S., 1899], ages 10–14).

1999   *Holes* by Louis Sachar. Farrar (Realism, ages 10–13).

HONOR BOOK

A Long Way from Chicago by Richard Peck. Dial (Historical fiction [U.S., 1930s], ages 9–12).

1998   *Out of the Dust* by Karen Hesse. Scholastic (Historical fiction [U.S., 1920–1934], ages 13–16).

HONOR BOOKS

Lily's Crossing by Patricia Reilly Giff. Delacorte (Historical fiction [U.S., 1944], ages 9–11).

Ella Enchanted by Gail Carson Levine. HarperCollins (Modern fantasy, ages 9–12).

Wringer by Jerry Spinelli. HarperCollins (Realism, ages 9–12).

1997   *The View from Saturday* by E. L. Konigsburg. Atheneum (Realism, ages 9–12).

HONOR BOOKS

A Girl Named Disaster by Nancy Farmer. Orchard (Realism/Multicultural [Black African], ages 12–14).

The Moorchild by Eloise McGraw. McElderry/ Simon & Schuster (Modern fantasy, ages 9–12).

The Thief by Megan Whalen Turner. Greenwillow (Modern fantasy, ages 12–16).

Belle Prater's Boy by Ruth White. Farrar (Realism, ages 10–12).

1996   *The Midwife's Apprentice* by Karen Cushman. Clarion (Historical fiction [England, 1200s], ages 10–14).

HONOR BOOKS

The Great Fire by Jim Murphy. Scholastic (Informational, ages 9–13).

The Watsons Go to Birmingham—1963 by Christopher Paul Curtis. Delacorte (Historical fiction [Southern U.S., 1960s; African-American], ages 10–14).

What Jamie Saw by Carolyn Coman. Front Street (Realism, ages 10–14).

Yolanda's Genius by Carol Fenner. McElderry (Realism/Multicultural [African-American], ages 10–14).

1995   *Walk Two Moons* by Sharon Creech. Harper-Collins (Realism [Native American], ages 11–14).

HONOR BOOKS

Catherine, Called Birdy by Karen Cushman. Clarion (Historical fiction [England, 1200s], ages 10–14).

The Ear, the Eye, and the Arm by Nancy Farmer. Orchard (Modern fantasy, ages 10–13).

1994   *The Giver* by Lois Lowry. Houghton (Modern fantasy, ages 10–12).

HONOR BOOKS

Crazy Lady by Jane Leslie Conly. HarperCollins (Realism, ages 10–12).

Dragon's Gate by Laurence Yep. HarperCollins (Historical fiction [China, Western U.S., 1860s], ages 12–14).

Eleanor Roosevelt: A Life of Discovery by Russell Freedman. Clarion (Biography, ages 10–14).

1993   *Missing May* by Cynthia Rylant. Orchard (Realism, ages 10–13).

HONOR BOOKS

The Dark-Thirty: Southern Tales of the Supernatural by Patricia McKissack. Knopf (Modern fantasy/Ghost stories/Multicultural [African-American], ages 8–12).

Somewhere in the Darkness by Walter Dean Myers. Scholastic (Realism/Multicultural [African-American], ages 11–14).

What Hearts by Bruce Brooks. HarperCollins (Realism, ages 11–14).

1992   *Shiloh* by Phyllis Reynolds Naylor. Atheneum (Animal realism, ages 8–10).

HONOR BOOKS

Nothing but the Truth by Avi. Orchard (Realism, ages 10–14).

The Wright Brothers: How They Invented the Airplane by Russell Freedman. Holiday (Informational/Biography, ages 9–12).

1991   *Maniac Magee* by Jerry Spinelli. Little, Brown (Realism, ages 9–13).

HONOR BOOK

The True Confessions of Charlotte Doyle by Avi. Orchard (Historical fiction [England, U.S., 1830], ages 10–13).

1990   *Number the Stars* by Lois Lowry. Houghton (Historical fiction [Denmark, 1940s], ages 8–10).

HONOR BOOKS

Afternoon of the Elves by Janet Taylor Lisle. Orchard (Realism, ages 10–13).
Shabanu, Daughter of the Wind by Suzanne Fisher Staples. Knopf (Realism, ages 12–16).
The Winter Room by Gary Paulsen. Orchard (Realism, ages 10–13).

1989   *Joyful Noise: Poems for Two Voices* by Paul Fleischman. Harper (Poetry, ages 9–14).

HONOR BOOKS

In the Beginning: Creation Stories from around the World by Virginia Hamilton. Harcourt (Traditional, ages 9–12).
Scorpions by Walter Dean Myers. Harper (Realism/Multicultural [African-American, Hispanic-American], ages 10–13).

1988   *Lincoln: A Photobiography* by Russell Freedman. Clarion (Biography, ages 8–12).

HONOR BOOKS

After the Rain by Norma Fox Mazer. Morrow (Realism, ages 12–16).
Hatchet by Gary Paulsen. Bradbury (Realism, ages 9–13).

Boston Globe–Horn Book Awards

These awards, established in 1967 and sponsored by *The Boston Globe* and *The Horn Book Magazine,* are given to an author for outstanding fiction or poetry for children, to an illustrator for outstanding illustration in a children's book, and, since 1976, to an author for outstanding nonfiction for children. Award winners and honor books since 1988 are listed here. For the complete list of award winners, go to www.hbook.com/bghb/past/past.asp.

2009   FICTION: *Nation* by Terry Pratchett. HarperCollins.

NONFICTION: *The Lincolns: A Scrapbook Look at Abraham and Mary* by Candace Fleming. Random.

ILLUSTRATION: *Bubble Trouble* by Margaret Mahy. Illustrated by Polly Dunbar. Clarion.

2008   FICTION AND POETRY: *The Absolutely True Diary of a Part-Time Indian* by Sherman Alexie. Little, Brown.

NONFICTION: *The Wall: Growing Up Behind the Iron Curtain* by Peter Sís. Farrar.

ILLUSTRATION: *At Night* by Jonathan Bean. Farrar.

2007   FICTION AND POETRY: *The Astonishing Life of Octavian Nothing, Traitor to the Nation, Volume I: The Pox Party* by M. T. Anderson. Candlewick.

NONFICTION: *The Strongest Man in the World: Louis Cyr* by Nicholas Debon. Groundwood.

ILLUSTRATION: *Dog and Bear: Two Friends, Three Stories* by Laura Vaccaro Seeger. Roaring Brook.

2006   FICTION AND POETRY: *The Miraculous Journey of Edward Tulane* by Kate DiCamillo. Illustrated by Bagram Ibatoulline. Candlewick.

NONFICTION: *If You Decide to Go to the Moon* by Faith McNulty. Illustrated by Steven Kellogg. Scholastic.

ILLUSTRATION: *Leaf Man* by Lois Ehlert. Harcourt.

2005   FICTION AND POETRY: *The Schwa Was Here* by Neal Schusterman. Dutton.

NONFICTION: *The Race to Save the Lord God Bird* by Phillip Hoose. Farrar.

ILLUSTRATION: *Traction Man Is Here!* by Mini Grey. Knopf.

2004   FICTION AND POETRY: *The Fire-Eaters* by David Almond. Delacorte.

NONFICTION: *An American Plague: The True and Terrifying Story of the Yellow Fever Epidemic of 1793* by Jim Murphy. Clarion.

ILLUSTRATION: *The Man Who Walked between the Towers* by Mordicai Gerstein. Roaring Brook.

2003 FICTION AND POETRY: *The Jamie and Angus Stories* by Anne Fine. Illustrated by Penny Dale. Candlewick.

NONFICTION: *Fireboat: The Heroic Adventures of the John J. Harvey* by Maira Kalman. Putnam.

ILLUSTRATION: *Big Momma Makes the World* by Phyllis Root. Illustrated by Helen Oxenbury. Candlewick.

2002 FICTION AND POETRY: *Lord of the Deep* by Graham Salisbury. Delacorte.

NONFICTION: *This Land Was Made for You and Me: The Life and Songs of Woody Guthrie* by Elizabeth Partridge. Viking.

ILLUSTRATION: *"Let's Get a Pup!" Said Kate* by Bob Graham. Candlewick.

2001 FICTION AND POETRY: *Carver: A Life In Poems* by Marilyn Nelson. Front Street.

NONFICTION: *The Longitude Prize* by Joan Dash. Illustrated by Dušan Petricic. Farrar.

ILLUSTRATION: *Cold Feet* by Cynthia DeFelice. Illustrated by Robert Andrew Parker. DK Ink.

2000 FICTION: *The Folk Keeper* by Franny Billingsley. Atheneum.

NONFICTION: *Sir Walter Ralegh and the Quest for El Dorado* by Marc Aronson. Clarion.

ILLUSTRATION: *Henry Hikes to Fitchburg* by D. B. Johnson. Houghton.

1999 FICTION: *Holes* by Louis Sachar. Farrar.

NONFICTION: *The Top of the World: Climbing Mount Everest* by Steve Jenkins. Houghton.

ILLUSTRATION: *Red-Eyed Tree Frog* by Joy Cowley. Illustrated with photographs by Nic Bishop. Scholastic.

1998 FICTION: *The Circuit: Stories from the Life of a Migrant Child* by Francisco Jiménez. University of New Mexico Press.

NONFICTION: *Leon's Story* by Leon Walter Tillage. Illustrated by Susan L. Roth. Farrar.

ILLUSTRATION: *And If the Moon Could Talk* by Kate Banks. Illustrated by Georg Hallensleben. Farrar.

1997 FICTION: *The Friends* by Kazumi Yumoto. Farrar.

NONFICTION: *A Drop of Water: A Book of Science and Wonder* by Walter Wick. Scholastic.

ILLUSTRATION: *The Adventures of Sparrow Boy* by Brian Pinkney. Simon & Schuster.

1996 FICTION: *Poppy* by Avi. Illustrated by Brian Floca. Orchard.

NONFICTION: *Orphan Train Rider: One Boy's True Story* by Andrea Warren. Houghton.

ILLUSTRATION: *In the Rain with Baby Duck* by Amy Hest. Illustrated by Jill Barton. Candlewick.

1995 FICTION: *Some of the Kinder Planets* by Tim Wynne-Jones. Orchard.

NONFICTION: *Abigail Adams: Witness to a Revolution* by Natalie S. Bober. Atheneum.

ILLUSTRATION: *John Henry* retold by Julius Lester. Illustrated by Jerry Pinkney. Dial.

1994 FICTION: *Scooter* by Vera B. Williams. Greenwillow.

NONFICTION: *Eleanor Roosevelt: A Life of Discovery* by Russell Freedman. Clarion.

ILLUSTRATION: *Grandfather's Journey* by Allen Say. Houghton.

1993 FICTION: *Ajeemah and His Son* by James Berry. Harper.

NONFICTION: *Sojourner Truth: Ain't I a Woman?* by Patricia and Fredrick McKissack. Scholastic.

ILLUSTRATION: *The Fortune-Tellers* by Lloyd Alexander. Illustrated by Trina Schart Hyman. Dutton.

1992 FICTION: *Missing May* by Cynthia Rylant. Orchard.

NONFICTION: *Talking with Artists* by Pat Cummings. Bradbury.

ILLUSTRATION: *Seven Blind Mice* by Ed Young. Philomel.

1991 FICTION: *The True Confessions of Charlotte Doyle* by Avi. Orchard.

NONFICTION: *Appalachia: The Voices of Sleeping Birds* by Cynthia Rylant. Illustrated by Barry Moser. Harcourt.

ILLUSTRATION: *The Tale of the Mandarin Ducks* retold by Katherine Paterson. Illustrated by Leo and Diane Dillon. Lodestar.

1990 FICTION: *Maniac Magee* by Jerry Spinelli. Little, Brown.

NONFICTION: *The Great Little Madison* by Jean Fritz. Putnam.

ILLUSTRATION: *Lon Po Po: A Red-Riding Hood Story from China* retold and illustrated by Ed Young. Philomel.

1989 FICTION: *The Village by the Sea* by Paula Fox. Orchard.

NONFICTION: *The Way Things Work* by David Macaulay. Houghton.

ILLUSTRATION: *Shy Charles* by Rosemary Wells. Dial.

1988 FICTION: *The Friendship* by Mildred Taylor. Dial.

NONFICTION: *Anthony Burns: The Defeat and Triumph of a Fugitive Slave* by Virginia Hamilton. Knopf.

ILLUSTRATION: *The Boy of the Three-Year Nap* by Diane Snyder. Illustrated by Allen Say. Houghton.

National Book Award for Young People's Literature

This award, sponsored by the National Book Foundation, is presented annually to recognize what is judged to be the outstanding contribution to children's literature, in terms of literary merit, published during the previous year. The award committee considers books of all genres written for children and young adults by U.S. writers. The award, which was added to the U.S. National Book Awards in 1996, carries a $10,000 cash prize.

2008 *What I Saw and How I Lied* by Judy Blundell. Scholastic.

2007 *The Absolutely True Diary of a Part-Time Indian* by Sherman Alexie. Little, Brown.

2006 *The Astonishing Life of Octavian Nothing, Traitor to the Nation, Vol. 1: The Pox Party* by M. T. Anderson. Candlewick.

2005 *The Penderwicks* by Jeanne Birdsall. Knopf.

2004 *Godless* by Pete Hautman. Simon & Schuster.

2003 *The Canning Season* by Polly Horvath. Farrar.

2002 *The House of the Scorpion* by Nancy Farmer. Atheneum.

2001 *True Believer* by Virginia Euwer Wolff. Atheneum.

2000 *Homeless Bird* by Gloria Whelan. HarperCollins.

1999 *When Zachary Beaver Came to Town* by Kimberley Willis Holt. Holt.

1998 *Holes* by Louis Sachar. Farrar.

1997 *Dancing on the Edge* by Han Nolan. Harcourt.

1996 *Parrot in the Oven: Mi Vida* by Victor Martinez. HarperCollins.

Great Britain

Kate Greenaway Medal

This award, established in 1955 and sponsored by the Chartered Institute of Library and Information Professionals, is given to the illustrator of the most distinguished work in illustration in a children's book first published in the United Kingdom during the preceding year. Award winners since 1988 are listed here. For the

complete list of winners, go to www.carnegiegreenaway
.org.uk/greenaway/full_list_of_winners.php.

2008   *Little Mouse's Big Book of Fears* by Emily
Gravett. Macmillan.

2007   *The Adventures of the Dish and the Spoon* by
Mini Grey. Jonathan Cape.

2006   *Wolves* by Emily Gravett. Macmillan.

2005   *Jonathan Swift's "Gulliver"* by Martin Jenkins.
Illustrated by Chris Riddell. Walker.

2004   *Ella's Big Chance* by Shirley Hughes. The
Bodley Head.

2003   *Jethro Byrd—Fairy Child* by Bob Graham.
Walker.

2002   *Pirate Diary* by Chris Riddell. Walker.

2001   *I Will Never Not Ever Eat a Tomato* by Lauren
Child. Orchard.

2000   *Alice's Adventures in Wonderland* by Lewis
Carroll. Illustrated by Helen Oxenbury.
Walker.

1999   *Pumpkin Soup* by Helen Cooper. Farrar.

1998   *When Jessie Came Across the Sea* by Amy Hest.
Illustrated by P. J. Lynch. Candlewick.

1997   *The Baby Who Wouldn't Go to Bed* by Helen
Cooper. Doubleday.

1996   *The Christmas Miracle of Jonathon Toomey* by
Susan Wojciechowski. Illustrated by P. J. Lynch.
Walker.

1995   *Way Home* by Libby Hathorn. Illustrated by
Gregory Rogers. Random.

1994   *Black Ships before Troy* retold by Rosemary
Sutcliff. Illustrated by Alan Lee. Frances
Lincoln.

1993   *Zoo* by Anthony Browne. Julia MacRae.

1992   *The Jolly Christmas Postman* by Janet and
Allan Ahlberg. Heinemann.

1991   *The Whale's Song* by Dyan Sheldon. Illustrated
by Gary Blythe. Dial.

1990   *War Boy: A Country Childhood* by Michael
Foreman. Arcade.

1989   *Can't You Sleep, Little Bear?* by Martin
Waddell. Illustrated by Barbara Firth. Walker.

1988   *Crafty Chameleon* by Mwenye Hadithi.
Illustrated by Adrienne Kennaway. Hodder &
Stoughton.

Carnegie Medal

This award, established in 1936 and sponsored by the
Chartered Institute of Library and Information Professionals, is given to the author of the most outstanding
children's book first published in English in the United
Kingdom during the preceding year. Award winners
since 1988 are listed here. For the complete list of winners, go to www.carnegiegreenaway.org.uk/carnegie/
full_list_of_winners.php.

2008   *Here Lies Arthur* by Philip Reeve. Scholastic.

2007   *Just in Case* by Meg Rosoff. Penguin.

2006   *Tamar* by Mal Peet. Walker.

2005   *Millions* by Frank Cottrell Boyce. Macmillan.

2004   *A Gathering Light* by Jennifer Donnelly.
Bloomsbury.

2003   *Ruby Holler* by Sharon Creech. Bloomsbury/
HarperCollins.

2002   *The Amazing Maurice and His Educated
Rodents* by Terry Pratchett. Doubleday/
HarperCollins.

2001   *The Other Side of Truth* by Beverly Naidoo.
Puffin/HarperCollins.

2000   *Postcards from No Man's Land* by Aidan
Chambers. Bodley Head.

1999   *Skellig* by David Almond. Delacorte.

1998   *River Boy* by Tim Bowler. Oxford.

1997   *Junk* by Melvin Burgess. Andersen.

1996   *His Dark Materials: Book 1, Northern Lights*
by Philip Pullman. Scholastic.

1995   *Whispers in the Graveyard* by Theresa Bresling.
Methuen.

1994   *Stone Cold* by Robert Swindells. Hamish
Hamilton.

1993   *Flour Babies* by Anne Fine. Hamish Hamilton.

1992   *Dear Nobody* by Berlie Doherty. Hamish Hamilton.

1991   *Wolf* by Gillian Cross. Oxford.

1990   *My War with Goggle-Eyes* by Anne Fine. Joy Street.

1989   *Pack of Lies* by Geraldine McCaughrean. Oxford.

1988   *The Ghost Drum* by Susan Price. Faber.

Canada

The Governor General's Literary Awards

The Governor General's Literary Awards were inaugurated in 1937, with separate prizes for children's literature (text and illustration) being added in 1987. The Canada Council for the Arts assumed responsibility for funding, administering, and adjudicating the awards in 1959, and added prizes for works written in French. Monetary prizes were introduced in 1951. The current prize to winners in each category—$15,000—dates from 2000. In addition, publishers of the winning books receive $3,000 to assist with promotion.

2008   ILLUSTRATION: *The Owl and the Pussycat* by Edward Lear. Illustrated by Stéphane Jorisch. Kids Can.

TEXT: *The Landing* by John Ibbitson. Kids Can.

2007   ILLUSTRATION: *The Painted Circus* by Wallace Edwards. Kids Can.

TEXT: *Carnation, Lily, Lily, Rose: The Story of a Painting* by Hugh Brewster. Kids Can.

2006   ILLUSTRATION: *Ancient Thunder* by Leo Yerxa. Groundwood.

TEXT: *Pirate's Passage* by William Gilkerson. Trumpeter.

2005   ILLUSTRATION: *Imagine a Day* by Sarah L. Thomson. Illustrated by Rob Gonsalves. Atheneum.

TEXT: *The Crazy Man* by Pamela Porter. Groundwood.

2004   ILLUSTRATION: *Jabberwocky* by Lewis Carroll. Illustrated by Stéphane Jorisch. Kids Can.

TEXT: *Airborn* by Kenneth Oppel. HarperCollins.

2003   ILLUSTRATION: *The Song within My Heart* by Dave Bouchard. Illustrated by Allen Sapp. Raincoast.

TEXT: *Stitches* by Glen Huser. Groundwood.

2002   ILLUSTRATION: *Alphabeasts* by Wallace Edwards. Kids Can.

TEXT: *True Confessions of a Heartless Girl* by Martha Brooks. Groundwood.

2001   ILLUSTRATION: *An Island in the Soup* by Mireille Levert. Groundwood.

TEXT: *Dust* by Arthur Slade. HarperCollins Canada.

2000   ILLUSTRATION: *Yuck, a Love Story* by Don Gillmore. Illustrated by Marie-Louise Gay. Stoddart Kids.

TEXT: *Looking for X* by Deborah Ellis. Groundwood.

1999   ILLUSTRATION: *The Great Poochini* by Gary Clement. Groundwood.

TEXT: *A Screaming Kind of Day* by Rachna Gilmore. Fitzhenry & Whiteside.

1998   ILLUSTRATION: *A Child's Treasury of Nursery Rhymes* by Kady MacDonald Denton. Kids Can.

TEXT: *The Hollow Tree* by Janet Lunn. Knopf Canada.

1997   ILLUSTRATION: *The Party* by Barbara Reid. Scholastic Canada.

TEXT: *Awake and Dreaming* by Kit Pearson. Viking.

1996   ILLUSTRATION: *The Rooster's Gift* by Pam Conrad. Illustrated by Eric Beddows. Groundwood.

TEXT: *Ghost Train* by Paul Yee. Groundwood.

1995   ILLUSTRATION: *The Last Quest of Gilgamesh* by Ludmila Zeman, reteller. Tundra.

TEXT: *The Maestro* by Tim Wynne-Jones. Groundwood.

1994 ILLUSTRATION: *Josepha: A Prairie Boy's Story* by Jim McGugen. Illustrated by Murray Kimber. Red Deer College Press.

TEXT: *Adam and Eve and Pinch-Me* by Julie Johnston. Lester.

1993 ILLUSTRATION: *Sleep Tight, Mrs. Ming* by Sharon Jennings. Illustrated by Mireille Levert. Annick.

TEXT: *Some of the Kinder Planets* by Tim Wynne-Jones. Groundwood.

1992 ILLUSTRATION: *Waiting for the Whales* by Sheryl McFarlane. Illustrated by Ron Lightburn. Orca.

TEXT: *Hero of Lesser Causes* by Julie Johnston. Lester.

1991 ILLUSTRATION: *Doctor Kiss Says Yes* by Teddy Jam. Illustrated by Joanne Fitzgerald. Groundwood.

TEXT: *Pick-Up Sticks* by Sarah Ellis. Groundwood.

1990 ILLUSTRATION: *The Orphan Boy* by Tololwa Mollel. Illustrated by Paul Morin. Oxford.

TEXT: *Redwork* by Michael Bedard. Lester & Orpen Dennys.

1989 ILLUSTRATION: *The Magic Paintbrush* by Robin Muller. Doubleday Canada.

TEXT: *Bad Boy* by Diana Wieler. Douglas & McIntyre.

1988 ILLUSTRATION: *Amos's Sweater* by Janet Lunn. Illustrated by Kim LaFave. Douglas & McIntyre.

TEXT: *The Third Magic* by Welwyn Wilton Katz. Douglas & McIntyre.

1987 ILLUSTRATION: *Rainy Day Magic* by Marie-Louise Gay. Stoddart.

TEXT: *Galahad Schwartz and the Cockroach Army* by Morgan Nyberg. Douglas & McIntyre.

Australia
Australian Children's Books of the Year Awards

The Children's Book Council of Australia sponsors five awards for excellence in children's books: the Picture Book of the Year Award (established in 1956); the Book of the Year for Early Childhood Award (established in 2001); the Book of the Year for Younger Readers Award (established in 1982); the Book of the Year for Older Readers Award (established in 1946); and the Eve Pownall Award for Information Books (not listed here). Award winners since 1988 are listed here. For the complete list of winners, go to http://cbca.org.au/awardshistory.

Australian Picture Book of the Year Award
(May be for mature readers.)

2008 *Requiem for a Beast* by Matt Ottley. Lothian.

2007 *The Arrival* by Shaun Tan. Lothian.

2006 *The Short and Incredibly Happy Life of Riley* by Colin Thompson. Illustrated by Amy Lissiat [AKA Colin Thompson]. Lothian.

2005 *Are We There Yet? A Journey around Australia* by Alison Lester. Viking.

2004 *Cat and Fish* by Joan Grant. Illustrated by Neal Curtis. Lothian.

2003 *In Flanders Fields* by Norman Jorgensen. Illustrated by Brian Harrison-Lever. Sandcastle.

2002 *An Ordinary Day* by Libby Gleeson. Illustrated by Armin Greder. Scholastic.

2001 *Fox* by Margaret Wild. Illustrated by Ron Brooks. Allen & Unwin.

2000 *Jenny Angel* by Margaret Wild. Illustrated by Anne Spudvilas. Penguin.

1999 *The Rabbits* by John Marsden. Illustrated by Shaun Tan. Lothian.

1998 *The Two Bullies* by Junko Morimoto. Translated by Isao Morimoto. Crown.

1997 *Not a Nibble* by Elizabeth Honey. Allen & Unwin.

1996 *The Hunt* by Narelle Oliver. Lothian.

1995 *The Watertower* by Gary Crew. Illustrated by Steven Woolman. Era.

1994 *First Light* by Gary Crew. Illustrated by Peter Gouldthorpe. Lothian.

1993   *Rose Meets Mr. Wintergarden* by Bob Graham. Viking/Penguin.

1992   *Window* by Jeannie Baker. Julia MacRae.

1991   *Greetings from Sandy Beach* by Bob Graham. Lothian.

1990   *The Very Best of Friends* by Margaret Wild. Illustrated by Julie Vivas. Margaret Hamilton.

1989   *Drac and the Gremlins* by Allan Baillie. Illustrated by Jane Tanner. Viking/Kestrel.

        The Eleventh Hour by Graeme Base. Viking/Kestrel.

1988   *Crusher Is Coming!* by Bob Graham. Lothian.

Australian Book of the Year for Early Childhood Award

2008   *Pearl Barley and Charlie Parsley* by Aaron Blabey. Viking.

2007   *Amy & Louis* by Libby Gleeson. Illustrated by Freya Blackwood. Scholastic.

2006   *Annie's Chair* by Deborah Niland. Viking.

2005   *Where Is the Green Sheep?* by Mem Fox. Illustrated by Judy Horacek. Viking.

2004   *Grandpa and Thomas* by Pamela Allen. Viking.

2003   *A Year on Our Farm* by Penny Matthews. Omnibus/Scholastic Australia.

2002   *"Let's Get a Pup!" Said Kate* by Bob Graham. Walker/Candlewick.

2001   *You'll Wake the Baby!* by Catherine Jinks. Illustrated by Andrew McLean. Penguin.

Australian Children's Book of the Year for Younger Readers Award

2008   *Dragon Moon* by Carole Wilkinson. Black Dog.

2007   *Being Bee* by Catherine Bateson. University of Queensland Press.

2006   *Helicopter Man* by Elizabeth Fensham. Bloomsbury.

2005   *The Silver Donkey* by Sonya Hartnett. Viking.

2004   *Dragonkeeper* by Carole Wilkinson. Black Dog.

2003   *Rain May and Captain Daniel* by Catherine Bateson. University of Queensland Press.

2002   *My Dog* by John Heffernan. Illustrated by Andrew McLean. Scholastic Australia.

2001   *Two Hands Together* by Diana Kidd. Penguin.

2000   *Hitler's Daughter* by Jackie French. Harper-Collins.

1999   *My Girragundji* by Meme McDonald and Boori Pryor. Illustrated by Meme McDonald. Allen & Unwin.

1998   *Someone Like Me* by Elaine Forrestal. Penguin.

1997   *Hannah Plus One* by Libby Gleeson. Illustrated by Ann James. Penguin.

1996   *Swashbuckler* by James Moloney. University of Queensland Press.

1995   *Ark in the Park* by Wendy Orr. HarperCollins.

1994   *Rowan of Rin* by Emily Rodda. Omnibus.

1993   *The Bamboo Flute* by Garry Disher. Collins/Angus & Robertson.

1992   *The Magnificent Nose and Other Marvels* by Anna Fienberg. Illustrated by Kim Gamble. Allen & Unwin.

1991   *Finders Keepers* by Emily Rodda. Omnibus.

1990   *Pigs and Honey* by Jeanie Adams. Omnibus.

1989   *The Best-Kept Secret* by Emily Rodda. Angus & Robertson.

1988   *My Place* by Nadia Wheatley and Donna Rawlins. Collins Dove.

Australian Children's Book of the Year for Older Readers Award

(For mature readers.)

2008   *The Ghost's Child* by Sonya Hartnett. Viking.

2007   *Red Spikes* by Margo Lanagan. Allen & Unwin.

2006   *The Story of Tom Brennan* by J. C. Burke. Random.

2005   *The Running Man* by Michael Gerard Bauer. Omnibus.

2004	*Saving Francesca* by Melina Marchetta. Viking.
2003	*The Messenger* by Markus Zusak. Pan Macmillan Australia.
2002	*Forest* by Sonya Hartnett. Viking.
2001	*Wolf on the Fold* by Judith Clarke. Allen & Unwin.
2000	*48 Shades of Brown* by Nick Earls. Penguin.
1999	*Deadly, Unna?* by Phillip Gwynne. Penguin.
1998	*Eye to Eye* by Catherine Jinks. Penguin.
1997	*A Bridge to Wiseman's Cove* by James Moloney. University of Queensland Press.
1996	*Pagan's Vows* by Catherine Jinks. Omnibus.
1995	*Foxspell* by Gillian Rubinstein. Hyland House.

1994	*The Gathering* by Isobelle Carmody. Penguin.
	Angel's Gate by Gary Crew. Heinemann.
1993	*Looking for Alibrandi* by Melina Marchetta. Penguin.
1992	*The House Guest* by Eleanor Nilsson. Viking.
1991	*Strange Objects* by Gary Crew. Heinemann Australia.
1990	*Came Back to Show You I Could Fly* by Robin Klein. Viking/Kestrel.
1989	*Beyond the Labyrinth* by Gillian Rubinstein. Hyland House.
1988	*So Much to Tell You* by John Marsden. Walter McVitty Books.

Awards for a Body of Work

Hans Christian Andersen Award

This international award, sponsored by the International Board on Books for Young People, is given every two years to a living author and, since 1966, to a living illustrator whose complete works have made important international contributions to children's literature.

2008	AUTHOR: Jürg Schubiger (Switzerland)
	ILLUSTRATOR: Roberto Innocenti (Italy)
2006	AUTHOR: Margaret Mahy (New Zealand)
	ILLUSTRATOR: Wolf Erlbruch (Germany)
2004	AUTHOR: Martin Waddell (Ireland)
	ILLUSTRATOR: Max Velthuijs (The Netherlands)
2002	AUTHOR: Aidan Chambers (United Kingdom)
	ILLUSTRATOR: Quentin Blake (United Kingdom)
2000	AUTHOR: Ana Maria Machado (Brazil)
	ILLUSTRATOR: Anthony Browne (United Kingdom)
1998	AUTHOR: Katherine Paterson (USA)
	ILLUSTRATOR: Tomi Ungerer (France)

1996	AUTHOR: Uri Orlev (Israel)
	ILLUSTRATOR: Klaus Ensikat (Germany)
1994	AUTHOR: Michio Mado (Japan)
	ILLUSTRATOR: Jörg Müller (Switzerland)
1992	AUTHOR: Virginia Hamilton (USA)
	ILLUSTRATOR: Kveta Pacovská (Czechoslovakia)
1990	AUTHOR: Tormod Haugen (Norway)
	ILLUSTRATOR: Lisbeth Zwerger (Austria)
1988	AUTHOR: Annie M. G. Schmidt (Netherlands)
	ILLUSTRATOR: Dušan Kállay (Czechoslovakia)
1986	AUTHOR: Patricia Wrightson (Australia)
	ILLUSTRATOR: Robert Ingpen (Australia)
1984	AUTHOR: Christine Nöstlinger (Austria)
	ILLUSTRATOR: Mitsumasa Anno (Japan)
1982	AUTHOR: Lygia Bojunga Nunes (Brazil)
	ILLUSTRATOR: Zbigniew Rychlicki (Poland)
1980	AUTHOR: Bohumil Riha (Czechoslovakia)
	ILLUSTRATOR: Suekichi Akaba (Japan)

1978   AUTHOR: Paula Fox (USA)

       ILLUSTRATOR: Otto S. Svend (Denmark)

1976   AUTHOR: Cecil Bödker (Denmark)

       ILLUSTRATOR: Tatjana Mawrina (USSR)

1974   AUTHOR: Maria Gripe (Sweden)

       ILLUSTRATOR: Farshid Mesghali (Iran)

1972   AUTHOR: Scott O'Dell (USA)

       ILLUSTRATOR: Ib Spang Olsen (Denmark)

1970   AUTHOR: Gianni Rodari (Italy)

       ILLUSTRATOR: Maurice Sendak (USA)

1968   AUTHORS: James Krüss (Germany) and José Maria Sanchez-Silva (Spain)

       ILLUSTRATOR: Jirí Trnka (Czechoslovakia)

1966   AUTHOR: Tove Jansson (Finland)

       ILLUSTRATOR: Alois Carigiet (Switzerland)

1964   René Guillot (France)

1962   Meindert DeJong (USA)

1960   Erich Kästner (Germany)

1958   Astrid Lindgren (Sweden)

1956   Eleanor Farjeon (Great Britain)

Laura Ingalls Wilder Award

This award, sponsored by the Association for Library Service to Children of the American Library Association, is given to a U.S. author or illustrator whose body of work has made a lasting contribution to children's literature. Between 1960 and 1980, the Wilder Award was given every five years. From 1980 to 2001, it was given every three years. Beginning in 2001, it has been given every two years.

2009   Ashley Bryan

2007   James Marshall

2005   Laurence Yep

2003   Eric Carle

2001   Milton Meltzer

1998   Russell Freedman

1995   Virginia Hamilton

1992   Marcia Brown

1989   Elizabeth George Speare

1986   Jean Fritz

1983   Maurice Sendak

1980   Theodor S. Geisel (Dr. Seuss)

1975   Beverly Cleary

1970   E. B. White

1965   Ruth Sawyer

1960   Clara Ingram Judson

1954   Laura Ingalls Wilder

NCTE Excellence in Poetry for Children Award

For the list of award winners, see Chapter 4, page 61.

Awards for Specific Genres or Groups

Mildred L. Batchelder Award

This award, established in 1968 and sponsored by the ALA's Association for Library Service to Children, is given to the American publisher of a children's book considered to be the most outstanding of those books originally published in a country other than the United States in a language other than English and subsequently translated and published in the United States during the previous year. Award winners since 1988 are listed here. For the complete list of winners, go to www.ala.org/ala/mgrps/divs/alsc/awardsgrants/bookmedia/batchelderaward/batchelderpast.cfm.

2009   *Moribito: Guardian of the Spirit* by Nahoko Uehashi. Translated from Japanese by Cathy Hirano. Scholastic.

2008   *Brave Story* by Miyuki Miyabe. Translated from Japanese by Alexander O. Smith. VIZ Media.

2007   *The Pull of the Ocean* by Jean-Claude Mourlevat. Translated from French by Y. Maudet. Delacorte.

2006   *An Innocent Soldier* by Josef Holub. Translated from German by Michael Hofmann. Arthur A. Levine.

2005   *The Shadows of Ghadames* by Joëlle Stolz. Translated from French by Catherine Temerson. Delacorte.

2004   *Run, Boy, Run* by Uri Orlev. Translated from Hebrew by Hillel Halkin. Houghton Mifflin.

2003   *The Thief Lord* by Cornelia Funke. Translated from German by Oliver Latsch. Scholastic.

2002   *How I Became an American* by Karin Gündisch. Translated from German by James Skofield. Cricket.

2001   *Samir and Yonatan* by Daniella Carmi. Translated from Hebrew by Yael Lotan. Levine/Scholastic.

2000   *The Baboon King* by Anton Quintana. Translated from Dutch by John Nieuwenhuizen. Walker.

1999   *Thanks to My Mother* by Schoschana Rabinovici. Translated from German by James Skofield. Dial.

1998   *The Robber and Me* by Josef Holub. Translated from German by Elizabeth D. Crawford. Holt.

1997   *The Friends* by Kazumi Yumoto. Translated from Japanese by Cathy Hirano. Farrar.

1996   *The Lady with the Hat* by Uri Orlev. Translated from Hebrew by Hillel Halkin. Houghton.

1995   *The Boys from St. Petri* by Bjarne Reuter. Translated from Danish by Anthea Bell. Dutton.

1994   *The Apprentice* by Pilar Molina Llorente. Illustrated by Juan Ramón Alonso. Translated from Spanish by Robin Longshaw. Farrar.

1993   No award

1992   *The Man from the Other Side* by Uri Orlev. Translated from Hebrew by Hillel Halkin. Houghton.

1991   *A Hand Full of Stars* by Rafik Schami. Translated from German by Rika Lesser. Dutton.

HONOR BOOK
Two Short and One Long by Nina Ring Aamundsen. Translated from Norwegian by the author. Houghton.

1990   *Buster's World* by Bjarne Reuter. Translated from Danish by Anthea Bell. Dutton.

1989   *Crutches* by Peter Härtling. Translated from German by Elizabeth D. Crawford. Lothrop.

1988   *If You Didn't Have Me* by Ulf Nilsson. Translated from Swedish by Lone Thygesen-Blecher and George Blecher. Illustrated by Eva Eriksson. McElderry.

Coretta Scott King Awards

These awards, founded in 1970 to commemorate Dr. Martin Luther King Jr. and his wife, Coretta Scott King, for their work in promoting peace and world brotherhood, are given to an African-American author and, since 1974, an African-American illustrator whose children's books, published during the preceding year, made outstanding inspirational and educational contributions to literature for children and young people. The awards are sponsored by the Social Responsibilities Round Table of the American Library Association. Award winners since 1988 are listed here. For the complete list of winners, go to www.ala.org/ala/mgrps/rts/emiert/cskbookawards/recipients.cfm.

2009   AUTHOR: *We Are the Ship: The Story of Negro League Baseball* by Kadir Nelson. Jump at the Sun.

ILLUSTRATOR: *The Blacker the Berry* by Joyce Carol Thomas. Illustrated by Floyd Cooper. HarperCollins.

2008   AUTHOR: *Elijah of Buxton* by Christopher Paul Curtis. Scholastic.

ILLUSTRATOR: *Let It Shine* by Ashley Bryan. Atheneum.

2007   AUTHOR: *Copper Sun* by Sharon Draper. Simon & Schuster/Atheneum.

ILLUSTRATOR: *Moses: When Harriet Tubman Led Her People to Freedom* by Carole Boston Weatherford. Illustrated by Kadir A. Nelson. Jump at the Sun/Hyperion.

2006   AUTHOR: *Day of Tears: A Novel in Dialogue* by Julius Lester. Jump At the Sun/Hyperion.

ILLUSTRATOR: *Rosa* by Nikki Giovanni. Illustrated by Bryan Collier. Holt.

2005   AUTHOR: *Remember: The Journey to School Integration* by Toni Morrison. Houghton.

ILLUSTRATOR: *Ellington Was Not a Street* by Ntozake Shange. Illustrated by Kadir A. Nelson. Simon & Schuster.

2004   AUTHOR: *The First Part Last* by Angela Johnson. Simon & Schuster.

ILLUSTRATOR: *Beautiful Blackbird* by Ashley Bryan. Atheneum.

2003   AUTHOR: *Bronx Masquerade* by Nikki Grimes. Dial.

ILLUSTRATOR: *Talkin' about Bessie: The Story of Aviator Elizabeth Coleman* by Nikki Grimes. Illustrated by E. B. Lewis. Orchard/Scholastic.

2002   AUTHOR: *The Land* by Mildred D. Taylor. Fogelman/Penguin Putnam.

ILLUSTRATOR: *Goin' Someplace Special* by Patricia McKissack. Illustrated by Jerry Pinkney. Atheneum.

2001   AUTHOR: *Miracle's Boys* by Jacqueline Woodson. Putnam.

ILLUSTRATOR: *Uptown* by Bryan Collier. Holt.

2000   AUTHOR: *Bud, Not Buddy* by Christopher Paul Curtis. Delacorte.

ILLUSTRATOR: *In the Time of the Drums* retold by Kim L. Siegelson. Illustrated by Brian Pinkney. Hyperion.

1999   AUTHOR: *Heaven* by Angela Johnson. Simon & Schuster.

ILLUSTRATOR: *i see the rhythm* by Toyomi Igus. Illustrated by Michele Wood. Children's Book Press.

1998   AUTHOR: *Forged by Fire* by Sharon M. Draper. Atheneum.

ILLUSTRATOR: *In Daddy's Arms I Am Tall: African Americans Celebrating Fathers* by Javaka Steptoe. Lee & Low.

1997   AUTHOR: *Slam!* by Walter Dean Myers. Scholastic.

ILLUSTRATOR: *Minty: A Story of Young Harriet Tubman* by Alan Schroeder. Illustrated by Jerry Pinkney. Dial.

1996   AUTHOR: *Her Stories: African American Folktales, Fairy Tales, and True Tales* by Virginia Hamilton. Illustrated by Leo and Diane Dillon. Blue Sky.

ILLUSTRATOR: *The Middle Passage: White Ships/Black Cargo* by Tom Feelings. Dial.

1995   AUTHOR: *Christmas in the Big House, Christmas in the Quarters* by Patricia C. McKissack and Fredrick L. McKissack. Illustrated by John Thompson. Scholastic.

ILLUSTRATOR: *The Creation* by James Weldon Johnson. Illustrated by James E. Ransome. Holiday.

1994   AUTHOR: *Toning the Sweep* by Angela Johnson. Orchard.

ILLUSTRATOR: *Soul Looks Back in Wonder* compiled and illustrated by Tom Feelings. Dial.

1993   AUTHOR: *The Dark-Thirty: Southern Tales of the Supernatural* by Patricia McKissack. Knopf.

ILLUSTRATOR: *Origins of Life on Earth: An African Creation Myth* by David A. Anderson. Illustrated by Kathleen Atkins Smith. Sight Productions.

1992   AUTHOR: *Now Is Your Time! The African-American Struggle for Freedom* by Walter Dean Myers. HarperCollins.

ILLUSTRATOR: *Tar Beach* by Faith Ringgold. Crown.

1991   AUTHOR: *The Road to Memphis* by Mildred D. Taylor. Dial.

ILLUSTRATOR: *Aïda* retold by Leontyne Price. Illustrated by Leo and Diane Dillon. Harcourt.

1990 AUTHOR: *A Long Hard Journey* by Patricia C. and Fredrick L. McKissack. Walker.

ILLUSTRATOR: *Nathaniel Talking* by Eloise Greenfield. Illustrated by Jan Spivey Gilchrist. Black Butterfly Press.

1989 AUTHOR: *Fallen Angels* by Walter Dean Myers. Scholastic.

ILLUSTRATOR: *Mirandy and Brother Wind* by Patricia McKissack. Illustrated by Jerry Pinkney. Knopf.

1988 AUTHOR: *The Friendship* by Mildred D. Taylor. Illustrated by Max Ginsburg. Dial.

ILLUSTRATOR: *Mufaro's Beautiful Daughters: An African Tale* retold and illustrated by John Steptoe. Lothrop.

Gryphon Award for Transitional Books

The Gryphon Award of $1,000 is given annually in recognition of an English language work of fiction or nonfiction for which the primary audience is children in kindergarten through grade 4. The title chosen best exemplifies those qualities that successfully bridge the gap in difficulty between books for reading aloud to children and books for practiced readers of books published in the preceding year. The award, established in 2004, is sponsored by the Center for Children's Books at the Graduate School of Library and Information Science at the University of Illinois in Urbana-Champaign.

2009 *Frogs* by Nic Bishop. Scholastic.

2008 *Billy Tartle in Say Cheese!* by Michael Townsend. Knopf.

2007 *The True Story of Stellina* by Matteo Pericoli

2006 *Stinky Stern Forever* by Michelle Edwards. Harcourt.

2005 *Little Rat Rides* by Monika Bang-Campbell. Harcourt.

2004 *Bow Wow Meow Meow: It's Rhyming Cats and Dogs* by Douglas Florian. Harcourt.

Pura Belpré Award

The Pura Belpré Award honors Latino writers and illustrators whose work best portrays, affirms, and celebrates the Latino cultural experience in a work of literature for youth. This biennial award is sponsored by the Association for Library Service to Children and the National Association to Promote Library Service to the Spanish Speaking.

2008 AUTHOR: *The Poet Slave of Cuba: A Biography of Juan Francisco Manzano* by Margarita Engle. Illustrated by Sean Qualls. Holt.

ILLUSTRATOR: *Los Gatos Black on Halloween* by Marisa Montes. Illustrated by Yuyi Morales. Holt.

2006 AUTHOR: *The Tequila Worm* by Viola Canales. Random.

ILLUSTRATOR: *Doña Flor: A Tall Tale about a Giant Woman with a Great Big Heart* by Pat Mora. Knopf.

2004 AUTHOR: *Before We Were Free* by Julia Alvarez. Knopf.

ILLUSTRATOR: *Just a Minute: A Trickster Tale and Counting Book* by Yuyi Morales. Chronicle.

2002 AUTHOR: *Esperanza Rising* by Pam Muñoz Ryan. Scholastic.

ILLUSTRATOR: *Chato and the Party Animals* by Gary Soto. Illustrated by Susan Guevara. Putnam.

2000 AUTHOR: *Under the Royal Palms: A Childhood in Cuba* by Alma Flor Ada. Atheneum.

ILLUSTRATOR: *Magic Windows: Cut-Paper Art and Stories* by Carmen Lomas Garza. Children's Book Press.

1998 AUTHOR: *Parrot in the Oven: Mi Vida* by Victor Martinez. HarperCollins.

ILLUSTRATOR: *Snapshots from the Wedding* by Gary Soto. Illustrated by Stephanie Garcia. Putnam.

1996 AUTHOR: *An Island Like You: Stories of the Barrio* by Judith Ortiz Cofer. Orchard.

ILLUSTRATOR: *Chato's Kitchen* by Gary Soto. Illustrated by Susan Guevara. Putnam.

Distinguished Play Award

This award, sponsored by the American Alliance for Theatre and Education, honors the playwright(s) and the publisher of the work voted as the best play for young people published during the past calendar year (January to December). Starting in 1989, two categories were instituted: Category A (plays primarily for upper and secondary school–age audiences) and Category B (plays primarily for elementary and middle school–age audiences). Beginning in 1998, Category C was established for adaptations. Award winners since 1988 are listed here. For the complete list of winners, go to http://aate.timberlakepublishing.com/content.asp?admin=Y&contentid=59#Dist_Play.

2008   Category A: *Brave No World: Community, Identity, Stand-Up Comedy* by Laurie Brooks. Dramatic Publishing.
Category B: No Award
Category C: *The Bluest Eye* adapted by Lydia R. Diamond from the novel by Toni Morrison. Dramatic Publishing.

2007   Category A: *Kara in Black* by Max Bush. Dramatic Publishing.
Category B: *La ofrenda* by Jose Casas. Dramatic Publishing.
Category C: *Roald Dahl's Danny the Champion of the World* adapted by David Wood. Samuel French, Ltd.

2006   Category A: No award
Category B: *The Forgiving Harvest* by Y York. Dramatic Publishing.
Category C: No award

2005   Category A: *Eric and Elliot* by Dwayne Hartford. Dramatic Publishing.
Category B: *In the Garden of the Selfish Giant* by Sandra Fenichel Asher. Dramatic Publishing.
Category C: *The Rememberer* by Steven Dietz, based on *As My Sun Now Sets* by Joyce Simmons Cheeka as told to Werdna Phillips Finley. Dramatic Publishing.

2004   Category A: *The Music Lesson* by Tammy Ryan. Dramatic Publishing.
Category B: No award
Category C: *Sarah, Plain and Tall* adapted by Joseph Robinette from the book by Patricia MacLachlan. Dramatic Publishing.

2003   Category A: *Paper Lanterns, Paper Cranes* by Brian Kral. Anchorage Press Plays.
Category B: *Salt and Pepper* by Jose Cruz Gonzalez. Dramatic Publishing.
Category C: *Spot's Birthday Party* adapted for the stage by David Wood, based on the book by Eric Hill. Samuel French.

2002   Category A: *Belongings* by Daniel Fenton. Dramatic Publishing.
Category B: No award
Category C: *Ezigbo, the Spirit Child* dramatized by Max Bush. Anchorage Press Plays.
Category C: *A Village Fable* by James Still, music by Michael Keck. Dramatic Publishing.

2001   Category A: *The Wrestling Season,* by Laurie Brooks. Dramatic Publishing.
Category B: No award
Category C: *Afternoon of the Elves* by Y York. Dramatic Publishing.

2000   Category A: *And Then They Came for Me: Remembering the World of Anne Frank* by James Still. Dramatic Publishing.
Category A: *The Taste of Sunrise* by Suzan Zeder. Anchorage Press.
Category B: *The Wolf Child* by Edward Mast. Anchorage Press.
Category C: No award

1999   Category A: *North Star* by Gloria Bond Clunie. Dramatic Publishing.
Category B: *Still Life with Iris* by Steven Dietz. Dramatic Publishing.
Category C: *Journey of the Sparrows* by Meryl Friedman. Dramatic Publishing.

1998   Category A: *Selkie* by Laurie Brooks. Anchorage Press.

Category B: *The Yellow Boat* by David Saar. Anchorage Press.

Category C: *Bambi: A Life in the Woods* by James DeVita. Anchorage Press.

1997   Category A: *The Less than Human Club* by Timothy Mason. Smith Kraus, Inc.

Category B: No award

1996   Category A: *Angel in the Night* by Joanna Halpert Kraus. Dramatic Publishing.

Category B: *The Prince and the Pauper* adapted for the stage by Aurand Harris. Anchorage Press.

1995   Category A: *T-Money & Wolf* by Kevin Willmott and Ric Averill. Dramatic Publishing.

Category A: *Scars and Stripes* by Thomas Cadwaleder Jones. Encore Publishing.

Category B: *Ramona Quimby* by Len Jenkins. Dramatic Publishing.

1994   Category A: *Song for the Navigator* by Michael Cowell. Dramatic Publishing.

Category B: *A Woman Called Truth* by Sandra Fenichel Asher. Dramatic Publishing.

1993   Category A: *This Is Not a Pipe Dream* by Barry Kornhauser. Anchorage Press.

Category B: *The Pinballs* by Aurand Harris. Anchorage Press.

1992   Category A: *The Secret Garden* by Pamela Sterling. Dramatic Publishing.

Category B: *Amber Waves* by James Still. Samuel French, Inc.

1991   Category A: *In the Middle of Grand Central Station* by Nancy Pahl Gilsenan. Dramatic Publishing.

Category A: *Jungalbook* by Edward Mast. Anchorage Press.

Category B: *Monkey Magic: Chinese Story Theatre* by Aurand Harris. Anchorage Press.

1990   Category A: *The Man-Child* by Arnold Rabin. Baker's Plays.

Category B: *The Chicago Gypsies* by Virginia Glasgow Koste. Dramatic Publishing.

Category B: *Aalmauria: The Voyage of the Dragonfly* by Max Bush. Anchorage Press.

1989   Category A: *A Separate Peace* by Nancy Pahl Gilsenan. Dramatic Publishing.

Category B: *Becca* by Wendy Kesselman. Anchorage Press.

1988   *Babies Having Babies* by Kathryn Montgomery and Jeffrey Auerbach. Baker's Plays.

Edgar Allan Poe Award (Mystery)—Best Juvenile Novel Category

This award, established in 1961 and sponsored by the Mystery Writers of America, is given to the author of the best mystery of the year written for young readers. Award winners since 1988 are listed here. For the complete list of winners, go to www.theedgars.com/edgarsDB/index.php and select "Best Juvenile" from the award category.

2009   *The Postcard* by Tony Abbott. Little, Brown.

2008   *The Night Tourist* by Katherine Marsh. Hyperion.

2007   *Room One: A Mystery or Two* by Andrew Clements. Simon & Schuster.

2006   *The Boys of San Joaquin* by D. James Smith. Simon & Schuster.

2005   *Chasing Vermeer* by Blue Balliett. Scholastic.

2004   *Bernie Magruder & the Bats in the Belfry* by Phyllis Reynolds Naylor. Atheneum.

2003   *Harriet Spies Again* by Helen Ericson. Random House/Delacorte.

2002   *Dangling* by Lillian Eige. Atheneum.

2001   *Dovey Coe* by Frances O'Roark Dowell. Simon & Schuster.

2000   *The Night Flyers* by Elizabeth McDavid Jones. Pleasant Company.

1999   *Sammy Keyes and the Hotel Thief* by Wendelin Van Draanen. Knopf.

1998   *Sparrows in the Scullery* by Barbara Brooks Wallace. Atheneum.

1997   *The Clearing* by Dorothy R. Miller. Atheneum.

1996   *Looking for Jamie Bridger* by Nancy Springer. Dial.

1995   *The Absolutely True Story . . . How I Visited Yellowstone Park with the Terrible Rupes* by Willo Davis Roberts. Atheneum.

1994   *The Twin in the Tavern* by Barbara Brooks Wallace. Atheneum.

1993   *Coffin on a Case* by Eve Bunting. HarperCollins.

1992   *Wanted . . . Mud Blossom* by Betsy Byars. Delacorte.

1991   *Stonewords* by Pam Conrad. Harper.

1990   No award

1989   *Megan's Island* by Willo Davis Roberts. Atheneum.

1988   *Lucy Forever and Miss Rosetree, Shrinks* by Susan Shreve. Holt.

Scott O'Dell Award for Historical Fiction

This award, donated by the author Scott O'Dell and established in 1984, is given to the author of a distinguished work of historical fiction for children or young adults set in the New World and published in English by a U.S. publisher. The author must be a citizen of the United States. Award winners since 1988 are listed here. For the complete list of winners, go to www.scottodell .com/odellaward.html.

2009   *Chains* by Laurie Halse Anderson. Simon & Schuster.

2008   *Elijah of Buxton* by Christopher Paul Curtis. Scholastic.

2007   *The Green Glass Sea* by Ellen Klages. Viking.

2006   *The Game of Silence* by Louise Erdrich. HarperCollins.

2005   *Worth* by A. LaFaye. Simon & Schuster.

2004   *The River between Us* by Richard Peck. Dial.

2003   *Trouble Don't Last* by Shelley Pearsall. Knopf.

2002   *The Land* by Mildred D. Taylor. Fogelman/ Penguin Putnam.

2001   *The Art of Keeping Cool* by Janet Taylor Lisle. Atheneum.

2000   *Two Suns in the Sky* by Miriam Bat-Ami. Front Street/Cricket.

1999   *Forty Acres and Maybe a Mule* by Harriette Gillem Robinet. Atheneum.

1998   *Out of the Dust* by Karen Hesse. Scholastic.

1997   *Jip: His Story* by Katherine Paterson. Dutton.

1996   *The Bomb* by Theodore Taylor. Harcourt Brace.

1995   *Under the Blood-Red Sun* by Graham Salisbury. Delacorte.

1994   *Bull Run* by Paul Fleischman. HarperCollins.

1993   *Morning Girl* by Michael Dorris. Hyperion.

1992   *Stepping on the Cracks* by Mary Downing Hahn. Clarion.

1991   *A Time of Troubles* by Pieter van Raven. Scribner's.

1990   *Shades of Gray* by Carolyn Reeder. Macmillan.

1989   *The Honorable Prison* by Lyll Becerra de Jenkins. Lodestar.

1988   *Charley Skedaddle* by Patricia Beatty. Morrow.

Orbis Pictus Award

This award, established in 1990 and sponsored by NCTE's Committee on Using Nonfiction in the Elementary Language Arts Classroom, is given to an author in recognition of excellence in writing of nonfiction for children published in the United States in the preceding year.

2009   *Amelia Earhart: The Legend of the Lost Aviator* by Shelley Tanaka. Illustrated by David Craig. Abrams.

2008   *M.L.K.: Journey of a King* by Tonya Bolden. Abrams.

2007   *Quest for the Tree Kangaroo: An Expedition to the Cloud Forest of New Guinea* by Sy Montgomery. Photographs by Nic Bishop. Houghton.

2006   *Children of the Great Depression* by Russell Freedman. Clarion.

2005   *York's Adventures with Lewis and Clark: An African-American's Part in the Great Expedition* by Rhoda Blumberg. HarperCollins.

2004   *An American Plague: The True and Terrifying Story of the Yellow Fever Epidemic of 1793* by Jim Murphy. Clarion.

2003   *When Marian Sang* by Pam Muñoz Ryan. Illustrated by Brian Selznick. Scholastic.

2002   *Black Potatoes: The Story of the Great Irish Famine, 1845–1850* by Susan Campbell Bartoletti. Houghton.

2001   *Hurry Freedom: African Americans in Gold Rush California* by Jerry Stanley. Crown.

2000   *Through My Eyes* by Ruby Bridges and Margo Lundell. Scholastic.

1999   *Shipwreck at the Bottom of the World: The Extraordinary True Story of Schackleton and the Endurance* by Jennifer Armstrong. Crown.

1998   *An Extraordinary Life: The Story of a Monarch Butterfly* by Laurence Pringle. Illustrated by Bob Marstall. Orchard.

1997   *Leonardo da Vinci* by Diane Stanley. Morrow.

1996   *The Great Fire* by Jim Murphy. Scholastic.

1995   *Safari beneath the Sea* by Diane Swanson. Photographs by the Royal British Columbia Museum. Sierra Club.

1994   *Across America on an Emigrant Train* by Jim Murphy. Clarion.

1993   *Children of the Dustbowl: The True Story of the School at Weedpatch Camp* by Jerry Stanley. Random.

1992   *Flight: The Journey of Charles Lindbergh* by Robert Burleigh. Illustrated by Mike Wimmer. Philomel.

1991   *Franklin Delano Roosevelt* by Russell Freedman. Clarion.

1990   *The Great Little Madison* by Jean Fritz. Putnam.

Robert F. Sibert Informational Book Medal

The Robert F. Sibert Informational Book Medal, established by the Association for Library Service to Children division of the American Library Association in 2001, is awarded annually to the author of the most distinguished informational book published during the preceding year.

2009   *We Are the Ship: The Story of Negro League Baseball* by Kadir Nelson. Jump at the Sun.

2008   *The Wall: Growing Up behind the Iron Curtain* by Peter Sís. Farrar.

2007   *Team Moon: How 400,000 People Landed Apollo 11 on the Moon* by Catherine Thimmesh. Houghton.

2006   *Secrets of a Civil War Submarine: Solving the Mysteries of the H. L. Hunley* by Sally M. Walker. Carolrhoda.

2005   *The Voice That Challenged a Nation: Marian Anderson and the Struggle for Equal Rights* by Russell Freedman. Clarion.

2004   *An American Plague: The True and Terrifying Story of the Yellow Fever Epidemic of 1793* by Jim Murphy. Clarion.

2003   *The Life and Death of Adolf Hitler* by James Cross Giblin. Clarion.

2002   *Black Potatoes: The Story of the Great Irish Famine, 1845–1850* by Susan Campbell Bartoletti. Houghton.

2001   *Sir Walter Ralegh and the Quest for El Dorado* by Marc Aronson. Clarion.

Other Notable Book Awards

New York Times Best Illustrated Children's Books of the Year

Sponsored by the *New York Times*, this list of ten books appears annually in the *Times*. A three-member panel of experts chooses the books.

International Reading Association Children's Book Award

Sponsored by the Institute for Reading Research and administered by the International Reading Association, this international award is given annually to an author for a first or second book that shows unusual promise in the children's book field.

International Board on Books for Young People Honor List

Sponsored by the International Board on Books for Young People (IBBY), this biennial list is composed of three books (one for text, one for illustration, and one for translation) from each IBBY National Section to represent the best in children's literature published in that country in the past two years. The books

selected are recommended as suitable for publication worldwide.

State Children's Choice Award Programs

Nearly all states have a children's choice book award program. Usually, a ballot of about twenty-five titles is generated from children's or teachers' nominations. Children from all over the state then vote for their favorite title. For information about your state children's choice award program, contact your state library association.

Professional Resources

Books

Barr, C., & Thomas, R. L. (2008). *Popular series fiction for K–6 readers* (2nd ed.). Santa Barbara, CA: Libraries Unlimited.

———. (2008). *Popular series fiction for middle school and teen readers* (2nd ed.). Santa Barbara, CA: Libraries Unlimited.

Guides to the best and most popular series, including series titles, all books in a given series, and suggestions for similar series.

Barstow, B., Riggle, J., & Molnar, L. (2007). *Beyond picture books: Subject access to best books for beginning readers* (3rd ed.). Santa Barbara, CA: Libraries Unlimited.

Subject guide to 3,600 titles for beginning readers ages 4 to 7. Includes a list of 200 outstanding first readers.

Bishop, R. S. (2007). *Free within ourselves: The development of African-American children's literature.* Westport, CT: Greenwood.

The evolution of fiction written for black children and by black authors and illustrators within the context of African-American social and literary history. Profiles of contemporary African-American authors and illustrators conclude the book.

Brozo, W. (2002). *To be a boy, to be a reader: Engaging teen and preteen boys in active literacy.* Newark, DE: International Reading Association.

Ideas for using literature with positive male archetypes to motivate boys to read.

Buss, K., & Karnowski, L. (2000). *Reading and writing literary genres.* Newark, DE: International Reading Association.

Offers readers and writers suggestions on how to understand and model a variety of different genres of literature and their elements.

The children's catalog (19th ed. with supplements in 2007, 2008, and 2009). (2006). New York: H. W. Wilson.

Part 1 lists books and magazines recommended for preschool children through sixth-graders, as well as useful professional resources. Part 2 helps the user locate entries through one alphabetical, comprehensive key that includes author, title, subject, and analytical listings.

De Las Casas, D. (2006). *Kamishibai story theater: The art of picture telling.* Illustrated by P. Chow. Santa Barbara, CA: Libraries Unlimited.

Practical information on developing a kamishibai program using large illustrated cards, based on the street art form seen from the 1920s to 1950s in Japan. See Allen Say's *Kamishibai Man* (Houghton, 2005) for a story about an itinerant storyteller.

Fox, D. L., & Short, K. G. (Eds.). (2003). *Stories matter: The complexity of cultural authenticity in children's literature.* Urbana, IL: NCTE.

Social responsibility of authors, cultural sensitivity and values, authenticity of content and images, and authorial freedom addressed by many contributors, including authors, illustrators, editors, publishers, educators, librarians, and scholars.

Freeman, J. (2007). *Once upon a time: Using storytelling, creative drama, and reader's theater with children in grades pre-K–6.* Santa Barbara, CA: Libraries Unlimited.

Tried-and-true stories, ideas, and activities for storytelling with children, including a bibliography of over 400 children's books to adapt for creative drama and/or readers' theatre.

Garcha, R., & Russell, P. Y. (2006). *The world of Islam in literature for youth: A selective bibliography for K–12.* Lanham, MD: Scarecrow.

Sixteen chapters present various aspects of Islam and the Muslim culture with annotated books; video and audio resources and teaching suggestions are included in separate chapters.

Gebel, D. J. (2006). *Crossing boundaries with children's books.* Lanham, MD: Scarecrow.

Includes annotations of nearly 700 international children's books published between 2000 and 2004, as well as selected American books set in countries other than the United States.

Hall, S. (1990, 1994, 2002). *Using picture storybooks to teach literary devices: Recommended books for children and young adults* (Vol. 1, 2, & 3). Phoenix, AZ: Oryx Press.

Offers strategies for using picture books to teach complex literary devices.

Jobe, R., & Dayton-Sakari, M. (1999). *Reluctant readers: Connecting students and books for successful reading experiences.* Markham, Ontario: Pembroke.

Activities and books for teachers and librarians to engage reluctant readers.

Leeper, A. (2006). *Poetry in literature for youth.* Lanham, MD: Scarecrow.

Innovative ways to integrate poetry into the K–12 curriculum and annotations of over 900 poetry books are included in this guide.

Lehman, B. (2007). *Children's literature and learning: Literary study across the curriculum.* New York: Teachers College Press.

Theories and methods for teaching literature across the curriculum.

Lehr, S. S. (Ed.). (2008). *Shattering the looking glass: Challenge, risk & controversy in children's literature.* Norwood, MA: Christopher-Gordon.

Politics, controversial issues, and recent change in the world of children's literature.

Lima, C. W., & Lima, J. A. (2006). *A to zoo: Subject access to children's picture books* (7th ed.). Westport, CT: Libraries Unlimited.

This index indicates the subject matter of 14,000 picture books for children with access through author, illustrator, and title, as well as 800 subjects.

Lukenbill, W. B. (2006). *Biography in the lives of youth: culture, society and information.* Englewood, NJ: Libraries Unlimited.

Varied uses of biography, types of biographies, their changes over time, and an extensive bibliography are presented, with age appropriateness indicated.

Moss, B. (2003). *Exploring the literature of fact: Children's nonfiction trade books in the elementary classroom.* New York: Guilford.

Discusses how to address children's literacy needs using children's nonfiction trade books.

NCTE bibliography series (National Council of Teachers of English):

Adventuring with books: A booklist for pre-K–grade 6 (13th ed.). (2002). Urbana, IL: NCTE.

Kaleidoscope: A multicultural booklist for grades K–8 (4th ed.). (2003). Urbana, IL: NCTE.

Your reading: An annotated booklist for junior high and middle-school students (11th ed.). (2003). Urbana, IL: NCTE.

All of these books include annotated listings of fiction and nonfiction books recommended for children and young people in the grades specified in each title.

Reynolds, M. (2004). *I won't read and you can't make me: Reaching reluctant teen readers.* Portsmouth, NH: Heinemann.

The author shares her many experiences, both as an author and as a teacher, with motivating reluctant young readers. Her techniques and suggestions include questionnaires and forms for guided response and book completion.

Robb, L. (2003). *Teaching reading in social studies, science, and math.* New York: Scholastic.

Provides practical ways to weave comprehension strategies into content-area teaching.

Stan, S. (Ed.). (2002). *The world through children's books.* Lanham, MD: Scarecrow.

A guide to international children's books published in the United States from 1996 to 2000, including a selection of children's books written by U.S. authors but set in other countries. An annotated bibliography is included.

Sullivan, M. (2003). *Connecting boys with books: What libraries can do.* Chicago: American Library Association.

Suggestions for program changes to address the problem of low reading skills among pre-adolescent boys.

———. (2009). *Connecting boys with books 2: Closing the reading gap.* Chicago: American Library Association.

A strategic plan for boys and reading through stimulating a sense of excitement in reading.

Tatum, A. W. (2005). *Teaching reading to black adolescent males: Closing the achievement gap.* Portland, ME: Stenhouse.

Practical suggestions for providing meaningful and culturally responsive reading strategies and assessment for black males and guidelines for selecting and discussing nonfiction and fiction texts with them.

Van Orden, P. (2000). *Selecting books for the elementary school library media center: A complete guide.* New York: Neal-Schuman.

An essential tool for new school libraries and useful for most libraries in balancing collections.

Vardell, S. M. (2008). *Children's literature in action: A librarian's guide.* Santa Barbara, CA: Libraries Unlimited.

Practical information for the preservice school or public librarian.

Books about the History of Children's Literature

Bingham, J., & Scholt, G. (1980). *Fifteen centuries of children's literature: An annotated chronology of British and American works in historical context.* Westport, CT: Greenwood.

Gillespie, M. C. (1970). *History and trends: Literature for children.* Dubuque, IA: Brown.

Hunt, P. (1995). *Children's literature: An illustrated history.* Oxford, England: Oxford University Press.

Hunt, P., & Ray, S. G. (1996). *International companion encyclopedia of children's literature.* London: Routledge.

Marcus, L. (2008). *Minders of make-believe: Idealists, entrepreneurs, and the shaping of American children's literature.* Boston: Houghton.

A 300-year history of children's book publishing, showing the evolution of the field from a local endeavor to an international, entrepreneurial business.

Marshall, M. R. (1988). *An introduction to the world of children's books: Books about the history of children's literature* (2nd ed.). Aldershot, England: Gower.

Bibliographies: Annual Lists

"CCBC Choices."

An annual spring annotated booklist, published by and for the members of the Friends of the CCBC, Inc. (Cooperative Children's Book Center). For information about CCBC publications and/or membership in the Friends, send a self-addressed stamped envelope to Friends of the CCBC, P.O. Box 5288, Madison, WI 53705-0288.

"Children's Choices."

This yearly list of newly published books, chosen by young readers themselves, appears each October in *The Reading Teacher* as a project of the International Reading Association/Children's Book Council Joint Committee.

"Notable Children's Books."

This annual American Library Association list appears in the March issue of *School Library Journal* and also in the March 15th issue of *Booklist.*

"Notable Children's Books in the Language Arts (K–8)."

This annual list of outstanding trade books for enhancing language awareness among students in grades K–8 appears in each October issue of *Language Arts.*

"Notable Social Studies Trade Books for Young People."

This list appears in the April/May issue of *Social Education* and at www.cbcbooks.org.

"Outstanding Science Trade Books for Students K–12."

This list appears in the March issue of *Science and Children* and at www.cbcbooks.org.

"Teachers' Choices."

This yearly list includes books recommended by teachers. It appears each November in *The Reading Teacher* and at www.reading.org.

"Young Adults' Choices."

The books on this annual list are selected by readers in middle, junior high, and senior high schools. It appears in the November issue of *Journal of Adolescent and Adult Literacy* and at www.reading.org.

Children's Magazines

The following list includes some of the most popular children's magazines available to young people today. It is organized by subject of primary emphasis.

Drama

Plays, the Drama Magazine for Young People. Scripts for plays, skits, puppet shows, and round-the-table readings (a type of readers' theatre). 8–10 scripts per issue. Ages 6–17. 7 issues/year. Order at www.playsmag.com

Health

Turtle. Articles, fiction, and activities with an emphasis on health, nutrition, and fitness. Ages 3–5. 6 issues/year. Similar magazines for different age groups by the same publisher include *Humpty Dumpty's Magazine* (ages 5–7) and *Jack and Jill* (ages 8–12). Order at www.cbhi.org

History

Calliope. Articles, stories, time lines, maps, and authentic photos to generate an interest in world history. Themed issues. Ages 9–14. 9 issues/year. Order at www.cobblestonepub.com

Cobblestone. Articles about U.S. history. Themed issues. Ages 9–14. 9 issues/year. Order at www.cobblestonepub.com

Language

Allons-Y. Topics of interest to 12- to 18-year-olds in French. Information and cultural details of French-speaking countries. Read-aloud plays and language CDs. 6 issues/year. Order at http://teacher.scholastic.com/products/classmags

Das Rad. Topics of interest to 12- to 18-year-olds in German. Information and cultural details of German-speaking countries. Read-aloud plays and language CDs. 6 issues/year. Order at http://teacher.scholastic.com/products/classmags

¿Qué Tal? Topics of interest to 12- to 18-year-olds in Spanish. Information and cultural details of Spanish-speaking countries. Read-aloud plays and language CDs. 6 issues/year. Order at http://teacher.scholastic.com/products/classmags

Language Arts

Read. Classic and contemporary fiction and nonfiction, plays, personal narratives, poetry; readers' theatre plays; articles on developing writing skills. Ages 11–16. 16 issues/year. Order at www.weeklyreader.com

Scholastic Scope. Plays, short stories, nonfiction, writing exercises, and skill builders. Ages 11–15. 17 issues/year. Order at http://teacher.scholastic.com/products/classmags

Stone Soup: The Magazine by Young Writers and Artists. Stories, poems, book reviews, and art by children. Ages 8–13. 6 issues/year. Order at www.stonesoup.com

Storyworks. Focuses on development of grammar, writing, vocabulary, test-taking. Includes read-aloud plays. Ages 8–11. 6 issues/year. Order at http://teacher.scholastic.com/products/classmags

Literature

Cricket. Fiction, nonfiction, book reviews, activities. Features international literature. Ages 9–14. 9 issues/year. Order at www.cricketmag.com

Lady Bug. Fiction, poems, songs, and games. Ages 3–6. 9 issues/year. Order at www.cricketmag.com

Spider. Fiction, poems, songs, and games for the beginning reader. Ages 6–9. 9 issues/year. Order at www.cricketmag.com

Mathematics

DynaMath. Humorously formatted word problems, computation, and test preparation; careers in mathematics feature. Ages 8–11. 8 issues/year. Order at http://teacher.scholastic.com/products/classmags

Scholastic Math Magazine. Math problems, computation, statistics, consumer math, real-life applications, career math, critical reasoning. Ages 11–15. 12 issues/year. Order at http://teacher.scholastic.com/products/classmags

Nature

National Geographic Explorer. Classroom magazines featuring nonfiction and nature photography aligned with science and social studies curriculum. Four levels (grades K–1, 2–3, 4–6, 6–12). 7 issues/year. Order at www.nationalgeographic.com/ngkids

National Geographic Kids. Nonfiction articles and nature photography. Promotes geographic awareness. Ages 6–14. 10 issues/year. Order at www.nationalgeographic.com/ngkids

Ranger Rick. Fiction and nonfiction, photoessays, jokes, riddles, crafts, plays, and poetry promoting the appreciation of nature. Superlative nature photography. Ages 7–12. 12 issues/year. Order at www.nwf.org/magazines

Your Big Backyard. Animal and nature stories and photography for the preschooler. Ages 3–7. 12 issues/year. Order at www.nwf.org/magazines

Recreation

Boys' Life. News, nature, sports, history, fiction, science, comics, Scouting, colorful graphics, and photos. Published by the Boy Scouts of America. Ages 7–18. 12 issues/year. Order at www.boyslife.org

Electronic Gaming Monthly. Gaming software and hardware previews and reviews. Ages 12 and up. 12 issues/year. Order at www.1UP.com

Highlights. General-interest magazine offering fiction and nonfiction, crafts, poetry, and thinking features. Ages 6–12. 12 issues/year. Order at www.highlights.com

Junior Baseball Magazine. Articles on baseball skills, sportsmanship, safety, and physical fitness. Ages 10–14. 6 issues/year. Order at www.juniorbaseball.com

New Moon: The Magazine for Girls and Their Dreams. An international magazine by and about girls. Builds healthy resistance to gender inequities. Ages 8–12. 6 issues/year. Order at www.newmoon.com

Nick Magazine. Nickelodeon television channel entertainment and humor magazine with television-related celebrity interviews, comics, puzzles, and activities. Ages 6–14. 10 issues/year. Order at www.nick.com/shows/nick_mag

Sports Illustrated for Kids. Stories about sports and sports celebrities, amateur sports, trivia. Poster included with each issue. Ages 6–10. 12 issues/year. Order at www.sikids.com

Science

Current Science. News in science, health, and technology; science activities; U.S. national science projects; science mystery photos; and kids in the news. Ages 11–16. 16 issues/year. Order at www.weeklyreader.com

Odyssey. Theme-based issues explore the latest science news. Ages 9–14. 9 issues/year. Order at: www.cobblestonepub.com

Science World. Articles, experiments, and news to supplement the science curriculum. Ages 11–16. 14 issues/year. Order at http://teacher.scholastic.com/products/classmags

SuperScience. Science concepts, critical thinking, and reasoning through hands-on activities and experiments; science news stories; interviews with scientists. Themed issues. Ages 8–11. 8 issues/year. Order at http://teacher.scholastic.com/products/classmags

Social Studies

Faces. Articles and activities exploring world cultures. Ages 9–14. 9 issues/year. Order at www.cricketmag.com

Junior Scholastic. Features U.S. and world history, current events, world cultures, map skills, and geography. Ages 11–14. 18 issues/year. Order at http://teacher.scholastic.com/products/classmags

Muse. Wide-ranging articles exploring ideas in science, history, and the arts. Ages 10–15. 9 issues/year. Order at www.cricketmag.com

Skipping Stones: An International Multicultural Magazine. Articles by, about, and for children about world cultures and cooperation. Multilingual. Ages 7–17. 5 issues/year. Order at www.skippingstones.org

Index to Children's Books and Authors

Subject Index

Credits and Acknowledgments

Illustration Credits